Foundations of
Distributed Artificial
Intelligence

Sixth-Generation Computer Technology Series

Branko Souček, Editor

Foundations of Distributed Artificial Intelligence

Edited by
G. M. P. O'Hare
N. R. Jennings

A Wiley-Interscience Publication

JOHN WILEY & SONS, INC.

New York • Chichester • Brisbane • Toronto • Singapore

This text is printed on acid-free paper.

Library of Congress Cataloging in Publication Data:
Foundations of distributed artificial intelligence/edited by G.M.P.
    O'Hare and N.R. Jennings.
        p.   cm. —(Sixth-generation computer technology series)
    "A Wiley-Interscience publication."
    Includes bibliographical references and index.
    ISBN 0-471-00675-0 (alk. paper)
    1. Electronic data processing—Distributed processing.
    2. Artificial intelligence. I. O'Hare, G. M. P. (Greg M. P.)
    II. Jennings, Nick. III. Series.
    QA76.9.D5F68 1996
    006.3—dc20   95-238

CONTENTS

CONTRIBUTORS

NIKOS M. AVOURIS
Department of Electrical
Engineering
University of Patras
GR 265 00 Rio-Patras, Patras
Greece

CRISTIANO CASTELFRANCHI
Istituto di Psicologia-CNR
00137 Rome
Italy

BRAHIM CHAIB-DRAA
Departement de Informatique
Faculte des Sciences
Universite Laval
Sainte-Foy, Quebec G1K 7P4
Canada

DAVID COCKBURN
EA Technology
Capenhurst
Chester CH1 6ES
United Kingdom

ROSARIA CONTE
Istituto di Psicologia-CNR
00137 Rome
Italy

KEITH S. DECKER
The Robotics Institute
Carnegie Mellon University
Pittsburgh, PA 15213

EDMUND H. DURFEE
Department of Electrical
Engineering and Computer Science
University of Michigan
Ann Arbor, MI 48109

JACQUES FERBER
Laforia-IBP
University Paris 6-B169
75252 Paris Cedex 05
France

KLAUS FISCHER
German Research Center for
Artificial Intelligence
Project AKA-Mod
D-66123 Saabrücken
Germany

AFSANEH HADDADI
Daimler-Benz AG
Research Systems Technology
Berlin
D-10559 Berlin 21
Germany

LYNNE E. HALL
Division de Organizacion y
Sistemas de Informacion
08201 Sabadell
Spain

SUSANNE KALENKA
Department of Electronic
Engineering
Queen Mary and Westfield College
London E1 4NS
United Kingdom

DENNIS KWEK
Department of Computer Science
University of Essex
Colchester CO4 3SQ
United Kingdom

NICK R. JENNINGS
Department of Electronic
Engineering
Queen Mary and Westfield College
London E1 4NS
United Kingdom

STEFAN KIRN
Westfälische Wilhelms-Universität
Münster
Institut für Wirtschaftsinformatik
D-48159 Münster
Germany

GEORGE KISS
Human Cognition Research
Laboratory
Faculty of Social Sciences
Open University
Milton Keynes MK7 6AA
United Kingdom

BERNARD MOULIN
Departement de Informatique
Faculte des Sciences
Universite Laval
Sainte-Foy, Quebec G1K 7P4
Canada

JÖRG P. MÜLLER
German Research Center for
Artificial Intelligence
Project AKA-Mod
D-66123 Saabrücken
Germany

H. JÜRGEN MÜLLER
University of Bremen
FB3-Computer Science, AG HI
D-28334 Bremen
Germany

GREG M. P. O'HARE
Department of Computation
UMIST
Manchester M60 1QD
United Kingdom

H. VAN DYKE PARUNAK
Industrial Technology Institute
PO Box 1485
Ann Arbor, MI 48106

MARKUS PISCHEL
German Research Center for
Artificial Intelligence
Project AKA-Mod
D-66123 Saabrücken
Germany

LORENZO SOMMARUGA
Departamento de Intelligencia
Artificial
Universidad Carlos III de Madrid
28911 Leganes, Madrid
Spain

DONALD D. STEINER
Siemens AG
Otto-Hahn-Ring 6
D-81739 Munich
Germany

KURT SUNDERMEYER
Daimler-Benz AG
Research Systems Technology
Berlin
D-10559 Berlin 21
Germany

RAIMO TUOMELA
Department of Philosophy
University of Helsinki
0014 Helsinki
Finland

MARC H. VAN LIEDEKERKE
Environment Institute Information
Unit
Commission of European
Community Joint Research Center
21020 Ispra (VA), Ispra
Italy

ERIC WERNER
Route 3, Box 181
Richland Center, WI 53581

MICHAEL WOOLDRIDGE
Department of Computing
Manchester Metropolitan University
Manchester M1 5GD
United Kingdom

PREFACE

Distributed artificial intelligence (DAI) is a subfield of AI concerned with distributing and coordinating knowledge and actions in multiple agent environments. In the 20 or so years since its inception the discipline has evolved quickly with research activity mushrooming around the globe. The quality and quantity of this research output has given birth to dedicated international conferences and workshops in Europe, America, and Japan.

Distributed artificial intelligence is a dynamic area of research, and this book constitutes the first comprehensive, truly integrated exposition of this exciting new discipline. It achieves this objective by bringing together influential contributions from leading authorities in the field. It combines introductory and review chapters with chapters which investigate specific research topics. The former act as a 'research map' enabling the reader to navigate through the general arena of DAI. The latter allows the reader to obtain a comprehensive appreciation of the key facets of DAI research. This approach enables *Foundations of Distributed Artificial Intelligence* to serve the dual role of a quality introductory text and a repository for current, yet seminal, research.

By providing a solid introduction to the theoretical and practical issues of DAI, this book is an essential companion to people who are new to the field, to practioners who wish to embrace DAI technologies, and to researchers already active in this arena.

Foundations of Distributed Artificial Intelligence comprises four parts. Each part begins with an introduction highlighting the similarities and differences between the approaches which are to be described. The first part, entitled "Formulative Readings," presents chapters which act as a foundation for the remainder of the book. These contributions provide a clear and thorough introduction to the discipline of distributed artificial intelligence, and study of these chapters is highly recommended for those new to the field.

The second part, entitled "Cooperation, Coordination, and Agency," addresses the core research topics of communication, coordination, and planning and describes how they are related to each other. This part further develops the key areas introduced within the formulative readings. Each contribution describes a problem, reviews approaches to that problem, and outlines the particular solution advocated by the author(s) together with its relationship to other work. Chapters 5 to 10 address the interplay between communication and belief revision, agent negotiation, the use of joint intentions, agent dynamics, and temporal logics for multiagent systems. While these chapters are generally concerned with reflective agents, the last chapter details the alternative paradigm of reactive systems.

The third part, entitled "DAI Frameworks and their Applications," describes a number of DAI testbeds. It illustrates particular strategies commissioned in providing software environments for building and experimenting with DAI systems. Specifically, two contributions review large ESPRIT projects, namely ARCHON and IMAGINE. The main aim of ARCHON is to define an architecture which provides a means of cooperation for preexisting semi-autonomous intelligent systems of coarse granularity. IMAGINE, on the other hand, integrates speech acts and basic agent plans and realizes these capabilities via a parallel logic programming paradigm. Four other toolkits are described: CooperA, AGenDA, TÆMS, and Agent Factory, each with their contrasting philosophies and enabling technologies.

The final part, entitled "Related Disciplines," contains contributions which consider DAI from different perspectives. It seeks to synthesize the field of DAI with other related areas of scientific endeavor, particularly philosophy, organizational science, cognitive science, and human computer interaction.

Our hope is that this book will rapidly enable the reader to gain an understanding of this broad and highly involved research area. It should stimulate interest and cultivate a thirst for further knowledge. To this end, the final contribution, "Distributed Artificial Intelligence References and Resources," provides a collection of useful information sources for DAI and multiagent systems in general.

GREGORY O'HARE
NICK JENNINGS

PART I

Formulative Readings

CHAPTER 1 ─────────────

An Overview of Distributed Artificial Intelligence

BERNARD MOULIN
BRAHIM CHAIB-DRAA

1 INTRODUCTION

Human groups, tribes, organizations, and societies have emerged and evolved as a result of collective and collaborative activities that sustained the progress of each individual as well as the groups to which they belong. Traditionally, tools and machines have been used by human beings as passive or mechanical artefacts that prolonged, enhanced, and multiplied their physical and mental abilities: a hammer is stronger than a human hand; a car can travel quicker than human legs; a book can memorize more information and for a longer time period than human memory. During the last decades, computers have been used as sophisticated tools, dramatically enhancing human abilities such as memory and calculation, as well as publishing and communication capabilities. Research in artificial intelligence has aimed at developing software to simulate so-called intelligent capabilities of human beings such as reasoning, natural language communication, and learning: with such programs, the computer's role departs from that of a mere tool to progressively become a kind of assistant to humans. The implementation of computer networks (long-range and local area networks) was a big step toward the development of computer organizations or "societies," since collaboration between individuals requires that communication links be established and used effectively. Distributed artificial intelligence (DAI) is a subfield of artificial intelligence which has, for more than a decade now, been investigating knowledge models, as well as communication and reasoning techniques that computational agents might need to participate

Foundations of Distributed Artificial Intelligence, Edited by G. M. P. O'Hare and N. R. Jennings.
ISBN 0-471-00675-0 © 1996 John Wiley & Sons, Inc.

in "societies" composed of computers and people. More generally, DAI is concerned with situations in which several systems interact in order to solve a common problem: computers and persons, sensors, aircrafts, robots, intelligent vehicles, etc.

DAI research is multidisciplinary in nature (see Part IV) and benefits from advances in various fields: artificial intelligence, social (see Chapter 20) and organizational sciences (Chapter 19), distributed computing, natural language processing, cognitive sciences, philosophy (Chapter 18), etc. Despite this di-,versity, several basic notions and techniques are fundamental to DAI (Chaibdraa et al., 1992). These techniques are presented along with an overview of the main research directions and some typical applications of DAI. Since DAI research is rapidly evolving, we do not pretend to provide an exhaustive coverage of the field. We simply propose a framework that will enable the reader *to navigate in the DAI seas and motivate her to explore new shores* with further readings and investigations.

This chapter is organized as follows. Section 2 identifies DAI's main research areas and characterizes the main problems addressed in this field. A framework consisting of four perspectives is proposed for conducting our review: agent perspective, group perspective, specific approaches, and designer's perspective. Section 3 deals with the agent perspective, covering several topics: agent categories, agent knowledge structures and knowledge maintenance, agent reasoning abilities, adaptation and learning abilities, and agent architectures. Section 4 analyzes the questions related to the organization of a group of agents and the modeling of societies of agents. Section 5 is concerned with the topics of cooperation, coordination, negotiation, coherent behavior, and planning among a group of agents. In Section 6 we study the problems related to agent communication and interaction: primitive communication, plan and message passing, information exchanges through a blackboard, high-level communication, and person/machine interaction. Section 7 presents specific approaches for DAI problems: open information systems semantics, ecosystems, reflection and autonomous agents, intelligent and cooperative information systems. Finally, Section 8 deals with the designer's perspective: analysis and design methods for DAI, design tools, and applications.

2   WHAT IS DAI?

Researchers in DAI are concerned with understanding and modeling action and knowledge in collaborative enterprises (Gasser, 1991). People usually distinguish two main areas of research in DAI (Bond and Gasser, 1988): distributed problem solving and multiagent systems.

Distributed problem solving (DPS) considers how the task of solving a particular problem can be divided among a number of modules (or "nodes") that cooperate in dividing and sharing knowledge about the problem and about its evolving solution(s). In a pure DPS system, all interaction (cooperation, coordination if any) strategies are incorporated as an integral part of the system.

Research in *multiagent systems* (MAS) is concerned with the behavior of a collection of (possibly preexisting) autonomous agents aiming at solving a given problem. A MAS can be defined as "a loosely-coupled network of problem solvers that work together to solve problems that are beyond their individual capabilities" (Durfee et al., 1989). These problem solvers, often called *agents*, are autonomous and may be heterogeneous in nature (characterized by various degrees of problem solving capabilities).

Durfee et al. (1989) observe that many applications are inherently distributed. Some applications are spatially distributed (such as interpreting and integrating data obtained from spatially distributed sensors, or controlling a group of robots). Other applications are functionally distributed as, for instance, a group of experts with different specialities collaborating to solve a difficult problem (see Chapter 4 for more details). A MAS has significant advantages over a single, monolithic, centralized problem solver: *faster problem solving* by exploiting parallelism; *decreased communication* by transmitting only high-level partial solutions to other agents rather than raw data to a central site; *more flexibility* by having agents with different abilities dynamically team up to solve current problems; and *increased reliability* by allowing agents to take on responsibilities of agents that fail. Gasser (1991) presents the following six problems as being inherent to the design and implementation of any system of coordinated problem solvers.[1]

1. How to formulate, describe, decompose, and allocate problems and synthesize results among a group of intelligent agents?
2. How to enable agents to communicate and interact? What communication languages and protocol to use? What and when to communicate?
3. How to ensure that agents act coherently in making decisions or taking action, accommodating the nonlocal effects of local decisions and avoiding harmful interactions?
4. How to enable individual agents to represent and reason about the actions, plans, and knowledge of other agents in order to coordinate with them: how to reason about the state of their coordinated process (e.g., initiation and completion)
5. How to recognize and reconcile disparate viewpoints and conflicting intentions among a collection of agents trying to coordinate their actions?
6. How to engineer and constrain practical DAI systems? How to design technology platforms and development methodologies for DAI?

Each of these problems appears in some form in DAI application domains. Gasser (1991) indicates that solutions to these problems are intertwined. "For example, different procedures for communication and interaction have implications for coordination and coherent behaviour. Different problem and task decompositions may yield different interactions or agent-modelling require-

---

[1]These problems were originally proposed in Bond and Gasser (1988).

ments. Coherent, coordinated behaviour depends on how knowledge disparities are resolved, which agents resolve them, etc.''

But DAI is not dealing with questions related to parallel or distributed processing. Bond and Gasser (1992) indicate: ''DAI is concerned with issues of coordination among concurrent processes at the problem-solving and representation levels. That is, we are not concerned with parallel processing for AI for reasons of improved efficiency in AI computations *per se.*'' So, we will not address issues related to parallel computer architectures, parallel programming languages or distributed operating systems designed for efficiency. DAI techniques have been applied to *distributed interpretation, distributed planning and control, cooperating expert systems, computer-supported cooperative work,* among other areas (a more detailed account of applications for DAI is given in Chapter 4).

DAI also brings about a new perspective in knowledge representation and problem solving, by providing richer scientific formulations and more realistic representations in practice. It sheds new light on cognitive sciences and artificial intelligence. Certain researchers, notably Nilsson (1980), believe that DAI could be crucial to our understanding of artificial intelligence. There are many arguments to support this claim. First, a system may be so complicated and contain so much knowledge that it is better to break it down into different cooperative entities in order to obtain more efficiency (i.e., modularity, flexibility, and efficiency). A second argument is based on the fact that DAI provides a practical framework for testing our intuitions about reasoning processes based on knowledge, actions, and planning. Currently, methods exist for representing beliefs, plans, actions, and reasoning about interactions of intelligent systems. Hence, knowing how an artificial system can reason about other agents could help us to better understand how such a system can reason about itself. A third argument is that methods used by an intelligent system to reason about other systems' actions can also be used to reason with other kinds of nonintelligent dynamic processes. Lastly, research in DAI may contribute to our understanding of communication processes based on natural language. Indeed, communicative acts between intelligent systems generally are an abstraction of certain aspects of the production and comprehension of natural language, and the study of this abstraction can help clarify certain problems studied in natural language.

DAI encompasses a fairly large body of research that can be studied from different perspectives. In order to organize our current review, we propose a framework that provides a structure for analysing and classifying most of DAI research activities (Figure 1.1). The themes that we will examine are

- The agent perspective, which includes all the elements characterizing an agent involved in a multiagent system.
- The group perspective, which gathers the elements that characterize a group of agents. Since this is a fairly large theme, we consider three subperspectives: organization of the group, coordination and planning, communication and interactions.

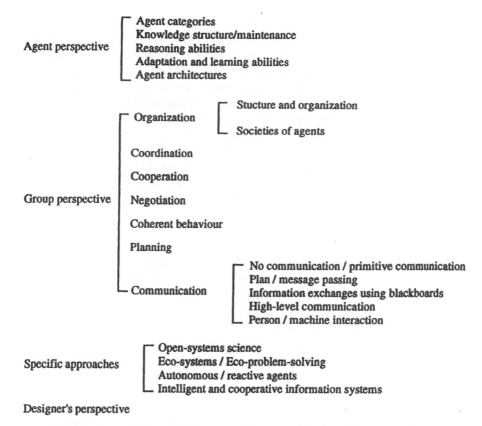

Figure 1.1 A framework for analyzing and classifying DAI research.

- A third perspective deals with specific approaches such as open systems, reflection, autonomous agents, and organizational information systems.
- The designer's perspective addresses topics, such as methods and implementation techniques for building MAS, testbeds, design tools and applications for DAI.

In the following sections we present the main research and development activities that are related to these different perspectives. Notice that Bond and Gasser (1992) contains a subject-indexed bibliography of more than 570 entries that are worth consulting. Throughout this chapter, when it is possible, we provide in footnotes a correspondence between the notions that we present and the list of subjects used by Bond and Gasser.

3 THE AGENT PERSPECTIVE

In a MAS, agents can present different degrees of *heterogeneity*. Agents may be identical, or they may differ only in the resources available to them (low heterogeneity). Agents may also differ in the problem solving methods and expertise they use (medium heterogeneity). They may only share a common interaction language, their other characteristics possibly being quite different (high heterogeneity). We distinguish different types of agents in a MAS: *artificial agents* (software modules) and *human agents* (users). In some MAS, we can introduce a *superagent* composed of several artificial agents and that may be considered as the representative of the group of elementary agents. This superagent itself behaves as an agent from the point of view of other agents or users interacting with it. When considering an agent involved in a MAS, several issues can be examined: *agent categories* (3.1), *knowledge structures* and *knowledge maintenance* (3.2), *reasoning abilities* (3.3), *learning abilities* (3.4), and *agent architecture* (3.5).

3.1   Agent Categories

In order to behave autonomously, agents should ideally possess several abilities: perception and interpretation of incoming data and messages, reasoning based upon their beliefs, decision making (goal selection, solving goal interactions, reasoning on intentions), planning (selection or construction of action plans, conflict resolution, resource allocation), and the ability to execute plans including message passing. However, in practical multiagent systems, agents may be characterized by various degrees of problem-solving capabilities. We distinguish reactive (Chapter 11), intentional (Chapter 5), and social agents[2] (Chapter 20).

A *reactive* agent reacts to changes in its environment or to messages from other agents. It is not able to reason about its intentions (goal manipulation). Its actions are performed as the result of triggering rules or of executing stereotyped plans: updating the agent's fact base (or belief space), and sending messages to other agents or to the environment. First-generation expert systems (composed of a knowledge base containing rule sets, a fact base, and an inference engine) are typical examples of reactive agents. Within a MAS, they should also be able to communicate with other agents: choosing and sending or receiving and interpreting relevant messages according to the current situation. Reactive agents may also be much more primitive as in actor systems (Hewitt, 1986, 1991).

An *intentional* agent (Chapters 2, 5, and Part II in general) is able to reason on its intentions and beliefs, to create plans of actions, and to execute those plans. Intentional agents can be considered as planning systems (Wilensky, 1983; Wilkins, 1988; Allen et al., 1991; Lizotte and Moulin, 1990; von Martial, 1992): they can select their goals (according to their motivations) and reason on them (detection and resolution of goal conflicts and coincidences),

---

[2]Reactive and intentional agents have been discussed in Demazeau and Müller (1991b). The distinction we propose here is slightly different and is based on a distinction between intentional and social agents.

select or create plans (action scheduling), detect conflicts between plans (resource allocation for instance), and execute and revise plans, if necessary. In a MAS, intentional agents coordinate themselves by exchanging information about their beliefs, goals, or actions. This information is eventually incorporated in their plans.

In addition to intentional agent capabilities, a *social* agent possesses explicit models of other agents. Hence, it must be able to maintain these models (updating beliefs, goals, and eventually plans), to reason on the knowledge incorporated in these models (intentions, commitments, expectations, anticipated reactions, and hypothetical behaviors), to make its decisions and create its plans with respect to other agents' models. The level of complexity of the models a social agent has of other agents (in the organization) is relative to the sophistication of that social agent.

3.2 Knowledge Structures, Knowledge Maintenance[3]

Agents can be thought of as knowledge-based systems that may be more or less sophisticated, depending on the characteristics of the MAS that is modeled. An agent may be characterized by different kinds of knowledge structures: facts (in expert system terminology) or beliefs (in planning system terminology); goals or intentions, preferences, motivations, desires, etc. Usually, an agent acquires new facts or beliefs as the result of messages sent by other agents or its environment. These messages can be thought of as speech acts (Searle, 1969).

In their pioneering work on modeling agents' interactions based on speech acts recognition and planning, Cohen and Perrault (1979) proposed an approach in which agents are considered as planning systems: their model provide structures that include agent's belief and goals, as well as beliefs related to other agents. Allen (1983) suggested that we can understand another agent's speech act as the result of the recognition of the agent's plans and obstacles to that plan. To that end, Allen defined a mechanism able to infer the goal and plan of an agent from the characteristics of the speech act. This mechanism used rules for inferring plans as well as some knowledge about the plans that agents could possibly share. Allen applied this approach to model cooperative behavior of agents in dialogues.

Cohen and Levesque (1990a,b) proposed a formal approach based on "principles governing the rational balance among an agent's beliefs, actions and intentions." By making explicit the conditions under which an agent can drop its goals (i.e., by specifying how an agent is committed to its goals), their formalism captures a number of important properties of intention. By relativizing one agent's intentions in terms of beliefs about another agent's intentions (or beliefs), they derive a preliminary account of interpersonal commitments.

---

[3]This section corresponds to the subject indexes belief modeling, commitment and intention, modeling others, rationality, truth maintenance, and incertainty in Bond and Gasser (1992).

Konolige and Pollack (1993) note that "most authors have employed *normal modal logics*, that is logics in which the semantics of modal operators is defined by accessibility functions over possible worlds." They argue that normal model logics are ill-suited to a formal theory of intention and propose an "alternative model of intention that is *representationalist*, in the sense that its semantic objects provide a more direct representation of cognitive states of the intending agent."

From another point of view, Shoham (1993) proposes a new approach for specifying agents that he calls *agent-oriented programming* by analogy with object-oriented programming (see also Chapters 3 and 17). In this framework, the (mental) states of an agent consist of components called beliefs, choices and capabilities. The agents' mental states are formally described using an extension of epistemic logic. Agents are controlled by *agent programs* which include primitives for communication. In this approach, agents are relatively simple, but they should be viewed as basic building blocks to create more complex MAS using a programming style equivalent to object orientation.

In a MAS, an agent only has a partial view of the situation and the problem to be solved. The information it manipulates is often partial, uncertain or even erroneous. Hence, an agent needs mechanisms to maintain the consistency of its knowledge bases or to revise its beliefs when new contradictory knowledge is acquired. Truth maintenance systems (Doyle, 1979; De Kleer, 1986) offer such belief revision mechanisms: they have been extensively applied in traditional AI systems such as expert systems. In DAI, truth maintenance systems have attracted the attention of researchers more recently. Mason presents a MAS composed of a number of expert systems and a distributed assumption-based truth maintenance system called DATMS (Mason and Johnson, 1989). Huhns and Bridgeland (1991) define the notion of logical consistency of beliefs among a group of computational agents. They consider several levels of consistency (inconsistency, local consistency, local-and-shared consistency, global consistency) and propose a distributed truth maintenance algorithm that guarantees local consistency for each agent and global consistency for data shared by agents. Galliers (1991) and Gaspar (1991) propose models for belief revision in dialogues.

3.3 Reasoning Abilities[4]

Usually, agents need to reason on different aspects of reality (see Chapters 4 and 10). They must deal with obligations, permissions and interdictions (*deontic logic*). Time is a factor that most systems must take into account (*temporal logic*). An agent may also need to explore various hypotheses (*hypothetical reasoning*) before making a decision (Werner, 1989, Chapter 2; Lizotte and Moulin, 1990; Mazer, 1991; Wooldridge and Fisher, 1992).

[4]This section corresponds to the subject indexes reasoning about action and knowledge in Bond and Gasser (1992).

In addition to its ability to reason on its own beliefs, desire and intentions, as agent needs to reason about other agents' knowledge and behavior, as demonstrated by Allen, Cohen and Perrault. Such reasoning may help an agent influence or even change the beliefs and behavior of other agents. According to Sycara (1989b), this ability is a must in multiagent negotiations. Let us consider the ability to reason about, and to change, beliefs and actions of other agents. In this area, most researchers have aimed at understanding the knowledge required to perform certain actions and how that knowledge can be acquired through communication.

McCarty and Hayes (1969) argued that a planning program needs to explicitly reason about its ability to perform an action. Moore (1980) took this argument one step further by emphasizing the crucial relationship between knowledge and action. Knowledge is necessary to perform actions, and new knowledge is gained as a result of performing actions. Moore went on to construct a logic with possible-worlds semantics that allowed explicit reasoning about knowledge and action, and then considered the problem of automatically generating deductions within the logic.

In the area of reasoning about another agent's beliefs, Halpern (1986) notes that most models of knowledge and belief are based on the possible-worlds model. In this model, an agent is said to know a fact if this fact is true in all worlds that he thinks are possible. Such situations are often formally described using a modal propositional logic and Kripke structures. Some of the problems that researchers have to deal with are logical omniscience (agents are able to derive all valid formulae and their logical consequences), and mutual knowledge (not only does everyone know that a fact is true, but they know everyone knows, etc.).

Shoham (1989a) considers the role played by the concept of action in AI. He first summarizes the advantages and limitations of past approaches which take the concept to be primitive, as embodied in situation calculus (McCarty and Hayes, 1969) and dynamic logic (Pratt, 1976). He also summarizes the alternative, namely adopting a temporal framework, and points out its complementary advantages and limitations. The author then proposes a framework that retains the advantages of both viewpoints and that ties the notion of action closely to that of knowledge. Specifically, Shoham proposes to start with the notion of time lines and to define the notion of action as the ability to make certain choices among sets of time lines. This framework sheds new light on the connection between time, action, knowledge, and on reasoning about the same events at different levels of detail. Shoham (1989b) complements this work by investigating the relation between the notions of knowledge and belief. In this context and contrary to the well-known slogan about "knowledge being true belief," the author proposes that belief should be viewed as defeasible knowledge. Specifically, he offers a definition of belief as knowledge-relative-to-assumptions, and ties this definition to the notion of nonmonotonicity. One of the main formalism of nonmonotonic reasoning is *autoepistemic logic* (Moore, 1985) whose basic idea is that agents' beliefs are "closed under perfect introspection''; that is, they know what they know and what they do not know. Levesque (1990) proposed a logic of *only-knowing* (OL), which is a classical modal logic extended by a new modality to express that a formula is *all* an agent believes. Lakemeyer (193) proposes a multiagent extension of OL that gives a semantic and proof-theoretic account of autoepistemic reasoning for several agents.

Galliers (1991) describes strategies that allow rational agents to change their beliefs during conversational interaction. Her approach includes (1) a foundation theory: beliefs are sustained by explicit justifications and are dropped if the justifications change; (2) a coherence theory: beliefs persist until challenged. Lizotte and Moulin (1990) extend this view to the connection between goals and beliefs. They introduce the notion of decision space where goals are bound to beliefs by preconditions and concurrent conditions. A goal can be activated only if concurrent conditions hold, and must be dropped if concurrent conditions change.

Behind the ability to reason about, and to change, beliefs and actions of other agents, intelligent agents must also reason about (and change) the behavior of others. In this respect, agents must reason about other agents' plans in order to recognize their potential actions. Many AI models of plan recognition have viewed it as a process of belief and *intention ascription* (Schmidt et al., 1978; Allen, 1983; Sidner, 1985; Litman and Allen, 1990). Such a plan recognition model could abstractly be viewed over a space of all plans that can be constructed from the known actions and states using causal relationships. Each plan that can be built in this search space could be viewed as a script structure. Kautz (1990) criticized this model for its failure to provide a formal analysis of the defeasible reasoning inherent in plan recognition. In particular, Kautz notes that this model presents only a space of possible inferences, and that little is said about why one should infer one conclusion instead of another, or what one should conclude if the situation is ambiguous. Kautz himself provides a plan recognition formalization, stated in terms of circumscription. However, his model relies upon two strong assumptions: (1) the observer— that is, the agent performing the plan recognition—is assumed to have complete knowledge of the domain; (2) the actor, which is the agent whose plan is being inferred, has a correct plan.

Pollack (1987, 1990) has shown that these assumptions are too strong for a useful model of plan recognition, particularly in the real world. Consequently, she proposes, with her colleague Konolige (Konolige and Pollack, 1989), an alternative formalization of plan recognition, one in which it is not necessary to assume that the actor's plan is correct from the perspective of the observer, but in which it is possible to specify in a precise way why certain conclusions should be preferred over others. This plan recognition model, which uses defeasible reasoning and direct argumentation for the ascription of belief, is actually used to support communication (Lochbaum et al., 1990).

Several authors applied *game theory* as a way of deciding future courses of action. Rosenschein and Genesereth (1985) proposed a framework for modeling agents' interactions that explicitly accounts for communication and promises and allows multiple goals among agents. They use the simple construct of "payoff matrix" of game theory, payoffs designating utility to the players of a particular joint move. Through the use of communication and binding promises, agents are able to coordinate their actions more effectively. Kraus and Wilkenfeld (1991) examine negotiation using game-theoretic techniques taking into account changes of agent's preferences over time. Gmytrasiewicz and his colleagues (1991) propose an approach, called the "recursive modeling method," which is based on metagame theory and allows an agent to recursively model another agent's decisions based on probabilistic views of how the agent perceives the multiagent situation. *Group voting* mechanisms can feasibly allow autonomous agents to reach consensus. Zlotkin and Rosenschein (1991) indicate that in designing such a mechanism several issues must be addressed: automatic generation of alternatives over which the group will vote; assessment by each agent of the value of each alternative; incorporation of an effective "incentive mechanism" for truth telling. They explore how the "Clarke tax" could be used as an effective "preference revealer" in the domain of automated agents, reducing the need for explicit negotiation (Ephrati and Rosenschein, 1991). Ephrati and Rosenschein (1993) propose a new multiagent planning technique that makes use of a dynamic iterative search procedure: agents incrementally construct a plan that brings the group to a state maximizing social welfare. Some researchers have also explored the impact of *lies on reasoning*: agents assess the possibility of transmitting incomplete or erroneous information to other agents in order to obtain some advantage over others or to reach some goal (Gmytrasiewicz and Durfee, 1992; Zlotkin and Rosenschein, 1990).

3.4 Adaptation and Learning Abilities[5]

An agent may also need to adapt to its environment and other agents' behavior. Hayes-Roth (1988) proposed several ways of making agents adaptive. In the MINDS project Huhns et al. (1987) developed a distributed information retrieval system in which agents share both knowledge and tasks to cooperate in retrieving documents for users. While in operation, agents are able to customize documents retrieval for each user by learning distribution patterns, as well as user interests and preferences. Shaw and Whinston (1989) present a method for incorporating machine learning capabilities in DAI systems based on two mechanisms of adaptation abstracted from human organizations (*market*) and natural systems (*evolution*). Weiss (1993) addresses the problem of how several agents can collectively learn to coordinate their actions such that they solve a given environmental task together. Two important constraints have been con-

---

[5]This section corresponds to the subject indexes adaptation and learning in Bond and Gasser (1992).

sidered: the "incompatibility constraint" (different actions may be mutually exclusive) and the "local information constraint" (each agent typically knows only a fraction of its environment).

Sian (1991) presented a MAS composed of several expert systems with diverse knowledge. A learning module based on inductive reasoning enables each agent to gain new knowledge after interacting with other expert systems. Namatame and Tsukamoto (1993) present an hypermedia system incorporating heterogeneous and composite learning agents.

3.5 Agent Architectures[6]

Among the agent categories we introduced in Section 3.1, the most sophisticated one is the social agent. Figure 1.2 describes our proposal for a general architecture of a social agent. Refer also to Chapter 3 and Part III for alternatives agent architectures and structures. The main functions that we associate with a social agent are perception (P1), interpretation and categorization of perceived information (P2), reasoning on beliefs and other agents' models (P3), decision making (P4), selection of predefined plans (P5) and/or plan construction (P6), simulation of plans and other agents' reactions (P8, optional), plan activation (P7), plan execution (P9), and plan learning (P10, optional). These various functions are opportunistically activated by the agent, thanks to an agenda for coordinating agent activities (A4): this is shown by the double arrows that link each function to A4 or to the grouping in which A4 is included. The knowledge (or *beliefs*) that an agent possesses about its environment, about other agents and about itself is partitioned in several "knowledge bases" or "worlds" (A3) that are used by the agent's functions. In addition, the agent may infer other agents' intentions (A13) and/or plans (A12). For decision making and planning its behavior, an agent uses its knowledge about the goals it can pursue (the decision space which is a network of predetermined goals; A5), the actions and plans that it can use (the action space which is a network of predetermined plans; A7) and the available resources (A19).

Now, let us examine how these functions typically support a social agent's behavior. The *perception function* (P1) receives messages from its environment or from other agents. The perceived information (A1) is then interpreted and categorized by *function P2*, using relevant rules from the interpretation-categorization knowledge base (A2): information is hence categorized in the relevant worlds and/or belief knowledge bases (A3). If needed, *function P3* is activated in order to reason on the agent's beliefs and/or on the models of other agents (A3). Function P3 can use metarules for reasoning on its beliefs (A14), as well as various rule bases that model evolution laws of the agent's environment (A16) and the anticipated or hypothesized behaviors of other agents (A15). Hypothetical reasoning and truth maintenance are examples of reasoning strat-

---

[6]This section corresponds to the subject index agent architecture in Bond and Gasser (1992).

Input message

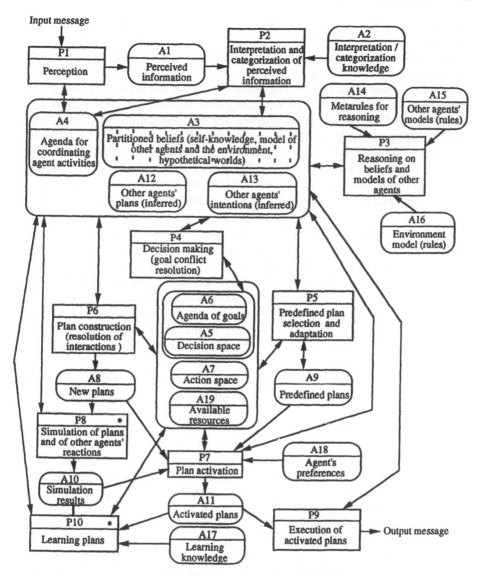

Figure 1.2 *General architecture of a social agent.*

egies that can be implemented in function P3. Function P3 can also be used
to infer other agents' intentions (A13) and/or plans (A12). *Function P4 is*
responsible for selecting from the decision space (A5) the goals that the agent
can try to reach, given the current state of its beliefs (A3) and the intentions
of other agents (A13): selected goals are put in the agenda of goals (A6) which
is also used by the planning functions P5, P6, and P10. Function P4 is also
responsible for resolving conflicts between activated goals. *Function P5 tries*

to select from the action space (and eventually adapt) predefined plans (A9) that can be used to reach the activated goals. If no predefined plan is available, *function P6* is activated in order to construct a new plan (A8). Function P6 is also responsible for solving eventual conflicts occurring between plans, based on available resources (A19). The agent may have the capacity of simulating the effects of its new plans (A8), taking into account the great beliefs (A3, A12, A13). *Function P8* is responsible for this simulation: it creates hypothetical worlds (in A3) which are used to record the effects of the simulation; it activates function P3 through the agenda for coordination (A4); it evaluates the results of the simulation (A10). *Function P7* is responsible for choosing the plans (A11) that will be activated, taking into account the agent's preferences (A18) and eventually the results of the simulation (A10). *Function P9* is responsible for executing activated plans (A11): messages are sent to the agent's environment and/or to other agents; relevant modifications are applied on the belief knowledge base (A3). Coordination between the various functions is again mediated by the coordination agenda (A4). An agent may have learning capabilities. *Function P10* uses learning knowledge or heuristics (A17) to analyze activated plans (A11) and their consequences on the agent's belief knowledge bases (A3, A12, A13), and eventually simulation results (A10). If successful, function P10 includes new plans in the action space (A7) and new learned goals in the decision space (A5). Other learning processes (not shown in Figure 1.2) can also be invoked to acquire new rules for the bases that model the agent's environment evolution laws (A16), the anticipated or hypothesized behaviors of other agents (A15) and the interpretation-categorization knowledge base (A2).

We do not claim that this agent architecture is perfect, complete and adequate for any DAI system (see Chapter 5 and Part III for alternative proposals). Our aim is far less modest: we propose this model as a framework for discussing the main issues that are related to an agent involved in a MAS. For example, a rule-based expert system can be considered as a reactive agent and would only have simplified versions of the following functions: perception (P1) and interpretation (P2) correspond to the acquisition of new facts in the fact base (A3); reasoning on beliefs (P3) would consist of inferring new facts (forward-chaining strategy); decision making (P4) corresponds to the selection of some hypothesis or fact to be demonstrated (backward-chaining strategy); selection, choice, and execution of relevant rules (simplified versions of P5, P7, and P9) complete the inference cycle by updating the fact base (A3) and eventually sending messages to other expert systems or to users.

Lizotte and Moulin (1990) proposed an architecture for an intentional agent, considered as a planning system dealing with temporal information.

A number of researchers have proposed general architectures for agents involved in MAS (see Chapter 5 and Part III). Bouron et al. (1991) propose an agent model taking into account social behaviors. This model comprises a central component (decision module) which interacts with three peripheral components (perception, communication, and organization modules). The organization module manages the agent's commitments. The model distinguishes several levels of social complexity: mobile perceiving agent (MP), MP communicating agent (MPC), MPC committed agent, MPC committed delegating agent, and MPC committed joined agent.

In the field of MAS, several agent architectures use *blackboard systems* (Nii, 1986a,b). For the DVMT project Lesser and Corkill (1983) used two blackboards (one for the data and the other for the agent's goals). In the MINDS project, Huhns et al. (1987) also used two specialized blackboards. Hayes-Roth and her colleagues (1989) proposed an architecture composed of three interacting ''subagents'': the ''perception agent,'' the ''control agent,'' and the ''reasoning agent.'' The control and reasoning agents have a similar architecture composed of three main components: an agenda manager, a scheduler and an executor. Nierenburg and Lesser (1986) developed OFFICE, an assistant system for supporting clerical tasks in offices based on the management of agents' agendas. In this system the agent's architecture clearly identifies the functions of perception, goal generation, scheduling, planning and execution as well as the main knowledge structures an agent needs (goals, plans, scheduling knowledge, object schemas and instances, agent agenda, and representation of other agents' agendas).

Recently, Ferguson (1992) presented a new multilayered architecture for controlling autonomous mobile agents that allows a resource-bounded, goal-directed agent to promptly react to unexpected changes in its environment. This architecture also allows an agent to predictively reason about conflicts by constructing and projecting theories that hypothesize other agents' intentions. Ferguson's architecture is composed of three concurrently operating layers: a reactive layer, a planning layer, and a ''reflective/predictive'' layer. Kiss (1992) also proposed a layered architecture in which higher-level layers are ''maximally decoupled from the world'' in order to support generality (''fully deliberative actions''), while lower-level layers are ''maximally coupled to the world'' in order to support power (''simple reflex actions'').

4 THE GROUP PERSPECTIVE: ORGANIZATION

4.1 Structure and Organization[7]

Several multiagent system characteristics are directly related to the group of agents: group organization (Chapter 19), cooperation, negotiation (Chapter 7), and agent roles. Planning and communication will be discussed in Sections 5 and 6. Historically, DAI systems have had very limited flexibility for adapting their global behaviour, since usually they were designed to handle a single

---

[7]This section corresponds to the subject indexes articulation work, organizational knowledge and modeling, organizational structures policies and architectures in Bond and Gasser (1992).

aspect of the problem at hand, such as task allocation (Cammarata et al., 1983; Davis and Smith, 1983; Durfee and Lesser, 1987). Today, it is critical to develop a useful framework to make DAI systems more adaptable, following some basic notions of *organization* and *organizational change*. Therefore, it is helpful to have a better idea of what we mean by "organization." We first distinguish an organization from a structure.

In a multiagent environment, a *structure* is the pattern of information and control relationships that exist between agents, and the distribution of problem-solving capabilities among them. In cooperative distributed problem solving for example, a structure gives each agent a high-level view of how the group solves problems and the role that each agent plays within this structure. With this view, the agents can ensure that they meet conditions that are essential to successful problem solving, including the following (Corkill and Lesser, 1983):

- *Coverage:* any necessary portion of the overall problem must be within the problem-solving capabilities of at least one agent.
- *Connectivity:* agents must interact in a manner that permits the covered activities to be developed and integrated into an overall solution.
- *Capability:* coverage and connectivity must be achievable within the communication and computation resource limitations, as well as the reliability specifications of the group.

Generally, the structure must specify *roles* and *relationships* to meet these conditions. For example, to ensure coverage, the structure could assign roles to agents according to their competence and knowledge for a given subproblem. The structure must also indicate the connectivity information to the agents so that they can distribute subproblems to competent agents. This connectivity information should also allow agents with overlapping competences to avoid duplication of effort when solving the same subproblem.

An *organization* for DAI is less structured in perspective and more related to current organization theory (Maines, 1984; Strauss, 1978 and Chapter 19). For example, Gasser (1986) views an organization as a "particular set of settled and unsettled questions about beliefs and actions through which agents view other agents. Organizational change means opening and/or settling some different set of questions in a different way, giving individual agents new problems to solve and a different base of assumptions about the beliefs and actions of other agents."

Clearly, an organization should not be conceived as a structural relationship among a collection of agents or as a set of externally defined limitations to their activities. In fact, it is relevant to view the concept of organization as embedded in the beliefs, intentions, and commitments of agents themselves. In other words, an organization is defined as a set of agents with mutual commitments, global commitments, mutual beliefs, and, eventually, joint intentions when these agents act together to achieve a given goal. Obviously, notions such as beliefs, intentions and commitment are driven by the degree of cooperation that exists between agents, and by the spectrum of communication strategies that is offered to an agent in order to exchange beliefs, intentions, and commitments (see Chapter 6).

Malone (1990) proposes a comprehensive study of *group organization*. "A group of agents is an organization if they are connected in some way (arranged systematically) and their combined activities result in something better (more harmonious) than if they were not connected. An organization consists of: a group of agents; a set of activities performed by agents; a set of connections among agents; and a set of goals or evaluation criteria by which the combined activities of the agents are evaluated." Hence, group organization depends upon the capacity of agents to coordinate their activities. At this point, it is relevant to consider human organizations as a source of inspiration for DAI researchers who investigate organizational problems for MAS.

Chapter 19 proposes a detailed account of the impact of organizational intelligence in DAI.

4.2 Societies of Agents in DAI[8]

Human organizations, which are naturally distributed systems, have developed various kinds of solutions for the problems faced by the individuals who belong to them: distributed decision making, hierarchical control, group coordination activities, etc.

Several researchers have found a source of inspiration in works done in social and organizational sciences (Fox, 1981). As a starting point for the development of organizational models for MAS, they proposed several "social metaphors" such as the *scientific community* metaphor (Kornfeld and Hewitt, 1981) and the *contract-net* protocol (Smith and Davis, 1981). Malone (1990) analyzed in a systematic way analogies between computer systems and human organizations. He proposed a framework for analyzing different ways of segmenting and coordinating tasks among a group of agents. Werner (1989) developed a unified theory of communication, cooperation, and social structure as the foundation for the design of systems of agents that behave as a social unit or group. He proposed a formal account of an agent's intentional states and related the linguistic messages with their effects on the planning process. This approach allowed him to give an account of social cooperative action, because agents' intentional states are mutually modified by communicative exchanges (i.e., a conversation or a discourse). This theory of communication and social structure was used to give a formal analysis of the contract-net (Smith and Davis, 1981).

[8]This section corresponds to the subject indexes societies of agents, social metaphors, and social modeling in Bond and Gasser (1992).

Another contribution is Star's (1989) work on the "structure of ill-structured solutions." Star argued that the development of DAI should be based on a social metaphor, rather than on a psychological one, and suggested that systems should be tested with respect to their ability to meet community goals. Star suggested to use the concept of "boundary objects" derived from analyses of organizational problem solving in scientific communities. Boundary objects are those objects that are plastic enough to be adaptable across multiple viewpoints, yet maintaining continuity of identity.

Gasser and his colleagues (1989) developed a framework for representing and using organizational knowledge in DAI systems. For these authors, organizational change means opening and/or settling some different sets of questions, giving individual agents new problems to solve, and, more importantly, different assumptions about the beliefs and actions of other agents. To test these ideas, they developed a testbed called the intelligent coordination experiment (ICE) in which two classes of agents, red and blue, may move in cardinal directions (north, south, west, east) on a rectilinear grid. Gasser (1991) suggested that social conceptions of knowledge and action be considered a foundation for DAI. Bond (1990) shares the same view of organization for DAI as Gasser and uses the concept of commitment introduced by Becker (1960) in sociology. In Becker's description, individual agents participate in several organizations or settings. Hence, to regard their behavior in any one setting as consistent lines of activity, we must introduce the notion of commitments consequent to the individual's participation in other settings. These commitments constrain the individual's action, and can be explicitly used in negotiation between agents. In this context, an organization is defined as a set of agents with consistent mutual commitments. Notice that the issues of agent integrity, plans and resources, and their representation are also discussed in Bond's work. Recently, Shoham and Tennenholtz (1992) proposed a formal approach to deal with "useful laws for artificial agents societies." These social perspectives of DAI greatly influenced the solutions proposed for modeling group activities such as cooperation or coordination of agents.

In order to describe the actions of a group of agents working collaboratively, the notion of *joint intention* (see Chapters 6 and 18) is needed to bind team members' actions together. Usually, researchers have concentrated on the description of joint intentions in terms of nested structures of beliefs and mutual beliefs about the goals and intentions of other agents within a society of agents (Rao and Georgeff, 1991, 1993). Jennings and Mamdani (1992) view joint responsibility as a metalevel description of how cooperating agents should behave when engaged in collaborative problem solving. Their formal account of joint responsibility uses modal and temporal logics to define preconditions that must be satisfied before joint problem solving can start and to prescribe how individual team members should behave once it has: agents agree that they will obey a "code of conduct" to guide their actions and interactions while performing the joint activity.

5 THE GROUP PERSPECTIVE: COOPERATION, COORDINATION, AND PLANNING[9]

5.1 Coordination[10]

Malone (1990) notes that two of the most fundamental components of *coordination* are the *allocation of scarce resources* and the *communication of intermediate results*.

> For example, *synchronizing interdependent activities* involves both of these components. If one activity requires as inputs the results of other activities, then synchronizing the communication of intermediate results in required. In nondivisible scarce resources (such as assembly line time) must be shared, then allocating these resources requires spreading demands out over time, . . . In order to fulfill the allocation and communication functions of coordination, agents must be connected to each other. In order to communicate intermediate results, information must be transferred over these *information links*. . . . In order to allocate shared resources, activities must be able to transfer control over the shared resources. This ability often leads to the ability to prescribe behaviour, as well. Therefore, it is sometimes useful to distinguish *control links* as a special kind of information link that carries information the recipients are motivated to follow as instructions.

Mintzberg (1979) considered three fundamental coordination processes. *Mutual adjustment* is the simplest form of coordination. It occurs whenever two or more agents agree to share resources to achieve some common goal. Agents usually must exchange a lot of information and make many adjustments in their own behavior, depending on the behaviour of other agents. In coordination by mutual adjustment, no agent has any prior control over the others, and decision making is a joint process. Coordination in peer groups and in markets is usually a form of mutual adjustment (see Chapters 6 and 8). *Direct supervision* occurs when two or more agents have already established a relationship in which one agent has some control over the others. This prior relationship is usually established by mutual adjustment (as when an employee or subcontractor agrees to follow directions given by a supervisor). In this form of coordination, the supervisor controls the use of shared resources (such as human labor, computer processing time and money) by the subordinates and may also prescribe certain aspects of their behavior. In some cases the supervisor coordinates by *standardization*, establishing standard procedures for subordinates to follow in a number of situations. Routine procedures in companies or computer programs are examples of coordination by standardization.

[9]Several items in this section correspond to the subject indexes social knowledge, social metaphors, and social power in Bond and Gasser (1992).

[10]This section corresponds to the subject indexes authority, coordination, hierarchical organization, and markets in Bond and Gasser (1992).

Malone (1990) suggests that using these fundamental coordination processes, it is possible to construct sophisticated systems for coordination, two of the most prevalent ones being hierarchies and markets. *Hierarchies* are based on the process of direct supervision. Mutual adjustment works well in small groups. However, as the size of the groups (and the number of tasks) grows, the number of information links and the amount of information to be exchanged become prohibitive very quickly. A large group can be efficiently divided into subgroups if most of the necessary information transfer can occur within subgroups, and if the few interactions between subgroups can be handled by supervisors. Hence, a hierarchy may be implemented within the group. Subgroups may be coordinated either by mutual adjustment or by hierarchical control, depending on the application domain and the task characteristics.

Markets can be considered as another form of group organization based on mutual adjustment. Agents, each of whom controls scarce resources (such as labor, raw material, goods and money), agree to share some of their respective resources to achieve some mutual goal. Valued resources are exchanged, either with or without explicit prices. Once a contract has been made, there is an agreement in which the buyer becomes the supervisor of the supplier.

Many organizations implement mixed coordination processes partly based on mutual adjustment, direct supervision and standardization. These organizational frameworks are used as a source of inspiration for choosing adequate organizational structures when developing multiagent systems. According to Malone (1990), there are two general criteria for evaluating how well the coordination scheme itself performs: there is a trade-off between *flexibility* and *efficiency* in multiagent environments. This trade-off involves moving between, on the one hand, highly coupled structures with formalized procedures for dealing with almost all eventualities, and on the other hand, loosely coupled structures that depend on massive amounts of informal communication and mutual adjustment to adapt to rapidly changing complex environments.

Of course, coordination is central to MAS and distributed problem solving. Without coordination, a group of agents can quickly degenerate into a chaotic collection of individuals, since an agent only has a partial and imprecise view of the overall system and its actions may interfere with rather than support other agents' actions. The easiest way of ensuring a coherent behavior seems to consist of providing the group with an agent which has a wider perspective of the system. This central controller could gather information from the agents of the group, create plans, and assign tasks to individual agents in order to ensure global coherence. However, such an approach is impractical in realistic applications because it is very difficult to create such a central controller informed of all agents' intentions and beliefs. In order to provide agents with a better idea about how their actions contribute to the group behavior, a number of approaches have been proposed such as techniques dealing with commitments and conventions (Jennings, 1993) or reasoning based on knowledge (Mazer, 1991).

5.2 Cooperation[11]

Implementing efficient ways of *cooperation* among agents is a central issue for MAS development (see Chapter 6). Durfee et al. (1989) propose four generic goals for cooperation among a group of agents: increase the task completion rate through parallelism; increase the set or scope of achievable tasks by sharing resources (information, expertise, physical devices, etc.); increase the likelihood of completing tasks by undertaking duplicate tasks, possibly with different methods of performing those tasks; decrease the interference between tasks by avoiding harmful interactions. Network control is difficult in a network of agents because limited interagent communication restricts each agent's view of network problem-solving activity. Durfee et al. (1989) suggest that effective MAS network control involves balancing efficient use of communication and processing resources, high reliability, responsiveness to unanticipated situations, and solution quality based on application-specific criteria.

Bond (1989) examines the cooperation of specialists with distributed knowledge, in the context of knowledge-based support for collaboration among different engineering departments in carrying out large design tasks. In reality, Bond examines the problem of *collaborative reasoning* in which intelligent systems cooperatively produce an agreed design. It is, however, closely related to Hewitt's organizational problem solving using the notion of *microtheories* (hewitt, 1986).

Conte et al. (1991) proposed characterizing cooperation in terms of agent goal adoption. Starting with a formal definition of *common goals*, they distinguish three categories of cooperation modes: accidental, unilaterally intended, and mutual cooperation.

In fact, there is a *degree of cooperation* that characterizes the amount of cooperation between agents that can range from fully cooperative (i.e., total cooperation) to antagonistic (Decker, 1987). *Fully cooperative* agents that are able to resolve nonindependent problems often pay a price in high communication costs. These agents may change their goals to suit the needs of other agents in order to ensure cohesion and coordination. Conversely, the *antagonistic* systems may not cooperate at all and may even block each others' goals. Communication costs required by these systems are generally minimal. In the middle of the spectrum lie traditional systems that lack a clearly articulated set of goals. Notice that most real systems have a weak degree of cooperation.

Total cooperation is applied in the *cooperative distributed problem-solving* (CDPS) studies (Durfee et al., 1989), where agents can work together in a loosely coupled network to solve problems that are beyond their individual capabilities. In this network, each agent is capable of resolving complex problems and can work independently, but the problems faced by the agents cannot

---

[11]This section corresponds to the subject indexes cooperation, distributed problem solving, and multiple perspectives in Bond and Gasser (1992).

be completed without total cooperation. Total cooperation is necessary because no single agent has sufficient knowledge and resources to solve a given problem, and different agents might have the expertise to solve its different parts (i.e., subproblems). Generally, CDPS agents cooperatively build a solution to a problem by using their local knowledge and resources to individually solve subproblems, and then by integrating these subproblems solutions into an overall solution. For example, geographically separated aircraft have different perceptions because their sensors pick up different signals. Only by combining information about their views are they able to form an overall picture of aircraft movements to resolve conflicts among them. Note that CDPS is particularly useful when distributed control becomes uncertain (Lesser and Corkill, 1981). The presence of other uncertainties such as incomplete or imprecise information, or an aggregation of information from multiple sources, makes the need for total cooperation even more crucial (Bonissone, 1986).

CDPS is also particularly useful when each agent has specific knowledge and does not have a clear idea of what it might do or what information it might exchange with others. In this context, Smith and Davis (1981) advocate the use of cooperative frameworks that minimize communication, allow load balancing, and distribute control, while also maintaining coherent behavior. Their proposed solution, contract-nets, is based on negotiation mechanism discussed in Section 5.3.

The fully cooperative-to-antagonistic spectrum has been surveyed by Genesereth et al. (1986) and Rosenschein and Genesereth (1985). They note that the situation of total cooperation, known as the *benevolent agent assumption*, is accepted by most DAI researchers, but that it is not always true in the real world where agents may have conflicting goals. Such conflicting goals are reflected, for example, by a set of personal meeting-scheduling agents where each agent tries to schedule a meeting at the best time for its particular owner. To study this type of interaction, Genesereth and Rosenschein define agents as entities operating under the constraints of various rationality axioms that restrict their choices.

5.3 Negotiation[12]

Negotiation plays a fundamental role in human cooperative activities, allowing people to resolve conflicts that could interfere with cooperative behavior (see Chapter 7). Durfee et al. (1989) define negotiation as the process of improving agreement (reducing inconsistency and uncertainty) on common viewpoints or plans through the structured exchange of relevant information. Generally, researchers in DAI use a negotiation mechanism to coordinate a group of agents. A number of very different approaches with varying techniques, but all embodying aspects of negotiation, have been developed by drawing on the rich

---

[12]This section corresponds to the subject indexes contract net and negotiation in Bond and Gasser (1992).

diversity of how humans negotiate in different contexts (Davis and Smith, 1983; Rosenschein and Genesereth, 1985; Conry et al., 1988; Sycara, 1989b).

One of the most studied protocols for negotiation goes back to the human organization metaphor (Davis and Smith, 1983). The *contract-net protocol* (Smith and Davis, 1981) has been one of the most influential negotiation approaches proposed for MAS. It was inspired by contracting processes in human organizations. Agents coordinate their activities through contracts to accomplish specific goals. An agent, acting as a *manager*, decomposes its contract (the task or problem it was assigned with) into subcontracts to be accomplished by other *potential contractor* agents. For each subcontract the manager announces a task to the network of agents. Agents receive and evaluate the announcement. Agents with appropriate resources, expertise, and information reply to the manager with *bids* that indicate their ability to achieve the announced task. The manager evaluates the bids it has received and awards the task to the most suitable agent, called the contractor. Finally, manager and contractor exchange information together during the accomplishment of the task. Parunak (1987) used this protocol to develop a manufacturing control system.

In another influential negotiation protocol, Cammarata et al. (1983) studied *cooperation strategies for resolving conflicts* among plans of a group of agents. They applied these strategies to the air traffic control domain, where the goal is to enable each agent (aircraft) to construct a flight plan that will maintain a safe distance with each of the aircrafts located in its flying area and satisfy other constraints such as reaching the desired destination with minimum fuel consumption. These authors chose a policy they called *task centralization*, in which agents involved in a potentially conflicting situation (airplanes becoming too close according to their current headings) choose one of the agents involved in the conflict to resolve it. The agent acts as a centralized planner (see Section 5.5) to develop a multiagent plan that specifies the concurrent actions of all the planes involved. The agents use negotiation to decide which of them is most able to do the planning. This ability can be evaluated on the basis of different criteria permitting to identify for instance the most-informed agent or the most-constrained agent.

Lâasri et al. (1992) describe a generic model, called the *recursive negotiation model*, that can serve as a basis for classifying and specifying where conflict resolution among multiple experts, viewpoints or types of reasoning is needed when building a sophisticated cooperative distributed problem-solving system. This model defines where and how negotiation can be applied and structures problem solving into four stages: problem formulation, focus of attention, allocation of goals or tasks to agents, and achievement of goals or tasks. Through this model Lâasri and her colleagues emphasize that negotiation may be a recursive, complex and pervasive process that is used to resolve conflicts in both domain-level and control-level problem solving.

The preceding negotiation protocols assume that agents are cooperative, hence pursuing some common goal. Sycara (1989b) has dealt with situations where cooperative behavior cannot be assumed and resolution of ensuing conflicts is necessary. Conflict resolution is achieved through direct negotiation among interacting agents or through a third party. She developed a system that resolves adversarial conflicts in the domain of labor relations. Three agents are involved: the employer, the employees' union representative, and a mediator. Employer and union agents usually have conflicting goals. The mediator generates offers and counteroffers in order to narrow the differences between the parties.

5.4 Coherent Behavior[13]

Assuming that a group of agents is cooperating to some extent, the problem is to know how these agents can achieve coherent behavior or global coherence. *Global coherence* means that actions of agents make sense with respect to the common goals of the entire group. Of course, the structure that is developed says something about how the group achieves coherence. For example, Kornfeld and Hewitt (1981) present a team structure they term a *scientific community metaphor* for cooperative distributed problem solving. This structure is based on the observation that "scientific communities are highly parallel systems." Agents are structured into loose classes that have general problem-solving goals. Proposers suggest possible solutions to the problem at hand. Proponents then collect and present evidence in favor of a proposal, while skeptics collect and present evidence to disprove this proposal. Evaluators examine proposals and balance the system so that more work is done on those proposals that seem to be more favorable. Note that evaluators, by controlling which proposals seem more favorable, provide *metalevel control* without altering the structure of agents.

The information communicated among agents also affects coherence. In this respect, Durfee and Lesser (1987) have shown that there are three major characteristics of communicated information that affect a coherent behavior: relevance, timeliness, and completeness. For a given message, *relevance* measures the amount of information that is consistent with the solution derived by the group of agents. Irrelevant messages may redirect the receiving agent into wasting its processing resources on attempts to integrate inconsistent information, so higher relevance of communicated information can result in more global coherence since this information stimulates work along the solution path. The *timeliness* of a transmitted message measures the extent to which a transmitted message will influence the current activity of the receiving agent. In this way, any transmitted information, which redirects the receiving agent to work in a more promising area, must be sent promptly. Finally, *completeness* of a message measures the fraction of a complete solution that the message represents. Completeness affects coherence by reducing the number of partially or fully redundant messages communicated between agents.

---

[13]This section corresponds to the subject indexes coherence, metalevel knowledge, and control in Bond and Gasser (1992).

These characteristics of communicated information are affected by both the agent's *social abilities* (which generate the potential information that can be transmitted), and the *communication policy* (which decides what information should be sent, to what agents, and when). So, increased global coherence could be achieved by improving only an agent's social abilities, by improving only communication policies, or by a combination of both. In each of these cases, more coherent decisions result if an agent has a better understanding of what it has already done, what it is likely to do, and the activities and intentions of other agents.

5.5 Planning[14]

Bond and Gasser (1988, p. 21) indicate that "we can achieve greater coordination by aligning behaviour of agents toward common goals, with explicit divisions of labour. Techniques such as centralized planning for multiple agents, plan reconciliation, distributed planning, organizational analysis, are ways of helping to align the activities of agents by assigning tasks after reasoning through the consequences of doing those tasks in particular orders."

A *multiagent plan* is a plan which has been generated for multiple executing agents. *Multiagent planning* is the process of creating a multiagent plan. Planning may be done by a single agent or by several agents (see Section 8). In *centralized multiagent planning* one agent is responsible for building a multiagent plan that specifies all the agents' planned actions. This approach has been chosen by Cammarata et al. (1983) for the air traffic control problem: Agents (aircrafts) first negotiate to choose a coordinator among them. The coordinator then creates a multiagent plan to be performed by the aircrafts involved in the conflict. Another way of implementing centralized multiagent planning was proposed by Georgeff (1988): the plans of individual agents are formed first; then a central planning agent collects the local plans and analyzes them to identify potential conflicts. This agent tries to solve the conflicts by modifying the local plans and introducing communication commands into them so that agents synchronize appropriately.

In *distributed multiagent planning*, the planning activities are divided among the group of agents. This approach is used when there is not a single agent with a global view of the group activities. Von Martial (1992) distinguishes two classes of subproblems of distributed planning: task-driven planning and plan coordination. In *task-driven planning systems*, there is an initial goal or task which is decomposed into subgoals or subtasks and distributed among several planners (top-down problem decomposition). In contrast, *plan coordination* deals with situations in which the agents' plans are preexisting (agent-

---

[14]This section corresponds to the subject indexes conflict resolution, constraints, distributed control, centralized control, distributed planning, distributed reasoning and search, functionally accurate/cooperative approach (FA/C), multiagent planning, representing action structures, task allocation, and task decomposition in Bond and Gasser (1992).

centered view) and the problem is to reconcile the given plans before they are performed in a common environment.

Generally, multiagent planning needs some kind of plan synchronization. This synchronization may be performed at several points: during the plan decomposition, during the plan construction, or after the plan construction. Agents' plans may be conflicting because of incompatible states, incompatible orders of activities or incompatible use of resources. Such conflicts can be solved by a particular agent (coordinator or mediator) or a solution may be reached through negotiation. Von Martial (1992) proposed a model for coordinating plans that are previously made by autonomous agents: plans are given and the approach aims at coordinating them by resolving conflicts. "Plan coordination is done via relations resolution and communication. The main contributions of this work include a detailed taxonomy of relations between multiagent plans, strategies for coordination based on these relations, and a communication framework for synchronizing plans." Multiagent plan relations imply a modification of agents' plans. In case of conflict, negative relations are handled by resolving the conflict; in case of reinforcement, positive relations are used to take advantage of converging plans. Klein (1991) proposed a model for conflict resolution based on the idea that "general conflict resolution expertise exists separately from domain-level design expertise, and that this expertise can be instantiated in the context of particular conflicts into specific advice for resolving those conflicts."

Conry et al. (1988, 1991) developed a negotiation protocol (called *multistage negotiation*) for cooperatively resolving resource allocation conflicts. The application domain was the monitoring and control of a complex communication system. The protocol starts with the generation of an initial plan and consists of several cycles of sending requests for secondary goals, local examination, generation of alternative plans, and sending responses.

Durfee and Lesser (1987) proposed an approach called *partial global planning* in which agents build local plans and share these plans to identify potential improvements in coordination (see Section 8 for more details). Unlike multiagent planning which assumes that a plan is formed before agents begin to act, partial global planning allows agents to interleave planning and actions: agents tentatively plan coordinated interactions and react to unanticipated situations by modifying their plans. This approach was applied to a multiagent testbed, called the *distributed vehicle monitoring testbed* (DVMT) (see Section 3).

Lesser (1991) notes that "the *Functionally Accurate/Cooperative* model (FA/C) was developed in what were perceived as deficiencies in the conventional model of how agents in a distributed system should interact. In the conventional model, tasks are decomposed to that each agent has sufficient data to solve its assigned sub-problems completely and accurately with little or no interaction with other agents." For many applications (distributed interpretation, distributed planning and resource allocation, etc.) this model of task decomposition is inappropriate. In the FA/C model, "agents need not have all the necessary information locally to solve their sub-problems, and agents interact through the asynchronous, co-routine exchange of partial results.'' A series of increasingly sophisticated cooperative control mechanisms for coordinating agents have been developed, including integration of data- and goal-directed control, use of static metalevel information specified by an organizational structure, and use of dynamic metalevel information developed in partial global planning.

In DAI, agents should manage their distributed *resources* which might be physical (such as communication capabilities) or informational (such as information about the problem decomposition). Agents must adapt their plans in order to take into account the availability of shared resources. Sathi and Fox (1989) examine the resource reallocation problem that requires multiagent choices under multiple criteria, most of which are based on qualitative attributes. Their work is motivated by human negotiation procedures such as logrolling, bridging, and unlinking. The reallocation process is viewed as being constraint-based, constraints being used both for evaluation of existing alternatives and for creating new ones. Sycara and her colleagues (1991) present the *distributed constraint heuristic search* model and mechanisms to guide concurrent, asynchronous distributed search. They use some measures of the search space characteristics, called ''textures,'' that are used to focus the attention of agents during search and allow them to make good decisions both in terms of quality of system solution and performance.

6 THE GROUP PERSPECTIVE: COMMUNICATION AND INTERACTIONS[15]

Agents may interact together either through explicit linguistic actions (communication) or through nonlinguistic actions modifying the world in which they are acting. Communication enables agents to exchange information and to coordinate their activities. In multiagent systems two main strategies may be used to support communication. Agents can exchange *messages* directly or they can access a shared data repository (called a *blackboard*) in which information can be posted and retrieved. In DAI the possible solutions to the communication problem range between those involving no communication to those involving high-level, sophisticated communication.

6.1 No Communication or Primitive Communications

In some cases an agent rationally infers other agents' plans without communicating with them. Schelling (1960) and Tubbs (1984) term this *tacit bargaining* and point out that it works best when agents' goals are not conflicting. To study this behavior, Genesereth et al. (1986) and Rosenschein (1986) used

---

[15]This section corresponds to the subject indexes interaction and communication, reasoning about communication, and message-passing semantics in Bond and Gasser (1992).

a game-theoretic approach characterized by payoff matrices that contain agents' payoffs for each possible outcome of an interaction. This approach also assumes that agents have common knowledge of the payoff matrix associated with the interaction, an assumption that may be unrealistic when considering that agents are nonbenevolent. Rosenschein and Breese (1989) extended this approach by providing agents with a mechansim for further refining agents' choice of rational moves: uncertainty about other players' moves is explicitly represented. However, there are difficulties with this approach. First, if all the agents are speculating on what others are going to do, the result could be an infinite nesting of beliefs, and the reasoning of each agent would be very difficult. Second, mutual rational deduction would lead to an enormous computational cost in a situation involving several agents. Indeed, agents must rely on sophisticated local reasoning compensating the lack of communication to decide on appropriate actions and interactions.

Primitive communication is restricted to some finite set of fixed signals (usually two) with fixed interpretations (Hoare, 1978). This communication strategy has been applied by Georgeff (1983) for multiagent planning to avoid conflicts between plans involving more than one agent. It has also been applied to coordinate parallel activities in robotic systems (Lozano-Perez, 1983). The limited number and types of signals available in this approach limit cooperation between agents. Hence, requests, commands, and complex intentions cannot be expressed using these signals.

6.2 Plan Passing and Message Passing

In the plan-passing approach, an agent A1 communicates its total plan to agent A2 and A2 communicates its total plan to A1. Whichever plan arrives first is accepted. While this method can achieve cooperation, it has severe problems (Rosenschein, 1986): total plan passing is computationally expensive; there is no guarantee that the resulting plan will be warranted by the recipient's knowledge base; total plan passing is not guaranteed by any medium of communication and is difficult to achieve in real world applications because there is a great deal of uncertainty about the present state of the world, as well as its future. Consequently, for real-life situations, total plans cannot be formulated in advance, and general strategies must be communicated to a recipient. The work by Hewitt and his colleagues (Hewitt, 1977; Kornfeld and Hewitt, 1981) an *Actor languages* is a significant application of *message passing* in DAI. The essential idea about actors is clearly summarized in the words of Agha and Hewitt (1988): "An actor is a computational agent which carries out its actions in response to processing a communication. The actions it may perform are: send communication to itself or to other actors; create more actors; specify the replacement behavior." The "replacement behavior" describes the new "Actor machine" produced after processing the communication, i.e., the new state of the Actor.

Note that Hewitt's intuition is fundamentally correct when he states that control of multiagent environments is best looked at in terms of communication structures. In his work, however, agents have an extremely simple structure, and the model gives no formal syntax, semantics, or pragmatics for such communication structures. Consequently, this model was rarely used as a theory of communication between complex agents.

Several other works in DAI have used classic message passing with a protocol and a precise content (Lesser and Corkill, 1981; Cammarata et al., 1983; Durfee et al., 1985). In a MAS, the complexity of communications depends upon the agents' characteristics. Reactive agents use sets of communication rules (or activities) that are triggered when specific states hold or predetermined events occur (these events may be messages received from other agents or changes perceived in the environment). The individual message types combined with their expected answers yield a protocol for interaction that spans more than one interaction. Such protocols have been developed for various systems such as the contract-net protocol (Smith and Davis, 1981) or cooperation protocols (Cammarata et al., 1983). Communication and action are usually interleaved. Hence, intentional agents must be able to create plans in which both linguistic and nonlinguistic actions are combined. Kreifelts and von Martial (1991) present a negotiation protocol that is used to coordinate the activities of planning agents.

Recently, Decker and Lesser (1993) proposed an approach to analyze the need for *metalevel communication* in DAI systems such as distributed sensor networks (see Chapter 16). They analyze static and dynamic organizational structures for naturally distributed, homogeneous, cooperative problem-solving environments. They specify how the performance of any static organization can be statistically described and under what conditions dynamic organizations do better or worse than static ones. They also show when metalevel communication about the actual state of problem solving will be useful to agents in constructing a dynamic organizational structure that outperforms a static one.

6.3 Information Exchanges through a Blackboard[16]

In AI, the *blackboard* is the model of shared memory that is most often used (Nii, 1986a,b; Corkill et al., 1986; Chaib-draa and Millot, 1987; Maitre and Lâasri, 1990). It is a repository on which agents write messages, post partial results, and obtain information. It is usually partitioned into several levels of abstraction appropriate for the problem at hand, and agents working at a particular level of abstraction have access to the corresponding blackboard level along with the adjacent levels. In that way, data that have been synthesized at any level can be communicated to higher levels, while higher-level goals can be filtered down to drive the expectations of lower-level agents. The simplicity with which the blackboard paradigm represents the classic problem of data-

---

[16]This section corresponds to the subject indexes blackboard systems and distributed blackboard systems in Bond and Gasser (1992).

driven versus goal-driven information flow is perhaps the reason why black-board models are widely used in existing distributed artificial intelligence systems.

Message passing and communication through a blackboard may be combined in complex systems. Each agent is composed of several subsystems (or "sub-agents") which exchange information using a local blackboard; agents communicate together by exchanging messages. Several MAS adopted this kind of architecutre. The DVMT uses a collection of identical blackboard-based systems to solve problems of monitoring and interpreting data from a set of sensors at spatially distributed locations which covers a region (Lesser and Corkill, 1983). In the MINDS system (Huhns et al., 1987) each user works with a blackboard-based agent to retrieve documents from its local data base or to get them from other agents.

6.4   High-Level Communication[17]

Research on natural language understanding, and, particularly, research on intentions in communication (Cohen et al., 1990) are relevant to DAI research because both research areas must investigate reasoning about multiple agents with distinct and possibly contradictory intentional states such as beliefs, facts, and intentions (see Chapters 12 and 13 for pragmatic examples of this approach). In natural language, examination of even simple dialogues illustrates the utility of mental states such as beliefs and intentions, and background knowledge. For example, to find missing sentences in a dialogue, a computer system needs to use background knowledge and likely intentions (i.e., plans) of the speaker. In this respect, Allen (1983, 1986) and Litman and Allen (1990) developed a natural language system using plans and goals to understand questions, generate helpful responses, and deal with indirect speech acts. However, their system did not give an explicit formal theory of how complex intentional states are formed during the communication process.

Cohen and Levesque (1990a,b) proposed a formal theory taking into account intentional states in the communication process. The basis of their communication theory is derived from a formal theory of rational interaction based on agents' intentions and commitments. Their major claim is that not all illocutionary acts (i.e., things you can do with an utterance) need be primitive, but rather can be treated as complex actions. Galliers (1988) extended this theory to situations involving conflicts between agents as well as cooperation. Her approach is based on a theory of agenthood, and considers multiagent and rational interaction as the basis for communication: it is no longer necessary to assume that agents are benevolent when participating in cooperative actions. Werner (1989, 1991) also takes an important step in this direction, proposing

---

[17]This section corresponds to the subject indexes modeling conversation, speech acts, metalevel communication, and natural language and DAI in Bond and Gasser (1992).

a general theoretical framework for designing agents with communicative and social competence. His framework is based on agent's cognitive states, such as knowledge and intentional states.

Winograd and Flores (1986) proposed to adopt a *"language/action perspective"* (see Chapter 20) where agents are seen as acting through the use of language. Hence, it is relevant to consider *speech-act theory* (Searle, 1969; Searle and Vanderveken, 1985) which provides a theoretical framework for studying the language used by persons when performing various kinds of *speech acts* such as requests, orders, promises. Social agents are able to reason about the mental states (beliefs, intentions, expectations) of other agents. For instance, to satisfy their own goals, they plan their speech acts to affect other agents' beliefs and intentions. Cohen and Perrault (1979) proposed a plan-based theory of speech acts which has been further extended in a theory of relationships among belief, intention, and rational communication (Cohen and Levesque, 1990a,b). Through an appropriate dialogue, agents can converge on shared mental plans (i.e., webs of mutual beliefs, commitments, and intentions) for how they should coordinate their activities (Chaib-draa, 1993; Grosz and Sidner, 1990).

Although speech-act theory has been widely applied to natural language processing such as dialogue systems or cooperative response systems (Kaplan, 1983), it has not been extensively used to implement communication interactions in MAS: several authors define the messages exchanged by MAS agents as speech acts, but still few systems provide their agents with capabilities to reason on mental states and speech acts (see Chapter 13).

From a larger perspective, interactions between social agents may be considered as taking place within *conversations*, and conversations may be viewed as coordinated cooperative interactions among agents (Gibbs and Mueller, 1990). Lewis (1969) emphasized the importance of *conventions* (regularities in behavior evolved by two or more people) to solve recurrent coordination problems. Grice (1975) proposed a theory of cooperation in conversation, considering that each participant in a conversation obeyed a *cooperative principle*: "make your conversational contribution such as required, at the stage it occurs, by the accepted purpose or the direction of the talk exchange in which you are engaged." These theories can provide important foundations for implementing sophisticated communication capabilities in MAS (Rousseau et al., 1993).

6.5 Person/Machine Interaction[18]

Usually, MAS involve both human and artificial agents (see Chapters 13 and 21). As for any software application, person/machine interaction in a MAS is a critical issue to make sure that the system will be effectively used by users.

---

[18]This section corresponds to the subject indexes person-machine collaboration, human-machine cooperation, DAI and interface in Bond and Gasser (1992).

Chang (1987) defined *participant systems* as computer systems that support collaborative intellectual tasks among a number of persons, possibly distributed in different locations. The proposed system provides mechanisms conducive to the establishment of social cohesiveness. Croft and Lefkowitz, (1988a,b) used the expert system shell KEE to build POLYMER, a system that supports users involved in cooperative activities that can be performed either by human or artificial agents. There are two main components in POLYMER: an "object management system" that maintains the objects relevant to the application and the "task manager," which assists users when they want to perform some tasks.

Pan and Tenenbaum (1991) describe an approach for integrating people and computer systems in large, geographically dispersed manufacturing enterprises. Their approach is based on a very large number of computerized assistants, called "intelligent agents (IAs)." Each IA supports "a clearly discernible task or job function, automating what it can and calling on the services of other IAs when necessary." Users participate in this society of agents through "personal assistants," a special kind of IA that knows how to communicate with humans (through multimedia interfaces), and with other IAs and a shared knowledge base (called the "knowledge service"; it is an object-oriented model of the enterprise).

There is a growing interest in computer systems which support group activities. This recent research field has been coined *computer-supported cooperative work* (CSCW) [Greif, 1988; Association for Computing Machinery (ACM), 1991], MAS can be used to enlarge the traditional perspective of team work: a team will be considered as a group of persons and computers that collaborate together in order to solve a common problem or to reach a common goal. In such a work organization, tasks are distributed among artificial and human agents in order to take advantage of the abilities of each team member (Steiner and Mahling, 1990). Artificial agents may thus be thought of as intelligent assistants to their users: they relieve human agents from tedious and time-consuming group activities such as searching and obtaining information from other team members, synchronizing agendas to organize a meeting, etc. In CSCW applications artificial agents can assist persons in different ways such as managing distributed data, filtering information, and coordinating activities among groups of users (Chang, 1987; Huhns et al., 1987; Malone, 1990; Pan and Tenenbaum, 1991).

7 SPECIFIC APPROACHES

In the preceding sections we have discussed several classical issues related to the involvement of agents and groups of agents in DAI systems. In this section we present some other approaches which shed new light on DAI problems.

7.1   From Open Information Systems Semantics to Ecosystems[19]

Hewitt (1986) proposed establishing the information processing foundations for taking action and making decisions in office work from an *open systems perspective*. He remarked that offices are inherently open systems because most information exchanges within the office and with its environment take place asynchronously. Open systems deal with large quantities of diverse information and exploit massive concurrency. Hewitt and Inman (1991) present a good overview of *open systems science* (OSS), its foundations and challenges. Hewitt and his colleagues identified primitives for concurrent systems, called *Actors*, and specified the laws that must hold for all Actor computations:

> Causality is local in Actor computations (there is no global entity or process). Computation is accomplished by Actors sending communications to one another. To send a communication to an Actor A, the sender must have a *handle* for A. Handles are somewhat like telephone numbers. When a communication arrives at an Actor, the actions of the Actor are determined by its current *Behaviour*. The Actor can process the message using any information available, but the available information is all local: the Actor's script, the Actor's *Acquaintances* (actors related to it), and any information in the message itself. An Actor may concurrently do any or all of the following: make local decisions; create more Actors, send more communications, replace its Behaviour (i.e., specify what Behaviour it will use to process the next communication it receives). All communications exist in the form of Actors, which are accessed only by sending messages along handles. Actor computations are conceived as *orchestrations of concurrent message-passes*. The Actor language was developed as a language independent characterization of concurrent systems. A *microtheory* is defined to be a derivational calculus, together with a prespecified automaton that can check the correctness of any individual derivation step, given only the step and no additional information. All conflicts are local in the sense that they occur at a particular time and place among local Participants. *Joint Activity* refers to any potentially-concurrent, interdependent activities. An activity is *self-reliant* to the extent that it can be carried out using only the resources that are local. Activities are *interdependent* to the extent that they are dependent on each other. Activities will be said to *conflict* if they interact in a way that prevents some of them from being completed. Self reliant and interpendent activities vary according to the following characteristics: *Late-arriving information* (participants have to take information into account as it arrives); *Multiple local authorities* (participants can react immediately to changing circumstances); *Division of labor* (involves the creation of sub-activities to physical distribute work and locally focus effort on a narrower range of joint activities); *Arm's length relationship* (enables participants to conceal internal activities from other participants). The trade-offs between self-reliant and interdependent activities is one of the most fundamental issues in OSS.

---

[19]This section corresponds to the subject index open systems, Actors in Bond and Gasser (1992). We will not quote the numerous papers that have been published in this area. We refer the reader to the papers published by Hewitt and his colleagues as a source of additional references.

Bond and Gasser (1988) note that

Actor models face (as other DAI approaches) the issues of coherence: the actor community must not degenerate into a society of bureaucrats that sends many messages but make little progress. Issues of Actor design, decisions on granularity of data and control representations, composition of actors into larger communities, constraints on actor behaviours, achieement of higher-level performance goals with only local knowledge, which are characteristics of other DAI approaches, still appear in Actor systems and have yet to be addressed comprehensively.

These issues have been addressed by Hewitt and Inman (1991). They proposed using an *organizational architecture*, called ORG, for organizing large-scale work. "Actors are universal primitives of concurrent computation. However, the design, construction, operation and maintenance of large-scale *Information Agencies* requires support for organization. *Organizations of Restricted generality (ORGs)* represent an extension of the Actor architecture, which provide support through the following facilities: the *Operations facility* provides resources (i.e. processing, storage, communications) for authorized tasks; the *Reporting facility* provides information for other facilities concerning what happened, when it happened and which participants were involved; the *Membership facility* keeps track of the ORG population, creates new memberships and terminates memberships as the ORG evolves; the *Liaison facility* controls communications crossing the ORG boundary; the *Management facility* controls the behavior of the ORG (it sets policies and procedures for ORG behaviour). These new features were presented in the *Open Information Systems Semantics* (OISS), a framework which integrates methods from Sociology and from Concurrent Systems Science (Hewitt, 1991).

Actors are very efficient when dealing with concurrent problems. However, they usually correspond to low-level processes composing a system and can be thought of as reactive agents. This low level of granularity of Actors can be an obstacle for the development of systems where agents need to implement complex behaviors based on reasoning on intentions, beliefs, plans, as well as on other agents' belief and intentions, etc. Usually, these systems are composed of a small number of complex agents interacting together. Hewitt's proposal of introducing special facilities for managing the organizational architecture of an open system can be considered as a step toward reducing the gap existing between the current use of Actors for constructing low-granularity systems and their application to the development of high-granularity systems. These facilities are also an important support for the designers using Actor languages.

Hogg and Huberman (1991) also considered DAI systems composed of a large number of agents, each agent having an individual, local view of the problem. They remark that

one of the difficulties in both the design and understanding of DAI systems comes from the lack of central controls and the ensuing conflicting, uncertain, imcomplete and delayed knowledge on the part of the agents. While considerable effort is being devoted to understanding the interactions among a few agents and developing operational DAI systems that can deal with simple problems, relatively little is known about the global behaviour of these systems as they are scaled up to deal with more realistic problems. This is an important issue since the individual agents must not only be designed to cooperate with each other, but also adapt appropriately to global consequences of their actions.

To evaluate the global dynamics of distributed systems, they consider them as *computational ecosystems* (Chapter 11), by analogy with similar biological and human organizations. Individual agents' choices correspond to the selection of appropriate resources for the solution of the problem. Since decisions are not centrally controlled, agents independently and asynchronously select from among the available choices the one with the highest payoff. Because the results of various choices can depend on what the other agents do, these payoffs will typically depend on the choices made by other agents. Imperfect information about the system state causes each agent's perceived payoff to differ from the actual value, with the difference increasing when there is more uncertainty in the information available to the agents. The authors describe a procedure for controlling *chaos* in distributed systems. It is based on a mechanism that rewards agents according to their actual performance. "Such a mechanism leads to the emergence of a diverse community of agents out of an essentially homogeneous one. This diversity in turn eliminates chaotic behaviour through a series of dynamical bifurcations that render chaos a transient phenomenon."

Ferber and Carle (1990) remarked that most Actor languages (like ABCL or Actalk) are not pure in the sense that several features have been incorporated in actor languages in order to make them easier to use. *Reflection* (Smith, 1982) is the ability for a system to model itself in terms of static description (by access to a representation) and dynamic execution (by controlling its execution mechanism). The goal of reflection is to define intelligent programs capable of reasoning and act upon themselves. Reflection is a useful tool for building complex and evolutionary languages, in which new constructs can be added using the language itself while the system is running. Ferber and his team developed MERING IV, an Actor language with reflection capabilities. MERING IV architecture is based on three levels: level M0 describes the virtual machine used for implementing the language; level M1 defines the core language based on the Actor model; level M2 provides abstract constructs through an object-oriented model (instances, classes, methods, etc.). Semantics of reflective systems is usually described using two functions: *reification* (the process of making explicit something usually implicit) and *reversion* (the process of making implicit an explicit structure). Ferber also indicates that reflection in object-oriented languages is based on a metaobject approach: every object has a metaobject that is its representation at the metalevel. Metaobjects and objects are causally related in such a way that all operations made at the metalevel have an impact on the structure and behavior of the basic-level objects. In MERING IV an agent's structure is specified by an actor/meta-

Actor pair: the actor is responsible for application domain actions, and the meta-Actor describes the agent's internal process and control. Meta-Actors are instances of classes defined at the metalevel: they describe the static and dynamic properties of objects seen as computing units. Message handling is performed by methods which are defined at the metalevel and executed as "self-methods" and the base level. Each object is responsible for its own way of handling messages and various message-handling schemes can be defined. Reflection has been used in different ways. New modes of message passing have been described in the language through the redefinition of metamethods. More complex agents can be built in MERING IV, using metamethods to describe the agents' behavioral model: thanks to the language reflexive properties, these agents are still able to communicate with elementary agents, which provides a solution to the general DAI problem of interactions between heterogeneous agents.

Ferber and Jacopin (1991) proposed *eco-problem solving* as an approach to solve a distributed problem by a technique involving agents representing the objects of the world on which the problem applies (see Chapter 11 for more details). These "eco-agents" are Actor-based and their behaviors are very simple. The interactions between agents with different behaviors allow the system to solve the problem. These authors show how to encode problems with eco-agents and illustrate their approach with classical AI problems (block world, robots, etc.).

Bouron and his colleagues (1991) present the MAGES system, which is a testbed for experimenting with different kinds of interactions between agents using heterogeneous architectures and behaviors. MAGES is implemented in ACTALK, a generic Actor language defined in Smalltalk. The language enables the designer to specify groups of agents as higher-level agents and to model the group's behavior as well as the behavior of its members.

7.2 Autonomous Agents

The approaches that we have presented up to now are developed in the main stream of current AI research. However, a group of researchers advocates a different approach to solve real life problems. Let us quote Brooks (1991):

> I, and others, believe that human level intelligence is too complex and little understood to be correctly decomposed into the right subpieces at the moment and that even if we knew the subpieces we still would not know the right interfaces between them. . . . I therefore argue for a different approach to creating artificial intelligence:
>
> - We must incrementally build up the capabilities of intelligent systems, having complete systems at each step of the way and thus automatically ensure that the pieces and their interfaces are valid.
> - At each step we should build complete intelligent systems that we let loose in the real world with real sensing and real action. Anything less provides a candidate with which we can delude ourselves.

Brooks adds: "We do claim that there need be no explicit representation of either the world or the intentions of the system to generate intelligent behaviour for the agents." In her editorial section of the book *Designing Autonomous Agents*, Maes (1990) summarizes the main lines of this research area:

Since 1970 the *Deliberative Thinking* paradigm has dominated AI research. Its main thesis is that intelligent tasks can be implemented by a reasoning process operating on a symbolic internal model. Emphasis is put on explicit knowledge, rational choice and problem solving. This approach has been proven successful in knowledge-based task areas such as expert level reasoning. However, only poor results have been obtained in its application to research on autonomous agents. The few systems built show deficiencies such as brittleness, inflexibility, no real time operation, etc. . ... For a few years, some researchers have been developing new ideas on how autonomous agents should be organized, which led to radically different architectures. The emphasis in these architectures is on more direct coupling of perception and action, distributedness and decentralization, dynamic interaction with the environment and intrinsic mechanisms to cope with resource limitations and incomplete knowledge.

Maes (1990) summarizes the main ideas advocated by Brooks:

One key idea in these new architectures is that of *emergent functionality*. The functionality of an agent is viewed as an emergent property of the intensive interaction of the system with its dynamic environment. ... A second important idea is that of *task-level decomposition*. An agent is viewed as a collection of modules which each have their own specific competence. These modules operate autonomously and are solely responsible for the sensing, modelling, computation or reasoning, and motor control which is necessary to achieve their specific competence. Communication among modules is reduced to a minimum and happens on an information-low level. There is no global internal model, nor is there a global planning activity with one hierarchical goal structure. Finally, the global behaviour of the agent is not necessarily a linear composition of the behaviours of its modules, but instead more complex behaviours may emerge by the interaction of behaviours generated by the individual modules.

Maes adds that a third idea becoming prevalent in much of this research domain is the exploitation of reasoning methods which operate on representations close to the raw sensor data. As an example, we will describe the work of Steels and his team on analogical representation. Steels (1990) compares symbolic representations which are based on a categorization of reality (a category is an invariant property of a set of objects) and analogical representations that represent a situation without prior categorization. An example is a spatial map in which the objects' positions are represented by locations on a map rather than coordinate descriptions or descriptions relative to the position of other objects. Steels indicates that analogical representations can be built for any kind of sensory information. Analogical representations have several advantages over symbolic representations: they do not assume a complex interpretation process to transform sensory data into symbolic representation; they contain more precision; they are easily mapped onto an "active" memory, i.e., the processing array of a data-level parallel computer; they allow the use of quite different operations during the problem-solving process. Steels remarks: "In a purely symbolic approach, sensory interpretation, planning, action selection and motor control take place by performing manipulations of symbolic structures. Analogical representations require a different approach. What we propose is to create various spatio-temporal structures which can then be used by other processes to make decisions." The model that has been used for manipulating analogical representations is similar to the Actor model in several respects, except that Actors are localized both in time and space. These Actors are called *agents* and the resulting model a *multiagent automaton*. Multiagent automata can be viewed as a generalization of cellular automata. A multiagent automaton operates on a grid of cells, its agents being located on specific cells of the grid. The agents' behavior is localized in both space and time. In an experiment Steels and his team conducted, a robot is wandering around in a place containing objects, some of which contain certain foods. The robot does not know the place, and after exploring it, it should recall where food sources are. The robot clearly needs to use some internal model of the world. The representation that is used is an analogical map on which obstacles as well as food sources are indicated using markers. These research activities on autonomous agents are obviously important for domains like robotics, the manipulation of analogical data and analogical reasoning. They may also have an impact on other DAI branches as well as on artificial intelligence in general.

7.3 Intelligent and Cooperative Information Systems[20]

Intelligent and cooperative information systems (ICIS) is a discipline that emerged during the early 1990s and gathers researchers from the fields of information systems, artificial intelligence, data bases, software engineering, and programming languages. They aim at integrating AI and information system technologies (Huff and Mylopoulos, 1992; Brodie and Ceri, 1992; Huhns et al., 1993, also Chapter 19).

Brodie and Ceri (1992) write that

> an information system (IS) can considered as *intelligent* when it incorporates reasoning mechanisms. Intelligence can be used to improve the quality of user interaction and IS functionality: explaining aspects of system's beahviour; reasoning about the results of computation; presenting conditional or hypothetical answers based on the existence of future events or guesses concerning incomplete information; allowing maximal abstraction from the physical realization of ISs; combining meta-information (i.e. the repository) with information in a simple and effective way; presenting the above features in the easiest and most effective

---

[20]This section corresponds to the subject index organizational information systems in Bond and Gasser (1992).

way for end-users. .... Intelligence can be added to the internal mechanisms of ISs to provide new or improved IS functionality and performance. Examples of these functionalities include: enhancing IS decision making or reasoning capabilities by means of features typical of expert systems and decision support systems; reactive (i.e. event-driven) behaviour within the IS; maintaining integrity constraints by means of active rules; supporting non-deductive forms of inference (e.g. induction of rules or constraints); supporting non-determinism which allows the IS to choose any of several answers to a given query; supporting case-based reasoning where information is structured according to previous cases; supporting forms of introspection (i.e. reasoning about IS meta-knowledge).

An ICIS is a system that provides forms of cooperation and intelligence. Cooperative ISs are defined in the terms of the ability of two or more systems to interact in order to execute tasks jointly (*interoperability*).

Examples of potential ICIS applications are organizations such as a hospital in which several persons and services (doctors, nurses, laboratories, etc.) collaborate to diagnose a patient illness, find and administrate the right treatment, to monitor a patient's progress, etc. This perspective is not far from the approach proposed by Pan and Tenenbaum (1991) to integrate people and computers in geographically dispersed manufacturing enterprises (see Section 6.5).

The interesting point about this research initiative is that it envisions the incorporation of DAI technology in future information systems. This trend may be a proof of the maturity of DAI as a research field. We can draw a parallel with the evolution of expert system (ES) technology during the 1980s. During the early 1980s ES technology migrated from research laboratories to industry: by that time expert systems were considered as prototypes or stand-alone systems. When ES technology matured during the 1980s, people in industry seriously considered the possibility to integrate expert systems in corporate information systems: companies were adopting ES technology in the same way they had adopted data base technology during the preceding decade. The 1990s could be the decade marking the integration of DAI technology in corporate information systems.

8. THE DESIGNER'S PERSPECTIVE

DAI literature is very abundant and covers a variety of topics, techniques and experiments. Facing such an abundance, a designer or a project manager may be confused by so many alternatives and may be wondering how to decide if DAI technology can bring about relevant solutions to corporate problems, how to start a project, how to make critical choices related to hardware and development software, how to analyze the current situation, how to select relevant DAI techniques, etc. These questions have not been addressed in literature in a comprehensive way yet and we think that they will become an important topic in the years to come. In this section we provide the reader with directions to investigate: analysis and design methods, design tools and testbeds, and applications.[21]

Before starting the development of a MAS, a designer may wonder if any analysis and design methods for DAI are available, as it is the case in domains such as software engineering, information system development, data base design or object-oriented system design. Surprising enough, analysis and design methods are quite rare in DAI literature.

Decker and his colleagues (1989) proposed a framework for evaluating research in CDPS. Their aim was to "provide a framework for understanding the interrelationships of disparate research efforts in order to assess progress in the field." They provide a "set of questions that relate to such things as the class of problem domains and environment that an approach can handle, the theoretical soundness of the approach, the software and hardware provided, and how the approach addresses the important issues of CDPS themselves." As an indication for the reader, we will only list the categories of questions (the number of questions is in parentheses) proposed by Decker and his colleagues: limit domain and environment assumptions (12); discover paradigms for building cooperating agents (6); develop methods or assessing global coherence (6); theories of organizational behavior and control (17); guaranteed responsiveness and fault tolerance (7); effective CDPS communication protocols (6); sophisticated agents (4); system and hardware support (7); develop general and representative hard-domain problems (8).

Werner (1992) proposes a framework that can be used to understand the relationships between users, programmers, designers, and the MAS to be designed or used (called the object system) (see Chapter 2). There are different ways of designing a MAS. A designer can create a MAS as a traditional piece of software. But in a given MAS the agents (called *object-agents*) may be able to evolve autonomously, creating their own plans, choosing goals, etc. Programming such a system can be viewed as a matter of influencing it by providing it with some initial knowledge, a given problem or directives. Werner distinguishes *meta-agents* such as a user, a programmer, or a designer, that are agents external to the object system, which is composed to *object-agents*. Using the notion of mode of interaction based on "well-defined channels," Werner tries to clarify various types of *metarelationships* between the meta-agents and the object system. Different modes of interaction correspond to different ways of changing and relating to the object system. Werner differentiates *invasive interactions* that could directly affect the inner mental state of an agent interactions that are compatible with exchanges occurring within the object system.

Woods and his colleagues (1990) present a design framework called "joint human-machine cognitive systems." They are concerned with the design of interaction computer programs which optimize the cognitive performance of the higher-order system made up of people and machines. Their primary focus

---

[21]This section corresponds to the subject indexes DAI architectures, DAI methodologies, observing modeling and describing distributed system behavior, and distributed knowledge and knowledge representation in Bond and Gasser (1992).

is on how the machine component should be designed to meet this system-level performance criterion. They perform an empirical examination of people interacting with an expert system for troubleshooting. They also develop a notation and a method for charting and analyzing interactive problem solving.

Goodson and Schmidt (1990) propose a method for decomposing a MAS problem into functional units, identifying units which the machine can perform well and the human poorly, and for building a machine problem solver for that unit. They also identify the need to design a joint problem-solving method in which the human and computer share responsibility. Their implicit metaphor is one of industrial engineering, in which a one-person job becomes too complex, and is so divided into a two-person job which requires a complete redesign of the job itself. They discuss in detail an application of this design strategy in a real-time problem domain where the main task is vehicle tracking via remote sensing.

Moulin and Cloutier (1994) present the "multiagent scenario-based method," a multiagent system design approach based on the analysis and design of scenarios involving human and artificial agents. This method is well suited to model systems supporting human/computer cooperative work. Different design techniques are proposed to describe scenarios and agents' behavior: beahvior diagrams, data models, transition diagrams, object life cycles, and object behavior diagrams. This approach proposes structured analysis and design steps following a philosophy familiar to software engineering or object-oriented design methods (Rumbaugh et al., 1991) or knowledge engineering (KADS methodology: Heyward et al., 1988; Hickman, 1989).

Knowledge acquisition for DAI systems is another area which has not been really investigated yet. What kind of problems face a knowledge engineer when studying collaborative activities among a group of persons? How can the activities that can be supported by a MAS be determined? What kind of system interface is suited for helping a group of users involved in a cooperative activity? It will be worth considering work done by researchers in various areas such as knowledge acquisition (see, for instance, Boose and Gaines, 1988) and distributed decision making (Rasmussen et al., 1991).

The designer of a DAI system must be aware of the large body of literature that presents *experimental testbed*, *design tools*, and *special-purpose languages* for DAI. For more information about these subjects we refer the reader to Bond and Gasser (1992)[22], Chapter 3, and Part III of this book.

DAI has been applied in several application domains. We list the domains that are indexed in Bond and Gasser (1992): air traffice control, design, diagnosis, distributed computing systems, distributed expert systems, distributed sensing and identification domains, information retrieval, manufacturing domains, medical domains, military domain, monitoring and control, network

---

[22]This section corresponds to the subject indexes systems by name, Actor languages, concurrent distributed and object-oriented languages, experimental test beds, integrative systems, logic programming, miscellaneous tools, parallel production systems and blackboard systems, and performance and modeling tools in Bond and Gasser (1992).

domains, research domains, allocation domains, robot domains, routing domains, scheduling domains, software engineering, telecommunication domains. Let us also mention the rapidly evolving domain of CSCW.

Some applications may benefit from the integration of neural networks in MAS. This is a relatively new research area that is worth the investigation (Gallant, 1988; Dunker et al., 1992).[23] Several other technical topics may be relevant for MAS designers and developers. We will not be able to discuss them in this chapter. However, we refer the reader to the following subject indexes in Bond and Gasser (1992): DAI architectures, hardware architectures, implementation platforms, real-time and time dependence and object-oriented concurrent programming.

9 CONCLUSION[24]

After this long review of DAI works, let us return to DAI foundations. Among DAI researchers, there is a large consensus for considering that DAI systems are social by nature, in the sense that the properties of a DAI system are not derivable or representable solely on the properties of its component agents. For example, Hewitt (1991) presented his new approach of open information system semantics as integrating methods from sociology and from concurrent system science. Gasser (1991) suggested that we need to begin to articulate the basis of knowledge and action for DAI in the light of their social character. He identified several principles that ought to underly the scientific and conceptual foundations for DAI systems from a social perspective.

- AI research must set its foundations in ways that treat the existence and interaction of multiple actors as a fundamental category.
- DAI theory and practice must address the basic tension between the local, situated and pragmatic character of knowledge and action, and the ways in which knowledge and action necessarily implicate multiple contexts.
- Representation and reasoning approaches used in DAI must 1) assume that multiple representations are recursively possible at any level of analysis or action, 2) assume that actors employ multiple representations individually and collectively, and 3) provide mechanisms for reasoning among multiple representations.
- DAI theory and practice must account for resource-limited activity.
- DAI theory and practice must provide account of and mechanisms for handling the three key problems of joint qualification, representation incommensurability and failure indeterminacy.

[23]This section corresponds to the subject index DAI and connectionism in Bond and Gasser (1992).
[24]Some other topics are categorized in Bond and Gasser (1992): DAI theory, experimental research, formal approaches-theories-methods, knowledge-based simulation, and surveys-collections-bibliographies.

- Overall, DAI theory and practice must account for how aggregates of agents can achieve joint courses of action that are robust and continuable (ongoing) despite indeterminate foolups, inconsistency, etc., which may occur recursively or any level of the system.

Adopting a social approach may change the way agents are modelled. For example, the usual way of modeling commitments is to define them in terms of an agent's beliefs and goals (Cohen and Levesque, 1990a). From a social perspective, a commitment is grounded in the actions of many agents' activities *taken together*: it is not a matter of individual choice. Gasser (1991) indicates that many other concepts that are associated with individual agents or problem solvers in typical AI systems, are, in sociological terms, *reifications* constructed through joint courses of actions and made stable by *webs of commitment*, or *alliances* among the agents using them. Some examples include concepts such as *problems*, *knowledge*, *facts* about the world and even *technical objects*.

In the same vein, Rosenschein (1993) presents his research as *social engineering for machines*: "we want to understand the kinds of negotiation protocols, and punitive and incentive mechanisms that would motivate designers to build machines that act in ways that all those designers find beneficial." Machines should interact flexibly. The agent that Rosenschein envisions should represent the interests of its owners and compromise when it is to their advantage. It should be secretive at times, not revealing all its information, and it should be able to recognize duplicity on the part of others, when possible. "In short, we want our agents to faithfully act as our surrogates in encounters with other agents."

In the conclusion of a recent invited talk, Gasser (1993) proposed ways of rethinking a number of familiar concepts such as fact, interaction, knowledge, and organization, raising questions about how well we can currently capture their social dimensions conceptually, representationally, and computationally. He suggested some directions to investigate:

- Learn to describe, build and experiment with communities of programs 1) that generate, modify, encode their local languages of interaction; 2) in which kinds and degrees of structure and reification and both increase and decrease with use; and 3) that modify both their knowledge and their activity structures at all levels of analysis.
- Define and demonstrate social mechanisms of dynamic category formulation, classification and concomitant reification.
- Investigate how these and similar reasoning, modeling, explanation and activity structures—e.g. dynamic aggregation, reification, etc.—appear in other fields and contexts, including biology, formulation of scientific knowledge, and social control/social change processes.

These few quotations will help the user to grasp some of the ideas that are proposed by leading DAI researchers to pave the way of future research projects. These orientations should not be considered exclusive. In every section of this chapter we tried to describe past and recent works in order to give the reader a feeling of the evolution that characterizes each research area. In addition to "traditional" DAI research domains such as coordination, planning, negotiation, and knowledge representation based on mental state, it is worth mentioning the growing influence of new research areas such as the impact of a social perspective on MAS as well as reification mechanisms, eco-problem solving, and autonomous agents mentioned in Section 7. It is also important to note that DAI technology is mature enough to motivate the incorporation of its techniques in so-called intelligent and cooperative information systems. As we saw in Section 8, if this trend proves true in the years to come, the need for practical analysis and design methods for DAI systems will be more acute, especially in industry.

ACKNOWLEDGMENTS

This research was supported by the Natural Sciences and Engineering Research Council of Canada (grant OGP 05518) and by FCAR.

BIBLIOGRAPHY

Adler, M. N., Davis, A. B., Weihmayer, R., and Worrest, R. W. (1989). Conflict-resolution strategies for non-hierarchical distributed agents. In *Distributed Artificial Intelligence* (L. Gasser and M. N. Huhns, eds.), Vol. 2, pp. 139–161. Morgan Kaufmann, Los Altos, CA/Pitman, London.

Agha, G., and Hewitt, C. (1988). Concurrent programming using actors. In *Object-Oriented Concurrent Programming* (Y. Yonezawa and M. Tokoro, eds.). MIT Press, Cambridge, MA.

Allen, J. F. (1983). Recognizing intentions from natural language utterances. In *Computational Models of Discourse* (M. Bradie and R. C. Berwick, eds.), Chapter 2, pp. 108–166, MIT Press, Cambridge, MA.

Allen, J. F. (1986). *Natural Language Understanding*, Benjamin/Cummings, Menlo Park, CA.

Allen, J. F., Kautz, H. A., Pelavin, R. N., and Teneberg, J. D. (1991). *Reasoning about Plans*. Morgan Kaufmann, San Mateo, CA.

Association for Computing Machinery (ACM) (1991). *Commun. ACM* (Special issue on Computer Supported Collaborative Work) **34**(12).

Becker, H. S. (1960). Notes on the concept of commitment. *Am. J. Sociol.* **66**, 32–40.

Bond, A. H. (1989). The cooperation of experts in engineering design. In *Distributed Artificial Intelligence* (L. Gasser and M. N. Huhns, eds.), Vol. 2, pp. 463–484. Morgan Kaufmann, Los Altos, CA/Pitman, London.

Bond, A. H. (1990). A computational model for organization of cooperating intelligent agents. *Proc. Conf. Off. Inf. Syst.*, Cambridge, MA, pp. 21–30.

Bond, A. H., and Gasser, L., eds. (1988). *Readings in Distributed Artificial Intelligence*. Morgan Kaufmann, San Mateo, CA.

Bond, A. H., and Gasser, L. (1992). A subject-indexed bibliography of distributed artificial intelligence. *IEEE Trans. Syst. Man Cybernet.* SMC-22(6) 1260–1281.

Bonissone, P. P. (1986). Plausible reasoning: Coping with uncertainty in expert systems. In *Encyclopedia of Artificial Intelligence* (S. C. Shapiro, ed.). Wiley, New York.

Boose, J., and Gaines, B., eds. (1988). *Knowledge Acquisition*, Vols. 1 and 2. Academic Press, San Diego, CA.

Bouron, T., Ferber, J., and Samuel, F. (1991). MAGES: A multi-agent testbed for heterogeneous agents. In *Decentralized Artificial Intelligence 2* (Y. Demazeau and J.-P. Müller, eds.), pp. 195–216. Elsevier/North-Holland, Amsterdam.

Brodie, M. L., and Ceri, S. (1992). On intelligent and cooperative information systems: A workshop summary. *Int. J. Intell. Coop. Inf. Syst.* 1(2), 249–290.

Brooks, R. A. (1991). Intelligence without representation. *Artif. Intell.* 47, 139–159.

Cammarata, S., McArthur, D., and Steeb, R. (1983). Strategies of cooperation in distributed problem solving. *Proc. J. Conf. Artif. Intell., 8th*, Karlsuhe, Germany, pp. 767–770.

Chaib-draa, B. (1993). Plans in natural language dialogues. *Knowl.-Based Syst.* 6(1), 67–75.

Chaib-draa, B., and Millot, P. (1987). Architecture pour les systèmes d'intelligence artificielle distribuée. *Proc. IEEE Compint*, Montreal, 1987, pp. 64–69.

Chaib-draa, B., Moulin, B., Mandiau, R., and Millot, P. (1992). Trends in distributed artificial intelligence. *Artif. Intell. Rev.* 6, 35–66.

Chang, E. (1987). Participant systems for cooperative work. In *Distributed Artificial Intelligence* (M. N. Huhns, ed.), pp. 311–339. Morgan Kaufmann, San Mateo, CA/Pitman, London.

Cohen, P. R., and Levesque, H. J. (1990a). Persistence, intention and commitment. In *Intentions in Communication* (P. R. Cohen, J. Morgan, and M. E. Pollack, eds.), pp. 33–69. MIT Press, Cambridge, MA.

Cohen, P. R., and Levesque, H. J. (1990b). Rational interaction as the basis for communication. In *Intentions in Communication* (P. R. Cohen, J. Morgan, and M. E. Pollack, eds.), pp. 221–255. MIT Press, Cambridge, MA.

Cohen, P. R., and Perrault, R. (1979). Elements of a plan-based theory of speech acts. *Cognit. Sci.* 3, 177–212.

Cohen, P. R., Morgan, J., and Pollack, M. E., eds. (1990). *Intentions in Communication*. MIT Press, Cambridge, MA.

Conry, S. E., Meyer, R., and Lesser, V. R. (1988). Multistage negotiation in distributed planning. In *Readings in Distributed Artificial Intelligence* (A. H. Bond and L. Gasser, eds.), pp. 367–36 . Morgan Kaufmann, San Mateo, CA.

Conry, S. E., Kuwabara, K., Lesser, V. R., and Meyer, R. A. (1991). Multistage negotiation for distributed constraint satisfaction. *IEEE Trans. Syst. Man Cybernet.* SMC-21(6), 1462–1477.

Conte, R., Miceli, M., and Castelfranchi, C. (1991). Limits and levels of cooperation: Disentangling various types of prosocial interaction. In *Decentralized Artificial Intelligence 2* (Y. Demazeau and J.-P. Müller, eds.). Elsevier/North-Holland, Amsterdam.

Corkill, D. D., and Lesser, V. R. (1983). The use of meta-level control for coordination in a distributed problem solving network. *Proc. Int. Jt. Conf. Artif. Intell., 8th*, Karlsruhe, Germany, *1983*, pp. 748–756.

Corkill, D. D., Gallagher, K. O., and Murray, D. E. (1986). GBB: A generic blackboard development system. *Proc. Am. Assoc. Artif. Intell.*, Philadelphia *1986*, pp. 1008–1014.

Croft, W. B., and Lefkowitz, L. S. (1988a). Knowledge-based support of cooperative activities. *Proc. 21st Annu. Hawaii Int. Conf. Syst. Sci.*, Vol. 3, pp. 312–318.

Croft, W. B., and Lefkowitz, L. S. (1988b). In *Readings in Distributed Artificial Intelligence* (A. H. Bond and L. Gasser, eds.), Morgan Kaufmann, San Mateo, CA.

Davis, R., and Smith, R. G. (1983). Negotiation as a metaphor for distributed problem solving. *Artif. Intell.* **20**, 63–109.

Decker, K. S. (1987). Distributed problem-solving techniques: A survey. *IEEE Trans. Syst. Man Cybernet.* **17**(5), 729–740.

Decker, K. S., Durfee, E. H., and Lesser V. R. (1989). Evaluating research in cooperative distributed problem solving. In *Distributed Artificial Intelligence* (L. Gasser and M. N. Huhns, eds.), Vol. 2, pp. 485–519. Morgan Kaufmann, Los Angeles, CA/Pitman, London.

Decker, K. S., and Lesser, V. (1993). An approach to analyzing the need for meta-level communication. *Proc. Int. Jt. Conf. Artif. Intell., 13th*, Cambéry, France, *1993*, pp. 360–366.

De Kleer, J. (1986). An assumption-based truth maintenance system. *Artif. Intell.* **28**, 127–162.

Demazeau, Y., and Müller, J.-P. eds. (1990). *Decentralized Artificial Intelligence*. Elsevier North-Holland, Amsterdam.

Demazeau, Y., and Müller, J-P., eds. (1991a). *Decentralized Artificial Intelligence 2*. Elsevier North-Holland, Amsterdam.

Demazeau, Y., and Müller, J.-P. (1991b). From reactive to intentional agents. In *Denctralized Artificial Intelligence 2* (Y. Demazeau and J.-P. Müller, eds.). Elsevier/North-Holland, Amsterdam.

Doyle, J. (1979). A truth maintenance system. *Artif. Intell.* **12**, 231–272.

Dunker, J., Scherer, D., and Schlageter, G. (1992). Integrating neural networks into a distributed knowledge based system. *Proc. Int. Conf. Expert Syst. Appl., 12th*, Avignon, France, *1992*.

Durfee, E. H. (1988). *Coordination of Distributed Problem Solvers*. Kluwer Academic Publishers, Boston.

Durfee, E. H., and Lesser, V. R. (1987). Using partial global plans to coordinate problem solvers. *Proc. Int. Jt. Conf. Artif. Intell., 10th, 1987*, pp. 875–883.

Durfee, E. H., Lesser, V. R., and Corkill, D. D. (1985). Increasing coherence in a distributed problem solving network. *Proc. Int. Jt. Conf. Artif. Intell., 9th*, Los Angeles, *1985*, pp. 1025–1030.

Durfee, E. H., Lesser, V. R., and Corkill, D. D. (1989). Trends in cooperative distributed problem solving. *IEEE Trans. Knowl. Data Eng.* **KOE-11**(1), 63–83.

Ephrati, E., and Rosenschein, J. S. (1991). The Clarke tax as a consensus mechanism among automated agents. *Proc. Am. Assoc. Artif. Intell.*, Anaheim, CA, *1991*, pp. 173–178.

Ephrati, E., and Rosenschein. J. S. (1993). Multi-agent planning as a dynamic search for social consensus. *Proc. Int. Jt. Conf. Artif. Intell., 13th,* Chambéry, France, *1993,* pp. 423–431.

Ferber, J., and Carle, P. (1990). Actors and agents as reflective concurrent objects: A Mering IV perspective. *IEEE Trans. Syst. Man, Cybernet.* **SMC-21**(6), 1420–1436.

Ferber, J., and Jacopin, E. (1991). The framework of eco-problem solving. In *Decentralized Artificial Intelligence 2* (Y. Demazeau and J.-P. Müller, eds.), pp. 181–194. Elsevier/North-Holland Amsterdam.

Ferguson, I. A. (1992). Toward an architecture for adaptive, rational, mobile agents. In *Decentralized Artificial Intelligence 3* (E. Werner and Y. Demazeau, eds.), pp. 249–261. Elsevier/North-Holland, Amsterdam.

Fox, M. S. (1981). An organizational view of distributed systems. *IEEE Trans. Syst. Man Cybernet.* **SMC-11**(1), 70–79.

Gallant, S. I. (1988). Connexionist expert systems. *Commun. ACM* **31**(2), 152–169.

Galliers, J. R. (1988). A strategic framework for multi-agent cooperative dialogue. *Proc. Eur. Conf. Artif. Intell., 8th,* Munich, Germany, pp. 415–420.

Galliers, J. R. (1991). Modeling autonomous belief revision in dialogue. In *Decentralized Artifical Intelligence 2* (Y. Demazeau and J.-P. Müller, eds.). Elsevier/North-Holland, Amsterdam.

Gaspar, G. (1991). Communication and belief changes in a society of agents: Towards a formal model of an autonomous agent. In *Decentralized Artifical Intelligence 2* (Y. Demazeau and J.-P. Müller, eds.). Elsevier/North-Holland, Amsterdam.

Gasser, L. (1986). The integration of computing and routine work. *ACM Trans. Off. Inf. Syst.* **4**(3), 205–225.

Gasser, L. (1991). Social conceptions of knowledge and action: DAI foundations and open systems semantics. *Artif. Intell.* **47,** 107–138.

Gasser, L. (1993). Social knowledge and social action: Heterogeneity in practice. *Proc. Int. Jt. Conf. Artif. Intell., 13th,* Chambéry, France, *1993,* pp. 751–757.

Gasser, L., and Huhns, M. N., ed. (1989). *Distributed Artificial Intelligence,* Vol. 2. Morgan Kaufmann, Los Angeles, CA/Pitman, London.

Gasser, L., Roquette, N. F., Hill, R. W., and Lieb, J. (1989). Representing and using organizational knowledge in distributed AI systems. In *Distributed Artificial Intelligence* (L. Gasser and M. N. Huhns, eds.), Vol. 2, pp. 55–78. Morgan Kaufmann, Los Angeles, CA/Pitman, London.

Genesereth, M. R., Ginsberg, M. L., and Rosenschein, J. S. (1986). Cooperation without communication. *Proc. Am. Assoc. Artif. Intell.,* Philadelphia, *1986,* pp. 51–57.

Georgeff, M. (1983). Communication and interaction in multi-agent planning. *Proc. Int. Jt. Conf. Artif. Intell.,* Karlsruhe, Germany, *1983,* pp. 125–129.

Georgeff, M. (1988). Communication and interaction in multiagent planning. In *Readings in Distributed Artificial Intelligence* (A. H. Bond and L. Gasser, eds.), pp. 200–204. Morgan Kaufmann, San Mateo, CA.

Gibbs, R. W., and Mueller, R. A. G. (1990). Conversation as coordinated cooperative interaction. In *Cognition, Computation and Cooperation* (W. W. Zachary and S. P. Robertson, eds.), pp. 95–114. Ablex, Norwood, NJ.

Gmytrasiewicz, P. J., and Durfee, E. H. (1992). Truth, lies, belief and disbelief in communication between autonomous agents. *Proc. Int. Workshop Distrib. Artif. Intell.*, *11th*, pp. 107–125.

Gmytrasiewicz, P. J., Durfee, E. H., and Wehe, D. K. (1991). A decision-theoretic approach to coordinating multiagent interactions. *Proc. Int. Jt. Conf. Artif. Intell.*, *12th*, Sydney, Australia, *1991*, pp. 62–68.

Goodson, J. L., and Schmidt, C. F. (1990). The design of cooperative person-machine problem-solving systems: A methodology and an example. In *Cognition, Computing and Cooperation* (W. W. Zachary and S. P. Robertson, eds.), pp. 187–223. Ablex, Norwood, NJ.

Greif, I., ed. (1988). *Computer-Supported Cooperative Work: A Book of Readings*. Morgan Kaufmann, San Mateo, CA.

Grice, H. P. (1975). Logic and conversation. In *Syntax and Semantics 3: Speech Acts* (P. Cole and J. Morgan, eds.). Academic Press, New York.

Grosz, B. J., and Sidner, C. L. (1990). Plans for discourse. In *Intentions and Communications*, P. R. Cohen, J. Morgan, and M. E. Pollack (eds.). MIT Press, Cambridge, MA.

Halpern, J. Y. (1986). Reasoning about knowledge: An introduction. In *Theoretical Aspects of Reasoning About Knowledge*, (J. Y. Hapern, ed.), pp. 1–18. Morgan Kaufmann, San Mateo, CA.

Hayes-Roth, B. (1988). Making intelligent systems adaptive. In *Architectures for Intelligence* (K. Van Lehn, ed.). Erlbaum, Hillsdale, NJ.

Hayes-Roth B., Hewett, M., Washington, R., Hewett, R., and Seiver, A. (1989). Distributed intelligence within an individual. In *Distributed Artificial Intelligence* (L. Gasser and M. Huhns, eds.), Vol. 2, pp. 385–412. Morgan Kaufmann, Los Altos, CA/Pitman London.

Hewitt, C. (1977). Viewing control structures on patterns of passing messages. *Artif. Intell.* **8**, 323–364.

Hewitt, C. (1986). Offices are open systems. *ACM Trans. Off. Inf. Syst.* **4**(3), 270–287.

Hewitt, C. (1991). Open information systems semantics for distributed artificial intelligence. *Artif. Intell.* **47**, 79–106.

Hewitt, C., and Inman, J. (1991). DAI betwixt and between: From "Intelligent Agents" to open systems science. *IEEE Trans. Syst., Man Cybernet.* **SMC-21**(6), 1409–1418.

Heyward, S. A., Wielinga, B. J., and Breuker, J. A. (1988). Structured analysis of knowledge. In *Knowledge Acquisition Tools for Expert Systems* (J. Boose and B. Gaines, eds.), pp. 149–160. Academic Press, San Diego, CA.

Hickman, F. (1989). *Analysis for Knowledge-Based Systems: A Practical Guide to the KADS Methodology*. Ellis Horwood, Chichester, UK.

Hoare, C. A. R. (1978). Communicating sequential process. *Commun. ACM* **21**, 666–677.

Hogg, T., and Huberman, A. (1991). Controlling chaos in distributed systems. *IEEE Trans. Syst. Man Cybernet.* **SMC-21**(6), 1325–1332.

Huff, K., and Mylopoulos, J. (1992). Developing intelligent information systems: A workshop summary. *Int. J. Intell. Coop. Inf. Syst.* **1**(2), 233–248.

Huhns, M. N., ed. (1987). *Distributed Artificial Intelligence*. Morgan Kaufmann, San Mateo, CA/Pitman, London.

Huhns, M. N., and Bridgeland, D. M. (1991). Multiagent truth maintenance. *IEEE Trans. Syst., Man Cybernet.* **SMC-21**(6), 1437-1445.

Huhns, M. N., Makhopadhyay, U., Stephens, L. M., and Bonnell, R. D. (1987). DAI for document retrieval: The MINDS Project. In *Distributed Artificial Intelligence* (M. N. Huhns, ed.), pp. 249-283. Morgan Kaufmann, San Mateo, CA/Pitman, London.

Huhns, M. N., Papazoglou, M. P., and Schlageter, G., eds. (1993). *Proceedings of the International Conference on Intelligent and Cooperative Information Systems*, Rotterdam, The Netherlands, *1993*.

Jennings, N. R. (1993). Coordination: Commitment and conventions, the foundation of coordination in multi-agent systems. *Knowl. Eng. Rev.* **8**(3), 223-250.

Jennings, N. R., and Mamdani, E. H. (1992). Using joint responsibility to coordinate collaborative problem solving in dynamic environments. *Am. Assoc. Artif. Intell., 1992*, pp. 269-275.

Kaplan, S. J. (1983). Cooperative responses from a portable natural language database query system. In *Computational Models of Discourse* (M. Bradie and R. C. Berwick, eds.). MIT Press, Cambridge, MA.

Kautz, H. A. (1990). A circumscriptive theory of plan recognition. In *Intentions in Communication* (P. R. Cohen, J. Morgan, and M. E. Pollack, eds.), pp. 105-133. MIT Press, Cambridge, MA.

Kiss, G. (1992). Variable coupling of agents to their environment: Combining situated and symbolic automata. In *Decentralized Artificial Intelligence 3* (E. Werner and Y. Demazeau, eds.), pp. 231-248. Elsevier/North-Holland, Amsterdam.

Klein, M. (1991). Supporting conflict resolution incooperative design systems. *IEEE Trans. Syst. Man Cybernet.* **SMC-21**(6), 1379-1390.

Konolige, K., and Pollack, M. E. (1989). Ascribing plans to agents: Prelmininary report. *Proc. Int. Jt. Conf. Artif. Intell., 11th*, Detroit, MI, *1989*, pp. 924-930.

Konolige, K., and Pollack, M. E. (1993). A representationalist theory of intention. *Proc. Int. Jt. Conf. Artif. Intell., 13th*, Chambéry, France, *1993*, pp. 390-395.

Kornfeld, W. A., and Hewitt, C. (1981). The scientific community metaphor. *IEEE Trans. Syst. Man Cybernet.* **SMC-11**(1), 24-33.

Kraus, S., and Wilkenfeld, J. (1991). Negotiation over time in a multi-agent environment. *Proc. Int. Jt. Conf. Artif. Intell., 12th*, Sydney, Australia, *1991*, pp. 56-61.

Kreifelts, T., and von Martial, F. (1991). A negotiation framework for autonomous agents. In *Decentralized Artificial Intelligence 2* (J. Demaeeau and J.-P. Müller, eds.), pp. 71-88. Elsevier/North-Holland, Amsterdam.

Lâasri, B., Lâasri, H., Lander, S., and Lesser, V. (1992). A generic model for intelligent negotiating agents. *Int. J. Intell. Coop. Inf. Syst.* **1**(1), 291-318.

Lakemeyer, G. (1993). All they know: A study in multi-agent autoepistemic reasoning. *Proc. Int. Jt. Conf. Artif. Intell., 13th*, Chambéry, France, *1993*, pp. 376-381.

Lesser, V. R. (1991). A retrospective view of FA/C distributed problem solving. *IEEE Trans. Syst., Man Cybernet.* **SMC-21**(6), 1347-1362.

Lesser, V. R., and Corkill, D. D. (1981). Functionally-accurate, cooperative distributed systems. *IEEE Trans. Syst., Man Cybernet.* **SMC-11**(1), 81-96.

Lesser, V. R., and Corkill, D. D. (1983). The distributed vehicle monitoring testbed: A tool for investigating distributed problem solving networks. *AI Mag.*, Fall, pp. 15-33.

Levesque, H. J. (1990). All I know: A study in autoepistemic logic. *Artif. Intell.* **42**, 263–309.

Lewis, D. (1969). *Convention*. Harvard Univ. Press, Cambridge, MA.

Litman, D. J., and Allen, J. F. (1990). Discourse processing and commensense plans. In *Intentions in Communication* (P. R. Cohen, J. Morgan, and M. E. Pollack, eds.), pp. 365–388. MIT Press, Cambridge, MA.

Lizotte, M., and Moulin, B. (1990). A temporal planner for modelling autonomous agents. In *Decentralized Artificial Intelligence* (Y. Demazeau and J.-P. Müller, eds.), pp. 121–136. Elsevier/North-Holland, Amsterdam.

Lochbaum, K. E., Grosz, B. J., and Sidner, C. L. (1990). Models of plans to support communication: An initial report. *Proc. Am. Assoc. Artif. Intell.*, Boston, MA, *1990*, pp. 485–490.

Lozano-Perez, T. (1983). Robot-programming. *Proc. IEEE* **71**(7), 821–841.

Maes, P., ed. (1990). *Designing Autonomous Agents*. MIT Press, Cambridge, MA/ Elsevier, Amsterdam.

Maines, D., ed. (1984). *Urban Life*, Special Issue on Negotiated Order Theory.

Maître, B., and Lâasri, H. (1990). Cooperating expert problem solving in blackboard systems: Atome case study. In *Decentralized Artificial Intelligence* (Y. Demazeau and J.-P. Müller, eds.), pp. 250–263. Elsevier/North-Holland, Amsterdam.

Malone, T. W. (1990). Organizing information processing systems: Parallels between human organizations and computer systems. In *Cognition, Computation and Co-operation* (W. W. Zachary and S. P. Robertson, eds.), pp. 56–83. Ablex, Norwood, NJ.

Mason, C. L., and Johnson, R. R. (1989). DATMS: A framework for distributed assumption based reasoning. In *Distributed Artificial Intelligence* (L. Gasser and M. N. Huhns, eds.), Vol. 2, pp. 293–317. Morgan Kaufmann, Los Altos, CA/Pitman, London.

Mazer, M. S. (1991). Reasoning about knowledge to understand distributed AI systems. *IEEE Trans. Syst., Man Cybernet* **SMC-21**(6), 1333–1346.

McCarty, J., and Hayes, P. (1969). Some philosophical problems from the standpoint of artifical intelligence. In *Machine Intelligence 4* (B. Meltzer and D. Mitchie, eds.), pp. 463–502. Edinburgh Univ. Press, Edinburgh.

Mintzberg, H. (1979). *The Structuring of Organizations*. Prentice-Hall, Englewoods Cliffs, NJ.

Moore, R. C. (1980). *Reasoning about Knowledge and Action*, Tech. Note 191. Artificial Intelligence Center, SRI International, Menlo Park, CA.

Moore, R. C. (1985). Semantic considerations on non monotonic logic. *Artif. Intell.* **25**, 75–94.

Moulin, B., and Cloutier, L. (1994). Collaborative work based on multiagent architectures: A methodological perspective. In *Artificial Intelligence: Theory and Applications* (F. Aminzadeh and M. Jamshidi, eds). Prentice-Hall, Englewood Cliffs, NJ.

Namatame, A., and Tsukamoto, Y. (1993). Learning agents for cooperative hyperinformation systems. *Proc. Int. Conf. Intell. Coop. Inf. Syst.*, Rotterdam, *1993*, pp. 124–133.

Nierenburg, S., and Lesser, V. R. (1986). Providing intelligent assistance in distributed office environments. In *Readings in Distributed Artificial Intelligence* (A. H. Bond and L. Gasser, eds.). Morgan Kaufmann. San Mateo, CA.

Nii, H. P. (1986a). Blackboard systems: The blackboard model of problem solving and the evolution of blackboard architectures. Part I. *AI Mag.*, pp. 38–53.

Nii, H. P. (1986b). Blackboard systems: Blackboard application systems, blackboard systems from a knowledge engineering perspective. Part II. *AI Mag.*, pp. 82–106.

Nilsson, N. J. (1980). Two heads are better than one. *Sigart Newl.*, pp. 43–43.

Pan, J. Y. C., and Tenenbaum, J. M. (1991). An intelligent agent framework for enterprise integration. *IEEE Trans. Syst. Man Cybernet.* **SMC-21**(6), 1391–1408.

Parunak, H. V. D. (1987). Manufacturing experience with the contract-net. In *Distributed Artificial Intelligence* (M. N. Huhns, ed.), pp. 285–310. Morgan Kaufmann, San Mateo, CA/Pitman, London.

Pollack, M. E. (1987). A model of plan inference that distinguishes between the beliefs of actors and observers. In *Reasoning about Actions and Plans* (M. P. Georgeff and A. L. Lansky, eds.), pp. 279–295. Morgan Kaufmann, Los Altos, CA.

Pollack, M. E. (1990). Plans as complex mental attitudes. In *Intentions in Communication* (P. R. Cohen, J. Morgan, and M. E. Pollack, eds.), pp. 77–103. MIT Press, Cambridge, Mass.

Pratt, V. R. (1976). Semantical consideration on Floyd-Hoare logic. *Proc. FOCS Conf., 17th*, pp. 109–121.

Rao, A. S., and Georgeff, M. P. (1991). Modeling rational agents within a BDI-architecture. In *Proceedings of the Second International Conference on Principles of Knowledge Representation and Reasoning* (J. Allen, R. Fikes, and E. Sandewall, eds.), Morgan Kaufmann, San Mateo, CA.

Rao, A. S., and Georgeff, M. P. (1993). A model-theoretic approach to the verification of situated reasoning systems. *Proc. Int. Jt. Conf. Artif. Intell., 13th*, Chambéry, France, *1993*, pp. 318–324.

Rasmussen, J., Brehmer, B., and Leplat, J., eds. (1991). *Distributed Decision Making*. Wiley, New York.

Rosenschein, J. S. (1986). Rational interactions: Cooperating among intelligent agents. Ph.D. Disertation, Computer Science Department, Stanford University, Stanford, CA.

Rosenschein, J. S. (1993). Consenting agents: Negotiation mechanisms for multi-agent systems. *Proc. Int. Jt. Conf. Artif. Intell., 13th*, Chambéry, France, *1993*, pp. 792–799.

Rosenschein, J. S., and Breese, J. S. (1989). Communication-free interactions among rational agents. In *Distributed Artificial Intelligence 2* (L. Gasser and M. N. Huhns, eds.), pp. 99–118. Morgan Kaufmann, Los Altos, CA/Pitman, London.

Rosenschein, J. S., and Genesereth, M. R. (1985). Deals among rational agents. *Proc. Int. Jt. Conf. Artif. Intell., 9th*, Los Angeles, *1985*, pp. 91–99.

Rousseau, D., Moulin, B., and Lapalme, G. (1993). Modélisation des conversations basée sur une perspective de systèmes multiagents. *Proc. Conf. Inf. Langage Nat.*, Nantes, France, *1993*.

Rumbaugh, J., Blaha, M., Premerlani, W., Eddy, F., and Lorensen, W. (1991). *Object-Oriented Modeling and Design*. Prentice-Hall, Englewood Cliffs, NJ.

Sathi, A., and Fox, M. S. (1989). Constraint-directed negotiation of resource reallocations. In *Distributed Artificial Intelligence 2* (L. Gasser and M. N. Huhns, eds.), pp. 163–193. Morgan Kaufmann, Los Altos, CA/Pitman, London.

Schelling, T. C. (1960). *The Strategy of Conflict*. Harvard Univ. Press, Cambridge, MA.

Schmidt, C. F., Sridharan, N. S., and Goodson, J. L. (1978). The plan recognition problem: An intersection of artificial intelligence and psychology. *Artif. Intell.* **10**(1), 45–83.

Serle, J. R. (1969). *Speech Acts*. Cambridge Univ. Press, Cambridge, UK.

Searle, J. R., and Vanderveken, D. (1985). *Foundations of Illocutionary Logic*. Cambridge Univ. Press, Cambridge, UK.

Shaw, M. J., and Whinston, A. B. (1989). Learning and adaptation in distributed artificial intelligence systems. In *Distributed Artificial Intelligence* (L. Gasser and M. N. Huhns, eds.), Vol. 2, pp. 413–429. Morgan Kaufmann, Los Altos, CA/ Pitman, London.

Shoham, Y. (1989a). Time for action: On the relation between time, knowledge and action. *Proc. Int. Jt. Conf. Artif. Intell.*, *11th*, Detroit, MI, *1989*, pp. 954–959.

Shoham, Y. (1989b). Beliefs as defeasible knowledge. *Proc. Int. Jt. Conf. Artif. Intell.*, *11th*, Detroit, MI, *1989*, pp. 1168–1173.

Shoham, Y. (1993). Agent-oriented programming. *Artif. Intell.* **60**, 51–92.

Shoham, Y., and Tennenholtz, M. (1992). On the synthesis of useful social laws for artificial agent societies. *Proc. Am. Assoc. Artif. Intell.*, *1992*, pp. 276–281.

Sian, S. S. (1991). Adaptation based on cooperative learning in multiagent systems. In *Decentralized Artificial Intelligence 2* (Y. Demazeau and J.-P. Müller, eds.), pp. 257–272. Elsevier/North-Holland, Amsterdam.

Sidner, C. L. (1985). Plan parsing for intended response recognition in discourse. *Comput. Intell.* **1**(1), 1–10.

Singh, M. P. (1991). Towards a formal theory of communication for multiagent systems. *Proc. Int. Jt. Conf. Artif. Intell.*, *12th*, Sydney, Australia, *1991*, pp. 69–74.

Smith, B. C. (1982). *Reflection in a procedural language*, Tech. Rep. 272. Computer Science Lab., MIT, Cambridge, MA.

Smith, R. G., and Davis, R. (1981). Frameworks for cooperation in distributed problem solving. *IEEE Trans. Syst. Man Cybernet.* **SMC-11**, 61–70.

Star, S. L. (1989). The structure of ill-structured solutions: Boundary objects and heterogeneous distributed problem solving. In *Distributed Artificial Intelligence* (L. Gasser and M. N. Huhns, eds.), pp. 37–54. Morgan Kaufmann, Los Altos, CA/ Pitman, London.

Steels, L. (1990). Exploiting analogical representation. In *Designing Autonomous Agents* (P. Maes, ed.), pp. 71–88. MIT Press/Elsevier, Cambridge, MA.

Steiner, D. D., and Mahling, D. E. (1990). Human computer cooperative work. *Proc. Workshop Distributed Artif. Intell.*, *10th*, Bandera, TX, *1990*.

Strauss, A. (1978). *Negotiations: Varieties, Processes, Contexts and Social Order*, Jossey-Bass, San Francisco.

Sycara, K. (1988). Resolving goal conflicts via negotiation. *Proc. Am. Assoc. Artif. Intell.*, St. Paul, MN, *1988*, pp. 245–250.

Sycara, K. R. (1989a). Argumentation: Planning other agents' plans. *Proc. Int. Jt. Conf. Artif. Intell.*, *11th*, Detroit, MI.

Sycara, K. R. (1989b). Multiagent compromise via negotiation. In *Distributed Artificial Intelligence* (L. Gasser and M. N. Huhns eds.), Vol. 2, pp. 119–137. Morgan Kaufmann, Los Altos, CA/Pitman, London.

Sycara, K. P., Roth, S., Sadeh, N., and Fox, M. (1991). Distributed constrained heuristic search. *IEEE Trans. Syst. Man Cybernet.* **SMC-21**(6), 1446–1461.

Tubbs, S. L., ed. (1984). *A System Approach to Small Group Interaction*, 2nd ed. Addison-Wesley, Reading, MA.

von Martial, F. (1992). *Coordinating Plans of Autonomous Agents*, Lect. Notes Artif. Intell. Springer-Verlag, Berlin.

Weiss, G. (1993). Learning to coordinate actions in multi-agent systems. *Proc. Int. Jt. Conf. Artif. Intell., 13th*, Chambéry, France, *1993*, pp. 311–317.

Werner, E. (1989). Cooperating agents: A unified theory of communication and social structure. In *Distributed Artificial Intelligence* (L. Gasser and M. N. Huhns, eds.), Vol. 2, pp. 3–36. Morgan Kaufmann, Los Altos, CA/Pitman, London.

Werner, E. (1991). A unified view of information, intention and ability. In *Decentralized Artificial Intelligence 2* (Y. Demazeau and J.-P. Müller, eds.), pp. 109–126. Elsevier/North-Holland, Amsterdam.

Werner, E. (1992). The design of multiagent systems. In *Decentralized Artificial Intelligence 3* (E. Werner and Y. Demazeau, eds.), pp. 3–30, Elsevier/North-Holland, Amsterdam.

Werner, E., and Demazeau, Y., eds. (1992). *Decentralized Artifical Intelligence 3*. Elsevier/North-Holland, Amsterdam.

Wilensky, R. (1983). *Planning and Understanding*. Addison-Wesley, Reading, MA.

Wilkins, D. (1988). *Practical Planning*. Morgan Kaufmann, San Mateo, CA.

Winograd, T., and Flores, F. (1986). *Understanding Computers and Cognition: A New Foundation for Design*. Ablex, Norwood, NJ.

Woods, D. D., Roth, E. M., and Bennett, K. B. (1990). Explorations in joint human-machine cognitive systems. In *Cognition, Computing, and Cooperation* (P. R. Cohen, J. Morgan, and M. E. Pollack, eds.), pp. 123–158, Ablex, Norwood, NJ.

Wooldridge, M., and Fisher, M. (1992). A first-order branching time logic of multi-agent systems. *Proc. Eur. Conf. Artif. Intell., 10th*, Vienna, Austria, pp. 234–238.

Zachary, W. W., and Robertson, S. P., eds. (1990). *Cognition, Computation and Cooperation*. Ablex, Norwood, NJ.

Zlotkin, G., and Rosenschein, J. S. (1990). Blocks, lies, and postal freight: The nature of deception in negotiation. *Proc. Int. Workshop Distributed Artif. Intell., 10th*, Bandera, TX.

Zlotkin, G., and Rosenschein, J. S. (1991). Cooperation and conflict resolution via negotiation among autonomous agents in noncooperative domains. *IEEE Trans. Syst. Man Cybern.* **SMC-21**(6), 1317–1324.

CHAPTER 2 ⎯⎯⎯⎯⎯⎯⎯⎯⎯⎯

Logical Foundations of Distributed Artificial Intelligence

ERIC WERNER

1 INTRODUCTION

1.1 Logic and Reductionism

Logic in this century has been primarily concerned with the foundations of mathematics, the formalization of the mathematical concepts. Mathematics was the child of physics focusing on the properties and relations of inanimate objects. In fact, the century started with the attempt by Whitehead and Russell (1910) to derive all of mathematics from logic. Later Tarski (1956) and Gödel (1931) showed this reductionist program was not possible. Yet, they too restricted their focus to the nonanimate world, and, thereby, excluded the observing subject. The mental and social realm of intentions was not real science; it had to be eliminated. Behaviorism and reductionism were two related philosophical movements that tried to reduce social concepts to physical, behavioral concepts. Chomsky (1969), Putnam (1975), and others, influenced in part by the early developments in computer science, began to realize that psychological states could not be reduced to behavioral properties, but instead required functional mental states. Thus, there was a movement by formalists from a pure concern with the physical world to understanding human psychology. Cognitive science was born.

1.2 Limitations of Cognitive Science and Artificial Intelligence

Cognitive science tried to take the notion of information processing from computer science and apply it directly to human mental processes. It tried to view

Foundations of Distributed Artificial Intelligence, Edited by G. M. P. O'Hare and N. R. Jennings
ISBN 0-471-00675-0 © 1996 John Wiley & Sons, Inc.

the human mind as an information processing system, a symbolic computer. With rare exceptions the work in cognitive science was not formal but relied on vague and sometimes strained analogies to what was happening in the field of computer science. One saw cognitive scientists writing programs whose input was claimed to be some analogue of perception (or the output of some previous, hypothesized mental process) and whose output was claimed to be a stage of mental processing.

Whether or not cognitive science as a paradigm has been successful is open to debate. The problem is that cognitive science is fundamentally an asocial science. The domain of cognitive science focused on one individual and his or her mental information processing. So, too, the related field of artificial intelligence was based on a similar individualistic paradigm of human mental processes. Artificial intelligence tried to apply this paradigm to enable computers to simulate human reasoning. Both cognitive science and artificial intelligence left out of consideration the social being and the social space in which social beings interact. They effectively ignored the social and economic sciences. Granted there were many exceptions (including Winograd, 1972; Schank and Abelson, 1977; Minsky, 1986), but I am addressing the paradigm, the conceptual structure underlying logic, cognitive science, and artificial intelligence.

This paradigm is breaking up. Information processing is just one level or view, a rather low-level view, of mental activity. It may not even be the most appropriate way to understand this activity. And, indeed, the information processing paradigm cannot account for most mental and social events.

1.3 A New Paradigm

The new paradigm is that of multiagent systems science. Multiagent science as a paradigm studies not just the physical world, nor agents in isolation, but the agent as part of a social space of other agents. The information processing paradigm tended to place the bits of information at the center of investigation, irrespective of their meaning (much like Shannon, 1948). The multiagent paradigm places *social information* and *communication* at the center. Social information includes information about values, strategies, and intentions, as well as, information about the state of the world. This essay is an attempt to introduce some of the concepts and the logical foundations for the science of social information and multiagent systems.

The importance of the new paradigm is evident when one considers that the world is undergoing a quite radical transformation from an information processing society where the information is acted on, to an extended social space that includes computers as part of its fabric. Here the information is not individualistic and passive, as it is in the paradigm of cognitive science. Instead, information becomes active social information that governs and constitutively creates the interactions between agents. Computers and robots are becoming part of the network of social life. The image of a single, intelligent mind in a vat, that answers questions, or a passive machine that mimics answers to pass the Turing test, is replaced by an active agent, a participating social being that contributes to the social space of interactions. The information highway coordinated by agents, and intelligent assistants are just indicators of the beginnings of this fundamental transition of social space and what constitutes a social being. It opens up new, problematic ethical issues and challenges the idea of a person as necessarily being human.

1.4 Comparisons to Other Formal Work

One of the first persons to envision the new paradigm and to understand that it was a new way of thinking was Carl Hewitt (1977). Hewitt realized that the interaction between agents was a new way of programming and understanding complex systems. Along the lines of Hewitt's paradigm the most significant work on agent control was probably that of Davis and Smith (1983) and Smith (1980) (Chapter 1). Others were approaching the new paradigm from a different direction by developing a new programming methodology they called distributed problem solving (Corkill, 1979; Corkill and Lesser, 1983; Lesser and Corkill, 1981; Durfee, 1988; Durfee et al., 1987) (Chapter 3). This empirically valuable work can be used as a springboard for theoretical work in distributed artificial intelligence. Barwise and Perry (1983) helped to break up the paradigm of standard logic and its semantics. They made the implementation of linguistic meaning appear to be possible. The work of Barwise provided a basis for the referential component of multiagent communication theory (Werner, 1988c, 1989a).

One cannot ignore the man whose ideas really preceded all of the above work. In 1921 John von Neumann (1961) wrote a mathematical essay formalizing games. Its significance to the most rigorous of the social sciences was displayed with the publication of his book (von Neumann and Morgenstern, 1947) linking game theory and economics. In spite of its vision in seeing the importance of agent interaction and in providing a formal conceptual framework for studying such interactions, von Neumann's work ignored communication and its relation to cooperation. He also ignored the cognitive structure of the agent and thus ignored the details of the social, interactive processes of coordination, cooperation, and communication. In some elegant formal work, Rosenschein (1986) applied some of von Neumann's ideas to multiagent systems. Like von Neumann, this early work ignored communication in multiagent cooperation, and limited itself to the study of agent interactions as regulated by economic rationality based on utilities. However, his more recent work (Rosenschein and Zlotkin, 1994) does address simple protocols of interaction. Also interesting is the use of voting in establishing agent consensus (Ephrati and Rosenschein, 1992).

Bratman (1987) gives a good philosophical account of intentions and of reasoning about intentions. The work is nonformal, but insightful and well worth reading. Perhaps the best-known attempt to formalize intentions is that of Cohen and Levesque (1987). However, there are problems with their theory

(Werner, 1990; Singh, 1992). Kraus has taken a syntactic approach to formalizing intentions (Grosz and Kraus, 1993). In spite of there being no semantics, I find her work interesting because of the detail of its syntactic formalization. Rao and Georgeff (1991) formalize the notion of intention in a somewhat similar approach to my own. However, in their formalization, they use accessibility relations for intentions that give little insight as to the relation of intentions to plans or to state information. This contrasts with their actual implementation of multiagent planning and team activity, which mirrors my own theory of cooperation through the coordination of intentional states (see Kinny et al., 1994; Werner, 1988c).

A number of investigators have been working on the problem of formalizing the concept of ability. Brown (1988) formalizes ability but ignores plans and strategies taking the perspective of an agent making one choice without the consideration of time. Singh (1990) tries to give semantics of ability but fails to relate abilities to plans and strategies, a serious shortcoming. He does give an interesting, though convoluted, account of skills and more permanent abilities. Thomas (1993) introduces time into the syntax, but, apparently unaware of my work, repeats some my studies yet at the same times suffers from not including strategies into the semantics of ability. All of the above authors restrict their theories of ability to the next time step. Such theories are unworkable in multiagent environments because they do not have a strategic theory of ability (Werner, 1990, 1991a). Wooldridge and Fisher (1992) extend my theory of strategic ability to include quantifiers (see Chapter 10).

Many investigators are beginning to see the importance of including time into the syntax and semantics of modal operators (as done originally in Werner, 1974, available as Werner, 1988a, 1989b, 1991b). Another problem is that none of the above authors integrate state information with strategic information. And, none of the above authors have a formal theory of uncertainty about information and intentions. Yet this is crucial for understanding multiagent communication as an interactive process. The representation of such uncertainties will be one of the concerns of this chapter.

While there are many authors who see that concepts from the social sciences are relevant to DAI and MAS, the only authors to do formal investigations into the logic of political interactions are Castelfranchi (1990), Castelfranchi et al. (1992) (see Chapter 20), and Werner (1983).

My own theory of multiagent systems developed out a fundamental question: What makes a society possible at all? This came as a natural development out of my study of communication and cooperation from a rigorous, formal perspective. I was interested in what I termed *open systems*, meaning dynamic systems of interacting agents. At first, I was interested in the dynamics of agent choices in a dynamic world of other agents. My methodology was to use logic and formal semantics. This led to a formalization of information and strategic action that turned out to have close links with von Neumann's work. I had developed the modal logic of games (Werner, 1988b). Later, as discussed below, the objective was to understand and formalize communication and cooperation in simple social systems. This led to the development of a general theory of multiagent communication and social organization (Werner, 1988c). It also resulted in a formalization of some of the Wittgensteinian language games (Wittgenstein, 1953, 1958; Werner, 1989a).

1.5 Outline of Things to Come

This chapter is a somewhat personal history and perspective of this new field. It focuses on concepts and does not attempt to give a detailed review of all of the literature. Most of the ideas presented here were developed by myself. This is not to say that others have not independently discovered or rediscovered some of the ideas presented here.

1.5.1 *Brief Overview.* We start by considering how communication may have evolved, how meaning and understanding evolved. The communication architecture of an agent is then described. Next, a conceptual, critical history of formal semantics (including Tarski, Kripke, Montague, and Situation semantics) is given in the light of the new theory of meaning, understanding and communication. Then, we dive into the deep subterranean world of types of uncertainty and their formalization. Simultaneous actions are explored. State uncertainty and uncertainty about plans are rigorously investigated. After the description of information states and the intentional states of individual agents and groups, we go on to an exploration of types of agent abilities, the logic of "can" or "is able to." We also present a novel, practical theory of utilitarian and probabilistic ability. Next, we look at types of intention in different social contexts. We conclude with an exploration of the concept of social entropy of organizations and groups.

1.5.2 *Advice to the Reader.* While the themes may appear to be diverse, they are all actually interconnected and necessary for an understanding of multiagent interaction. One of my main goals in introducing these concepts is for you, the reader, to gain a view of these interconnections and, thereby, help you to understand this fascinating field.

In terms of presentation style, I try to strike a balance between intuitive, informal descriptions of some of the key foundational concepts, on the one hand, and more rigorous formal definitions of these concepts, on the other hand. Thus, intuitive, philosophical, and historical conceptual description is mixed with a rigorous development of key concepts. For those who find the formal terrain difficult to traverse, please do not be intimidated and concentrate on the ideas, which are the basis of the formal concepts anyway. You can choose to skip or just briefly view the formal parts of the chapter on the first reading. Those who want a longer, deeper, and easier introduction to the field, as well as more details on the formalism, will hopefully enjoy my upcoming book on these and other issues.

2 THE EVOLUTION OF COMMUNICATION

My fundamental assumption is that coordination and cooperation is only possibly by way of the exchange of information. Isolated agents that are truly autonomous with no interactions are assumed to have no coordinated behavior. There may be relationships between their behavior because they may have a similar structure or experience. However, similar structure is a result of the phylogeny of the organism in its interaction over generations with the environment. Similar experience is a result of the ontogeny of the organism resulting from the interactions of the organism with its environment over its lifetime. In both cases the environment can be viewed as another agent, an agent common to both our original agents. Their common structure is then a result of an interaction with the same environment.

2.1   The Solipsistic and Alien Agents

A *solipsistic agent* is a single agent with no interaction with other agents or with the environment because it accepts no input. Such an agent may be difficult to imagine, but we include it for the sake of completeness in our logical space of possible agents as classified by their interactions. Such an agent may be a robot gone out of control having lost its senses and acting only on its internal imagined representations. Note, such an agent is still phylogenetically speaking couched in its environment. Even its ontogenetic structure may be intact. An *alien agent* is one whose phylogeny and ontogeny is not from the multiagent world in question and with a concomitant lack of commonality of ways of being with and understanding the world. Thus, its degree of alienation is relative to a multiagent system which in turn is part of a more general ecology.

2.2   Reactive Agents and Reactive Conversations

A *purely reactive agent* is one whose strategic state is purely reactive to its environment (cf. Chapter 11). If there are other agents in the environment it treats them on a par with other objects and not as harbingers of meaning. As such agents gain the faculty of memory, their reactions can become more and more sophisticated, and coordination may even be possible if the reactive strategies of the agents have coevolved so as to achieve some social end. The coordination in this case was achieved with Mother Nature being the common agent of interaction. Mother Nature weeded out all the reactive strategies that did not fit together. Consciously programming such agents to have coordination "emerge" can be very difficult. Since the agents change the properties of the world in some way, these properties if unique enough may be a stimulus for another agent including the agent who generated the stimulus. In this way a *reactive conversation* may emerge. One particular and popular beginning programming project is to have the agents interact by leaving a scent (Hussmann and Werner, 1990) or dropping pebbles. In these cases the environment can be viewed as being the program that the agents react to. The agents program each other and themselves by changing their common environment.

2.3 User-Guided Evolution of Reactive Coordination

A different approach to programming agents can be taken by extending the work of Karl Sims (1993) as motivated by Daniel Hillis (1990) and Holland (1975). Transferring and slightly generalizing these thoughts on graphics to agents, let the agents strategies evolve over time and let the user play Mother Nature in selecting those reactive strategies that suit him. Here the coordination that evolves is the result of the user as common agent. The user's tastes influence the phylogenically induced strategic control structure of the agents. Reactive interactions that are coordinated in space time may evolve quite naturally instead of being coerced by the more conscious and painful efforts of a programmer who directly and explicitly tries to design and program coordinated single and multiagent interaction strategies.

Simple reactive agents are extremely limited in the kinds of coordination that they can achieve. Real coordination and cooperation only become possible if we have communication (see also Chapter 6).

2.4 Where Does Meaning in Communication Come from?

Historically, attempts at a theory of meaning have been dominated by referential theories of meaning. These are theories that view meaning as a relationship between the language as syntax and the world as a set of objects (as well as properties and relations, in more sophisticated later versions). The meaning of a language token is what it refers to. For example, "mouse" refers to a mouse. "On top of" refers to a relation. The point is that an object or event, e.g., a sound or a stone, or a picture, represents something else. And the information content of this something else is usually much greater than and/or different from its symbolic representative object. This is the core of referential communication. It allows the transfer of information about an object, situation, or event without transferring all the information of the actual object or its original perception.

2.5 What Makes Communication Possible?

How is such a transfer possible? How can we transfer information in a conduit that is clearly incapable of actually representing the information it is to transfer? The answer lies in the nature of understanding. To understand a symbolic communicative object or event (e.g., a symbol, sound or gesture) means that the subject interprets the symbol. The subject has a capacity to relate the symbol to previously stored information. The symbol's meaning lies in its association with a representation in the subject and how the subject transforms his representation of the world in response to the symbol's representation. This is what I have called the pragmatic meaning of a symbolic object or event.

2.6 Pragmatic Meaning

Meaning, in this view, is not a passive representation that pictures the original object. Instead, it is associated with an operator that transforms the mental state of the subject. The subject brings more or different information to the meaning and interpretation of the symbol than can ever be informationally possible in the symbol, as conduit, itself. If we take the subject's information state I to be his representation of the state of the world, then I gives partial information about the world that is gotten by direct perception and by communication. A symbol α communicated to the agent transforms the agent's information state I to a new state J, where $J = \alpha I$. Here, the symbol α acts as an operator on the receiver's information state.

The point of the above philosophical discussion is that if α is just a syntactic symbol, or noise, or gesture, it could have any arbitrary meaning. Since its effect as an operator the symbolic object or event α must be given a pragmatic interpretation by the subject. If our subject is Dany, then let $Prag_{Dany}(\alpha)$ be Dany's subjective interpretation of α. If Dany accepts the message α, say that Sophie is in the kitchen, then the message α transforms her representation to one where Sophie is in the kitchen. Dany's information state becomes $J_{Dany} = Prag(\alpha) (I_{Dany})$, which says that the Dany's new information state J_{Dany} results from her previous information state I_{Dany} as transformed by the operator $Prag(\alpha)$, which is the pragmatic interpretation of the message α. It is actually a bit more complex, because the pragmatic interpretation function $Prag$ is relativized to Dany, $Prag_{Dany}$ since Dany's interpretation of messages like α may differ from that of other agents.

2.7 Referential Agents

Given that reactive agents have the ability to partially represent the world, at least one capacity that distinguishes communicating agents from purely reactive agents is the capacity to interpret messages pragmatically in the above sense. Such a capacity will give the agents a capacity to engage in referential pragmatic interpretations of symbols. A referential pragmatic interpretation changes the information state I_A of the agent A. Let us call such agents *referential agents*.

What do referential agents gain from such pragmatic capacity? We will see that information about state increases the capabilities of an agent as well as the capabilities of groups. Furthermore, in so far as vision is an interpreting process of visual information, vision itself can be taken to be a pragmatic operator that interprets visual information and transforms the information state of the seeing subject. Vision is in this sense like a language that transforms the information state I_A of the observer-agent A. Like a language we learn to see more with experience. With learning, the pragmatic visual operator changes. In fact, the visual pragmatic interpretive capacity, as well as the cognitive capacities this presupposes, may have been necessary for the evolution of the linguistic pragmatic interpretive capacity.

2.8 Intentional Agents

If all that agents could do was to talk about the state of the world, in the sense that their pragmatic operators were restricted to referential interpretations, then agents might be able to describe and to react to this information. For example, an agent may report a bear is coming toward the cave and the agents might react to this new information state by running away, given they have evolved such a strategy. However, if the agents wanted to kill a mammoth they may have had to coordinate their activities. And, reactive strategies to communication of state information will in general not be sufficient to elicit the complex coordination required in hunting activities.

Coordination requires something not found in a referential account of meaning. It requires the coordinated formation of strategic information states or intentions (see Chapters 5 and 6). By a *strategic information state* or *intentional state* I mean a mental state of the agent that represents and constitutes her control state. It is the state that guides and controls her actions in the world.

2.9 Evolution of Communication about Intentions

In itself, without communicative interactions, a control state may be reactive, as well as being tactical and strategic. It may have sophisticated planning capabilities associated with it. This is much like animals who have both reactive, tactical, strategic and planning capabilities. A key event in the evolution of meaning was when symbols began not just to have referential meanings, but to have strategic pragmatic meaning. A symbol (e.g., sound, object, picture, text) began to be associated with an action as well as with whole strategies of action. These symbols required a different sort of pragmatic interpretation. Instead of changing the information state, the operator associated with the symbol transformed the strategic control state of the agent. It transformed her intentions. And, by transforming her intentions it allowed the agent's actions to be directly influenced, controlled and coordinated. This fundamental development was crucial to all further human and animal organization, and it is the basis for complex coordination and cooperation in multiagent systems generally (see Chapter 6).

To systematically distinguish a message that has a primarily strategic meaning let us use the exclamation mark (!) to indicate a request or command. Thus, if $\beta!$ is a strategic symbol, the pragmatic interpretation of $\beta!$ is $Prag_A(\beta!)$, where A is the receiving, interpreting agent. We assume that the agent has a capacity to represent its intentions (see Chapter 5 for example of how this can be realized in software systems). Let us call this representation the agent A's *intentional state* and symbolically denote it as S_A.

2.10 The Architecture of Social Agents

Social agents have not only intentions that guide their actions but also the ability to take on various roles in social settings. These may range from very particular roles in action situations to complex responsibilities and permissions in an organization (see Chapters 18–20). As described in my work on communication and social structure (Werner, 1988c, 1989a) such roles can involve both state information I, strategic information S and evaluative information V. Together these basic types of information constitute the agent's *representational state $R = (I, S, V)$*. The adoption of a role then forms and constrains the agent's overall representational state. In order to be able to adopt a role the agent must have the abilities required by the role (see the section on abilities).

2.11   Communication Theory and the Force of Speech Acts

In the theory of communication that I developed (Werner, 1988c, 1989a), I distinguished between the syntax, the semantics and the pragmatics of a language. The *syntax* consists of a set of rules that generate the grammatical sentences of the language. The *semantics* relates language to situations in the world or representations of situations in the world. The *pragmatics* defines how language transforms the mental state of the communicators. The speaker's pragmatic competence is given by a compositional semantics and pragmatics that gives a semantic and pragmatic meaning to every sentence of the language generated by the syntax. This is different from the categorization made by Morris (1946, 1964, 1972).

For those familiar with speech act theory as developed by Austin (1962a,b) and Searle (1985), the pragmatics of a language, in my sense of the term, is not a theory of the perlocutionary effects as those are more like side effects of an utterance. The pragmatics is, instead, a theory of how language manipulates the representational state of the agent. For those not familiar with speech act theory, a speech act consists of a force plus a propositional content. The force indicates whether we are dealing with a request or assertion, for example. The propositional content is the referential component of the speech act that links it to the world. For example, "Open the door!" and "The door is open" are said to have the same propositional content but different force.

The theory of representations and pragmatic meaning outlined above allows us to give a novel and noncircular definition of the force of a speech act (Werner, 1988a). The *force* of a speech act is the focus of the pragmatic transformation. This focus can be directed at one of the following three fundamental types: the information state, the intentional state or the evaluative state. Thus, for example, assertives such as "He is in the kitchen" focus on the information state, while commands and requests like "Please give me some more cable" focus on the strategic, intentional state. Evaluatives or emotives like "I like that" focus on the evaluative state. Thus, the force of a speech act indicates the dominant part of the representational state of the agent that is to be changed by that speech act's pragmatic meaning, given that the message is accepted by the receiver. This theory of force has several advantages over the previous theory of Vandervecken and Searle as their definition is essentially circular, syntactic with no semantics, and does not relate force to mental states in a systematic way (see Werner, 1988a, for details).

3 MEANING IN MULTIAGENT SYSTEMS

3.1 The Meta-Observer and the Object System

The designer of a multiagent system Γ as observer and agent can and usually does take a meta perspective with regard to that system. By *meta-perspective* I mean that the system is viewed and acted on from the outside, from a perspective and action space external to the system. Let us call the agent that is observing the system from the meta-perspective the *meta-observer* and the observed system the *object system*. The agents in the object multiagent system will be called *object agents*. The *object world* is the world in which the agents act. This world contains the object agents as well. The *state* of a multiagent object system minimally consists of the object space-time world state (physical environment), the state of the agents as objects in that world, as well as the internal (informational, intentional and evaluational) state of the agents.

3.2 Object and Meta-Language

Our notion of meta-perspective was motivated by the logician Alfred Tarski. Tarski (1956) made a distinction between the *object language* that the logician is investigating, e.g., the formulas of first-order logic, and the *meta-language* that the logician uses to talk and prove things about the object language. The typical meta-language was a natural language such as English supplemented with a mathematical language such as set theory. A proof in the object language was different than a proof in the meta-language. The meta-language is typically more powerful than the object language. This allows the object language to be translated into the meta-language. Hence, to each term $\bar{\alpha}$ in the object language there corresponds a term α in the meta-language.

3.3 Multiagent Object and Meta-Languages

We propose making an analogous distinction for the study of multiagent systems. Hence, we distinguish the *agent object language* (AOL) that the agent's use to communicate, from the designer's *agent meta-language* (AML), that the system designer uses to talk about the agents and their communication. Distinguishing the AOL from the meta-language has the important consequence that it keeps the communication interface between the agents precise. Agent linguistic communication is restricted to the agent object language AOL. When this is not done one can observe that the programmer designing and implementing the system has a difficult time maintaining the boundaries between his program (the meta-language) and the interaction language between the agents.

Indeed, most often the programmer is totally unaware that he is mixing the two. The result is a possibly poor, messy design that is not modular and also difficult to extend and maintain.

3.4 Object Semantics and Object Pragmatics

As we saw, *semantics* relates language to the world, *pragmatics* relates language to how it transforms the mental state of the agent. The pragmatics is realized through *pragmatics operators* that act on the information state, intentional state and evaluative state of the agent. A pragmatic interpretation of a language associates operators with sentences of the language. For each sentence α of the language the associated operator $Prag(\alpha)$ indicates how the intentional state, the information state, and the evaluative state of the agent is to be updated or transformed (see Werner, 1989a, for more details).

For Tarski, semantics was part of the meta-language. He took the role of the meta-observer who provides a theory of meaning for the given object language by giving it a formal semantics where the terminology used to describe the semantics was part of the meta-language. He did not consider agents or their communication. He was concerned with the semantics of logical formulas. We, however, are interested in understanding the process of communication between agents. In communication it is the *agent* who interprets and gives meaning to the agent object language AOL. So, for us, the semantics and pragmatics become part of the agent, and, thus, they become part of the agent as objects of meta-observation.

Therefore, from our meta-perspective (you the reader and I), we distinguish the meta-language and its *meta-semantics* used by an observer of a multiagent system Γ from the agent object language AOL with its associated *object semantics OS_B* and *object pragmatics OP_B* which is used by the object agents within that system Γ. Thus, if we want to be very precise, consider a meta-agent A observing a multiagent system Γ containing an object agent B. We can distinguish between the agent A's meta-language AML_A and its associated meta-semantics MS_A, from the agent object language AOL_Γ and the associated object semantics OS_B and object pragmatics OP_B for AOL_Γ.

For example, the designer, and possibly the user, can communicate with the agents at their level if he communicates with those agents using the agent object language. The designer must interpret the agent object language, by way of the object semantics, in terms of a meta-linguistic description and its corollary meta-interpretation.

The situation is a bit complicated because the object semantics when studied by the meta-observer is described in the meta-language of the meta-observer. And, this meta-language is meaningful to the meta-observer because he has a meta-semantics and pragmatics to interpret the meta-language. These are the considerations that arise when we (you the reader and I) are the meta-meta-observers observing the combined system of meta-observer (now as object agent relative to us) observing an object agent community. As an aside, it is interesting to note that this is just the situation in Everett's many-worlds interpretation of quantum mechanics where Everett assumes the role of meta-meta-observer and adds the meta-observer (which von Neumann kept separate from the observed system) to be part of the system under observation (see von Neumann, 1961; Everett, 1957; Wheeler, 1957).

The notion of *object semantics/pragmatics* is needed because the capacity of the agent to understand the agent object language AOL is given locally by the agent's object structure. This concept is important since the object semantics and pragmatics is local to the agent. The agent object language together with its object semantics and pragmatics encapsulate the linguistic communicative properties of the agent and, thereby, allow a well-defined communication interface to the agent. They make the agent part of a linguistic community.

If we imagine a group of robots building a space station, their agent object language might be a simplified natural language of directives, requests, commands, informatives, and simple evaluatives. The robots would have an object semantics and pragmatics to interpret this object language. Furthermore, they would be able to execute the new intentional states that result from the communicative interchange. That is, there are two levels of interpretation happening. One level interprets the object language with the object pragmatics by acting on the agent's intentions (plan states). The level below is an *object plan interpreter*, which may be local to the agent, that executes the active intentional state.

3.5 The Relativity of Semantics and Pragmatics

Traditionally, formal theories of meaning, such as model theory or possible world semantics, have failed to distinguish the object semantics from the meta-semantics. Even Tarski, who first made the distinction of the object and meta-language failed to recognize the distinction of object and meta-semantics. This failure resulted in the implicit projection, of part or all of the meta-semantics, onto all agents as the universal object semantics. That meant that within these theoretical frameworks one could not give an account of inter- and intracommunity linguistic variance in meaning and understanding. Both Tarski semantics, as well as possible world semantics, are not defined with regard to agents. The point of view, i.e., the meta-perspective, is external and global. It is that of a meta-observer having a clear and correct understanding of the semantics. As a consequence, they could not explain misunderstanding. Once the distinction between object and meta-semantics is made, however, it becomes clear that there may be variance and divergence in the object semantics/pragmatics within and between communities of agents. Furthermore, we are now in a position to give a precise account of inter- and intracommunity variance of language meaning and understanding.

In a multiagent system, each agent has his own realization of the object semantics and object pragmatics of the agent object language AOL. It is, therefore, possible that each agent has different object semantics and pragmatics from every other agent. This means that the pragmatic operators $Prag_A(\alpha)$ are relativized to the agent A that is interpreting the sentence α of the agent object language AOL. It can happen that for two agents A and B, it is possible that for the same sentence α in their common agent object language the pragmatic interpretations differ:

$$Prag_A(\alpha) \neq Prag_B(\alpha) \tag{1}$$

Thus, each agent has his own local interpretation of any given message α.

3.6 Misunderstanding and Learning a Language

It is a different question as to how the commonality and divergence of meaning arises. The relativization of the object semantics and pragmatics to agents makes misunderstanding possible. Now, as we would like our agents to understand each other, one might also want an agent to be gradually integrated into a society of agents by learning their norms, roles, and their language (see Werner, 1992). But, that implies that the agent starts out in a state where he only has a partial understanding of that language. Hence, the agent's starting object semantics and object pragmatics may be different from that of the community.

A theory of language learning needs to give an account of how the object pragmatics of the learning agent, e.g., a child, changes to be in line with the object pragmatics of the community. Such a theory requires a relativization of the semantics and pragmatics to the agent. This relativity of semantics and pragmatics to the agent is just a natural extension of the relativity of knowledge of the agent. For, each agent A has his own information state I_A, intentional state S_A, and evaluative state V_A. These states are dynamic, changing with time as the agent interacts with other agents in the world. The relativization of semantics and pragmatics to the agent allows the object semantics and pragmatics to be dynamic as well.

The communicative interaction of agent and social context results in a gradual acquisition of the capacity to understand the language; the agent learns the semantics and pragmatics of the language. Note, Chompsky (1969) really only addressed the problem of how speakers learn the syntax of a language. Here we are confronting the problem of how speakers learn to understand a language. Winogard in his early work on a robot controlled by language clearly saw the difference (1972) as did Schank and Abelson (1977).

4 A GENERAL COMMUNICATION ARCHITECTURE ICE

Based on the above conceptual developments, let us outline the general architecture of agents with a communicative competence. We call it the ICE architecture which is short for $I^2C^2E^2$, or information, intention, communication, cooperation, evaluation, and empowerment architecture for dynamic interacting agents.

4.1 Agent Cognitive Architecture

The ICE architecture for the mental or *representational state* of an agent A consists of tuple $R_A = (I_A, S_A, V_A)$, where

1. I_A is the agents *information state*. We allow nesting, I_A^B is A's state information about B's information. I_A^A is A's information about its own information state. The information state gives the agent's information about its world at a given time.
2. S_A is the agent's *strategic or intentional state*. Again we allow nesting as with information states. It consists of a partial strategy or, equivalently, a set of strategies that guide the agent's choices of action (see also Chapters 6–9, 18, and 20).
3. V_A is the *evaluation state* of the agent. It can consist of a utility function over objects, situations and states. It may be discreet, indicating wants or desires (see Chapter 9).

The representational state R and its components I, S, and V are all dynamic changing in time and modified by the dynamic interactions with the environment and with other agents.

4.2 The Space of Possible Representations of an Agent

The agents can form concepts, plans, and evaluations dynamically while they are in some goal-directed process. Part of the competence of the agent's real time planning and strategic capabilities comes from a repertoire of plans and concepts (see Chapter 8). This repertoire is combined dynamically to form the given actual intentional state of the agent.

1. $PC(\Omega)_A$ is the *absolute plan competence space* of the agent. It is the set of possible partial (including complete) plans and strategies of the agent given the action space Ω. It sets the limits of what is logically possible for the agent given his action space. All competencies that follow are within this space.
2. PR_A^t is the *plan repertoire* also called a *plan library* of the agent A at time t. These are the basic skill fragments, tactics or strategies the agent has inherited or learned and are available dynamically to construct a much larger set of real time available dynamic plans. Note, this repertoire is itself dynamic since the agent can learn a new skill or strategy while attempting some goal-directed process.
3. $PC(PR)_A^t$ is the *plan competence* of the agent given his plan repertoire at some time t. It consists of the space of possible plans as limited by

A's repertoire. It allows unbounded computation time but no new skill development.

4. $\Delta(R_A)'_A$ is the set of *dynamic strategies* available to the agent in real time relative to his plan repertoire PR'_A at time t. Here "real time" depends on the time of activity in which an agent can adjust his plan state dynamically in a goal-directed process. This dynamic competence will in general depend on what the agent knows and so also depends of his representational state R_A.

We have introduced a dynamic plan space Δ_A because a plan library does not indicate the real-time plan competence of the agent. For the agent may not, and need not, have a full representation of the abstract, partial plan he is executing. He will usually fill in the details as he performs the plan depending on the local circumstances, surprises, failures, and opportunities.

4.3 Communicative Competence

Given an agent architecture with $R_A = (I_A, S_A, V_A)$ and a dynamic repertoire $\Delta(R_A)$ we can define the communicative competence of the agent:

1. *Syntax.* The agent has a language L, the *agent object language* AOL, with a syntax to generate the sentences of the language. This syntax can range from being very basic consisting of a very few symbols to being an advanced natural language like English.

2. *Semantics OS_a.* The agent has an *object semantics Semantics^L_A* for the language L. The semantics provides a situational meaning to the basic expressions and sentences of the language relating the language to the agent's world.

3. *Pragmatics OP_A.* The agent has an *object pragmatics Prag^L_A* for the language L. The agent's object pragmatics associates with each sentence α of the language L an operator $Prag_A(\alpha)$ on the representational capacity of the agent. It takes a representational state $R_A = (I_A, S_A, V_A)$ and transforms it to a new representational state:

$$Prag_A(\alpha) (R_A) = R'_A$$

$$= (Prag_A(\alpha) (I_A), Prag_A(\alpha) (S_A), Prag_A(\alpha) (V_A)) \quad (2)$$

4. *Linguistic Strategies.* The agent has a *dialogue competence* that allows him to interact in conversations. These consist of linguistic protocols and strategies. These may be dynamically formed from a repertoire.

If we let α be shorthand for both the sentence and the operator, this states $\alpha(R) = \alpha R = R'$. We can then easily chain communication operators $\alpha_1\alpha_2\alpha_3 R$ which represents a series of pragmatic messages starting with α_3 then α_2 and ending with α_1 operating on R. The *force* of the message (speech act) is that subrepresentation of R that is the primary focus of the operator. For example, a command or request will have as its primary focus the strategic intentional state S_A with a secondary focus on the information state I_A indicating that a message has arrived, etc. So, the force of a command or request is strategic. The focus of assertions is on the information state I_A and its force is informative.

4.4 Cooperation or Social Architecture

Beyond a basic communicative competence to pragmatically understand a language the agent will have a social competence to interact with the language. It is usually not recognized by linguists that this is a fundamental additional linguistic and social skill of an agent. Additionally, the capacity to interact socially in organizations with roles and networks of such are additional social competencies that agents may or may not have.

1. *Social Roles.* The social agent has the capacity to participate in, take on, and recognize social roles. Roles include permissions and responsibilities. Roles may also have associated linguistic strategies of interaction (see Chapter 20).

2. *Organizational Competence.* The agent has the competence to functionally represent and participate in organizations. Organizations consist of complexes of roles and suborganizations (see Chapter 19).

3. *Networks of Organizations.* The agent has the competence to represent and participate in networks of organizations. The networks are linked by special network roles (see Chapter 19). These may involve special linguistic protocols.

5 MOTIVATION AND DEVELOMENT OF THE ICE ARCHITECTURE

5.1 Conceptual History of the ICE Architecture

The ICE architecture was developed independently in the mid- to late 1970s as a basis for understanding communication and cooperation among multiple agents. The theory behind ICE was developed in three major phases.

Operators on Information States. First, in my work on the temporal modal logic of games, I had developed a formal dynamic semantics that included information states as part of the semantics. I realized that one should be able to use the formalization of information within semantics to develop a theory of how information is communicated by language. More particularly, I became interested in understanding how the information state of agents changes as they communicate. I developed a theory of how communication changes information states. This is what I called a pragmatic theory of the meaning of informative messages. The subject or agent had a mental state, his information state and this state were transformed by the communicative messages he received and interpreted.

Relations to Observables in Quantum Mechanics. This led to a view that meaning is like an operator on the information state of the subject changing the information state by operating on it to form a new information state. Independently, I had been reading in quantum mechanics, in particular von Neumann's mathematical foundations of quantum mechanics and the theory of how observations act as operators on the state (as a vector in a Hilbert space) of the wave function (von Neumann, 1959). By viewing the observer's state itself as a wave function, we can view the observation as changing the state of the observer and the observed. Physicists had studied interesting properties of such operators, and I realized that they had analogues in normal communication. Furthermore, the gaining of information about a phase space in statistical mechanics, with its reduction of entropy, as the reduction of the phase space (see, for example, Khinchin, 1949, and Boltzmann, 1981), was similar to the way communication operators reduce the information set defining the information state of the agent. These similarities with other seemingly dissimilar theories suggested that there was some fundamental, universal aspect of information that had been captured by the theory of information states and their operators.

The Influence of Sociology and Intentional States. This representational operator model of communication was extended, when, stimulated by the writings of the sociologist Jürgen Habermas (1981), it became obvious to me that the most important aspects of human communication, namely communication in social cooperative activity, could not be explained by communication about state information alone. Some other representational structure was needed, something that controlled the agent's actions: control information. So, I developed the theory of intentional states with the explicit aim that such states must be dynamically transformable (operated on) by communicative interactions. The idea was that communication between agents dynamically form the intentions of agents setting up their intentional states so that coordinated activity and cooperation were possible. This I saw as the foundation for a theory of society. I viewed the intentional state as that which controls the agent's activity on the basis of the evaluations and state information the agent has about the world.

Language Games. Habermas also reminded me of my student readings of Wittgenstein (1953, 1958). Wittgenstein had actually made a similar discovery, that state information cannot adequately account for all the functions of language. In his terms the meaning of language lies in its use. His examples of various language games show that the meaning of the expressions used in the games (e.g., "brick!" when uttered by a mason to his apprentice to mean "bring me a brick!") could not be reduced to an assertion that was true or false. They are good examples of self-contained mini social situations of agents engaged in communication and cooperative activity. It is for this reason that I formalized some of his language games to test my theory of communication. For one of the simpler formalizations, see Werner (1989a).

5.2 Motivations for BDI

How does the ICE architecture differ from the BDI (for beliefs, desires, intentions) architecture? The BDI architecture was based on the work of Bratman (1987), and described more thoroughly in Chapter 5. It was developed after Bratman had independently developed a theory of intentions. His intuitions and discoveries about intentions were strikingly similar to mine. However, our original motivations were different. He was more interested in capturing the properties of human intentions and their function in human reasoning and decision making, whereas I was interested in the function of intentions in communication and social coordination. My ultimate motivation was an abstract theory of what makes social cooperation possible. I viewed communication as playing a central role in social cooperation. It should also be noted that the BDI architecture is not a formal theory but rather a verbal description that beliefs, desires, and intentions ought to be part of the mental states of the agent. It says nothing of how to precisely integrate these notions into a coherent theory.

5.3 Requirements of a Theory of Animal and Robotic Communication

Since I was trying to develop a general theory, I was not only interested in human communication and cooperation but in animal and robotic communication and cooperation as well, for animals exhibit quite sophisticated social coordination and signaling. A theory of communication and coordination should be able to explain such phenomenon as well. Since they are probably simpler phenomenon than human communication and social coordinations, I saw them as an interesting area to test a theory of communication and cooperation.

   If one wanted to build robots with various degrees of abilities, communicative and social competence, then a theory of representational states (such as the ICE architecture), communication, and cooperation should be abstract enough to permit the design of very simple communicating and cooperating robots. Such robots may not reason symbolically and may lack sophisticated intentions and beliefs, but they still need strategic control states and information states that are manipulable by some form of primitive communication. More generally reactive agents might have very simple, nonsymbolic, nonanthropomorphic strategic control states (see Chapter 11). Yet these might still respond to a primitive, or even complex, pragmatically interpreted language.

5.4   Problems with Belief and Desire

This is one reason I stayed away from the notion of belief. The logic and semantics of belief and knowledge have been controversial since their inception. Information states are more abstract and make use of solid theory about the nature of information, control, entropy, and game theory. Indeed, the way the "belief" predicate is actually used by adherents to the BDI architecture, it is little different than a symbolic way of indicating what state information the agent has. Similarly, I preferred the notion of evaluations to desires because, again I did not want to make anthropomorphic projections on the evaluations of utility that animals, humans, or robots may be making.

5.5   Universality: BDI as a Special Case of ICE

In a further demand for universality, my notion of intentional state as a set of possible strategies that control an agent, allows a formalization of control information that has nice properties that make it fit well with a general theory of information and communication. Also, it allows an integration of state information, strategic-intentional information, and evaluative-utility information. This integration allows the explanation and formalization of interesting social phenomena. It is necessary to explain the relation of state information, abilities of an agent and the intentions of the agent (Werner, 1990, 1991a). Furthermore, the abstract ICE architecture allows the inclusion of the BDI architecture as a special case. Namely, beliefs correspond to and are one way to define information states, desires are particular sorts of evaluations, and the informal notion of intention corresponds to the more rigorous notion of plan state and intentional state. Finally, the ICE architecture allows but does not require a commitment to a symbolic representation of information (including beliefs), intentions, or evaluations (including desires). A connectionist or other theory of mental representational states is allowed by the ICE architecture.

6   A BRIEF CONCEPTUAL HISTORY OF FORMAL SEMANTICS

We now look at the work in formal semantics that has had an influence on the formal study of multiagent systems and formal communication theory.

6.1   Tarski Semantics

First, there is the tradition of modern mathematical logic which began with Boole and continued in this century with its emphasis on formal axiomatic systems (Whitehead and Russell, 1910). The work of Tarski is significant because it was the first formalization of the semantics of first-order logic with quantifiers over individuals. Tarski (1956) viewed *semantics* as establishing a relationship between the language of logic which he called the *object language* and the world which he called a *model*. Tarski distinguished the object language from the meta-language. Recall, for Tarski, the object language is the language the logician is studying. The *meta-language* is the language the logician uses to investigate the object language. The meta-language contains the object language but it also consists of ordinary English and any other mathematical language that the logician chooses to use. Thus, the semantics of the object language is described in a semiformal meta-language. The object language has explicit and rigorous rules of syntax which specify precisely what sentences and expressions are part of the object language and which are not. In contrast, the meta-language need have no precise syntax since it is usually an informal mixture of natural language and formal mathematical language.

To be termed a *formal semantics*, there must be a precise mathematical description of the world, called the *model*, consisting of objects, their properties and relationships. There must also be a precise mapping between the object language's terms and predicates, on the one hand, and the objects, properties, and relations in the model, on the other hand. And there must be a precise definition of the conditions under which any given sentence of the object language is true or false. The latter are called the *truth conditions* (also satisfiability, validity conditions) of the semantics. More formally, a Tarski model for a language L consists of $\langle O, R^n, \Phi \rangle$, where O is a set of objects, R^n is a set of properties and relations on O, and Φ is an evaluation function that assigns truth and falsity to sentences of the object language L.

With Tarski's work, one starts to have a feeling or intuition that it is the beginnings of a formal theory of meaning for a language. In fact, the work of Tarski has had a tremendous influence on formal logic, linguistics, and computer science. Its dominant influence in computer science and linguistics has been by way of the semantics for modal logic (which investigates operators like "it is possible that," "it is necessary that," "it will be the case that," "A believes that," etc.) The syntax and some of the axiomatic systems of modal logic were first investigated by Lewis and Langford (1959). But it took some 30 years before semantics of modal logics developed. Hintikka (1962), Prior (1967), and Kripke (1963) made some ground breaking investigations into the semantics of modal logic. Kripke's work is perhaps the most abstract and generally applicable.

6.2 Possible-Worlds Semantics

Kripke semantics (1963) adds possible worlds to Tarski models (1956). Instead of having a model represent a world, a model now contains many possible worlds and an *accessibility relationship* R between possible worlds indicates what other worlds are possible from a given world. For example, suppose our model M contains a set of possible worlds W with w_1 and w_2 member worlds in W. Furthermore, our model will contain an accessibility relationship R that holds if one world can be reached from another world. Let Φ be a function that assigns truth T and falsity F to sentences depending on the conditions that hold in the model M. Then the truth condition for the sentence $\Diamond \alpha$ (read "it is possible that α'') can be written as

$$\Phi(\Diamond\alpha, w_1) = T \text{ iff } \exists w_2 \in W, \text{ if } w_1 R w_2 \text{ then } \Phi(\alpha, w_2) = T \qquad (3)$$

This states the sentence "It is possible that α" is true in the world w_1 if and only if there is some world w_2 that is accessible from w_1 and α is true in that world. In effect, the truth condition repeats the intuitive meaning of the sentence but in a formal description that relates the sentence to the conditions of the model that represents the structure of the universe (which in this case consists of many possible worlds).

6.3 Semantics of Temporal Logic

More informally, A. N. Prior (1967) investigated the semantics of tense operators like "It will be the case that α," $F\alpha$, before Kripke. But, it turned out that one can reinterpret the accessibility relationship in Kripke semantics in many ways. One way is to interpret the accessibility relationship as a temporal ordering relationship. In the case of linear time R is just $<$, the less-than relationship between time points. This can then be used to give a formal semantics to the Prior tense operators as well as others. Summing up, in Kripke's extension to Tarski semantics a model is a tuple $\langle W, R, O, P^n, \Phi \rangle$ where W is a set of *possible worlds* and R is an accessibility relationship between possible worlds. The subportion $\langle W, R, O, P^n \rangle$ is called a *model structure* as it is somewhat independent of the particular truth conditions function Φ of the complete model.

6.4 Limitations of Kripke Possible-Worlds Semantics

Note, there are no agents in a Kripke model. A further subtlety is that any sophisticated object language contains both tense operators and modal operators. For example, one can speak of what *was possible* or what *will be necessary*. Such mixed modal systems that contain several types of modal operators are becoming increasingly common and being used in the formal specification and verification of distributed and multiagent systems. They were first investigated in Werner (1974). The main results were republished and are available in Werner (1988b, 1989b). Both modal operators with temporal indices, as well as logics with both tenses and modal operators were investigated.

Modal operators with temporal indices allow one to express things like $\Box_{t_1}\alpha(t_2) \rightarrow \Box_{t_3}\alpha(t_2)$ where $t_1 \leq t_3$. This states that if it is necessary at time t_1 that sentence α holds at time t_2 then it will be necessary at any later time t_3 that α holds at time t_2. Tensed modal systems allow a similar sentence: $P\Box\alpha \rightarrow \Box P\Box\alpha$ where P is the past operator for "it was the case that" and $\Box$ is the necessity operator. The formula states "If it was necessary that α then it is necessary that was necessary that α." Since the above two axioms hold in models where the information that an agent has does not decrease over time, I called these axioms the NDI axioms (nondiminishing information axioms). These were part of a systematic investigation of logics for agents acting in a changing open world of choices given only partial information about the world.

6.5 Problems with Branching Time

The semantics for these multimodal systems become more complex. Now we need to include not just possible worlds but also time. In a Kripke model the worlds are static. However, as we noted above, the accessibility relation R can be interpreted as a temporal relationship. Thus, if R is linear we can interpret it as a linear time ordering. Particular temporal axioms then hold. Many authors attempt to use Prior's original solution to modeling choices in a temporal framework by using his notion of *branching time*. In branching time the temporal relationship is not linear but allows branches into the future (given the appropriate assumptions about the temporal relation R.) We then get a treelike temporal structure where each path in the tree from start to finish (given a finite tree) represents a possible history of the world.

There are difficulties with branching time, as Prior himself recognized. First, it is very counterintuitive to the normal view of time as linear. Second, times in distinct possible histories are incomparable. Yet, we regularly reason, both hypothetically and counterfactually, about possibilities that involve comparing times in distinct possible futures and pasts. Third, a more subtle, but central point is that the semantic representation of uncertainty about time becomes difficult. Fourth, the computation of temporal comparisions becomes more complex because one has to check the partial ordering relationships versus checking direct linear numerical relationships. Fifth, the use of time to represent indeterminism forces an identification of possibilities with time points. This is not only an ontological confusion but also a category mistake that jeopardizes the semantics of both time and world states. For these and other reasons, I rejected the use of branching time in favor of linear time with indeterministic worlds.

6.6 Dangers of Whimsical Accessibility Relations

A scientist who blindly adheres to Kripke semantics may try to introduce a separate accessibility relation for each new operator he comes across without trying to understand the function and structure of those relations. We have seen how Kripke introduced an accessibility relation for the necessity and possibility operators, and we have noted the use of an accessibility relation for representing branching time.

One might also be tempted to postulate an accessibility relation for the "believes that" operator and the "intends that" operator. Unfortunately, in doing this all hope of actually understanding the relationship between such operators, e.g., "believes that" and "intends that," becomes problematic, for, without giving an accessibility relation properties, one accessibility relation is no better than and no different from any other accessibility relation holding between possible worlds. Discovering those properties of accessibility relations is one of the key problems in developing formal semantics. Furthermore, in postulating that an operator's semantics is given by an accessibility relation between possible worlds one may actually no longer be making any sense. To say that "*A* intends that *α*" holds if the "intends that" accessibility relation holds for some set of worlds fails to relate the logic of intends to plans. It, instead, is based on a false and blind analogy with the "necessary that" and "possible that" operators.

For this reason I try to integrate the concepts of time, information, ability and intention as constitutive parts of the semantics and pragmatics. I do so not by blindly adding accessibility relations between possible worlds but constructing the specific formal semantic objects that are appropriate to the meaning of the operator. Providing this meaning is, after all, the purpose of a semantics. Because of this, I will, for example, define "can" and the "intends that" operators in terms of plans and strategies and structures constructed from or derived from such plans and strategies. We, thereby, are more likely to get at the actual meaning of these operators.

The failure to provide structure to the intends and belief accessibility relations by connecting the semantics with the actual meaning makes, for example, the relationship of intentions with abilities very difficult if not impossible to see. Just as difficult to formulate is the relationship of information (beliefs) with intentions, as well as, with abilities. Furthermore, our semantics allows the investigation of what happens in cases of partial information about the world, as well as the more difficult topic of partial information about plans. The reason we are able to formalize these relationships is because the semantics I developed, in contradistinction to other semantics, integrates dynamic plans and dynamic information states into a temporal possible-worlds semantics.

7 DYNAMIC POSSIBLE-WORLD SEMANTICS

7.1 Avoiding Branching Time

How do we avoid using branching time? We simply refuse to identify time points with world states or situations. Instead, we associate world states with times, both having equal ontological status but being of different categories of entities. Thus, a world history becomes a function from the set of times to the set of possible states. More formally, let T be a set of times linearly ordered by a relation $<$. Let Σ be the set of all possible states of the system. Then a *history* H is a function from T to Σ. Let H_t represent the state of the world H at time t in T. That is, $H_t = H(t)$. Let H^t be the *partial history* of the world H up to and including time t. Intuitively, H^t is the history of the world up to the time t; it is not defined after time t. But prior to and including time t the partial history H^t behaves just like H. This is because they are identical prior to time t; i.e., $H_{t_0} = H'_{t_0}$ for all times $t_0 \leq t$. A branch into the future at time t consists of two histories H and K such that H and K are identical up to the time t but diverge thereafter. We then say the worlds H and K are *backwards identical* at time t. Let Ω be the set of all possible histories H that are allowed by the system, universe, or model in question. We now are able to represent indeterministic situations without using branching time.

7.2 Dynamic Accessibility Relationships

In Kripke semantics the accessibility relationship is static; it does not change with time. Yet, in the real world possibilities change with time and intuitively the worlds that are accessible even from the same world can change over time. In chess, you have the classic example that you cannot castle the king if the king has been moved before, even if the king has been moved back to its original position. Thus, what is possible after the king has moved is no longer possible in the future even if the state of the chess game is identical to one where one could otherwise castle. More generally, it is helpful to consider relationships that change with time when investigating the dynamic situations that agents find themselves in, especially when the agents no longer have perfect information about the state of the world.

A world history, much like the world line in phsyics, can be viewed as a world that changes in time. So, analogous to world histories, a changing relationship can be defined as a function from times to possible static relationships. The result is a dynamic relation that changes with time. In particular, we can generalize the Kripke accessibility relationship to one that changes with time. More formally, a dynamic accessibility relation $\Re$ is a function from times T to relations on Ω. Let $\Re^t$ be the value of the dynamic accessibility relation $\Re$ at time t. Two histories H and K are related by $\Re$ at time t if $H\Re^t K$. Recall a normal static relation is just a set of ordered pairs. On this view, two objects a, b stand in a static relationship R if the ordered pair (a, b) is a member of R. A *dynamic relation* $\Re$ is a changing set of ordered pairs. So the value of a dynamic relationship at a time t, in symbols $\Re^t$, is a static set of ordered pairs. Hence, H is related to K by $\Re^t$ if and only if the ordered pair (H, K) is a member of $\Re^t$ which is what $H\Re^t K$ says.

7.3 Models with Dynamic Worlds in Changing Relationships

So far so good. We now have changing indeterministic worlds that can be in changing relationships to one another. Time is still linear. We have extended the Kripke model significantly. Given a temporal modal language L (still unspecified) a *semantics* for temporal modal logic consists of a dynamic open model structure

$$MS = ((T, <), \Sigma, \Omega, \Re, O, P^n) \tag{4}$$

together with an evaluation function Φ where

1. T is a set of times linearly ordered by a temporal ordering relation $<$.
2. Σ is a set of possible states.
3. Ω is a set of dynamic world histories.
4. $\mathfrak{R}$ is a dynamic accessibility relation between the elements of Ω.
5. O is a set of objects.
6. P^n is a set of properties and relations of order $n = 0$ to some finite N.
7. Φ is an evaluation function giving the truth (and satisfiability) conditions for the given temporal modal language L.

7.4 Dynamic Semantics for Temporal Modal Logics

We already have a quite powerful semantics. We can investigate the dynamic modal logics of agents in changing circumstances. The logics can be temporally indexed modal operators, like $\Box_t$. Or we have tenses combined with modal operators, as in $\neg F \neg \Box \alpha$, where $\neg$ is the negation operator ("it is not the case that"), F is the future operator ("it will be the case that"), and $\Box$ is the necessity operator ("It is necessary that"). Thus, literally this formula states "It is not the case that it will be the case that it is not the case that it is necessary that α." Equivalently and more succinctly this says "It will always be necessary that α."

The truth condition for $\Box_t$ is as follows:

$$\Phi(\Box_t \alpha(t'), H) = T \text{ iff for all } K \in \Omega, H\mathfrak{R}^t K, \Phi(\alpha(t'), K) = T \qquad (5)$$

Translating into English, this says that "It is necessary at time t that α is true (T) at time t'" is true in the world history H if and only if for all world histories K such that K is possible in the history H at time t relative to the dynamic conditions $\mathfrak{R}^t$, α holds in K at time t'. The time-dependent relationship $\mathfrak{R}^t$ expresses conditions such as information conditions in the world H that determine what is possible at that point in time.

The analogous truth condition for the tense modal language is

$$\Phi(\Box \alpha, H, t) = T \text{ iff for all } K \in \Omega, H\mathfrak{R}^t K, \Phi(\alpha, K, t) = T \qquad (6)$$

Intuitively, this is like the Kripke interpretation except now what is possible and necessary depends on the time t and changing accessibility relation $\mathfrak{R}$ holding over changing worlds H and K. The properties of the accessibility relationship determine the kind of modal axioms that hold (Hughes and Cresswell, 1968), except now those properties include temporal properties of changing relationships. We now look at what is possible in a changing world at a given point in time. Temporal relationships are evaluated distinctly from modal relationships in the case of tense operators. If, for example, α is a tense formula of the form $F\beta$ then $\Phi(\Box F\beta)$, H, t) holds if and only if for all K, $H\Re'K$, $\Phi(F\beta, K, t)$ holds. And this holds if and only if for each K, $H\Re'K$, there is a time t' where $t < t'$ and $\Phi(\beta, K, t')$ holds. Hence, $\Box F\beta$ holds in world H at time t if β holds in every possible future K at some future time t'. In other words, β is inevitable in the world H at time t, but the exact time at which β will hold is not specified.

7.5 Properties of the Dynamic Accessibility Relation

Interestingly, some general axioms hold depending on the dynamic properties of the dynamic accessibility relation. Two of the most important properties are backwards identity and backwards consistency. Later we will also see that the information conditions of an agent generate a dynamic, information relation that is also a dynamic, accessibility relation. There is an interesting relation between the information conditions of an agent and the properties of the dynamic, accessibility relation.

7.5.1 *Backwards Identical Dynamic Relations* A dynamic relation $\Re$ is *backwards identical* if for all worlds H and K in Ω and for all times t in T, $H\Re'K$ if and only if for all times $t_0 \le t$, $H_t = K_t$. This just says the two worlds are identical prior to and including time t. We will see that when an agent in a system has perfect information, in the sense of knowing his complete past and present states, then the accessibility relation generated by the information conditions is backwards identical.

7.5.2 *Backwards Consistent Dynamic Relations* A dynamic relation $\Re$ has *nondiminishing information* or *satisfies the NDI-condition* if for all times t and t' in T where $t \le t'$, if $H\Re'K$ then $H\Re'K$. This says the dynamic relation $\Re$ cannot grow larger in the future. We will see why this implies information is not lost. Note, this does not say that more options cannot be available in the future. Indeed, the opposite can be true. Rather it only says the world *histories* that are related cannot increase under the backwards consistency condition. Note, also, that the backwards consistency condition is implied by the backwards identity condition. Later we will see the informational analogue of this, namely, perfect information implies nondiminishing information.

8 SITUATION SEMANTICS AND PRAGMATICS

8.1 From Montague to Situation Semantics

In the 1970s Montague semantics was king of the hill. It was a systematic extension and application of the Tarski, Kripke semantics to give a semantic analysis of language (see Montague, 1976). Because of its extensive use of possible worlds and accusations of computational intractability, it fell out of favor in the 1980s. Taking its place was the challenger, situation semantics, developed by Barwise and Perry (1983). It is this challenger that held the world of computer science captive for almost a decade. It was the semantics embraced by the "Fifth Generation Project" in Japan, the project that was to produce a thinking expert machine by the end of the 1980s.

8.2   Motivations for Situation Semantics

Besides many counterintuitive complex structures in Montague semantics, one motivation Barwise and Perry may have had was the following idea: Why use possible worlds if we can build up semantic structures directly in terms of world objects, properties, and relations. Meaning then becomes a direct relation of language with the world and is not mediated by way of truth conditions and possible worlds. More deeply, one may view situation semantics as an attempt to represent information positively, and not extensionally, about the world. Instead of looking at the set of possible worlds where Bill sits on a horse and concluding the sentence "Bill sits on a horse" is known with certainty if Bill sits on a horse in all accessible possible worlds, one just represents it as a direct situation, e.g., **sits-on (Bill, Horse)**. For simplicity, I have left out time and other details. The basic idea is there though, to represent meaning as a set of situations that a sentence refers to. This avoids a nondenumerable set of possible worlds and makes the representation of semantics in a computer at least feasible. The goal is then to map a situation with each possible sentence of the language, instead of the earlier truth conditions.

8.3   Problems with Situation Semantics

Unfortunately, there are difficulties with the approach. They involve exactly what situation semantics tried to avoid, namely, possibilities. Consider, for example, negation. What does "Bill is not sitting on a horse" mean? It is not a unique situation where Bill is not sitting on a horse, for there are infinitely many such possible situations. Also disjunctions were a problem. For, there again we have possibilities, e.g., "Bill is sitting on a horse or Bill is in the kitchen." Quantifiers are also difficult. The result was that Barwise and Perry were forced to include sets of possible situations into the semantics. While situation semantics is still interesting, it began to look suspiciously like a more encompassing possible-worlds semantics (possible worlds were just complete situations). A further, more subtle, but very important problem is that the attempt to represent all information positively without the use of possibilities is not as powerful as the possible states approach because there will always be information states that are not representable as positive situations. Yet, these possible information states are, of course, representable by sets of possibilities in the information as possibilities approach.

The above problems are faced by any theory meaning that tries to represent information positively instead of extensionally in terms of possibilities. Yet another problem with situation semantics is that it is restricted to situations; it fails to include the subject or agent and his mental life into the theory of meaning. However, to understand social cooperation by use of linguistic interactions, we need a theory of representations of intentions. And, we need a theory of how language transforms such representations. For this we need a theory of pragmatics.

Still the idea that referential meaning and simple propositional content can be positively or directly represented is I believe a good one and has a place as a component in a general theory of meaning.

8.4 Situations by a Different Route

Around the late 1970s at about the same time Barwise was developing situation semantics, I was intrigued with speech acts, like commands and requests. Since such speech acts are not true or false, giving commands and requests a classical truth-conditional semantics appeared questionable and inappropriate. I realized that the theory of meaning for commands, requests, and questions was going to be fundamentally different from the semantics of true and false sentences that researchers had concentrated on previously. While assertions focus on the world, commands and requests focus on controlling or influencing the actions of another agent. My hypothesis was that they control or influence another agent by changing the intentions of the agent, since the intentions were plan like states that guided the agent. I developed the concept of intentional state. These states were to be like information states (the formal theory of which I had already developed) in that they must be dynamically changeable by communication with other agents. Taking my theory of information states and my theory of communication for information states as a basis, the next key step for me was to develop the formal theory of intentional states.

The development of such a theory involved keeping in mind the requirements of a theory of communication and cooperation. The theory of intentional states was thus developed simultaneously with the pragmatic theory of meaning and communication for such intentional states (outlined above). I decided to test the developing theory on larger and larger fragments of English, including directives, requests, and informatives as well as prepositions and tensed verbs. In the attempt to provide a semantics for such English sentences, it became evident that it was useful to give verbs and basic sentences a referential meaning that directly refers to objects having properties and standing in various relationships with one another. My idea was to give a basic referential semantics to atomic sentences in terms of what I called *relational structures* (including relational space time structures or events).

8.5 Deep Referential Situation Semantics and Pragmatics

Later, while I was investigating a large but relatively flat fragment of English (English for foreigners), I saw quickly that negation, disjunctions, quantifiers, etc., were going to cause difficulties if one tried to give a direct relational structure semantics to all sentences of English. Since, however, language does refer to and link up with the world, I needed to formalize the propositional or referential content of sentences. To solve the problem I divided the theory of meaning into two layers. The first layer, which I called the *deep semantics*, was a semantics referring to situation-like, relational space-time structures. A second layer, the *pragmatics*, allowed the interpretation of more complex sentences by describing their effect on the information and intentional states of the agent. The deep semantics was actually developed out of the need to give a full compositional pragmatics for English like fragments. The compositional pragmatics arose out of the attempt to understand communication. The theory of communication arose out of the attempt to understand cooperation between groups of agents. This methodology of having one discipline constrain another is quite useful for the development of ideas.

9   INFORMATION AND UNCERTAINTY

If we consider planning and action from the perspective of an agent A who is acting in not just a physical environment Ω but also in a social environment of other groups G of agents, then the state of uncertainty, or what the agent knows and does not know, can be very complex. Fundamental to a clearer understanding the complex relationships of uncertainty to action and intention is the rigorous description of these kinds of uncertainty.

But before we do this, it is important to note that information and uncertainty are two sides of the same coin. Each type of uncertainty (e.g., state, temporal, intention, plan uncertainty), has a corresponding type of information state (e.g., state information, temporal information, intentional state, plan state) that positively describes the uncertainty in terms of information the agent possesses.

9.1   Imperfect and Perfect Information

We will say an agent is in a *state of imperfect information* or, simply, the agent has *imperfect information* about the world, the consequences of an action, his own plans or the plans of others, or the consequences of a plan or set of plans, if that agent has state uncertainty, action uncertainty, plan uncertainty, or plan consequence uncertainty, respectively. Otherwise, the agent has *perfect information* about state, action consequences, or plans.

An agent in a state of imperfect information may either have some information or no information. To say an agent has *total uncertainty* is equivalent to saying the agent has no information. If the agent has perfect information of some kind, it is equivalent to saying the agent has no uncertainty of the kind in question.

9.2 Relating Information States and States of Uncertainty

Thus, we get the following equivalences: *no information* ↔ *total uncertainty, partial information* ↔ *partial uncertainty, perfect information* ↔ *no uncertainty*. A minimal requirement of any theory of information and uncertainty is that it be able to define and distinguish perfect information (no uncertainty), from imperfect information (partial uncertainty), and no information (total uncertainty). In what follows we will talk either of uncertainty or information depending on which side of the coin we want to emphasize.

In the following sections, we will formally define these different types of information and uncertainty by defining the different categories of states of information and uncertainty of agents. This will make possible the investigation of the precise interrelationships between these types of uncertainty and information. We start with describing state information and uncertainty about state and, later, we will give a formal characterization of strategic uncertainty (information about intentions, strategies, and plans). This will then give formal substance to the more abstract summary of the ICE agent architecture described above.

10 STATE UNCERTAINTY

Agents acting in a world will generally not have full information about the state of the world. The semantics of Tarski, and also Kripke semantics, make no provisions for partial information about the world. This is because those semantics were never intended to deal with problems of agent cooperation and communication. The dynamic semantics provides a framework for describing changing accessibility relationships in a dynamic changing world of possibilities. However, the exact interpretation of the properties of a dynamic accessibility relation is left open. We now extend the semantic framework to include partial states of information about the world.

10.1 Possible Situations Over Time

First, we need some preliminary concepts. Let Ψ be the set of *macro time instants* ordered by a relation $<$. Let TP be the set of time periods over Ψ. We will use t to represent instants and τ to represent time periods. Let s be a situation at a given instant. A situaion is a partial representation of the state of the world (Barwise and Perry, 1983). Let *Sit* be the set of all possible situations. An *event e* is a partial function from the set of times into the set of possible situations, $e: \Psi \rightarrow Sit$. Let EVENTS be the set of all possible events.

Let a *world state* σ be a total description of the state of the world at a given instant. Hence, a world state will be a totally defined situation. Let Σ be a set of states. A *(total) history H* is a function from Ψ into Σ. A history is thus a series of complete situations over the time period Ψ. We will also refer to histories as possible worlds, possible past and futures, or as world lines. Let Ω be the set of all total histories each indexed by Ψ. If $H \in \Omega$, then let H_t be the value of the function H at $t \in \Psi$. H_t represents the state of the world H at time t. Ω then represents the set of all possible changes the system can undergo given the constraint that these changes are allowed by the rules or laws governing the system. A given history H *realizes* an event e over period $\tau \in TP$ iff $Domain(e) = \tau$ and $\forall t \in Domain(e)$, $e_t \subseteq H_t$.

A *partial history* H^t of H is a partial function from Ψ into Σ such that $H_{t_0}^t = H_{t_0}$ if $t_0 \le t$ and undefined if $t < t_0$. $V(\Omega)$ represents the class of all partial histories in Ω. These $H^t \in V(\Omega)$ are also called the *vertices* of Ω.

10.2   Information States

State information is that which reduces state uncertainty. By state information we mean information about the state of the world. For example, information about the state of the cards in a game of cards or the location of a robot in a room at a particular point in time is state information. We distinguish it from strategic information, which is information about agent plans and intentions.

An *information set* or *I-set* on Ω is a nonempty class I of partial histories in Ω such that for any $t, t' \in \Psi$ and any $H \in \Omega$, if $H^t \in I$ and $H^{t'} \in I$ then $t = t'$. We will use the letter I, J with and without superscripts to denote information sets. For a given agent A the information set I_A represents the information state of the agent at some time in a given world. If I is any information set on Ω, let I^* be the class of worlds intersected by I. I^* is the set of histories allowed by the information I.

$$I^* = {}_{df}\{H : H \in \Omega \text{ and there is a } t \in \Psi \text{ such that } H^t \in I\} \qquad (7)$$

With each information set I we associate a set of *alternatives* $Alt(I)$. Alternatives are the choices available to the agent given the information I. These alternatives are generated from the effect of microactions on the present state (see the section on simultaneous choices). Note, the alternatives leaving an information set are different from the possibilities H^t within the information set.

10.3   Information and Possibility

Information sets have an interesting property, which we call the *entropy principle*: The information available to an agent is inversely related to the number of possibilities in the information set. A corollary principle, which we call the *principle of possibility reduction* (PPR), is the following: The more information becomes available the fewer the possibilities. This principle also holds for information sets. To illustrate this principle consider an example: Mary, who is playing cards with Joe, knows Joe has the queen of hearts ($Q\heartsuit$), but she does not know if Joe has the king of hearts ($K\,\heartsuit$) or the jack of spades ($J\,\spadesuit$). Mary's information state $I_1 = \{\sigma_1, \sigma_2\}$ is one where she does not know if Joe's hand is in state $\sigma_1 = \langle Q\heartsuit, J\spadesuit \rangle$ or in state $\sigma_2 = \langle Q\heartsuit, K\heartsuit \rangle$. The information that Joe has the king of hearts reduces the information set I_1 (by the possibility reduction principle) to the information state $I_2 = \{\sigma_2\}$ where Mary knows with certainty (has perfect information) that Joe has the hand $\sigma_2 = \langle Q\heartsuit, K\heartsuit \rangle$. Note, here information sets consist of states σ which are partial histories that are one instant of time in length (see Werner, 1991a, for further discussion about these and other principles). Starting from very similar intuitions, a complementary approach to state information in planning is taken by Steel (1991).

10.4 Temporal Uncertainty

Imperfect Information about Time. Let $Time(I_A) = \tau$ be the time period specified by the information state I. It is the temporal information given by I. An information set I is *straight* if for any H, $K \in \Omega$, if $H^t \in I$ and $K^{t'} \in I$ then $t = t'$. An information set that is not straight will be said to be *slanted*. Straight information sets give perfect temporal information about the $Time(I)$ because any two partial histories in I pick out the same unique present time t. Slanted information sets give imperfect information about time. Formally, this means that for two partial histories H^t and $K^{t'}$ that are possibilities in I, their present times t and t' may differ. This means that given this information I, we do not know if the present time is t or t'.

Perfect Temporal Information. An information set is *thin* if $H^t \in I$ and $H^{t'} \in I$ then $t = t'$. Intuitively, this means that for a given history H the agent has no uncertainty about time. In effect, perfect information about the history and state of the world gives the agent perfect information about time. The general restriction on information sets is that they are thin. But, one could imagine situations where the agent is uncertain about the time of the world even though he knows exactly what has occurred up to his range of uncertainty. He just does not know if he is in the future or in the past relative to his temporal uncertainty. This situation may hold if the world can have two successive states that are absolutely identical. The only difference is the time. An example might be an agent who sits passively in a room without a clock and who loses track of the time.

10.5 Information Conditions

The following is used to represent all possible information conditions of a given agent: An *information ensemble* for Ω is a class Ξ of information sets on Ω such that the following conditions hold:

1. For any $H^t \in V(\Omega)$, there is an information set $I \in \Xi$ such that $H^t \in I$.
2. For any $I, J \in \Xi$, if $I \neq J$ then $I \cap J = \Lambda$, the null set.

We will use the symbols Ξ, Ξ' to denote information ensembles.

An information ensemble is a complete partition of the vertices in Ω. It follows immediately from the definition that if Ξ is any ensemble for Ω then, for any partial history $H^t \in V(\Omega)$, there is a unique information set I in Ξ such that $H^t \in I$. Let this unique information set be denoted by $I(H^t)$. Let the *information history* $I(H)$ be a function from Ψ to Ξ where $I(H)(t) = I(H)_t =_{df} I(H^t)$ for each $t \in \Psi$.

An information set $I(H)$ represents the information available to an agent in the world H at time t. $I(H)$ represents the changing information conditions throughout the history H. An information ensemble Ξ then gives the information conditions for an observer for all possible developments of the given system. We interpret an ensemble as relativized to an observer-agent. The information conditions for n agents are then given by n distinct information ensembles $\Xi_1, \ldots, \Xi_n$.

10.6 Nondiminishing Information

Let Ξ be any ensemble for Ω, then there is *nondiminishing information* in Ξ if for all $H \in \Omega$ and all $t, t' \in \Psi$, if $t \leq t'$ then $I(H^{t'})^* \subseteq I(H^t)^*$. If there is nondiminishing information in Ξ, we call Ξ an *NDI-ensemble*. An increase in size of an information set $I(H)$ represents a decrease in available information. For, an increase in the size of $I(H)$ is an increase in the possibilities. By insuring that the information set $I(H)$ does not expand in the future, the condition of nondiminishing information guarantees that no information is lost once it is stored. A different way of putting this is that no new, unforseen possibilities may arise.

10.7 Perfect State Information

The condition of nondiminishing information is the weakest information condition one can place on an ensemble and still have no loss of stored information. We now define the strongest condition one can place on the information.

Let Ξ be any ensemble for Ω, then there is *perfect state information* in Ξ if for each $I \in \Xi$, I is a unit set; i.e., if $\forall v_1, v_2 \in V(\Omega)$, if $v_1 \in I$ and $v_2 \in I$ then $v_1 = v_2$.

A decrease in the size of the information set represents an increase of information. When $I(H^t)$ is a unit set for some $H \in \Omega$, the observer has total knowledge of the history of the system up to and including the time t. Chess and checkers are examples of games with perfect information; most card games are games of imperfect information.

10.8 Definition of an Information Relation

The information conditions of an agent generate a Kripke-like accessibility relation with the difference that it is a dynamic relation that varies with time and information. Given an ensemble Ξ for Ω, the variable *information relation* $\mathfrak{I}^{\Xi}$ generated by Ξ is defined as follows: For any H, $K \in \Omega$ and any $t \in \Psi$, $H\mathfrak{I}_t^{\Xi}K$ if and only if $K \in I(H^t)*$.

Intuitively, $\mathfrak{I}^{\Xi}$ is a relation that varies with time. $H\mathfrak{I}_t^{\Xi}K$ says that K is a possible outcome of H given the information available in H at time t. K is an associated world of H but need not be accessible to H in the sense of being an *actual possibility*. K may only appear to be possible because of the limited information available in H. We can abstract away from the reference to the information ensemble Ξ and state information conditions as properties of a temporal accessibility relation (Werner, 1988b).

11 INFORMATION, SEMANTICS, AND TEMPORAL LOGIC

11.1 Information-Based Semantics

The dynamic information relation $\mathfrak{I}^{\Xi}$ can be used to define *information-based semantics* for both tensed and temporally indexed modal logics. To do this we simply replace, or better, instantiate the more abstract dynamic accessibility relation $\mathfrak{R}^t$ with the information relation $\mathfrak{I}_t^{\Xi}$. For the temporally indexed necessity-information operator we have

$$\Phi(\Box_t\alpha(t'), H) = T \text{ iff for all } K \in \Omega, H\mathfrak{I}_t^{\Xi}K, \Phi(\alpha(t'), K) = T \quad (8)$$

For the tensed modal version of the necessity-information operator we have

$$\Phi(\Box\alpha, t, H) = T \text{ iff for all } K \in \Omega, H\mathfrak{I}_t^{\Xi}K, \Phi(\alpha, t, K) = T \quad (9)$$

Note how the time index has been moved from the formulas of the object language to the semantic truth conditions.

11.2 Relating Logic, Information, and Time

The surprising discovery made in Werner (1974) (see Werner, 1988b, 1989b) was that the properties of the dynamic, accessibility relation have direct correlates in properties of the information conditions holding in open multiagent systems. Thus, the axioms that hold can be interpreted as corresponding to abstract properties of time-dependent accessibility relations or as reflecting types of information conditions of agents.

Let me put this last, important point another way. We have seen that the information conditions of an agent generate an information-relative, dynamic, accessibility relation between possible histories. This information relation was used to construct a semantics. Earlier we saw that dynamic accessibility relations can have various properties. These properties determine what temporal modal axioms hold of a system. But, since these properties correspond to information conditions, the axioms are also informational principles.

11.3   Temporal, Information-Based, Modal Logics

We now look at some important axioms that hold for various information conditions. We will look at both temporally indexed versions and tensed versions of the axioms. The mixed tensed modal systems resulting from axioms that correlate both tenses and modal operators are of special interest because they cannot be generated by simply combining standard modal and tense logics.

Axioms for Nondiminishing Information.   The following schemata of a temporally indexed modal language is valid in every model for the language when the dynamic, accessibility relation is backwards consistent. But, since we have the theorem that any system with nondiminishing information has a dynamic accessibility relation that is backwards consistent, it follows that these axioms also hold for any system with the nondiminishing information condition holding.

For *NDI axiom for temporally indexed formulas*: For all t, t', t'' where $t \le t'$,

$$\Box_t \alpha(t'') \rightarrow \Box_{t'} \alpha(t'') \tag{10}$$

The axiom says if it is necessary at time t that α holds at time t'' then it is necessary at time t' where $t \le t'$ that α holds at time t''. In other words, once an assertion is known then it continues to hold. This is just the condition that information is not lost or forgotten; it does not diminish. Note, though, that α refers to a specific time t''.

NDI *axiom (tensed version)* for P and $\Box$:

$$P\Box_A \alpha \rightarrow \Box_A P\alpha \tag{11}$$

The axiom reads "If it was necessary that α then it is necessary that α was the case." Or "If agent A had the information that α then A has the information that α was the case." Again, it holds only for the case where the information is nondiminishing (Werner, 1974, 1988b). Also there are special conditions on α.

Analogous to temporally indexed modal axioms (Werner, 1974, 1988b), the axioms of tensed modal logics can be interpreted as informational principles that give constraints on the information states of an agent. For example, the above tensed modal axiom for P and $\Box$ is a partial monotonicity constraint. Informationally, it asserts that if an agent has had the information that α in the past, then the agent will continue to have the information that he had the information that α. Note, this is a weaker information condition than complete monotonicity, i.e., no information loss. For the agent may no longer have the information that α, if $\neg \Box \alpha$ holds. Yet, the agent will still have the information that it was the case that α, $P\alpha$, since the axiom implies $\Box P\alpha$ still holds.

Axioms for Perfect Information.   There is also a theorem that states that the following axioms hold if the accessibility relation is backwards identical. Furthermore, there is a theorem that the information relative accessibility relation generated by a system with perfect information conditions is backwards identical. Therefore, these axioms also hold for systems with perfect information. The temporally indexed axiom that holds under condition of perfect information is:

PI axiom for temporally indexed formulas: For all t, t' where $t \leq t'$,

$$\alpha(t) \rightarrow \Box_{t'}\alpha(t) \tag{12}$$

As an informational principle it says that if $\alpha(t)$ is true at time t, then it is and will continue to be known. Note, this does *not* imply that $\alpha(t') \rightarrow \Box_t\alpha(t')$ when $t \leq t'$. This says that if α holds at time t' then it was the case that it was known at time t that α will hold at t'. This is not guaranteed by the condition of perfect information, since it allows uncertainty about the future.

Perfect information axiom (tensed version) for P and $\Box$:

$$\alpha \rightarrow \Box_A\alpha \tag{13}$$

Note, there are restrictions on α, in particular, that it contains no future tenses. This axiom only holds if there is perfect information about the state of the world. As an informational principle it expresses exactly that: If some fact α is true of the present or a past state of the world, then the agent has the information that α holds. It puts no constraints on the agent's uncertainty about the future.

Note, too, since we are in a time-dependent system, these axioms do not result in the collapse of the modal operator as it would in a nontensed system.

These axioms are important because their conditions of validity are based on fundamental dynamic, information relationships. These relationships are universal holding for any multiagent system with the requisite properties of their dynamic, accessibility relationships. For proofs of consistency and completeness theorems for dynamic modal logics as well as more details on other systems, their semantics, and the relationship to more classical nondynamic modal systems, see Werner (1974, 1988b, 1989b). There it is also shown that von Neumann games satisfy particular temporal modal logics.

12 ACTIONS

12.1 Action Types

An action is a type of event. At the lowest level (in macrotime) we have *token actions* consisting of objects with properties and standing in various relations that vary in time. There is a distinguished object called the *agent* who is the initiator of the action. They are partial situations over time called *events*. An *action type* **a** is then a class of such token actions. A token action a is *realized* in a world H if the only if $a \subseteq H$. An action type **a** is *realized* in a world H if and only if for some token $a \in \mathbf{a}$, a is realized in H. With an action and an agent and a given situation we associate a set of possible *consequence events*. An action type's uncertainty will be the union of all the possible consequences of each of its possible token actions.

12.2 Action Uncertainty

The agent A may be uncertain about the consequences of an action. This uncertainty may have different causes:

Action Uncertainty from Indeterminism. There may be *inherent action uncertainty* where the agent is uncertain about the consequences of an action because the world itself is indeterministic. In an indeterministic universe, multiple possible consequences may be an objective feature of an action.

Action Uncertainty from Computational Limits. There is also a *subjective action uncertainty* that results from the lack of information the agent has about the effects of the action given his computational limitations.

Action Uncertainty from State Uncertainty. However, even if we assume a deterministic universe, and no subjective uncertainty about an action's consequences for a given state, the agent may still be uncertain about the action's consequences since his information state I may not tell the agent his exact state in the world. Since the action's effects depend on the given state, the agent will not know all the consequences of his action. This is represented formally by the fact that an alternative leaving an information set I is a whole set of individual choices or alternatives, one for each possible state of the world given the information I.

Multiagent Action Uncertainty. Action uncertainty may also be due to a *multiagent setting*. In a multiagent social world a given agent's actions will never fully determine the next state, because this state is dependent on what the other agents do as well. Only strategic knowledge about the other agent's intentions or plan states can reduce this kind of *socially induced action uncertainty*.

Socially induced action uncertainty is a natural part of our theory. For, in a multiagent world the state is determined only after all agents have made some choice. The *do-nothing* or *null choice* being, of course, always one of the options available to an agent. Formally, any given pure agent strategy π_A will not have a unique outcome in a multiagent social world. Indeed, the more agents there are the less determined is the result of the strategy π_A. let us look at this phenomenon in more detail for the case of simultaneous actions by one or more agents.

12.3 A Theory of Simultaneous Choices

When agents act they act simultaneously with all the other agents. Since the null action is an action, we can assume that each agent makes a choice at each moment of time.

Why Actions Cannot Be Functions from States to States. Traditionally, an action by an agent was viewed as a function from states to states. It is viewed as transforming a given state σ_1 to a new state σ_2 that results from applying the action a to σ_1. While this appears to work in the case of a single agent making a single choice at any given time, this approach has problems when one considers multiagents acting simultaneously or even a single agent performing two actions at the same time.

More formally, it is common to view an action a as an operator that takes a state σ and transforms the state into a new state $\sigma' = a(\sigma)$. As soon as we allow the possibility of simultaneous actions, an agent's action can no longer be a function or operator taking one state to a new state. Why? Consider two agents A and B where A does action a and B does action b. Then given the agents are in state σ, $a(\sigma)$ need not equal $b(\sigma)$. If both operators are applied to σ the result is not a unique state. Yet, intuitively, we want to allow two operators to act on a state simultaneously, but if they do so, the operators are no longer functions from states to states. We need a new framework.

The Problem of Interference in Simultaneous Actions. The above problem with the traditional theory of action is rooted in the deeper problem of how to represent action *interactions* (interference or emergence). Simultaneous actions may influence and interfere with one another. An action taken by an agent alone may have a different effect than if another agent interferes or helps. For example, in basketball Joe may be perfect at making a basket if he is playing alone. When, however, Ray is defending the basket, Joe's performance may suffer. Similarly, Ray may not be able to lift the couch himself, but with Joe's help they can lift it. In a larger context of many agents, an agent's action, including communication, may set off a diverse pattern of actions resulting in a large-scale multiagent event. For example, a single command such as "Attack!" when issued by the appropriate agent may start a war. We need a theory of simultaneous actions that allows the description of such interferences and emergent effects.

Turn Taking to Solve Agent Action Interference. One way of solving the problems is to have the agents take turns. First, the action of agent A is applied and then the action of agent B is applied. The idea is that agents never really act at the same time and so cannot interfere with each other. A good example of this is the function of traffic lights and stop signs to make drivers take turns at intersections. Unfortunately, and fortunately, the real world has simultaneous events and activities. In fact, many actions only have their effect if the actions are applied simultaneously. For example, when Dany lifts the heavy vase she needs to act with both hands at the same time. She cannot lift with one hand and then lift with the other hand. The vase would never be lifted. In the multiagent case if we are to represent cooperative and noncooperative interactions, simultaneous interactions are again required. Thus, we must have a theory of simultaneous actions for single and multiple agents.

The Ultrastructure of Time Points. My solution is to have the agents act in a virtual sequence, not in real, macro time but in microtime. By *macrotime* I mean normal linear time which we will, for simplicity, consider to be discrete. *Microtime* is the virtual time that makes up the fine structure of a time point. Note, it is not a time in between two macro time points. That would lead to problems with dense and real time since there is no next time point if we have dense or real time. Furthermore, micro time is similar to, but not identical to, an interleaved process used to simulate simultaneous, parallel actions on a single processor computer, for that is just turn taking in small time steps.

Instead, we consider the time point itself to have structure. Its structure is a tree of microactions taken by agents. We will call it the *microtime tree* associated with a time *t*. Any path in the tree leads to a new state when the time is over. With discrete time this is easier to see. At any time point t_1 an agent has a finite number of simultaneous *microchoice points* available. Each microchoice point gives the agent a set of possible microactions.

Micro Actions In Micro Time. A *microaction* is a primitive act that the agent can do. At each choice point the agent must choose one microaction. At each choice point there may also be a *do-nothing* or *null microaction*. The result is a complete subpath in the microtime tree which we will call the agent's *complete choice*. We might call this a *complete personal choice* or *complete single-agent choice* to emphasize its individual nature. Each agent makes a complete choice by making a microchoice at each of his choice points. The result is a *complete multiagent microtime path* through the multiagent microtime tree. Each complete path of microchoices leads to a world state.

Micro Events In Macro Time. Actions occur in a world history *H*. Each microaction a_i at time *t* is realized as an event in a next possible state $K_{t'}$, where *K* is backwards identical with *H* at time *t*. The world *K* corresponds to the choice a_i made by the agent. In fact, the actual next state will contain a complete choice event corresponding to the agents complete choice. A way to think of this is that actions are first played out in microtime but then actually realized as events in macrotime. In fact the world itself is one of the agents that makes a complete choice as well, in the sense that its possibly indeterministic move is part of the interactivity that generates the next state in a multiagent system. The simultaneous actions literally occur within a time point. The effect is on the next possible states.

Simultaneous Actions. Micro time allows the formalization of simultaneous actions for a single agent and for multiple agents. Each of the agents may make their own personal simultaneous micro choices to construct their simultaneous action or complete choice. What is important is that the microtime tree relates the initial states to the possible next states. In doing so, it specifies the interactions that occur between simultaneous microactions by way of the effect on the resulting state. Let us note, we have said nothing about what the agent actually knows about his microchoices. He may make some micro choices without being aware of it. And, his choices may only be partially determined. We will discuss this case below.

13 INTENTIONS AND UNCERTAINTY

In a plan-based theory of intentional states, we must confront the fact that agents are uncertain about their own intentions and plans, as well as the intentions and plans of other agents and groups of agents (see Chapters 5–9). We now present a theory of plan uncertainty. This is a theory of how to represent partial information about the plans and intentions of single agents and groups of agents. The key step that I made, when I first developed the theory of intentional states, was to see the analogy between uncertainty about states of the world and uncertainty about plans and intentions. Thus, we can represent uncertainty about plans, strategies and intentions as *sets* of possible strategies S. Such a set corresponds to partial information about the strategy of an agent, or, from a different perspective, it corresponds to a partial plan the agent may be following. Once we have a representation of partial information about are intentions, we can represent perfect information about intentions, imperfect information about intentions, and total uncertainty about intentions in a way analogous to state information. Except, now the possibilities are not histories of the world, but possible strategies that an agent or group might follow. This allows the formalization of a semantics of ability and intention where the agents have partial knowledge of intentions. Furthermore, it turns out that there are interesting conceptual and practical relationships among state information, strategic information (information about intentions), and ability (Werner, 1991a). State information creates possible strategies for an agent. It, thereby, also creates abilities and enables possible intentions an agent may achieve.

Just as state information reduces the agent's state uncertainty, so strategic information reduces the agent's plan uncertainty. An agent's plan state gives information and describes the uncertainty about the agent's plans.

13.1 Strategic Information

In order to formally define plan uncertainty, we need some formal preliminaries. Let *Inf* be the class of all possible information states. A *pure strategy* π

is a function from information sets I in *Inf* to the alternatives at I. Thus, $\pi(I)$ $\in Alt(I)$. *Strat* is the set of all possible strategies. If π is a pure strategy, let π^* be those histories H in Ω that are compatible with that strategy. We refer to the class X^* generated by the star operator $*$ on X as the *potential* of X. The star operator $*$ denotes the set of possible histories (past, present, and future) allowed by the strategy or plan state. π^* is then the potential of a strategy π and consists of all those possible histories that are not excluded by the strategy π^*; i.e.,

$$\pi^* =_{df} \{H: H \in \pi_A(I), \forall I \in \Xi_A(H)\} \tag{14}$$

where

$$\Xi_A(H) =_{df} \{I: I \in \Xi_A \text{ and } \exists t \in \Psi, H^t \in I\} \tag{15}$$

Since action occurs in the context of information I possessed by the agent, let $\pi^*[I]$ be the set of worlds allowed by the strategy π given the information I. Thus,

$$\pi^*[I] =_{df} \pi^* \cap I^* \tag{16}$$

13.2 Single-Agent Plan Uncertainty

Given Perfect State Information. Recall when A has perfect information his information sets I are unit sets of the form $I(H^t) = \{H^t\}$. Given perfect information we need to describe the agent's plan state S_A for each of A's possible information states $I = \{H^t\}$, or, more simply, for each state H^t.

We describe an agent A's partial plans by a class of strategies S_A that govern that agent's actions. Any strategy π in S_A is one of the agent's possible strategies that may be guiding his actions. Analogous to information sets, if π is not in S_A, then it is known π is not guiding A's actions. We refer to $S_A(H^t)$ as the *plan state* of agent A at time t in the world H. More formally: Let Π_A be the set of all possible strategies of agent A. For each $H^t \in V(\Omega)$, let $S_A(H^t) \subseteq \Pi_A$. $S_A(H^t)$ is the set of A's possible strategies that are guiding A's actions at time t in the world H.

$$S_A(H^t)^* =_{df} \bigcup_{\pi \in S_A(H^t)} \pi^* \tag{17}$$

describes the potential worlds, past, present and future, that are allowed given strategic information S_A in the world H at time t. $S_A(H)$ is the *plan history* of the agent A in the world history H. It describes the changing plan states in the world H.

$S_A^B(H^t) \subseteq \Pi_B$ is the strategic information that agent A has about agent B's plans in the world H at the time t. $S_B(H^t) \subseteq S_A^B(H^t)$ when A's strategic information is correct.

$$S_A^B(H^t)^* =_{df} \bigcup_{\pi \in S_A^B(H^t)} \pi^* \tag{18}$$

is the set of worlds that are possible given what agent A knows about B's plans in the world H at time t. Thus, $S_A^B(H^t)$ and $S_A^B(H^t)^*$ are two ways of representing A's strategic information about B's plans Π there is perfect information about the state of the world up to time t.

With the above semantic structures we are able to formally represent the case where agent A may have perfect state information, but only partial plan, intentional, or strategic information.

Given Imperfect State Information. When an agent A has imperfect state information, we need to extend the above definitions of knowledge about plan states. Let

$$S_A(I) =_{df} \bigcup_{H^t \in I} S_A(H^t) \tag{19}$$

This represents A's plan state given the partial state information I. Since each world state $H^t \in I$ is indistinguishable for A, each plan state $S_A(H^t)$ is identical for each state H^t in I. Hence, $S_A(I_A) = S_A(H^t)$ for H^t in I_A.

As for A's strategic information about another agent's plan states, A may be able to distinguish B's plan states over different world state I^t in I. Let

$$S_A^B(I) =_{df} \bigcup_{H^t \in I} S_A^B(H^t) \tag{20}$$

when $S_A^B(I_A(H^t))$ represents A's strategic information about B's plans relative to A's state information $I_A(H^t)$.

$$S_A^B(I_A(H^t))^* =_{df} \bigcup_{\pi \in S_A^B(I(H^t))} \pi^* \tag{21}$$

describes the potential worlds (past and future) that are possible given agent A's strategic information about B's plans given A has imperfect state information about the world at time t.

We can now represent agents having imperfect state information and imperfect intentional, strategic information. Next, we look at the multiagent cases.

13.3 Multiagent Plan Uncertainty

Given Perfect State Information. In order for an agent to determine what he can do, the agent must be able to represent the plans not just of other individual agents, but of whole groups of agents. Let Ag be a group of agents, $Ag = \{1, \ldots, n\}$. Then

$$S_A^{Ag}(H^t) =_{df} \{S_A^i(H^t)\}_{i \in Ag}$$
$$= \{\langle 1, S_A^1(H^t)\rangle, \ldots, \langle n, S_A^n(H^t)\rangle\} \tag{22}$$

This represents the strategic knowledge that agent A has about the plans of other agents Ag in the world H at time t given A has perfect state information. It is the strategic information that the agent A has under the assumption that he has perfect information about the state of the world. The potential

$$S_A^{Ag}(H^t)^* =_{df} \{S_A^{Ag}(H^t)\}^* =_{df} \bigcap_{i \in Ag} S_A^i(H^t)^* \tag{23}$$

Note, we take the set intesection of the potential strategy classes of the individual agents, because those are the worlds possible given the combined plans of the agents in Ag.

Given Imperfect State Information. The *plan state* $S_{Ag}(I_{Ag}(H^t))$ of a group of agents Ag given imperfect information $I_{Ag}(H^t) = \{I_1(H^t), \ldots, I_n(H^t)\}$ is defined as

$$S_{Ag}(I_{Ag}(H^t)) = \{S_1(I_1(H^t)), \ldots, S_n(I_n(H^t))\} \tag{24}$$

Here the potential is defined as

$$S_{Ag}(I_{Ag}(H^t))^* =_{df} \bigcap_{i \in Ag} S_i(I_i(H^t))^* \tag{25}$$

It is the set of possibilities allowed by the plan state S_{Ag} of the group given the state information I_{Ag} of the group.

To define the strategic information an agent A has about a group's plans, given his imperfect state information, we proceed as follows:

$$S_A^{Ag}(I_A(H^t)) =_{df} \{S_A^i(I_A(H^t))\}_{i \in Ag}$$
$$= \{\langle 1, S_A^1(I_A(H^t))\rangle, \ldots, \langle n, S_A^n(I_A(H^t))\rangle\} \tag{26}$$

Here, $S_A^{Ag}(I_A(H^t))$ describes agent A's information about the plans of all other agents Ag given A's state information I_A in the world H at time t.

The potential is defined by

$$S_A^{Ag}(I_A(H^t))^* =_{df} \{S_A^{Ag}(I_A(H^t))\}^* =_{df} \bigcap_{i \in Ag} S_A^i(I_A(H^t))^* \tag{27}$$

Here, $S_A^{Ag}(I_A(H^t))^*$ represents the set of pasts, presents, and futures that are possible given what agent A knows about the plans S_A^{Ag} of the other agents Ag relative to A's state information I_A in the world H at time t. Intuitively, it describes the effects of plans of the other agents given the available information at the time t in the world H. The agent A can then play what-if scenarios about what would happen if A adopts the plan Π_A as part of his plan state. Then

$$\Pi_A \cap \{S_A^A(I_A(H'))\}* \cap S_A^{Ag}(I_A(H'))* \tag{28}$$

is the set of possible futures of what would happen if A adopts Π_A.

13.4 Plan Consequence Uncertainty

With any partial or total strategy π we associate, relative to an agent A with information state I_A, a set $\pi*$ of possible worlds that are possible consequences of the strategy. These are the actually or really possible, consequence worlds of the strategy given the information available to the agent. An agent will in general not be able to compute $\pi*$. Instead, the agent will associate expected consequences (a class of possible events) with the strategy. These expectations generate a set of possible futures $C_{A,I}(\pi)*$ thought possible by the agent A relative to information I. We say the agent's expectations for π are *correct* if and only if $\pi* \subseteq C_{A,I}(\pi)*$. This states that if an agent does not know the exact consequences of a strategy, his assessment is correct if it does not contradict the actual possible consequences of the strategy.

14 INFORMATION AND ABILITY

When we get up in an unfamiliar hotel room in the middle of the night, our first reaction is to find the light switch and turn on the light. Without the light we can do very little. We might bump into furniture or we may fall down because of some other obstacle. When we turn on the light, suddenly all is clear and we can take control of the situation; we can take a great deal more than before. How is this possible? You will recall that an increase of information leads to a decrease in possibilities.

14.1 Possibilities Generated by Information

The solution to this problem is that, formally, while the number of possibilities decreases, the number of strategies available to an agent increases with an increase of state information. There are literally more choices than there are without the information. Furthermore, the *specificity* of the consequences of those choices increases with more state information. A simple example of the game of matching pennies played once with perfect information and once with imperfect information makes this obvious (see examples in Werner, 1991a).

More generally, an increase in state information makes more actions possible for the agent. Often a message may only convey state information such as "the door is unlocked." The receiving agent, however, has more abilities as the result of the message. He now can, for example, "open the door" without requiring a key. Another example is the function of the senses. Vision, in humans and animals, increases the state information about local space-time tremendously, reducing the state uncertainty, increasing state information and increasing strategic action possibilities.

In fact, we can view space as an action possibility manifold that presents action possibilities to the agent. As the philosopher Berkeley observed, vision is the language of God. It presents world state information to the agent so that the agent can act at all. It was Kant who recognized the human contribution of the visual apparatus to the construction of the space time manifold of action possibilities. The action space is constituted by the state information resulting from visual information as interpreted by the categories and processes of the mind (see Kant, 1956, and later, Bohr, 1972; Marr, 1983). Perception in this abstract sense can be described as an operator on the information state of the observer. This state information is used to construct the action possibility space for the agent.

14.2   What Is the Connection between Communication and Abilities?

Communication translates into abilities. We saw there are at least two basic types of information communicated: state information and strategic information. The communication of state information translates into abilities by making more strategies available to the agent. This expands the agents sphere of abilities.

The communication of strategic information can be of two types. First, strategic information can also create strategies by showing the agent how to do something. This creates a dynamic, accessible strategy. It may have existed as a logically possible strategy in Π; however, the agent must actually have that strategy in his dynamic repertoire Δ. Second, communication of strategic information can give information about the intentions of other agents. This can be utilized by the agent to coordinate or cooperate by adjusting his own intentions to achieve his ends.

15   TYPES OF ABILITY

The use of the word "can" has many senses and its meaning varies in different contexts of use. These kinds of ability turn out to be related to the social context of state and strategic information that is available and utilized by the agent in his reasoning about his own and others abilities. Abilities are also central in agent reasoning and in the formation of dependencies and power relations between agents (see Chapter 20). Because of their importance, we will analyze various senses of the word "can" and more generally the concept of ability.

The general theory of ability underlying the logic and semantics of "can" and "is able to" that I developed is based on a simple hypothesis, namely an agent A can do or achieve α if A has a strategy that leads to α being the case. Many variants of this basic idea emerge if one considers different physical and social contexts in which the abilities of single and multiple agents are ascertained. Now in ordinary English we sweep most of these semantic and pragmatic differences under one syntactic rug. That is to say, we use the same word "can" to cover a variety of different semantic and pragmatic meanings. For clarity of formalization and implementation of the notion of ability, however, it is best to be aware of the differences. Thus, we artificially construct different types of "can" operators by giving them labels to make it easier to recall and distinguish their meanings. Yet in ordinary English usage all of these forms are just referred to by "can" or "is able."

15.1 Subjective and Objective Ability

I use the term *objective* to mean that which is judged from a perspective external to the agent. This may be the perspective of another agent with information different from that available to the agent or it may be the meta-perspective of an all knowing being. This is contrasted with the term *subjective* which is used to refer to the subjective, intrinsic perspective of the agent himself as limited by his local information whether this be state information, strategic information or evaluative information.

Throughout this essay we distinguish between the objective strategies Π_A available to an agent A and the subjective strategies Δ_A that are actually available given the agent's actual know-how and limited capacities. The subjective strategies are those generable dynamically from a "library" of substrategies. For example, in a game of chess it may be true that Boris has an objective strategy π_{Boris} in Π_{Boris} to win the game against Bobby, but since Boris is just an average chess player he does not actually have this strategy available in Δ_{Boris}. Bobby, however, is a grand master and knows the strategy π_{Boris} that would allow Boris to win against him.

For any strategy π_A that an agent A has π_A generates a set of possibilities that are consistent with that strategy. We denote the set of possibilities allowed by the strategy π_A by π_A^*. Any world history H in π_A^* is a possible outcome of the strategy.

Let α be any sentence of a language that talks about events and actions in our multiagent space-time world. α may be a tensed modal formula or a temporally indexed formula. Given any strategy π_A of some agent A, we say that strategy is *a strategy for* α if for all possible outcomes K in π_A^*, α is realized in K. Note, a partial strategy for α is just a more general version of a strategy for α that many particular instance strategies may satisfy. Thus, if π is a partial strategy for α then any more specific instance of π will also be a strategy for α.

Given these preliminaries about strategies we now defined the objective and subjective abilities of an agent in terms of available strategies.

15.2   Objective Ability or Logical can

When an agent objectively or logically can do something, then judged objectively, from an external perspective, there is a strategy in the logical space of possible strategies for some goal α. The strategy is not necessarily in the space of realizable dynamic plans Δ.

An agent A *objectively can* α at time t in the world H if A has a strategy π_A in Π_A and for all future possibilities K in π^* from the time t, α holds in K. In effect, this says no matter what the other agents do, a strategy for α ensures that α will hold in any case.

$$\Phi(A \text{ o-can } \alpha, H, t) = T \text{ iff } \exists \pi \in \Pi_A \text{ such that } \forall K \in \pi^*, \Phi(\alpha, K, t) = T$$

$$(29)$$

15.3   Subjective Ability

An agent subjectively **can** α if the agent has a strategy for α and that strategy is part of the space of realizable dynamic plans Δ of the agent. For example, Joan is grand master in chess and can see that she can win. She has a realizable strategy for α. There is the subjective component here in that the agent must realize she is able to do the action based on her available strategies.

An agent A *subjectively can* α at time t in the world H if A has a strategy π_A in Δ_A and for all future possibilities K from the time t, α holds in K. Like the case of objective ability, no matter what the other agents do, a subjective strategy for α ensures that α will hold in any case.

$$\Phi(A \text{ s-can } \alpha, H, t) = T \text{ iff } \exists \pi \in \Delta_A \text{ such that }$$

$$\forall K \in \pi^*, \Phi(\alpha, K, t) = T \qquad (30)$$

Note that there is an added complexity here, for the agent may have a dynamic plan for some event, but not realize it. We could distinguish between what the agent can dynamically do, from what the agent can dynamically know that he can do. This distinction is conflated in the notion of the possible dynamic plans Δ. Thus, we could distinguish the *logically possible abilities* of the agent from the *real abilities* of the agent and this in turn from the *subjective abilities* the agent is aware of that he has them. The two types of objective abilities, the logically possible and the real abilities, is in part due to the fact that the agent must actually have a representation of the strategy to be able to use it. Thus, comes in the importance of experience and training in building the repertoire or basis for dynamically generating real strategies.

15.4   Coordinative Ability or cocan

In the objective and subjective forms of **can**, if A **can** α holds in the world H at time t, then A has a strategy where α will eventually hold no matter what the other agents do. A softer version of **can** is not so absolute and depends on the agent's knowledge or expectations of the intentions of other agents. The agent utilizes this knowledge of the intentions of other agents to increase his ability.

In other words, the agent has a strategy that is dependent for its success on the intentional plan structure of the social space. The strategy by itself with different social information may not succeed in achieving the goal. For example, Henry loves Sue. He knows she will be at the chess match at 10 A.M. tomorrow. So, Henry **co-can** meet Sue, because of his knowledge of her intentions. Sue does not like Henry and would not show up if she knew of Henry's intentions. But, since Sue does not have this knowledge of Henry's intentions, Sue is not **co-able** to avoid this. She **co-could** avoid Henry if she knew of his intentions.

Indeed, a lot of human effort is spent in trying to determine the intentions of other persons, groups and nations without them knowing that their intentions are partially known. For once those intentions are known that strategic knowledge gives a form of power to the knowing agent. This form of power is captured by our formalization of **co-can**.

$$\Phi(A \textbf{ cocan } \alpha, H, t) = T \text{ iff } \exists \pi \in \Delta_A \text{ such that}$$

$$\forall K \in \pi^* \cap [S_A^{\text{Group}}]^*, \Phi(\alpha, K, t) = T \quad (31)$$

Here, Δ_A consists of the possible dynamic plans that are dynamically constructible from his repertoire of basic plans. **cocan** as well as the forms of **can** below have both a subjective and objective form. For brevity we present only the subjective form.

15.5 Cooperative Ability or coopcan

A group coop can achieve some goal α if each member of the group has a strategy such that the combined (possibly coordinated) space-time effect of the strategies results in the achievement of α. For example, Joan likes Fred and Fred likes Joan, so they arrange to meet at the chess tournament at 12 P.M. tomorrow. Each independently can (in the single agent sense of **can** above) be at the tournament at 12 noon, and the combined effect is the joint space-time event of meeting at 12 noon.

More generally, mutual communicative interaction by linguistic communication, gesture and observation of each others actions, can be used to form the intentional states S_A and S_B of two (or more) agents A and B. The superposition of the resulting intentional states of a group of cooperating agents can achieve events that are not achievable by any subgroup, including individual agents. These events can be of any form, including helping and hindering events. Sometimes an event meant to hinder can have the effect of helping, and vice versa. These are situations repeated over and over again in novels and films.

$$\Phi(\text{Group}_1 \ \textbf{coopcan} \ \alpha, H, t) = T \text{ iff } \forall A \in \text{Group}_1 \ \exists \pi_A \in \Delta_A \text{ such that}$$

$$\forall K \in \bigcap_{A \in \text{Group}} \pi_A^*, \Phi(\alpha, K, t) = T$$

This states that group *Group*$_1$, **coopcan** the event α if they have strategies whose superimposed interaction results in α being achieved. This means that α is inevitable if the agents set up their strategies using communication of some form. Below we will refer to **coopcan**$_{Group}$ by **can**$_{Group}$ where single agent **can** is just a special case of group **can**.

15.6 Coordinative Cooperative Ability or co-coopcan

A group *Group*$_1$ can cooperatively achieve some event α using their knowledge of the intentions of other groups of agents *Group*$_2$. In fact, each agent A of group *Group*$_1$ uses his individual strategic knowledge of the intentions of group *Group*$_2$. In this case we have a form of **co-coopcan**. The agents can interact to form intentions that superimposed will interact with the co-intentions of a second group *Group*$_2$ to achieve their ends.

$$\Phi(\text{Group}_1 \ \textbf{co-coopcan} \ \alpha, H, t)$$

$$= T \text{ iff } \forall A \in \text{Group}_1 \ \exists \pi_A \in \Delta_A \text{ such that}$$

$$\forall K \in \bigcap_{A \in \text{Group}_1} \pi_A^* \cap [S_A^{\text{Group}_2}]^*, \Phi(\alpha, K, t) = T$$

Note, **can** in all of its above forms only says that the appropriate subjective and objective strategies exist. It does not say or imply that such strategies will be adopted and, hence, does not imply that the corresponding strategic intentional states will be formed. Indeed, in the case of **coopcan** there may be a heavy coordination cost associated with the formation of such interlocking strategic intentional states.

16 A THEORY OF UTILITARIAN ABILITY

The above forms of ability of single and multiple agents do not consider the cost or utility of performing or achieving some event described by α. We now formalize forms of ability that make the utility an explicit part of the operator. We restrict our discussion to the subjective and objective forms of **can**. The **cocan** and **coopcan** forms also exist.

Let us denote the *utility* that α has for an agent A in the world H at time t by $U_A(\alpha, H, t)$. Thus, the utility of some event described by α is relative to the agent A, the history H, and the time t. If the utility is negative, $U_A(\alpha, H, t) < 0$, then we call the utility the *cost* or *negative utility* of α. If the utility is positive, it is called the *value* or *positive utility* of α for the agent

A. If the utility is equal to 0 we say that α has *no utility* for *A* or that the utility is *neutral* or that there is *no cost* or *no value* for *A*.

16.1 Pessimistic But Safe Utilitarian Ability

For strategy π, we say π *forces* α, in symbols $\pi \| \mapsto \alpha$ if and only if for all $H \in \pi^*$, α holds in H. Let $\Psi_t = \{t': t' \in \Psi \text{ and } t' > t\}$. Then we can define utilitarian ability as follows:

A **can**$_t^u$ $\alpha(t')$ in *H* iff $\exists$ strategy $\pi \in \Pi_A$ such that $\pi \| \mapsto \alpha$ and the utility

$$u = \min_{H \in \pi^*, t' \in \Psi_t} [U_A(\alpha(t'), H, t)] \qquad (32)$$

Note, this gives the minimal positive utility or value or the maximal possible negative utility or cost of attaining α given the strategy π_A is followed. Thus, this sense of utility relativized ability is a *pessimistic* but *safe* minimal damage assessment. If the utility u is positive then it is the minimum that the agent can gain if he follows the strategy π_A. If the utility is negative, representing a cost, then it is the most the agent can lose given that he follows the strategy.

16.2 Optimistic But Unsafe Ability

An *optimistic* but unsafe assessment of ability is obtained if we substitute *max* for *min* in our semantic definition.

A **can**$_t^u$ $\alpha(t')$ in *H* iff $\exists$ strategy $\pi \in \Pi_A$ such that $\pi \| \mapsto \alpha$ and the utility

$$u = \max_{H \in \pi^*, t' \in \Psi_t} [U_A(\alpha(t'), H, t)] \qquad (33)$$

If the optimistic utility u is positive it represents the greatest possible benefit that may result from the strategy π. If the optimistic utility u is negative, it is the least costly result possible under the strategy π.

16.3 Probabilistic Ability

Often agents act with the outcome of the action being only probable and not certain. This is actually the most prevalent case for everyday human action. It is, therefore, interesting to formalize this more realistic sense of ability. In probabilistic ability an agent can do α with probability p if there is a strategy π_A that ensures α will be the case with probability p. Let $\alpha(\pi_A^*) = \{K: K \in \pi_A^* \text{ and } \alpha \text{ holds in } K\}$. Intuitively, $\alpha(\pi_A^*)$ is the set of futures allowed by the strategy where α is true.

$$A \ \mathbf{can}_t^p \ \alpha \ \text{in } H \text{ iff } \exists \text{ strategy } \pi \in \Pi_A \text{ such that } \sum_{K \in \pi_A^* \cup \alpha(pi_A)} p(K) = p \quad (34)$$

Here, $p(K)$ is the probability that the possible future K will be actually realized.

16.4 Probabilistic Expected Utilitarian Ability

Assume we have a probability distribution p over the choices of the agents where $\Sigma_{K \in \pi_A^*} p(K) = 1$. Furthermore, we say a strategy π_A *forces* an event α *with probability* p, in symbols, $\pi \Vert \rightarrow_p \alpha$, if and only if $\Sigma_{K \in \pi_A^*} p(K) = p$. Then we can define the expected utility of α in the world H at time t as follows:

$$A \ \mathbf{can}_t^{xu} \ \alpha(t') \ \text{in } H \text{ iff } \exists \text{ strategy } \pi \in \Pi_A \text{ such that } \pi \Vert \overrightarrow{p} \ \alpha \text{ and}$$

$$\text{the expected utility } xu = \sum_{K \in \pi_A^*} p(K)U(\alpha(t'), K, t) \quad (35)$$

This says that the agent A can do α and can expect to have a payoff or cost depending on whether the expected utility xu of α is positive or negative, respectively. The strategy π_A generates a set of possible futures which we denote by π_A^*. This set of futures has probabilities associated with each possible course of action H. These probabilities are then used to calculate the average or expected utility of the action-event described by α.

The expected utility can be a positive benefit or a negative cost or a neutral value of zero. Thus, if $A \ \mathbf{can}_t^{xu} \ \alpha$ and xu is negative then agent A can do α but he expects it to cost him xu. If xu is positive A expects to gain benefit xu. And, if xu is zero, then A expects no benefit but also no cost in doing α. Note, since we are dealing with both probabilities and utilities, very unlikely but very costly events may have more weight than a less costly and more likely event. The point is that the utility can be positive in one possible future and negative in another possible future. Which future has more influence on the expected utility depends on the probability multiplied by the utility of α in that future.

Probabilistic utilitarian ability is less pessimistic than pessimistic utilitarian ability and less optimistic than optimistic utilitarian ability. Thus, probabilistic utilitarian ability lies between pessimistic and optimistic utilitarian ability. A true and careful pessimist will not use expected utilities to assess his abilities. For no matter how unlikely, a very costly possible outcome is still possible even if the expected utility is very good.

Our motivation for defining the above ability operators is because they are useful. First, they reflect a more realistic and pragmatic approach to ability. Second, they are useful for understanding dependency and power relations between agents.

17 TYPES OF INTENTION

Throughout, for each operator we distinguish the consequences of a plan state that are independent of the actions of other agents and the consequences that depend on the social intentional state of the social space. We add the **co-** prefix to the operator if the social context is part of the computation of its consequences.

17.1 Intends or Plans

For a single agent, A **plans** α if A's intentional state in the world H at time t relative to his information state I leads to the achievement of α no matter what the other agents do.

$$A \text{ plans}_t \, \alpha(t') \text{ in } H \text{ iff } \forall K \in S_A(I_A(H'))^*, \, \alpha(t') \text{ holds in } H \qquad (36)$$

Here, **plans** implies **can**. To make this realistic, background assumptions about the expected circumstances are usually added. An example might be Boris in a game of chess plans to win if his plan state that is guiding him realizes a winning strategy. Note, this sense of intends and plans is neutral with respect to beliefs, desires, and awareness. But, it is dependent on the information and plan state of the agent.

17.2 Coordinated Intentions

For single agents, the agent plans to achieve α by using his information about the intentions of others.

$$A \text{ co-plans}_t \, \alpha(t') \text{ in } H \text{ iff}$$

$$\forall K \in S_A(I_A(H'))^* \cap S_A^{Ag}(I_A(H'))^*, \, \alpha(t') \text{ holds in } H \qquad (37)$$

The agent is in an intentional state such that in conjunction or in superposition with the social space in which the agent acts, the intentional state of the agent plus the intentional structure of the social space results in the realization of the event described by α.

17.3 Cooperatively Intending

A group of agents cooperatively intends to achieve some event α if they each have the appropriate intentional states such that when these intentional states are applied or executed, the event described by α is realized.

$$\text{Group plans}_t \alpha(t') \text{ in } H \text{ iff}$$

$$\forall K \in S_{\text{Group}}(I_{\text{Group}}(H'))^*, \, \alpha(t') \text{ holds in } H \qquad (38)$$

Cooperative intentions are different from coordinate intentions, in that cooperative intentions require the active cooperation of the agents involved (see Chapters 6 and 18), whereas coordinate intentions can be executed by a single agent who makes use of his knowledge of the social space, such as, for example, his knowledge of the intentions of others.

17.4   Third-Person Predictions

This might be called the "will result in" operator. For it has to do with the logical and physical consequences of a plan that the agent himself may not be aware of, but which another agent may be aware of because of additional strategic or state information. It is meant to be neutral with regard to the intentions of the agent. For example, when Sue goes to the tournament she does not realize that one consequence will be that she **will** run into Henry whom she wants to avoid. Note, here this is a consequence in the social context of other intentions, such as Henry's and that of the tournament organizers. It is a social context about which our agent, Sue, does not possess perfect intentional information.

B has the information that A **will**$_t$ $\alpha(t')$ in H iff

$$\forall K \in S_B^A(I_B^A(H'))^*, \; \alpha(t') \text{ holds in } H \tag{39}$$

This states that from the perspective of agent B, agent A will do α at time t'. Note, the agent A may make assessments about what he himself will do. In this case $B = A$.

17.5   Probabilistic Intentions

Assume that we have a probability distribution over the possible outcomes of a partial strategy S_A. Let $\alpha(S_A^*) = \{K: K \in S_A^* \text{ and } \alpha \text{ holds in } K\}$. Intuitively, $\alpha(S_A^*)$ is the set of futures allowed by the strategy where α is true. A partial strategy S_A *forces* an event α with probability p; in symbols, $S_A \Vdash_{\overrightarrow{p}} \alpha$ if and only if $\Sigma_{K \in \alpha(S_A^*)} p(K) = p$. In other words, a partial strategy forces α with probability p if, under the constraints of the strategy, the sum of the probabilities where α holds is equal to p. Given this definition, we can then define the probabilistic plan state of an agent as follows:

$$A \text{ **plans**}_t^p \alpha(t') \text{ in } H \text{ iff } S_A \Vdash_{\overrightarrow{p}} \alpha(t') \tag{40}$$

17.6   Utilitarian Intentions

People often break their best intentions. Often, when the path becomes too difficult, or another alternative is too tempting, some people stray from promises, commitments, and intentions (see Chapter 6).

$$A \text{ **plans**}_t^u \alpha(t') \text{ in } H \text{ iff } \forall K \in S_A \text{ if } U(\alpha, K, t) \geq u \text{ then } \alpha(t') \text{ holds in } K$$

$$\tag{41}$$

Thus, an agent with a utilitarian intentions is committed to α only to the degree that the utility does not decrease below the value u. This means an unexpected cost or an enticement can lead the agent astray from his intention to do α.

18 THE ENTROPY OF PLANS AND ORGANIZATIONS

Fascinating is the thought of being able to give a measure of the uncertainty of control in a multiagent system. Put differently, can we come up with a measure of the control information in a multiagent organization? Can we come up with measures of the entropy of an organization? We now take some preliminary steps that take us in the direction of measuring the entropy of multiagent systems.

Beyond defining state uncertainty, we have also been able to define control uncertainty formally and explicitly. Historically, a formal account of state uncertainty made a formal definition of the *entropy* of a system possible. Thus, given a set of states $\sigma \in I$ and a probability distribution p over I we can define the entropy of I to be $H(I) = -\Sigma_{\sigma \in I} p(\sigma) \log p(\sigma)$. This definition was, in its essence, first given by Boltzmann (1981) in his statistical foundations of thermodynamics (Khinchin, 1949) and later by many others including Shannon (1948) in his mathematical theory of communication (Khinchin, 1957). Without probabilities, the entropy is simply the log of the magnitude of the set I.

18.1 Entropy of Intentional States

Because we have constructed a formal definition of plan or control uncertainty, we can now also give an analogous definition of *control entropy*:

$$H(S) = -\sum_{\pi \in S} p(\pi) \log p(\pi) \tag{42}$$

where $p(\pi)$ is the probability that the agent is following the strategy π and S is the control information of the agent.[1] This gives a mathematical measure of the control uncertainty of an agent. Alternatively, it gives a measure of the *control information content* if that control uncertainty were removed. To distinguish the new concept of control entropy from the traditional notion of entropy, we call the former *control entropy* (also, *plan entropy*) and the latter *state entropy* since it is concerned with measuring state uncertainty or, positively, the state information content if that uncertainty is removed. The plan state S may be for a single agent or for a whole multiagent system.

---

[1]The strategic information or plan state S is not to be confused with the S in the Boltzmann formula for state entropy: $S = k \ln P$, where P is the thermodynamic probability of the system being in a given state and k is the Boltzmann constant (1981). Furthermore, it should be obvious from the context that the notation $H(\ )$ for entropy and the notation H for world history are two very different things.

18.2 Conditional Control Entropy

Given the definition of control entropy we can define other concepts concernng control information that are analogous to some of the traditional concepts in Shannon's communication theory. Thus, given two agents A and B,[2] with plan states S_A and S_B, the *conditional control entropy* is defined as

$$H_{S_A}(S_B) = \sum_{\pi \in S_A} p(\pi) H_\pi(S_B) \tag{43}$$

where

$$H_\pi(S_B) = -\sum_{\theta \in S_B} p_\pi(\theta) \log p_\pi(\theta) \tag{44}$$

where $p_\pi(\theta)$ is the conditional probability that B has plan θ when A has plan π. Expressed in terms of control information $H_A(B)$ indicates how much control information is contained on the average in the partial plan state S_B given it is known that agent A is following plan state S_A.

18.3 Strategic Entropy Due to Multiagent Side Effects

We have already seen above that actions and strategies, in the context of a social world of other agents, are not fully determined. We can actually measure the entropy of a strategy due to multiagent side effects.

$$H(\pi_A) = -\sum_{K \in \pi_A} p(K) \log p(K) \tag{45}$$

where π_A is a strategy of agent A and $p(K)$ is the probability of the future world K given the strategy π_A. This measures the uncertainty of the strategy given no information about the strategies of the other agents. The relations among state entropy, plan entropy, and strategic entropy will be the subject of another publication.

19 CONCLUSION

We have tried to understand the relationship of an agent to his social space. How is coordination and cooperation in social activity possible? How is the information about the state of the world related to the agent's intentions? How are the intentions of agents related? What role does communication play in this coordination process? Such questions led to fundamental hypotheses and theories about the nature of social agents.

---

[2]It should be clear from the above that these may be groups as well.

What is an agent? By an agent I mean an entity that is guided by some strategy that controls its behavior. We have seen that there are many different types of agents possible. But the core of all agents reduces to three fundamental components: the information state I that gives the agent's information about the world, the strategic state S that gives the agent's control information that guides his actions, and an evaluative state V that gives the agent's evaluations and guides his reasoning. A solipsistic agent need not even have external inputs. In simple agents, the strategic state may simply be a reactive strategy that is directly linked to the agent's information state, with the information state being determined by immediate perceptions. The evaluative component may be nonexistent. As the agents gain more social abilities, the representational states of the agent become more and more complex. The agent now has dynamic properties constraining the information and strategic states including properties such as nondiminishing information and perfect information.

We also investigated the abilities of the agent and saw that what an agent can do is definable in terms of the existence of strategies in various contexts of state, strategic, and social information. The existence of strategies, and, therefore, what an agent or group can do and intend, depends on the available state information. Thus, communication of state information was seen to have a fundamentally important function for individual and social action. The intentions of an agent and a group of agents was investigated and the relationship to state information has several important functions in the social space of agents: First, strategic information can create real abilities from logically possible abilities through training or by simply making the agent aware of their existence. Second, strategic information creates new coordinate abilities since the agent can use strategic information about other agents to plan his actions. Third, strategic information creates cooperative abilities, leading to the possibility of cooperation in multiagent activity. This is because the communication of strategic information is a fundamentally important function in the formation of coordinated intentional states between agents, and, thereby, forms the basis of cooperation.

The formal modeling of state and plan uncertainty is important for a deeper understanding of the social space of agents, including the processes of communication, cooperation, and coordination. This has a direct effect on the design and implementation of single agents and of multiagent systems. In this chapter, we hope we have gone further in the direction of providing a conceptual and logical foundation for work in the area of planning and distributed artificial intelligence. In addition, we have extended the concept of entropy to include the entropy of intentional states. The entropy of intentions may provide a measure of the entropy of organizations in their dynamic activity. Multiagent system science and the formalization of social processes between agents will, I believe, lead to a revolution in the psychological, social, economic, and biological sciences. By providing a new foundation for these sciences we hope to contribute to the future understanding of social beings and multiagent social systems.

ACKNOWLEDGMENTS

This chapter is dedicated to Jacques Picard and his family.

REFERENCES

Austin, J. L. (1962a). In *Sense and Sensibilia* (G. J. Warnock, ed.). Clarendon Press, Oxford.

Austin, J. L. (1962b). *How to do Things with Words*. Harvard Univ. Press, Cambridge, MA.

Barwise, J., and Perry, J. (1983). *Situations and Attitudes*. Bradford Books, MIT Press, Cambridge, MA.

Bohr, N. (1972). In *Collected Works of Niels Bohr* (L. Rosenfeld, ed.). North-Holland Publ., Amsterdam.

Boltzmann, L. (1981). In *Gesamtausgabe: Ludwig Boltzmann* (U. S. von Roman, ed.). Akademische Druck und Verlagsanstalt, Braunschweig.

Bratman, M. (1987). *Intentions, Plans, and Practical Reason*. Harvard Univ. Press, Cambridge, MA.

Brown, M. A. (1988). On the logic of ability. *J. Philos. Logic* **17**, 1-26.

Castelfranchi, C. (1990). Social power: A point missed in multi-agent, dai and hci. In *Decentralized Artificial Intelligence* (Y. Demazeau and J.-P. Müller, eds.), pp. 49-61. Elsevier/North-Holland, Amsterdam.

Castelfranchi, C., Miceli, M., and Cesta, A. (1992). Dependence relations among autonomous agents. In *Decentralized Artificial Intelligence 3* (E. Werner and Y. Demazeau, eds.), pp. 215-227. Elsevier/North-Holland, Amsterdam.

Chomsky, N. (1969). *Syntactic Structure*. Mouton, The Hague.

Cohen, P., and Levesque, H. (1987). Intention = choice + commitment. *Proc. Am. Assoc. Artif. Intell.*, Seattle, WA, pp. 410-415.

Corkill, D. D. (1979). Hierarchical planning in a distributed environment. *Proc. Int. J. Conf. Artif. Intell. 6th*, Cambridge, MA, *1979*, pp. 168-175.

Corkill, D. D., and Lesser, V. R. (1983). The use of meta-level control for coordination in a distributed problem solving network. *Proc. Int. J. Conf. Artif. Intell.*, *8th*, Karlsruhe, Germany, *1983*, pp. 748-756.

Davis, R., and Smith, R. G., (1983), Negotiation as a metaphor for distributed problem solving. *Artif. Intell.* **20**, 63-109.

Demazeau, Y., and Müller, J.-P., eds. (1991). *Decentralized Artificial Intelligence 2*. Elsevier/North-Holland, Amsterdam.

Durfee, E. H. (1988). *Coordinating Distributed Problem Solvers*. Kluwer Academic Purblishers, Boston.

Durfee, E. H., Lesser, V., and Corkill, D. (1987). Coherent cooperation among communicating problem solvers. *IEEE Trans. Comput.* **C-36**, 1275-1291.

Ephrati, E., and Rosenschein, J. S. (1992). The Clarke tax as a consensus mechanism among automated agents. *Proc. Eur. Conf. Artif. Intell.*, *10th*, Vienna, Austria, pp. 173-178.

Everett, H. (1957). Relative state formulation of quantum mechanics. *Rev. Mod. Phys.* **29**, 454–462.

Gödel, K. (1931). Über formal unentscheidbare Sätze der Principia Mathematica und verwandter Systeme I. *Monatsh. Math. Phys.* **38**, 173–198.

Grosz, B., and Kraus, S. (1993). Collaboration plans for group activities. *Proc. Int. Jt. Conf. Artif. Intell.*, Chambéry, France, *1993*.

Habermas, J. (1981). *Theorie des Kommunikativen Handelns.* Suhrkamp, Frankfurt am Main.

Hewitt, C. (1977). Control structures as patterns of passing messages. *Artif. Intel.* **8**, 323–363.

Hillis, W. D. (1990). Co-evolving parasites improve simulated evolution as an optimization procedure. *Physica D* **42**, 228–234.

Hintikka, J. (1962). *Knowledge and Belief.* Cornell Univ. Press, Ithaca, NY.

Holland, J. H. (1975). *Adaption in Natural and Artificial Systems.* University of Michigan, Ann Arbor.

Hughes, G. E., and Cresswell, M. J. (1968). *Introduction to Modal Logic.* Methuen, London.

Hussmann, M., and Werner, E. (1990). *AgentS: An Agent Simulation Development System for the Macintosh*, Research Report. University of Hamburg, Hamburg, Germany.

Kant, I. (1956). *Kritique der Reinen Vernumft.* Felix Meiner Verlag, Hamburg.

Khinchin, A. I. (1949). *Mathematical Foundations of Statistical Mechanics.* Dover, New York.

Khinchin, A. I. (1957). *Mathematical Foundations of Information Theory.* Dover, New York.

Kinny, D., Ljungberg, M., Rao, A., Sonnenberg, E., Tidhar, G., and Werner, E. (1994). Planned team activity. In *Artificial Social Systems* (C. Castelfranchi and E. Werner, eds.). Springer-Verlag, Berlin.

Kripke, S. A. (1963). Semantic analysis of modal logic i, normal propositional calculi. *Z. Math. Logic Grundlagen Math.* **9**, 67–96.

Lesser, V., and Corkill, D. (1981). Functionally accurate, cooperative distributed systems. *IEEE Trans. Syst., Man Cybernet.* **SMC-11**(1); 81–96.

Lewis, C. I., and Langford, C. H. (1959). *Symbolic Logic.* Dover, New York.

Marr, D. (1983). *Vision.* Freeman, San Francisco.

Minsky, M. (1986). *The Society of Mind.* Simon & Schuster, New York.

Montague, R. (1976). In *Formal Philosophy* (R. H. Thomason, ed.). Yale Univ. Press, New Haven, CT.

Morris, C. W. (1964). *Signification and Significance: A Study of the Relations of Signs and Values.* MIT Press, Cambridge, MA.

Morris, C. W. (1946). *Signs, Language, and Behavior.* G. Braziller, New York.

Morris, C. W. (1972). *Writings on the General Theory of Signs.* Mouton, The Hague.

Prior, A. N. (1967). *Past, Present and Future.* Oxford Univ. Press, London.

Putnam, H. (1975). *Philosophical Papers.* Cambridge Univ. Press, London and New York.

Rao, A. S., and Georgeff, M. P. (1991). Modeling rational agents within a bdi-architecture. In *Proceedings of the Second International Conference on Principles of Knowledge Representation and Reasoning* (J. Allen, R. Fikes, and E. Sandewall, eds.), pp. 473–484. Morgan Kaufmann, San Mateo, CA.

Rosenschein, J. S. (1986). *Rational Interaction: Cooperation among Intelligent Agents.* Ph.D. Thesis, Stanford University, Stanford, CA.

Rosenschein, J. S., and Zlotkin, G. (1994). *Rules of Encounter: Designing Conventions for Automated Negotiation among Computers.* MIT Press, Cambridge, MA.

Schank, R., and Abelson, R. P. (1977). *Scripts, Plans, Goals, and Understanding: An Inquiry into Human Knowledge Structures.* Erlbaum, Hillsdale, NJ.

Searle, J. R., (1985). *The Philosophy of Language.* Oxford Univ. Press, London.

Shannon, C. E. (1948). The mathematical theory of communication. *Bell Syst. Tech. J.* **27**, 379–423, 623–656.

Sims, K. (1993). Interaction evolution of equations for procedural models. *Visual Comput.* **9**, 466–476.

Singh, M. P. (1990). Towards a theory of situated know-how. *Proc. Eur. Conf. Artif. Intell., 9th*, Stockholm, Sweden, *1990*.

Singh, M. P. (1992). A critical examination of the cohen-levesque theory of intentions. *Proc. Eur. Conf. Artif. Intell., 10th*, Vienna, Austria, p. 364–368.

Smith, R. G. (1980). The contract net protocol: High-level communication and control in a distributed problem solver. *IEEE Trans. Comput.* **C-29**(12), 1104–1113.

Steel, S. (1991). Knowledge subgoals in plans. *Eur. Workshop Planning*, Sankt Augustine, Germany, *1991*.

Tarski, A. (1956). *Logic, Semantics, Metamathematics: Papers from 1923 to 1938.* Clarendon Press, Oxford.

Thomas, B. (1993). *A Logic for Representing Actions, Beliefs, Capabilities, and Plans*, Tech. Rep. Computer Science Department, Stanford University, Stanford, CA.

von Neuman, J. (1961). In *Collected Works of John von Neumann* (A. H. Taub, ed.). Pergamon, New York.

von Neumann, J. (1955). *Mathematical Foundations of Quantum Mechanics.* Princeton Univ. Press, Princeton, NJ.

von Neumann J., and Morgenstern, O. (1947). *The Theory of Games and Economic Behavior.* Princeton Univ. Press, Princeton, NJ.

Werner E. (1974). *Foundations of Temporal Modal Logic.* University of Wisconson, Out of print, available from the author upon request.

Werner, E. (1983). *Euro Notebooks.*

Werner, E. (1988a). A formal computational semantics and pragmatics of speech acts. *Proc. Int. Conf. Comput. Linguistics, 12th*, Budapest, Hungary, *1988*.

Werner, E. (1988b). *The Modal Logic of Games*, WISBER Rep. B48. University of Hamburg, Hamburg, Germany.

Werner, E. (1988c). Toward a theory of communication and cooperation for multiagent planning. In *Theoretical Aspects of Reasoning about Knowledge II* (M. Vardi, ed.), pp. 129–142. Morgan Kaufmann, San Mateo, CA.

Werner, E. (1989a). Cooperating agents: A unified theory of communication and social structure. In *Distributed Artificial Intelligence* (L. Gasser and M. N. Huhns, eds.), vol. 2, pp. 3–36. Morgan Kaufmann, Los Altos, CA/Pitman, London.

Werner, E. (1989b). *Tensed Modal Logic*, WISBER Rep. B49. University of Hamburg, Hamburg, Germany.

Werner, E. (1990). What can agents do together? a semantics of cooperative ability. *Proc. Eur. Conf. Artif. Intell., 9th*, Stockholm, Sweden, *1990*, pp. 694–701.

Werner, E. (1991a). A unified view of information, intention, and ability. In *Decentralized Artificial Intelligence 2* (Y. Demazeau and J.-P. Müller, eds.). Elsevier/North-Holland, Amsterdam. (Originally WISBER Rep. No. B37, University of Hamburg, 1988).

Werner, E. (1991b). Planning and uncertainty. In *SYSTEMS91, Verteilte Künstliche Intelligenz, Proceedings of the 4th International GI Kongress*. Springer-Verlag, Munich.

Werner, E. (1992). Ontogeny of the social self. In *Symposium on Social Simulation*. University of Surrey, UK.

Wheeler, J. A. (1957). Assessment of relative state formulation of quantum theory. *Rev. Mod. Phys.* **29**, 463–465.

Whitehead, A. N., and Russell, B. (1910). *Principia Mathematica*. Cambridge Univ. Press, Cambridge. UK.

Winograd, T. (1972). *Understanding Natural Language*. Academic Press, New York.

Wittgenstein, L. (1958). *The Blue and Brown Books*. Blackwell, Oxford.

Wittgenstein, L. (1953). *Philosophical Investigations*. Basil Blackwell, Oxford.

Wooldridge, M., and Fisher, M. (1992). A first order branching time logic of multi-agent systems. *Proc. Eur. Conf. Artif. Intell., 10th*, Vienna, Austria.

CHAPTER 3

Distributed Artificial Intelligence Testbeds

KEITH S. DECKER

1 INTRODUCTION

Since the inception of the field, distributed artificial intelligence researchers have used testbeds as a stepping-stone between formal theory and applications. These testbeds have provided both development environments for DAI applications and abstract, customizable problem solving domains in which agents can participate. As the term implies, they have been used to test, develop, and analyze the performance of various communication, coordination, and negotiation mechanisms, as well as experiment with new agent architectures. This chapter will discuss what a testbed is and how it can be used, using as examples two historically influential systems, the Distributed Vehicle Monitoring Testbed (DVMT) and the MultiAgent Computing Environment (MACE). Finally, we will briefly discuss the current ideas and systems you will read about in detail in Part III.

2 WHAT IS A DAI TESTBED?

The main purpose of a DAI testbed is to support the implementation of ideas so that they can be evaluated in a useful context. Often theoretical ideas need to be operationalized in order to test them fully; sometimes they only cover some of the complex issues that make up a full DAI system. A testbed provides the means to implement these ideas, and can provide support facilities to elaborate hypotheses about a particular system characteristic, such as a new coordination algorithm or negotiation protocol (see Chapter 1). With this purpose in mind, most DAI testbeds provide three classes of facilities:

Foundations of Distributed Artificial Intelligence, Edited by G. M. P. O'Hare and N. R. Jennings.
ISBN 0-471-00675-0 © 1996 John Wiley & Sons, Inc.

1. *Domain Facilities.* representation and simulation of the problem being solved
2. *Development Facilities.* an environment or tools for building the agents that will solve the problem
3. *Evaluation Facilities.* tools for display, data collection, and analysis to understand how well the agents perform

DAI testbeds do not have to actually run on distributed hardware; many use simulated concurrent execution to allow repeatable, detailed evaluations. On the other hand, most distributed computing platforms come with at least some development facilities, but are not DAI testbeds *per se*, because they do not provide facilities for representing and simulating problem domains, and often provide only weak evaluation facilities. DAI testbeds can be built successfully on distributed computing platforms, as is demonstrated by both MACE and DVMT.

Before we discuss these types of facilities in detail we will introduce the DVMT and MACE as examples.

3   THE DISTRIBUTED VEHICLE MONITORING TESTBED

The DVMT, developed at the University of Massachusetts under the direction of Dr. Victor R. Lesser, is arguably the oldest, largest, and most-cited distributed AI testbed. Work on the DVMT, which began in 1981 and continued through 1991, has resulted in over 50 papers and Ph.D. theses in areas such as meta-level control (Corkill and Lesser, 1983), performance modeling (Pavlin, 1983), distributed diagnosis (Hudlická and Lesser, 1987), and coordination (Durfee and Lesser, 1991). The DVMT has also supported research into parallel scheduling (Decker et al., 1993a), real-time problem solving (Lesser et al., 1988; Decker et al., 1990, 1993b), incremental planning (Durfee and Lesser, 1988b), organizational design (Pattison et al., 1987), and many other issues of sophisticated control, distributed search, and blackboard architectures (Lesser and Corkill, 1981, 1983; Lesser et al., 1987; Lesser, 1991).[1] Over those 10 years, more than 20 people have contributed to five distinct implementations of the testbed on platforms ranging from the DEC VAX to the TI Explorer Lisp machine and the Sequent multiprocessor. The idea for the DVMT came from experiments done with a distributed version of the HEARSAY-II speech understanding system (Lesser and Erman, 1980), which was difficult to use because it took large amounts of computation time and had too many inflexible, single-agent design choices. Today the spirit of the DVMT lives on through two other testbeds: DRESUN, a distributed version of the RESUN blackboard-based architecture for planning to resolve uncertainties in sensor interpretation

---

[1]The Lesser et al. (1987) technical report should be considered the most recent complete description of the "classic" DVMT.

(Carver et al., 1991), and TÆMS, a framework for building models of multiagent task environments at multiple levels of abstraction and supporting environment-centered analysis and design of coordination and scheduling mechanisms (see Chapter 16).

The DVMT simulates a network of vehicle monitoring *nodes* (agents), where each node is a problem solver that analyzes acoustically sensed data to identify, locate, and track patterns of vehicles moving through a two-dimensional space. Each problem-solving node is associated with a sensor or sensors. In the simulated domain environment, each vehicle generates sounds (at particular locations and discrete times) that are described by a *grammar* in terms of signal groups, which are then described in terms of low-level, detectable signal frequencies. A particular class of vehicle may be more likely to generate some signal groups than others, and signal groups may have multiple or uncertain definitions. Signal strength is related to vehicle loudness and velocity. Signals generated by vehicles may degrade over distance or be reflected and cause ghosting or acoustic masking by atmospheric effects. The simulated sensors at each node may have different accuracies for different ranges of signals, exhibit directional sensitivity, or introduce random or correlated errors in the incoming signals.

Each problem-solving node is responsible for a specific area and attempts to recognize and eliminate erroneous sensor data as it integrates the correct data into an answer map. These responsibilities are indicated by *interest areas* that indicate the nodes' organizational roles and direct communication. Each problem solver has a blackboard architecture with blackboard levels and knowledge sources appropriate for vehicle monitoring. Figure 3.1 (from Durfee and Lesser, 1988a) demonstrates a few of the set of potential cooperative interactions engendered by the testbed. The figure shows four nodes and four associated sensors (sensor *i* is connected to node *i*). The sensor ranges overlap somewhat, such that a vehicle in the overlapping area will be heard by more

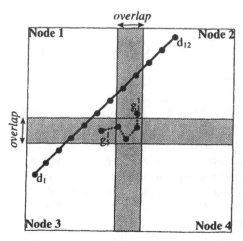

Figure 3.1 *Four DVMT nodes tracking a vehicle. All data arrives in a single burst at the start of a run. Assume that node 2 has a faulty sensor, and that the g track is spurious and is seen only by node 1.*

than one sensor. Sensor 2 is faulty and not only detects signals at the correct frequencies for each location (according to the grammar) but also detects noisy signals at spurious frequencies for each location. The track $d_1 \rightarrow d_{12}$ was made by a real vehicle, but the data associated with points $g_1^1 \rightarrow g_5^1$ is a spurious "ghost" track and is only detected by the sensor at node 1. Several types of cooperative interactions are possible in this scenario:

- *Exploiting Predictive Information.* Node 1 should send information to node 2 to help resolve ambiguity and speed up processing (information from node 1 about the vehicle's class and likely heading could be used by the domain knowledge sources at node 2 to disambiguate the noisy data).
- *Avoiding Redundant Activity.* Nodes 1 and 3 should avoid redundant work on overlapping sensor data (typically overlapping work served no purpose in the DVMT's domain).
- *Sharing Tasks.* Node 4 should take on some tasks because it is idle (either domain tasks such as integrating partial results into the complete track, or perhaps coordination tasks).
- *Resolving Ambiguity.* Nodes 1 and 4 can work together to eliminate the ghost track data (or at least delay work on it until the more promising full track is completed).
- *Constructing Answers.* The nodes might develop a plan, based on their relative load, about how to integrate the results into an areawide map (who should communicate what information to whom and when).

This should give you some idea about the general domain and structure of the DVMT; later we discuss the DVMT in terms of its domain, development, and evaluation facilities.

4   MACE

MACE was developed at the University of Southern California under the direction of Dr. Les Gasser, between 1985 and 1990. It has supported research in coordination, organizational structuring, parallel production systems, blackboard architectures, visual scene analysis, distributed diagnosis, and distributed planning (Gasser et al., 1987, 1988, 1989). MACE was implemented serially on the TI Explorer lisp machine and in parallel on the Intel SYM-1 hypercube.

MACE provided tools for constructing DAI systems at different levels of abstraction, from fine-grained, rule-base-like systems where each "rule" was an agent that could potentially execute in parallel, to coarse-grained systems with large-scale agents that could carry out coordination mechanisms like the contract net protocol (Davis and Smith, 1983). In contrast to the DVMT, MACE had no fixed domain for problem solving activity, and provided a language for describing and instantiating agents quite different from the blackboard-based agents of the DVMT. The MACE language is based on the Actors paradigm (Hewitt and Lieerman, 1984) of parallel object-oriented systems communicating via message passing. This paradigm is somewhat different from today's common object-oriented language paradigms because it was expressly designed for concurrent execution—each object could execute actions independently of the others, and sending a message to another object did not entail waiting for a reply. Common object-oriented languages today assume sequential execution—sending a message or invoking a generic function causes the single thread of control to transfer to the called function, essentially the caller waits until control returns. The MACE environment provided a set of *kernels* for low-level message routing and I/O on different kinds of hardware; *system agents* to build or destroy other agents, allocate agents to processors, monitor execution, and interface to users; a distributed *description database* of agents from which agent instantiations can be built; and a collection of useful problem-solving facilities to be used by the agents such as pattern matchers, error handlers, etc. Each MACE agent has an *engine*, often a production system, that decides what action the agent should take next.

The Intelligent Coordination Experiment (ICE) was implemented on MACE, and serves as a good example of the type of research the testbed could support (Gasser et al., 1989). The ICE domain, which has been a fruitful one for Distributed AI researchers since introduced in 1986 (Benda et al., 1986), is usually called the pursuit problem and involves two classes of agents, predators and prey, moving in four possible directions on a rectilinear grid. The goal of the predactors is to surround the prey on all four sides. How might the predators go about coordinating their actions (if, indeed, they need to be coordinated at all)? Several papers describing solutions to this problem have appeared in the (mostly unpublished) proceedings of the ninth, tenth, and eleventh international workshops on DAI. For the ICE in particular, the inherently dynamic and reorganizable nature of the MACE agent-building and communication facilities allowed Gasser and his group to experiment with creating computational versions of noncomputational social theories of *negotiated order*. In the context of representing and using organizational knowledge in the ICE environment, the pursuing agents would dynamically alter their organizational roles to adapt to the current situation. Using MACE's ability to build agents at different levels of abstraction, each ICE agent comprised six simpler MACE agents to handle different functions.

We will now turn to describing the three classes of facilities provided by DAI testbeds.

5 DOMAIN FACILITIES

Most DAI testbeds provided facilities for representing and simulating the domain, or problem-solving environment, of which the agents are a part. For example, the DVMT simulated vehicle monitoring, ICE simulated the pursuit problem, researchers at Rand simulated an air traffic control task (Cammarata et al., 1983). Sometimes, as in the Rand example, simulation is used because the real process would be too expensive or dangerous to use. Sometimes, as in the ICE environment, it is used to reduce or control the real-time nature of the task. Sometimes, as in the DVMT, researchers want more extensive control over aspects of the problem being solved. Finally, testbeds such as MACE, or MICE (Michigan Intelligent Coordination Environment) (Durfee and Montgomery, 1989) focus on providing tools to model many domains, as opposed to a single representative domain. MICE generalizes the pursuit game to the general actions of agents on a grid and so can simulate environments with, for example, fire agents and fire-fighting agents. The resulting domains are interesting but simple enough to allow MICE to be used for teaching as well as research purposes.

Another way to contrast these testbeds is by the relative importance they put on domain facilities versus development facilities (to be discussed in the next section). The DVMT provides a strong domain simulator and a strong agent architecture. MACE only provides basic tools for developing a domain simulator and agents, using its own Actors like language. ICE provides a strong domain, and fairly free construction of the agents via MACE. MICE generalizes the ICE pursuit problem, but is otherwise architecturally neutral, allowing agents to be written in any language and with any architecture.

The four domain simulation characteristics mentioned earlier of *cost, non-real-time performance, better control*, and *generalization* are important because the purpose of this component of a testbed is to drive the evaluation process. Whether you are trying to test a theory or engineer a solution to a particular problem, the domain facilities of a testbed interact closely with the evaluation facilities (described in Section 7). The simulation cost needs to be low enough so that runs can be made quickly enough to get useful feedback—some researchers have run hundreds of pursuit experiments with random starting positions to evaluate their algorithms.[2] Non-real-time performance is not simply the ability to ignore real-time control issues, which in a real-time problem would be a mistake (Dean and Boddy, 1988; Russell and Wefald, 1991; Garvey and Lesser, 1993), but the ability to examine the effect of the *relative* speeds of the external environment and the agent's computations. For example, while evaluating a soft real-time architecture for the DMVT, Decker et al., (1993b) varied the speed of the external environment relative to the speed of the agent's domain knowledge source executions (see also Tileworld and Phoenix, below). Better control over an environment means that you can replicate scenarios (more about replications in Section 7), measure important features of the scenario or domain that might otherwise be hard to measure and even control the parts of the problem-solving process itself. For example, the DVMT had a feature— one of many that were never used to their full extent—that allowed the experimenter to control the strength of the "knowledge" available in the agent's knowledge sources. Thus, one could create "dumber" agents and "smarter"

---

[2]Unfortunately, the DVMT could, for a large problem, take several hours to terminate. The largest DVMT experiments were run with 13 agents; most were with 4.

agents, or agents whose areas of expertise did not entirely overlap, and examine directly the effects of knowledge on coordination. Unfortunately, the DVMT probably had too many controls—configuring all the parameters and ensuring their consistency was a daunting job. Some tools were created to help in scenario generation (see Section 7).

The characteristic of generalization in the domain representation or simulation facility has two different qualities: broad applicability and abstraction. MACE, by allowing the experimenter to build his own domain from the tools provided, has broad applicability (but at the price of the implementation work involved), while the DVMT with its prespecified domain provided abstraction from the detailed sensor interpretation problem. In particular, the DVMT abstracted away thorny details of the real sound understanding problem such as the various signal processing algorithms used in low-level speech understanding (i.e., Hearsay-II) (Erman et al., 1980) or the geometric and hydrographic models used in low-level underwater sonar processing.[3] The clear and careful separation of domain problem-solving knowledge from the control and coordination knowledge in the DVMT was the key to providing the flexibility needed to answer many different questions. It was difficult to create domain knowledge of the DVMT that would work for agents in arbitrary organizational contexts.

Generalization as abstraction is the key to building useful (and, one hopes, testable) theories (Cohen, 1991). Consider the difficulties facing an experimenter asking under what environmental conditions a particular local scheduler produces acceptable results, or when the overhead associated with a certain coordination algorithm is acceptable given the frequency of particular subtask interrelationships. A testbed domain facility should provide useful characterizations of the important environmental features, which can be used to state theories or to test them within some defensible methodological framework.

Doran (1993) has suggested a third type of domain generalization possible in DAI testbeds that he calls "targeted" modeling—modeling a very specific situation to determine a solution. Targeted modeling is the opposite of the abstract (or "theory building") approach taken by the DVMT. Most testbeds with the "broad applicability" generalization characteristic *could* be used for targeted modeling. Examples of targeted testbeds that have been used to model particular domain problem instances or episodes include CADDIE and the VDT (see below).

6 DEVELOPMENT FACILITIES

The second key feature of distributed AI testbeds is their development facilities. Regardless of whether agent executions are real or simulated, building agents can be a complicated and time-consuming process. Testbed development fa-

---

[3]Because realistic modeling of problem solving requires a strong domain model, Lesser et al. (1993) eventually returned to true low-level signal processing in the IPUS system for understanding household sounds, which is built on the RESUN architecture.

cilities may include a *language* for expressing agent-oriented concepts simply and directly, prespecified agent problem-solving *architectures*, special support for message *communication* between agents, *translation* facilities for helping agents to understand one another, *debugging* support for the resulting concurrent distributed system, and *graphics* for visualization of execution and evaluation. Testbeds often include at least some of these facilities.

6.1 Language

Language support is the most basic development facility. Many testbeds have been implemented using only standard languages (usually Lisp), but more recent testbeds at least use object-oriented languages (like CLOS, the Common Lisp Object System), which are naturally expressive for the type of programming involved in building distributed agents. The approach of MACE is different in that the objects have simultaneous, concurrent existence [a feature developed by the Actor family of languages (Hewitt and Lieerman, 1984; Agha, 1986)]. MACE objects include

- *Demons* that monitor external events and send messages about these events to agents
- *Imps* that monitor an agent's internal events and can execute any arbitrary Lisp function
- *Agents* themselves that comprise an execution engine and various knowledge structures (such as models of other agents in the system).

Language development for multiagent programming has been an active area, whether tied to a DAI testbed or development environment or not. MERING-IV (Ferber and Carle, 1990) (Chapter 11) is an Actor-type language that has as its unique feature a mechanism for reflection, i.e., the ability to model itself at a meta-level. The reflective mechanisms can be invoked at runtime to change the structure and behavior of classes of objects. ABCL (Yonezawa et al., 1988) is also a descendent of Actor languages and has as one of its distinguishing characteristics three types of message passing (send and no wait, send and wait for reply, send and no wait but expect a reply later) and two message-passing modes (ordinary and express, the later allowing interruption of the former). Shoham has produced Agent0 (Shoham, 1991), a simple interpreter based on the more general idea of *agent-oriented programming* (AOP). AOP specializes the ideas of object-oriented programming (in the Actor sense) so that objects become agents that have a formally defined mental state (beliefs, commitments, and capabilities) and that send messages to one another with types inspired by speech act theory (inform, request, offer, etc.). OZ (Henz et al., 1993) is not an Actor-derived language (Chapter 15) but rather one derived from concurrent constraint programming and logic programming. Its innovations include a higher-level facility for communicating constraints than other concurrent constraint programming languages, and a facility for higher-order (meta-object) programming.

6.2 Architecture

The prespecified knowledge structures of MACE go beyond language constructs toward support for a problem-solving *architecture* (Chapters 1 and 5). MACE provides a fairly sophisticated structure for each agent's models of itself and other agents, as well as a set of system agents that handle common system-level tasks such as the creation of new agents, user interaction, and support for error handling and debugging. Each MACE agent keeps a model of its *acquaintances* that includes the other agents skills, goals, (partially ordered) plans, communication address, and roles (the relationships between the modeling agent and the agent being modeled, such as "creator," "co-worker," "my-organization-manager," etc.).

DVMT agents used the Generic BlackBoard architecture (GBB) (Corkill et al., 1986) as their base. Three key components make up a blackboard-based agent:

1. *Cooperating Knowledge Sources.* The cooperating knowledge source paradigm is used as the agent's basic problem-solving model. Each knowledge source is a black box that can contain any kind of problem-solving system, algorithm, rule-base, etc.

2. *Separate Control Component.* This is where most of the "AI" (and coordination) in a blackboard system resides—in choosing the order in which to execute knowledge sources. Knowledge sources often contribute to this function by providing triggering conditions and preconditions.

3. *The Blackboard Itself.* A partitioned shared memory often organized using database principles for efficient retrieval. The blackboard provides communication for knowledge sources through common representations, facilities to trigger knowledge source applications, and a locus of community memory for the knowledge sources).

DVMT knowledge sources were divided into three basic classes, two of which were associated with domain problem solving (these classes were called *synthesis* and *track extension*) and one for communication between agents. Experiments in coordination dealt not only with the communication knowledge sources but also with various meta-control mechanisms that were part of, or on top of, the blackboard control component. In contrast, testbeds like MICE are architecturally neutral, in that they only provide an agent interface, and no particular agent architecture (or language) is assumed or provided. If one wished, one could use GBB to construct blackboard-based agents to interact in MICE, for example. The BB1 blackboard system shell (Hayes-Roth, 1985) is another architectural base that has been used for the construction of distributed AI systems (Hayes-Roth et al., 1989), as is ABE (Hayes-Roth et al., 1988) (ABE, however, is not a blackboard shell).

Note that the discussion of "architecture" here has related to *if* and *to what extent* the testbed provides (or prescribes) a particular *agent* architecture. Another sense of "architecture" that can usefully be applied to distributed AI testbeds is the way in which the testbeds themselves support multiple agents. If the testbed runs on a uniprocessor, do agents share a single process and address space (complete simulation), or do agents have individual address spaces and are multiplexed, or perhaps a single address space with language-supported process control. If the testbed is truly distributed, then which choice was made for each processor (can more than one agent run on a processor, like MACE)? Of course the form of the hardware also comes into play here, such as the hypercube hardware used by MACE, or the DVMT implementations on multiple VAX (Durfee et al., 1984) or the Sequent multiprocessor.

6.3   Communication

Although the field has made formal studies of noncommunicative approaches to distributed coordination (Genesereth et al., 1986) (Chapter 6), most testbeds rely heavily on communication between agents. Communication support may be general, so that the researchers can define their own communication protocols, or may be based on a formal model that predefines all or certain classes of communication actions. Both the DVMT and MACE follow the first approach, while AGENT-0 is an example of the second. AGENT-0 uses speech act theory (Searle, 1969) as a base for communication, where messages are preclassified as to the agent's intent: informing, requesting, offering, etc. Often a particular coordination or negotiation scheme will fix the type and contents of messages, for example, the contract net protocol and its announcements, bids, awards, reports, etc.

6.4   Translation

The communication problem can of course be more complex than just providing the necessary facilities to the agents. This is brought out clearly by work on distributed expert systems, enterprise integration, and like endeavors where very heterogeneous groups of agents are working together on a problem. How can they understand the content of one another's communications? Testbeds oriented toward these types of problems (like Archon or CooperA, below) often provide some type of translation facilities for agent communication. Work on this problem often involves three major components:

- Some *facilitator* that interfaces or "wraps around" a problem solver, expert system, or "legacy system"[4] in order to make it into an "agent"
- A communication protocol, as discussed in the previous section
- An *interlingua*, translated into and out of by the facilitators, constructed from the agents' shared ontologies (like KIF) (Genesereth et al., 1992)

Neither MACE nor the DVMT support translation directly.

---

[4]A program that does something important but was written long ago and cannot easily be rewritten.

6.5 Debugging

Debugging a truly distributed system is a complex process due to the inherent asynchrony (Bates et al., 1983)—that is why so many testbeds either are simulated or provide simulation capabilities. MACE provides both simulated distributed execution and true distributed execution on an Intel hypercube; different versions of the DVMT also simulated distributed execution, ran truly distributed across multiple machines and ran in parallel (intranode parallelism) on the Sequent multiprocessor. One of the most important aspects of a testbed simulation is *repeatability* (for more than one reason—see also the section on evaluation); debugging can be a nightmare if problems cannot be reliably reproduced. Simulation of truly distributed systems can overcome some of these problems by providing a shared centralized clock.

DAI testbeds often support sophisticated tracing facilities. There is a tremendous amount of information generated, and possibly collected, during a run, and the users of the testbed need to be able to filter out the information that is particularly relevant to the problem at hand. The DVMT, for example, used a hierarchical, event-based trace structure that allowed groups of related tracing messages to be turned on or off together, and new groups to be defined in relation to others as the capabilities of the system were expanded. For example, the information needed to debug a new coordination policy may be quite different from the information needed to debug a new local scheduling policy. Understanding the coordination policy may require knowing when certain coordination-related meta-communications are sent and to whom, and when they are noticed by the remote nodes and how they are acted upon. Understanding the local scheduling mechanism in a blackboard system, for example, may require detailed information about what knowledge sources were activated at a certain time and which knowledge source activation was actually chosen for execution. The DVMT also allowed side-by-side agent traces. Automated tools for analyzing DVMT performance based on a simple model of blackboard-based problem solving (Pavlin, 1983) and other explanation tools met only limited success, either because of the inability to model the complex interaction of the system or the weak domain model.

MACE, in its predefined community of system agents, provided several tools for debugging, among them *monitor* agents for tracing and logging data based on demon and imp requests, and *user-interface* agents for controlling terminal I/O. The MACE tracing system could maintain temporal links between data even when executing concurrently on separate processors. The MACE distributed simulation could model arbitrary logical processor speeds, interconnection topologies, and even simulate errors with a specified probability.

6.6 Graphics

Finally, many DAI testbeds provide some kind of development facility for graphical visualization; these facilities can be used for both debugging and evaluation (Chapter 21). MACE provided access to such a facility through the predefined system user-interface agents, but did not support any particular graphical interface. The DVMT, after it moved to the Lisp machine, sported a domain-level interface that showed the progress of each agent in terms of the hypotheses and goals of the agents. The content of the hypothesis or goal was displayed by a physical shape (rectangle), the blackboard level by color, and the degree of belief by brightness level. When combined with a view of the "consistency blackboard," where the true solution was stored, one could tell by visual inspection when, for example, an agent was distracted. A graphical view was also available of the solution construction graph at a node—the solution construction graph was used by the partial global planning algorithm to indicate *how* nodes should interact, including specifications about what partial results to exchange and when to exchange them.

7 EVALUATION FACILITIES

The third and final set of facilities we will discuss are evaluation facilities. Since the main purpose of a DAI testbed is to support the evaluation of ideas, evaluation facilities are very important. Historically, they have focused on the collection of data, and not very much on the analysis of that data.

All testbeds have some kind of data collection or instrumentation facility, often tied to the debugging and graphical facilities that were described in the previous section. MACE uses the demon and imp mechanisms to collect data on message traffic, queue and data base sizes, work done by an agent (for several definitions of "work"), and processor load. Collecting other types of data is possible, but more detailed data can be collected only during MACE's simulated distributed execution (as opposed to parallel execution on the hypercube). The DVMT can also collect data on a variety of events at the systemwide, domain problem solving, and coordination levels.

The earlier section on domain facilities talked some about scenario generation, and this is also important for evaluation. Because of the nature of the DVMT vehicle tracking problem (and remember, it was simplified from a completely realistic task) scenarios had to be specified in a high-level language which was then used to generate the low-level sensor data and noise that served as input to the system. Often it was difficult to generate certain high-level behaviors in the agents with this amount of scenario control. One of the problems of the DVMT was that arbitrary environments could not be automatically generated, and thus at least some information about the scenarios was not explicitly available to the agents.

An important facility that was discussed earlier in the context of debugging is replication. Replication is important for evaluation in that it allows the use of paired-response experiments across treatments (for example, applying different scheduling or coordination algorithms to the same domain scenario). Such experiments often have greater power in separating out treatment effects than nonpaired response experiments with random, nonreplicated runs for each treatment. The MACE distributed execution simulator was deterministic; the DVMT used scenario definitions that were repeatable. For a complete evaluation, the generation of new scenarios is important too: both carefully constructed scenarios that highlight certain problems and randomly generated scenarios to test average performance. For example, a graphical system could also be used to interactively construct individual DVMT scenarios; ICE randomly generated initial conditions for pursuit problems.

The most important part of evaluation is the analysis of the results, but DAI testbeds have not historically supported internal analysis tools. This situation comes about in part because the testbed designers do not want to make strong methodological commitments for their users. This situation may change as DAI develops stronger evaluative methodologies.

8 OTHER TESTBEDS

There have been many other testbeds used in distributed AI research, although they are often only peripherally described in the most visible published literature. This is because the testbed itself must take a backseat to the results and advances that researchers achieve through its use. We have already mentioned MACE, DVMT, MICE, DRESUN, and the Rand air traffic control simulator, languages like the Actors framework, MERING-IV, and AGENT-0, and development environments like GBB, BB1, and ABE. Other testbeds and development tools that have been or are used for distributed AI include the following (the last five are discussed in Part III; see also Buoron et al., 1991; Doran et al., 1991).

Tileworld. Tileworld (Pollack and Ringuette, 1990) is a domain simulator more similar in spirit to the DVMT than MACE. Although not originally a distributed AI testbed, it has more recently been used as one (Goldman and Rosenchein, 1993). Tileworld agents are simulated robots that fill up simulated "holes" in the gridworld they occupy. Various extensions include different costs and benefits for filling holes, the frequency with which holes appear, and obstacles in the world that agents must travel around. Tileworld's use of a domain simulator is due to the need for better control and precise instrumentation (like the DVMT), and for experimentation with real-time response (by varying the relative speeds of the environment and agents). Tileworld does not have a suite of development facilities and thus is architecturally neutral toward the agents. Evaluation facilities include the collection, automatic generation, and replication of scenarios as well as graphical displays.

Phoenix. The Phoenix fire-fighting testbed (Cohen et al., 1989) is another domain simulator. Although not primarily a DAI testbed, it does have multiple agents (firebosses and bulldozers) operating semiautonomously in a highly dynamic environment (a fairly complex fire simulation based on weather conditions, Yellowstone National Park's physical features, and fire-fighting data of the burn rates of various land types). Some work has been done on coordinating multiple firebosses (Moehlman et al., 1992) through negotiation over bulldozers considered as resources. The Phoenix use of a domain simulator is due to the cost associated with the real application, need to control real-time responsiveness (again, by varying the relative speed of environmental change and agent actions versus agent deliberation), and better control and more precise instrumentation. The Phoenix testbed uses Lisp as its implementation language and promotes a flexible high-level agent architecture, an extensible set of communication primitives, but no translation facilities. Due to the environment's complexity and size, extensive and detailed debugging and graphical visualization tools are used with the system, as well as tools for collecting and analyzing the data. These data collection and analysis tools were generalized into CLIP (Common Lisp Instrumentation Package) and CLASP (Common Lisp Analysis and Statistics Package), which are not tied to Phoenix (see T*Æ*MS below).[5]

CADDIE. CADDIE (Control And Direction of Distributed Intelligent Agents) (Farhoodi et al., 1991) is a testbed for examining questions about organizational structures and procedures. Rather than simulate a specific domain, CADDIE provides tools to build particular scenarios in a particular domain of interest, such as urban emergency services or air traffic management. CADDIE's development tools are based on general languages (C++, Prolog) and provide an architecture for describing agents (and organizations of agents called FUNs—FUNctional units) and their communications. Since it was designed to evaluate organizational structures and procedures, CADDIE provides evaluation tools for defining scenarios, collecting data (many performance metrics are predefined), and analyzing it (both sensitivity analysis and "what-if" question-answering are supported). CADDIE has been used for targeted modeling of the response of emergency services to accidents.

VDT. The VDT (Virtual Design Team) (Levitt et al., 1994) is a targeted testbed for examining the effect of organizational structure, communication facilities, and project policies on the duration of engineering facility design and construction projects. It focuses on providing strong domain modeling facilities, and strong-built evaluation facilities. Domain specification and agent development are done via a high-level OPDL (organization and project description language). The VDT has been validated on real projects such as petroleum refinery design and the design of a subsea oil drilling module.

Articulator. Articulator (Mi and Scacchi, 1990) is a testbed for examining questions about software engineering processes. It provides tools to model

---

[5]Although some work on Phoenix continues, Cohen's lab is now working with the transportation planning testbed for the ARPA knowledge-based planning and scheduling initiative.

software engineering tasks and the agents involved, and tools to adapt existing multiagent software engineering processes and develop new ones. These processes represent both software development tasks and surrounding coordination work including "articulation" tasks—negotiation or accommodation tasks needed when things do not go as planned. The testbed allows users to simulate their processes to determine likely problems and bottlenecks. Articulator provides language and architecture support—the emphasis is not developing agents, but rather the processes that the agents will take part in.

EOS. EOS (Doran et al., 1994) uses a DAI testbed with abstractly generalized domain to explore theories about the emergence of centralized decision making in early human society. EOS is used to build computational models of anthropologic theories, similar to the way CADDIE, the VDT, or TÆMS build computational models of sociological theories. The EOS simulations attempt to link cognative and environmental factors to the emergence of hierarchical groupings among small sets (10–20) of agents.

ARCHON. ARCHON (see Chapter 12) is a complete development environment for building small communities of cooperating heterogeneous systems, thus closer to MACE than the DVMT. It is built on a traditional language base (C++ and CLOS (common Lisp object system)), and provides a fully developed agent architecture (the Archon layer). ARCHON does not dictate the problem solving architecture of an agent below this layer. Communication facilities include predefined services and message types built on those services. Translation facilities are sometimes provided (depending on the application). ARCHON does not provide facilities to simulate or model problem-solving domains nor does it provide built-in evaluation facilities—but of course it does not preclude the development of such facilities. ARCHON has been used in the development of several real applications in areas such as electrical power management; individual domain models have been built, and evaluation methodologies followed, for each of these applications separately.

IMAGINE. IMAGINE (integrated multiagent interactive environment; see Chapter 13) is also a development environment. Its focus is on developing systems where computer applications and humans work together to solve problems, and thus it also draws on the area of computer-supported cooperative work as well as DAI. Applications that are being developed include urban traffic control (distributed parking lot allocation) and distributed meeting scheduling.

CooperA. The CooperA testbed, described in Chapter 14, is primarily a development testbed, more similar to MACE than the DVMT. It uses a general language (Knowledge-Craft's CRL-Lisp, which is Lisp extended with a frame (schema) knowledge representation language) and a well-defined agent structure. CooperA provides a uniform message structuring protocol for communication, and communication translation facilities for heterogeneous agents. A special user interface agent provides graphics and debugging facilities that allow the user to see and trace the flows of interactions among the agents. CooperA is implemented on a Symbolics, as a simulated distributed system and encourages experimentation with alternative communication and domain problem-solving strategies. An example CooperA domain is DChEM, the distributed chemical emergencies manager for establishing the threat level of a chemical emergency.

TÆMS. TÆMS (Task Analysis, Environment Modeling, and Simulation), described in Chapter 16, is a framework for exploring questions about coordination, scheduling, and organization that includes as a component a simulation testbed. The framework provides a language for building general models of many different domains that can be then analyzed mathematically or simulated; the domain models include a generative component. Understanding real-time performance is a key feature, and both the analytical and simulation components include detailed temporal information. Because TÆMS focuses on domain modeling it remains architecturally neutral with respect to the agents—it provides no separate development language or specific agent architecture—and is intended to work with any of the current formal and informal agent descriptions. Because communication uses resources and potentially changes the state of the external environment, TÆMS does define several classes of communication actions; developers of coordination algorithms need to indicate the mapping between the messages in their specific protocol and these communication classes. TÆMS provides an extensible trace facility similar to the DVMTs, and graphical display of domain scenarios (called task structures). Other graphical views can be constructed for a particular domain (such as one mimicking the original DVMT interface). TÆMS supports data collection facilities using CLIP and analysis using CLASP or standard statistical packages. Special attention is paid to describing the statistical characteristics of the external environment for generation of scenarios (called *episodes*); repetition is supported including support for paired response studies. While the creators of TÆMS have an analysis methodology in mind (Decker and Lesser, 1993), TÆMS does not yet support it directly (or force one to use it).

The Agent Factory. The Agent Factory (see Chapter 17) supports the construction of multiagent systems through their algebraic specification as abstract data types. It is being developed on top of the Paradox system, which generates implementations that adhere to the abstract specifications.

9 SUMMARY

Distributed AI testbeds have been and will continue to be a feature in the DAI research landscape, although their use as research tools often keeps them in the background. In this chapter we discussed two testbeds of historical importance, the DVMT and MACE. These two testbeds exemplify two different styles: one focused on the controlled and instrumented simulation of a domain in order to study general questions in research areas such as coordination, the other focused on development facilities for building physically distributed systems. The systems are not at opposite ends of this spectrum, but somewhere toward the midpoints—each has informed and learned from the other. This chapter also presented three classes of questions to think about when reading about or implementing a testbed: questions about the *domain* facilities, such as why the domain is being simulated—cost, real-time control, precise instrumentation, and/or generalization; questions about the *development* facilities— special languages, agent architectures, communication and translation of messages, debugging, and graphics; questions about the *evaluation* tools—data collection, generation and replication of scenarios, analysis. Keep these questions in mind when you read about a testbed in this book or elsewhere, and look for testbeds to be used both for research and as tools for educating students about the problems and solutions of the distributed AI research community.

REFERENCES

Agha, G. (1986). *Actors—A Model of Concurrent Computation for Distributed Systems.* MIT Press, Cambridge, MA.

Bates, P. C. Wileden, J. C., and Lesser, V. R. (1983). A debugging tool for distributed systems. *Proc. Annu. Phoenix Conf. Comput. Commun.*, pp. 311–315.

Benda, M., Jagannathan, V., and Dodhiawala, R. (1986). *On Optimal Cooperation of Knowledge Sources*, Tech. Rep. BCS-G2010-28. Boeing AI Center, Boeing Computer Service, Seattle, WA.

Buoron, T., Ferber, J., and Samuel, F. (1991). MAGES: A multi-agent testbed for heterogeneous agents. In *Decentralized Artificial Intelligence 2* (Y. Demazeau and J.-P. Müller, eds.). Elsevier/North-Holland, Amsterdam.

Cammarata, S., McArthur, D., and Steeb, R. (1983). Strategies of cooperation in distributed problem solving. *Proc. Int. Joint. Conf. Artif. Intell. 8th*, Karlsruhe, Germany, *1983*, pp. 767–770.

Carver, N., Cvetanovic, Z., and Lesser, V. (1991). Sophisticated cooperation in FA/C distributed problem solving systems. *Proc. Nat. Conf. Artif. Intell.*, *9th*, Anaheim, *CA*, pp. 191–198.

Cohen, P. R. (1991). A survey of the Eighth National Conference on Artificial Intelligence: Pulling together or pulling apart? *AI Mag.* **12**(1), 16–41.

Cohen, P. R., Greenberg, M., Hart, D., and Howe, A. (1989). Trial by fire: Understanding the design requirements for agents in complex environments. *AI Mag.* **10**(3), 33–48.

Corkill, D. D. and Lesser, V. R. (1983). The use of meta-level control for coordination in a distributed problem solving network. *Proc. Int. Jt. Conf. Artif. Intell.*, *8th*, Karlsruhe, Germany, *1983*, pp. 748–755.

Corkill, D. D., Gallagher, K. Q., and Murray, K. E. (1986). GBB: A generic blackboard development system. *Proc. Nat. Conf. Artif. Intell.*, *5th*, Philadelphia, pp. 1008–1014.

Davis, R., and Smith, R. G. (1983). Negotiation as a metaphor for distributed problem solving. *Artif. Intell.* **20**(1), 63-109.

Dean, T., and Boddy, M. (1988). An analysis of time-dependent planning. *Proc. Nat. Conf. Artif. Intell.*, *7th*, St. Paul, MN, pp. 49-54.

Decker, K. S., and Lesser, V. R., (1993). An approach to analyzing the need for meta-level communication. *Proc. Int. Jt. Conf. Artif. Intell.*, *13th*, Chambéry, France, *1993*, pp. 360-366.

Decker, K. S., Lesser, V. R., and Whitehair, R. C. (1990). Extending a blackboard architecture for approximate processing. *J. Real-Time Syst.* **2**(1/2), 47-79.

Decker, K. S., Garvey, A. J., Humphrey, M. A., and Lesser, V. R. (1993a). Control heuristics for scheduling in a parallel blackboard system. *Int. J. Pattern Recognition Artificial Intell.* **7**(2), 243-264.

Decker, K. S., Garvey, A. J., Humphrey, M. A., and Lesser, V. R. (1993b). A real-time control architecture for an approximate processing blackboard system. *Int. J. Pattern Recognition Artif. Intell.* **7**(2), 265-284.

Doran, J. (1993). Using DAI software testbeds. *Proc. Comp. Knowl. Based Syst. SIG Workshop*, University of Keele, Keele, UK, 1993.

Doran, J., Carvajal, H., Choo, Y., and Li, Y. (1991). The MCS multi-agent testbed: Developments and experiments. In *Cooperating Knowledge Based Systems 1990* (S. Deen, ed.), pp. 240-251. Springer-Verlag, Berlin.

Doran, J., Palmer, M., Gilbert, N., and Mellars, P. (1994). The EOS project: Modelling upper palaeolithic social change. In *Simulating Societies* (N. Gilbert and J. Doran, eds.). UCL Press (to be published).

Durfee, E., and Lesser, V. (1988a). Predicability vs. responsiveness: Coordinating problem solvers in dynamic domains. *Proc. Nat. Conf. Artif. Intell.*, *7th*, St. Paul, MN, pp. 66-71.

Durfee, E. H., and Lesser, V. R. (1988b). Incremental planning to control a time-constrained, blackboard-based problem solver. *IEEE Trans. Aerosp. Electron. Sys.* **AES-24**(5), 647-662.

Durfee, E., and Lesser, V. (1991). Partial global planning: A coordination framework for distributed hypothesis formation. *IEEE Trans. Syst. Man Cybernet.* **SMC-21**(5), 1167-1183.

Durfee, E., and Montgomery, T. (1989). MICE: A flexible testbed for intelligent coordination experiments. *Proc. Int. Workshop Distributed Artif. Intell.*, *9th*, Rosario, WA.

Durfee, E. H., Corkill, D. D. and Lesser, V. R. (1984). Distributing a distributed problem solving network simulator. *Proc. IEEE Comput. Soc. Real-Time Syst. Symp.*, *5th*, pp. 237-246.

Erman, L. D., Hayes-Roth, F., Lesser, V. R., and Reddy, D. R. (1980). The Hearsay-II speech-understanding system: Integrating knowledge to resolve uncertainty. *Comput. Surv.* **12**(2), 213-253.

Farhoodi, F., Proffitt, J., Woodman, P., and Tunnicliffe, A. (1991). Design of organizations in distributed decision system. *Proc. Am. Assoc. Artif. Intell. Workshop Coop. Heterogeneous Intell. Syst.*, Anaheim, CA.

Ferber, J., and Carle, P. (1990). Actors and agents as reflective concurrent objects: A MERING IV perspective. *Proc. Int. Workshop Distributed Artif. Intell.*, *10th*, Bandera, TX.

Garvey, A., and Lesser, V. (1993). Design-to-time real-time scheduling. *IEEE Trans. Syst., Man Cybernet.* **SMC-23**(6), 1491–1502.

Gasser, L., Braganza, C., and Herman, N. (1987). MACE: A flexible testbed for distributed ai research. In *Distributed Artificial Intelligence* (M. N. Huhns, ed.), pp. 119–152. Morgan Kaufmann, San Mateo, CA/Pitman, London.

Gasser, L., Braganza, C., and Herman, N. (1988). Implementing distributed AI systems using MACE. In *Readings in Distributed Artificial Intelligence* (A. H. Bond and L. Gasser, eds.), pp. 445–450. Morgan Kaufmann, San Mateo, CA.

Gasser, L., Rouquette, N. F., Hill, R. W., and Lieb, J. (1989). Representing and using organizational knowledge in distributed AI systems. In *Distributed Artificial Intelligence* (L. Gasser and M. N. Huhns, eds.), Vol. 2, pp. 55–78. Morgan Kaufmann, Los Altos, CA/Pitman, London.

Genesereth, M. R., Ginsberg, M. L., and Rosenschein, J. S. (1986). Cooperation without communication. *Proc. Nat. Conf. Artif. Intell., 5th*, Philadelphia, pp. 51–57.

Genesreth, M. R., Fikes, R. E. *et al.* (1992). *Knowledge Interchange Format, Version 3.0 Reference Manual*, Tech. Rep. Logic-92-1. Computer Science Department, Stanford University, Stanford, CA.

Goldman, C., and Rosenschein, J. R. (1993). Emergent coordination through the use of cooperative state-changing rules. *Proc. Int. Workshop Distributed Artif. Intell., 12th*, Hidden Valley, PA.

Hayes-Roth, B. (1985). A blackboard architecture for control. *Artif. Intell.* **26**, 251–321.

Hayes-Roth, F., Erman, L., Fouse, S., Lark, J., and Davidson, J. (1988). ABE: A cooperative operating system and development environment. In *Readings in Distributed Artificial Intelligence* (A. H. Bond and L. Gasser, eds.), pp. 457–490 Morgan Kaufmann, San Mateo, CA.

Hayes-Roth, B., Washington, R., Hewett, R., and Hewett, M. (1989). Intelligent monitoring and control. *Proc. Int. Jt. Conf. Artif. Intell., 11th*, Detroit, *1989*, pp. 250–255.

Henz, M., Smolka, G., and Würtz, J. (1993). Oz—a programming language for multi-agent systems. *Proc. Int. Jt. Conf. Artif. Intell., 13th*, Chambéry, France, *1993*, pp. 404–409.

Hewitt, C., and Lieerman, H. (1984). Design issues in parallel architectures for artificial intelligence. *Proc. IEEE Comput. Soc. Int. Conf., 28th*, San Francisco, pp. 418–423.

Hudlická, E., and Lesser, V. R. (1987). Modeling and diagnosing problem-solving system behavior. *IEEE Trans. Syst., Man Cybernet.* **SMC-17**(3), 407–419.

Lesser, V. R. (1991). A retrospective view of FA/C distributed problem solving. *IEEE Trans. Syst., Man, Cybernet.* **SMC-21**(6), 1347–1363.

Lesser, V. R., Nawab, H., Gallastegi, I., and Klassner, F. (1993). IPUS: An architecture for integrated signal processing and signal interpretation in complex environments. *Proc. Nat. Conf. Artif. Intell., 11th*, Washington, DC, pp. 249–255.

Lesser, V. R., and Corkill, D. D. (1981). Functionally accurate, cooperative distributed systems. *IEEE Trans. Syst., Man Cybern.* **SMC-11**(1), 81–96.

Lesser, V. R., and Corkill, D. D. (1983). The distributed vehicle monitoring testbed. *AI Mag.* **4**(3), 63–109.

Lesser, V. R., and Erman, L. D. (1980). Distributed interpretation: A model and an experiment. *IEEE Trans. Comput.* **C-29**(12), 1144–1163.

Lesser, V. R., Corkhill, D. D., and Durfee, E. H. (1987). *An Update on the Distributed Vehicle Monitoring Testbed*, Comput. Sci. Tech. Rep. 87-111. University of Massachusetts, Amherst.

Lesser, V. R., Pavlin, J., and Durfee, E. (1988). Approximate processing in real-time problem solving. *AI Mag.* **9**(1), 49–61.

Levitt, R., Cohen, P., Kunz, J., Nass, C., Christiansen, T., and Jin, Y. (1994). The virtual design team: Simulating how organizational structure and communication tools affect team performance. In *Computational Organization Theory* (K. Carley and M. Prietula, eds.). Erlbaum, Hillsdale, NJ.

Mi. P., and Scacchi, W. (1990). A knowledge-based environment for modeling and simulating software engineering processes. *IEEE Trans. Knowl. Data Eng.* **KDE-2**(3), 283–294.

Moehlman, T., Lesser, V., and Buteau, B. (1992). Decentralized negotiation: An approach to the distributed planning problem. *Group Decis. Nego.* **1**(2), 161–192.

Pattison, H. E., Corkill, D. D., and Lesser, V. R. (1987). Instantiating descriptions of organizational structures. In *Distributed Artificial Intelligence* (M. N. Huhns, ed.). Morgan Kaufmann, San Mateo, CA/Plenum, London.

Pavlin, J. (1983). Predicting the performance of distributed knowledge-based systems: A modeling approach. *Proc. Nat. Conf. Artif. Intell.*, *3rd*, Washington, DC, pp. 314–319.

Pollack, M. E., and Ringuette, M. (1990). Introducing Tileworld: Experimentally evaluating agent architectures. *Proc. Nat. Conf. Artif. Intell.*, *8th*, Boston, pp. 183–189.

Russell, S., and Wefald, E. (1991). *Do the Right Thing: Studies in Limited Rationality.* MIT Press, Cambridge, MA.

Searle, J. R. (1969). *Speech Acts: An Essay in the Philosophy of Language.* Cambridge Univ. Press, Cambridge, UK.

Shoham, Y. (1991). AGENT0: A simple agent language and its interpreter. *Proc. Nat. Conf. Artif. Intell.*, *9th*, Anaheim, CA, pp. 704–709.

Yonezawa, A., Briot, J., and Shibayama, E. (1988). Object-oriented concurrent programming in ABCL/1. In *Readings in Distributed Artificial Intelligence* (A. H. Bond and L. Gasser, eds.), pp. 434–444. Morgan Kaufmann, San Mateo, CA.

CHAPTER 4

Applications of Distributed Artificial Intelligence in Industry

H. VAN DYKE PARUNAK

1 INTRODUCTION

In many industrial applications, large centralized software systems are not as effective as distributed networks of relatively simpler computerized agents. For example, to compete effectively in today's markets, manufacturers must be able to design, implement, reconfigure, resize, and maintain manufacturing facilities rapidly and inexpensively. Because modern manufacturing depends heavily on computer systems, these same requirements apply to manufacturing control software, and are more easily satisfied by small modules than by large monolithic systems.

This chapter reviews industrial needs for distributed artificial intelligence (DAI),[1] giving special attention to systems for manufacturing scheduling and control. It describes a taxonomy of such systems, gives case studies of several advanced research applications and actual industrial installations, and identifies steps that need to be taken to deploy these technologies more broadly.

2 THE DEMAND FOR MULTIAGENT SYSTEMS

This section describes the vision of agile manufacturing, outlines challenges that conventional CIM systems face in reaching toward this vision, and suggests why systems of autonomous agents may be particularly well suited to overcoming these challenges.

---

[1]In the sense used here, DAI systems may include simple reactive modules that would not individually be considered artificially intelligent, as well as humans integrated electronically into the overall system.

Foundations of Distributed Artificial Intelligence, Edited by G. M. P. O'Hare and N. R. Jennings.
ISBN 0-471-00675-0 © 1996 John Wiley & Sons, Inc.

TABLE 4.1.   Characteristics of Agility

	Cost	Response Time	Quality	Scope	Relation to Agility
Agile	Low	Quick	Self-Healing	Limitless	
Flexible	Low	Fast	Strong	Limited	Superseded
Lean	High	Slow	Fragile	Little	Complemented

2.1   The Challenge of Agility[2]

Agility, the ability to thrive in an environment of continuous and unanticipated change, provides competitiveness in global markets. Manufacturers with shorter product cycles can track customer desires more closely and thus capture market share. Firms that can change volume of production rapidly can avoid sinking large amounts of capital in excess inventory, while still maximizing returns in periods of rapidly increased demand. With the demise of the cold war, agility is also the foundation for dual-use strategies that permit high levels of preparedness without diverting industrial investment into dedicated defense facilities.

Table 4.1 compares agility with other manufacturing objectives along four dimensions: cost, time, quality, and scope.

Agility requires systems that are low in cost, quick to respond, able to correct themselves in the presence of faults, and unlimited in scope. The first two characteristics have been explored in the context of *flexible* systems (systems engineered to switch rapidly among predefined members of a family of products), but only within predefined limits, and quality has been guaranteed by brute strength rather than the ability for self-correction. *Lean* manufacturing invests heavily, in both time and money, to obtain a facility that is optimized for a particular task but deteriorates rapidly outside the design envelope.

Agility impacts the entire manufacturing organization, including product design, customer relations, and logistics, as well as production. For the sake of concreteness, this discussion focuses on production systems, but occasionally mentions applications of multiagent systems to other manufacturing functions as well.

2.2   Problems with Conventional CIM Systems

Conventional systems for computer-integrated manufacturing (CIM) are often highly centralized. At the least, a central data base (DB) provides a consistent global view of the state of the enterprise, both for internal reference and as an interface to the rest of the organization. Typically, a central machine also computes schedules for the facility, dispatches actions throughout the factory in keeping with the schedule, monitors any deviations from plan, and dispatches corrective action.

---

[2]This section relies heavily on Dove (1992).

TABLE 4.2. Challenges to Traditional Manufacturing
Scheduling and Control

	Centralized	Planned	Sequential
Stochasticity		X	X
Tractability	X	X	X
Decidability		X	
Formal chaos		X	

This approach has three characteristics that impede agility. It is centralized; it relies on global plans; and it precedes execution with planning and scheduling. These characteristics aggravate four operational challenges to manufacturing scheduling and control (MSC): stochasticity (the impact of noise and randomness, such as machine breakdown), tractability (the combinatoric impact of large numbers of interacting entities), decidability (the operational implications of the factory's formal equivalence to a Turing machine, making most of its interesting properties undecidable) and formal chaos (sensitivity to initial conditions resulting from nonlinearities) (Parunak, 1991), as outlined in Table 4.2.

A *centralized* MSC approach is especially susceptible to problems of tractability, because the number of interacting entities that must be managed together is large and leads to combinatorial explosion.[3] All four challenges to MSC make it difficult to predict what will happen, and thus to form a global detailed *plan* that can be executed after it is computed. The need for *sequential* planning and execution is particularly difficult in the face of stochasticity (which changes the state of the world in ways unanticipated in the plan and thus makes the plan invalid) and tractability (which increases the computational resources needed to derive a schedule, to the extent that there may not be enough time available to complete a schedule before it is needed).

In addition to these operational challenges, it is difficult to implement agile systems with conventional technology in the first place. Centralized software is large, complex, and expensive. It is difficult to bring on-line. The resulting credo "If it ain't broke, don't fix it!" is a strong disincentive to change. Because each installation requires extensive customization, it is difficult to realize economies of scale that would make new installations less expensive and easier to bring on-line.

2.3 Conventional MSC Approaches

The major technologies used today for MSC, particularly for scheduling and planning, are heuristic dispatching verified by simulation, numerical programming, traditional AI, and advanced heuristics.

[3]Some multiagent systems rely on some sort of central control to coordinate their agents, often through a NASREM-type hierarchy (Albus et al., 1987). While this approach lends itself well to conventional control techniques, the hierarchy induces a strong binding among agents that makes agile reconfiguration difficult.

Heuristic Dispatching. For many practical applications, shop floor control is dominated by heuristic dispatching, in which a simple decision rule determines the next job to be processed at a given workstation. Typical rules are select the job with the shortest remaining processing time, select the job with the earliest due date, and process jobs in the order received. Dozens of simulation studies have examined the performance of hundreds of such rules with respect to parameters such as total cost per job, number of late jobs, machine and labor utilization, and mean and variance of job residency in the shop (Panwalkar and Iskandar, 1977).

The simplicity and robustness of dispatching rules makes them attractive in the real world. However, there are regions of the solution space of schedules that cannot be generated by applying a single dispatching rule to every workstation in the plant (Blackstone et al., 1982).

Numerical Programming. Techniques such as linear and integer programming offer clean analytical formulations of scheduling problems, and the combination of new algorithms and more powerful hardware makes them feasible for solving fairly substantial problems. Their great advantage is that they can find true optima. The disadvantage is that they are combinatorially explosive and computationally intensive and so require either a large investment in supercomputers or an environment that can wait for slow answers. Thus their main value is in relatively static situations such as long production runs. Even there, plans can be rendered useless by equipment breakdowns or the arrival of a priority order.

Because of the time required to schedule a large facility completely by numerical programming methods, two techniques have been developed to permit partial rescheduling: DEDS (Ho and Cao, 1983; Ho and Cassandras, 1983) and turnpike theory (Bean and Birge, 1985). DEDS (discrete event dynamic systems) adopts the techniques of perturbation analysis from continuous systems to the requirements of a discrete environment. Once a nominal trajectory of the system has been obtained (by simulation or exhaustive scheduling), limited deviations from the trajectory can be analyzed without complete recomputation. Thus predictions can be corrected within certain limits without recomputation. Turnpike theory derives its name from the problem of a traveler who has detoured off the highway before nearing the destination. Under certain conditions, it is easier and cheaper to find a way back to the highway than it is to replan the entire trip from the current location to the destination. Applied to scheduling, the challenge is to find ways to return to a previously computed schedule.

DEDS and turnpiking can help reduce rescheduling for a large facility that drifts off schedule, but are of relatively little use in the kinds of reconfiguration and capacity shifts anticipated in agile manufacturing. Agility requires machine configurations that can be changed daily and batch sizes approaching unity, not just small incremental shifts from present practice. The need to tailor the program to the facility being scheduled, as well as the time-consuming scheduling process, both make numerical programming less than ideal for an agile environment.

Traditional AI. Traditional artificial intelligence (AI) has devoted considerable attention to problems of manufacturing scheduling and control (Smith, 1991). By taking into account semantic information about the domain that does not lend itself to numerical computation, by applying heuristics judiciously and selectively (rather than globally as with dispatch rules), and by adopting a "satisficing" approach that does not insist on a theoretically perfect optimum, symbolic computation has led to systems that are somewhat faster than numerical programming and are more flexible and able to accommodate richer constraints, while yielding results superior to dispatch rules. However, these systems still tend to be large, complex, and specific to a particular installation, thus making them expensive to construct and difficult to maintain and reconfigure. Furthermore, while they are faster than some numerical programming codes, they are not fast enough for a facility whose configuration and load changes daily.

Advanced Heuristics. Recent research in operations research (Morton and Pentico, 1993) combines heuristics, simulation techniques, and mathematical optimization theory in various ways to address scheduling problems. Such techniques overcome the restrictions of simple heuristics, and have many characteristics in common with AI approaches. Implementations with an industrial track record are successful in some but not all contexts [for example, OPT (Meleton, 1986; Lundrigan, 1986; Vollman, 1986) has difficulty with shifting bottlenecks], and some of the newer theories are still untested in industrial conditions.

2.4 How Can Multiagent Systems Help?

This section briefly reviews the characteristics of multiagent systems and, based on the business context outlined above, suggests the kinds of applications where they are most likely to be valuable.

Characteristics of Multiagent Systems. Multiagent systems offer a way to relax the constraints of centralized, planned, sequential control, though not every multiagent system takes full advantage of this potential. They offer production systems that are decentralized rather than centralized, emergent rather than planned, and concurrent rather than sequential.

The autonomous agent approach replaces a centralized data base and control computer with a network of agents, each endowed with a local view of its environment and the ability and authority to respond locally to that environment. The overall system performance is not globally planned, but emerges through the dynamic interaction of the agents in real time. Thus the system does not alternate between cycles of scheduling and execution. Rather, the

TABLE 4.3. Agent-Based vs. Conventional Technologies

Issue	Autonomous Agents	Conventional
Model	Economics, biology	Military
Issues favoring conventional systems		
Theoretical optima?	No	Yes
Level of prediction	Aggregate	Individual
Computational Stability	Low	High
Issues favoring autonomous agents		
Match to reality	High	Low
Requires central data?	No	Yes
Response to change	Robust	Fragile
System reconfigurability	Easy	Hard
Nature of software	Short, simple	Lengthy, complex
Time required to schedule	Real time	Slow

schedule emerges from the concurrent independent decisions of the local agents (Schelberg, 1992).

Autonomous agent systems are inspired by models from biology (ecosystems) (see Chapter 11) and economics (markets), in contrast with the military patterns of hierarchical organization manifested by traditional approaches (see Chapter 1). Table 4.3 contrasts some of the advantages and disadvantages of the two philosophies.

On the one hand, the autonomous agent approach may face some disadvantages. Theoretical optima cannot be guaranteed. Predictions for autonomous systems can usually be made only at the aggregate level. In principle, systems of autonomous agents can become computationally unstable. The degree of seriousness of these challenges needs to be assessed empirically: the optima computed by conventional systems may not be realizable in practice, and the more detailed predictions that conventional approaches permit are often invalidated by the real world.

On the other hand, an autonomous approach appears to offer some significant advantages over conventional systems. Because each agent is close to the point of contact with the real world, the system's computational state tracks the state of the world very closely, without need for a centralized data base. Because overall system behavior emerges from local decisions, the system readjusts itself automatically to environmental noise or the removal or addition of agents. The software for each agent is much shorter and simpler than would be required for a centralized approach, and as a result is easier to write, debug, and maintain. Because the system schedules itself as it runs, there is no separate scheduling phase of operation, and thus no need to wait for the scheduler to complete.

When Should Multiagent Systems Be Used? Agent-based systems offer the greatest promise in applications with several characteristics.

Distribution. Agents are an inherently distributed mechanism, and are a promising strategy when other constraints make a centralized architecture undesirable. Thus they are the technology of choice for interaction among widely distributed shops, or when for other reasons a centralized control computer is undesirable in a single shop (for example, when the single point of failure it presents is not acceptable).

Factorization. Much of the power of an agent comes from its identification with some entity (such as an information source, a machine, a part, or a tool) that makes sense in the application domain. When the problem is easily conceived in terms of such naturally occurring entities, agents can be applied fairly easily. However, factorizations that are suggested by traditional analysis but do not correspond to naturally occurring entities (such as the hierarchical decomposition of a factory) can lead to very inefficient agent architectures.

Variability. A system whose parameters do not vary widely can be optimized through a carefully planned traditional scheduling and control system. A population of agents can reconfigure itself as it runs, an important advantage for systems that must respond to a wide range of different conditions. For example, a classical approach may be competitive in a paint shop for a factory that makes only one color of car, but a case to be described below shows the benefits of an agent architecture when many colors must be supported.

Change. Using conventional techniques, the most expensive part of a manufacturing system is not the machinery, tooling, or energy to operate it, but software creation and maintenance. When a system has a long lifetime, this expense can be amortized over many years. When systems are expected to change frequently, the agent approach shifts the software effort from integrated systems that depend on a particular configuration to the individual agents that can be swapped in and out as the entities they represent are shuffled around.

3 A TAXONOMY OF MULTIAGENT SYSTEMS

Several taxonomies of multiagent systems have been published (Bond and Gasser, 1988; Decker et al., 1989; Demazeau and Müller, 1990; Durfee et al., 1989; Grant, 1992; Huhns, 1987). The taxonomy presented here has been developed from these, giving special attention to features that are most relevant from an application perspective, based on an extensive survey of applied research and development in industrial applications of MAS. (This chapter does not cite all of the cases considered, but only representative examples.) Three groups of perspectives are important: the manufacturing function to which MAS technology is applied, the architecture of an individual agent, and the architecture of the system within which agents interact.

3.1 Application Function

In manufacturing, most MASs are applied to two functions: production and design. By far the most common application of MASs to manufacturing is in production, mostly in scheduling and control and to a lesser extent in monitoring and diagnosis. The fit of such systems to production lies in their ability to represent the distributed entities on the shop floor and endow each with some level of local intelligence.

Several systems (e.g., Klein, 1991) support the design function. Here, multiple agents help designers to interact with one another and with their production counterparts to avoid design conflicts and ensure manufacturability. A few systems (e.g., ARCHON/GRATE; Wittig, 1992; Cockburn and Jennings, this volume) deal with other manufacturing functions, such as power distribution, information integration, and logistics.

3.2   Individual Agent Architecture

In considering individual agents, we consider how similar they must be with one another in order to interact, and how sophisticated the reasoning is within each agent.

How Diverse Are Agents from Each Other?   If agents are to interact with one another, they must have something in common. In most research systems, agents have differing functions, but share a common architecture (see Chapter 5). Sometimes this commonality extends to every aspect of an agent except for a few parameters that it manipulates (Morley and Schelberg, 1993). At the other extreme are "body-head" architectures, where agents' bodies can have radically different architectures, even being different off-the-shelf products, but with a common "head" to permit communications among agents (Jennings et al., 1992). (In the simplest case the "head" takes the form of a standard language, such as SQL.) Body-head architectures are a common mechanism for incorporating humans as peer agents in a system. Systems whose agents differ from one another by more than parametric variation may be termed "heterogeneous" (see Chapter 13).

While communications usually takes the form of digital messages over a network, this is not the only possible coordination mechanisms. Agents may coordinate solely through their effects on a shared environment. In this case, the head of a body-head architecture consists of common sensor-effector modalities.

How Sophisticated Is an Individual Agent's Reasoning?   Different levels of sophistication can be used by different agents, or even by the same agent at different times and under different circumstances. (Demazeau and Müller, 1991) offers a variety of studies along this important dimension.

Levels of Sophistication.   In theory, an agent's sophistication can range from a simple *sensing* agent that reacts to its environment but has no memory and no model of other agents, all the way up to full *human* capabilities (see Chapter 1). In practice, actual implementations add at least *memory* to sensing, so that the agent maintains local state. The next level of sophistication is *self-consciousness*, in which each agent knows of the existence of other agents distinct from itself, and thus can carry on rudimentary communication. A *social* agent goes a step further and models other agents' states, goals, and plans. Higher capabilities yet include such functions as making commitments to one another (Chapter 6), planning tasks (Chapter 8), and learning from experience (Shoham, 1993).

Few industrial applications of artificial agents at present go beyond self-conscious agents. In industry, more complex functions are usually provided by using artificial agents as an interface for a human operator, to whom they furnish information and from whom they take commands (see Chapter 21). Thus the main point of the system is to agument, rather than replace, the human operator. From an industrial perspective, it is both expensive and technically complex to automate the controls on much existing production equipment to the point that a human operator could be replaced, and social and political concerns also challenge the wisdom of eliminating the human. Thus the most direct route for many firms to using DAI on the factory floor may be via products that are emerging under the rubric of "manufacturing execution systems" [Advanced Manufacturing Research (AMR), 1993; Gillespie, 1992]. These systems provide human staff throughout a manufacturing enterprise with electronic connectivity, data access, and decision support, and may be considered "groupware for the shop floor."

Combining Reaction and Planning. In some systems, the various levels of sophistication within each agent are separately accessible. For example, sensing capabilities provide a rapid reflex response, while higher-level planning capabilities are invoked if there is time. The term "subsumption architecture" for this technique was introduced by (Brooks, 1986), who eschews any symbolic representation within an agent (Brooks, 1991), but the term can be extended to apply to architectures that include symbolic representations as well.

When we do add more sophisticated reasoning capabilities to a reactive agent, we would like to do so in a way that does not forfeit the benefits of simple reaction. Systems for reactive planning fall along a continuum from pure reaction (which is fast but inflexible) to pure planning (which is slow but highly adaptive (Table 4.4).

The top three cases fall in the "reactive planning" category.

TABLE 4.4. From Reaction to Planning

	Fastest
Pure Reaction	Flavors (Morley and Schelberg, 1993; Steels, 1990; Brooks, 1986)
Reaction modified by plan	RS (Lyons and Hendriks, 1992)
Reaction overridden by plan	Phoenix (Cohen et al., 1989)
Pure planning	BOSS (Smith and Hynynen, 1987)
	Slowest

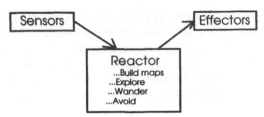

Figure 4.1 Pure reaction (e.g., Brooks).

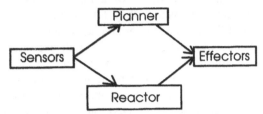

Figure 4.2 Overridden reaction (e.g., Cohen).

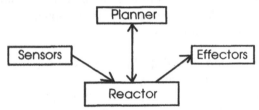

Figure 4.3 Modified reaction (e.g., Lyons' RS).

In *pure reaction* (Figure 4.1), there is no way to alter the behavior of the reactor. No planning takes place at run time. The system is inflexible, but fast (Brooks, 1986, 1991). Such an architecture is most appropriate in tasks where the overall envelope of possible tasks is understood well in advance. Brooks applies the model to a mobile robot, and it would be appropriate for intelligent mobile vehicles used to transport materials around a factory.

In *reaction overridden by plan* (Figure 4.2), the planner monitors the external world in parallel with the reactor, and when it disagrees with the reactor, pushes its own instructions out to the actuators, thus overriding the reactor for the nonce. However, the next time the situation arises, the reactor will still react the same way. (The planner may cache the preferred response so that the reactor can be overridden more efficiently the next time.) Because the preferred response comes via the planner rather than the reactor, it is slower (Cohen et al., 1989). The developers of this model apply it to unmanned bulldozers used in fighting forest fires, emphasizing its suitability where the domain presents considerable uncertainty. It would be useful for agents that support interaction of human designers. Reactions can take care of anticipated requirements, while the system can plan around unanticipated situations without jeopardizing system security.

In *reaction modified by plan* (Figure 4.3), the planner can rewire the reactor in real time so that in the future a new behavior will be performed at reaction speeds. This rewiring is in software, thus reactors of this class may be slower than hardware-wired reactors *à la* Brooks, but the response is still faster than invoking a planner (Lyons and Hendriks, 1992). This approach is useful for agents that must handle uncertainty in real time, such as applying emergency corrections to system failures.

3.3 System Architecture

Individual agents require the support of an overall system within which to interact. This system must provide a means for agents to communicate with one another, and define protocols for the resulting conversations. The special case when some agents are artificial and others are human merits special consideration.

How Do Agents Communicate with Each Other? The notion of a multi-agent system presumes that individual agents can change their shared environment, sense changes in this environment, and alter their behavior in response to these changes. These interactions via environmental change fall into two categories: *performance* and *convention*.

Performance interactions are those defined by the environmental changes that an agent must make in performing its domain function, whether or not there are other agents in the system. For example, a manufacturing cell can only run when its input buffers contain parts and there is room in its output buffer. As observers, we may interpret the action of placing a part in an input buffer or removing one from an output buffer as a "message" to the cell to begin execution, but there need be no intentionality on the part of the suppliers and consumers of these parts to convey a message. The cell is simply performing its manufacturing function in response to changes in its environment. Usually, performance interactions take place through the physical environment rather than by way of digital communications.

Most applications in manufacturing production manipulate the physical environment (for example, changing the state of a part or the population of a buffer), and thus have performance interactions with each other.

Convention interactions rely on environmental changes that are independent of the problem domain, and whose meaning is assigned by convention. For example, the difference between "Start" and "Stop" messages to a workstation from an area controller is defined entirely by convention, not by the mechanics of the manufacturing domain. In one system, a 1 bit could mean "Start," while in another, the same 1 bit could mean "Stop." Usually, convention interactions take place over a digital communications medium.

"Communications" usually refers to convention interactions. Various communication strategies differ depending on whether a message is addressed to a

TABLE 4.5.   Communication Strategies

Do Messages Persist after Being Sent?	Are Messages Addressed to Specific Agents?	
	Yes	No
Yes	Interactive Transaction Net (Lee et al., 1993)	Blackboards (Nii, 1986)
No	Directed	Broadcast

specific agent or broadcast to the entire population, and whether messages persist after being sent. All combinations of these options have been explored (Table 4.5), and a single system will sometimes use more than one.

What Protocols Govern the Interaction?   A protocol defines the structure of the dialogue among agents. Most commonly, agents *react* without question or discussion to messages or commands from one another. This simple technique can produce surprisingly complex behavior (Steels, 1990). At the next level of sophistication (but one used only rarely in research systems), agents express their opinions to a central moderator, who counts or weighs their *votes* in order to select a course of action (Fordyce et al., 1992). The contract net (Davis and Smith, 1983; Müller, this volume) uses a *negotiation* among a limited set of participants and with a fixed protocol in order to select a course of action. *Constraint propagation* permits decisions to be made on the basis of multidirectional discussions among agents, without the rigid structure implicit in negotiation. A growing body of research permits agents to embody a model of *speech acts* that enables them to reason about messages in such categories as assertions, directives, declarations, and commitments (Shoham, 1993; Jennings and Mamdani, 1992). While the resulting discussions may be considered negotiation, the degree of complexity is much higher than in the cases labeled "Negotiation" or "Constraint Propagation."

Hybrid Systems: Communities of Humans and Machines.   In some cases (Pan and Tenenbaum, 1992) humans function as peer agents, rather than just as operators (see Chapter 13). That is, other agents do not distinguish between interactions with humans and interactions with artificial agents. All such hybrid systems are heterogeneous (as defined above), but there are heterogeneous systems that are not hybrid. This section describes hybrid systems as a natural outcome of the history of manufacturing technology, outlines two directions from which one can approach such an architecture and raises some challenges for further research and development.

The Changing Roles of People and Machines.   Throughout the history of manufacturing, the relative roles of people and their equipment has been changing. Multiagent systems make possible yet another change in these roles (Kirn, this volume; Hall, this volume).

Before the industrial revolution, tools are mostly manual. People supply both the power to operate the tool and the intelligence to guide its application; the tool is both passive and ignorant. The role of the human is that of artisan, closely coupled to the material being transformed through relatively simple and inactive tools.

The industrial revolution moves from passive tools to active machines. New sources of energy supplement and even replace human strength, but human intelligence remains dominant. The strength and activity of the machine stand between the human and the material; the worker's interaction is more with the machine than with the material, and humans move from being artisans to operators.

With the advent of computers and the multiagent paradigm, equipment in the factory gains intelligence in addition to strength, and machines become colleagues and partners to humans. People still remain in overall charge of the process, but the paradigm of emergent control presumes that equipment assumes much more responsibility than before. Hybrid architectures explicitly support this partnership of human and machine.

Two Approaches to Human-Machine Communities. Two areas of computer science have been developing techniques that can implement the partnership between people and machines toward which technical history is leading. Classical work in multiagent systems builds systems of artificial agents, into which we can introduce people. Computer-supported collaborative work (CSCW) uses computer technology to integrate communities of humans, and opens the door to adding in artificial agents (see Chapter 1).

Both MAS and CSCW rely on the body-head architecture to integrate dissimilar agents (whether different people as in CSCW, or heterogeneous artificial agents in some MAS work). The head contains knowledge of the individual agent (which is customized for each class of agent), and knowledge of the rest of the community (common to all heads). It is responsible for translating between the individual agent's language and the *lingua franca* of the community.

While multiagent systems open the door to a partnership between humans and machines, they do not guarantee it. Many multiagent systems still model people as operators [for example, ARCHON (Wittig, 1992) and PACT (Cutkosky et al., 1993)]. But several others seek closer integration.

In theory, there are two ways to incorporate people into a network of agents. Either artificial agents can be made so intelligent that people come to view them as peers, or people can be represented in the network by artificial agents that make them look to other agents like computers (see Chapter 13 and 14). The first approach is the objective of classical AI's Turing test, but most engineering applications of multiagent systems take the second approach.

For example, the MKS system (Pan and Tenenbaum, 1992) integrates a variety of human and artificial agents through a central model of the enterprise. Some of the agents implement conventional automation functions, such as monitoring and control, and their integration through the shared model bears a close architectural resemblance to conventional distributed systems. However, the system also assigns a computerized personal agent (PA) to each human in the network, and the other computerized agents see only this PA, not the human directly.

Traditional CSCW develops computer mechanisms (such as electronic mail, computer conferencing, interactive videoconferencing, and shared data bases) to help networks of humans interact more efficiently. In our terms, such systems provide each human with an electronic "head" that provides connectivity to other humans. Once such a network is in place, nonhuman bodies can be incorporated by giving them a head that is compatible with the others in the system. For example, DCSS (Klein, 1991) supports collaboration among designers of local area networks by providing them with a protocol for representing and justifying design decisions, mechanisms for detecting conflicts among proposals, and resources for suggesting alternative solutions. The system offers valuable support for purely human teams of designers, but once the protocols are defined, it can be augmented by the inclusion of automated design consultants as well.

4. CASE STUDIES

Most of the cases considered in the survey that led to this taxonomy are laboratory prototypes that demonstrate feasibility but are not currently functioning in commercial environments. Five cases, described in this section, are either detailed simulations based on data from real applications (rather than toy problems) or in fact on-line systems in daily commercial use. These examples are restricted to those that have been discussed in the open literature. Other commercial applications exist, but cannot be described because of proprietary restrictions. In general, these systems rely much more on reaction than on sophisticated planning, and the contract net is the most common protocol among agents. Shop-floor scheduling and control is the most common manufacturing application of distributed agents.

4.1   GE Power Generation Job Shop

Baker (1991) describes a detailed simulation of a contract net against data from 35 workstations in a job shop that produces parts for steam turbines for the General Electric Power Generation business. The shop as a whole includes 115 machine tools and produces 350,000 parts of 25,000 different designs each year. The case study covered 491 orders of 184 unique products, with an average of 8.2 operations per job (and a maximum of 18 operations per job). Each workstation is represented by an agent in the system, whether it is automated or staffed by a human. Other agents represent the customer and the shop purchasing department.

The customer enters a request for bid for the final product. Agents that can deliver that product post requests for the input parts or assemblies that they need, and their suppliers repeat the process in turn with the next layer of supplying workstations, until the supply chains that emerge extend to the purchasing agent. Then bids percolate back to the customer. Bids are not single numbers but functions that give cost per unit as a function of delivery time and lot size. The customer can then place a firm order for specific lots at specific delivery times.

Computationally, Baker's agents are identical with one another, all implementing the same algorithmic costing function. No sophisticated reasoning, modeling of other agents, or learning is involved. All messages are broadcast among all agents. Both humans and automatic machines are represented by agents, yielding a hybrid system. There is no central control, and the population of agents does not change as the system operates.

There are at least five different ways in which the agents in a contract net can be mapped onto the application domain. Baker's system illustrates one of them.

1. YAMS (Parunak, 1987), perhaps the original implementation of multi-agent systems in manufacturing, assigns an agent to each node in a NASREM-type control hierarchy (factory, cell, workstation, machine) (Albus et al., 1987). An agent at one level uses negotiation to identify agents under its control at the next lower level to whom to assign tasks. This basic approach has been followed by numerous other researchers. Unfortunately, it inherits the overhead of the classical centralized hierarchical structure. Probably because of this centralization, YAMS experienced severe communications bottlenecks.

2. Shaw and Whinston (1985) and Baker (1991) describe schemes in which agents are workstations. In Shaw's scheme, workstations try to find consumers for their outputs, while in Baker's, they seek needed inputs. The CASCADE material-handling architecture (Parunak, 1990) models each segment of a transport system as an agent that can both push and pull.

3. Maley (1988) and Duffie et al. (1988) each build negotiating systems around smart parts that carry their process plans with them and at each state negotiate with transport and processing equipment to get the next step done. Maley goes through a central bulletin board; Duffie simply broadcasts requests.

4. P. Müller (personal communication, 1992) at Neuchatel is designing MARS, which models each behavior as an agent. This system focuses on assembly problems, where there may not be a distinguished part, and thus looks at the Operation as the agent.

5. Linguistic case theory (Parunak, 1992) provides a theoretical integrating framework that permits workstations, parts, tools, operators, and operations to function as agents.

Compared with the actual performance of the shop as scheduled by classical techniques, the schedule that emerged in real time in Baker's simulation reduced work-in-process inventory (WIP) by 47%, shop residency time by 59%, and average job tardiness by 92%, and came within 0.2% of the theoretically optimal cost per job. Such improvements provide an important competitive edge to a job shop.

4.2 ARCHON

The ARCHON project (see Chapter 12) is developing an architecture for integrating multiple preexisting expert systems. While the original application domain is electrical power distribution systems, the architecture has also been applied to realistic prototype problems in robotics and the control in the domains of cement manufacture and particle accelerators. ARCHON is a prototypical example of a heterogeneous body-head architecture. The head of each agent maintains models of its own state and that of other agents with which it is acquainted, and uses speech act theory to negotiate task assignments with other agents.

ARCHON addresses one of the major challenges in introducing DAI to industry, the challenge of "legacy systems," systems that were put in place before an agent-based architecture was adopted. Although in the long run the agent architecture may eliminate the need for some of these systems, it is usually necessary, both economically and politically, to introduce agents in a small, focused area, and then extend their scope. When preexisting systems can be cast in the role of information sources, ARCHON provides a mechanism for turning them into agents and incorporating them in a DAI paradigm.

4.3. The Flavors Paint Shop

The Flavors PIM [parallel inference machine—a MISD (multiple-instruction, single-datum) supercomputer] has been used to simulate a paint shop in a truck plant (Morley and Schelberg, 1993). Finished truck bodies enter the shop, each to be painted a specific color. There are only seven paint booths, fewer than the total number of colors that the factory can produce. A booth must be set up to spray a particular color. Thus it is sometimes necessary to change the color that a given booth is spraying. Changing color increases the idle time of the booth, wastes paint that must be purged from the plumbing, and increases environmental contamination. However, refusing to change color may delay the delivery of a truck whose color is not currently available.

Each booth is represented by its own processor in the PIM, and an additional processor represents in turn each truck that arrives at the paint shop. The implementation uses a negotiation protocol to assign trucks to booths.

1. When a truck arrives at the broker, the broker announces to the paint booths that a truck is available.
2. Each booth that has at least empty position in its input buffer responds to this announcement, reporting its current color and the number of trucks currently in its buffer.

3. The broker assigns the new truck to a booth on the basis of three rules.

> If a booth of the required color has responded (and therefore has space), send the truck to that booth. (This rule avoids color changes.)
>
> Otherwise, if a booth reports that its input buffer is empty, send the truck there. (This rule avoids idle equipment.)
>
> Otherwise, send the truck to any responding booth. (This rule avoids holding up trucks).

All booth agents run the same code. Booths do not model one another. While they communicate directly with the broker, their interaction with one another is indirect, through the effect of their actions on the incoming flow of trucks. Their reasoning is extremely simple, consisting of "If-Then" rules that read and write directly to the common environment. Both broadcast (for truck announcements) and directed messages (for bids) are used. The use of a broker imposes a primitive hierarchy on the system. Humans do not participate in the system. Booths can be added and removed as the system runs.

In spite of the extreme simplicity of this model, it cuts the number of paint changes in half in comparison with a centralized control code, resulting in annual savings of about $1 million. The required code is less than one-tenth the length of the conventional program, resulting in easier maintenance and upgrading.

4.4 LMS

The logistics management system (LMS) (Fordyce et al., 1992) supports shop dispatching at a semiconductor fabrication facility operated by IBM. The fab produces 13,000 different kinds of circuits, each of which requires between 200 and 400 operations on a variety of processing equipment (including oxidation, photolithography, and diffusion/ion tools). The system handles some 240,000 transactions per day.

The LMS system as a whole is not agent oriented, but one component of the system uses a voting protocol among expert advisors. Each lot of wafers makes multiple passes through each kind of tool, and the specific routing within a tool group frequently depends on which pass is currently taking place. Several lots may be available when a tool group becomes available. The selection of the next lot depends on four goals.

1. Completing each batch as close to its promised schedule as possible
2. Meeting daily production quotas for certain types of products
3. Satisfying the demands of downstream workstations
4. Reducing setup time and increasing the utilization of individual machines

Each of these goals is represented by a separate agent that maintains the data and heuristic functions necessary to evaluate a given lot from the perspective of its specific goal. When a tool group becomes available, each of the goal advocates issues a vote for each of the available lots. The votes range from 0 (vetoing the lot from the perspective of the goal) to 1 (indicating that the goal "must have" this lot next). Any lot vetoed by any advocate is dropped. If a single lot receives a 1 vote it is chosen. Otherwise the lot with the highest average vote is chosen.

The voting goal advocates in LMS are not homogeneous, since they implement different decisions functions, but their architecture is the same. Their reasoning includes simple heuristics, but they do not model their associates or learn over time. They communicate only with a centralized judge via directed messages, imposing a shallow hierarchy, and the decision protocol is voting. Humans are not incorporated directly in the architecture, although the entire LMS system provides sophisticated operator interfaces that can be used to override system decisions. The population of agents is fixed.

4.5 Hitachi ADS

The ADS (autonomous distributed systems) architecture (Mori et al., 1986) is in operation at two steel coil processing lines at Kawasaki Steel (Mori et al., 1988) and the traffic control system for the 1070 km Shinkansen, or Bullet Train, which carries 400,000 passengers per day between Tokyo and Hakata, Japan (Ihara and Mori, 1984).

ADS is a data-driven architecture for real-time control. Its design was motivated by the need to be able to modify specific software control modules without bringing down the entire system, and the functions it supports reflect this motivation. The system at Kawasaki Steel is reported to have been in nonstop operation since 1988.

Each agent ("atom" in ADS terminology) consists of a head with five standard functions, and a body containing one or more modules of application code. Messages are not addressed to a specific agent, but are broadcast into a "data field" and contain a content code that individual agents use to identify messages of interest to them. An agent's head includes five standard functions:

1. Data field management registers the content codes of interest to the applications currently resident in the agent, traps relevant messages from the data field and brings them into view of the applications, and passes messages from application modules back out to the data field.
2. Construction management receives new or upgraded application modules through the data field and installs them in the agent's body.
3. Built-in test generates test data and exercises resident applications. During testing, an application can see operational data, but its messages are not passed back onto the data field. Thus applications can be validated in the actual operating environment.
4. Execution management authorizes the execution of specific application modules when all of their necessary data is available.

5. Data consistency arbitrates between duplicate application modules when their results differ.

ADS supports heterogeneous agents through its body-head architecture. The available literature does not discuss the internal complexity of agents (and, in particular, of application modules), but considering the languages in which they are implemented (Fortran at Kawasaki, Cobol at the Shinkansen), one may reasonably conclude that they are fairly traditional. Agents communicate through the global data field. There is no evidence of any sophisticated negotiation among agents. The agents are embedded in a traditional centralized hierarchy that is scheduled each day in advance of operations. Humans interact with the system through operator consoles, but are not represented as separate agents.

5 MOVING MULTIAGENT SYSTEMS INTO INDUSTRIAL PRACTICE

The examples discussed in the last section show that simple techniques from MAS and DAI are being applied now in industrial settings. Nevertheless, many industrial firms find it difficult to justify the expense and risk of installing such systems. This section identifies ways that researchers, technology vendors, and end users can accelerate the deployment of multiagent technologies into commercial use, and closes with some speculation about directions that the market will lead research in applied DAI.

5.1 Researcher Issues

Researchers can help by directing their attention to industrial problems. Much DAI research concentrates on elegant theories and structures that are applied only to highly abstract, toy problems. Such toy problems face one or more of four shortcomings: they may not address a realistic industrial problem; they may not scale up well, their scope may be inadequate, and they may not provide an adequate level of demonstration.

Often DAI research problems sacrifice *realism* for research orientation. For example, the navigation of unmanned vehicles is a rich source of DAI problems, but a comparatively minor problem in manufacturing. While some plants do use automatic guided vehicles (AGVs), these vehicles operate in a structurally stable, engineered environment, and navigation and map building are not their major challenges. Reliability and resource allocation are much more critical. While DAI could be applied to these problems, such application still does not offer the greatest industrial benefit, since by far most industrial material handling is with various forms of conveyor system. Far more promising applications for DAI, though less dramatic, are in the allocation and coordination of various pieces of shop-floor equipment.

Problems of *scale* arise when algorithms that work well for relatively few agents in a laboratory environment are transferred to realistic numbers of agents that must interact with the real world. While computer scientists have powerful tools for calculating the impact of combinatorics on algorithms, few researchers have the industrial experience to know the number of entities (machines, parts, workers) in a typical plant or the rates at which decisions must be made, and so cannot formulate realistic scenarios in which to apply these tools. In addition to combinatoric challenges, communities of interacting agents are susceptible to complex dynamic behavior that often is not adequately analyzed in the laboratory context, but that can lead to unexpected and unacceptable behavior in application.

Scope issues result from the necessary process of abstracting from the real world to a research domain, and sometimes abstracting away necessary constraints. For example, the usefulness of vision in coordinating machining operations is severely limited in environments liable to contamination with cutting fluid (which can block camera lenses), and an algorithm that requires a Sun workstation will be useless if the computational resources available at a machine tool consist of an 8-bit processor. The research community should value the contribution of those researchers who are willing to grapple with the complexities of real problems.

The level of *demonstration* provided in the research laboratory is usually inadequate to justify commercial investment for further development. Researchers should demand, and research funders and industry associations should provide, realistically detailed models of actual manufacturing problems, both static (detailed shop-floor performance data) and dynamic (sophisticated simulations), against which DAI research can be tested and exercised to evaluate its industrial potential.

5.2 Vendor Roles

Industry will not place a technology into regular commercial use without vendor support. In a few very large firms, the vendor may be an internal department that has implemented the technology itself, but in most cases, a technology will not be broadly deployed until it can be purchased off-the-shelf from a recognized vendor with documentation and a hot line to call with problems.

The vendor community is beginning to recognize the potential of multiagent systems. The PIM parallel computer from Flavors Technology in Andover, New Hampshire, is being marketed as a platform for MAS applications, and Hitachi's ADS architecture is available at least in Japan. Numerous hardware vendors, including Allen-Bradley, Honeywell, Mitsubishi, Echelon, and ZWorld, are developing small controllers and buslike communication architectures that are designed to turn small groups of sensors and actuators into autonomous agents. While some of these steps seem mundane from a research perspective, vendor support is critical to the deployment of this technology, and researchers who test their ideas in close partnership with a vendor and using industrial-strength platforms will find the transition path much shorter.

Perhaps the greatest challenge for the vendor community is managing the technology transition so that users can upgrade incrementally. Conventional manufacturing software tends to be structured according to functions (for example, scheduling, material management, resource planning) that span shop-floor entities such as people, parts, and machines. DAI techniques are most readily applied to these entities, from whose interactions the distributed functions will emerge dynamically. Systems vendors need to develop strategies for migrating from selling scheduling modules to providing intelligent parts.

5.3 User Challenges

Some of the greatest challenges faced by potential users of multiagent technologies are social and organizational, not technical (see Chapter 19 and 21). Users need to address these issues up front if they are to succeed in implementing these technologies. For example:

- Multiagent technologies can drastically change the roles and importance of such traditional manufacturing functions as scheduling, management information systems (MIS), and systems engineering. Staff in these functions may perceive a threat to their jobs from the new technologies, and may seek to sabotage them in order to preserve their own security, unless their concerns are recognized and addressed up front.
- People can be notoriously difficult to "reprogram," and years in the "operator" role have conditioned most workers to think of the machine as a tool rather than a partner. Effective implementation of hybrid systems will require careful attention to human work customs.
- Assignment of credit and blame can be difficult enough in a purely human organization. When automatic partners are introduced, how does credit allocation work? In conventional automation, there is precedent for focusing attention on the programmer of the system. With relatively simple agents whose behavior is emergent, the situation is much more complex. The sociology of the workplace will change greatly as a result of such systems.
- Moving from a conventional centralized system to one that uses distributed agents poses a considerable risk, especially for "early adopters," those rare industrial users who are willing to be the first among their competitors in trying out a new technology. Special attention needs to be given to building the business case that justifies such risks. The potential impact on operations and the resulting financial benefits must be quantified in a persuasive manner if users are to be persuaded to make the shift.

5.4 Market and Research Directions

Agent research spans a broad spectrum in the granularity of agents, from complex agents that possess individual intelligence down to simple agents whose individual behavior is not intelligent but whose interactions yield overall system behavior that can be termed intelligent. Current industrial applications tend to favor the latter over the former approach. Usually, the nature of the decisions to be made by a given manufacturing entity (such as a part, a machine, or a worker) are fairly simple. Research in artificial life and emergent systems has shown that acceptable overall performance can be achieved from the local interactions of such simple agents, without the need or expense of more sophisticated reasoning and global data support. This tendency does not mean that more sophisticated inferencing will not find a place in industry. However, it is likely to be deployed as an enhancement of previously installed simple agents, rather than as the first step in an industry's adoption of agent technology.

One of the most challenging visions for capital-intensive industries is that of the self-configuring system. More than half of the cost associated with a piece of computer-controlled manufacturing equipment (such as a stamping press) is in the preparation and maintenance of its software. Manufacturing strategists anticipate "brilliant machines" that come from the vendor with an understanding of their own capabilities. Once such a machine is placed on the shop floor and plugged into a multiplexed source of power and communications, the only configuration necessary is to key in its physical location and orientation. By itself, it will identify the other machines in the shop, and together with them determine how to execute the various work orders that appear on the network.

A critical issue for agent research is the issue of aggregation: how simple individual agents team up to form more complex entities that then can act as a single more complex agent. Tomorrow's economy will favor teams of smaller firms over large monolithic companies (Nagle and Dove, 1991), and there will be strong demand for agent architectures that can encompass the entire scope from machine components on the shop floor to aggregates of organizations that behave as though they were single entities.

While autonomous agents will continue to make steady inroads in traditional industry, their most dramatic deployment over the next decade will be in information networks. The emerging information economy has two advantages over many other industries that make it fertile ground for agents. First, it is a relatively new industry and so has little of the tradition and inertia associated with industries such as manufacturing, transportation, construction, or mining. Second, information applications are entirely computational in nature, unlike (say) manufacturing, in which digital manipulations must be coupled with material transformations through elaborate control schemes. The Digital Equipment Corporation is developing agent-based network management mechanisms, and a Silicon Valley startup called General Magic will soon begin selling agents that will roam through information networks to execute tasks specified by their masters (Markoff, 1994). While all industrial applications of agents rely on network technology, those industries that live mostly on networks will see the most rapid deployment of DAI technology.

6 CONCLUSIONS

The increasing demands for agility in manufacturing are imposing limits on classical approaches to manufacturing scheduling and control. Multiagent systems, particularly networks of autonomous agents with emergent rather than imposed behavior, offer significant promise in addressing these challenges. A few systems using these technologies have been fielded in industrial settings, but concerted effort on the part of researchers, vendors, and industrial users will be necessary to deploy DAI more broadly in industry.

REFERENCES

Advanced Manufacturing Research (AMR) (1993). *The AMR Report on Manufacturing Information Systems.* AMR, Boston.

Albus, J. S., McCain, H. G., and Lumia, R. (1987). NASA/NBS Standard Reference Model for telerobot control system architecture (NASREM). *NBS Tech. Note (U.S.)* **1235.**

Baker, A. (1991). *Manufacturing control with a market-driven contract net.* Ph.D. Dissertation, Dept. of Electrical Engineering, Rensselaer Polytechnic Institute, Troy, NY.

Bean, J. C., and Birge, J. R. (1985). *Match-Up Real-Time Scheduling*, Tech. Rep. 85-22. Department of Industrial and Operations Engineering, University of Michigan, Ann Arbor.

Blackstone, J. H., Jr., Phillips, D. T., and Hogg, G. L. (1982). A state-of-the-art survey of dispatching rules for manufacturing job shop operations. *Int. J. Prod. Res.* **20**(1), 27–45.

Bond, A. H., and Gasser, L. (1988). An analysis of problems and research in DAI. In *Readings in Distributed Artificial Intelligence* (A. H. Bond and L. Gasser, eds.), pp. 3–36. Morgan Kaufmann, San Mateo, CA.

Brooks, R. A. (1986). A robust layered control system for a mobile robot. *IEEE J. Robotics Autom.* **RA-2**(1), 14–23.

Brooks, R. A. (1991). Intelligence without representation. *Artif. Intell.* **47**, 139–159.

Cohen, P. R., Greenberg, M. L., Hart, D. M., and Howe, A. E. (1989). Trial by fire: Understanding the design requirements for agents in complex environments. *AI Mag.* **10**(3), 34–48.

Cutkosky, M., Engelmore, R., Fikes, R., Genesereth, M., Gruber, T., Mark, W., Tenebaum, J., and Weber, J. (1993). PACT: An experiment in integrating concurrent engineering systems. *IEEE Comput.* **26**(1), 28–37.

Davis, R., and Smith, R. G. (1983). Negotiation as a metaphor for distributed problem solving. *Artif. Intell.* **20**, 63–109.

Decker, K. S., Durfee, E. H., and Lesser, V. R. (1989). Evaluating research in cooperative distributed problem solving. In *Distributed Artificial Intelligence* (L. Gasser and M. Huhns, eds.), Vol. 2, pp. 487–519. Morgan Kaufmann, Los Altos, CA/Pitman, London.

Demazeau, Y., and Müller, J. P. (1990). Decentralized artificial intelligence. In *Decentralized Artificial Intelligence* (Y. Demazeau and J.-P. Müller, eds.), pp. 3–13. Elsevier-North Holland, Amsterdam.

Demazeau, Y., and Müller, J.-P., eds. (1991). *Decentralized Artificial Intelligence 2*. Elsevier/North-Holland, Amsterdam.

Dove, R. (1992). Putting agility in perspective: A profiling tool. Unpublished material presented at Agile Manufacturing Enterprise Forum 2nd Annual Conference, Orlando, FL.

Duffie, N. A., Chitturi, R., and Mou, J. I. (1988). Fault-tolerant heteroarchical control of heterogeneous manufacturing system entities. *J. Manuf. Syst.* **7**(4), 315–328.

Durfee, E. H., Lesser, V. R., and Corkill, D. (1989). Cooperative distributed problem solving. In *The Handbook of Artificial Intelligence* (A. Barr, P. R. Cohen, and E. A. Feigenbaum, eds.), Vol. 4, pp. 83–147. Addison-Wesley, Reading, MA.

Fordyce, K., Dunki-Jacobs, R., Gerard, B., Sell, R., and Sullivan, G. (1992). Logistics management system: An advanced decision support system for the fourth decision tier dispatch or short-interval scheduling. *Prod. Oper. Manage.* **1**(1), 70–86.

Gillespie, D. M. (1992). The architecture of an execution system. *Autofact '92*, pp. 18-7 to 18–20.

Grant, T. (1992). Agents that learn to plan. *DECUS Newsl.*, February, AI-3 to AI-29.

Ho, Y. C., and Cao, X. (1983). Perturbation analysis and optimization of queueing networks. *J. Optim. Theory Appl.* **40**(4), 559–582.

Ho, Y. C., and Cassandras, C. (1983). A new approach to the analysis of discrete event dynamic systems. *Automatica* **19**(2), 149–167.

Huhns, M. N. (1987). Foreword. In *Distributed Artificial Intelligence* (M. N. Huhns, ed.), pp. v–ix. Morgan Kaufmann, San Mateo, CA/Pitman, London.

Ihara, H., and Mori, K. (1984). Autonomous decentralized computer control systems. *IEEE Comput.* **17**(8), 57–66.

Jennings, N. R., and Mamdani, E. H. (1992). Using joint responsibility to coordinate collaborative problem solving in dynamic environments. *Proc. Am. Assoc. Artif. Intell.*, San Jose, CA, pp. 269–275.

Jennings, N. R., Mamdani, E. H., Laresgoiti, I., Perez, J., and Corera, J. (1992). GRATE: A general framework for co-operative problem solving. *J. Intell. Syst. Eng.* **1**(2), 102–114.

Klein, M. (1991). Supporting conflict resolution in cooperative design systems. *IEEE Trans. Syst., Man Cybernet.* **SMC-21**(6), 1379–1390.

Lee, C. K., Mansfield, W. H., Jr., and Sheth, A. P. (1993). A framework for controlling cooperative agents. *IEEE Comput.* **26**(7), 8–16.

Lundrigan, R. (1986). What is this thing they call OPT? *Prod. Inventory Manage.* **27** (2nd Q.), 2–12.

Lyons, D. M., and Hendriks, A. J. (1992). Planning, reactive. In *Encyclopedia of Artificial Intelligence* (S. C. Shapiro, ed.), 2nd ed., pp. 1171–1181. Wiley, New York.

Maley, J. (1988). Managing the flow of intelligent parts. *Robotics Comput.-Integr. Manuf.* **4**(3/4), 525–530.

Markhoff, J. (1994). Hopes and fears on new computer organisms. *New York Times*, January 6. p. C1.

Meleton, M. P. (1986). OPT—Fantasy or breakthrough? *Prod. Inventory Manage.* **27**(2nd Q.), 13–21.

Mori, J., Torikoshi, H., Nakai, K., Mori, K., and Masuda, T. (1988). Computer control system for iron and steel plants. *Hitachi Rev.* **37**(4), 251–258.

Mori, K., Ihara, H., Suzuki, Y., Kawano, K., Koizumi, M., Orimo, M., Nakai, K., and Nakanishi, H. (1986). Autonomous decentralized software structure and its application. *Proc. Fall J. Comput. Conf.*, Dallas, TX, pp. 1056–1063.

Morley, R. E., and Schelberg, C. (1993). An analysis of a plant-specific dynamic scheduler. *Proc. NSF Workshop Dyn. Schedul.*, Cocoa Beach, FL.

Morton, T. E., and Pentico, D. W. (1993). *Heuristic Scheduling Systems.* Wiley, New York.

Mueller, J. P. (1992), personal communication.

Muller, H. J. (1994). "Negotiation Principles." O'Hare and Jennings, eds., *Foundations of Distributed Artificial Intelligence* (this volume).

Nagle, R., and Dove, R. (1991). *21st Century Manufacturing Enterprise Strategy: An Industry-Led View*, Vol. 1. Iacocca Institute, Lehigh University, Bethlehem, PA.

Nii, H. P. (1986). Blackboard systems. *AI Mag.* **7**(3, 4), 40–53, 82–107.

Pan, J. Y. C., and Tenenbaum, J. M. (1992). An intelligent agent framework for enterprise integration. In *Artificial Intelligence Applications in Manufacturing* (A. Famili, D. Nau, and S. Kim, eds.), pp. 349–383. AAAI/MIT, Menlo Park, CA.

Panwalken, S. S., and Iskander, W. (1977). A survey of scheduling rules. *Operations Research* **25**(1), 45–61.

Parunak, H. V. D. (1987). Manufacturing experience with the contract net. In *Distributed Artificial Intelligence* (M. N. Huhns, ed.), pp. 285–310. Morgan Kaufmann, San Mateo, CA/Pitman, London.

Parunak, H. V. D. (1990). Distributed AI and manufacturing control: Some issues and insights. In *Artificial Intelligence* (Y. Demazeau and J.-P. Müller, eds.), pp. 81–104. Elsevier/North-Holland, Amsterdam.

Parunak, H. V. D. (1991). Characterizing the manufacturing scheduling problem. *J. Manuf. Syst.* **10**(3), 241–259.

Parunak, H. V. D. (1992). How do describe behavior space. *Work. Pap. Int. Workshop Distributed Artif. Intell.*, 1992, pp. 303–316.

Schelberg, C. (1992). Parallel scheduling of random and of chaotic processes. In *Dynamic, Genetic, and Chaotic Programming* (B. Soucek, ed.), pp. 535–549. Wiley, New York.

Shaw, M. J., and Whinston, A. B. (1985). Task bidding and distributed planning in flexible manufacturing. *Proc. IEEE Int. Conf. Artif. Intell.* pp. 184–189.

Shoham, Y. (1993). *Artif. Intell.* Agent-oriented programming. *Artif. Intell.* **60**(1), 51–92.

Smith, S. F. (1991). *Knowledge-Based Production Management: Approaches, Results and Prospects* CMU-RI-TR-91-21. Robotics Institute, Carnegie Mellon University, Pittsburgh, PA.

Smith, S. F., and Hynynen, J. E. (1987). Integrated decentralization of production management: An approach for factory scheduling. In *Intelligent and Integrated Manufacturing Analysis and Synthesis* (C. R. Liu, A. Requicha, and S. Chandrasekar, eds.), pp. 427–439. ASME, New York.

Steels, L. (1990). Cooperation between distributed agents through self-organization. In *Decentralized Artificial Intelligence* (Y. Demazeau and J.-P. Müller, eds.), pp. 175–196. Elsevier/North-Holland, Amsterdam.

Vollman, T. E. (1986). OPT as an enhancement to MRP II. *Prod. Inventory Manage.* **27**(2nd Q.), 38–47.

Wittig, T., ed. (1992). *ARCHON: An Architecture for Multi-Agent Systems.* Ellis Horwood, New York.

PART II

Cooperation, Coordination, and Agency

This section builds upon the formulative readings of section one and is concerned with identifying the mechanisms and structures which are central to the functioning of DAI systems. It addresses issues related to the design and implementation of intelligent agents and in particular how they are able to coordinate and cooperate with one another. In more detail, the following key topics are addressed: the design of belief, desire, and intention agent architectures (Chapter 5), the mechanisms which are essential for managing coordination (Chapter 6), the principles of interagent negotiation (Chapter 7), the main approaches to planning in DAI systems (Chapter 8), the role of agent dynamics (Chapter 9), the use of temporal belief logics for modeling DAI systems (Chapter 10), and the principles of reactive DAI systems (Chapter 11). Many of these issues are elaborated upon and given precise operational semantics by the specific DAI frameworks described in Part III of this book. Part IV examines how some of these key issues are viewed in disciplines such as philosophy, social psychology and organisational science, thus providing a truly multidisciplinary perspective.

Haddadi and Sundermeyer examine how the approach of conceptualizing agents in terms of their mental state (i.e., their beliefs, their desires and their intentions) can lead to well designed and implemented DAI architectures and systems. The key components which make up an agent's mental state are described in detail before four exemplar systems (IRMA, PRS, COSY and GRATE*) are compared and contrasted. After this analysis, the authors reflect on this general approach to building DAI systems and outline some key open issues which need to be addressed before the full potential of this approach can be realized.

Jennings addresses the problem of coordination in DAI systems. The operation of DAI systems is conceptualized as a distributed graph search with multiple loci of control, the notions of commitments (pledges to undertake a specific course of action) and conventions (means of monitoring commitments in changing circumstances) are defined, and then these two notions are shown to be the central concepts for managing interagent coordination. To further justify this stance, a number of extant coordination models are examined and it is shown how they can be reduced to the primitive notions of commitments and conventions.

Müller presents a comprehensive review of negotiation which is one of the most important forms of interactions in DAI systems. As a consequence of its ubiquity, negotiation has been used to describe a number of different social phenomena and so the first task in this chapter is to offer a clear definition. From this definition, research into negotiation is divided into three categories each of which is explored in detail: (i) work on the negotiation language which is concerned with the communication primitives and their semantics; (ii) work on negotiation decision making where the algorithms to compare negotiation topics and correlation functions are discussed; and (iii) work on the negotiation process itself where several general models are investigated and the global behavior of the participants are examined.

Durfee discusses a number of approaches which have been used to plan the actions of multiple agents in DAI systems, dealing in particular with the underlying assumptions about agents, tasks, and environments that stimulated their development. A more detailed study of partial global planning, one of the most influential approaches to distributed planning, is then presented. This analysis concludes with a discussion of the limitations and opportunities which are present in this important subfield of DAI.

Kiss presents a wide-ranging and multidisciplinary examination of the role of dynamics, both within a single agent and within DAI systems as a whole. After some brief background on agent theory, the chapter discusses how some of its central concepts (e.g., information, knowledge, actions, goals, and desires) can be formulated using an abstract model of the dynamics of processes in distributed systems.

Wooldridge presents, in an easy to follow manner, the use of formal methods for reasoning about DAI systems. Particular emphasis is placed upon the twin problems of specifying and verifying such systems. A critical review of several types of formalism (intentional logics, temporal logics and process algebras), emanating from AI and mainstream computer science, is undertaken. To circumvent the weaknesses highlighted in the aforementioned methods, a hybrid approach which involves constructing a model of DAI systems and then defining an execution model (which defines how agents act and interact) is proposed. The author then reflects upon the use of logic in DAI systems and highlights a number of future research topics.

Ferber describes the reactive approach to building DAI systems. This approach differs from all of the others described in this section in that the agents have no representation of their environment or one another and their behavior is programmed solely in terms of stimulus-response pairings which are grounded in the environment. The chapter concentrates on the basic issues behind the design of such reactive agents and how they can be used in various domains such as simulation (e.g., studying the emergence of division of labor patterns within a society of primitive ants) and problem solving (e.g., collecting rock samples in an unpredictable environment and taking them back to a home base).

CHAPTER 5

Belief-Desire-Intention Agent Architectures

AFSANEH HADDADI
KURT SUNDERMEYER

1 INTRODUCTION

Research in "artificial agency" has borrowed extensively from the folk psychological studies of mind and human behavior. One influential work is due to Dennett (1987), who employed the term *intentional systems* (Chapters 2, 6–10) to refer to systems whose behavior can be described by attributing to the system, mental attitudes such as "belief," "preference," "intention," and the like. These attitudes seem to play different roles in determining an agent's behavior. For example Kiss (1992) groups them into three categories: (i) *cognitive*, such as belief and knowledge; epistemic issues in general; (ii) *conative*, such as intention, commitment and plan; issues related to action and control; and (iii) *affective*, such as desires, goal, and preference; issues referring to the motivations of an agent.

Belief, desire and intention have been generally taken to be the representatives of the three classes, respectively. There is a whole pool of literature concerning belief and knowledge, and by now their meaning is more or less well understood. Generally belief of an agent is taken to be whatever it holds about its environment and about itself. Attention to the role of desires and intentions is rather more recent. While both refer to a state of affairs that an agent wishes to bring about, they are generally distinguished in that with intentions there is a measure of commitment associated which leads and controls future activities of the agent (see Chapter 6). Therefore while an agent may have certain desires, it may never set out to fulfil them. However, once an

Foundations of Distributed Artificial Intelligence, Edited by G. M. P. O'Hare and N. R. Jennings. ISBN 0-471-00675-0 © 1996 John Wiley & Sons, Inc.

agent intends some state of affairs, this intention will lead the agent into finding the appropriate means of arriving at those intended ends. In other words intentions move an agent to act. Furthermore, intentions are conduct-controllers, meaning that they guide future activities of the agent and anything that it chooses to perform. A good philosophical view on this topic is given by Tuomela (Chapter 18) and Bratman (1990).

There is also a wide range of theoretical and logical work on these topics (see Chapter 4). The first attempt to formalize these concepts was due to Cohen and Levesque (1990), who based their logical foundation on the philosophical work of Bratman. Their work has set the grounds for many other formalisms that has since been developed (e.g., Rao and Georgeff, 1991; Singh, 1994; and Wooldridge and Jennings, 1994). In general, all these theories attempt to describe, analyse and specify an agent's behavior by describing the relationship between beliefs, desires and intentions (or some other attitudes which play similar roles).

The motivation for such theoretical analysis has been very diverse. Some for instance take an observer's perspective (or according to Werner "metaperspective;" see Chapter 2) and aim to explain and predict an agent's behavior from the outset (Dennett, 1987). Some on the other hand, need such theories for design of agent architectures, or even to characterize introspective agents, i.e., agents who reason about their own beliefs, intentions and so forth. For *social agents* (see Chapter 1), such theories encompass reasoning about other agents in the system and their intentional attitudes and, further, characterize intentional attitudes of a group of agents who, for instance, engage in a group activity (e.g., joint intentions).

In some agent architectures intentional attitudes of an agent are represented explicitly. A subset of these architectures are known as BDI architectures, in which the triple structure of ⟨belief, desire, intention⟩ take an active role in the cognitive processes of the agent. First such conscious attempts were due to Bratman et al. (1988) in the design of IRMA, and Georgeff and Lansky (1987) in their PRS architecture. In effect, both architectures are aimed at accommodating real-time constraints for a single, rational, reasoning agent. Using the terminology in Chapter 1, these architectures are concerned with *intentional agents* but not (as yet) *social agents*. Inevitably, existence of other agents in the system sheds light to additional problems. COSY (Burmeister and Sundermeyer, 1992) and GRATE* (Jennings, 1993) agents have been designed to address some of these problems. While the COSY system augments a BDI structure with specific capabilities for interacting agents, GRATE* agents stress aspects of joint intentions for collaborative team activities.

A brief review of each of these architectures are provided in the four sections that follow. A brief survey of other related approaches and an evaluation and comparison of the different systems are made in Section 6. Preliminary to the discussions on these systems, it may be justified here to give some argument as to what benefits is expected to be gained from taking the intentional systems perspective and architectures explicitly based on them.

In support of viewing agents as intentional systems (Singh, 1994) argues that

> taking intentional stance makes available abstractions such as intentions and know-how of agents which not only have conceptual appeal but also there is simple pragmatic and technical reasons for considering them seriously. They (i) are natural to us, as designers and analysers; (ii) provide succinct descriptions of, and help understand and explain, the behaviour of complex systems; (iii) make available certain regularities and patterns of action that are independent of the exact physical implementation of the agent in the system; and (iv) may be used by the agents themselves in reasoning about each other.

When we consider a system with perceptive and effectoric capabilities, we require to bind these capabilities by means of some say "cognitive" capabilities which determine the agent's actions with respect to tasks it is expected to accomplish and the states of the environment within which it is situated (see Chapter 20). In other words actions of the agent should be in accordance to what is possible in the given situation. It is more natural to us as human to take advantage of the abstractions provided by intentional notions and model the required cognitive capabilities in terms of attitudes such as beliefs, desires and intentions and the interrelationship between them. Most of the architectures based on such concepts have a well-founded philosophical and theoretical background. It will be argued in the conclusion in Section 7 that the architectures which make explicit use of intentional attitudes are more flexible than purely deliberative or reactive systems. Since such concepts and the intentional abstractions are natural to us, they simplify the design of agents for a wide variety of applications, in particular those in which agents are situated in a dynamic environment and which have to act rationally while responding to the changes in the system in a timely manner.

2 IRMA

IRMA stands for *intelligent resource-bounded machine architecture*, an implementation based on the design of a "resource-bounded rational agent," where the resource boundedness primarily refers to computational power (Bratman et al., 1988). The authors note that the design of an architecture for a rational agent should allow for means-end reasoning and for weighing alternative courses of actions while recognizing the fact that agents are resource bounded. They present a high-level specification of the "practical reasoning" component of IRMA which includes a fairly direct representation of beliefs, desires, and intentions. The underlying principles of this design is based on Bratman's work which appeared in Bratman (1987, 1990).

The architecture (see Figure 5.1) has different information stores (indicated as ovals in the figure) and processes (indicated as rectangles). The information

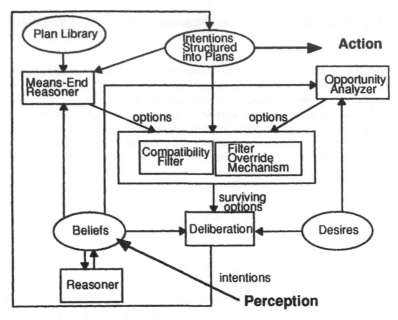

Figure 5.1 *IRMA architecture (from Bratman et al., 1988).*

stores are *beliefs, desires, plan library, intentions structured into plans*. There is a distinction between plans as recipes and plans that an agent has adopted to execute. The *plan library* contains plans as recipes and can be seen as a subset of the agents beliefs about what plan is applicable for accomplishing which task and under what circumstances. The latter type of plans are those which an agent currently follows, corresponding to intentions that are stored in the *intentions structured into plans*.

The authors argue that "a rational agent is committed to what she plans. The nature of this commitment is quite complex but involves at least certain characteristic roles in further practical reasoning," and they illustrate at least three roles: (i) they drive means-end reasoning, (ii) they provide constraints on what options need to be seriously considered, and (iii) they influence the beliefs on which further practical reasoning will be based.

This is accomplished through the processes *means-end reasoner, opportunity analyzer, filtering mechanisms*, and *deliberation*, which have access to the beliefs, desires, intentions, and the plans in the information stores. Options (plans) are proposed by two processes: the *means-end reasoner* and the *opportunity analyzer*.

Once an intention is formed, the means-end reasoner is invoked for each of the existing partial plans, to propose subplans that complete it. Means-end reasoning may occur at any time up to the point at which a plan is in danger of becoming means-end incoherent; at that point new options are proposed which may serve as subplans for the already intended plans.

The opportunity analyzer is the component that proposes options as a result of changes in the environment. Such opportunities may be welcome or unwelcome, in the sense that some of these changes may refer to unexpected opportunities for satisfying desires, and others to opportunities for avoiding possible threats.

The means-end reasoner may propose a number of options for satisfying the same means. These options together with those given by the opportunity analyzer are passed into the filtering mechanisms. The *compatibility filter* checks if an option is compatible with the agent's existing intentions, and if so it passes them to the *deliberation* process. An option which is deemed to be incompatible may pass through the *filter override mechanism* which runs in parallel. Only those options are subject to this reconsideration which satisfy one of the conditions encoded by the override mechanism. These are conditions under which some of the already intended plans should be suspended and weighed against some other option. The main purpose of this mechanism is to limit the amount of computation required by the deliberation in practical reasoning. The authors note that the design of such a mechanism should ensure that the override mechanism is neither too sensitive about the changes in the environment nor too benevolent.

Surviving options after filtering are passed along to the *deliberation* process. This process weighs the competing options against one another and updates the *intentions structured into plans*.

The theory behind IRMA was tested and evaluated in a series of experiments in the context of a Tileworld example, a simple simulated robot agent in a dynamic and unpredictable environment (Pollack and Ringuette, 1990). The main result of the experiments was that a strict filtering coupled with an appropriate overriding mechanism is viable (at least under certain circumstances); in other words, commitment to already adopted plans is a valuable strategy for an agent in a changing environment.

3 PRS

The *procedural reasoning system* (PRS) (Georgeff and Lansky, 1987; Georgeff and Ingrand, 1989) is a system for reasoning about and performing tasks in dynamic environments. It was developed within a reaction control system of a NASA Space Shuttle project. This work is based on a well-founded theoretical background presented in Rao and Georgeff (1991, 1992).

In PRS the attitudes of beliefs, desires, and intentions are represented explicitly and together determine actions of the system at any given instance. These attitudes are reasoned upon and modified dynamically by a reasoning mechanism as presented in the shaded area in Figure 5.2. The components constituting this architecture are *database*, *goals*, *knowledge area library*, *intention structure*, and *interpreter*.

The *database* contains current beliefs or facts about the world. The knowledge about how to accomplish tasks and how to react in certain circumstances are encapsulated in a declarative procedure specification called *knowledge area*

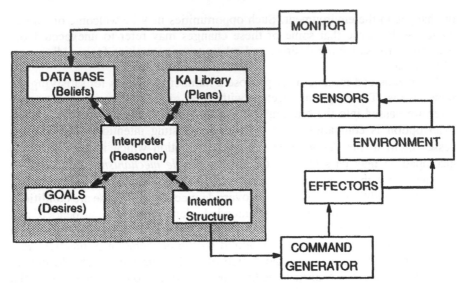

Figure 5.2 *PRS Architecture (from Georgeff and Ingrand, 1989).*

(KA). Each KA has a "body" that consists of the steps of the procedure and an "invocation condition" which describes under which conditions the KA is applicable. In the KA library, in addition to the KAs related to the application domain, there are "metalevel" KAs and a set of system-dependent default KAs. The metalevel KAs perform the reasoning on and manipulation of beliefs, desires, and intentions of the PRS itself. They embody the type of metalevel knowledge required for choosing among multiple relevant KAs, performing additional reasoning that can be undertaken given the real-time constraints of the system and so forth. Selection of a metalevel KA can also be through other metalevel KAs.

Goals represent the desired behavior of the system, rather than static world states to be achieved. They appear both in the representation of KAs and in the system's *goal stack* and that is how KAs corresponding to a goal become applicable. The authors distinguish between *intrinsic* goals and *operational* goals in that, intrinsic goals are not related to an already existing goal and are considered as a result of obtaining new beliefs about the world.

Intentions of PRS are the tasks the system has chosen to execute either immediately or sometime in the future. A single intention consists of some initial KA to accomplish a task, together with all the other (sub-) KAs invoked to accomplish that task. Intentions of the system are inserted into the *intention structure* according to their precedence. This ordering may change as a result of execution of some metalevel KAs. An intention earlier in the ordering must be either realized or dropped before intentions appearing in the ordering can be executed. An intention may be in one of three possible states of "active," "suspended," or "conditionally suspended." An intention that is adopted, but no decisions has been made as when it should be carried out, is in a suspended state; one that has to be executed next or immediately is in an active state; and one that awaits execution until some specified condition is satisfied is in a conditionally suspended state.

The operation of the PRS interpreter which runs the entire system can be conceptually described as follows: At any given time the system has some active goals and holds some beliefs in its data base. Based on these goals and beliefs a subset of KAs become applicable, and then one of these KAs will be chosen for execution and thus will be placed on the *intention structure*. As a reminder, this decision is made by relevant metalevel KAs or some default procedures. In the course of executing a KA, new (sub-) goals will be produced and pushed into the system's *goal stack* for which another cycle of means-end reasoning takes place. In the light of new beliefs, the interpreter performs consistency-checking procedures and possibly activates other relevant KAs. During this process various metalevel KAs may be invoked to make decisions like choosing among alternative means, decomposing a goal into achievable components, and so forth.

Unless some new belief or goal activates some new KAs, the system tries to fulfil the intentions that were previously decided upon. It does this in a focused, goal-directed manner in which through reasoning KAs are expanded analogous to the execution of subroutines in procedural programming systems. In light of new information or a new goal, PRS will reason on its current intentions and beliefs and perhaps choose to work on some other goal. Therefore, KAs are invoked not only as a result of pursuing goals but as a reaction to certain conditions in the environment. This ensures that the agent does not overcommit to an intention and that it takes the changes in the environment into consideration.

The Tileworld simulation environment was also used by Kinny and Georgeff (1991) to investigate how commitment to goals contributes to effective behavior and to compare the properties of different strategies for reacting to changes. As a result of their experiments, the authors claim that despite the simple nature of PRS's planning and control mechanisms, reactive metalevel control of deliberation for resource-bounded agents situated in dynamic domains is very important. Furthermore, as with Pollack and Ringuette (1990) they found that in such settings, commitment with intelligent reactive replanning results in optimal behaviors. A useful reading on testbeds, experimentation, and the design of agent architectures is provided in Hanks et al. (1993; see also Chapters 3 and 15) where the validity of simple simulated experiments for proving concepts (such as those behind IRMA and PRS) in a larger context is questioned and argued.

4 COSY

COSY started off as a project for investigating a methodology for cooperating knowledge-based systems. Current direction of COSY is toward development of a frame for agent-oriented design and implementation. The COSY concepts, as will be described in this section, have been tested in various domains like traffic management, logistics and layout, and material flow in a manufacturing domain.

The COSY agent model (Burmeister and Sundermeyer, 1992) describes an agent by its intentions, behaviors (actions and perception), and the resources required for fulfilling intentions and executing the behaviors. Two kinds of intentions are distinguished, namely "strategic intentions" standing for long-term goals, attitudes, roles, responsibilities, and the like (which control an agent's decision making), and "tactical intentions," which are directly bound to the actions of an agent.

The COSY agent architecture is modular, with modules ACTUATORS, SENSORS, COMMUNICATION, INTENTION, and COGNITION (see Figure 5.3). The nature of the first three modules is obvious. The INTENTION module comprises the strategic intentions. The commitment to tactical intentions, their formation, revision, or abandoning is part of COGNITION. The COGNITION module, implemented as a knowledge-based system, evaluates the perceptual knowledge and prepares an appropriate action for the given situation by consulting the INTENTION module. It consists of a knowledge base (KB), script execution component (SEC), protocol execution component (PEC), and a "reasoning, deciding, and reacting" component (RDRC).

The triple ⟨belief, desire, intention⟩ is represented in the COSY approach fairly directly: KB contains the beliefs, desires are represented in the INTENTION module (i.e., the strategic intentions), chosen scripts, and protocols encode intentions (i.e., the tactical intentions).

Domain-independent problem solving is based on scripts and cooperation protocols. A script is a stereotypical recipe or plan of achieving a specific task. It contains calls to other scripts, protocols, and primitive behaviors. Primitive behaviours are "acting" behaviors which are executed by the ACTUATORS. The COGNITION component SEC, administers the execution of scripts, delegating the execution of primitive behaviors to the ACTUATORS and the execution of cooperation protocols to the PEC.

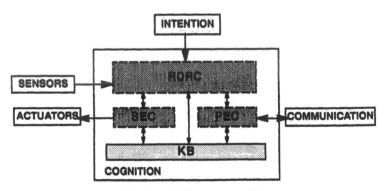

Figure 5.3   *COSY agent architecture.*

Cooperation protocols represent a stereotypical dialogue in a specific co-operation pattern like contracting. Correspondingly, the PEC monitors and administers execution of cooperation protocols by preparing messages to be sent and processing received messages related to a particular protocol (see Burmeister et al., 1993, for more details).

As its name entails, RDRC is responsible for reasoning about the world, reacting if the situation demands and deliberating as how best to achieve goals and fulfill intentions. Part of this task is handling decisions arising during interactions, i.e., intraprotocol decisions.

RDRC consists of an *agenda*, an *intention-structure* and procedures for operating on these data structures (see Figure 5.4). The agenda and the intention-structure consist of scripts required as input to the procedures. Scripts are put on the agenda as a result of the agent's perception of the current situation, by SENSORS and COMMUNICATION. A script that enters the agenda is classified based on (i) whether it is directly in the plan of achieving the agent's current goal, (ii) whether it is applicable as a reaction to the current (unforeseen) situation, or (iii) whether it refers to a new goal to be considered. The scripts put on the agenda by the PEC, as a result of interactions with other agents, can be of any of the aforementioned categories. The intention-structure contains scripts which the agent has already committed itself to execute some time in the future. These are the scripts whose execution was interrupted, those await-ing resources, and the script being currently executed by the SEC.

The reasoning, deciding, and reacting within RDRC are carried out by spe-

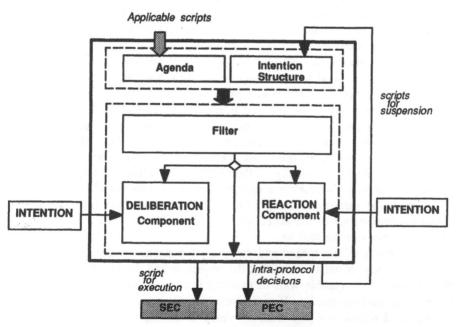

Figure 5.4 *The structure of RDRC.*

cialized procedures called *filter*, *reaction*, and *deliberation*. At every interpreter cycle, the RDRC first calls the filter procedure after which the control is divided into two directions, one led by the deliberation procedure and the other by the reaction procedure. The decision on the competing scripts referring to the first two classes of scripts described above is made by the reaction procedure by looking at the script and event priority structure in the INTENTION module. The filter gives priority to the second class of scripts before even considering those referring to the agent's existing plans of current goal. Scripts of the last category require deliberation, which is performed by the deliberation procedure by referring to the strategic intentions in the INTENTION module. This procedure has access to application specific decision-making mechanisms as well as generic intraprotocol decision-making procedures (see Haddadi, 1993, for more details).

5   GRATE*

The functional agent architecture of the GRATE* (Jennings, 1993) greatly resembles IRMA with additional components to incorporate collaborative problem solving. It utilizes the concepts of joint intentions and joint responsibility (Jennings, 1992) to establish a collaborative activity and monitor the execution of the joint activity. GRATE* has been implemented and tested on the real-world application of electricity transportation management.

As shown in Figure 5.5, the functional architecture on GRATE* is indeed a BDI architecture. In what follows we will first describe the functional architecture of GRATE* and later briefly denote how this architecture is realized at the implementation level.

Events occurring as a result of local problem solving or changes in the environment, in addition to the events occurring elsewhere in the community, are monitored by the *monitor events* process. Events signify a potential need for a fresh activity and therefore a new objective. This new objective serves as input to the *means-end analysis* process. Upon existence of a new objective for consideration, the means-end analyzer refers to the *recipe library* to find appropriate plans to fulfill the objective. These plans indicate whether the objective can be satisfied locally, collaboratively, or whether a choice between the two is required. In making a decision as to whether the objective should be adopted, the means-end analyzer also considers the existing intentions to weigh the importance of the objective as compared to the activities the agent has already been committed to.

If as a result of the means-end analysis, the agent decides to pursue the objective locally, it must ensure that the objective and the means of satisfying the objective is compatible with its existing intentions. This task is performed by the *compatibility checker*. If as a result of compatibility checking an inconsistency is detected, the *inconsistency resolver* attempts to either modify the existing commitments or alter the objective to remove the conflict. The controlling elements in this process are the agents' preferences or *desires*. Usually the less important task is subject to modification. In many cases the outcome of the conflict resolution process will require a further round of means-end analysis. Any modifications made by the resolution mechanism is reflected in the intention representation.

If the result of the means-end analysis is a decision to fulfill the objective collaboratively, a social action must be established. The first phase is to identify those agents in the community who are potentially interested in being involved (team formation). Once the potential members have been identified a skeletal joint intention exists in which potential participants have registered their interest, but no firm selection of either the final team or the common solution has been made. The second phase is finalising the outline of the proposal (social plan generation) and mapping between the actions to be carried out and the individuals within the group who can undertake them (role assignment). The result of the plan selection/generation and role assignment is passed onto each member of the group and ultimately requires them to perform local means-end reasoning to fit the primitive actions in with their existing commitments whilst satisfying the relationships with their associated actions. Every time a new individual or a joint action is proposed, the consistency checker checks if there is a coherence between individual and joint intentions.

In GRATE* intentions not only provide means for coordinating actions, but

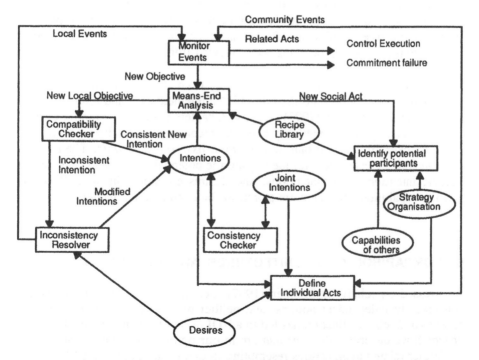

Figure 5.5 *GRATE* functional architecture (from Jennings, 1993).*

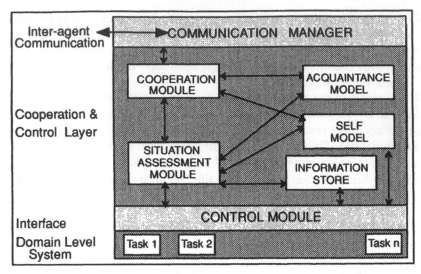

Figure 5.6   GRATE* implementation architecture (from Jennings, 1993).

also act as a guide for task execution and monitoring. Jennings (1993) contains a description of how this is achieved.

The functional agent architecture outlined above describes the computational processes necessary to support such a model. Figure 5.6 gives the implementation architecture of GRATE*. Problems of the domain level are presented as tasks—atomic units of processing when viewed from the *cooperation and control layer*.

Here we will only outline the mapping from the functional architecture presented in Figure 5.5 onto the GRATE* implementation and refer the interested readers to Jennings (1993) (see also Chapters 6 and 18). Monitor events, means-end analysis, compatibility checker, inconsistency resolver, and consistency checker are mapped onto the *situation assessment module*. The *cooperation module* is responsible for identifying the potential participants. The recipe library, intentions, joint intentions, and desires are stored in the *self-model*, and the capabilities of others are stored in the *acquaintance model*.

6   COMPARISON OF ARCHITECTURES AND RELATED WORK

As stressed especially by Bratman (1987), beliefs, desires, and intentions are conceptually independent notions, and neither of them can be reduced to the other two. Such a distinction has led to a BDI design for computational agents, of which we described the four that are in our opinion fair representatives.

Further related architectures resembling in one form or another a BDI structure are those by Brustoloni (1991), Chaib-draa and Millot (1990), and Shoham (1993). The *hybrid agent architecture* of Brustoloni has been inspired by the PRS but puts more emphasis on how goals are formed from an agents' *drives*. Chaib-draa and Millot's agent model is based on the logical system of Cohen and Levesque (1990), where desires and beliefs lead to the choice of goals and to the generation of commitments, intentions, and plans within a reasoning module. AGENT0 of Shoham (1993) and Chapter 1 and 3, although it does not directly deal with beliefs, desires and intentions, employs similar intentional notions. However, the stress is more on the design of an agent-oriented programming language than an agent architecture.

Although the terms *belief*, *desire*, *intention*, and related ones have became well respected in the DAI community, there is so far no common agreement on the exact syntax and semantics of these notions. This has had an apparent influence on the design of architectures mentioned in this chapter. As a consequence, any comparison with respect to the role of each of the related intentional notions in the architecture, should be made more on conceptual and theoretical level than design.

The design of IRMA seems to have pioneered the work on BDI architectures, but with the aim of designing an agent with bounded computational resources. So the articles related to IRMA stress the central role of the filtering process and the cost of various deliberation strategies. They also pay a special attention to "cautious" and "bold" agents and their performance in environments with varying rate of changes. Apart from the philosophical analysis of intentions by Bratman (1990), there is no logical foundations in support of the theory and specification in terms of beliefs, desires, and intentions that is directly bound to IRMA.

Just like IRMA, PRS is an architecture for a single "situated" agent, also inspired by Bratman's work. In Kinny et al. (1992) one finds a formal extension of the central ideas of PRS to the multiple-agent context, but no implementation has been reported thus far. Of all the systems described, PRS is the one with the most-founded theoretical background. The logical system of Rao and Georgeff (1991), which gives the syntax and semantics of beliefs, desires, goals, and intentions was made operational and bound to an interpreter module to construct a BDI architecture in Rao and Georgeff (1992). In these more recent theoretical works, the authors improve upon the loose notion of goals and desires which they had employed in the architecture described here. Desires are a set of tasks, state of affairs, or system behavior that an agent is expected to accomplish. This means that the goal stack now corresponds to the agent's desires. Goals are then defined to be the chosen desires of the agent. In this respect, intentions of an agent in a given time, are a subset of its goals or in other words they are commitment to certain goals (or desired future state of affairs).

Embedded in the system interpreter of PRS are certain fixed decision-making processes that are stringently bounded in execution time, yet which can be overridden whenever the system can bring more powerful decision-making knowledge to bear. This is comparable to the filter override mechanism of IRMA. In PRS, the fixed decision-making processes are hard-coded into the basic system interpreter, whereas the knowledge to override or elaborate these decisions is contained in appropriate metalevel KAs.

COSY takes elements both of IRMA and PRS. Some of the modules have been given names (and functionality) of these architectures, for instance, *intention structure* from PRS and *filter* and *deliberation* from IRMA. Other components can clearly be identified with components in IRMA and PRS, like scripts which correspond to plans in the plan library of IRMA and to KAs in PRS. However, the COSY architecture extends their underlying concepts by incorporating cooperation protocols to enable a high-level multiagent communication and interactions. A semiformal theory behind the COSY agent model was developed in Burmeister and Sundermeyer (1992) describing internal processes of an agent in terms of state transitions and functional mappings. In light of many new insights and worked out theories of intentionality, currently a formal theory behind the COSY agent model is being worked out which will be largely based on the logical works encompassing beliefs, desires, and intentions of an agent and a society of agents. It is expected that this theory will lead to new modifications and extension of the model. In particular the theory will concentrate on the role of intentional notions in planning communication and coordination.

GRATE*, based in many respects on IRMA, was the first implemented BDI architecture treating joint mental states. However, there is a gap both between the underlying descriptive theory and the architecture and between the functional and the implementation architecture. As Jennings himself points out: "... the architecture does not specify how intentions are represented, how commitment is described, what circumstances are used to obtain agreements nor how to develop the common solution." The architecture of GRATE* does not sketch out the details of team formation, social plan generation, and role assignment. These processes are left to the application designers to define appropriate mechanisms based on the organizational strategies and belief of an agent about capabilities of the others. It is hard to see, anyhow, how these largely application-dependent mechanisms could possibly be structured in general terms. Some of the underlying concepts such as social conventions (Chapter 6) and cooperative problem solving have been recently formalized in Wooldridge and Jennings (1994).

In none of the architectures presented is the formation of intentions from desires satisfactorily described (see Chapter 9). This is probably because desires have different semantics for different authors. In IRMA and GRATE* this seems to be hidden, although it is not clear where. In PRS this happens in the metalevel KAs, without being further specified. Similarly in COSY it is the responsibility of the INTENTION module which is currently largely application dependent. Brustoloni (1991) claims however that his model "... explicitly tackles the question of how goals are formed and manipulated."

7 CONCLUSION

We sketched the philosophical and logical background for modeling agents' internal states by mental categories based on the notion of intentionality. We also described some architectures which at the functional and implementation level more or less explicitly make use of the intentional states belief, desire, and intentions. The functionality and data repositories of these architectures can be mapped onto the related parts of the conceptual architecture described in Chapter 1, but more precisely defined. In these architectures, although the actual use of the mental states is different, the common understanding is that of belief standing for epistemic notions, intention standing for chosen plans and actions, and desires describing the motivation of an agent.

BDI architectures lie somewhere in between purely reactive and purely deliberative planning systems. The limits of purely deliberative planning systems in their inability to cope with a dynamic environment has been pointed out for some time now. It is important to observe that in the presence of other autonomous agents the environment of an agent is dynamic per se. Consequently the purely reactive approach received a lot of publicity; see Chapter 11. Its strength was demonstrated among others by the "creatures" of R. Brooks and the "ecoproblem solving" approach of J. Ferber and their groups. Although the reactive conceptualization might be useful for modeling the internal operations of robots or for modeling entities in games like Pengi or the N-puzzle, we doubt that basic instincts are the appropriate means to model coarse-grained enterprises, which need both elements of reactiveness and deliberativeness (see Chapter 15). The motivation behind the BDI architectures has been to enable a reasonable and rational behavior for limited computational agents situated in dynamic environments. These architectures exhibit a measure of flexibility that neither of the two approaches alone could offer. However, experiments have shown that for highly dynamic environments these systems currently come short of rapid response and performance that is more likely to be achieved by purely reactive systems. On the other hand, they allow for both reaction and reflection for environments with a "reasonable" rate of change, the measure of which for any application can be only determined through experimentation. Various experiments have also shown that the performance of the system can be increased by tuning the reasoning and deliberation strategies to the specific requirements of the application in question.

Recently "agent-oriented techniques" has generated a large interest as a new paradigm in systems and software technology. They promise to offer adequate means to handle complex systems, with distributed autonomous subsystems interacting in a flexible manner, coping with the dynamics of the environment they live in. Many agent architectures have been proposed without making any implicit or explicit reference to intentional notions. These systems may even be in certain ways more powerful than the BDI architectures. But in our experience, the design principles behind such architectures are somewhat ad hoc. In order to overcome this weakness, one needs (1) theories of agents. For this, belief-desire-intention logics are promising candidates; (2) efficient programming languages realizing part of the theories [in this respect, the first results on the expressiveness and complexity of BDI logics (Rao and Georgeff, 1991) are encouraging]; (3) analysis and design techniques in which a natural conceptualization of complex systems and enterprises can support the user of the language. Again, beliefs, desires, and intentions are adequate concepts. In our own experience, we found that abstractions provided by intentional notions and the theories that relate them together has eased the design process. This has proved even more useful for designing social agents, because social agents are "autonomous" and therefore have to reason about other agents in the system in order to coexist, compete, or cooperate with them. Design methods based on intentionality offer natural means for an agent to reason about other agents and their behavior.

As a last remark, it is worth stating that although the term "agent" is central to DAI, so far there has been no commonly accepted definition of what constitutes a social agent and an agent society. We not only doubt that a universal agent definition will be established one day, but also do not believe that it is mandatory to rely on a specific agent architecture. In the spirit of Hewitt's "open systems" it is more important that DAI provides means that societies of different kinds of agents, irrespective of their internal structure, be able to coordinate their activities to fulfill both individual and common goals.

REFERENCES

Bratman, M. (1987). *Intentions, Plans, and Practical Reasoning.* Harvard Univ. Press, Cambridge, MA.

Bratman, M. (1990). What is intention? In *Intentions in Communication* (P. R. Cohen, J. Morgan, and M. E. Pollack, eds.), pp. 15–31. MIT Press, Cambridge, MA.

Bratman, M., Israel, D. I., and Pollack, M. E. (1988). Plans and resource-bounded practical reasoning. *Comput. Intell.* **4,** 349–355.

Brustoloni, J. (1991). *Autonomous Agents: Characterization and Requirements*, Rep. CMU-CS-91-204. School of Computer Science, Carnegie-Mellon University, Pittsburgh, PA.

Burmeister, B., and Sundermeyer, K. (1992). Cooperative problem-solving guided by intentions and perception. In *Artificial Intelligence 3* (E. Werner and Y. Demazeau, eds.), pp. 77–92. Elsevier/North-Holland, Amsterdam.

Burmeister, B., Haddadi, A., and Sundermeyer, K. (1993). Configurable cooperation protocols for multi-agent systems. *Proc. Eur. Workshop Modell. Auton. Agents Multi-Agent World (MAAMAW-83), 5th*, Neuchatel, Switzerland.

Chaib-draa, B., and Millot, P. (1990). A framework for cooperative work: An approach based on the intentionality. *Artif. Intell. Eng.* **5**(4), 199–205.

Cohen, P. R., and Levesque, H. J. (1990). Intention is choice with commitment. *Artif. Intell.* **24,** 213–261.

Dennett, D. C. (1987). *The Intentional Stance*. Bradford Books/MIT Press, Cambridge, MA.

Georgeff, M. P., and Ingrand, F. F. (1989). Decision-making in an embedded reasoning system. *Proc. Int. Jt. Conf. Artif. Intell., 11th,* Detroit, MI, pp. 972–978.

Georgeff, M. P., and Lansky, A. L. (1987). Reactive reasoning and planning. *Proc. Nat. Conf. Artif. Intell., 6th,* pp. 677–682.

Haddadi, A. (1993). A hybrid architecture for multi-agent systems. *Proc. Coop. Knowl. Based Syst. SIG Workshop,* University of Keele, Keele, UK, pp. 13–25.

Hanks, S., Pollack, M. E., and Cohen, P. R. (1993). Benchmarks, test beds, controlled experimentation, and the design of agent architectures. *Proc. of the 11th Am. Assoc. Artif. Intell.,* Washington, DC, pp. 17–41.

Jennings, N. R. (1992). On being responsible. In *Decentralized Artificial Intelligence* (E. Werner and Y. Demazeau, eds.), pp. 93–102. Elsevier/Holland, Amsterdam.

Jennings, N. R. (1993). Specification and implementation of a belief-desire-joint-intention architecture for collaborative problem solving. *Int. J. Intell. Coop. Inf. Syst.,* **2**(3), 289–318.

Kinny, D., and Georgeff, P. G. (1991). Commitment and effectiveness of situated agents. *Proc. Int. Jt. Conf. Artif. Intell., 12th,* Sydney, Australia.

Kinny, D., Ljungberg, D. M., Rao, A., Sonenberg, E., Tidhar, G., and Werner, E. (1992). Planned team activity. In *Artificial Social Systems* (C. Chastelfranchi and E. Werner, eds.), pp. 226–256. Springer Verlag.

Kiss, G. (1992). Variable coupling of agents to their environment: Combining situated and symbolic automata. In *Decentralized Artificial Intelligence 3* (E. Werner and Y. Demazeau, eds.), pp. 231–248. Elsevier/North-Holland, Amsterdam.

Pollack, M. E., and Ringuette, M. (1990). Introducing the tileworld: Experimentally evaluating agent architectures. *Proc. Nat. Conf. Artif. Intell., 8th,* Boston, pp. 183–189.

Rao, A. S., and Georgeff, M. P. (1991). Modeling rational agents within a BDI architecture. In *Proceedings of the Second International Conference on Principles of Knowledge Representation and Reasoning* (J. Allen, R. Fikes, and E. Sandwall, eds.), pp. 473–484. Morgan Kaufmann, San Mateo, CA.

Rao, A. S., and Georgeff, M. P. (1992). An abstract architecture for rational agents. In *Proceedings of the Third International Conference on Principles of Knowledge Representation and Reasoning* (B. Nebel, C. Rich, and W. Swartout, eds.), pp. 439–449. Morgan Kaufmann, San Mateo, CA.

Shoham, Y. (1993). Agent-oriented programming, *Artif. Intell.* **60**(7), 51–92.

Singh, M. P. (1994). *Multiagent systems: A theoretical Framework for Intentions. Know-how, and Communication*. Springer-Verlag, Berlin.

Wooldridge, M. J., and Jennings, N. R. (1994). Formalising the cooperative problem solving process. *Proc. Eur. Workshop Modell. Auton. Agents Multi-Agent World (MAAMAW-94), 6th,* Odense, Denmark, pp. 403–417.

Dennett, D. C. (1987). The Intentional Stance. Bradford Books/MIT Press, Cambridge, MA.

Georgeff, M. P., and Ingrand, F. F. (1989). Decision-making in an embedded reasoning system. Proc. Int. J. Conf. Artif. Intell., 11th, Detroit, MI, pp. 972-978.

Georgeff, M. P., and Lansky, A. L. (1987). Reactive reasoning and planning. Proc. Nat. Conf. Artif. Intell., Am., pp. 677-682.

Haddadi, A. (1995). A BDI architecture for manager-or operator... Proc. Coop. Based Syst, SIG Workshop, University of Keele, Keele, UK, pp. 12-27.

Hanks, S., Pollack, M. E., and Cohen, P. R. (1993). Benchmarks, test beds, controlled experimentation, and the design of agent architectures... AI Mag. Winter, pp. 17-41.

CHAPTER 6 ————————————

Coordination Techniques for Distributed Artificial Intelligence

NICK R. JENNINGS

1 INTRODUCTION

Coordination, the process by which an agent reasons about its local actions and the (anticipated) actions of others to try and ensure the community acts in a coherent manner, is perhaps the key problem of the discipline of distributed artificial intelligence (DAI). In order to make advances it is important that the theories and principles which guide this central activity are uncovered and analyzed in a systematic and rigorous manner. To this end, this chapter models agent communities using a distributed goal search formalism, and argues that *commitments* (pledges to undertake a specific course of action) and *conventions* (means of monitoring commitments in changing circumstances) are the foundation of coordination in all DAI systems.

2 THE COORDINATION PROBLEM

Participation in any social situation should be both simultaneously constraining, in that agents must make a contribution to it, and yet enriching, in that participation provides resources and opportunities which would otherwise be unavailable (Gerson, 1976). Coordination, the process by which an agent reasons about its local actions and the (anticipated) actions of others to try and ensure the community acts in a coherent manner, is the key to achieving this objective. Without coordination the benefits of decentralised problem solving vanish and

Foundations of Distributed Artificial Intelligence, Edited by G. M. P. O'Hare and N. R. Jennings.
ISBN 0-471-00675-0 © 1996 John Wiley & Sons, Inc.

the community may quickly degenerate into a collection of chaotic, incohesive individuals. In more detail, the objectives of the coordination process are to ensure that all necessary portions of the overall problem are included in the activities of at least one agent, that agents interact in a manner which permits their activities to be developed and integrated into an overall solution, that team members act in a purposeful and consistent manner, and that all of these objectives are achievable within the available computational and resource limitations (Lesser and Corkill, 1987). Specific examples of coordination activities include supplying timely information to needy agents, ensuring the actions of multiple actors are synchronised and avoiding redundant problem solving.

There are three main reasons why the actions of multiple agents need to be coordinated.

1. There are dependencies between agents' actions. Interdependence occurs when goals undertaken by individual agents are related, either because local decisions made by one agent have an impact on the decisions of other community members (e.g., when building a house, decisions about the size and location of rooms impacts upon the wiring and plumbing) or because of the possibility of harmful interactions among agents (e.g., two mobile robots may attempt to pass through a narrow exit simultaneously, resulting in a collision, damage to the robots, and blockage of the exit).

2. There is a need to meet global constraints. Global constraints exist when the solution being developed by a group of agents must satisfy certain conditions if it is to be deemed successful. For instance, a house-building team may have a budget of £250,000, a distributed monitoring system may have to react to critical events within 30 seconds, and a distributed air traffic control system may have to control the planes with a fixed communication bandwidth. If individual agents acted in isolation and merely tried to optimize their local performance, then such overarching constraints are unlikely to be satisfied. Only through coordinated action will acceptable solutions be developed.

3. No individual has sufficient competence, resources, or information to solve the entire problem. Many problems cannot be solved by individuals working in isolation because they do not possess the necessary expertise, resources, or information. Relevant examples include the tasks of lifting a heavy object, driving in a convoy, and playing a symphony. It may be impractical or undesirable to permanently synthesize the necessary components into a single entity because of historical, political, physical, or social constraints; therefore, temporary alliances through cooperative problem solving may be the only way to proceed. Differing expertise may need to be combined to produce a result outside of the scope of any of the individual constituents (e.g., in medical diagnosis, knowledge about heart disease, blood disorders, and respiratory problems may need to be combined to diagnose a patient's illness). Different agents may have different resources (e.g., processing power, memory, and communications) which all need to be harnessed to solve a complex problem. Finally, different agents may have different information or viewpoints of a

problem (e.g., in concurrent engineering systems, the same product may be viewed from a design, manufacturing, and marketing perspective).

Even when individuals can work independently, meaning coordination is not essential, information discovered by one agent can be of sufficient use to another that the two agents can solve the problem more than twice as fast. For example, when searching for a lost object in a large area it is often better, though not essential, to do so as a team. Analysis of this "combinatorial implosion" phenomena (Kornfield and Hewitt, 1981) has resulted in the postulation that cooperative search, when sufficiently large, can display universal characteristics which are independent of the nature of either the individual process or the particular domain being tackled (Clearwater et al., 1991).

If all the agents in the system could have complete knowledge of the goals, actions, and interactions of their fellow community members and could also have infinite processing power, it would be possible to know exactly what each agent was doing at present and what it is intending to do in the future. In such instances, it would be possible to avoid conflicting and redundant efforts and systems could be perfectly coordinated (Malone, 1987). However such complete knowledge is infeasible, in any community of reasonable complexity, because bandwidth limitations make it impossible for agents to be constantly informed of all developments. Even in modestly sized communities, a complete analysis to determine the detailed activities of each agent is impractical—the computation and communication costs of determining the optimal set and allocation of activities far outweighs the improvement in problem-solving performance (Corkill and Lesser, 1983).

As all community members cannot have a complete and accurate perspective of the overall system, the next easiest way of ensuring coherent behavior is to have one agent with a wider picture. This global controller could then direct the activities of the others, assign agents to tasks and focus problem solving to ensure coherent behavior. However, such an approach is often impractical in realistic applications because even keeping one agent informed of all the actions in the community would swamp the available bandwidth. Also the controller would become a severe communication bottleneck and would render the remaining components unusable if it failed.

To produce systems without bottlenecks and which exhibit graceful degradation of performance, most DAI research has concentrated on developing communities in which both control and data are distributed. Distributed control means that individuals have a degree of autonomy in generating new actions and in deciding which tasks to do next. When designing such systems it is important to ensure that agents spend the bulk of their time engaged on solving the domain-level problems for which they were built, rather than in communication and coordination activities. To this end, the community should be decomposed into the most modular units possible. However, the designer should ensure that these units are of sufficient granularity to warrant the overhead inherent in goal distribution—distributing small tasks can prove more expensive than performing them in one place (Durfee et al., 1987).

The disadvantage of distributing control and data is that knowledge of the system's overall state is dispersed throughout the community and each individual has only a partial and imprecise perspective. Thus there is an increased degree of uncertainty about each agent's actions, meaning that it is more difficult to attain coherent global behavior; for example, agents may spread misleading and distracting information, multiple agents may compete for unshareable resources simultaneously, agents may unwittingly undo the results of each others activities and the same actions may be carried out redundantly. Also the dynamics of such systems can become extremely complex, giving rise to nonlinear oscillations and chaos (Huberman and Hogg, 1988). In such cases the coordination process becomes correspondingly more difficult as well as more important.[1]

To develop better and more integrated models of coordination, and hence improve the efficiency and utility of DAI systems, it is necessary to obtain a deeper understanding of the fundamental concepts which underpin agent interactions (see Chapters 2 and 5). The first step in this analysis is to determine the perspective from which coordination should be described. When viewing agents from a purely behavioristic (external) perspective, it is, in general, impossible to determine whether they have coordinated their actions. Firstly, actions may be incoherent even if the agents tried to coordinate their behavior. This may occur, for instance, because their models of each other or of the environment are incorrect. For example, robot$_1$ may see robot$_2$ heading for exit$_2$ and, based on this observation and the subsequent deduction that it will use this exit, decide to use exit$_1$. However if robot$_2$ is heading toward exit$_2$ to pick up a particular item and actually intends to use exit$_1$ then there may be incoherent behavior (both agents attempting to use the same exit) although there was coordination. Second, even if there is coherent action, it may not be as a consequence of coordination. For example imagine a group of people are sitting in a park (Searle, 1990). As a result of a sudden downpour all of them run to a tree in the middle of the park because it is the only available source of shelter. This is uncoordinated behavior because each person has the intention of stopping themselves from becoming wet and even if they are aware of what others are doing and what their goals are, it does not affect their action. This contrasts with the situation in which the people are dancers and the choreography calls for them to converge on a common point (the tree). In this case the individuals are performing exactly the same actions as before, but it is coordinated behavior because they each have the aim of meeting at the central point as a consequence of the overall aim of executing the dance. For these two reasons, the coordination process is best studied by examining the internal structure of the individual agents (i.e., the agents' beliefs, desires, preferences, intentions, and so on).

---

[1]Similar experiences have also been noted in organizational science: the greater the task uncertainty, the greater the amount of information which must be processed among decision makers during task execution in order to achieve a given level of performance (Galbraith, 1973).

Having decided upon a perspective, the next decisions concern the model that will be used to describe the problem and the structures that will be used to describe the agents. Here a distributed goal search formalism is used to characterize DAI systems (Section 3) and the key agent structures are *commitment* and *convention* (Section 4). This model of coordination is founded upon the *Centrality of Commitments and Conventions Hypothesis*, which states that *all coordination mechanisms can ultimately be reduced to commitments and their associated (social) conventions*. Commitments are viewed as pledges to undertake a specified course of action, while conventions provide a means of monitoring commitments in changing circumstances. The former provide a degree of predictability so that agents can take the (future) activities of others into consideration when dealing with interagent dependencies, global constraints or resource utilization conflicts. The latter provide the flexibility which cooperating agents need if they are to cope with being situated in dynamic environments. To operate effectively when the external world and their own beliefs are constantly changing, agents must possess a mechanism for evaluating whether existing commitments are still valid. Conventions provide this mechanism: defining the conditions under which commitments should be reassessed and specifying the associated actions which should be undertaken in such situations. Finally, Section 5 investigates three prominent coordination techniques (organizational structuring, meta-level information exchange and multiagent planning) and shows how they can all be reformulated in terms of commitments and conventions, thus providing further evidence for the main claim of this chapter.

3 MODELING DAI SYSTEMS AS A DISTRIBUTED GOAL SEARCH PROBLEM

Several authors have recently characterized DAI as a form of distributed goal search with multiple loci of control (Durfee and Montgomery, 1991; Gasser, 1992; Jennings, 1993; Lesser, 1991). Adopting Lesser's basic formalism, the actions of Agent$_1$ and Agent$_2$ in solving goals G_0^1 and G_0^2 respectively can be expressed as a classical AND/OR goal structure search[2] (Figure 6.1). The classical graph structure has been augmented to include a representation of the interdependencies between the goals and to indicate the resources needed to solve the primitive goals (leaf nodes). Interdependencies can exist between high-level sibling goals, such as G_1^1 and G_2^1, or they can be more distant in the goal structure (e.g., between $G_{1,1}^1$ and $G_{p,2}^2$). In the latter case, G_1^1 and G_p^2 become interacting goals if $G_{1,1}^1$ is used to solve G_1^1. Indirect dependencies exist between goals through shared resources (e.g., $G_{m,1,2}^1$ and $G_{p,2,2}^2$ through re-

---

[2]Figure 6.1 represents a typical multiagent situation in which each individual has its own goals, but it must interact with others to achieve them. In contrast, a distributed problem-solving system would have a single root node corresponding to the common objective.

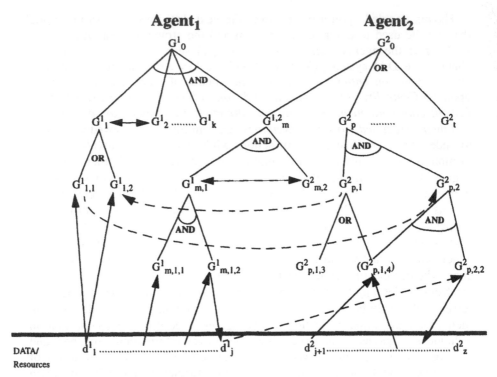

Figure 6.1 *A distributed goal search tree involving Agent₁ and Agent₂. The dotted arrows indicate interdependencies between goals and data in different agents, solid arrows dependencies within an agent. The superscripts associated with goals and data indicate the agent which contains them (Jennings, 1993).*

source d_j^1). Resource dependencies can be removed simply by providing more of the resource in question; dependencies between goals, on the other hand, cannot be circumvented as they are a logical consequence of the community's environment. In all other aspects, the two types of dependency are identical.

Interdependencies can be classified along two orthogonal dimensions: whether they are weak or strong, and whether they are unidirectional or bidirectional. *Strong dependencies* must be satisfied if the dependent goal is to succeed; *weak dependencies* facilitate or constrain problem solving but need not be fulfilled for the dependent goal to succeed. An example of a strong dependency is where the output of a goal (G) is a mandatory input (I) for the dependent goal (DG) and where G is the only source of I in the community. A weak dependency exists if there is more than one source for I or if I is an optional input for *DG*. A *unidirectional* dependency (written $G_{1,1}^1 \rightarrow G_{p,2}^2$) means that agent₂'s goal $G_{p,2}$ is dependent (either strongly or weakly) on agent₁'s goal $G_{1,1}$, but $G_{1,1}^1$ is unaffected by $G_{p,2}^2$; with *bidirectional* dependencies (written $G_{m,1}^1 \leftrightarrow G_{m,2}^2$) the goals of both agents are affected. The provision of information I by goal G for DG is an example of a unidirectional dependency

$(G \rightarrow DG)$; a bidirectional dependence occurs, for example, when two goals need to be performed simultaneously.

The nature of the interagent dependencies is the critical determinant of the type of coordination which will take place. For example, if Agent$_1$ knows that $G^2_{p,2,2}$ requires resource d^1_j before it can start (strong dependency, unidirectional), then it may decide to execute $G^1_{m,1,2}$ (to produce the necessary resource) before $G^1_{m,1,1}$ if there is no other information distinguishing between these two alternatives. Second, the relationship between $G^1_{m,1}$ and $G^2_{m,2}$ may stipulate that both actions need to be performed simultaneously (strong dependency, bidirectional) in which case the two agents need to reach an agreement about the respective execution times. Finally, if Agent$_1$ chose $G^1_{1,1}$ as a means of satisfying G^1_1 the result of this task may provide valuable information (weak dependency, unidirectional) which Agent$_2$ could use when solving $G^2_{p,2}$ (e.g., it may provide a partial result which enables $G^2_{p,2}$ to be significantly shorter). Knowing this, Agent$_1$ will invoke an information-sharing form of cooperation to supply Agent$_2$ with the necessary result when it becomes available.

It was necessary to extend Lesser's graph formalism to allow joint goals (e.g., $G^{1,2}_m$) because joint goals are the basis of joint action (i.e., there can be no joint action unless there is first a joint goal) (see also Chapter 18). Joint actions are a sophisticated form of cooperation in which a team of agents decide to pursue a common goal in a cooperative manner (this contrasts with simpler forms of cooperation such as asking an agent to perform a single task or spontaneously volunteering relevant information to interested acquaintances). This form of interaction can be characterized as having the following properties: (i) the team members are mutually responsive to one another; (ii) the team members have a joint commitment to the joint activity; and (iii) the team members are committed to be mutually supportive of one another during the pursuit of their joint objective (Bratman, 1992). Joint goals differ from individual goals in that they are not directly associated with actions. For this reason, they must be mapped onto individual goals as only individual agents have the ability to act (perform domain-level tasks). However joint goals can be in the mind of each individual which is acting as part of the collective, implying that everything necessary for team behavior can be possessed by individual agents, even though the aim makes reference to the collective. Thus the joint goal $G^{1,2}_m$ is internalized within Agent$_1$ and Agent$_2$ and results in Agent$_1$ performing $G^1_{m,1}$ and Agent$_2$ performing $G^2_{m,2}$.

Lesser (1991) makes the following general observations about the graph formalism. The entire goal structure need not be fully elaborated in order for problem solving to begin, it may be constructed as problem-solving progresses. Developing the graph can be a complex social activity involving negotiation, persuasion, and the resolution of conflicts or it may be undertaken centrally by one agent. Construction can involve a top-down elaboration based on higher-level goals, a bottom-up process driven by the data, or a mixture of the two. Finally, the formalism says nothing about whether the structure is statically defined or evolves dynamically from a composite view of the current, local goal structures of the individual agents.

Formulating a multiagent system in this manner allows the activities which may require coordination to be clearly identified. Such activities include (i) defining the goal graph (including identification and classification of interdependencies); (ii) assigning particular regions of the graph to appropriate agents; (iii) controlling decisions about which areas of the graph to explore; (iv) traversing the goal structure; and (v) ensuring that successful traversal of the search space is reported. Some of these activities may be collaborative and some may be carried out by an individual acting in isolation. Determining the approach adopted for each of the various phases is a matter of system design. It will depend upon the nature of the domain (e.g., in applications in which agents have distinct expertise, assignment of goals simply becomes a matter of identifying the individual capable of performing the activity), the type of agents included in the community (e.g., with autonomous agents, the global search space is given by the union of the local search spaces and each agent works on its own local goals), and the desired solution characteristics (e.g., to increase the likelihood of an important result being produced, the same area of the search space may be redundantly assigned to multiple agents, whereas if the desire is to optimize agent usage then such an arrangement is inefficient). This chapter concentrates on the problems of deciding which areas of the graph to explore, actually executing the goal structure and ensuring that successful traversal of the goal graph is reported.

4 THE COMMITMENT AND CONVENTION MODEL OF COORDINATION

This section describes the process of coordination in terms of the distributed goal graph of the previous section and shows that commitments and conventions are the key mechanisms controlling this activity. This section also argues for the Centrality of Commitments and Conventions Hypothesis which states that "all coordination mechanisms can ultimately be reduced to commitments and their associated conventions" (Jennings, 1993).

4.1 Detailing Commitments and Conventions

This subsection provides a more precise characterisation of the properties of commitments, joint commitments, conventions, and social conventions before Section 4.2 shows how they are the key to the coordination process. See also the discussion in Chapters 1, 2, 5, 18, and 20 on various aspects of intention and commitments.

Commitments. Commitments can be seen to have a number of important properties (Becker, 1960; Bond, 1989; Bratman, 1987; Dennett, 1987; Fikes, 1982; Searle, 1983). Agents can make pledges about both actions and beliefs, and these pledges can either be about the future or the past. Thus agent A can commit itself to play cricket tomorrow (object of commitment = action, time = future) and agent B can commit itself to believe a particular version of events about the reasons for the start of World War I (object of commitment = belief, time = past). For the purposes of coordination, however, the most important commitments are related to present and future beliefs and actions. No fundamental differences between pledges which are internalized within an agent (e.g., I will lose 12 pounds in weight) and pledges which are made to a second party (e.g., I will fix your car for you) are assumed. Commitments may be conditional. For example, A will play cricket tomorrow if the weather is sunny. Finally, a pledge to undertake an activity involves an associated commitment about the resources required to carry out that action. If A pledges to play cricket tomorrow, then it is also devoting its resources of time and energy to this activity.

If an agent commits itself to perform a particular action then, provided that its circumstances do not change, it will endeavor to honor that pledge. This obligation constrains an agent's subsequent decisions about undertaking fresh activities since it knows that sufficient resources must be reserved to honor its existing commitments. If an agent had infinite resources which could be freely allocated to any permutation of its commitments then there would be no such restrictions. However, as most resources are finite, and constraints are often imposed by the environment, an agent is limited in the number and type of commitments it can make. For this reason, an agent's commitments should, as far as it is aware, be both internally consistent and consistent with its beliefs.

Commitments can be made at many different levels and have correspondingly different time horizons. When Agent$_1$ pledges to perform G_0^1 this will invariably be a high-level objective (e.g., diagnose faults in an electricity network) to which it will probably remain committed for some considerable amount of time. The leaf nodes, on the other hand, will involve fairly specific courses of action (e.g., see if there is a fault in low-voltage line$_1$) and will have a correspondingly shorter duration.

Generally, the greater the degree of accuracy to which an agent knows its acquaintances' commitments, the more detailed its predictions can be and so the more coherently the community will behave. However it is not always desirable to transmit all of the low-level details about commitments. Agents should communicate at a sufficiently detailed level to promote satisfactory coordination, but at a sufficiently abstract level to ensure agents retain a degree of flexibility in achieving their objectives in an uncertain environment. For example, knowing that Agent$_2$ is committed to G_0^2, gives no indication of whether $G_{p,1}^2$ will be performed. However knowing that Agent$_2$ is committed to G_p^2 means that it is possible to predict that $G_{p,1}^2$ will indeed be performed and that Agent$_1$ can delay its processing of $G_{1,2}^1$ to benefit from the weak, unidirectional dependence. Even if Agent$_2$ communicated a more detailed description of its commitments, for instance that it will perform $G_{p,1,3}^2$, this information will be of no additional benefit to Agent$_1$ since it is not dependent on how $G_{p,1}^2$ is achieved. Not sending details of how $G_{p,1}^2$ will be achieved also leaves Agent$_2$ unconstrained as to whether it will use $G_{p,1,3}^2$ or $G_{p,1,4}^2$.

Joint Commitments. When agents decide to pursue a joint action (see Chapters 2, 18, and 20), they must jointly commit themselves to a joint goal which will bring about the desired state of affairs (Cohen and Levesque, 1991; Grosz and Sidner, 1990; Jennings, 1992; Kinny et al., 1992; Rao et al., 1992; Searle, 1990; Tuomela and Miller, 1988). This joint commitment has all the aforementioned properties of individual commitment, but it has the additional constraint that it involves more than one agent.[3] This means the overall state of the joint commitment is distributed. (In contrast, with individual commitments the agent which has made the pledge is aware of its exact status as it forms part of its internal state.) So, for example, the state of the joint commitment to the joint goal $G_m^{1,2}$ is distributed between Agent$_1$ in its processing of $G_{m,1}^1$ and Agent$_2$ in its processing of $G_{m,2}^2$. Ideally all team members should have access to a shared mental state related to the joint commitment as this would ensure that they all have the same experiences and beliefs simultaneously. In such cases there would be no divergence among the group's members. However since joint actions are undertaken by individuals, and not the team *en masse*, it is the individuals which have first exposure to events related to the joint commitment. Thus a shared mental state is impossible, unless all the agents possess a single common structure which records all of their beliefs about the joint commitment (i.e., agents cannot have any local or private beliefs about the joint action). For example in a team search, if one agent satisfies the group's objective by finding the target item, then at that precise instant in time it is the only one which knows that the joint commitment has been fulfilled. This agent may subsequently inform the others of its achievements, meaning they all share a common perspective once more; however, in the meantime, the cooperating agents have diverged in their beliefs about the joint commitment.

Conventions. An agent should honor its commitments provided that its circumstances do not change. However, in the majority of realistic scenarios agents are situated in time-varying and unpredictable contexts—the external world may change, the agent may become aware of new information, another agent may attempt to interact with it, and so on (Jennings, 1995). Therefore in many cases an agent's beliefs and desires will change between the making of a commitment and the associated intention actually being performed. In fact, the longer the time between these two events, the greater the likelihood of a change occurring. In some instances these changes will leave the agent's commitments unaffected, but in other cases commitments may need to be reviewed. For example, if agent A is informed that the first customer at a new garage opening tomorrow will receive a Ferrari, then it may indeed revise its commitments about playing cricket. Therefore commitments should be relatively stable over time, but they should not be irrevocable.

To operate successfully and intelligently, agents need general policies for governing the reconsideration of their commitments. These *conventions* de-

---

[3] A joint commitment involving one agent is equivalent to an individual commitment.

scribe circumstances under which an agent should reconsider its commitments. They also indicate the appropriate course of action to retain, rectify, or abandon these commitments. An agent may have several different conventions at its disposal, although each of its commitments should be tracked using precisely one convention.

When specifying conventions a balance needs to be reached between constantly reconsidering all commitments (which will enable the agent to respond rapidly to changing circumstances, but will mean that it spends a significant percentage of its time reasoning about action rather than actually carrying out useful tasks) and never reconsidering commitments (which means agents spend most of their time acting, but what they are actually doing may not be particularly relevant in the light of subsequent changes). Kinny and Georgeff (1991) carried out a series of experiments in which different conventions were examined in environments exhibiting different rates of change. In all cases it was found that the "bold" agents (those which never reconsidered their commitments) performed better than the "normal" agents (those which are slightly more open to reconsideration) which were better than the "cautious" agents (those which were prone to reconsideration). However in rapidly changing and uncertain contexts, the utility of a relatively sophisticated convention is significantly increased. Indeed empirical evaluation has shown that in such circumstances conventions play a pivotal role in ensuring the community acts in a coherent manner (Jennings and Mamdani, 1992).

The lists of both the situations under which commitments should be reassessed and the actions which should be taken in such circumstances can be empty. So an agent can remain permanently committed to a goal even if it has been achieved or an agent can take no action as a result of changes in its circumstances. Figure 6.2 shows a convention based upon Cohen and Lev-

```
CONVENTION: Cohen and Levesque Model

REASONS FOR RE-ASSESSING COMMITMENT:
        • COMMITMENT SATISFIED
        • COMMITMENT UNATTAINABLE
        • MOTIVATION FOR COMMITMENT NO LONGER PRESENT

ACTIONS:

    R1:  IF   COMMITMENT SATISFIED OR
              COMMITMENT UNATTAINABLE OR
              MOTIVATION FOR COMMITMENT NO LONGER PRESENT
         THEN DROP COMMITMENT
```

Figure 6.2 *Sample convention.*

esque's (1990) model of individual rational behavior. It shows that an agent can renege upon a commitment if it believes that the commitment is satisfied or unattainable or if the motivation for the commitment is no longer present.

Social Conventions. Although conventions play an important role in DAI systems, they are essentially asocial constructs. They describe how an agent should monitor its commitments, but they do not specify how an agent should behave towards its fellow community members if it alters or modifies its commitments. For goals which are unrelated to other activities this stance is sufficient. However for goals which are interdependent, it is essential that the relevant acquaintances are informed of any substantial change which affects their processing, if the community is to act in a coherent manner. For this reason, agents need social conventions which specify how to behave with respect to the other community members when their commitments alter. Designing such conventions is a skillful activity. On the one hand it is important that relevant information pertaining to changes in commitment is disseminated at the earliest possible opportunity; on the other hand, agents should not broadcast information about their commitments each and every time they change because this will overburden the communication resources and needlessly distract the recipients. A sample social convention which reflects this trade-off is shown in Figure 6.3.

Ideally the participants should be mutually aware of the convention which governs their interaction. Such awareness is needed if the agents are to minimize the uncertainty in their collaboration and maximize the benefit of the joint

```
SOCIAL CONVENTION: Limited-Bandwidth

INVOKE WHEN:
            • LOCAL COMMITMENT DROPPED
            • LOCAL COMMITMENT SATISFIED
ACTIONS:

  R1:  IF LOCAL COMMITMENT SATISFIED
       THEN INFORM ALL RELATED COMMITMENTS

  R2:  IF LOCAL COMMITMENT DROPPED BECAUSE UNATTAINABLE OR MOTIVATION
              NOT PRESENT
       THEN INFORM ALL STRONGLY RELATED COMMITMENTS

  R3:  IF LOCAL COMMITMENT DROPPED BECAUSE UNATTAINABLE OR MOTIVATION
              NOT PRESENT
          AND COMMUNICATION RESOURCES NOT OVERBURDENED
       THEN INFORM ALL WEAKLY RELATED COMMITMENTS
```

Figure 6.3 Sample social convention.

action. Thus, for example, if $Agent_2$ must have resource d_j^1 to perform $G_{p,2,2}^2$, then it will invoke a task-sharing form of cooperation and ask $Agent_1$ to make this resource available. However, merely asking for d_j^1 to be produced is not sufficient because $Agent_2$ also wants to be informed when it is available. To ensure the necessary dissemination occurs, $Agent_2$ must request that the resource be produced using an appropriate social convention (e.g., that of Figure 6.3). Whether $Agent_1$ accepts this proposal will depend upon its personal preferences and the relative authority of the two agents. If the proposal is acceptable, or if $Agent_2$ can force $Agent_1$ to use it, then the convention will be adopted. If the proposal is unacceptable, then the two agents will have to enter a negotiation phase to decide upon an acceptable solution. Alternatively, rather than having to determine the social convention for each and every interdependent goal at run time, which will significantly slow down processing, the system designer may stipulate that when two agents interact they will always use a particular convention. He may even specify that the whole community must use a particular convention for all their joint actions.

The social conventions specified up to this point have all been concerned with interrelated individual goals. However, all joint actions must have an overarching joint goal and a corresponding joint commitment. This begs the question: how does the social convention for a joint commitment differ from the social convention of an individual commitment which is related to other goals? The answer to this question lies in the mutual support requirement of joint actions. The minimum form of mutual support that a team of cooperating agents should provide to one another is to share information about (i) the status of their commitment to the shared objective; (ii) the status of their commitment to the given team framework.[4] If an agent's beliefs about either of these issues change, then it is part of the intuitive semantics of joint commitments that all team members are informed. As many joint actions depend upon the participation of all their team members, a change of commitment by one participant can also jeopardize the whole group's efforts. Hence, if an agent comes to believe that a fellow team member is no longer jointly committed, it also needs to reassess its own position with respect to the joint action. These three basic assumptions are encoded in a convention which represents the minimum state of affairs for joint commitments (Figure 6.4). Thus, whereas any convention can be used for individual commitments (even for those which have related goals), joint commitments require each team member to adhere to the basic joint action convention. In some applications it may be desirable to have more sophisticated joint action conventions, but in every case they must still incorporate these fundamental ideals.

---

[4]This stipulation covers the situation in which an agent which is initially committed to the joint action decides to leave the team, but continues to pursue the joint objective in an individualistic manner. Detecting this situation is important because the agent which is no longer committed to the team framework will follow its own solution path, without considering its effects on those remaining in the original team.

```
┌─────────────────────────────────────────────────────────────────────┐
│  BASIC JOINT ACTION CONVENTION                                        │
│                                                                       │
│  INVOKE WHEN:                                                         │
│            • STATUS OF COMMITMENT TO JOINT GOAL CHANGES               │
│            • STATUS OF COMMITMENT TO ATTAINING JOINT ACTION IN        │
│                  PRESENT TEAM CONTEXT CHANGES                         │
│            • STATUS OF JOINT COMMITMENT OF A TEAM MEMBER CHANGES      │
│                                                                       │
│  ACTIONS:                                                            │
│                                                                       │
│     R1:    IF STATUS OF COMMITMENT TO JOINT ACTION CHANGES OR        │
│                  STATUS OF COMMITMENT TO PRESENT TEAM CONTEXT CHANGES │
│            THEN INFORM ALL OTHER TEAM MEMBERS OF CHANGE              │
│                                                                       │
│     R2:    IF STATUS OF JOINT COMMITMENT OF A TEAM MEMBER CHANGES    │
│            THEN DETERMINE WHETHER JOINT COMMITMENT STILL VIABLE      │
│                                                                       │
└─────────────────────────────────────────────────────────────────────┘
```

Figure 6.4   Basic joint action convention.

4.2   Commitments and Conventions: The Cornerstones of Coordination

Durfee et al. (1989) identify three major ingredients which must be present for successful coordination: (i) there must be structures which enable the agents to interact in predictable ways; (ii) there must be flexibility so that agents can operate in dynamic environments and can cope with their inherently partial and imprecise viewpoint of the community; and (iii) the agents must have sufficient knowledge and reasoning capabilities to exploit the available structure and the flexibility. The final component, which they fail to explicitly mention, is the necessity of structures to provide mutual support to the cooperating agents. In the remainder of this subsection it is shown that commitments provide the necessary structure for predictable interactions, conventions provide the flexibility needed to operate in dynamic environments, and social conventions provide the necessary degree of mutual support. Thus,

$$\text{Coordination} = \text{Commitments} + \text{conventions}$$
$$+ \text{ social conventions} + \text{local reasoning}$$

These assertions are demonstrated by examining the multifarious social interactions which occur as a consequence of the various types of goal relationships and goal interdependencies (see Chapters 2 and 18). For each distinct case the central role of commitments, conventions, and social conventions is highlighted.

Commitments in Goal-Subgoal Relationships.   If the goal being undertaken by a group of cooperating agents involves an AND relationship, then all commitments to the subgoals must be honored if the parent goal is to succeed. If just one agent reneges, then the other agents' activities are doomed in their present form. Therefore it is only the belief that others will honor their commitments that makes it rational for an agent to carry out its part. Without this confidence no agent would carry out its individual processing, since achievement of the subgoals in isolation is unlikely to bring it any benefits. Hence, AND goals cannot be achieved by cooperative problem solving without the notion of commitment.

If a goal is composed of a number of subgoals, organized in an OR relationship, and these are each assigned to different agents which all carry out their activities in parallel, then failure of one agent to fulfill its commitment will not jeopardize achievement of the parent goal. However if all the agents renege upon their obligations then the parent goal will not be achieved; thus the commitment of at least one agent must be guaranteed. If agents coordinate their activities more closely and arrange for only one of the alternate subgoals to be carried out at any one time (to avoid needless duplication), then commitment failure can have serious repercussions for the community's overall level of coherence. For example, if a team agrees that $Agent_1$ will carry out the subgoal which fulfills the parent goal G, then the remaining agents can continue with their processing and can make subsequent commitments based on the fact that G will indeed be achieved and that they do not have to expend resources toward this end. However if $Agent_1$ does not honor its pledge, then provided that G is still desired, one of the other agents will have to carry out some unexpected processing activity. This additional work may conflict with commitments which the agent has subsequently made and may result in it having to delay, or even abandon, some of them because additional resources are unexpectedly required to achieve G. Such delays may have a knock-on affect to other agents, causing the community to operate ineffectively and requiring it to undertake a significant amount of replanning.

Commitments in Goal-Dependency Relationships. Consider the situation in which $Agent_1$ and $Agent_2$ have the respective interrelated goals G_1^1 and G_1^2. If there is a strong bidirectional dependence then both agents must honor their commitments, otherwise neither of them will be able to achieve their objectives. If the relation is strong but unidirectional $(G_1^1 \rightarrow G_1^2)$, then failure of $Agent_1$ to honor its commitment means that $Agent_2$ will be unable to achieve G_1^2 and it will either have to find an alternative path for achieving the parent goal or abandon it completely.

With weak dependencies, the agents involved may still be able to proceed but this may be in a suboptimal manner. For example, an agent may have delayed processing an action on the premise that an acquaintance will provide it with sufficient information to significantly speed up its problem solving. If this information is no longer forthcoming, because the acquaintance changed its commitments, then the agent has wasted potentially useful processing time. As another example, an agent may select a certain path through the search space in the belief that information which will be provided through a weak dependency will make this path less expensive than its alternatives. But if the agent providing the information reneges upon its commitment and the information is not forthcoming, then the chosen path may be suboptimal.

If the relationship is bidirectional and one agent fails to fulfill its pledge, the agent which is still committed to its side of the bargain may be adversely affected since it chose to undertake the goal believing that it would be able to profit from the commitment of the other agent. In the unidirectional case $(G_1^1 \rightarrow G_1^2)$ if Agent$_1$ changes its mind, Agent$_2$'s processing of G_1^2 will be adversely affected for the reason described above.

In both the weak and the strong unidirectional cases, if Agent$_2$ drops its commitment to G_1^2 then this may have a detrimental effect on Agent$_1$. This is the case if Agent$_1$ chose G_1^1, even though it was locally suboptimal, because the net utility to the community of the performance of the pair $\{G_1^1, G_1^2\}$ while satisfying the specified relationship was higher than if Agent$_1$ chose an alternative to G_1^1 and Agent$_2$ chose G_1^2. However, the potential benefits of Agent$_1$'s sacrifice were not observed because Agent$_2$ failed to carry out its pledge about G_1^2.

Social Conventions in Goal-Subgoal Relationships. Social conventions report changes in commitments to dependent agents and are especially important when there is an AND relationship between a goal and its constituent subgoals. Without adequate information dissemination the other agents will remain committed to performing their subgoals even though they will not satisfy their original purpose of fulfilling the parent goal. This is also the case for OR relationships in which only one of the subgoals is active at any one time. Adherence to a suitable convention provides a secondary degree of confidence in joint actions—the group believes that each individual will do their best to perform their subpart, but if they are unable to keep their commitment then they must inform their fellow team members of their change in state.

Social Conventions in Goal-Dependency Relationships. In terms of interagent goal dependencies $(G_1^1 \rightarrow G_1^2)$, reports of changes in the status of commitments are essential if the relationship is strong and bidirectional, and if Agent$_1$ reneges on its goal and the relation is strong and unidirectional. In all other cases reports on changes in commitments are desirable in that they may enable the agent which is still committed to reassess its position. This may result in it choosing a different path through the graph, either because it is freed from the constraint of having to honor the relationship or because it can no longer benefit from the interaction with the agent which is no longer committed.

The Basic Joint Action Convention, Joint Commitments, and Joint Goals. With respect to joint actions, the most important feature of joint commitments and social conventions is that they enable individuals to make assumptions about the actions of other community members. They provide a degree of predictability to counteract the uncertainty caused by the distribution of control. So for the joint goal $G_m^{1,2}$, Agent$_2$ can carry out $G_{m,2}^2$ in the knowledge that Agent$_1$ is probably performing $G_{m,1}^1$ and that, if it is not, then it will at least be trying to inform it of this change (because of the basic joint action convention). Without this assurance there would be no point in Agent$_2$ even starting $G_{m,2}^2$ since it is only carrying out this activity to achieve the joint goal and the joint goal requires both subgoals to be fulfilled. Thus, each agent is only carrying out its respective action because it believes that the other is also doing its bit.

5 COMMON COORDINATION TECHNIQUES AND THEIR USE OF COMMITMENTS AND CONVENTIONS

In this section, three of the most common mechanisms for managing the coordination process in DAI systems are presented and analyzed. These include organizational structuring (Section 5.1), exchanging meta-level information (Section 5.2), and multiagent planning (Section 5.3). For each technique there is a brief statement about how it facilitates the coordination of behavior, what its main characteristics are and how it can be reformulated in terms of the Centrality of Commitments and Conventions Hypothesis.

5.1 Organizational Structures

In the context of DAI systems, an organizational structure can be viewed as a pattern of information and control relationships between individuals (Gasser, 1992) (see Chapters 1, 2, and 18 for more detailed discussions of these points). These control relationships, be they hierarchical, heterarchical or flat, are responsible for designating the relative authority of the agents and for shaping the types of social interaction which can occur. For example, when building a community of agents for diagnosing faults in an electricity network (Cockburn and Jennings, this volume), the system designer may specify a functional organization (Agent$_1$ works on high-voltage faults, while Agent$_2$ works at the low-voltage level) or a spatial organization (Agent$_1$ deals with all types of faults in region$_1$, Agent$_2$ with all types of faults in region$_2$). Concentrating on the spatial distribution, and assuming the interest areas of the agents overlap, the authority relationships determine how redundances are avoided. In a hierarchy, high-level nodes inform the lower-level ones of the activities they are to pursue; whereas in a flat structure this process is only achievable through direct negotiation between the parties concerned.

The relationships specified by the organizational structures give general, long-term information about the agents and the community as a whole. They aid the coordination process by specifying which actions an individual will undertake and by providing a means of dividing up the search space without having to go into detail about the particular subtrees. Other authors have followed this basic approach using different terminology. Singh (1990) employs the notion of "strategies" to provide an abstract specification of the behavior of an agent or a group and Werner (1989) uses "roles" for describing expectations about individual behavior. Shoham and Tennenholtz (1992) propose a more detailed organizational form which they term a "social law." With this approach, the society adopts a set of laws (e.g., road traffic rules) which specify how individuals should behave. Each programmer is then committed to obeying these laws when building his individual agent. The design process is simplified because it can be assumed that all the other agents will adhere to the specified law.

As a specific illustration of this approach consider the distributed vehicle monitoring testbed (see Chapter 3) which simulates a spatially organized community of agents performing a distributed interpretation to track vehicles moving among them. Each agent decides which areas of the search space to explore based upon its current local view and its organizational knowledge of its role in the community. In this context, coordination consists of two concurrent activities: the construction and maintenance of a communitywide organizational structure, and the continuous elaboration of this structure into precise activities using the local knowledge and control capabilities of each agent. The organization itself is specified as a set of "interest areas" and as a set of priority ratings. The former indicate what, when, and to whom information should be sent; the latter indicate how to evaluate the importance of processing different types of goals. The authority relationships indicate the relative priorities which should be attached to processing externally generated goals versus local goals.

When an agent undertakes a particular role within an organization, it is, in fact, making a high-level commitment about the types of activity it will pursue. For instance, in the electricity management scenario, if Agent$_1$ undertakes the role of diagnosing high-voltage faults, other agents will expect it to undertake work in this area. They will make subsequent decisions in their local problem solving based on the assumption that Agent$_1$ will indeed be dealing with all the faults on the high-voltage network.

Although they are relatively long-term structures, it has been shown that different organizations are appropriate for different problem situations and performance requirements (Malone, 1987 and Chapter 19). Hence, as a situation evolves, the community may need to periodically reassess its structure to determine whether it is still appropriate or whether a rearrangement would be beneficial. See the work of Ishida et al. (1990) for an illustration of the dynamic reorganization of a group of cooperating agents in response to changes in the environment. In the electricity management scenario, for example, the community may decide that it is best to replace the agent carrying out high-voltage diagnosis with several spatially distributed agents so that the load and the reliance upon any one individual is reduced. This evaluation corresponds to a convention for the organizational structure.

5.2 Meta-Level Information Exchange

Meta-level information exchange involves agents sending each other control-level information about their current priorities and focus (Gasser, 1992). For example, in the functionally distributed electricity management scenario described in the previous subsection, $agent_1$, which is working on the low-voltage network, may indicate that it believes the most important fault is in $region_1$. Upon receiving this information, $agent_2$, which is working on the high-voltage network, may also decide to concentrate its efforts on this region to determine whether the fault being experienced on the low-voltage network is in fact a manifestation of a problem with the high-voltage system (e.g., no supply is getting through).

Durfee (this volume) has developed a meta-level information exchange mechanism, called partial global planning, in which agents build and share local plans as a means of identifying potential improvements to coordination (see Chapter 8). These partial global plans (PGPs) are exchanged by agents as a means of building representations of their acquaintances' activities. They indicate which goals will be pursued and in what order, what results will be achieved and how long each goal is likely to take. Individual community members then use a model of themselves and a representation of their acquaintances to identify when agents have PGPs whose objectives are part of some larger community effort. If such complementary activities are detected, the related PGPs are combined into a single, larger PGP which provides a more complete view of the group's activities. Agents can then revise their other PGPs to reflect the new position. As a specific example, a PGP could indicate that the outcome of one agent's task provides useful predictive information for an acquaintance. This expectation, together with the accompanying transmission of the information, would then be explicitly represented in the PGP, resulting in a plan to use information resources more effectively. As a second example, an agent may survey its current view of communitywide PGPs and identify acquaintances which are being under utilized, while there are others which are overburdened. By modifying the relevant PGPs, the agent could propose how the community could transfer subproblems so as to work better as a team.

Meta-level information exchange is a medium-term source of knowledge about an agent's commitments, shorter than organization structures but longer than multiagent planning approaches (Section 5.3). It enhances coordination only to the degree to which it is accurate. Indeed inaccurate information may be more detrimental than no information at all. Again it can be seen that once an agent indicates it will work in a particular region of the search space, it is important to honor that commitment. Failure to do so will result in misleading information being spread around the network and incoherent problem solving. However, as with the other approaches, commitments should not be irrevocable; some form of convention is needed for monitoring their progression. With the PGP approach, for example, agents often altered their local plans, either because new tasks arrived or because actions took longer than expected, and so their commitments needed to be updated. However if agents informed each other of every minor change in their commitments, it could cause a chain reaction which spreads throughout the system. Therefore, agents adopted an implicit convention in which they informed their acquaintances only when the deviations were deemed significant.

5.3 Multiagent Planning

With the multi-agent planning approach to coordination, agents usually form a plan which specifies all their future actions and interactions with respect to achieving a particular objective (see Chapter 8). It details, before execution commences, the areas of the search space that will be traversed and the route each agent should take at each decision point in the activity.[5] Multiagent plans are typically built to avoid inconsistent or conflicting actions, particularly with respect to the consumption of scarce resources.

Multiagent planning differs from organizational structuring and meta-level information exchange in terms of the level of detail to which it specifies every agent's activities. With this approach, agents know in advance exactly what actions they will take, what actions their acquaintances will take and what interactions will occur. By requiring such a complete specification of behavior, the plans can only realistically have a short time horizon because of problems with the unpredictability and dynamicity of events in the environment. As plan construction has to take into account all the possible choice points the agent would have reached, without the benefit of constraining information from actual execution, this approach often requires substantially more computational and communication resource than the other two mechanisms.

There are two basic approaches to multiagent planning: centralized and distributed. Georgeff (1983) built a system in which the plans of individual agents were developed separately and then sent to a central coordinator which analyzed them to identify potential interactions. The coordinator then identified those interactions which had the potential to cause conflicts and grouped the sequences of unsafe actions to create critical regions. Finally, communication primitives were inserted into the individual plans so that the agents synchronized their activities appropriately. Cammarata et al. (1983) also devised a centralised multiagent planning system (for the air traffic control domain). In their system, each aircraft (agent) sends the coordinator information about its intended actions. The coordinator then builds a plan which specifies all of the agents' actions, including the actions that they, or some other node, should take to avoid collisions. With distributed multiagent planning, the plan is developed by several agents. This means there may be no individual with a view

---

[5]Partial global planning differs from multiagent planning in that the former does not require the agents to reach mutual agreements about all of their activities before they start acting. Indeed because the partial plans can change so fluidly and because it takes time to propagate changes such agreements may never be attained.

of the entire community's activities, and hence detecting and resolving undesirable interactions become significantly more difficult. Corkill (1979) devised a distributed hierarchical planner based on NOAH (Sacerdoti, 1977) where agents represent each other using MODEL nodes and plan execution is coordinated by using explicit synchronization primitives. Rosenschein and Genesereth (1985) used a logic-based approach to study how agents with a common goal, but different local knowledge, could exchange information to converge on identical plans.

Once a plan has been devised, the agents involved are committed to performing the specified actions. If they believed that their acquaintances are unlikely to keep their pledges, then they would not enter the planning phase in the first place because it is such a resource-consuming activity. Commitments are, therefore, the foundation of this approach. There is no latitude for deviation from the agreed course of action because it may introduce resource conflicts or other undesirable side effects which would impair the community's performance. However, the situation may change so radically between generation and execution that if the plan was performed the benefit would be negligible or even negative. In this case it is worth entering a replanning phase to produce a more profitable alternative (Kambhampati and Hendler, 1992; Pollack, 1992). Hence, there is a need for conventions to determine when replanning is necessary and whether the existing plan should be reused or whether a fresh plan should be devised.

6 CONCLUSIONS

This chapter has argued that the process of coordination is built upon four main structures: commitments, conventions, social conventions, and local reasoning capabilities. Furthermore it has hypothesised that *all* coordination mechanisms can be expressed using these concepts; to demonstrate this point three of the most common coordination techniques have been reformulated in these terms.

Having posited the key structures it is important that the model is refined in order to more precisely discriminate between a number of different types of social interaction. This refinement should be undertaken by two parallel strands of work: (i) by building DAI applications which explicitly use these concepts (see Huang et al., 1994, for an illustration from the domain of distributed patient care); and (ii) by producing more precise models of some of the key concepts (see Wooldridge and Jennings (1994) for a first formulation of commitments and conventions using a quantified multimodal logic). This subsequent work should aim to address the following issues:

- Produce a finer grain classification of the types of goal interdependency
- Provide a methodology for designing appropriate conventions and social conventions

- Characterize the process by which social conventions are agreed
- Provide mechanisms which support robust coordination in the face of uncertainty about the social convention which is in operation during a given interaction
- Provide empirical evidence of the effectiveness of different conventions in various environmental and domain circumstances
- Provide a means of characterizing the local reasoning which is required to support coordinated behavior

ACKNOWLEDGMENTS

This is a refined and updated version of the paper which appeared in *The Knowledge Engineering Review*.

REFERENCES

Becker, H. S. (1960). Notes on the concept of commitment. *Am. J. Sociol.* **66**(1), 32–40.

Bond, A. H. (1989). Commitment: Some DAI insights from symbolic interactionist society. *Proc. Int. Workshop Distributed Artif. Intell.*, *9th*, Bellevue, WA, pp. 239–261.

Bratman, M. E. (1987). *Intention, Plans and Practical Reason*. Harvard Univ. Press, Cambridge, MA.

Bratman, M. E. (1992). Shared cooperative activity. *Philos. Rev.* **101**(2), 327–341.

Cammarata, S., McArthur, D., and Steeb, R. (1983). Strategies of cooperation in distributed problem solving. *Proc. Int. J. Conf. Artif. Intell.*, *8th*, Karlsruhe, Germany, *1983*, pp. 767–770.

Clearwater, S. H., Huberman, B. A., and Hogg, T. (1991). Cooperative solution of constraint satisfaction problems. *Science* **254**, 1181–1184.

Cohen, P. R., and Levesque, H. J. (1990). Intention is choice with commitment. *Artif. Intell.* **42**, 213–261.

Cohen, P. R., and Levesque, H. J. (1991). Teamwork. *Noûs* **25**(4), 487–512.

Corkill, D. D. (1979). Hierarchical planning in a distributed environment. *Proc. Int. J. Conf. Artif. Intell.*, *6th*, Cambridge, MA, *1979*, pp. 168–175.

Corkill, D. D., and Lesser, V. R. (1983) The use of meta-level control for coordination in a distributed problem solving network. *Proc. Int. J. Conf. Artif. Intell.*, *8th*, Karlsruhe, Germany, *1983*, pp. 748–756.

Dennett, D. C. (1987). *The Intentional Stance*. MIT Press, Cambridge, MA.

Durfee, E. H., and Montgomery, T. A. (1991). Coordination as distributed search in a hierarchical behaviour space. *IEEE Trans. Syst., Man Cybernet.* **SMC-21**, 1363–1378.

Durfee, E. H., Lesser, V. R., and Corkill, D. D. (1987). Coherent cooperation among communicating problem solvers. *IEEE Trans. Comput.* **36**, 1275–1291.

Durfee, E. H., Lesser, V. R., and Corkill, D. D. (1989). Trends in cooperative distributed problem solving. *IEEE Trans. Knowl. Data Eng.* **1**(1), 63–83.

Fikes, R. E. (1982). A commitment-based framework for describing informal cooperative work. *Cognit. Sci.* **6**, 331–347.

Galbraith, J. (1973). *Designing Complex Organizations.* Addison-Wesley, Reading, MA.

Gasser, L. (1992). DAI approaches to coordination. In *Distributed Artificial Intelligence: Theory and Praxis* (N. M. Avouris and L. Gasser, eds.), pp. 31–51. Kluwer Academic Publishers, Boston.

Georgeff, M. P. (1983). Communication and action in multi-agent planning. *Proc. Nat. Conf. Artif. Intell., 3rd,* Washington, DC, pp. 125–129.

Gerson, E. M. (1976). On quality of life. *Am. Sociol. Rev.* **41**, 793–806.

Grosz, B. J., and Sidner, C. L. (1990). Plans for discourse. In *Intentions in Communication* (P. R. Cohen, J. Morgan, and M. E. Pollack, eds.), pp. 417–444. MIT Press, Cambridge, MA.

Huang, J., Jennings, N. R., and Fox, J. (1994). Cooperation in distributed medical care. *Proc. Int. Conf. Coop. Inf. Syst.,* Toronto, Canada, pp. 255–263.

Huberman, B. A., and Hogg, T. (1988). The behaviour of computational ecologies. In *The Ecology of Computation* (B. A. Huberman, ed.), pp. 77–115. North-Holland Publ., Amsterdam.

Ishida, T., Yokoo, M., and Gasser, L. (1990). An organisational approach to adaptive production systems. *Proc. Nat. Conf. Artif. Intell., 8th,* Boston, pp. 52–58.

Jennings, N. R. (1992). Towards a cooperation knowledge level for collaborative problem solving. *Proc. Eur. Conf. Artif. Intell, 10th,* Vienna, Austria, pp. 224–228.

Jennings, N. R. (1993). Commitments and conventions: The foundation of coordination in multi-agent systems. *Knowl. Eng. Rev.* **8**(3), 223–250.

Jennings, N. R. (1995). Controlling cooperative problem solving in industrial multi-agent systems using joint intentions. *Artif. Intell.* **75**(2), 195–240.

Jennings, N. R., and Mamdani, E. H. (1992). Using joint responsibility to coordinate collaborative problem solving in dynamic environments. *Proc. Nat. Conf. Artif. Intell., 10th,* San Jose, CA, pp. 269–275.

Kambhampati, S., and Hendler, J. A. (1992). A validation structure based theory of plan modification and reuse. *Artif. Intell.* **55**, 193–258.

Kinney, D. N., and Georgeff, M. P. (1991). Commitment and effectiveness of situated agents. *Proc. Int. Jt. Conf. Artif. Intell., 12th,* Sydney, Australia, pp. 82–88.

Kinny, D. N., Ljungberg, M., Rao, A., Sonenberg, E., Tidhar, G., and Werner, E. (1992). Planned team activity. *Proc. Eur. Workshop Model. Auton. Agents Multi-Agent World, 4th,* Rome, Italy.

Kornfield, W. A., and Hewitt, C. E. (1981). The scientific community metaphor. *IEEE Trans. Syst., Man Cybernet.* **11**(1), 24–33.

Lesser, V. R. (1991). A retrospective view of FA/C distributed problem solving. *IEEE Trans. Syst. Man and Cybern.* **21**, 1347–1363.

Lesser, V. R., and Corkill, D. D. (1987). Distributed problem solving. In *Encyclopedia of Artificial Intelligence* (S. C. Shapiro, ed.), pp. 245–251. Wiley, New York.

Malone, T. W. (1987). Modelling coordination in organizations and markets. *Manage. Sci.* **33**, 1317–1332.

Pollack, M. E. (1992). The uses of plans. *Artif. Intell.* **57**, 43–68.

Rao, A. S., Georgeff, M. P., and Sonenberg, E. A. (1992). Social plans: A preliminary report. In *Decentralized Artificial Intelligence 3* (E. Werner and Y. Demazeau, eds.), pp. 57–76. Elsevier/North-Holland Amsterdam.

Rosenschein, J. S., and Genesereth, M. R. (1985). Deals among rational agents. *Proc. Int. J. Conf. Artif. Intell.*, *9th*, Los Angeles, *1985*, pp. 91–99.

Sacerdoti, E. D. (1977). *A Structure for Plans and Behaviour*. Elsevier, Amsterdam.

Searle, J. R. (1983). *Intentionality: An Essay in the Philosophy of Mind*. Cambridge Univ. Press, Cambridge, UK.

Searle, J. R. (1990). Collective intentions and actions. In *Intentions in Communication* (P. R. Cohen, J. Morgan, and M. E. Pollack, eds.), pp. 401–416. MIT Press, Cambridge, MA.

Shoham, Y., and Tennenholtz, M. (1992). On the synthesis of useful social laws for artificial agent societies. *Proc. Nat. Conf. Artif. Intell.*, *10th*, San Jose, pp. 276–281.

Singh, M. P. (1990). Group intentions. *Proc. Workshop Distributed Artif. Intell.*, *10th*, Bandera, TX, MCC Tech. Rep. ACT-AI-355-90.

Tuomela, R., and Miller, K. (1988). We-intentions. *Philos. Stud.* **53**, 367–389.

Werner, E. (1989). Cooperating agents: A unified theory of communication and social structure. In *Distributed Artificial Intelligence* (L. Gasser and M. N. Huhs, eds.), Vol. 2, pp. 3–36. Morgan Kaufmann, Los Altos, CA/Pilman, London.

Wooldridge, M. J., and Jennings, N. R. (1994). Formalising the cooperative problem solving process. *Proc. 13th Int. Distributed Art. Int. Workshop*, Seattle, WA, pp. 403–417.

CHAPTER 7 ⸻⸻⸻⸻⸻⸻⸻

Negotiation Principles

H. JÜRGEN MÜLLER

1 INTRODUCTION

Negotiation is one of the notions most often stressed in DAI (see Chapter 1). The general aims of negotiation are *modification* of local agent plans, in the case of negative (harmful) interactions, and *identification* of situations where potential interactions are possible. Modification and identification situations trigger the process of negotiation in the sense that agents communicate in a certain way to reach a common decision. Negotiation is used more specifically for task and resource allocation, the recognition of conflicts, the resolution of goal disparities, the determination of organizational structure, and hence for the coherence of the agent society. Though negotiation is highly important for the modeling of multiagent systems, there is no clear and common definition of what negotiation is.

The common idea in all DAI contributions to negotiation is that agents use negotiation for conflict resolution and coordination. There were investigations to negotiation as a *language* problem, where syntax and semantics of the "messages" are analyzed. Others explored the *process* of negotiation and another group considered the *behavioral* aspects of the negotiators. Since the points of view are so different, it is clear why there is no common definition of negotiation, nor a formal theory. And it is obvious, too, that we will not find *the* common negotiation theory on the following pages.

The aim of this chapter is to clarify the different views, to fix the various perspectives and to work out principles of negotiation, which will be presented

Foundations of Distributed Artificial Intelligence, Edited by G. M. P. O'Hare and N. R. Jennings. ISBN 0-471-00675-0 © 1996 John Wiley & Sons, Inc.

as categories and classes. The language category handles the interagent part of negotiation, the decision category deals with the intra-agent part of negotiation, and the process category is concerned with the global negotiation behavior of the individual agent and the negotiating society.

For each category a detailed example and a brief discussion of the literature will be given. Eventually, literature on the different aspects of negotiation is classified according to the categories and classes.

2 FIRST DEFINITIONS

Let us start with the work of Davis and Smith (Smith and Davis, 1980; Smith, 1988) on the contract net protocol (CNP). They viewed negotiation as an ''organizing principle'' used to effectively match tasks and problems solvers. They wrote:

> By negotiation, we mean a discussion in which the interested parties exchange information and come to an agreement. For our purposes negotiation has three important components: (a) there is a two-way exchange of information, (b) each party to the negotiation evaluates the information from its own perspective, (c) final agreement is achieved by mutual selection.

Their definition contains two main elements for negotiation, namely communication [see (a)] and decision making [(b) and (c)]. They worked out a fixed protocol (the CNP) for the information exchange, which works essentially as follows: There is an offer by one agent which is answered by bids of other agents. The offer is granted to the best bidder and the other bids are rejected.

From the point of view of negotiation there is a major shortcoming: In the view of Smith and Davis there must not be a conflict at all between the agents, to start the CNP. Hence, there is no possibility of bargaining between the agents. The contractor does not communicate its minimal condition, nor do the bidders have a second choice. Moreover a mutual agreement (not necessarily reached in each negotiation!) is eventually given by the decision of the offer. Hence, the CNP is more like a standardized coordination method than a negotiation principle.

Pruitts' (1981) definition is based on psychosociological considerations (see also Bartos, 1974; Gulliver, 1979). Again the elements of communication and decision making are motivated, but now a conflict comes in as a starting point and a whole process of concession follows:

> Negotiation is a process by which a joint decision is made by two or more parties. The parties first verbalize contradictory demands and then move towards agreement by a process of concession or search for new alternatives.

Following this discussion the main ingredients of negotiation can be fixed: the *communication* aspect without which negotiation would not be possible at

Figure 7.1 The structure of the negotiation categories.

all, the *decision* aspect which is necessary to model the reasoning of the negotiators during the negotiation, and the procedural model and global behavior of the negotiators during the whole negotiation cycle. Hence, the following classification of negotiation categories is suggested:

- *Negotiation Language Category.* Research is concerned with the communication primitives for negotiation, their semantics and their usage in terms of a negotiation protocol. This category also comprises the investigation of the structure of the negotiation topics.
- *Negotiation Decision Category.* Algorithms to compare the negotiation topics and correlation functions for them are discussed. The definition of utility functions and the representation and structure of the agents' preferences are fixed. Negotiation strategies fall in this category, too.
- *Negotiation Process Category.* General models of the negotiation process are investigated and the global behavior of the negotiation participants analyzed

Figure 7.1 shows the three main categories plus their respective classes. They will now be discussed in detail.

3 THE NEGOTIATION LANGUAGE CATEGORY

Almost every investigation of negotiation contains at least a short paragraph which deals with the communication part of negotiation: usually the primitives of the negotiation language are described together with their intended meaning.

However, there are also deeper investigations in the formal semantics of the language and discussions of the context information transmitted with the language primitives (for linguistic approaches, cf. Ballmer and Brennstuhl, 1981; Bach and Harnish, 1979).

The negotiation language category spans over four subcategories:

- Negotiation language primitives
- Negotiation object structure
- Negotiation protocols
- Negotiation language semantics

which are discussed in the following sections.

3.1 Negotiation Language Primitives

One of the basic forms of communication between agents is simple message passing as in the Actor model (Hewitt, 1977; Agha, 1986). But simple send/receive operations are far too weak for negotiation purposes, and of course most work on negotiation language primitives takes the conversational aspects pointed out by Winograd and Flores (1986) into account. They are built on the theory of speech acts (Searle, 1969; Austin, 1962) and handle the illocutionary aspects of utterances, which convey the speaker's intent to the hearer. However, our grouping of negotiation primitives, which are used by artificial agents, are orthogonal to the classes (Assertives, Directives, Commissives, Permissives, and Prohibitives) defined in speech act theory. The primitives are divided into three groups corresponding to whether they initiate a negotiation, whether they react on a given statement or whether they complete a negotiation:

- *Initiators*, such as Propose, Arrange, Request (of Resources), Inform, Query (for Information), Command, Inspect
- *Reactors*, such as Answer, Refine, Modify, Change, Bid, Send, Send Value, Reply, Refuse, Explain
- *Completers*, such as Confirm, Promise, Commit, Accept, Reject, Grant, Agree

The primitives exemplified above are taken from various investigations (Campbell and d'Inverno, 1990; Huhns et al., 1990; Kakehi and Tokori, 1993; Sablayrolles and Schupeta, 1993; Fischer et al., 1995; Werkman, 1990). Ignoring differences in names, which often depend on an application for the primitives, the groups are always the same. Interactions begin with negotiation initiative primitives, which are followed by reactors used during the mutual exchange in the bargaining phase. They are eventually finished by the use of completing primitives (cf. also Figure 7.2).

3.2 Negotiation Object Structure

Together with a negotiation language primitive a special context is always transmitted. Besides context information like sender, receiver, message number, reference number, time, etc. the important contents are the negotiation topic or object. This may be plans (i.e., action sequences) (as in Kakehi and Tokoro, 1993; von Martial, 1992b), time intervals for possible appointments (Sablayrolles and Schupeta, 1993), offers or tasks (Fischer et al., 1995), or costs and prices depending on the application. The negotiation topic is important, because the agents use them for their local calculations (cf. negotiation decision category) which in turn influence the negotiation performance. Since the object structure mainly depends on the application, it is not discussed further here. The fundamental point is a precise definition of the syntax of the language used, as discussed for instance in Bussmann and Müller (1993b) for a negotiation language used for a bargaining game, where the agents have to negotiate on the exchange of letters. In the following this bargaining language will be described. For the formal definition the Backus-Naur form is used.

Note that the language divides into an application independent part (up to deny) and an application-specific part, which has to be redefined according to the negotiation topics.

⟨speech-act⟩	⇒ ⟨speaker⟩ ⟨addressee⟩ ⟨speech-act-type⟩ ⟨id⟩ ⟨message⟩
⟨speaker⟩	⇒ ⟨agent-name⟩
⟨addressee⟩	⇒ ⟨agent-name⟩
⟨speech-act-type⟩	⇒ inform|question|answer|propose| accept|deny
⟨message⟩	⇒ ⟨inform⟩|⟨question⟩|⟨answer⟩| ⟨propose⟩|⟨accept⟩|deny
⟨inform⟩	⇒ ⟨predicate⟩ +
⟨question⟩	⇒ ⟨question-predicate⟩
⟨answer⟩	⇒ ⟨answer-list⟩ ⟨speech-act-reference⟩
⟨propose⟩	⇒ ⟨proposal⟩
⟨accept⟩	⇒ ⟨speech-act-Reference⟩
⟨deny⟩	⇒ ⟨speech-act-Reference⟩
⟨predicate⟩	⇒ ⟨have⟩|⟨have-not⟩|⟨give-not⟩| ⟨want-not⟩
⟨question-predicate⟩	⇒ ⟨have?⟩
⟨answer-list⟩	⇒ (⟨numbered-list-of-letters⟩)
⟨proposal⟩	⇒ ⟨give⟩ ⟨give⟩
⟨have⟩	⇒ (have ⟨agent⟩ ⟨numbered-list-of-letters⟩)
⟨have-not⟩	⇒ (have-not ⟨agent⟩ ⟨list-of-letters⟩)
⟨give⟩	⇒ (give ⟨agent⟩ ⟨numbered-list-of-letters⟩)
⟨give-not⟩	⇒ (give-not ⟨agent⟩ ⟨numbered-list-of-letters⟩)

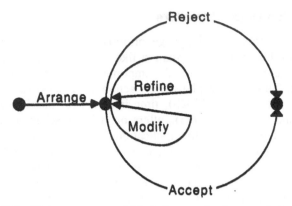

Figure 7.2   Finite automata which defines a simple negotiation protocol.

⟨want-not⟩	⇒	(want-not ⟨agent⟩ ⟨numbered-list-of-letters⟩)
⟨have?⟩	⇒	(have ⟨agent⟩ ⟨numbered-list-of-letters⟩)
⟨list-of-letters⟩	⇒	(⟨letter⟩*)
⟨numbered-list-of-letters⟩	⇒	((⟨letter⟩ ⟨number⟩))*)
⟨numbered-list-of-letters?⟩	⇒	((⟨letter⟩ ?)+)
⟨speech-act-reference⟩	⇒	(id ⟨number⟩)
⟨agent⟩	⇒	⟨agent name⟩ |I| you

⟨x⟩ denotes a nonterminal symbol, | denotes the alternative, + denotes the repetition (at least once), and * denotes the unspecified repetition. ⟨speech-act⟩ is the starting symbol of the language.

The following properties complete the language definition:

1. The message type must correspond to the speech act type.
2. ⟨speaker⟩ must be the name of the uttering agent. The symbol *I* refers to the speaker, and the symbol *you* refers to the addressee.
3. ⟨number⟩ must be a nonnegative integer.

The above specification of the bargaining language allows us to use a deterministic finite automaton for the language recognition. It is based on a kernel automaton which provides the application independent part. The kernel can then be extended for the needs of the application.

We now come to the allowed sequences of utterances.

3.3 Negotiation Protocols

Negotiation protocols specify the possibilities of initiating a negotiation cycle and of responding to a message. The simple way is that negotiation protocols define the possible sequences of negotiation actions given for example by pairs

(⟨negotiation primitive⟩, ⟨message contents⟩)

In most cases the protocols are defined as finite automata (Chang and Woo, 1991; Kogan, 1993) and hence are highly nonmonotonic. Figure 7.2 shows a simplified one used in the context of appointment scheduling (Sablayrolles and Schupeta, 1993). It states that after an Arrange proposal a series of Refine and Modify *actions* can be exchanged which will eventually be followed by a Reject or Accept of the final date.

Often the negotiation protocol is intermixed with the negotiation process description by including extra descriptions of the decision making into the states of the automata (Sablayrolles and Schupeta, 1993; Chang and Woo, 1991). Singh even defined generally (M. P. Singh, 1991):

> Protocols can be taken as specifying the policies that the agents would follow with regard to their interactions with other agents; e.g. these policies would determine the conditions under which a request would be acceded to or a permission issued or a statement believed.

However, a clear division between the decision and the language level should be preferred.

A formal approach to negotiation protocols was investigated by Singh (1994). His concern was to clarify the objective conditions of satisfaction for different kinds of messages. He used the speech act classifiers together with a possible worlds semantics to formalize protocols. For example, the CNP may be described as

$$\langle \text{directive, co } mm(y, x,$$
$$\langle \text{commissive, comm}(x, y,$$
$$\langle \text{directive, comm}(y, x, \langle \text{assertive, result}(T)\rangle)\rangle\rangle$$
$$\rightarrow F \text{ comm}(y, x, \langle \text{assertive, result}(T)\rangle)$$
$$\rangle)\langle$$

where $\langle i, p \rangle$ is a message consisting of the illocutionary force i and the proposition p, and comm(x, y, z) is a predicate applying to two agents x, y and a message z to be true if message z is satisfied in the context of the illocutionary force and uttered to y by x. With the semantics in mind, the above definition says that the call for bids is a directive asking the hearer to commit to sending the manager the result of the task T. The assertive with the result T is satisfied only if the contractor produces the right result, and does so while intending to and having the required know-how. The contractor must commit to producing the result, if assigned the task. Thus the task assignment directive is satisfied if the contractor produces the result when asked to M. P. Singh (1991, 1994).

3.4 Negotiation Semantics Category

Though a first glance at a semantics is given for the protocol above and with the choice of the words for the negotiation primitives, little work has been done on the pure semantics of negotiation primitives. Mostly the semantics are given informally as in the following example (Kakehi and Tokoro, 1993):

Reject (plan-set): A message used when there are no acceptable plans in the other agent's plan set.

In contrast to that informal definition of the semantic of Reject, the negotiation primitives can be defined in a very precise way as is done in Numaoka and Tokoro (1990). They use situation semantics as a basis, together with various modal operators, as the following example shows:

INFORM (S, R, L)

preconditions:

$\ll$ believe, S, $\ll$ know, R, $\ll$ believe, S, σ; 1 $\gg$; 0 $\gg$; 1 $\gg$

$\wedge \ll$ want, S, $\ll$ know, R, $\ll$ believe, S, σ; 1 $\gg$; 1 $\gg$

effect:

$\ll$ speak, S, R, σ; 1 $\gg$ $\rightsquigarrow$

$\ll$ hear, R, σ; 1 $\gg$ $\rightarrow$ $\ll$ know, R, $\ll$ believe, S σ; 1 $\gg$; 1)

Informally, this means the following:

Suppose that an agent S believes that an agent R does not know that

S believes that a sentence σ is true **and**

that S wants that R knows that S believes σ then it holds that after S

spoke to R, R knows that S believes σ provided R heard σ

Cohen and Perrault (1988) and Werner (1989) use pure modal logics to define the semantics of the negotiation primitives.

4 THE NEGOTIATION DECISION CATEGORY

Suppose the negotiation language, the protocols, the semantics and the negotiation object structures are fixed. Then the agents are able to communicate about certain topics. However, they must still decide which protocol to choose and which of the primitives to choose inside a protocol. The negotiation decision category addresses these problems and it contains the four classes of decision aspects for negotiation:

- Utility functions
- Comparing and matching functions

- Preferences
- Negotiation strategies

In the following the details of the classes will be discussed.

4.1 Utility Functions

Utility functions are best known for the game-theoretic approaches to multi-agent systems (Zlotkin and Rosenschein, 1990, 1991, 1992, 1993a,b,c). The utilities are given as decision matrices, where an agent looks up a value for a certain action. Corresponding to the general strategy, it will perform the action with the lowest or highest value. In the context of negotiation, utility functions represent the prices or costs for activities.

As an example of the calculation of utilities the theoretical framework of Kuhn and Müller (1993) will be discussed in detail. In this framework the price P_r^t of a resource r at a time t is given by the base price G_r and a certain addition or difference as follows. Suppose the addition corresponds to the number of agents which like to get access to r. Further let l be the length of the queue Q_r. Hence the price will be $P_r^t \approx G_r + l(Q_r^t)$. While G_r is usually constant the addition or difference should vary over time depending on whether the queue grows or shrinks. So let ϵ_r be the extra factor for resource r per element in the queue. Hence, the relative price of a resource r at time t is

$$P_r^t := G_r + (\Sigma_{1,\dots,t} \, (l(Q_r^t) - l(Q_r^{t-1}))\epsilon_r)$$

The cost $K_{a,r}^t$ of a resource r at a time t for an agent will then consist of P_r^t and disposability cost for agent a to get r at t. Hence

$$K_{a,r}^t := P_r^t + Z_{a,r}^t$$

Suppose an agent a has n tasks $A_1, \dots, A_n$ with corresponding values $W_1, \dots, W_n$. The utility N_a^t of a at a time t after finishing each task is given by

$$N_a^t := \Sigma_{i=1\dots n} \, (W_i - \min_r \{K_{a,r}^t\})$$

An agent tries to optimize its utility over time; i.e., it tries to maximize the total utility

$$N_a := \max_t \{N_a^t\}$$

The negotiation process depends heavily on the agents' (internal) goal to maximize its utilities. The various costs, prices, and values might serve as negotiation objects, but the decisions are settled on the basis of the utility optimization.

4.2   Comparing and Matching Functions

As mentioned before the term negotiation is often used in the context of conflict resolution (as in Kakehi and Tokoro, 1993) and task sharing (as in von Martial, 1992a). In these cases the negotiation decisions of an agent are based on complex negotiation objects like plans in the first line. The plans have to be evaluated and the final decision is settled on the computed utility. In this sense, a major question is how to design comparing functions for the objects.

Kakehi and Tokoro used plans as complex objects to negotiate about. A plan is a sequence of actions which are represented in the classical STRIPS (Fikes and Nilson, 1971) notation:

$$\text{action (resources):}$$

precond: state_o (resources), ...

delete list: state_i (resources), ...

add list: state_p (resources), ...

During the negotiation process the actual plan sets of the agents are exchanged. If an agent receives a set of plans, it matches its favorite plan with the received plans to compute the set of maximal, nonconflicting plans. The matching function thus computes the maximal sequences of actions starting with the action of the favorite plan. For example, let

$$\underline{\text{act}_1 \ \text{act}_m} \ \underline{\underline{\text{act}_1 \ \text{act}_p}} \ \text{act}_n$$

be the reference plan and let the plan set consist of two plans

$$\underline{\underline{\text{act}_1 \ \text{act}_p}} \ \text{act}_q$$

and

$$\text{act}_q \ \text{act}_p$$

With respect to the reference plan, there are two common starting subsequences act_1 and $\text{act}_1 \ \text{act}_p$ from the first plan and a complete disagreement on the second plan. Hence, $\text{act}_1 \ \text{act}_p$ will serve as the starting sequence of a most convenient common activity.

4.3   Preferences

The negotiators often have an expectation about the outcome of the negotiation (e.g., to maximize gain, to minimize risk, to find a fair (50/50) solution, etc.) (Bussmann and Müller, 1992). They might prefer one solution over another (see Chapter 9), which in turn provides to them an agreement criterion for solutions. In general, preferences might be expressed absolutely or relatively, i.e., a certain property (predicate) is present (true), or it is less than, equal to, or greater than a certain value, respectively. Preferences can be expressed as first-order formulas like

```
Meet (Susan) v (Today (Sunday) → Goto (Stadium))
```

A preference defined as the formula above states that either the agent prefers to meet Susan or if it is a Sunday it equally prefers to go to the football stadium. If the preferences of the opponent are known, strategies can be applied to propose a solution that is most likely to be accepted. In Kraus et al. (1993) and Sycara (1989) argumentations are used to change the opponents preferences in order to find a mutually agreed upon solution.

4.4 Negotiation Strategies

Negotiation behavior and negotiation strategies are obviously important topics in sociology and psychology. Hence, elements from these disciplines should influence the modeling of negotiation mechanisms for artificial agents, too. The work of Pruitt (1981) is significant to this enterprise. He distinguished five negotiation strategies:

1. Concede unilaterally
2. Being **competitive:** stand firm and employ pressure tactics
3. Being **cooperative:** search for a mutually acceptable solution
4. Inaction
5. Breaking

Conceding unilaterally will not improve the benefit of all participants. It may only be interesting if the negotiation becomes pointless or superfluous to a party (e.g., due to parallel events). It is obvious that *inaction and breaking* will not push the negotiation. *Competitive and cooperative* behavior are the two extreme points in the spectrum of negotiation behavior and will now be discussed in more detail.

At the beginning of a negotiation, a conflict (from a set of conflicts) to be resolved has to be chosen by one of the following strategies:

1. Take one by one
2. Take the most important one
3. Take the less different one
4. Reduce all criteria to one (e.g., honor, money)
5. Packaging, i.e., two (or more) issues are regarded as equivalent in value and will be resolved together (see trading)

Which of the tactics is the most suitable cannot be determined beforehand and often depends on the situation itself. In situations where negotiation seems to fail, one might choose the least different conflict in order to revive the negotiation. A reduction of all the topics may not always be possible, and packaging should make sense. One of the ordinary tactics is to choose the most important conflict or take them one by one. Packaging may be employed successfully if the resolution of a conflict implies that one party must concede unilaterally. The goals of the conflict resolution can be chosen by either

1. Equal division, e.g., 50/50.
2. Argumentation; the opponent has to be convinced to pursue a certain proposal, either by argument or by evidence.
3. Trading of packages, exchanging one preference for another one.
4. Appeal to authority, rules, ideology, or common goals.

Note that with respect to the classes utility functions and preferences, this last class in the negotiation decision category represents a meta level of decision making. However, it influences the decisions and it has therefore its place in this category.

Up to now the aspects for modeling the negotiation abilities of artificial agents were discussed. The negotiation language category provides the agents for the communicational tasks. It describes how to communicate if a conflict situation arises. The negotiation decision category defines the control level of negotiation. It describes how to find the "right words" in the communication. What remains is the meta level of negotiation, namely the holistic view of the process of negotiation and its valuation by nonparticipating parties.

5   THE NEGOTIATION PROCESS CATEGORY

While the language and the decision categories dealt with the micro considerations of the negotiation, the negotiation process category is dedicated to the macro level. Its focus lies on the description of the whole process and in the system analysis from the viewpoint of the negotiation society. Concretely, the following two classes will be discussed:

- Procedural negotiation model
- System behavior and analysis

The procedural negotiation model defines the behaviour of an agent during the negotiation process. It can be defined abstractly using notions of strategies and preferences like above or it can be precisely presented as an algorithm, which basically describes the interaction of the communication module, the decision level, the planner, and the knowledge base (Bussmann and Müller, 1993a; Griffeth and Velthuijsen, 1993).

Into the system behavior and analysis class fall the works which analyze the behavior of the negotiating society. Problems which were considered are the quality of the problem-solving process in the context of negotiation versus central processing and fairness/deadlock problems.

5.1 Procedural Negotiation Model

In Bussmann and Müller (1992) a negotiation algorithm was presented as a two-level process model. The pure negotiation cycle starts with proposing solutions to a certain conflict, the critical analysis of other solutions with respect to the own preferences, and the update of the solution space and their own preference list. In parallel to this runs the conflict resolution cycle by determining conflicts, selecting high-priority conflicts, and planning conflict resolution. It describes the essential steps each agent will go through during negotiation, leaving the choice of language and decision to the agent designer.

Lander and Lesser (1993) reported about a similar approach called negotiation search: A set of states is defined which represent the states of the negotiation process with respect to the quality of the actual solution. The states are changed by applying negotiation search operators to initiate, critique, extend, and relax solutions, and to terminate the search. As in the former model the choice of the micro implementation is left to the designer, though the operators do not provide many variations.

5.2 System Behavior and Analysis

Beside the work of Burkhard (e.g., 1993) on the analysis of properties of multiagent systems like liveness and fairness for different kinds of agent societies, there has been little work in this class.

Kosoresow (1993) tried to gain complexity results in analyzing the algorithms which implement the agents' interactions. He showed that the total work (TW) to be done in a multiagent system with negotiation is less or equal to the total work in coordinated, centralized on-line, and centralized off-line systems. On-line and off-line means here, that given a queue of tasks, in an on-line system the agents decide who will do which task as tasks are coming in, with the requirement that each task be completed before the next task arrives. The off-line case means that all tasks are known a priori and the tasks are assigned to the agents in an optimal order.

In Zlotkin and Rosenschein (1993b) the field of task-oriented domains, i.e., domains in which negative interactions among agents' goals are not allowed, are analyzed with respect to negotiation protocols. Different kinds of deals between agents, domain attributes, and types of deception are investigated. The results show that there exist distributed consensus mechanisms with simple and stable strategies that lead to efficient outcomes, even when agents have incomplete information about their environment.

6 CONCLUSION AND OUTLOOK

In this overview on the principles of negotiation an investigation was made toward a clear structure for the research field of negotiation. The division into several categories and classes not only serves as a classification, but also provides a methodology for the designer of negotiation based multiagent systems. Let us summarize our results from that point of view in the following list. A sequential top-down development will first define the agents' negotiation communication abilities at the language level, which is then followed by the design of the control capabilities at the decision level. The parts are connected then by a process model, which (ideally) provides a tool for analyzing the system behavior.

Language Level
   Negotiation topics
   Language primitives and types of messages
   Semantic
   Protocols
Decision Level
   Utility functions
   Preferences
      Global behavior and roles
      Strategies
Process Level
   Negotiation cycle
   Conflict processing cycle
      Structure of the society
      Ascription and valuation

Future research in the area of negotiation in multiagent systems will comprise recognition (i.e., learning) of preferences and strategies to improve the negotiation behavior, argumentation and persuasion with fuzzy values, and formal specification and validation of negotiation processes.

ACKNOWLEDGMENTS

The starting point for this overview was my project AKA-Mod on modeling cooperating agents and thus I have to thank the whole AKA-Mod team for the intensive discussions on the topic negotiation. Particular thanks are dedicated to Norbert Kuhn, Stefan Bussmann, and Kurt Sundermeyer for the ideas on the decision part and language level, and to Al Burt, Jörg Müller, and Munindar Singh for reading and investigating in earlier drafts.

BIBLIOGRAPHY

The bibliography contains not just the references mentioned in the text, but it also gives an overview on the current literature in the field. Though emphasis is on articles in recent DAI conferences and books, important classical and psychosociological literature is also included.

Agha, G. A. (1986). *Actors: A Model of Concurrent Computation in Distributed Systems.* MIT Press, Cambridge, MA.

Austin, J. L. (1962). *How to do Things with Words.* Harvard Univ. Press, Cambridge, MA.

Ballmer, T., and Brennenstuhl, W. (1981). *Speech Act Classification.* Springer, New York.

Bach, K., and Harnish, R. M. (1979). *Linguistic Communication and Speech Acts.* MIT Press, Cambridge, MA.

Bartos, O. J. (1974). *Process and Outcome of Negotiation.* Columbia Univ. Press, New York.

Burkhard, H. D. (1993). Liveness and fairness in multi-agent systems. *Proc. Int. Jt. Conf. Artif. Intell., 13th,* Chambéry, France, *1993,* 325–337.

Burmeister, B., Haddadi, A., and Sundermeyer, K. (1993). Generic configurable co-operation protocols for multi-agent systems. In *Pre-Proceedings of the Fifth European Workshop on Modelling Autonomous Agents in a Multi-Agent World* (Ghedira and K. Sprumont, eds.), Cote No. RI-93/8-1. Inst. Inf. Intell. Artif., Université de Neuchatel, Switzerland.

Bussmann, S., and Müller, H. J. (1992). A negotiation framework for cooperating agents. *Proc. Spec. Interest Group Coop. Knowl. Based Syst., SIG Workshop,* University of Keele, Keele, UK, pp. 1–18.

Bussmann, S., and Müller, H. J. (1993a). A communication architecture for cooperating agents. *Comput. Artif. Intell.* **12**(1), 37–54.

Bussmann, S., and Müller, H. J. (1993b). Bargaining agents (ext. abstr.). In *Progress in Artificial Intelligence* (M. Filgueiras and L. Damas, eds.), Lect. Notes Artif. Intell., vol. 727. Springer-Verlag, Berlin.

Campbell, J. A., and d'Inverno, M. P. (1990). Knowledge interchange protocols. In *Decentralized Artificial Intelligence 2* (Y. Demazeau and J.-P. Müller, eds.), Elsevier/North-Holland, Amsterdam.

Cawsey, A., Galliers, J. R., Reece, S., and Jones, K. S. (1992). A comparison of architectures for autonomous multi-agent communication. *Proc. Eur. Conf. Artif. Intell., 10th,* Vienna, Austria, pp. 249–256.

Chang, M. K., and Woo, C. C. (1991). Sanp: A communication level protocol for negotiations. In *Decentralized Artificial Intelligence 3* (E. Werner and Y. Demazeau, eds.), pp. 31–56.

Cohen, P. R., and Perrault, C. R. (1988). Elements of a plan-based theory of speech acts. In *Readings in Distributed Artificial Intelligence* (A. H. Bond and L. Gasser, eds.). Morgan Kaufmann, San Mateo, CA.

Conry, S. E., Meyer, R. A., and Lesser, V. R. (1988). Multistage negotiation in distributed planning. In *Readings in Distributed Artificial Intelligence* (A. H. Bond and L. Gasser, eds.). Morgan Kaufmann, San Mateo, CA.

Crott, H., Kutschker, M., and Lamm, H. (1977). *Verhandlung I: Individuen und Gruppen als Konfliktparteien Ergebnisse aus sozialpsychologischer Verhandlungsforschung*, p. 20. Sozioökonomie, Stuttgart, Germany.

Davis, R., and Smith, R. G. (1988). Negotiation as a metaphor for distributed problem solving. In *Readings in Distributed Artificial Intelligence* (A. H. Bond and L. Gasser, eds.). Morgan Kaufmann, San Mateo, CA.

Decker, K., and Lesser, V. (1993). Analyzing the need for meta-level communication. *Proc. Int. Workshop Distributed Artif. Intell, 12th*, Hidden Valley, PA, *1993*, pp. 51-65.

Durfee, E. H., Lesser, V. R., and Corkill, D. D. (1987). Cooperation through communication in a distributed problem solving network. In *Distributed Artificial Intelligence* (M. N. Huhns, eds.). Morgan Kaufmann, Los Altos, CA/Pitman, London.

Durfee, E. H., Lesser, V. R., and Corkill, D. D. (1988). Coherent cooperation among communicating problem solvers. In *Readings in Distributed Artificial Intelligence* (A. H. Bond and L. Gasser, eds.). Morgan Kaufmann, San Mateo, CA.

Fikes, R. E., and Nilson, N. J. (1971). STRIPS: A new approach to the application of theorem proving to problem solving. *Artif. Intell.* 2, 189-208.

Fischer, K., Kuhn, N., Müller, H. J., and Müller, J.-P. (1995). Modeling the transportation domain. *Computational Economics* 8, 8-93.

Genesereth, M. R., Ginsberg, M. L., and Rosenschein, J. S. (1988). Cooperation without communication. In *Readings in Distributed Artificial Intelligence* (A. H. Bond and L. Gasser, eds.). Morgan Kaufmann, San Mateo, CA.

Georgeff, M. P. (1988). Communication and interaction in multi-agent planning. In *Readings in Distributed Artificial Intelligence* (A. H. Bond and L. Gasser, eds.). Morgan Kaufmann, San Mateo, CA.

Ginsberg, M. L. (1987). Decision procedures. In *Distributed Artificial Intelligence* (M. N. Huhns, ed.). Morgan Kaufmann, Los Altos, CA/Pitman, London.

Gmytrasiewicz, P., and Durfee, E. H. (1992). Decision-theoretic recursive modeling and the coordinated attack problem. *Work. Pap. Int. Workshop Distributed Artif. Intell. 11th*, The Homestead, Glen Arbor, MI, pp. 95-106.

Griffeth, N., and Velthuijsen, H. (1993). Win/win negotiation among autonomous agents, *Proc. Workshop Distributed Artif. Intell., 12th*, Hidden Valley, PA, pp. 187-202.

Gulliver, P. H. (1979). *Disputes and Negotiations—A Cross-Cultural Perspective*. Academic Press, New York.

Hewitt, C. E. (1977). Viewing control structures as patterns of passing messages. *J. AI* 8(3), 323-364.

Huhns, M. N., Bridgeland, D. M., and Arni, N. V. (1990). A DAI communication aide. *Proc. Int. Workshop Distributed Artif. Intell., 10th*, Bandera, TX, Chapter 29, ACT-AI-355-90.

Kakehi, R., and Tokoro, M. (1993). A negotiation protocol for conflict resolution in multi-agent environments. *Proc. Int. Conf. Intell. Coop. Info. Syst.*, Rotterdam, The Netherlands, *1993*, pp. 185–196.

Kogan, D. (1993). Design and implementation of CB lite. *Proc. Conf. Organ. Comput. Syst.*, Milpitas, CA, *1993*.

Kosoresow, A. P. (1993). On the efficiency of agent-based systems. *Proc. Intell. Auton. Syst.*, Chapter 55, pp. 551–560.

Kraus, S., Nirkhe, M., and Sycara, K. (1993). Reaching agreements through argumentation: A logical model. *Proc. Int. Workshop Distributed Artif. Intell., 12th*, Hidden Valley, PA, *1993*, pp. 233–247.

Kreifelts, T., and von Martial, F. (1991). A negotiation framework for autonomous agents. In *Decentralized Artificial Intelligence 2* (Y. Demazeau and J.-P. Müller, eds.), pp. 71–88. Elsevier/North-Holland, Amsterdam.

Kuhn, N. (1993). Comparing rankings of heterogeneous agents. *Proc. Conf. Organ. Computing Syst.*, Milpitas, CA, *1993*.

Kuhn, N., and Müller, H. J. (1993). Preisgesteuerte Multiagentenkoordination. In *Informatik, Wirtschaft, Gesellschaft* (H. Reichel, ed.). Springer Informatik Aktuell, Berlin.

Laasri, B., Laasri, H., and Leser, V. R. (1990). Negotiation and its role in cooperative distributed problem solving. *Proc. Workshop Distributed Artif. Intell., 10th*, Bandera, TX, Chapter 9, ACT-AI-355-90.

Lander, S., and Lesser, V. R. (1992). Negotiated search: Cooperative search among heterogeneous expert agents. *Proc. Am. Assoc. Artif. Intell.*, San Jose, CA, pp. 74–83.

Lander, S., and Lesser, V. R. (1993). Understanding the role of negotiation in distributed search among heterogeneous agents. *Proc. Int. Workshop Distributed Artif. Intell., 12th*, Hidden Valley, PA, *1993*, pp. 249–262.

Levin, J. A., and Moore, J. A. (1988). Dialogue-games: Metacommunication structures for natural language interaction. In *Readings in Distributed Artificial Intelligence* (A. H. Bond and L. Gasser, eds.). Morgan Kaufmann, San Mateo, CA.

Lux, A., Steiner, D. D., and Bomarius, F. (1992). A model for supporting human computer cooperation. *Proc. Am. Assoc. Artif. Intell.*, San Jose, CA, pp. 84–88.

Moses, Y., and Tennenholtz, M. (1992). On computational aspects of artificial social systems. *Work. Pap. Int. Workshop Distributed Artif. Intell. 11th*, The Homestead, Glen Arbor, MI, *1992*, pp. 267–284.

Numaoka, C. (1992). Conversation for organizational activity. In *Decentralized Artificial Intelligence* (E. Werner and Y. Demazeau, eds.), pp. 189–198. Elsevier/North-Holland, Amsterdam.

Numaoka, C., and Tokoro, M. (1990). Conversation among situated agents. *Proc. Int. Workshop Distributed Artif. Intell., 10th*, Bandera, TX, Chapter 13, ACT-AI-355-90.

Okamura, K. (1993). Combining local negotiation and global planning in cooperative software development projects. *Proc. Conf. Organ. Comput. Syst.*, Milpitas, CA, *1993*.

Parunak, H. V. D. (1987). Manufacturing experience with the contract net. In *Distributed Artificial Intelligence* (M. N. Huhns, ed.). Morgan Kaufmann, Altos, CA/Pitman, London.

Pruitt, D. G. (1981). *Negotiation Behaviour*. Academic Press, New York.

Sablayrolles, P., and Schupeta, A. (1993). Conflict Resolving Negotiation for Cooperative Schedule Management Agents (COSMA). *DFKI Tech. Memo* **TM-93-02.**

Sandholm, T. (1993). An implementation of the contract net protocol based on marginal cost calculations. *Proc. Int. Workshop Distributed Artif. Intell., 12th*, Hidden Valley, PA, pp. 295–308.

Searle, J. R. (1969). *Speech Acts: An Essay in the Philosophy of Language*. Cambridge University Press, England.

Searle, J. R., and Vanderveken, D. (1985). *Foundations of Illocutionary Logic*. Cambridge Univ. Press, New York.

Sen, S., and Durfee, E. (1992). A formal analysis of communication and commitment in distributed meeting scheduling. *Working Pap. Int. Workshop Distributed Artif. Intell., 11th*, The Homestead, Glen Arbor, MI, pp. 333–344.

Shechory, O., and Kraus, S. (1993). Coalision formation among autonomous agents, strategies and complexity. In *Pre-Proceedings of the Fifth European Workshop on Modelling Autonomous Agents in a Multi-Agent World* (Ghedira and K. Sprumon, eds.), Cote No. RI-93/8-1. Ins. Inf. Intell. Artif., Université de Neuchatel, Switzerland.

Sidner, C. L. (1992). Using discourse to negotiate in collaborative activity: An artificial language. *Proc. Am. Assoc. Artif. Intell.*, San Jose, CA, pp. 121–128.

Singh, M. P. (1991). On the semantics of protocols among distributed intelligent agents. *DFKI Tech. Memo* **TM-91-09.**

Singh, M. P. (1994). *Multiagent Systems: A Theoretical Framework for Intentions, Know-How, and Communications*. Springer, New York.

Singh, S. S. (1991). Adaptation based on cooperative learning in multi-agent systems. In *Decentralized Artificial Intelligence 2* (Y. Demazeau and J.-P. Müller, eds.), pp. 257–272. Elsevier/North-Holland, Amsterdam.

Smith, R. G. (1988). The contract net protocol: High-level communication and control in a distributed problem solver. In *Readings in Distributed Artificial Intelligence* (A. H. Bond and L. Gasser, eds.). Morgan Kaufmann, San Mateo, CA.

Smith, R. G., and Davis, R. (1980). Frameworks for cooperation in distributed problem solving. In *Readings in Distributed Artificial Intelligence*, (A. H. Bond and L. Gasser, eds.). Morgan Kaufmann, San Mateo, CA.

Stainiford, G., Bench-Capon, T. J. M., and Dunne, P. E. S. (1993). Cooperative dialogues with the support of autonomous agents. *Proc. Int. Conf. Intell. Coop. Info. Syst.*, Rotterdam, The Netherlands, *1993*, pp. 144–151.

Steeb, R., Cammarata, S., Hayes-Roth, F., Thorndyke, P., and Wesson, R. (1988). Architectures for distributed air-traffic control. In *Readings in Distributed Artificial Intelligence* (A. H. Bond and L. Gasser, eds.), Morgan Kaufmann, San Mateo, CA.

Stirling, W. (1992). Multi agent coordinated decision-making using epistemic utility theory. *Pre-Proc. Eur. Workshop Model. Auton. Agents Multi-Agent World, 4th*, Rome, Italy, pp. 1–18.

Sycara, K. P. (1989). Multiagent compromise via negotiation. In *Distributed Artificial Intelligence* (L. Gasser and M. Huhns, eds.), Vol. 2, pp. 119–137. Morgan Kaufman, San Mateo, CA/Pitman, London.

Urzelai, K., and Garijo, F. J. (1992). Makila: A tool for the development of cooperative societies. *Pre-Proc. Eur. Workshop Model. Auton. Agents Multi-Agent World, 4th*, Rome, Italy, pp. 1–14.

Velthuijsen, H., and Griffeth, N. D. (1992). Negotiation in telecommunication systems, cooperation among heterogeneous intelligent systems. *Proc. Am. Assoc. Artif. Intell.*, San Jose, CA. pp. 138–147.

von Martial, F. (1992a). Coordination by negotiation based on a connection of dialogue states with actions. *Work. Pap. Int. Workshop Distributed Artif. Intell., 11th*, The Homestead, Glen Arbor, MI, pp. 227–246.

von Martial, F. (1992b). *Coordinating Plans of Autonomous Agents*, Lect. Notes Artif. Intell, No. 610. Springer-Verlag, Berlin.

Werkman, K. J. (1990). Knowledge-based model of negotiation using shareable perspectives. *Proc. Workshop Distributed Artif. Intell., 10th*, Bandera, TX, Chapter 6, ACT-AI-355-90.

Werner, E. (1989). Cooperating agents: A unified theory of communication and social structure. In *Distributed Artificial Intelligence*, L. Gasser and M. Huhns, eds., Vol. 2, pp. 3–36. Morgan Kaufmann, Los Altos, CA Pitman, London.

Winograd, T., and Flores, C. F. (1986). Understanding Computers and Cognition: A New Foundation for Design. Ablex, Norwood, NJ.

Zlotkin, G., and Rosenschein, J. S. (1990). Blocks, lies, and postal freight: The nature of deception in negotiation. *Proc. Int. Workshop Distributed Artif. Intell., 10th*, Bandera, TX, Chapter 8, ACT-AI-355-90.

Zlotkin, G., and Rosenschein, J. S. (1991). Negotiation and goal relaxation. In *Decentralized Artificial Intelligence 2* (Y. Demazeau and J.-P. Müller, eds.), pp. 273–286. Elsevier/North-Holland, Amsterdam.

Zlotkin, G., and Rosenschein, J. S. (1992). A domain theory for task oriented negotiation. *Proc. Am. Assoc. Artif. Intell.*, San Jose, CA, pp. 148–153.

Zlotkin, G., and Rosenschein, J. S. (1993a). Negotiation with incomplete information about worth: Strict versus tolerant mechanisms. *Proc. Int. Conf. Intell. Coop. Inf. Syst.*, Rotterdam, the Netherlands, *1993*, pp. 175–184.

Zlotkin, G., and Rosenschein, J. S. (1993b). A domain theory for task oriented negotiation. *Proc. Int. Jt. Conf. Artif. Intell., 13th*, Chambéry, France, *1993*, pp. 416–422.

Zlotkin, G., and Rosenschein, J. S. (1993c). One, two, many, coalitions in multi-agent systems. In *Pre-Proceedings of the Fifth European Workshop on Modelling Autonomous Agents in a Multi-Agent World* (Ghedira and K. Sprumont, eds.), Cote No. RI-93/8-1. Inst. Inf. Intell. Artif., Université de Neuchatel, Switzerland.

CHAPTER 8

Planning in Distributed Artificial Intelligence

EDMUND H. DURFEE

1 INTRODUCTION

While many everyday tasks (such as avoiding collisions with people in a hall-way) can be accomplished by taking immediate reactions to a situation, many other tasks (such as picking up milk on the way home from work) can require some amount of forethought to determine effective actions to take given desirable future actions and goals. In artificial intelligence, planning research has concentrated on how to construct sequences of actions that, when executed correctly and in order, will bring about a desired state of the world (goal). Classical planning research has assumed that the single agent doing the planning is the only source of change in its environment, and so concurrent, unexpected actions are not possible. Extensions to classical planning have allowed that events beyond the control of the agent are possible, so plans must be monitored and revised in the face of such events.

But actions taken by another agent, which is presumably acting to achieve its goals, are not necessarily unpredictable and uncontrollable. In a multiagent environment, an agent should at least try to plan its own actions so as to be effective despite the concurrent actions that it predicts that others will be taking. Better yet, an agent can attempt to exert some control over other agents' actions, just as those agents are influencing its actions, by providing information that leads them to act in a more coordinated way.

Planning is thus a crucial component in coordinated behavior. While some forms of coordination can take place purely through reactions to current situations (such as swerving to avoid collision), more generally the success of coordination hinges on anticipating how agents' courses of action will affect the world, determining the desirability of various states of the world, identifying

Foundations of Distributed Artificial Intelligence, Edited by G. M. P. O'Hare and N. R. Jennings.
ISBN 0-471-00675-0 © 1996 John Wiley & Sons, Inc.

which worlds to strive toward, and changing agents' plans (and hence often their current actions) to achieve their goals better (see Chapter 6). For example, in transportation tasks, a vehicle peforming its pickups and deliveries might be able to impact another vehicle either through interference (it might tie up resources—roadways or parcels—needed by the other) or through assistance (it might transport parcels needed by the other vehicle to a more convenient pickup point). But since pickups and deliveries require sequences of actions, and current choices of actions (such as roads taken) can influence what future actions and interactions can take place, coordination requires vehicles to anticipate future interactions among alternative plans, identify interactions to strive for or avoid, build and commit to appropriate plans, and change current behaviors suitably.

Distributed planning thus addresses the problems of how an agent should formulate a course of action that takes into account the desired and undesired actions that others might concurrently take, how an agent should ascertain what those courses of action that others might take are, how an agent should model how its actions are being anticipated by others, how an agent can influence others by changing their models of its actions, and how an agent should commit to such models of itself. Thus, whereas planning for a single agent is a process of constructing a sequence of actions considering only goals, capabilities, and environmental constraints, planning in an environment populated by multiple agents considers also the constraints that their activities place on an agent's choice of action, the constraints that an agent's commitments (Chapters 2 and 6) to others place on that agent's options over courses of action, and the less than fully predictable evolution of the world caused by other unmodeled agents.

2 APPROACHES TO DISTRIBUTED PLANNING

In this chapter, we will survey a variety of distributed planning approaches, and we will focus on one approach to distributed planning that provides some answers to these questions by explicitly considering that an agent's plans will change over time due to outcomes of its actions, outcomes of others' actions, changes in the environment, changes to the agent's goals, or changes in the agent's perception of the multiagent context. As a consequence of this, and of the limitations agents have in what they can sense, communicate, and reason about at any instant of time, we begin from the assumption that plans are formed (and reformed) based on an agent's current partial model of the environment and of the other agents, and this model is continuously revised during an agent's course of action. This in turn means that planning must be interleaved with plan execution, that plans are inherently uncertain of achieving their effects, and that plan optimality must be traded off in the interests of timely execution, lest the agent fail to take action because its model of the world changes faster than its formation of plans in response to a particular model of the world.

Our partial global planning (PGP) approach (Durfee, 1988; Durfee and

Lesser, 1991) views individual and group planning activities as being ongoing and tightly intertwined. In deciding what action to take next, an agent should refer to its local plans that elaborate courses of action that lead to desired individual goals, and in deciding among its possible local plans (for different goals), an agent should refer to collective (multiagent) plans that elaborate concurrent, intertwined courses of action for all agents that lead to desired global goals. However, without any central, global controller to guide them, agents must construct their collective plans from their local plans, and their local plans must in turn be constructed from the actions that they are capable of taking in the current situation. As the situation that agents find themselves in evolves, so will their candidate local actions, their local plans, and their collective plans; as their collective plans change, so will their local plans and their actions.

Coordinated planning thus involves a continuing flow of information upward and downward at different levels of decision making. Action in a dynamic world involves reaching decisions based on the best information available. Partial global planning accommodates the need for both planning and action by giving agents the ability to construct local plans, exchange information about their plans, construct partial global plans with the information they currently have received, revise local plans based on partial global plans, and choose actions accordingly. As information flows among agents, partial global plans (and hence coordination decisions) will evolve. The goal of partial global planning is thus not to construct, once and for all, a collective blueprint of actions that agents are to follow to the letter, but rather to provide agents with the most current and complete model of the dynamically changing activities in the network to guide them into making good decisions.

2.1 Earlier Approaches

Work in distributed planning before PGP had generally taken the former view, of complete planning before action. The collective plan could be formed centrally and then distributed, such as using a partial order planner like NOAH (Sacerdoti, 1977) and distributing unordered sequences of actions to be executed in parallel. An advantage of this kind of approach is that standard nonlinear planning techniques can be employed for distributed planning, but a disadvantage is that the number of plans to distribute is only dependent on the goals and actions, and not on the available agents.

An alternative approach, therefore, is to begin by decomposing the global conjunctive goal into subgoals that can be assigned to individual agents. This ensures that each available agent has some part of the global activity to pursue. However, because the subgoals might interact (most usually, that accomplishing one will interfere with accomplishing another, although more positive interactions are also possible), each agent cannot simply plan and act on its subgoal independently. Somehow, the agents must recognize subgoal interactions and modify their plans to avoid them.

There are two basic approaches to this process of recognition and repair of interactions. One approach is to designate, either statically (as in Georgeff, 1983) or dynamically (as in Cammarata et al., 1983; Steeb et al., 1988), an agent that is to perform the recognition and repair activities. All of the other agents send it their separate plans, and this agent examines the plans for critical regions where contention between the plans of the agents (for reusable but nonsharable resources, for example) could lead to failure. Repair of the plans could take one of several forms. In Georgeff's work, where the application involved access to workcells in a job shop, synchronization messages were inserted into plans such that one agent would wait for a workcell until it was released by another. In contrast, the approach of Cammarata, Steeb, and colleagues in the air traffic control domain would attempt to find one of the aircraft (preferably that one that was acting as the central coordinator) which could alter its (flight) plan so as to remove the interaction (predicted collision).

The other approach to the recognition and repair problem is to execute this process itself in a distributed manner. In his distributed NOAH system (Corkill, 1979), Corkill developed distributed versions of the traditional NOAH critics. As above, the conjunctive subgoals are assigned to different agents, and each agent builds a plan for its subgoal. However, each agent also represents the fact that other agents are concurrently carrying out their plans (using MODEL nodes in the procedure net), and as plans are constructed locally the effects (postconditions) of those plans are propagated so that ordering constraints on plan steps to prevent interference can be identified and resolved (using synchronization messages).

Each of these earlier approaches relies on the same assumptions as classical planning systems for single agents, namely, that actions have reliable outcomes and that the only changes to the environment are those that are planned. Thus, detailed planning, followed by execution, is an appropriate method. In fact, for some of the application domains for which these approaches have been developed, such as air traffic control and factory floor automation, these assumptions might be realistic, since the environment in these kinds of domains can be carefully monitored and generally well controlled. However, these assumptions do not hold in other applications of interest, both for single-agent planning and multiagent planning, leading to more incremental and reactive planning approaches.

2.2   Approaches to Distributed Planning in Dynamic Environments

Partial global planning assumes that unexpected events are going to happen and thus interleaves planning and execution at each of the agents. Because events can happen asynchronously and propagation of changes across the network of agents takes time, PGP assumes that agents might never have complete and consistent views of the collective situation, but instead must make decisions on partial knowledge of the current global situation.

Other more recent work in distributed planning has also been concerned with planning coordinated actions in dynamic environments, such as the work on planned team activity (Kinney et al., 1992). Building off of Georgeff's work on the procedural reasoning system (PRS) (Chapter 5), which allows the flexible execution of existing routine plans, Kinney and colleagues considered cases where existing routine plans for multiple agents are available. In other words, existing procedures can involve the concurrent activity of multiple agents, each playing some role in the planned team activity. A challenge in this approach, as addressed by Kinney and colleagues, is in developing general, robust mechanisms by which agents can form a team and assign roles in a multiagent procedure (Chapter 2). Once this is done, each agent can then execute its role flexibly by adopting individual subprocedures based on the current context. Because this approach is more oriented to the dynamic execution of existing procedures rather than the formulation of those procedures in the first place, it is different from most traditional planners. In application domains where such procedures exist ahead of time and might even be codified (such as military procedures), this approach can be very effective.

During the execution of multiagent plans, one or more agents might determine that the context has changed so much that the current collective plan should be abandoned, possibly in favor of a different collective procedure. Foundations for modeling joint intentions (Levesque et al., 1990), and, building upon these, joint responsibility (Jennings and Mamdani, 1992) can provide a rigorous underpinning to plan execution systems in dynamic domains. Specifically, Jennings has distinguished between commitments among agents, and conventions for resolving situations when commitments cannot be honored by, for example, insisting that an agent which abandons a joint intention must alert others to this fact (see Chapters 6 and 18 for more details). Thus, whereas most distributed planning work has concentrated on the process of formulating a plan for agents to commit to in the first place, the work of Jennings has instead focused on how agents with this capability should use it in dynamic environments as the plans they had previously formulated become obsolete or ineffective.

By updating others about significant changes in local plans, agents using partial global planning also adopt such a strategy. The idea that only *significant* changes to local plans need be discussed among agents ties into other recent distributed planning research, which has focused on partitioning the planning space into localized regions such that planning within each region can be pursued nearly independently of planning in other regions (Lansky, 1990; Pope et al., 1992). Localization of planning leads to substantial reductions in complexity, both in terms of computation and communication, but requires knowledge engineering to identify nearly independent planning problems.

For example, localization can be achieved by identifying particular coordination relationships of interest (Decker and Lesser, 1992; von Martial, 1992). The work of Decker and colleagues identifies coordination relationships such as enabling (one agent is performing a task whose results will enable another agent to pursue its tasks), facilitating (one agent's task, once performed, could help another agent perform its task better or faster), inhibiting, and so on (see

Chapter 16). Von Martial's work concentrates predominantly on what he calls the *favor* relationship: in contrast to the bulk of distributed planning work which has concentrated on resolving conflicts among plans, Von Martial has focused instead on developing mechanisms for identifying opportunities for agents to help each other accomplish their goals and for modifying their plans accordingly. In applications where the goal is for the system as a whole to work as effectively as possible, the assumption that the agents can be designed to assist (facilitate, favor) each other is valid, and these approaches can be gainfully employed. While partial global planning did not represent the synergistic task relationships as clearly and explicitly as this more recent work, it is based on the same assumption.

The assumption that informed agents would choose to help each other is violated in more competitive applications, such as when individual delivery firms are competing for business and profit. While there might be opportunities for mutually beneficial collaboration, agents cannot be assumed to be cooperative unless it is in their own self-interests. Coordination and cooperation among self-interested agents can be achieved through rational choices of actions (Gmytrasiewicz et al., 1991) and deal-making behavior (Zlotkin and Rosenschein, 1991). Furthermore, engineering the deal-making environment appropriately can lead self-interested agents that truthfully reveal information about their plans and goals to converge on collective plans that benefit them all, despite being individually self-interested (Ephrati and Rosenschein, 1993).

In summary, a variety of distributed planning approaches have been developed for different assumptions about agents (how inherently cooperative they are), environments (how predictable they are), and tasks (how clearly defined and decomposable they are). While none is appropriate for all applications, each attempts to balance the costs of planning with its benefits in the particular agent-environment-task combination for which it was developed. Partial global planning is no exception, assuming that agents will adhere to some minimal set of properties that give predictability to their actions; that the environment can change dynamically leading to the arrival of new tasks over time and deviations from existing plans; and that tasks, while dynamically changing, all conform to a basic, repetitive problem-solving paradigm.

3 PARTIAL GLOBAL PLANNING: THE DETAILS

3.1 Task Decomposition

Partial global planning starts with the premise that tasks are inherently decomposed—or at least that they could be. Therefore, unlike planning techniques that assume that the overall task to be planned for is known by one agent, which then decomposes the task into subtasks, which themselves might be decomposed, and so on, partial global planning assumes that an agent with a task to plan for might be unaware at the outset as to what tasks (if any) other agents might be planning for, and how (and whether) those tasks might be related to its own. A fundamental assumption in partial global planning is that no individual agent might be aware of the global task or state, and the purpose of coordination is to allow agents to develop sufficient awareness to accomplish their tasks nonetheless.

3.2 Local Plan Formulation

Before an agent can coordinate with others using partial global planning, it must first develop an understanding of what goals it is trying to achieve and what actions it is likely to take to achieve them. Hence, purely reactive agents, which cannot explicitly represent goals that they are trying to achieve and actions to achieve them, cannot gainfully employ partial global planning. Moreover, since most agents will be concurrently concerned with multiple goals (or at least will be able to identify several achievable outcomes that satisfy a desired goal), local plans will most often be uncertain, involving branches of alternative actions depending on the results of previous actions and changes in the environmental context in carrying out the plan.

3.3 Local Plan Abstraction

While it is important for an agent to identify alternative courses of action for achieving the same goal in an unpredictable world, the details of the alternatives might be unnecessary as far as the agent's ability to coordinate with others. That is, an agent might have to commit to activities at one level of detail (to supply a result by a particular time) without committing to activities at more detailed levels (specifying how the result will be constructed over time). Abstraction plays a key role in coordination, since coordination that is both correct and computationally efficient requires that agents have models of themselves and others that are only detailed enough to enhance collective performance. In partial global planning, for example, agents are designed to identify their major plan steps that could be of interest to other agents.

3.4 Communication

Since coordination through partial global planning requires agents to identify how they could and should work together, they must somehow communicate about their abstract local plans so as to build models of joint activity. In partial global planning, the knowledge to guide this communication is contained in the meta-level organization (MLO). The MLO specifies information and control flows among the agents: who needs to know the plans of a particular agent, and who has authority to impose new plans on an agent based on having a more global view. The declarative MLO provides a flexible means for controlling the process of coordination.

3.5 Partial Global Goal Identification

Due to the inherent decomposition of tasks among agents, the exchange of local plans (and their associated goals) gives agents an opportunity to identify when the goals of one or more agents could be considered subgoals of a single global goal. Because, at any given time, only portions of the global goal might be known to the agents, it is called a partial global goal. Construction of partial global goals is, in fact, an interpretation problem, with a set of operators that attempts to generate an overall interpretation (global goal) that explains the component data (local goals). The kinds of knowledge needed are abstractions of the knowledge needed to synthesize results of the distributed tasks. And, just as interpretations can be ambiguous, so too is it possible that a local goal can be seen as contributing to competing partial global goals.

3.6 Partial Global Plan Construction and Modification

Local plans that can be seen as contributing to a single partial global goal can be integrated into a partial global plan, which captures the planned concurrent activities (at the abstract plan step level) of the individuals. By analyzing these activities, an agent that has constructed the partial global plan can identify opportunities for improved coordination. In particular, the coordination relationships emphasized in PGP are those of facilitating task achievement of others by performing related tasks earlier, and of avoiding redundant task achievement. PGP uses a simple hill-climbing algorithm, coupled with an evaluation function on ordered actions, to search for an improved (although not necessarily optimal) set of concurrent actions for the partial global plan (see Figure 8.1). The evaluation function sums evaluations of each action, where the evaluation of an action is based on features such as whether the task is unlikely to have been accomplished already by another agent, how long it is expected to take, and on how useful its results will be to others in performing their tasks.

3.7 Communication Planning

After recording the major local plan steps of the participating agents so as to yield a more coordinated plan, an agent must next consider what interactions should take place between agents. In PGP, interactions, in the form of communicating the results of tasks, are also planned. By examining the partial

1. For the current ordering, rate the individual actions and sum the ratings.
2. For each action, examine the later actions for the same agent and find the most highly rated one. If it is higher rated, then swap the actions.
3. If the new ordering is more highly rated than the current one, then replace the current ordering with the new one and go to step 2.
4. Return the current ordering.

Figure 8.1 Algorithm for PGP plan step reordering.

1. Initialize the set of partial task results to integrate.
2. While the set contains more than one element:
   for each pair of elements, find the earliest time and agent at which they
      can be combined
   for the pair that can be combined earliest:
      add a new element to the set of partial results for the combination
       and remove the two elements that were combined.
3. Return the single element in the set.

Figure 8.2 *Algorithm for planning communication actions.*

global plan, an agent can determine when a task will be completed by one agent that could be of interest to another agent, and can explicitly plan the communication action to transmit the result. If results need to be synthesized, an agent using PGP will construct a tree of exchanges such that, at the root of the tree, partially synthesized results will be at the same agent which can then construct the complete result (see Figure 8.2).

3.8 Acting on Partial Global Plans

Once a partial global plan has been constructed and the concurrent local and communicative actions have been ordered, the collective activities of the agents have been planned. What remains is for these activities to be translated back to the local level so that they can be carried out. In PGP, an agent responds to a change in its partial global plans by modifying the abstract representation of its local plans accordingly. In turn, this modified representation is used by an agent when choosing its next local action, and thus the choice of local actions is guided by the abstract local plan, which in turn represents the local component of the planned collective activity.

3.9 Ongoing Modification

As agents pursue their plans, their actions or events in the environment might lead to changes in tasks or in choices of actions to accomplish tasks. Sometimes, these changes are so minor that they leave the abstract local plans used for coordination unchanged. At other times, they do cause changes. A challenge in coordination is deciding when the changes in local plans are significant enough to warrant communication and recoordination. The danger in being too sensitive to changes is that an agent that informs others of minor changes can cause a chain reaction of minor changes, where the slight improvement in coordination is more than offset by the effort spent in getting it. On the other hand, being too insensitive can lead to very poor performance, as agents' local activities do not mesh well because each is expecting the other to act according to the partial global plan, which is not being followed very closely anymore (see Chapter 6). In PGP, a system designer has the ability to specify parametrically the threshold that defines significant temporal deviation from planned activity.

3.10 Task Reallocation

In some circumstances, the exogenous task decomposition and allocation might leave agents with disproportionate task loads. Through PGP, agents that exchange abstract models of their activities will be able to detect whether they are overburdened, and to find candidate agents that are underburdened. By generating and proposing partial global plans that represent others taking over some of its tasks, an agent essentially suggests a contracting relationship among the agents. A recipient has an option of counter proposing by returning a modified partial global plan, and the agents could engage in protracted negotiations. If successful, however, the negotiations will lead to task reallocation among the agents, allowing PGP to be useful even in situations where tasks are quite centralized.

4 AN EXAMPLE

To illustrate partial global planning, and to make the operational details more concrete, consider the example task for which PGP was initially developed, the task of distributed vehicle monitoring (see Chapter 3). In this task, a set of agents are distributed geographically, each capable of sensing some portion of the overall area to be monitored. As vehicles move through its sensed area, an agent detects characteristic sounds from those vehicles at discrete time intervals. By analyzing the combination of sounds heard from a particular location at a specific time, an agent can develop interpretations of what vehicle(s) might have created those sounds. Furthermore, by analyzing temporal sequences of vehicle interpretations, and using knowledge about mobility constraints on various vehicles, the agent can generate tentative maps of vehicle movements in its area.

Of course, in moving through the entire area, vehicles will move from the area of one agent to the area of another. By communicating about partial interpretations, the agents can not only converge on mappings of vehicular movements through the whole area (which is their goal), but can also help each other process their data by providing related interpretations (such as warning another agent that a vehicle of a particular kind has just entered its area, so that agent need not consider all of the possible interpretations of the data since it knows what kind of vehicle to expect). Finally, because agents might have overlapping sensors (to ensure coverage), they might need to coordinate to avoid redundant tracking in overlapping regions.

A simple example of the vehicle-monitoring task, involving only two agents with overlapping sensors, is shown in Figure 8.3. In this example, a vehicle is sensed over eight discrete time points. Agent A detects the signals for times

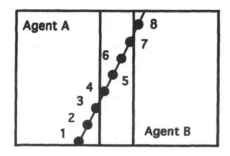

Figure 8.3 *Example two-agent vehicle monitoring scenario.*

1 through 7; Agent B detects the signals for times 4 through 8. Moreover, Agent B has a relatively noisy sensor, which introduces spurious frequencies into the data collected, making the interpretation process more difficult and time consuming.

Left on its own, Agent A would process its data sequentially, taking several actions to process the various pieces of data at each time point, and then actions to link them together into tracks. So would Agent B. Clearly, the agents will be able to formulate the whole track faster if they avoid redundant work in their overlapping area (data points 4 through 7). But Agent B has noisy data and will require more time to process it. As a result, one way that they can work together more effectively is to have Agent A take on more of the work in the overlapping area, since its data is less noisy. But, in addition, if Agent A were to work in an area next to where agent B is working first, and supply B with an interpretation that B then can use to constrain the interpretations that it is trying to form, then A can provide B with information that facilitates B's task. However, since A, if acting alone, would work from the earliest data forward, A must change its plans to provide the facilitating information earlier.

Here is how it happens with agents using PGP. First, each performs a quick analysis of its data to determine that it looks like the data could be part of a single local track, and each thus formulates a local goal of verifying and characterizing the track. The detailed plan for doing this involves sequences of interpretation knowledge sources that apply knowledge of how different frequencies together are indicative of certain vehicle components, and various components are indicative of certain vehicle types. At the abstract level, however, each agent forms a plan that simply identifies the order in which it plans to construct the track associated with the goal: Agent A has a plan to apply its various knowledge sources to the data sensed at time 1, then at time 2, and so on. B plans on working on data sensed at time 4 first, and finishing with data sensed at time 8.

By exchanging these abstract summaries of their local plans and comparing the goals being achieved, the agents recognize (with the same knowledge that allowed them to hypothesize that the data they had locally could be part of the same track) that their goals could be part of a single, more global goal, of forming a track for sensed times 1 through 8. They thus each can formulate a partial global plan that interleaves their actions. Each then performs the hill-climbing search to see if a better ordering can be found, and discovers that A's actions for processing data at times 4 and beyond, being done after B expects to already have processed that data, are lowly rated where they stand now in terms of providing new results to the growing solution, but are considered to be important actions from the perspective of providing predictive information to Agent B, as detected by the fact that B expects to require much more time to process the same data. With these considerations, Agent A's actions are reordered such that it will start with data at time 5 and work backward, sharing its partial track for sensed times 4 and 5 with B as soon as it is done. Agent B will begin processing data at sensed time 6 and then move to subsequent sensed times. It expects to process those more rapidly once it receives the partial track from Agent A. Consistently with this view, when the agents plan their interactions, they identify that Agent A should send the short partial track to Agent B as soon as it is done, and then send its more complete track to Agent B once that is done. Agent B will put the pieces all together.

Once this partial global plan is complete, the agents incorporate the changes into their local plans and proceed to apply their knowledge sources as appropriate. As they proceed, Agent A detects that it will generate partial tracks at slightly different times than had been planned, but these deviations are not substantial enough to warrant the coordination overhead of replanning. However, once Agent B receives the short partial track from Agent A and discovers that it has already formed a suitable interpretation for data at time 6, and hence will build the remaining parts of its track much sooner than expected, it sends its updated abstract local plan to A. The agents employ the PGP algorithms again, with the only major change to their partial global plans being that now B expects to form its part of the overall solution first and the planned interactions now involve Agent B sending its piece to A rather than the other way around. The agents then continue to follow this partial global plan until the solution is created.

While this example explained what the agents do and in broad brushstrokes how they do it, there are many details of the algorithms and knowledge representations that have been glossed over here, due to space limitations. The interested reader is referred to Durfee (1988) and Durfee and Lesser (1991) for more details, and to Durfee and Lesser (1988, 1989) for more discussion on task sharing using PGP and on balancing quality and cost of coordination using PGP, respectively.

5 DIRECTIONS IN PGP AND DISTRIBUTED PLANNING

While PGP has served to bring together concepts of coordinating for both task sharing and result sharing and has illustrated how distributed planning can occur incrementally and continuously in an evolving task domain, it has several limitations that have triggered further research in order to apply PGP to other application domains.

One limitation of PGP is that it follows an implicit assumption that it is permissible to proceed with actions before converging on agreed global plans. While this assumption works well for dynamic domains where recovery from incorrect actions is straightforward, it might be a bad choice in some physical domains (like air traffic control) where it is better to be sure about others before taking actions yourself. PGP is being extended for such situations, where associated with actions are the expected utilities of such actions. Actions that "burn important bridges behind the agent" without high probability of eventual success will not be taken until the eventual outcome (based on the actions of others) is predicted with sufficient certainty.

A second limitation is that the choice of relationships between the goals and actions of the different agents that was considered in the original PGP implementation was specific to the needs of the vehicle-monitoring task. Since that time, substantial effort has gone into defining more general coordination relationships and developing generic PGP algorithms to be applied under a wider variety of conditions for a broader range of coordination problems (Decker and Lesser, 1992b).

Finally, a third limitation of PGP is that it assumes that coordination should occur at a specific level of abstraction over agent activities. This leads to considerable scale-up difficulties, as partial global plans involving tens of agents consider the major plan steps of all of them. To counter this, we have been investigating the use of abstraction along a variety of dimensions as a means for agents to represent individual and collective activity flexibly, so as to balance the costs and benefits of coordination activity. We call the space of abstractions a "behavior space" and have been examining representations for it and algorithms for searching it, such that coordination at different levels of abstraction—resembling organizational plans, short-term plans, or even immediate schedules—can all be treated as a search through the hierarchical behavior space (Durfee and Montgomery, 1991; Montgomery and Durfee, 1993).

More generally, with the current renewed interest in multiagent systems, studies of distributed planning have increased. Several of these have already been mentioned. Increasingly, the emphasis has been on flexible communication in complex, dynamic environments. Some work emphasizes dynamics of the population of agents, including agents that might be hostile, or at least self-interested, and how to get such agents to plan or take actions that lead to certain properties for the set of agents (Ephrati and Rosenschein, 1993; Shoham and Tennenholtz, 1992; Hogg and Huberman, 1991). Other work emphasizes the need for agents to perform well in dynamically changing environments or when tasks change unexpectedly (Kinney et al., 1992); PGP represents one of the first steps in this latter direction. Progress is being made on both of these fronts, but has been hampered by the lack (shared with single agent planning) of a clear way of characterizing the features that make a (distributed) planner appropriate for a particular application domain. Thus, the field needs both the continued exploration of alternative planning paradigms for novel applications, as well as a consolidation of the knowledge gained from past and current explorations into foundational principles for distributed planning.

REFERENCES

Cammarata, S., McArthur, D., and Steeb, R. (1983). Strategies of cooperation in distributed problem solving. *Proc. Int. Jt. Conf. Artif. Intell.*, *8th*, Karlsruhe, Germany, *1983*, pp. 767–770.

Corkill, D. D. (1979). Hierarchical planning in a distributed environment. *Proc. Int. Jt. Conf. Artif. Intell.*, *6th*, Cambridge, MA, *1979*, pp. 168–175.

Decker, K. R., and Lesser, V. R. (1992a). The analysis of quantitative coordination relationships. *Proc. Int. Workshop Distributed Artif. Intell.*, *11th*, The Homestead, Glen Arbor, MI, pp. 59–76.

Decker, K. S., and Lesser, V. R. (1992b). Generalizing the partial global planning algorithm. *Int. J. Intell. Coop. Inf. Syst.* 1(2), 319–346.

Durfee, E. H. (1988). *Coordination of Distributed Problem Solvers*. Kluwer Academic Publishers, Boston.

Durfee, E. H., and Lesser, V. R. (1988). Predictability versus responsiveness: Coordinating problem solvers in dynamic domains. *Proc. Natl. Conf. Artif. Intell.*, *7th*, St. Paul, MN, pp. 66–71.

Durfee, E. H., and Lesser, V. R. (1989). Negotiating task decomposition and allocation using partial global planning. In *Distributed Artificial Intelligence* (L. Gasser and M. N. Huhns, eds.), Vol. 2, pp. 229–243. Morgan Kaufmann, Los Altos, CA/ Pitman, London.

Durfee, E. H., and Lesser, V. R. (1991). Partial global planning: A coordination framework for distributed hypothesis formation. *IEEE Trans. Syst. Man Cybernet.* **SMC-21**(5), 1167–1183.

Durfee, E. H., and Montgomery, T. A. (1991). Coordination as distributed search in a hierarchical behavior space. *IEEE Trans. Syst. Man Cybernet.* **SMC-21**(6), 1363–1378.

Ephrati, E., and Rosenschein, J. S. (1993). Multi-agent planning as a dynamic search for social consensus. *Proc. Int. J. Conf. Artif. Intell.*, *13th*, Chambéry, France, *1993*, pp. 423–429.

Georgeff, M. (1983). Communication and interaction in multi-agent planning. *Proc. Natl. Conf. Artif. Intell.*, *3rd*, Washington, DC, pp. 125–129.

Gmytrasiewicz, P. J., Durfee, E. H., and Wehe, D. K. (1991). A decision theoretic approach to coordinating multiagent interactions. *Proc. Int. Jt. Conf. Artif. Intell.*, *12th*, Sydney, Australia, pp. 62–68.

Hogg, T., and Huberman, B. (1991). Controlling chaos in distributed systems. *IEEE Trans. Syst. Man Cybernet.* **SMC-21**(6), 1325–1331.

Jennings, N. R., and Mamdani, E. H. (1992). Using joint responsibility to coordinate collaborative problem solving in dynamic environments. *Proc. Natl. Conf. Artif. Intell.*, *10th*, San Jose, CA, pp. 269–275.

Kinney, D., Ljungberg, M., Rao, A., Sonenberg, E., Tidhar, G., and Werner, E. (1992). Planned team activity. *Pre-Proc. Eur. Workshop Modell. Auton. Agents Multi-Agent World*, *4th*, Rome, Italy, *1992*.

Lansky, A. L. (1990). Localized search for controlling automated reasoning, *Proc. DARPA Workshop Innovative Approaches Planning, Sched. Control*, pp. 115–125.

Levesque, H. J., Cohen, P. R., Nunes, J. H. T. (1990). On acting together. *Proc. Natl. Conf. Artif. Intell.*, *8th*, Boston, pp. 94–99.

Montgomery, T. A., and Durfee, E. H. (1993). Search reduction in hierarchical distributed problem solving. *Group Dec. Negot.* **2,** 301–317.

Pope, R. P., Conry, S. E., and Mayer, R. A. (1992). Distributing the planning process in a dynamic environment. *Proc. Int. Workshop Distributed Artif. Intell. 11th,* The Homestead, Glen Arbor, MI, pp. 317–331.

Sacerdoti, E. D. (1977). *A Structure for Plans and Behavior.* Elsevier, Amsterdam.

Shoham, Y., and Tenninholtz, M. (1992). On the synthesis of useful social laws for artificial agents societies (preliminary report). *Proc. Nat. Conf. Artif. Intell., 10th,* San Jose, CA, pp. 276–281.

Steeb, R., Cammarata, S., Hayes-Roth, F., Thorndyke, P., and Wesson, R. (1988). Architectures for distributed air-traffic control. In *Readings in Distributed Artificial Intelligence* (A. H. Bond and L. Gasser, eds.), Morgan Kaufman, Los Altos, CA.

von Martial, F. (1992). Coordination by negotiation based on a connection of dialogue states with actions. *Proc. Workshop Distributed Artif. Intell., 11th,* The Homestead, Glen Arbor, MI, pp. 227–246.

Zlotkin, G., and Rosenschein, J. S. (1991). Cooperation and conflict resolution via negotiation among autonomous agents in non-cooperative domains. *IEEE Trans. Syst., Man Cybernet.* **SMC-26**(6).

CHAPTER 9 ━━━━━━━━━━━━━━━━

Agent Dynamics

GEORGE KISS

1 INTRODUCTION

In this chapter I shall look at distributed AI through the metaphor of agent
theory. In this kind of approach to distributed AI, systems are pictured as
collectives of entities that are autonomous and intelligent to some degree. These
entities are often called agents, and the system is then called a multiagent
system. Among the many issues that are relevant to a theory of multiagent
systems I shall concentrate on their dynamics. The main objective is to show
that the perspective of dynamics gives an intuitively coherent interpretation of
many concepts in agent theory. This is particularly the case of multiagent,
distributed systems.

The chapter starts by restating some overall objectives of agent theory in
general and of complex agents in particular. Possible foundations for agent
theory in a number of disciplines are briefly enumerated. A basic framework
of concepts is then set out in preparation for talking about the dynamics of
agents. Finally, some of the agent-theoretic concepts reviewed at the start of
the paper are reinterpreted in the dynamics framework. Because of this structure, some concepts are repeatedly discussed from different points of view, but
we have tried to reduce redundancy to a minimum.

2 WHAT ARE AGENTS?

Agents are the "active ingredients" in nature. They are the sources of changes
of states, i.e., events. *Action* is the central characteristic of agents. They bring
about change through action.

It is useful to distinguish complexity classes of agents: from subatomic
particles to autonomous intelligent human beings. While ultimately the most

Foundations of Distributed Artificial Intelligence, Edited by G. M. P. O'Hare and N. R. Jennings.
ISBN 0-471-00675-0 © 1996 John Wiley & Sons, Inc.

interesting agents are the most complex ones, much useful work can be done, both theoretical and applied, at lower levels.

2.1 What Are the Issues in General Agent Theory?

The literature on agents appears to concentrate on clusters of issues such as having information, making decisions, and taking action (see Chapter 1). Much of this can be discussed in terms of the concept of possibility. For the moment we shall use possibility as an informal commonsense term. Later it will be used in the same sense as in formal semantics which use possible worlds as a primitive concept (see, for example, Moore, 1975). For the time being, the reader should take possibilities to mean "the ways things could be." How then can we relate possibilities to the concepts of information, decision, and action?

> *Information:* this concept can be formulated in terms of possibilities and constraints on possibilities. In classical information theory information is taken to reduce uncertainty, that is, the number of possibilities. The more information we have, the fewer the remaining possibilities. Information thus constrains the possibilities.
>
> *Decision:* can be interpreted as choice between possibilities.
>
> *Action and Change:* can be interpreted as realizing possibilities.

In a theory of complex agents (comparable to humans or similarly evolved animals or machines) many of the interesting issues can be grouped into three classes according to this classification:

Cognitive issues (informational)
Affective issues (choice)
Conative issues (action)

Example issues in complex agent theory are

Agent action (doing, willing, intending)
Freedom and determinism
Attitudes (beliefs, desires, emotions)
Self
Subjectivity (qualia)
Consciousness

All these are bewilderingly complex phenomena. Many disciplines might contribute to making progress with them. Where should we look for foundations? Here is a partial list of some disciplines and some hints at the contributions they might make, without going into details (for a more detailed survey, see Kiss, 1988):

Logic (see Chapters 2 and 10)

Descriptions in formal languages
Specialized (often modal) logics: dynamic, temporal, epistemic, etc.
Proof theory
Semantics and model theory

Mathematics

Theories of information and probability
Theories of structure: topology, graphs, lattices
Descriptions of temporal change, differential equations
Theories of approximation
Tools for describing fields

Computer Science

Computation in distributed systems
Analysis of processes and temporal structures
Analysis of (data) structures

Physics (and Chemistry)

Concepts of action in physics
Concepts of constraint (and degree of freedom), least-effort and other extremum principles, classification of variables (effort and flow, intensive and extensive, etc.)
Treatment of lumped *nonlinear* systems
Distributed systems composed of large numbers of low-complexity agents: multiparticle motion, gases, liquids, magnetism, etc.

Philosophy (see Chapter 18)

Conceptions of *complex* agency in philosophy of mind
Philosophy of action, the attitudes, intentionality, the self, volition, the will, intending

Biology (see Chapter 11)

Insect societies
Evolution
Ontogenesis of form

Psychology (see Chapter 20)

Motivation
Emotion
Cognition
Social structures and processes

Artificial Intelligence

Knowledge representation and reasoning in machines
Theories of action in problem solving; search
Planning
Pattern recognition

Economics

Equilibrium theory in economics
Group behavior, e.g., group decision making

It is not the purpose of this chapter to offer a survey or overview. What we want to do is argue the case for concentrating on a discipline which cuts across many in this list: it is dynamics. The rest of the chapter is devoted to indicating its central role in a theory of agents and multiagent systems.

2.2 Agent Dynamics

One might characterize the majority of work in agent theory at the present time as being focused on kinematics: the major theme is the interaction between knowledge and action (this is still true of approaches like dynamic logic, where the procedural aspects of action are treated; see van Benthem 1990; Harel, 1984).

There are very few attempts to produce a systematic theory of another cluster of phenomena surrounding what might be termed desires. Notions like goals, values, preferences, utility are members of this cluster (see Chapter 20). We think that the extension of agent theory into this area is analogous to the extension of physics to dynamic phenomena. Dynamics is the study of why and how things change in nature. In agent theory, too, we need a theory of why and how an agent changes its environment and itself through the actions it takes.

It is natural to look to well-understood theories of dynamics in physics for the first steps in this direction. We propose therefore to borrow concepts from physical nonlinear dynamics in taking some steps towards an integrated agent theory that would offer a uniform foundation for knowledge, action, and desires in agents (for introductions to nonlinear dynamics, see Thompson and Stewart, 1986; Devaney, 1986). The exercise is essentially integrative: we combine recent developments from a number of areas, including artificial intelligence, computer science, and physics. We also attempt to formalise some of our intuitions about agent dynamics. Our concerns in this chapter are with the description and analysis of agents. We do not propose approaches to implementation, although the point of view we adopt opens some interesting possibilities in that direction which will be discussed elsewhere. Some brief remarks are made in the concluding section.

Briefly, our program is as follows. First, we construct an abstract model of agents as distributed information processing systems. We justify our emphasis on distributed systems in a number of ways. We review how the concepts of knowledge and action can be interpreted in this model and how such an interpretation can link to physics through the concept of state. We observe that the notion of a trajectory (state transition sequence) is central in such a model. We then motivate the study of the asymptotic behavior of trajectories through our interest in questions of stability, equilibrium or persistence over time in relation to agents. We offer an interpretation of goals and values as attractors in the state space on which trajectories converge from a basin of attraction. An abstract potential function is introduced as a basis for analyzing how goals and values steer the behavior of an agent and how the effects of multiple attractors are combined.

3 SOME BASIC CONCEPTS

3.1 Space

We shall need to adopt an appropriate model of space, as required by the framework, having some stated topological properties. Since in this book we are interested in distributed systems, we shall explicitly model space rather than leave spatial concepts implicit in the system implementations only. For the moment, we shall assume a set of atomic locations L, with a topology suitable for modeling physical space, and additional structuring can be given by a *pairs(L)* operation, such that $x, y \epsilon pairs(L)$ implies $(x, y) \epsilon pairs(L)$ and there is a distinguished element $nil_L \epsilon pairs(L)$.

3.2 Time

Since we are interested in real-time performance and in reasoning about time in general, we shall explicitly model time rather than leave temporal concepts implicit in the system implementations only. For the moment we shall assume an ordered set of instants, T.

3.3 Generalization of the Distributed System Concept

We generalize the notion of a distributed system to cover time in addition to space. We shall call a system distributed if either spatial or temporal or both kinds of properties are explicitly modeled in describing the system. We borrow heavily from the frameworks of Rosenschein (1986), Rosenschein and Kaelbling (1986), and of Halpern and Moses (1990) for the epistemic modeling of distributed systems.

3.4 Possibility

Possibility is handled in the usual way by distinguishing possible histories of the world (often called a possible world; see, e.g., Moore, 1975). These histories are called trajectories in dynamics. A trajectory is, for example, a possible computation in a computer system, or the temporal evolution of a physical system.

3.5 State

In general, states are functions from locations, possible worlds, and times to data values. This sense of state is a localized notion. It can be generalized to the state of a structured collection of locations by associating data values with each of the locations in the collection.

However, in addition to talking about the state of a location, we also want to talk about the state of a process. We define processes below through the locations they occupy at any given time. The state of a process is then determined by the states of the locations occupied by the process at that time.

3.6 Processes

In their most general conception, processes extend over both space and time, or in other words, processes occupy a spatiotemporal region. It is also a common intuition to think of processes as a temporal sequence of localized states. We capture these intuitions in two parts. First, we identify the locations occupied by a process, i.e., its spatial trajectory. Second, we identify the states of the locations occupied by the process.

The conception of a process as a spatial region, i.e., a temporal sequence of sets of atomic locations that are occupied by the process, is formally captured by regarding a process as a mapping $\pi: W \times T \rightarrow 2^L$ from world-time pairs to sets of atomic locations.

The simplest case is an atomic process, which is a process such that for every world w and time t, $\pi(w, t)$ is an atomic location. An atomic process occupies one atomic location at a time and the evolution of the atomic process is pictured as the movement of the occupied location over space.

The states of a processes π will be modeled by data values taken from some data domain D_π. The atomic data value domain will be denoted by D_0 and is defined to be the union of the data value domains of the set of atomic processes.

The complete data value domain D is the union of the data value domains of all processes π. The notions of state and data value will be used synonymously.

The evolution of a process over time is therefore described by the locations it occupies and the data values of those locations at each instant of time. Formally, the function $\pi: W \times T \to 2^L$ determines the atomic locations the process occupies, while the function $q: L \times W \times T \to D_0$ assigns atomic states to atomic locations at every world-time pair.

In many applications it is sufficient to work with processes occupying a fixed location or sets of locations (perhaps with some internal structuring of that location). When this is the case, we can treat locations and processes as synonymous. We shall call such processes (spatially) localized. A spatially localized process is just a time series of data values occurring at a fixed location. In what follows, we shall generally assume such localized processes, unless otherwise stated. If a location is labeled x, then the state of the localized process occurring at x is modeled by the value, $*x$, at that location.

3.7 Process Interactions

We shall analyze complex systems into sets of (localized) processes. This is the usual picture of a distributed, concurrent computing system. The component processes in such a system interact with each other through constraint relationships, implemented as message or signal passing. The occurrence of states in one process constrains the states of another process.

Much work has been done recently in computer science on the formal analysis of such systems at various levels of granularity.

One example is the general model of Halpern and Moses (1990) in which there are a set of processors connected by a communication network. The processors communicate by sending messages along the links in the network. The system is characterized by the set of runs R which are all possible computations in such a system. A run r is characterized by describing for every instant of time t every processor's local history $h(p_i, r, t)$. The history is the sequence of events that processor p_i has observed up to time t in the run r. The history includes the processor's initial state and the sequence of messages sent and received by it up to time t. The processor's local state at any time is determined by its history. The runs are generated by running a protocol, which defines what actions a processor takes (i.e., what messages it sends) at any point as a function of its local state. At any point in a run each processor has a *view* of the system which is a function of its history.

Other models, concentrating on concepts of concurrency, are usually described in terms of sets of communicating processes [the CSP system of Hoare (1984), the CCS system of Milner (1983) and the work described in Chapters 2, 10, and 17). Communication is usually through message passing or the exchange of synchronization signals.

Connectionist architectures can also be interpreted in such a model, and here the messages are values, usually in the real number or Boolean data domains.

3.8   Observer and Observation

The notion of an observer (sometimes also referred to as the "designer") is an essential element in many treatments of intentionality in agents (Shoham, 1991; Rosenschein, 1986; Dennett, 1978). We do not want to digress into a discussion of intentionality here (refer to Chapter 1 and 5 for more details), but as a preliminary, we would like to sharpen our intuitions about observers as follows.

We again model an observer as a localized process, i.e., as a set of locations. Data values at these locations define the observer's state. Abstractly, observations are functions from observed states to observer states. An observed state exists at a set of environmental locations at the time of the observation. Environmental locations are disjoint from the locations of the observer. More concretely, observations consist in sending and receiving signals or messages, i.e., communication between the observer locations and environment locations. This process of communication is assumed to determine, at least partially, the state of a location. [It is interesting to note that Halpern and Moses (1990) do not assume any internally caused changes of local state in a processor other than those due to sending and receiving messages! Such an assumption would leave no room for agent autonomy.]

3.9   Facts and Propositions

Following Carnap (1950), we introduce facts as functions from sets of states to truth values. A fact about the environment is the set of environment states in which the fact is true. A fact about an observer is the set of observer states in which the fact is true. The fact is normally expressed by a statement in a language and is then a proposition.

3.10   Information

The terminology of information and knowledge has a confusing usage in the literature (see Chapter 2 for more details). The usage we adopt is that information is a weaker and knowledge is a stronger epistemic concept in terms of the constraints they impose on systems. (In Shannon's classical information theory the quantificational issues are central. We shall not be concerned with quantification issues in this paper at all.)

As hinted at the beginning of this chapter, we interpret the notion of "having information" in terms of constraints on the states of a system. One process has information about another if its state is constrained by the state of the other.

Information about a fact is contained in the state of a process (or the state of a location for fixed-location processes). The state carries (or encodes) the information.

If a state carries information about a fact, it also automatically carries information about all other facts that are implied by that fact. The implied facts are more general facts in the sense of a Boolean algebra of classes.

There is thus an ambiguity about the information carried by a state. In order to eliminate this ambiguity, we can choose to take the most specific fact as the information carried by the state (Dretske, 1981). But this would be just a convention.

3.11 Process Dynamics

The temporal evolution of a process is referred to as its dynamics (for a general introduction to dynamical systems, see Thompson and Stewart, (1986). This is a behavioral description of processes. The dynamics is defined by the constraints operating on the state-to-state transitions of the process. Formally, these constraints can be captured by a transition (or next-state) function. We shall be particularly interested in the asymptotic behavior of processes over time.

The temporal evolution is normally described in terms of a trajectory in a state space. This can be modeled in the framework of Halpern and Moses by a *run* of a system where a run is a function from time to a global system state. The global system state is a tuple of the local states of each process in the system. The runs of a system may terminate or continue indefinitely. However, useful computations are usually taken as convergent in some sense, even if they are nonterminating. We shall see examples of such ongoing computations below. The notion of convergence will lead us to goal directedness in agents which will be discussed later, based on ideas originally proposed by Kiss (1991).

3.12 Agents as Discrete Event Systems

We model agents as instances of discrete event systems in a computational context. Examples of computational real-time discrete event systems are process control, flexible manufacturing, robotics, communication networks, traffic control, human-computer interaction, etc.

Typical characteristics are

Events occur at discrete times and states are discrete values.

Nondeterministic processes occur.

Processes are event driven.

Processes have internal dynamics and interact with other processes in a nonterminating manner.

There are concurrent events.

Real-time constraints apply.

In discrete event systems information and dynamics are brought together. The problem is often stated as the design of a controller which would ensure that no unsatisfactory behavior occurs in some controlled object (the "plant"). In agent theory, the plant is the environment and the controller is the agent.

In the study and implementation of discrete event systems there is a need for several kinds of languages:

A representation language to describe plant and controller behavior. The representation language can be a system like CSP, extended state machines (Ostroff, 1989) or other types of generalized transition systems, logic circuits with delays (Rosenschein, 1986), or temporal automata (Shoham, 1991).

An assertion language for describing desired specifications (see Chapter 17). The assertion language can be used to prove things about the behavior described in the representation language (see Chapter 10). Typically some form of temporal logic is used as the assertion language.

A programming language which can be executed on a computer and with an easy translation from/to the representation language. This is used for implementing the controller. The programming language can be a suitable real-time language such as ADA, Occam, or REX.

4   EPISTEMIC ISSUES AND AGENT DYNAMICS

4.1   Truth Values and Trajectories

As the representative point of the trajectory moves to different points in the phase space, different propositions will be true. As is usual in formal semantics making use of topological models (e.g., intuitionistic logic, Lewis's model for counterfactuals, etc.), truth values are assigned to propositions at points of a topological space. We adopt this point of view (also taken by Halpern and Moses, 1990) and associate truth values of propositions with points of trajectories.

4.2   Epistemic Interpretation of Merging and Branching Trajectories

In conservative systems trajectories can neither merge nor branch. In dissipative systems trajectories can asymptotically merge and branch at limit points.

In real systems state descriptions have to be of finite size, resulting in an uncertainty about the state. Two regions of uncertainty can overlap in which case they can be considered to have merged since they cannot be distinguished.

Loss of information occurs when trajectories converge to such an extent that the fixed finite accuracy of observation cannot distinguish them. Intuitively, the loss occurs since we lose the ability to associate different propositions to separate states. When states become indistinguishable, they must carry the same information. Some degree of freedom is lost and hence information is lost.

Our general conclusion is that merging reduces and branching increases information *from an observer's point of view*. See Chapter 10 for a specific treatment of branching temporal logics.

In a later major section on goals, values, and agent dynamics we shall argue the case for goals and values to be modeled by attractors in the state-space of a process. Since attractors are areas of convergence, it follows that *epistemically* attractors are minimal information states (or rather state sets). In contrast, repellors are maximal information state sets. Goal-directed behavior can therefore be described as information minimization. This is of course again from an observer's point of view. These considerations lead to the conclusion that describing an agent's behavior through its goals is informationally economical. This makes intuitive sense, since the goal is a very compact specification of a whole equivalence class of behaviors, i.e., those that terminate in the goal state. The goal-related issues will of course be discussed in more detail later. In this section our main concern is with informational and epistemic issues and we have just mentioned in passing this epistemic aspects of goals.

4.3 Information

To recapitulate, information about an environment is obtained by making observations. The concept of information is a relation between states in our framework. Normally we say that an observer acquires information about its environment if the observer state is systematically constrained by the environment states. As mentioned, most often this constraining will be done by sending signals or messages between locations. Specifically, a location is said to have information about a fact in a given global state S, if the fact holds in all global states that the location cannot distinguish from S, on the basis of its local state. The local state is in turn determined by the locations' past communicative interactions with its environment, i.e., its communication history. Halpern and Moses call this history the *view* of the location. Two global states are indistinguishable to a location if it has the same view in both.

Thus, the dynamics-based approach provides us with an epistemic interpretation of process states. It is important that this notion of information is external and can only be used by a designer or observer to analyze what is known by a physical system. The system itself cannot describe, analyze, or reason about its information, or answer questions based on it. In many cases it cannot even "compute its information" (Halpern and Moses, 1990).

4.4 Knowledge

It has already been mentioned that knowledge is a stronger epistemic state than having information. We shall now discuss this is in detail.

Physical agents must obey the laws of physics. The physical constraints impose some requirements on what an agent can and cannot do. Doing is movement at least in the sense of change of state. The agent cannot be in incompatible states or carry out incompatible changes of state. In this sense an agent that is composed of parts must ensure that its parts act in a coordinated way. This is the requirement for *agent unity*.

Coordination of parts requires communication between them. Communication in turn requires common information. Common information is based on shared environments. Simple examples of shared environments are semaphores in computer programming or shared locations in cellular automata.

Shared environments give rise to the logical concept of common information through a circularity as follows. Suppose that s is a situation and p is a fact. Then we use the notation $s \mid= p$ to say that p is a fact of situation s. Suppose we have two agents, $a1$ and $a2$. Then $a1$ and $a2$ have the common information that p if

$$s \mid= p$$

$s \mid= a1$ has the information that s is the case

$s \mid= a2$ has the information that s is the case

The characterization is circular, since agents $a1$ and $a2$ having information about s are themselves parts of the situation s about which they have the information.

This circularity can also be expressed by a more directly recursive definition. Let us label the fact that $a1$ and $a2$ have common information by t. Then we can define t as

$$t = (a1 \text{ and } a2 \text{ have the information that } (p \text{ and } t))$$

Barwise (1988) calls this the *fixed-point approach*, since t is a fixed point of the expression.

Finally, common information can also be characterized by unwinding the recursive definition into an infinite sequence of facts that are all implied by t:

$a1$ has the information that p.

$a2$ has the information that p.

$a1$ has the information that $a2$ has the information that p.

etc.

Barwise labels this the *iteration approach*, because of the iterative occurrence of the "has the information that" operator.

Rosenschein (1986) has shown that the circularity involved in these definitions for the "having information" operator is not vicious, i.e., does not lead to infinite requirements in space or time. The reason for this is that in physical systems having information is encoded into states of processes. A single state can have information about infinitely many facts, provided that all those facts are implied by some specific fact. When such implicational relations hold, the information can be "compressed" into a single state.

On the other hand, Barwise also shows that for finite situations the iteration approach is equivalent to the fixed-point approach and that a finite set of iterations form an approximation to the fixed point.

Information and knowledge are related concepts. But knowledge is a stronger notion. A necessary condition for knowing is to have information. The physical implementation of having information is straightforward through the use of constraints between states of processes, as shown by Rosenschein's work. What then is the physical implementation of knowledge?

The proposal of this chapter is that the appropriate physical implementation of knowledge is common information between the constituent components of an agent. When the constituent parts have the common information that p, the agent as a whole *knows* that p, and each component of the agent also *has the information* that p.

What requirements need to be imposed on a system to be able to know in this sense? It follows from Barwise's analysis that there are three requirements if we wish to replace common information by common knowledge. First, the situations of interest must be finite. For people and machines this is satisfied. Second, the components must be perfect reasoners with respect to informational facts. Rosenschein's work shows that this is satisfied under the state-based representation of information: the behavior of physical components satisfies the axioms of *S5* modal logic. Here we take this logic to characterize *information*, not knowledge as is more usually the case. Therefore physical components are perfect reasoners about information. Third, the fact that the components are perfect reasoners should be common information between the components. This is the only requirement that is difficult to satisfy. One possibility is that it should be satisfied through a shared environment architecture. Although Barwise (1988), Halpern and Moses (1990), and Clark and Marshall (1981) all seem to think that this is how common information becomes available, it is not easy to see how this works in a physical system. One scenario is that the participants need to be co-present when a message is displayed. They then all see the message, see that they all see it, etc. Presumably the idea is that they instantaneously go into a state representing this situation as a whole. It is not clear what this state is wired to as a detector of a situation. A more likely scenario is that the state of common information needs to be computed jointly by the participants from the information that is directly available to them. We know from the work of Halpern and Moses and from Moses and Tuttle (1988), that under some conditions a system of components can compute whether it is in a state of common information. In the case of failures of components or of communication, only approximations can be computed.

Nevertheless, it seems that for our purposes even approximations are sufficient, if we are content with an agent being in a state that approximates knowing, or with the state of knowing being reachable only in special cases.

5 ACTION AND AGENT DYNAMICS

In general, we model action as a change of state. However, more specifically, we need to distinguish changes due to agent action from spontaneous changes of the environment (or of the world as a whole). We model this distinction by associating separate dynamics with the agent, A_d, and with the environment, E_d. Agent actions will be modeled by movement along agent trajectories in an agent state-space, while environmental changes are modeled by movement along environment trajectories in an environment state-space. The total world dynamics W_d will be a composition of these two dynamics, $W_d = A_d \| E_d$. Normally we shall take the point of view that the agent exerts a controlling influence on the environment dynamics through its actions, in the manner of control system theory.

To an observer of the environment, agent action seems to modify the environment trajectories. The effect of agent action can be modeled as jumps between environment trajectories. Of course, this appearance is due to the incomplete observation. When the agent is included in the observations, the trajectories are well behaved.

Intuitively, agent action has also something to do with choice (see the justification in Shoham, 1989). This intuition is captured in our model by interpreting jumps as choices between environment states: the agent chooses to "ride" on one or another environment trajectory. Alternatively, we can interpret agent actions as setting up different initial starting states for the environment dynamics.

The treatment of the external (environmental) effects of agent action is thus straightforward and does not differ in principle from the point of view adopted in control system theory. The internal aspects of agent action are a different matter, and we shall return to them in a moment.

6 GOALS, VALUES, AND AGENT DYNAMICS

6.1 Goal-Directed Agents

In general, we identify agents with processes or sets of processes. In contrast to previous work, we wish to emphasize the role of dynamics in interpreting an agent's goals and values (see also Kiss, 1991). We shall therefore specialize the notion of an agent to systems with particular types of dynamics, those in which *attractors* of various types occur. Attractors are compact regions of the state-space and nearby trajectories converge to them.

In order to show how goals determine action in our framework, we now introduce abstract computational analogues of some physical concepts. We shall call these abstract analogues, since we do not want to interpret them in mechanical, electrical, or other physical terms, but want to apply them in a computational or even epistemic context.

The introduction of such analogies has some precedents in the literature, e.g., by Kiss and Savage (1971) for computational work in cognitive science; by Manthey and Moret (1983) for computational mass, distance, velocity, and momentum in distributed computing systems as models of physics; and by Fredkin (1990) for energy, momentum, and mass in cellular automata as models of physics.

Assume that the state of a process can be described as a tuple of values, as stated in our general model. Then

Mass is some measure of the size of the state tuple.

Distance is the distance between state tuples in a suitable metric.

Velocity is the rate of change of state.

Momentum is mass times velocity.

Force is mass times acceleration.

Potential energy is $V = \frac{1}{2} Cf^2$, where C is the analogue of a capacitance or compliance parameter.

In physical dynamics it is customary to introduce dynamics through a velocity or force vector field. The intuition is that the change of system state is caused by the force vector field, e.g., gravitation.

We shall assume that for each point x of the state space a potential $V(x)$ can be computed. The state transitions of the system can then be interpreted as rolling down the potential surface gradient. In potential gradient systems the only stable limit sets are fixed points located at minima of the potential surface. These are sufficient for our purpose of illustrating the interpretation of simple goals, but of course more complicated limit sets like cyclic and chaotic attractors will be of interest in the future.

In general, we identify goals and values with attractors. We picture the agent as moving under the influence of a potential field created by the presence of such attractors. Notice that the notion of a subgoal corresponds to a lower-dimensional region of the state space. This can be seen by thinking of the goal as specified by a tuple of coordinates. Subgoals correspond to subsets of elements of the tuple.

We propose to handle multiple goals by superimposing the potential fields created by them, using some function to represent differences in strengths. The overall potential is then some function of the component potentials, for example a linear combination.

The internal structure of the agent and the influence of the environment will normally impose some constraints on the agent state-space, excluding certain regions of it. We can imagine these to be obstacles to movement in the state space. Generating agent behavior then becomes analogous to a navigation or route-finding problem among obstacles to a goal state. When multiple goals exist, agent behavior is driven by a minimization of potential through movement, constrained by the obstacle regions which are to be avoided. Clearly, this formulation is that of a constrained optimization problem, well known in the optimization literature.

This is where we make contact with the third area of agent-theoretic issues, that of affect. The potential is interpreted in agent-theoretic terms as a "hedonic," or "satisfaction" metric (Kiss and Reichgelt, 1992). The intuition we have about this is that an agent's state of pleasure or displeasure, or satisfaction and dissatisfaction, is a function of this hedonic metric. In other words, we interpret the agent's hedonic state as the degree to which the agent has succeeded in optimizing its state with respect to its positive and negative goals and values. Whether or not the hedonic metric is available for inspection by the agent itself, is a question of the agent architecture. For complex agents like people subjective experience of pain and pleasure is only too real. We are less sure in the case of insects, and fairly certain that it is not available to thermostats and other simple agents. These questions relate closely to issues about the agent's self and consciousness, to which we now turn.

7 THE AGENT'S SELF

We postulate the existence of a subsystem (a set of locations) within each agent with special properties. We shall refer to this subsystem as the agent's *self*. The special properties we shall postulate are (a) the ability to compute common-information states between its locations, and (b) that its internal dynamics are chaotic.

The self subsystem is delimited on the basis of distinguishing three different kinds of locations: internal, boundary, and external locations.

The distinctions between these locations is based on their corresponding (local) transition functions. The transition function of an internal location takes as arguments only the states of internal and boundary locations. Similarly, the transition function of an external location takes as arguments only the states of external and boundary locations.

Since we want the self subsystem to be able to influence the external world and, conversely, to be sensitive to the external world, we assume that the self subsystem has boundary elements whose transition functions take arguments, some of which are states of internal locations and some are states of external locations. These locations act as interfaces between the agent and the rest of the world.

It is to be emphasized that all these transition functions are assumed to be deterministic.

We attribute to the agent the capability of changing the state of the self subsystem directly, without doing anything else. This corresponds to philosopher's notion of "basic agent action." These actions are thus modelled as state transitions of the self subsystem. They are determined "mostly" by the internal dynamics of the self subsystem. The boundary elements influence the internal dynamics, but do not determine it completely.

When dealing with the epistemic aspects of an agent, we also attribute to the agent the capability of knowing the state of the self subsystem directly and explicitly, because this knowledge will be encoded explicitly in the state of the self subsystem as common information between the elements. It is postulated as a special property of the self subsystem that it is capable of computing at least approximations to the state of common information. We postulate this as the mechanism which corresponds to our intuitions about the *unitary* nature of agents with respect to phenomena like knowing and making commitments.

We now make the additional assumption that the self subsystem is a *chaotic* dynamic system (Devaney, 1986). The major property of chaotic systems that we wish to appeal to is that although deterministic, they are unpredictable. Therefore, chaotic systems can be regarded as generators of information. A finite external observer cannot predict what a chaotic system will do. To that observer it will seem that the chaotic system is making free choices as to its state transitions. In this sense the chaotic system is informationally opaque to the observer. We wish to use this property to account for the phenomena of subjectivity and free will in agents. Subjective phenomena too, are informationally opaque to an external observer. The only way to experience them is to *be* the system. The phenomenon of free will is also due to this informational opacity. The chaotic system cannot be controlled because of its sensitive dependence on the starting state: small errors in setting up (i.e., knowing) the starting state have massive consequences later (this is the famous "butterfly effect": a butterfly flapping its wings in London may cause a hurricane in Miami). This lack of controllability is, however, not nondeterminism. The transition function of the chaotic system is deterministic.

It is proposed that the unpredictability of agent action and hence the impression of free will are due to the fact that chaotic processes act as generators of information. This resolves the ontological conflict between determinism and free agent action. Chaotic processes are deterministic but are informationally decoupled and hence opaque, unpredictable, from an observer's point of view.

8 DECOUPLING, ARCHITECTURE, AND AUTONOMY

In another paper (Kiss, 1992) I have identified *generality* (robustness) and *power* (processing work per unit time) as two major but conflicting requirements for the design of autonomous intelligent agents. A separation of these two concerns leads to the notion of a *variable degree of causal coupling* between parts of a mechanism and its environment in terms of space and time. Recent controversies surrounding subsymbolic processing, symbol grounding, situated agents and reactive architectures can all be interpreted as manifestations of the pressure toward power by *close coupling* to the environment. Classical AI approaches based on symbolic processing, planning, general problem-solving methods, the use of logic can all be interpreted as manifestations of the pressure toward generality by loose coupling or *decoupling* from the environment. An implementation strategy for variable coupling can be a layered architecture, where the decoupled higher layers support generality and the close-coupled lower layers support power (see Chapters 12 and 15).

It has also been postulated that the role of consciousness is to support generality by being a modality-independent representation system in the architecture. Representations within this layer correspond to the subjective meaning extracted from the incoming information. Consciousness as a representation system is assumed to be a function of the agent's self subsystem and is located at the highest levels of the layered architecture. These architecture issues are discussed in more detail in Kiss (1992). Here our main concern is with dynamics.

Chaotic attractors in the self subsystem offer a mechanism for variable coupling of the agent to its environment. The reason for this is the same as that for epistemic opacity. Recall that an external observer cannot predict what a chaotic system will do. To that observer it will seem that the chaotic system is making free choices as to its state transitions. Recall also that I have interpreted information in terms of constraints between processes. To the degree that a process is chaotic it is also less constrained by inputs acting on it and is therefore decoupled from those inputs. Another way of saying all this is that chaotic processes are *autonomous*. And this is one of the central characteristics of agents we have stated at the outset.

9   CONCLUSIONS

This chapter has made a case for adopting dynamics as a unifying theoretical framework in which to interpret agent-theoretic concepts in a distributed systems context. We have identified some of the fundamental cognitive, conative, and affective characteristics people attribute to complex agents, and we have shown how these characteristics can be given an interpretation in the dynamics framework. Some of these interpretations also appear to require some assumptions to be made about agent architectures.

It is of interest that the dynamics based framework is equally at home with models of computation ranging from neural networks to object-oriented programming or to closely and loosely coupled multiprocessor systems. The framework is thus quite general and is in line with many current trends in computer science.

A practical advantage of this framework is that using the central notions of state and state transitions, it is easy to move from the theory to physical implementations in machines and living systems. The current trends in neurocomputing and fine-grained, massively parallel computation (for examples see Kosko, 1992; Amit, 1989; Hopfield, 1990), are encouraging from this point of view. There is an increasing emphasis on the *dynamics* of computation in such systems, as shown by a voluminous literature. Interesting related developments are also taking place in the areas of artificial life (Langton, 1986) and in the use of cellular automata (see, for example, Goles and Martinez, 1990; Demongeot et al., 1985; Fredkin, 1990) as dynamical models of physical and biological systems.

The dynamics-based framework is increasingly used, explicitly or implicitly, in the design of multiagent systems for image processing (Demazeau, 1991) and in robotics (Overgaard, 1991), making use of the notion of force.

Implementation in the form of *discrete event systems* is also a going concern and also links this framework to temporal logics for descriptive purposes (Ostroff, 1989). This close link with implementation concerns contrasts with frameworks based on multimodal symbolic logics (e.g., Cohen and Levesque, 1990) which give no direct hint about implementation, although they are useful for description and specification. Implementation by doing theorem proving in the corresponding multimodal logics, or their transformations into first-order logic, tends to be inefficient if at all possible. Theorem provers for multimodal logics are not "off the shelf."

We conclude that it is reasonable to assign a central role to dynamics in the theoretical treatments of distributed computer systems, distributed AI, and multiagent systems. It gives a unified framework for the analysis of the various concerns, epistemic, motivational, and affective, in a theory of agents. It leads in a natural way into issues about architectures and implementations in distributed form.

REFERENCES

Amit, D. J. (1989). *Modelling Brain Function*. Cambridge Univ. Press, Cambridge, UK.

Barwise, J. (1988). Three views of common knowledge. In *Reasoning About Action and Plans* (M. Y. Vardi, ed.), pp. 365–379. Morgan Kaufmann, Los Altos, CA.

Carnap, R. (1950). *The Logical Foundations of Probability*. Chicago Univ. Press, Chicago.

Clark, H., and Marshall, C. (1981). Definite reference and mutual knowledge. In *Elements of Discourse Understanding* (A. Joshi, B. Webber, and I. Sag, eds.). Cambridge Univ. Press, Cambridge, UK.

Cohen, P. R., and Levesque, H. J. (1990). Intention is choice with commitment. *Artif. Intell.* **42**, 213–261.

Demazeau, Y. (1991). Coordination patterns in multi-agent worlds: Applications to computer vision and robotics. *Proc. IEE Colloq. Intell. Agents*, London.

Demongeot, J., Goles, E., and Tchuente, M., eds. (1985). *Dynamical Systems and Cellular Automata*. Academic Press, New York.

Dennett, D. (1978). *Brainstorms*. Bradford, Cambridge, MA.

Devaney, R. L. (1986). *An Introduction to Chaotic Dynamical Systems*. Benjamin/Cummings, Menlo Park, CA.

Dretske, (1981). *Knowledge and the Flow of Information*. MIT Press, Cambridge, MA.

Fredkin, E. (1990). Digital mechanics: An informational process based on reversible universal cellular automata. *Physica D* **45**, 254–270.

Goles, E., and Martinez, S. (1990). *Neural and Automata Networks: Dynamical Behavior and Applications.* Kluwer Academic Publishers, Dordrecht, The Netherlands.

Halpern, J. Y., and Moses, Y. (1990). Knowledge and common knowledge in a distributed environment. *J. Assoc. Comput. Mach.* **37**(3), 549–587.

Harel, D. (1984). Dynamic logic. In *Handbook of Philosophical Logic* (D. Gabbay and F. Guenthner, eds.), Vol. 2. Reidel, Dordrecht, The Netherlands.

Hoare, C. A. R. (1984). Communicating sequential processes. *Commun. ACM* **21**, 666–677.

Hopfield, J. (1990). Dynamics and neural computation. *Int. J. Quantum Chem.: Quantum Chem. Symp.* **24**, 633–644.

Kiss, G. R. (1988). *Some Aspects of Agent Theory* (A paper commissioned by Philips UK Research Laboratories), HCRL Tech. Rep., The Open University, Walton Hall, Milton Keynes, England.

Kiss, G. R. (1991). Autonomous agents, AI and chaos theory. In *From Animals to Animats* (J.-A. Meyer and S. W. Wilson, eds.), pp. 518–526. MIT Press, Cambridge, MA.

Kiss, G. R. (1992). Decoupling of agents from their environment: Combining symbolic and reactive architectures. In *Decentralized Artificial Intelligence 3* (E. Werner and Y. Demazeau, eds.) pp. 231–237. Elsevier/North-Holland, Amsterdam.

Kiss, G. R., and Reichgelt, H. (1992). Decoupling of agents from their environment: Combining symbolic and reactive architectures. In *Decentralized Artificial Intelligence 3* (E. Werner, and Y. Demazeau, eds.), pp. 115–127. Elsevier/North-Holland, Amsterdam.

Kiss, G. R., and Savage, J. (1971). Computational work and power: The limits to human information processing. *J. Math. Psychol.* **16**, 68–90.

Kosko, B. (1992). *Neural Networks and Fuzzy Systems: A Dynamical Systems Approach to Machine Intelligence.* Prentice-Hall, Englewood Cliffs, NJ.

Langton, C. G. (1986). Studying artificial life with cellular automata. *Physica D* **22**, 120–149.

Manthey, M. J. and Moret, B. M. E. (1983). *Commun. ACM.* **26**, 137–145.

Milner, R. (1983). Calculi for synchrony and asynchrony. *Theor. Comput. Sci.* **25**, 267–310.

Moore, R. C. (1975). *Reasoning about knowledge and action.* Ph.D. Thesis, MIT Artificial Intelligence Laboratory, Cambridge, MA.

Moses, Y., and Tuttle, M. R. (1988). Programming simultaneous actions using common knowledge. *Algorithmica* **3**, 121–169.

Ostroff, J. S. (1989). *Temporal Logic for Real-Time Systems.* Research Studies Press, Taunton, England.

Overgaard, L. (1991). Pseudo-force methods for generating collision-free motion of multi-agent systems in unpredictable environments. Master's Thesis, Odense University, Denmark.

Rosenschein, S. (1986). Formal theories of knowledge in AI and robotics. *New Generation Comput.* **3**, 345–357.

Rosenschein, S., and Kaelbling, L. (1986). The synthesis of digital machines with provable epistemic properties. In *Proceedings of the 1986 Conference on Theoretical Aspects of Reasoning About Knowledge* (J. Halpern, ed.), pp. 83–98. Morgan Kaufmann, Los Altos, CA.

Shoham, Y. (1989). Time for action. *Proc. Int. Jt. Conf. Artif. Intell., 11th*, Detroit, MT, pp. 954–959.

Shoham, Y. (1991). *Agent Oriented Programming*, Tech. Rep. Computer Science Department, Stanford University, Stanford, CA.

Thompson, J. M. T., and Stewart, H. B. (1986). *Nonlinear Dynamics and Chaos*. Wiley, Chichester, UK.

van Benthem, J. (1990). *General Dynamics*, Tech. Rep. Institute for Language, Logic and Information, University of Amsterdam.

CHAPTER 10

Temporal Belief Logics for Modeling Distributed Artificial Intelligence Systems

MICHAEL WOOLDRIDGE

1 INTRODUCTION

This chapter discusses the use of *formal methods* for reasoning about DAI systems. By formal, we really mean *mathematical*, and in particular, this chapter is concerned with using *logics* for reasoning about multiagent systems. Now the use of formal methods to reason about computer systems is not universally accepted as both worthwhile and practicable, even in mainstream computer science (where such techniques have been the object of study since the late 1960s). The article therefore begins, in the following section, by motivating the work. Following this, a critical review is presented of three types of formalism that suggest themselves as being appropriate to the task. These formalisms are (i) intentional logics, developed by researchers in AI and philosophy to describe systems with beliefs, goals, intentions, and so on; (ii) temporal logics, developed by researchers in computer science for reasoning about "reactive" systems; and (iii) process algebras, developed for modeling concurrent activity. The review concludes that none of these types of formalism are ideal for the task. However, it is suggested that a *hybrid* approach might be suitable. Specifically, the chapter proposes the following three-stage research program:

1. Develop a formal model of the type of multiagent system you wish to reason about.

Foundations of Distributed Artificial Intelligence, Edited by G. M. P. O'Hare and N. R. Jennings.
ISBN 0-471-00675-0 © 1996 John Wiley & Sons, Inc.

2. For the model developed in (1), construct an *execution model*, which states formally how the execution of such a system may proceed.

3. Use the *histories* traced out in the execution of a system as defined in (2) as the semantic basis for a logic, which can then be used to represent and reason about the systems modeled in (1).

In Section 3, we give an example, worked in as much detail as space allows, to illustrate this program; this section results in the definition of a *temporal belief logic* called AL, which, it is claimed, can be used to express the properties of multiagent systems. The use of this logic is discussed in Section 4, and some conclusions are presented in Section 5.

1.1 Motivation

There are a number of reasons why one should study formal methods for multiagent systems. The first, and most obvious reason, is that they might provide a tool to help manage the complexity of such systems. Such a tool is highly desirable, as designing, implementing, and debugging multiagent systems is not easy: Gasser et al. (1987, p. 148) observed that

> Concurrency, problem domain uncertainty and non-determinism in execution together conspire to make it very difficult to understand the activity within a distributed intelligent system.

To counter such problems, the authors advocated the development of

> ... graphic displays of system activity linked to intelligent model based tools which help a developer reason about expected and observed behavior. (p. 148)

The work described by Gasser and colleagues is firmly and unashamedly in the experimental tradition of AI, hence the call for practical tools to aid understanding. However, given the software experience of the past two decades, it seems surprising that no similar plea was made for principled techniques for specifying and verifying multiagent systems.

In addition to providing a tool to help understand and manage multiagent systems, it is to be expected that a suitable formalism would provide a framework in which general questions about cooperation and social interaction might be posed, and solutions developed. For example, a number of theories of social activity have been developed by workers in DAI (see Chapters 1, 2, 6, 18) of which probably the best known is the Levesque-Cohen model of joint intentions (Levesque et al., 1990). And yet such theories are typically expressed in formalisms that cannot be related to "real" DAI systems, as they make unreasonable assumptions about the deductive capabilities of agents. So, more realistic formalisms for representing multiagent systems might be used as the basis of more pragmatic theories of social activity.

2 BACKGROUND

If one aims to develop formal methods for reasoning about multiagent systems, a good place to start is by observing how the mainstream AI/DAI community has gone about building intelligent (social) agents. Unfortunately, one immediately runs into difficulties, as the issue of intelligent agent architecture (Chapters 2, 3, 5 and Part III) is the subject of a somewhat heated ongoing debate in AI. Interesting and important though this debate is, it is not the aim of this chapter to become embroiled in it (see, e.g., Brooks, 1991, for one view). Despite the intense interest—and controversy—that alternative approaches have evoked, the majority of work in DAI lies in the "classical" or "deliberative" camp, and it is on such work that this chapter focuses. Briefly, this camp proposes that individual agents are symbolic AI systems in the classical sense, with some "knowledge" (expressed in a symbolic language), some reasoning ability, and so on. Examples of classical approaches to DAI are Agent0 (Shoham, 1993), Concurrent Metatem (Fisher and Wooldridge, 1993a), MACE (Gasser et al., 1987), and MCS/IPEM (Doran et al., 1991) (see Chapter 3 and Part III).

How is one to go about reasoning about such systems? What techniques are appropriate, and/or available for the task? There are three resources which initially suggest themselves as suitable: intentional logics, temporal logics, and process algebras.

1. *Intentional Logics.* Researchers in AI, philosophy, and economics have developed many logics for representing and reasoning about the *intentional* notions: belief, desire, and so on. If it is accepted that the agents we wish to reason about may be described in such terms (see, e.g., Shoham, 1993 and Chapters 2 and 5), then one might use such a logic to reason about them.

2. *Temporal Logics.* Researchers in mainstream computer science have for some time used temporal logics for reasoning about *reactive* systems, of which DAI systems are a subset (see below). Therefore, some variant of temporal logic might be suitable for reasoning about DAI systems.

3. *Process Algebras.* In order to model concurrency, a variety of process algebras have been developed; since DAI systems are by definition concurrent, it may be that some formalism of this type may be used (see Chapters 2 and 17).

In the remainder of this section, we discuss these formalisms in more detail.

Intentional Logics. There is a well-established tradition in AI/philosophy of devising logics of the mentalistic, *intentional* notions: belief, knowledge, intention, and so on (Hintikka, 1962; Moore, 1985; Konolige, 1986a; Cohen and Levesque, 1990). Such logics identify an agent with an *intentional system*:

> *intentional systems* . . . [are] entities whose behaviour can be predicted by the method of attributing beliefs, desires, and rational acumen . . . . (Dennett, 1987, p. 49)

The prevalent method for defining the semantics of intentional logics has been to give them a *possible-worlds* interpretation (Halpern and Moses, 1992). Possible-worlds semantics have the advantage of a well-established, theoretically attractive foundation, (see, e.g., Chellas, 1980), but suffer from several disadvantages. Chief among these is the famous "logical omniscience" problem, which seems to imply that agents are perfect reasoners. Another difficulty is that unless the worlds in the semantics are in some way "grounded" (i.e., given some concrete interpretation in terms of agents), then they must remain a theoretical nicety. Given that standard possible-worlds semantics are not suited to the task of reasoning about multiagent systems, one seems to be faced by three options. If one wishes to retain possible-worlds semantics, (they are, after all, highly attractive from a theoretical point of view), then one might attempt to find some way of *grounding* the possible worlds. The second option is to try to weaken the possible-worlds model in some way. The final option is to reject possible worlds altogether and seek an alternative semantic base.

Epistemic logics with grounded possible-worlds semantics have recently become the object of study for researchers in mainstream computer science, who found that the notion of knowledge is a valuable one for analyzing distributed systems and protocols (see Halpern, 1987, for an overview). However, it is not clear how these approaches are related to the classical model of agents—if at all. So, while distributed systems models of knowledge are an important research topic in their own right, they are, at the moment, only of tangential interest to DAI.

Another possibility is to weaken possible worlds semantics in some way; Levesque suggested one way of doing this (Levesque, 1984), by borrowing some ideas from situation semantics (Barwise and Perry, 1983). Another scheme is described in Fagin and Halpern (1985). However, these methods have been criticized for their essentially ad hoc nature (Konolige, 1986b). Also, they suffer from one of the key problems of standard possible worlds approaches: they are not grounded.

Some researchers have rejected possible worlds altogether, and looked instead to the possibility of developing an alternative semantics. The best-known example of this work is the *deduction model of belief* developed by Kurt Konolige (1986a). The deduction model defines a belief system as a tuple containing a "base set" of formulae in some internal, logical language of belief, together with a set of *deduction rules* for deriving new beliefs. Konolige argued that an agent with such a belief system could be said to believe something if it was possible to derive that thing from its base set using its deduction rules. Logically incomplete reasoning may be modeled by giving the agent logically incomplete deduction rules. Interestingly, the deduction model can be viewed as an abstract model of the beliefs of classical AI systems. For this reason, the deduction model seems to be the best candidate out of all the intentional logics mentioned so far for the purposes of this research.

Temporal Logics. The second resource that may possibly be used for reasoning about multiagent systems is the Pnuelian tradition of using temporal logics to reason about *reactive systems*:[1]

> Reactive systems are systems that cannot adequately be described by the *relational* or *functional* view. The relational view regards programs as functions . . . from an initial state to a terminal state. Typically, the main role of reactive systems is to maintain an interaction with their environment, and therefore must be described (and specified) in terms of their on-going behaviour. . . . [E]very concurrent system . . . must be studied by behavioural means. This is because each individual module in a concurrent system is a reactive subsystem, interacting with its own environment which consists of the other modules. (Pnueli, 1986)

There are good reasons for supposing that multiagent systems of the type this chapter is interested in modeling are reactive:

- The applications for which a multi-agent approach seems well suited (e.g., air traffic control; Cammarata et al., 1983) are typically nonterminating, and therefore cannot be described by the functional view.
- Multiagent systems are necessarily concurrent, and as Pnueli observes (above) each agent should therefore be considered a reactive system.

In a 1977 article, Pnueli proposed the use of temporal logic for reasoning about reactive systems. Much research effort has subsequently been devoted to investigating this possibility (see, e.g., Emerson, 1990, for a good overview and references). Unfortunately, naive attempts to adapt such techniques to DAI seem doomed to failure, as Pnuelian models of concurrency typically deal with the execution of individual program instructions, a grain size too fine for our purposes.

---

[1]There are at least three current usages of the term *reactive system* in computer science. The first, oldest usage is that by Pnueli and followers (see, e.g., Pnueli (1986), and the description above). Second, researchers in AI planning take a reactive system to be one that is capable of responding dynamically to changes in its environment—here the word "reactive" is taken to be synonymous with "responsive" (see, e.g., Kaelbling, 1986). More recently, the term has been taken to denote systems which respond directly to the world, rather than reason explicitly about it (see, e.g., Connah and Wavish, 1990, chapter 11). In this article the term is used in its Pnuelian sense.

Process Algebras. Process algebras are model-based formalisms developed by researchers in computer science to allow reasoning about concurrency in systems. Probably the best-known examples of process algebras are Milner's calculus of communicating systems (CCS) (Milner, 1989) and its recent off-spring, the π-calculus (Milner et al., 1992). In a formalism such as CCS, the behavior of an agent[2] is defined as a set of equations; an algebra is provided for manipulating these equations, and so proving properties of agents (see also Chapter 17). CCS and its relatives are the subject of much ongoing work in computer science, and together they form a rich family of techniques for modeling and understanding concurrency. However, the abstract properties of systems that we wish to reason about are often difficult to express using process algebras. Also, at the time of writing, process algebras are not in the mainstream of (D)AI research at all; in fact the author is aware of no published work which applies them to the problems of (D)AI. For these reasons, we do not consider CCS-like formalisms any further in this chapter.

Comments. None of the formalisms described above are directly applicable to our problem. However, there are elements of both intentional logics and temporal logics that are appealing. In an ideal formalism, a temporal component would seem useful to describe the reactive nature of DAI systems; and a model of belief such as Konolige's deduction model could be used to represent the beliefs that agents have. However, simply combining formalisms in an unprincipled way would not be helpful. Instead, we must be careful to develop a temporal belief logic and establish a precise relationship between that logic and the systems we wish to reason about. This leads us to the three-stage research program mentioned earlier.

3 AN APPROACH TO REASONING ABOUT MULTIAGENT SYSTEMS

Recall the three-stage program of research we sketched earlier: (i) define a formal model of the multiagent systems about which we wish to reason; (ii) define an execution model for such systems, which describes how agents may act and interact; and (iii) use runs of such a system as a model for a temporal-based logic. This program is illustrated, by means of a worked example, in this section, which concludes with the definition of a logic called AL. Although AL has superficial syntactic similarities to logics such as that described in Cohen and Levesque (1990), it is closely linked to the systems we are modeling. We can thus begin to realistically claim that we have a logic for reasoning about the kind of system we might actually build.

---

[2]We stress that in process algebras, the term ''agent'' is used in a much looser sense than it is used here.

3.1 A Model of Multiagent Systems

In this section, we define a simple formal model that captures the following key properties of classical multiagent systems:

- *Agents Have Names.* Each agent is uniquely identified by an *agent id*, drawn from the set *Ag*. We usually write *i* and *j* for agent ids.

- *Agents Have Beliefs.* As we observed, it is reasonable to model the "knowledge" of a classical AI system as a belief set, after Konolige (1986a). We assume for our model that agent's beliefs are expressed in some *internal* language *L*; this language could be a frame or semantic net language, but we shall suppose it is a *logical language*. We write *Form(L)* for the set of (well-formed) formulae of *L*, and we let *BS* be the set of possible belief sets that an agent could have

$$\overset{\text{def}}{BS} = \wp(Form(L))$$

- *Agents Can Perform Actions.* The problem of modeling and reasoning about actions performed in the physical world is the subject of much ongoing work in AI. To avoid the problems inherent in any treatment of such actions, we shall assume that agents can only perform *private* actions; that is, they can only perform actions which operate on their own state. We let *Ac* be the set of all such actions.

- *Agents can send messages.* Although communication is not universally assumed in DAI, it is, nevertheless, a common assumption. We therefore suppose that agents can communicate by sending messages. A message is a triple $\langle i, j, \phi \rangle$, where $i \in Ag$ is the *sender* of the message, $j \in Ag$ is the *recipient*, and $\phi \in Form(L)$ is the message content. (We could assume a different communication language if required.) Let *Mess* be the set of all messages:

$$\overset{\text{def}}{Mess} = \{\langle i, j, \phi \rangle | i, j \in Ag \text{ and } \phi \in Form(L)\}$$

It is useful to assume a function *rcv*, with the signature

$$rcv : Ag \times \wp(Mess) \rightarrow \wp(Mess)$$

such that if $i \in Ag$ and $m \subseteq Mess$, then $rcv(i, m)$ is that subset of *m* in which *i* is the recipient.

We now define an agent to be a 4-tuple:

$$\langle \mathcal{B}^0, \mathcal{A}, \mathcal{M}, \mathcal{N} \rangle$$

where

$\mathcal{B}^0 \in BS$ is the agent's *initial belief set*.

$\mathcal{A} : BS \rightarrow Ac$ is the agent's *action function*.

$\mathcal{M} : BS \rightarrow \mathcal{P}(Mess)$ is the agent's *message generation function*.

$\mathcal{N} : BS \times Ac \times \mathcal{P}(Mess) \rightarrow BS$ is the agent's *next state function*.

The idea is that on the basis of its initial beliefs, an agent selects an action to perform using the function $\mathcal{A}$, and some messages to send, using the function $\mathcal{M}$. The function $\mathcal{N}$ then transforms the agent from one state to another, on the basis of the messages it receives, and action it has just performed.

A multiagent system is then just an indexed set of such agents:

$$\{\langle \mathcal{B}_i^0, \mathcal{A}_i, \mathcal{M}_i, \mathcal{N}_i \rangle : i \in Ag\}$$

We must now consider how the execution of such a system may proceed.

3.2 Execution Models

The execution model we present in this section hinges on the notion of the *state* of a system, and of changes in state being caused by *transitions*. Crudely, a state is a "snapshot" of the belief set of every agent in the system at some moment in time. These belief sets are assumed to be in some kind of "equilibrium" (cf. Gärdenfors, 1988). A state change, or transition, occurs when one or more agents receive some messages and perform actions.

Let us return to our model of multiagent systems. The initial state of the system is given by every agent i having its initial belief set $\mathcal{B}_i^0$. The next state of agent i depends upon the action that i performed, the messages that were sent to it, and its initial state. Formally, the state $\mathcal{B}_i^1$ of agent i at time 1 is given by the equation

$$\mathcal{B}_i^1 \stackrel{def}{=} \mathcal{N}_i\left(\mathcal{B}_i^0, \mathcal{A}_i(\mathcal{B}_i^0), rcv\left(i, \bigcup_{j \in Ag} \mathcal{M}_j(\mathcal{B}_j^0)\right)\right)$$

We can thus deduce the state of the system at time 1. This equation can easily be generalized to give the belief set of agent i for an arbitrary time $u \in \mathbb{N}$ such that $u > 0$:

$$\mathcal{B}_i^u \stackrel{def}{=} \mathcal{N}_i\left(\mathcal{B}_i^{u-1}, \mathcal{A}_i(\mathcal{B}_i^{u-1}), rcv\left(i, \bigcup_{j \in Ag} \mathcal{M}_j(\mathcal{B}_j^{u-1})\right)\right) \tag{1}$$

The execution of a system thus proceeds, according to this very simple execution model, with each agent picking an action to perform, sending messages, receiving messages, shifting into its next state, and so on. Note that this execution model does not really describe *concurrency* at all, as it assumes that agents act in synchrony (see Section 5).

As it executes, a system traces out an *execution history*, which describes each agent's state, the actions it performed, and the messages it sent at each moment in time. Without going into formal details, we shall assume that Σ is the set of all such execution histories, and we shall use σ to denote a member of this set. If we write s_u for the uth state of σ, and τ_u for the uth transition of σ, then we can visualize σ as follows:

$$\sigma: s_0 \xrightarrow{\tau_0} s_1 \xrightarrow{\tau_1} s_2 \xrightarrow{\tau_2} s_3 \xrightarrow{\tau_3} \cdots \xrightarrow{\tau_{u-1}} s_u \xrightarrow{\tau_u} \cdots$$

It is assumed that executions are nonterminating.

3.3 A Linear Time Temporal Belief Logic

This section introduces a logic for reasoning about multiagent systems of the type described by the model developed above. The logic is called AL, which stands for Agent Logic. The logic is propositional, in that it does not allow quantification,[3] and it contains three atomic operators: **Bel**, for describing the beliefs of agents; **Send**, for describing the messages that agents send; and **Do**, for describing the actions that agents perform. Additionally, AL contains a set of modal temporal operators, which allow the description of the dynamic properties of agents. Finally, note that AL is based on a model of time that is *linear* (i.e., each moment in time is assumed to have just one successor), *bounded in the past* (i.e., there is a "beginning of time"), and *infinite in the future* (i.e., there is no "last moment" of time). For alternative versions of AL, based on a *branching* model of time, see Wooldridge (1992) and Wooldridge and Fisher (1992).

Syntax. AL is intended to allow reasoning about agents: their beliefs, their actions, and the messages they send. Since it is not possible to actually put an action or agent directly into a formula of the language, there must be a way of referring to them. This is achieved by putting symbols into the language whose denotation is an agent identifier or action. Since quantification is not allowed in AL, these symbols will be constants. Also, to express the beliefs of agents, the internal language L must appear in AL somewhere.

More formally, the language of AL based on L contains the following symbols:

1. The symbols {**true, Bel, Send, Do**}
2. A countable set of constant symbols *Const* made up of the disjoint sets *Const*$_{Ag}$ (agent constants), and *Const*$_{Ac}$ (action constants)

---

[3]There is no special reason why we should not define a quantified language other than the space restrictions of this chapter; for quantified versions of AL, see Wooldridge (1992).

3. All closed formulae of the internal language L

4. The unary propositional connective $\neg$ and binary propositional connective $\lor$

5. The unary temporal connectives $\{\bigcirc, \bigcirc\}$ and the binary temporal connectives $\{\mathfrak{U}, \mathcal{S}\}$

6. The punctuation symbols $\}), (\}$

AL is thus parameterized by the internal language, L. The set of (well-formed) formulae of AL based on internal language L is defined by the following rules:

1. If i, j are agent ids, ϕ is a closed formula of L, and α is an action constant, then the following are atomic formulae of AL:

$$\textbf{true} \quad (\textbf{Bel } i \; \phi) \quad (\textbf{Send } i \; j \; \phi) \quad (\textbf{Do } i \; \alpha)$$

2. If ϕ, ψ are formulae of AL, then the following are formulae of AL:

$$\neg \phi \quad \phi \lor \psi$$

3. If ϕ, ψ are formulae of AL, then the following are formulae of AL:

$$\bigcirc \phi \quad \bigcirc \phi \quad \phi \mathfrak{U} \psi \quad \phi \mathcal{S} \psi$$

Table 10.1 summaries the meaning of the nonstandard operators in AL.

Semantics. A model for AL is a structure:

$$M = \langle \sigma, Ag, Ac, bel, action, sent, I \rangle$$

where

$\sigma \in \Sigma$ is an execution history.
Ag is a set of agent ids.
Ac is a set of actions.

TABLE 10.1. Schematic Rules for AL

(Bel i ϕ)	Agent i believes ϕ
(Send i j ϕ)	Agent i sent j message ϕ
(Do i α)	Agent i performs action α
$\bigcirc \phi$	Next ϕ
$\bullet \phi$	Last ϕ (strong)
$\phi \mathfrak{U} \psi$	ϕ Until ψ (not strict)
$\phi \mathcal{S} \psi$	ϕ Since ψ (strict)

bel : $\Sigma \times Ag \times \mathbb{N} \rightarrow BS$ is a function that takes an execution history, an agent identifier, and a time, and returns the belief set of the agent in the execution history at that time.

action: $\Sigma \times Ag \times \mathbb{N} \rightarrow Ac$ is a function that takes an execution history, an agent identifier, and a time, and returns the action performed by the agent in the execution history at that time.

sent : $\Sigma \times \mathbb{N} \rightarrow \mathcal{P}(Mess)$ is a function that takes an execution history and a time, and returns the set of messages sent in the execution history at that time.

I : *Const* $\leftrightarrow$ $(Ag \cup Ac)$ interprets constants.

There is a close relationship between the formal model of multiagent systems developed earlier, and logical models for AL. We can characterize this relationship by stating precisely the conditions under which a model for AL can be considered to represent an execution of a multiagent system.

A model

$$\langle \sigma, Ag, Ac, bel, action, sent, I \rangle$$

for AL represents a run of the system

$$\{\langle \mathcal{B}_i^0, \mathcal{C}_i, \mathfrak{M}_i, \mathfrak{N}_i \rangle : i \in Ag\}$$

iff the following condition obtains:

$$\forall u \in \mathbb{N} \cdot \forall i \in Ag \cdot bel(\sigma, i, u) = \mathcal{B}_i^u \wedge action(\sigma, i, u)$$

$$= \mathcal{C}_i(\mathcal{B}_i^u) \wedge sent(\sigma, u) = \bigcup_{j \in Ag} \mathfrak{M}_j(\mathcal{B}_j^u)$$

(Recall that $\mathcal{B}_i^u$ is defined in Eq. (1).) The satisfaction relation $\models$ for AL holds between pairs of the form $\langle M, u \rangle$ (where M is a model for AL, and $u \in \mathbb{N}$ is a temporal index into M) and formulae of AL. The semantic rules for AL are given in Figure 10.1.

The first four rules deal with atomic formulae, (or *atoms*), of AL. The formulae **true** is a logical constant for truth; it is always satisfied. The formula (**Bel** i ϕ) is read "agent i believes ϕ." **Bel** is essentially the belief operator from Konolige's logic L^B (Konolige, 1986a). The formula (**Do** i α) is read "agent i performs the action α." The formula (**Send** i j ϕ) describes the sending of messages, and will be satisfied if agent i has sent j a message with content ϕ.

The propositional connectives $\neg$ (not) and $\vee$ (or) have standard semantics. The remaining propositional connectives ($\Rightarrow$ (if ... then ...), $\wedge$ (and), and $\leftrightarrow$ (iff)) are defined as abbreviations in the usual way.

For convenience, the abbreviations in Table 10.2 are assumed. $\bigcirc$ and $\bigcirc$

$\langle M, u \rangle \models \text{true}$

$\langle M, u \rangle \models (\text{Bel } i \; \varphi)$	iff	$\varphi \in bel(\sigma, I(i), u)$
$\langle M, u \rangle \models (\text{Do } i \; \alpha)$	iff	$action(\sigma, I(i), u) = I(\alpha)$
$\langle M, u \rangle \models (\text{Send } i \; j \; \varphi)$	iff	$\langle I(i), I(j), \varphi \rangle \in sent(\sigma, u)$
$\langle M, u \rangle \models \neg\varphi$	iff	$\langle M, u \rangle \not\models \varphi$
$\langle M, u \rangle \models \varphi \vee \psi$	iff	$\langle M, u \rangle \models \varphi$ or $\langle M, u \rangle \models \psi$
$\langle M, u \rangle \models \bigcirc\varphi$	iff	$\langle M, u + 1 \rangle \models \varphi$
$\langle M, u \rangle \models \bullet\varphi$	iff	$u > 0$ and $\langle M, u - 1 \rangle \models \varphi$
$\langle M, u \rangle \models \varphi\,\mathcal{U}\,\psi$	iff	$\exists v \in \mathbb{N}$ s.t. $v \geq u$ and $\langle M, v \rangle \models \psi$ and $\forall w \in \mathbb{N}$ s.t. $u \leq w < v, \langle M, w \rangle \models \varphi$
$\langle M, u \rangle \models \varphi\,\mathcal{S}\,\psi$	iff	$\exists v \in \{0, \ldots, u - 1\}$ s.t. $\langle M, v \rangle \models \psi$ and $\forall w \in \mathbb{N}$ s.t. $v < w < u, \langle M, w \rangle \models \varphi$

Figure 10.1 *Semantic rules for AL.*

TABLE 10.2 Derived Temporal Operators

$\bullet\phi \stackrel{\text{def}}{=} \neg\bullet\neg\phi$	(Weak) last ϕ
$\text{start} \stackrel{\text{def}}{=} \neg\bullet\text{true}$	Initially ...
$\Diamond\phi \stackrel{\text{def}}{=} \text{true}\,\mathcal{U}\phi$	Sometime ϕ
$\Box\phi \stackrel{\text{def}}{=} \neg\Diamond\neg\phi$	Always ϕ
$\phi\mathcal{W}\psi \stackrel{\text{def}}{=} \Box\varphi \vee \phi\,\mathcal{U}\psi$	ϕ Unless ψ
$\blacklozenge\phi \stackrel{\text{def}}{=} \text{true}\,\mathcal{S}\psi$	Was ϕ
$\blacksquare\phi \stackrel{\text{def}}{=} \neg\blacklozenge\neg\phi$	Heretofore ϕ
$\phi\mathcal{Z}\psi \stackrel{\text{def}}{=} \blacksquare\phi \vee \phi\mathcal{S}\psi$	ϕ Zince ψ
$\phi\beta\psi \stackrel{\text{def}}{=} \neg((\neg\phi)\mathcal{U}\psi)$	ϕ Before (precedes) ψ

are the *next* and (strong) *last* operators respectively: $\bigcirc\phi$ is satisfied if ϕ is satisfied at the next time; $\bullet$ is the past time version of this operator, so that $\bullet\phi$ is satisfied if ϕ was satisfied at the last time. $\bullet$ is said to be *strong* because it is never satisfied at the beginning of time. The $\bullet$ operator is the weak version of $\bullet$: it is always satisfied at the beginning of time. The formula **start** is *only* satisfied at the beginning of time.

The symbols $\square$ and $\blacksquare$ are the *always* and *heretofore* operators respectively: $\square\phi$ will be satisfied iff ϕ is satisfied now and in all future moments $\blacksquare$ is the past time version. $\diamond$ and $\blacklozenge$ are the *sometime* and *was* operators respectively: $\diamond\phi$ will be satisfied if ϕ is satisfied now, or becomes satisfied at least once in the future; $\blacklozenge$ is the past version, so $\blacklozenge\phi$ will be satisfied if ϕ was satisfied at least once in the past. $\mathcal{U}$ and $\mathcal{W}$ are the *until* and *unless* operators respectively ($\mathcal{W}$ is sometimes called the *weak until* operator): $\phi\mathcal{U}\psi$ will be satisfied if ϕ is satisfied at all times until ψ becomes satisfied—ψ must eventually be satisfied. $\mathcal{W}$ is similar to $\mathcal{U}$, but allows for the possibility that the second argument never becomes satisfied. Finally, the $\mathcal{S}$ (since) and $\mathcal{Z}$ (zince) operators are the past time versions of $\mathcal{U}$ and $\mathcal{W}$ respectively.

Satisfiability and *validity* for AL are defined in the usual way.

Proof Theory. The proof-theoretic aspects of the linear discrete temporal logic upon which AL is based have been examined at length elsewhere, and we will not, therefore, discuss them here. The reader is referred to Gough (1984), Fisher (1991), Manna and Pnueli (1992), and Emerson (1990) for references and overviews.

4 REASONING ABOUT MULTIAGENT SYSTEMS

Having developed, in the preceding sections, a logic which may be used to represent the properties of multiagent systems, we now turn to the issue of actually *using* the logic. There are two obvious ways in which the logic might be used: for *specification* and for *verification*.

4.1 Specification

A system's specification is a statement describing those properties that it is intended the system should exhibit. A *formal* specification is one which is expressed (for the most part) in the language of mathematics. It is possible to use AL as a formal specification language for multiagent systems, in a way that we shall now illustrate.[4]

It was pointed out in Section 2 that temporal logics have for some time been used as a specification language for reactive systems, of which DAI systems

---

[4]Examples are actually presented using the quantified version of AL developed in Wooldridge (1992).

are a subset. There are two types of properties of such systems that we normally wish to specify:

- Liveness properties, which assert that "something good will happen"
- Safety properties, which assert that "nothing bad happens"

To illustrate such properties, and the way in which they might be expressed using AL, we shall consider a trivial example of a protocol for cooperative activity. In this protocol, agents communicate through just two message types (cf. Shoham, 1993):

$$Request(\alpha) \quad \text{a request for action } \alpha \text{ to be performed}$$
$$Inform(\phi) \quad \text{sender informs recipient of "fact" } \phi$$

Two domain predicates are assumed:

$$Friend(i) \quad \text{agent } i \text{ is a friend}$$
$$Trust(i) \quad \text{agent } i \text{ is trusted}$$

An agent that receives a *Request* from a friendly agent to do some action will eventually do it, but not otherwise (i.e., actions will *only* be done at the request of a friendly agent). If an agent receives an *Inform* message, it will add the "fact" to it beliefs only if the sender is trusted.

This simple protocol may be specified with ease. First, we state that an agent that receives a *Request* from a friendly agent will do the action; this is a liveness property.

$$\Box \forall i \cdot \forall j \cdot \forall \alpha \cdot (\textbf{Send } i\, j\, Request(\alpha)) \wedge (\textbf{Bel } j\, Friend(i)) \Rightarrow \Diamond(\textbf{Do } j\, \alpha)$$

That is, it is always true that if i sends j a *Request* for α, and j believes i to be friendly, then j will eventually do α.

The following expresses a safety property, namely that if an agent does some action, then the performance of the action must have been preceded by a *Request* from a friendly agent to do the action.

$$\Box \forall i \cdot \forall j \cdot \forall \alpha \cdot \begin{bmatrix} \neg((\textbf{Send } i\, j\, Request(\alpha)) \wedge (\textbf{Bel } j\, Friendly(i))) \\ \mathcal{Z} \\ (\textbf{Do } j\, \alpha) \wedge \neg(\textbf{Send } ij\, Request(\alpha)) \end{bmatrix}$$
$$\Rightarrow \neg(\textbf{Do } j\, \alpha)$$

We now move on to the properties of *Inform* messages. The following liveness property asserts that an agent receiving an *Inform* message from a trusted agent will eventually come to believe the content of the message.

$$\Box \forall i \cdot \forall j \cdot (\textbf{Send } i\, j\, Inform(\phi)) \wedge (\textbf{Bel } j\, Trusted(i)) \Rightarrow \Diamond(\textbf{Bel } j\, \phi)$$

In this case, there is no corresponding safety property: we do not want to specify that an agent will only believe something if it has previously been informed of it by a trusted agent.

This example is admittedly simple, but at least demonstrates how one might go about the specification process. In Wooldridge (1992), several more detailed examples are provided.

4.2 Verification

Verification is the process of showing that an implemented system is correct with respect to its specification. *Formally* verifying a system involves proving (in the mathematical sense) that it is correct. Just as it is possible to use AL for specification, so it is possible to use it for verification. However, verification is generally regarded as a much more complex process than specification, and although the principles of formal verification have been fairly well understood for some time, it is quite rare to find examples of its use outside textbooks and research papers. We will therefore only touch on the subject here.

To verify that a system $\mathcal{SYS}$ is correct with respect to a specification $\mathcal{SPEC}$ (where $\mathcal{SPEC}$ is expressed as a set of formulae of AL, as described above), one first derives the *theory* of $\mathcal{SYS}$, which we shall denote by $\mathcal{JJC}(\mathcal{SYS})$. Then, one attempts to prove that $\mathcal{SPEC}$ follows from $\mathcal{JJC}(\mathcal{SYS})$, i.e., that $\mathcal{JJC}(\mathcal{SYS}) \vdash \mathcal{SPEC}$, using the proof theory of AL. $\mathcal{JJC}(\mathcal{SYS})$ will be a set of formulae of AL which capture both *general* properties of the type of system being modeled, and *specific* properties of $\mathcal{SYS}$. Examples of how one goes about deriving the theory of a system are provided in both Wooldridge (1992, Chapter 6) and Fisher and Wooldridge (1993b).

5 DISCUSSION

This chapter has described a research program, directed at developing formal methods for reasoning about multiagent systems. This program was illustrated by means of a simple worked example. The emphasis throughout the chapter has been on developing the ideas in an intelligible way. This has meant that in order to avoid confusion, a number of important issues have been glossed over, or ignored completely. Future work must focus particularly on the following topics:

Realistic Treatments of Concurrency. The issue of concurrency has scarcely been addressed in formal treatments of DAI, and yet concurrency is at the very heart of the area. The reluctance to address this issue is understandable, however: DAI systems are *not* simply concurrent systems. DAI researchers have quite rightly focused on such issues as coordination, as these are peculiar to the domain. Nevertheless, if we ever hope to claim that we have a formalism which truly captures the properties of a DAI system, then we must deal with this issue. There are some signs that work is being done in this area (Burkhard, 1993).

Modeling More Complex and Realistic Agents and Systems. The model of agents presented in this chapter was intended to be general, and yet its very generality makes it unrealistically simple. All but the most basic applications have a much richer internal structure. Our theories and models must be able to represent this structural and operational complexity, while remaining conceptually tractable. In this area too, there are signs that some work is being done (Rao and Georgeff, 1992; Wooldridge, 1994).

(Semi-)automated Theorem Proving. We cannot hope to use logics such as AL for reasoning about realistic multiagent systems without some kind of theorem proving support for them. Unfortunately, this kind of logic tends to be extraordinarily complex in computational terms; some similar logics are so complex as to be undecidable, *even in the propositional case* (Halpern and Vardi, 1989). However, work is underway to find proof methods for simplified variants of these logics (Wooldridge and Fisher, 1994).

Bridging the Gap between Theory and Practice. There is an intrinsic value in formal models and theories of the world that makes them a worthwhile exercise even if they have no immediately obvious practical application. However, it is hoped that the research program sketched in this chapter *does* have some practical applications. One important possibility for the near future involves bringing the practice of DAI closer to its theory by using logics such as AL to program agents directly; this is, in essence, what the "agent-oriented" paradigm is all about (Shoham, 1993; Thomas, 1993; Fisher and Wooldridge, 1993a).

ACKNOWLEDGMENTS

This chapter is a condensed and simplified version of part of the author's Ph.D. thesis (Wooldridge, 1992), and as such this work was supported by (what was) the SERC; a revised and much extended version of the review material presented here has appeared in Wooldridge and Jennings (1994). Thanks to Michael Fisher for his time and suggestions and to Greg O'Hare for his encouragement and enthusiastic support.

REFERENCES

Barwise, J., and Perry, J. (1983). *Situations and Attitudes.* MIT Press, Cambridge, MA.

Brooks, R. (1991). Intelligence without reason. *Proc. Int. Jt. Conf. Artif. Intell, 12th,* Sydney, Australia, *1991,* pp. 569–595.

Burkhard, H.-D. (1993). Liveness and fairness properties in multi-agent systems. *Proc. Int. Jt. Conf. Artif. Intell., 13th,* Chambéry, France, *1993,* pp. 325–330.

Cammarata, S., McArthur, D., and Steeb, R. (1983). Strategies of cooperation in distributed problem solving. *Proc. Int. Jt. Conf. Artif. Intellig., 8th*, Karlsruhe, Germany, *1983*.

Chellas, B. (1980). *Modal Logic: An Introduction.* Cambridge Univ. Press, Cambridge, UK.

Cohen, P. R., and Levesque, H. J. (1990). Intention is choice with commitment. *Artif. Intell.* **42**, 213–261.

Connah, D., and Wavish, P. (1990). An experiment in cooperation. In *Decentralized Artificial Intelligence* (Y. Demazeau and J.-P. Müller, eds.), pp. 197–214. Elsevier/North-Holland, Amsterdam.

Dennett, D. C. (1987). *The Intentional Stance.* MIT Press, Cambridge, MA.

Doran, J., Carvajal, H., Choo, Y. J., and Li, Y. (1991). The MCS multi-agent testbed: Developments and experiments. In *Proceedings of the International Working Conference on Cooperating Knowledge Based Systems* (S. M. Deen, ed.), pp. 240–254. Springer-Verlag, Berlin.

Emerson, E. A. (1990). Temporal and modal logic. In *Handbook of Theoretical Computer Science* (J. van Leeuwen, ed.), pp. 996–1072. Elsevier, Amsterdam.

Fagin, R., and Halpern, J. Y. (1985). Belief, awareness, and limited reasoning. *Proc. Int. Jt. Conf. Artif. Intell., 9th*, Los Angeles, CA, *1985*, pp. 480–490.

Fisher, M. (1991). A resolution method for temporal logic. *Proc. Int. Jt. Conf. Artif. Intell., 12th*, Sydney, Australia, *1991*.

Fisher, M., and Wooldridge, M. (1993a). Executable temporal logic for distributed A.I. *Proc. Int. Workshop Distributed Artif. Intell., 12th*, Hidden Valley, PA, pp. 131–142.

Fisher, M., and Wooldridge, M. (1993b). Specifying and verifying distributed intelligent systems. In *Progress in Artificial Intelligence* (M. Filgueiras and L. Damas, eds.) Lect. Notes Artif. Intell., Vol. 727, pp. 13–28. Springer-Verlag, Berlin.

Gärdenfors, P. (1988). *Knowledge in Flux.* MIT Press, Cambridge, MA.

Gasser, L., Braganza, C., and Hermann, N. (1987). MACE: A flexible testbed for distributed AI research. In *Distributed Artificial Intelligence* (M. N. Huhns, ed.), pp. 119–152. Morgan Kaufmann, San Mateo, CA/Pitman, London.

Gough, G. D. (1984). Decision procedures for temporal logic. Master's Thesis, Department of Computer Science, Manchester University, Manchester, UK.

Halpern, J. Y. (1987). Using reasoning about knowledge to analyze distributed systems. *Annu. Rev. Comput. Sci.* **2**, 37–68.

Halpern, J. Y., and Moses, Y. (1992). A guide to completeness and complexity for modal logics of knowledge and belief. *Artif. Intell.* **54**, 319–379.

Halpern, J. Y., and Vardi, M. Y. (1989). The complexity of reasoning about knowledge and time. I. lower bounds. *J. Comput. Syst. Sci.* **38**, 195–237.

Hintikka, J. (1962). *Knowledge and Belief.* Cornell Univ. Press, Ithaca, NY.

Kaelbling, L. P. (1986). An architecture for intelligent reactive systems. In *Reasoning About Actions and Plans* (M. P. Georgeff, and A. L. Lansky, ed.), pp. 395–410. Morgan Kaufmann, San Mateo, CA.

Konolige, K. (1986a). *A Deduction Model of Belief.* Morgan Kaufmann, San Mateo, CA/Pitman, London.

Konolige, K. (1986b). What awareness isn't: A sentential view of implicit and explicit belief (position paper). In *Proceedings of the 1986 Conference on Theoretical As-*

pects of Reasoning About Knowledge (J. Y. Halpern, ed.), pp. 241–250. Morgan Kaufmann, Los Altos, CA.

Levesque, H. J. (1984). A logic of implicit and explicit belief. *Proc. Natl. Conf. Artif. Intell.*, *4th*, Austin, TX, *1984*, pp. 198–202.

Levesque, H. J., Cohen, P. R., and Nunes, J. H. T. (1990). On acting together. *Proc. Natl. Conf. Artif. Intell.*, *8th*, Boston, MA, pp. 94–99.

Manna, Z., and Pnueli, A. (1992). *The Temporal Logic of Reactive and Concurrent Systems*. Springer-Verlag, Berlin.

Milner, R. (1989). *Communication and Concurrency*. Prentice Hall, Englewood Cliffs, NJ.

Milner, R., Parrow, J., and Walker, D. (1992). A calculus of mobile processes. *Inf. Comput.* **100**(1), 1–77.

Moore, R. C. (1985). A formal theory of knowledge and action. In *Formal Theories of the Commonsense World* (J. R. Hobbs and R. C. Moore, eds.). Ablex, Norwood, NJ.

Pnueli, A. (1977). The temporal logic of programs. *Proc. Symp. Found. Comput. Sci.*, *18th*.

Pnueli, A. (1986). Specification and development of reactive systems. In *Information Processing 86.* Elsevier/North-Holland, Amsterdam.

Rao, A. S., and Georgeff, M. P. (1992). An abstract architecture for rational agents. In *Proceedings of the Third International Conference on Knowledge Representation and Reasoning* (C. Rich, W. Swartout, and B. Nebel, eds.), pp. 439–449. Morgan Kaufmann, San Mateo, CA.

Shoham, Y. (1993). Agent-oriented programming. *Artif. Intell.* **60**(1), 51–92.

Thomas, S. R. (1993). *PLACA, an agent oriented programming language*. Ph.D. Thesis, Computer Science Department, Stanford University, Stanford, CA. (available as Tech. Rep. STAN-CS-93-1487).

Wooldridge, M. (1992). *The logical modelling of computational multi-agent systems*. Ph.D. Thesis, Department of Computation, UMIST, Manchester, UK (also available as Tech. Rep. MMU-DOC-94-01, Department of Computing, Manchester Metropolitan University, Manchester, UK).

Wooldridge, M. (1994). This is MYWORLD: The logic of an agent-oriented testbed for DAI. In *Pre-Proceedings of the 1994 Workshop on Agent Theories, Architectures, and Languages* (M. Wooldridge and N. R. Jennings, eds.), pp. 147–163. Amsterdam.

Wooldridge, M., and Fisher, M. (1992). A first-order branching time logic of multi-agent systems. *Proc. Eur. Conf. Artif. Intellig.*, *10th*, Vienna, Austria, pp. 234–238.

Wooldridge, M., and Fisher, M. (1994). A decision procedure for a temporal belief logic. In *Temporal Logic, Proceedings of the First International Conference* (D. M. Gabbay and H. J. Ohlbach, eds.), Lect. Notes Artif. Intell., Vol. 827, pp. 317–331. Springer-Verlag, Berlin.

Wooldridge, M., and Jennings, N. R. (1994). Agent theories, architectures, and languages: A survey. In *Pre-proceedings of the 1994 Workshop on Agent Theories, Architectures, and Languages* (M. Wooldridge and N. R. Jennings, eds.), pp. 1–32. Amsterdam.

CHAPTER 11

Reactive Distributed Artificial Intelligence: Principles and Applications

JACQUES FERBER

1. INTRODUCTION

The field of distributed artificial intelligence (DAI) distinguishes between cognitive and reactive multiagent systems (Demazeau and Müller, 1991). Cognitive agents have a symbolic and explicit representation of their environment on which they can reason and from which they can predict future events. Cognitive agents are driven by intentions, i.e., by explicit goals that conduct their behavior and make them able to choose between possible actions (see Chapters 1, 2, 5, 6, 8, and 9). Examples of this approach are given by L. Gasser with the MACE system (Gasser et al., 1987), by J. Doran (Doran et al., 1994) who uses cognitive agents to model social changes in paleolithic societies, by V. Lesser and E. Durfee who have studied cooperative work between agents at the cognitive level (Durfee et al., 1987a), by A. Haddadi and K. Sundermeyer who construct intelligent agent architectures for cooperative work (Haddadi and Sundermeyer, this volume), and by Castelfranchi and Conte (Conte et al., 1991) who build a theory of cognitive emergence by virtue of cognitive dependence, using the formal apparatus of Cohen and Levesque (1990). Most DAI industrial systems such as ARCHON (Jennings and Wittig, 1992, Chapter 12) are related to the cognitive paradigm. Fundamental issues of cognitive multiagent systems can be found in Gasser (1991, 1992, as well as Chapters 5, 6, 8, and 9).

Reactive agents on the contrary do not have representation of their environment and act using a stimulus/response type of behavior: they respond to the

Foundations of Distributed Artificial Intelligence, Edited by G. M. P. O'Hare and N. R. Jennings.
ISBN 0-471-00675-0 © 1996 John Wiley & Sons, Inc.

present state of the environment in which they are embedded. Thus, reactive agents follow simple patterns of behavior which can easily be programmed. Studies on reactive agents can be traced to the works of Agre and Chapman (1987), Brooks (Brooks and Connell, 1986), Connah and Wavish (Wavish and Connah, 1990), and Steels (1989).

Many architectures or theories about reactive actions have been proposed. The *subsumption architecture*, defined by Brooks, the *task competition approach* which is described below in the context of the EthoModeling Framework, or the situated action theory proposed by Suchman (1987) and pursued by Agre and Chapman. But the most interesting part of reactive agents does not lie in their achitecture, but in their ability to interact with other agents in a simple way from which global complex patterns of activities can emerge.

Reactive agents have been applied in a few domain areas, where the most important are simulation, robotics, and problem solving. In the simulation area, reactive agents have been mainly used to represent animal behavior as in the work of Hogeweg (Hogeweg and Hesper, 1985), Collins and Jefferson (1991a), Deneubourg (Deneubourg et al., 1987; Deneubourg and Goss, 1989), and Maruichi and Tokoro (Maruichi et al., 1987). Reactive agents have been proposed in robotics by Brooks (1990) and Steels (1989) but many examples of reactive agents can be considered as simulations of little robots moving around in some environment. They have also been proposed as a way to solve diverse kind of problems by Ferber (1989) and Connah (1991).

This chapter describes the basic issues behind the design of reactive agents systems, and their use in various domains such as simulation and problem solving. This chaper is not an exhaustive survey of approaches conducted in reactive agents systems, but its aim is to give a better understanding of the way reactive agents can be used for different purposes. It is divided in three parts: Section 2 gives a general presentation of the main characteristics of reactive agent systems. In particular the importance of topological structures and of feedback mechanisms are pointed out. Section 3 introduces the field of multi-agent simulation. Section 4 presents the MANTA project which is an example of the use of reactive agents for simulating insect societies. Section 5 presents the field of collective problem solving as both a problem decomposition approach and a set of problem-solving methods based on simple and reactive interacting agents.

2   BASIC ISSUES OF REACTIVE MULTIAGENT SYSTEMS

2.1   Behavior-Based Activity

Reactivity is a behavior-based model of activity, as opposed to the symbol manipulation model used in planning (Chapman, 1987). This leads to the notion of cognitive cost, i.e., the complexity of the overall architecture needed to achieve a task. Cognitive agents support a complex architecture which means that their cognitive cost is high. Cognitive agents have an internal representation of the world which must be in adequation with the world itself. The process of relating the internal representation and the world is considered as a complex task. On the otherhand, reactive agents are simple, easy to understand and do not support any internal representation of the world. Thus their cognitive cost is low, and tend to what is called cognitive economy, the property of being able to perform even complex actions with simple architectures.

Because of their complexity, cognitive agents are often considered as self-sufficient: they can work alone or with only a few other agents. On the contrary, reactive agents need companionship. They cannot work isolated and they usually achieve their tasks in groups. Reactive agents are situated: they do not take past events into account, and cannot foresee the future. Their action is based on what happens *now*, on how they sense and distinguish situations in the world, on the way they recognize world indexes and react accordingly. Thus, reactive agents cannot plan ahead what they will do. But what can be considered as a weakness is one of their strengths because they do not have to revise their world model when perturbations change the world in an unexpected way.

Robustness and fault tolerance are two of the main properties of reactive agent systems. A group of reactive agents can complete tasks even when one of them breaks down. The loss of one agent does not prohibit the completion of the whole task, because allocation of roles is achieved locally by perception of the environmental needs. Thus reactive agent systems are considered as very flexible and adaptive because they can manage their resources abilities (the agents) in unpredictable worlds, and complete the tasks they are engaged in even in the case of partial failures of the system.

2.2 Importance of Topological Structures

The structure of the environment agents live in is highly important for organizing a society, because spatial differences are transformed into organizational structures and social differentiation of agents. Spatial relations provide major opportunities and constraints to self-organization. Because stimuli propagation and reciprocal influences decrease as a function of the distance between agents, behaviors of agents are strongly dictated by their relative positions in a topological structure (see Chapter 9).

Figure 11.1 exemplifies this process. Let us assume that we are in a reactive multiagent system, and that a stimulus S produced by a source S_0 can trigger a behavior P into agents A and B of the same kind. Let us suppose also that agent A is closer to the source S_0 than agent B. Because stimulus intensity decreases as an inverse function (either linear or square root) of the distance between the source and its receiver, the stimulus level of S is such that $level_s(A) > level_s(B)$. Then the impact of S will be stronger on A than on B, and the behavior P will be triggered more easily on A than on B. If a reinforcement takes place as on the EMF model described in Section 4, A will tend to be

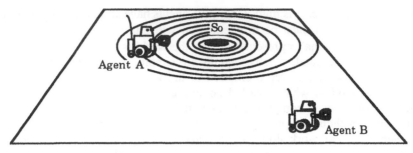

Figure 11.1   *Importance of spatial relations.*

more specialized than B in dealing with actions triggered by the stimulus S, thus providing a social differentiation of the agents roles in the society.

2.3   Feedback

Emergence of functionality and of stable states are produced by the joined forces of different feedback mechanisms. Positive feedback tends to create diversities among agents, whereas negative feedback regulates societies, imposing a conservative force upon their social structures. In multiagent systems, feedback can be classified in two categories:

1. Local feedback which is built by the agent designer, and is part of the primitive constructs of agents
2. Global feedback, which is the result of interactions between agents and whose action is not explicitly described at the agent level

For instance, a reinforcement process that makes an already specialized agent more inclined to perform the same tasks is a type of positive feedback that can be set up at the agent level. Its effect is to strengthen any differentiation and create disparities among agents. Regulations such as the distribution of roles in the society is a negative feedback that can be observed as an emergent functionality of agents interaction, as we will see below. Whereas local feedback loops are deterministic because they have been designed as such by a programmer, global feedback is not always deterministically predictable. They often result from autocatalytic processes which result from interactions in open systems (Prigogine and Stengers, 1979).

2.4   Architectures of Reactive Agents

Many architectures have been proposed to define reactive agents and allow them to perform their tasks autonomously.

Situated Rules.   The simplest reactive architecture is provided by a finite number of rules which relate perceptions to actions and provide a means to describe reactions to situations. This architecture follows from the work of Suchman (1987) and Agre and Chapman's theory of action (1987). Wavish and Connah (Wavish, 1990; 1992) have implemented their theory of situated action by describing the behaviour of an agent as a set of rules which directly relates perceived situations to specific actions in the following manner:

```
if <perceived situation>
then <specific actions>
```

For instance, let us suppose that we want to describe the behavior of an agent which has to fetch a hammer from a shed and bring it to a workroom. One way is to describe its behavior using the following set of rules:

```
Rule fetch-hammer
    if I don't carry anything
    and I am not at the shed location
    then go to the shed

Rule take-hammer
    if I don't carry anything
    and I am at the shed location
    then take a hammer

Rule go-workroom
    if I carry something
    and I am not at the workroom
    then go to the workroom

Rule drop-thing
    if I carry something
    and I am at the workroom
    then drop it
```

Architectures made of rules are very handy for simple behaviors, but they tend to be inadequate for more complex forms of action control. Situated rules suppose that an agent does not have any memory of past states, and that action comes only from perception. It is also generally assumed that the rules are mutually exclusive and that the system does not contain any rule conflict. This assumption imposes severe restriction on the way to write such a rule system. In order to bypass this limitation, Rosenchein and Kaelbling (1986), have proposed a language based on a logical formalism called situated automata. Expressions of this language can be traansformed into a combinatorial circuits which perform an input to output transformation from sensors to actuators.

Finite-State Automata and Subsumption Architectures. In order to provide agents with more elaborate architectures and behavior descriptions, R.

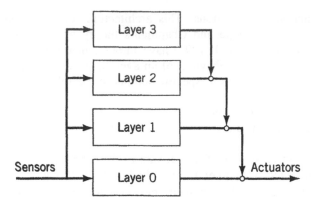

Figure 11.2   *Structure of a typical subsumption architecture.*

Brooks, proposed a specific architecture for his robots called the subsumption architecture (Brooks and Connell, 1986). A subsumption architecture is made of a set of modules, represented as augmented finite-state machines, which are linked through a master/slave relationship of inhibition. A higher-level module can inhibit that input values flow into a lower module or that output informations are sent to actuators. Modules are combined into layers, where each layer is responsible for some level of competence of the agent, as in Figure 11.2. The subsumption architecture has been used to implement various robots of different abilities, from simple *wall-followers* to more complex *can-finder* robots. Steels (1989) used it to study self-organization of cooperative simulated robots collecting samples (see Section 5.1. below) and Mataric (1992) to build her own set of cooperative robots. The subsumption architecture can be considered as a typical architecture to build a behavior-based agent. However, complex behaviors, such as conflicts between tendencies of the same level, tends to be very tricky to design by simple inhibitory mechanisms.

Competing Tasks. A different approach is to consider the behavior of an agent as the result of competing entities which tries to get control over the actuators of the agent. This idea comes in direct line from the Society of Mind of Minsky (1986), and has been realized differently by Maes (1991), Travers (1988), and Drogoul and Ferber (1992c). An agent is defined as a set of conflicting tasks where only one can be active simultaneously. A task is a high-level behavioral sequence opposed to the low-level actions performed directly by actuators, and are considered here as primitives. The selection and suspension of a task is triggered by stimuli proceeding from the environment or the internal parts of the agent. A reinforcement mechanism is used as a basic learning tool to help the agent to be more sensitive to stimuli that have already triggered a task. This helps the agent to be more efficient in tasks that are often used and to discard the others. We will see in Section 4 the use of a competing task architecture to simulate the behavior of ants.

Neural Networks. In order to get smoother behavior, neural networks have been broadly used to implement action decisions. Many proposals come directly from ideas gained in neuroethology. For instance Beer (1990) showed how to build an insect-like agent made of ''neurons'' to perform various tasks (wandering, edge following, feeding) and survive in a simulated environment. Usually a simple network cannot accommodate complex task performances. More elaborate architectures are needed to differenciate between tasks and control intricate actions. Pfeifer and Vershure (1992) have realized a layered architecture were each layer is made of artificial neurons (Fig. 11.3). Arbib and colleagues (Lyons and Arbib, 1989) have also specified a hierarchical architecture derived from biology. It is also possible to integrate neural networks and genetic algorithms, encoding weights of the networks into the agent's genome. Genetic algorithms are then used as an optimizing function to adapt the structure of networks to their environmental conditions (Belew et al., 1991; Werner and Dyer, 1991; Cliff et al., 1993).

The major interest of neural network architectures is their ability to directly learn from their previous actions. Some architectures make a distinction between learning and performance phases. This assumes that an operator has to decide when the agent should start and stop the learning phase, which makes the agent less autonomous than is advocated. A better solution lies in systems whose dynamics lead to an equilibrium when the environment is stable and start again their learning when changes happen in the environment (see Chapter 1). However, it is still difficult to control complex task coordination

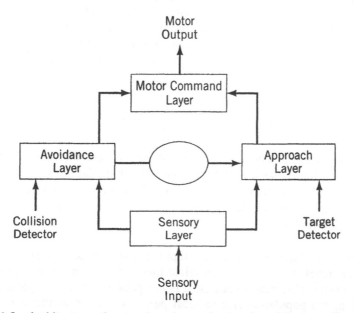

Figure 11.3 *Architecture of a structured neural network architecture. (From Pfeifer and Verschure, 1992.)*

when decisions have to be made at different level (see Chapters 6 and 8). Such systems still exhibit very simple behaviors, mainly because researchers want to start from zero, leading to a huge global search which makes higher-level behaviors very unlikely to appear.

3 MULTIAGENT SIMULATION

Understanding the process of evolution in population is important in the study of ecological and sociological systems. Simulation is both a design tool and an analytic device which is used to experiment on a model. Simulation consists in artificially reproducing natural phenomena using a model, which is an abstract representation of a studied system based on a theory. The representation link is an abstract function that maps individuals and/or properties of individuals to elements of the model. The tool is a computational device (usually a computer), and evaluation procedure is a methodology for evaluating the results and comparing them to the real system.

3.1 Traditional Simulation Techniques

Traditional techniques of simulation are based on mathematical or stochastic models, usually differential equations which relates various parameters and describe the dynamics of the systems. They examine the cause-and-effect relationships during the simulation by relating output variables to input ones. For instance, ecological simulations can relate the population size of specific species to the growth of different species and the number of predations. The following simple differential equations shows the well-known formulas defined by Lotka and Volterra (Volterra, 1926) which express the rate of growth of predator and prey populations:

$$\frac{dN_1}{dt} = r_1 N_1 - P N_1 N_2 \qquad \frac{dN_2}{dt} = a P N_1 N_2 - d_2 N_2$$

where P is the coefficient of predation, N_1 and N_2 are the prey and predator populations, a represents the efficiency with which predators converts food into offspring, r_1 is the birthrate of preys and d_2 is the death rate of predators. Differential equations have been intensely used for simulating societies but they present severe limitations:

1. *Micro to Macro Relationship.* Input and output parameters are defined at the same level; i.e., they do not relate global parameters to local ones. For instance, from differential equations, it is not possible to relate a global parameter such as the population size to local parameters such as the decision processes of the individuals. Individual behaviors, i.e., decisions made at the individual or group level, cannot be incorporated into these simulations.

2. *Complexity and Realism of Parameters.* Complexity in models leads to the definition of new parameters whose relation to reality is not obvious. For instance, in the above equations (which are very simple differential equations though), the parameter a, which relates the food taken to the offspring does not model reality in a very accurate way, where offspring are the results of many complex processes and behaviors (e.g., mating, nesting, foraging, etc.) where the group structure is of primary importance. Detailed simulations require complex differential equations leading to the definition of awkward parameters.

3. *Taking Behaviors into Account.* Differential equations, and numerical methods in general, do not represent actions, i.e., activities resulting in a modification of the world. Actions are only seen by their measurable achievement and in terms of their probability to happen.

4. *Multitask Behaviors and Conditional Task Switching.* In numerical modeling, actions cannot be considered as proceeding from evaluation decisions whose outcome depends on conditions of the world, i.e., perceived situations and/or stimuli. For instance in numerical modeling, a feeding and hunting process can be described by an equation relating the number of preys to the probability for a predator to find a prey, and the number of predators. This kind of equations does not show the different kind of strategies by which a predator can find and hunt a prey. Its does not describe the behavior of the predator but only relations between the number of predators and number of preys in a delimited data.

5. *Qualitative Information.* Lastly, numerical simulations cannot cope with qualitative data such as the relation between a stimulus and the behavior of an individual. These relations, which are typical of ethological models, are beyond the scope of analytical equations and numerical simulations. They require new computing models and tools that can capture the local interactions from which a global behavior of the population emerges.

3.2 Multiagent Simulation

The life of an individual can be characterized by its behavior, where the term behavior means the set of actions an agent performs in response to its environmental conditions, its internal states and its drives.

The multiagent simulation model is based on the idea that programs do exhibit behaviors that can be entirely described by their internal mechanisms, the program instructions (see Chapter 10). By relating an individual to a program, it is possible to simulate an artificial world populated with interacting computational entities. This is what is called multiagent systems in the field of computing sciences. Simulation can be achieved by transposing the population of a real biosystem to its artificial counterpart. Each individual organism of the population is separately represented as a computing process, an agent. The behavior of an agent during all its stages of life (e.g., birth, feeding, mating, reproduction, and death) is programmed with all the required details.

Multiagent simulations are primarily used to represent complex situations in which individuals have complex and different behaviors, and to analyze the global situations as emergent structures of the interaction processes. The purpose of such simulations is to consider both quantitative (e.g., numerical parameters) and qualitative (e.g., individual behaviors) properties of a system in the model, as opposed to traditional simulation in which the representation link only relates properties to quantitative parameters. Multiagent simulation is also called *microanalytic* simulation meaning that each individuals behavior and environmental conditions are effectively represented (Collins and Jefferson, 1991b). Such simulations are based on the construction of a microworld where particular hypotheses can be explored, and experiments can be repeated and controlled in a similar way that real experiments are done in a real laboratory.

In a multiagent simulation, each biological and sociological individual (or a group of individuals) is analogically represented as a computational agent, i.e., an autonomous computational process capable of performing local actions in response to various stimuli and/or communications with other agents. The behavior of an agent is a consequence of its observation and interactions with other agents, whereas interactions means communications, stimuli influences, or direct actions of other agents. Therefore, there is a one-to-one correspondence between individuals (or groups) of the world to be described and agents.

In a multiagent simulation, the model is not a set of equations as in mathematical models, but a set of entities that can be described by the quadruple

⟨**agents, objects, environment, communications**⟩

where **agents** is the set of all the simulated individuals (defined by their ability to perceive specific kind of communications, by their skills in performing various actions, their deliberation model if any, and their way to relate perception to action), **objects** is the set of all represented passive entities that do not react to stimuli (e.g., furniture, etc.), **environment** is the topological space where agents and objects are located, where they can move and act upon, and where signals (e.g., sounds, smells, etc.) propagate, **communications** is the set of all communications categories, such as voice, written materials, media, scent, signs, etc.

3.3   Goals of Multiagent Simulation

Multiagent simulation can be used for different purposes.

a. *Test hypothesis* about the emergence of social structures from the behavior of each individual and its interactions. This can be done by experimenting about the minimal conditions given at the microlevel which are necessary to observe phenomena at the macrolevel.

b. *Build theories* that contribute toward the development of a general understanding of ethological, sociological, and psychosociological systems by relating behaviors to structural and organizational properties.

c. *Integrate different partial theories* coming from various disciplines (i.e., sociology, ethology, ethnology, cognitive psychology) into a general framework by providing tools that allows for integration of disjointed studies.

Multiagents and numerical analysis are not contradictory, but they are intended to be used at different levels. Multiagent models are used at a local level as analogical mappings of a real system. From this description, one can derive global parameters which can be studied and be incorporated into a mathematical model. In multiagent simulations, numerical data and statistics are not eliminated, but they are used as evaluation procedures to compare the results coming from the simulation tool to the observation data coming from the "real" world. Thus mathematical models are used at the macrolevel, whereas multiagent simulation models are used to cross the micro-macro bridge by letting global configuration emerge from the local agent interactions.

4 THE MANTA PROJECT: AN EXAMPLE IN MULTIAGENT SIMULATION

The purpose of the MANTA (Modeling an ANThill Activity) project is to study the emergence of a division of labor within a society of primitive ants. It has been developed as an application of the EthoModeling Framework (EMF for short), a multiagent modeling system whose features are briefly described in the next section. More details about its implementation and its use can be found in Drogoul and Ferber (1992c). The MANTA project can be seen as an example of the use of multiagent systems to help in the study of collective behaviors of real animals. Other examples can be found in Hogeweg and Hesper (1985). Deneubourg et al. (1987), Collins and Jefferson (1991a), Theraulaz et al. (1991), and Theraulaz (1991).

4.1 The EMF Model

EMF gives the user a domain-independent kernel that allows him to design simulations including different species of individuals and an environment. In this model, the species are called *classes*. Classes are defined by inheritance of the kernel class **EthoAgent** and define the default behaviours and knowledge of their agents. The creation process of an agent from its class is called *instanciation*. **EthoAgent** rules describe the default functioning of the agents and the interactions between them and their environment. From this object-oriented approach, it is possible to define

1. New species of agents by creating new classes that inherit from **EthoAgent**
2. Subspecies by inheritance, modification of the behaviors, or addition of new ones

3. An individual differentiation among the agents by allowing specific instanciations

Environment and Communication. The environment consists of a large set of entities that are called *places*. *Places* are divided into two categories: free places and obstacles. The main difference between them is that *obstacles* cannot accept agents and do not propagate stimuli. The agents communicate by propagating signals in the environment. The class **EthoAgent** provides each agent with personal stimuli, a set of "pheronome-like" signals working as personal "signatures." Modification in the state of an agent is recursively propagated to adjacent places, the signal intensity decreasing with distance. Thus neighboring agents becomes "aware" of this transformation, and can respond to these new stimuli.

Agent Structure. An agent architecture is comprised of two levels of actions using a task competition architecture. Contrast this with the approaches described in Chapter 5 and other chapters in Part III.

1. *Primitives* are low-level actions directly related to physiological possibilities. We assume that they cannot be decomposed into lower-level actions. Agents of the same species share the same primitives. The primitives are not related to stimuli and cannot be directly used by the agent and are composed in *tasks*.

2. *Tasks* are high-level behaviors that coordinate primitives calls in response to a *stimulus*. Agents of the same species do not necessarily own the same tasks. From an ethological point of view, tasks are close to *fixed-action patterns*. Each task is defined by a *name weight* which specifies its relative importance inside the agent, a *threshold* and an *activity level* when it becomes active.

Agents are initially provided with a mechanism of behavior reinforcement. When a task calls a primitive, the agent performs the *task-selection process*, to figure out if another task would be more appropriate to its environment than the current one. This process is made up of three steps (Figure 11.4) and based on a task competition principle:

1. *Sensing.* An agent acquires stimuli from its environment and eliminates those that do not match with a task name.

2. *Selection.* An agent computes the *activation level* a_i of a task i as follows:

$$a_i(t) = \frac{w_i(t)}{\sum\limits_{j=1}^{n} w_j(t)} x_i(t)$$

where w_i is the weight and x_i is the intensity stimulus of a task. A task is selectable if $a_i(t) > \sigma_i$ their threshold.

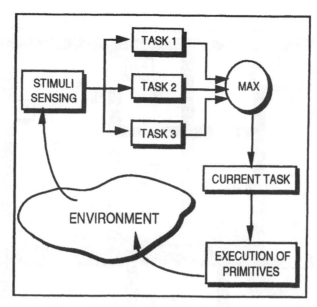

Figure 11.4 The task selection process.

3. *Activation.* Whenever there are selectable tasks whose activation level is higher than the one of the current task, the agent chooses the one with the higher *activation level*, suspends the *current task*, activates the selected one and increment its weight. When no tasks have been selected, then the current task simply goes on, and its activity level is decremented to provide for a kind of "boredom" process and make other task able to win the subsequent task competitions.

4.2. Simulating Ant Societies with MANTA

The species modeled in the MANTA project, *Ectatomma ruidum*, has a geographical distribution extending from southern Mexico to northern Brazil. The colonies contain a small number of ants (less than 300). This species is usually monogynous and a clear dimorphism distinguishes the queen from the workers. There are no physiological distinctions between the workers. The social organization of this species has been fully studied in Corbara et al. (1989) from the foundation of a society to its maturity, through

1. An individual analysis of the behavior of each member of a society
2. The establishment of an inventory of behavioral acts, combined into behavioral categories
3. The determination of "functional groups" by comparing and aggregating the behavioral profiles of the ants

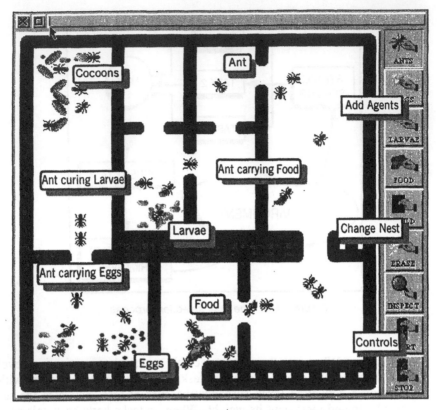

Figure 11.5 *Simulation environment of MANTA.*

MANTA Features. The environment of the simulation, depicted in Figure 11.5, reproduces a laboratory nest, with a large place not shown here representing the "outside" in which food can be placed. MANTA first defines some *environmental agents*, which are only used for propagating *environmental informations*. The classes that have been defined are **LightAgent** and **HumidityAgent,** which propagate stimuli name **#light** and **#humidity.**

The ants involved in the model are instances of two classes: **EctatommaAnt** and **EctatommaQueen** (which inherits from **EctatommaAnt**). An instance of these classes can respond to five stimuli (**#egg, #larva, #cocoon, #food, #ant**). The weight and thresholds of the related tasks are arbitrarily fixed (but may easily be modified).

These tasks can manage eight primitives. Here is the code of the task **#doEgg** which is called when an ant senses some eggs.

```
doEgg
   positiveTaxis(#egg)
   if there is an egg then
      take it
      do positiveTaxis(#egg) and negativeTaxis(#humidity)
      drop it
   else
      stop doEgg
```

The primitive **positiveTaxis** makes the agent follow the maximum gradient path to find the source of the corresponding stimulus (here **#egg**). The primitive **negativeTaxis** works in the opposite direction by making the agent flee from the source of the stimulus (here **#humidity**). The primitives **take** and **drop** are used to hold something or to leave it where the agent stands.

Experimenting with MANTA. As an illustration of the use of multiagent simulation, we will report some simple experiments using MANTA where ants are provided only with three tasks (**#doEgg, #doLarva** and **#doFood**) whose initial weight and threshold are identical for all tasks. The case study is composed of 30 identical ants, 50 larvae, 50 eggs, and 50 pieces of food randomly scattered in the nest. The simulation ends when the eggs, larvae and pieces of food are totally sorted into three separate clusters. Although this example does not intend to simulate a real nest, because the ants are not provided with all their behaviors, two lessons can be drawn from it:

1. The average distribution of the global working time between the three tasks equals the initial distribution between eggs, larvae and pieces of food (this has been checked in other examples; Drogoul and Ferber, 1992a), which indicates that the whole society adapts its means to the demand, and act as a good distributed regulating system.
2. A division of labor appears within the nest, characterized by several functional groups (see Figure 11.6 for the sociogram of the population)
   a. Eggs nurses (group 1, eight ants): distinguished by a high level of care of eggs and a low level of inactivity
   b. Unspecialized (group 2, eight ants): distinguished by a high level of inactivity. The ants nevertheless contribute to the other activities in the nest
   c. Feeders (group 3, seven ants): distinguished by a high level of feeding activities. The members of this group also show an important level of inactivity
   d. Larvae inactive (group 4, three ants): distinguished by a high level of care of larvae, a high level of inactivity and a very low level of care of the eggs

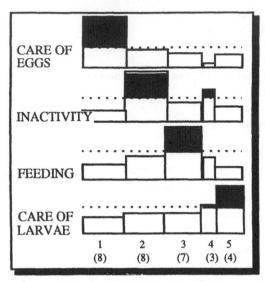

Figure 11.6 *Sociogram of the population of ants. Rows show the tasks and the columns give the distribution of tasks between ants.*

    e. Larvae nurses (Group 5, four ants): distinguished by a high level of care of larvae and low level in the other actvities.

    This labor division is simpler than what is observed in a real nest because of the simplification of the ants behavior. However, the structure is very stable throughout the various simulations we have made, which confirms the global negative feedback we talked about in Section 2.3: demands issued from eggs and larvae is reduced by the work supplied by ants in this small marketlike activity.

5 COLLECTIVE PROBLEM SOLVING

Reactive multiagent systems can be used to solve problems in multiple domains. Here are some examples of their use to perform tasks in a very robust and flexible way. Sometimes, these methods are also more efficient than classical methods in terms of time spent to solve a problem, because of their ability to compute locally and directly the "right" solution without exploring a large state-space. Application of these systems can be found in the field of robotics where a system consisting of many simple robots are somehow cheaper, more efficient, more adaptive, and less prone to break down than a single robot. For instance, an aircraft collision avoidance system can be defined using only reactive agents (Zeghal, 1994).

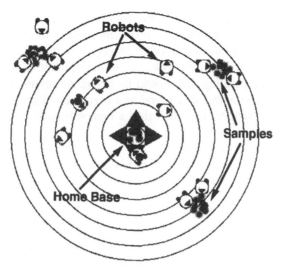

Figure 11.7 *Diagram of collective sample application.*

5.1 Collecting Samples

The "explorer robots application" appears to be one of the most common examples found to illustrate the capacity of a population of poorly intelligent creatures to handle with a global goal.

The key idea of the collective sample experiments is to make a set of little robots collect rock samples in an unpredictable environment and take them back to a home base. These robots usually operate independently and behave in quite a simple way. They can sense the samples, the home base and some other environmental signs (possibly left by other robots) and, of course, pick up and put down samples (Figure 11.7).

The first report about the "collecting samples" application has been made in Steels (1989) and was derived from the work of Deneubourg on simulation of foraging ants. This application, appears to be very popular because of its use in the three most important fields of artificial life, namely the simulation of the animal's behavior, with the works of Deneubourg et al. (1986), genetic algorithms and genetic programming (see, e.g., Koza, 1990, with the Santa-Fe trail), and robotics where it has been used to introduce the idea of using small cheap robots for exploring planets or dangerous locations (Brooks, 1990). Furthermore, it is now widely accepted as the best illustration of "swarm intelligence," along with the collective sorting example (Deneubourg et al., 1991).

This application is well adapted to reactive agents. If we suppose that it is not possible to plan the whole activity because of the lack of detailed maps of the terrain, robots should act autonomously to avoid obstacles and crevasses while achieving the global task. The general problem can be expressed as follows: how can these robots coordinate their tasks to explore, collect, and carry samples to the home base in order to get the best possible result (in terms of amount of samples collected within a certain amount of time)?

A simple noncooperating task would be to ask all agents to explore the area at random, collect samples once found and carry them back home, drop them, and go back to its random search, using a behavior such as the following:

```
simple collecting behavior
   if I detect an obstacle in front of me
   then I change my direction
   else
      if I carry a sample
      then if I am at the base location
            then I drop the samples I was holding
            else I go back to the base
      else if I find a sample
            then I pick it up
            else if I sense a sample
                  then I follow the gradient of this stimulus
                  else I move randomly
```

Obviously, this would not lead to very good results, because the time to get all samples is just the quotient of the time spent by one agent divided by the number of agents. Agents do not use their ability to cooperate to get better results. This method could be used when samples are scattered uniformly among the area, but when samples are clustered in a certain spot it would be more interesting to make several robots collect samples from a found spot. When one robot finds a spot with samples, it should communicate its location to others. With *cognitive agents*, this communication would be carried on by messages and the location would be given by its coordinate. But simple reactive agents do not possess such abilities.

However, a method inspired by the foraging behavior of ants, allows for agents to communicate by considering the environment as the transmission medium. By dropping "crumbs" on their way back to their home base, agents mark their environment and inform others of the spot position. We have called this technique *Tom Thumb* behavior because of the resemblance with Charles Perrault's tale (Drogoul and Ferber, 1992b).

To operate properly, crumbs have to persist while the spot contains samples and disappear when there is none. Many solutions can be proposed. One could think of slowly vanishing crumbs, whose intensity decay with time, or imagine agents with cleaning behaviors. They drop two crumbs when they carry samples and pick up one crumb if not (Steels, 1989). Thus, while a spot hold samples, agents which carry samples back home increase the number of crumbs and create trails made of crumbs. But when a spot is emptied, agents do not grasp any more samples and they quickly transform the trail into a land without crumbs:

```
Tom Thumb collecting behavior
   if I detect an obstacle in front of me
   then I change my direction
   else
      if I carry a sample
      then if I am at the base location
            then I drop the samples I was holding
            else I go back to the base and I drop two crumbs
      else if I find a sample
            then I pick it up
            else if I find crumbs
                  then I pick up one crumb
                  else if I sense a sample or a crumb
                        then I follow the gradient of this  stimu-
                        lus
                        else I move randomly
```

It has been shown that the crumb method is optimum when the competition between agents is low. When competition increases and leads to conflicts (e.g., traffic jams due to overcrowd) new techniques can be used. For instance, in Drogoul and Ferber (1992b) agents make chains from the samples spot to the home base, passing samples from one agent to the next. Chains emerge from a simple behavior which can be described as follows:

```
1. when I hold nothing and come from the base,
      if I encounter an agent carrying a sample,
      I take its sample and bring it back to the base.

2. When I hold something coming back to the base,
      if I encounter an agent carrying nothing,
      I give it my sample and go back to the samples' spot.
```

Figure 11.8 shows a simulation of chain-making robots in progress. Chains are dynamic structures that emerge from local actions of transferring samples from one agent to another. When the density of agents is high, agents do not move any more. They take samples from agents standing closer to the spot, and pass them to those which are closer to the base. When a spot becomes empty, agents cannot carry samples and the chain soon vanishes. Thus, chains are very robust and flexible: the discovery of new spots can lead to the creation of new chains and incidental destruction of agents lead to a dynamical reconstruction of a chain.

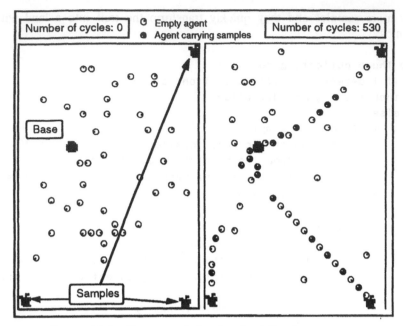

Figure 11.8   *Two snapshots of a simulation in progress.*

Reactive agents can be used to perform classical computer tasks such as sorting. Deneubourg et al. (1991) have shown that simple agents can partition elements in segregated piles using only local behaviors such as pick up or drop elements, where the probability to pick up (or drop) an element is a decreasing (increasing) function of the similarity of other objects in the vicinity. This continuous modification of the environment due to the ongoing collective actions acts as a positive feedback which transforms the scattered elements into piles of similar elements.

5.2.   Solving Classical Problems with Collective Behaviors

Since the beginning of artificial intelligence, problem solving has been seen as a state-space search. This fact is so deeply imbedded into the deep core of AI, that it seems somehow impossible to conceive another line of reasoning. However, this technique has weaknesses due to the combinatorial explosion. To overcome this difficulty, traditional approaches try to reduce the size of the state-space by using appropriate constraints propagation and heuristics. The lack of performance of these methods can be found in that they do not use the properties of the problem domain. Indeed, exploring a state-space is a way to recognize its own incapacity to use more elaborate methods, but reactive agents can be used to solve many classical AI problems.

For instance, our approach, which we call *eco-problem solving* (EPS) (Ferber and Jacopin, 1991), is based on the paradigm of ''computational ecosystems'' (Huberman and Hogg, 1988): problem solving is seen as the production of stable or stationary states in a dynamic system, where evolution is due to the behavior of simple agents. The effect of intelligence (the solution of a problem) is seen as an emerging process of interacting and communicating simple agents. By "simple" we mean agents that do not have goals or plans, but just behave according to their specific program, that we call its *eco-behavior*, which is just a simple "tropism," i.e., a behavior made of reactions to the environment. In that respect, this approach differs from other distributed approaches, such as "distributed planning" (Durfee et al., 1987b) or "planning for multiple agents" (Katz and Rosenschein, 1988) where a solution is obtained by coordination of the agents local plans.

In the ecoproblem-solving approach, a problem is defined by a population of autonomous agents whose interaction leads to a particular state (usually a stable state) that is called the solution of the problem. Each agent follows the principles of locality and autonomy, i.e., it can only take decisions from its own local information, without knowing about any global state of the world.

While behaving, these agents can execute specific actions, which are directly related to actions that could have been performed by a centralized system (e.g., a planning program) to obtain the result. Thus the solution is obtained as a side effect of the agents' behavior.

The Structure of Eco-Agents. Eco-agents are continuously questing for a satisfaction state. In this undertaking, they can be disturbed by other agents called *intruders*. Then the former attacks the later which has the obligation to flee and become *runaway*. The runaways are inclined to recursively attack other intruders that keep them from fleeing. Each eco-agent can be characterized by

1. A goal, i.e., which is defined as another agent with which it must be related (by what is called a *satisfaction relation*) to be satisfied.
2. An internal state which is a member of the following set: *satisfied, looking for satisfaction, fleeing, looking for flight*.
3. A set of elementary actions which are domain dependent and correspond to the satisfaction and flight behaviors.
4. A perception function returning the set of intruders for an agent that either looks for satisfaction or for flight.
5. A dependency agent which is the goal agent of an agent. We say that an agent is satisfied if its dependency is also satisfied and if it is connected by a satisfaction relation to its dependency.

An eco-agent can be modeled as a finite state automation with four states which represent the four internal states of the agent: *satisfied (S), looking for satisfaction (LS), looking for flight (LF), and fleeing (F)*. The starting state is LS. Inputs of the automaton are made of detection of aggression and intrusion. Outputs are commands to the domain-dependent actions (DoActionFlee and DoActionSatisfaction) and to the sending of an aggression message to another

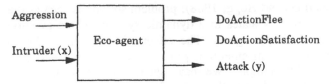

Figure 11.9 *Inputs/outputs of an eco-agent.*

agent (Figure 11.9). The graph of the automaton is given Figure 11.10. Each state transition is defined by a pair of input variables $\langle a, x \rangle$, where a means that the agent is attacked by another agent (and $\neg a$ means no aggression), and where x means that an agent x is an intruder ($\varnothing$ means no intruders and ? means indifferent) and by a triple of output variables $\langle$DoActionFlee, DoActionSatisfaction, Attack(y)$\rangle$, where 1 means that the command is performed.

Examples of Eco-Problem Solving. An eco-problem is given by a triple $\langle A, C, T \rangle$ where A is a set of agents characterized by their goal and their behavior, C is an initial configuration defined by a set of agents (whose automaton is in a starting state), and T is a terminating criterion, which corresponds generally to the satisfaction of every agent. The most difficult part is solving a problem using EPS is to figure out the set of agents and their behavior. This needs an analysis method differing radically from classical problem solving. Whereas the latter uses state transition operators, EPS uses interacting entities as basic

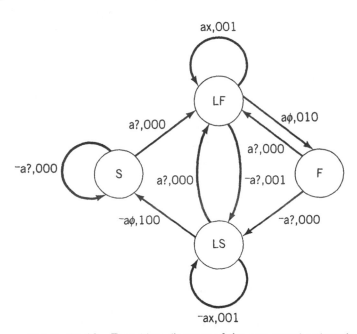

Figure 11.10 *Transition diagram of the eco-agent automaton.*

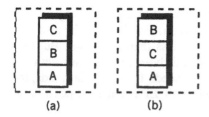

Figure 11.11 *Initial and final configuration of a cube problem.*

(a)   (b)

building blocks. *This approach is to problem solving what object oriented methods are to procedural programming.* The center of interest shifts from operators to objects described by their methods and their relation to other objects.

The Cube World. The cube world is very well known, and one of the most-studied problems in planning. A cube problem can be described as follows (Figure 11.11): what is the set of actions that must be executed in order to get a final configuration (b) from an initial one (a), moving only one cube at a time. Traditional approaches explore the state-space obtained by applying a set of operators on the initial state. Within EPS each cube is considered as an agent and the goal state is given as a set of local satisfaction of the cubes. Cubes A, B and C will be satisfied when they will stand respectively on the table, on C and on A. Fleeing means for a cube to go on the table or on another cube. The set of satisfaction conditions is

$$\{on(B,C), \ on(A,Table), \ on(C,A)\}$$

From which we can compute that B depends on C, A depends on the table, and C depends on A. As each cube (and the table) is an eco-agent, they all try to be satisfied. Because the table is always satisfied, the cube A is also satisfied (it is already on the table). Then B wants to go on C and C on A. Because B depends on C, C tries to go on A. But B is intruder for C, because it is above and is an obstacle to the satisfaction of C. Thus, C aggresses B and B flees on the table. Then C can go on A, and B can follow by jumping on C, satisfying the terminating condition.

The n-Puzzle. EPS has been shown to be capable of solving the *n*-puzzle problem. The *n*-puzzle has inspired many studies in problem solving. It consists of a square frame containing *N* square tiles and an empty position called "the blank." Authorized operations slide any tile next to the blank into the blank position. The task is to rearrange the tiles from some random initial configuration into a particular designed goal configuration.

The best results obtained before EPS, are those of R.E. Korf, started in 1985 with the use of the IDA* algorithm (Iterative-Deepening A*) (Korf, 1985) followed with the research algorithms RTA* (Real-Time A*) and its followers like LRTA* (Learning Real Time A*) (Korf, 1988). These algorithms have improved the A* algorithm, whose major drawback is to need both exponential space and time to run, using limited search horizon. Problems as far as a 5 × 5 puzzle can be solved in reasonable time (i.e., less than a human). But they still appear to be very limited because the search horizon increases with the size of the puzzle, and their heuristic function needs to be specially adapted for each size of the puzzle. We have shown with EPS that it is possible to derive an efficient algorithm which

1. Is linear with the number of tiles
2. Does not have to be modified with the size of the puzzle
3. Can be applied to other forms of n-puzzles such as n-puzzles with k blanks or n-puzzles with no-square shape

Drogoul has produced the best results so far, for different size of n-puzzle as large as 30 by 30 puzzles (time: 20 minutes on a Sparc station 10 in Smalltalk 4.1) (Drogoul, 1993). More examples and explanations about how EPS works and its comparison with classical planning systems can be found in Bura et al. (1991), Ferber and Jacopin (1991), and Ferber and Drogoul (1992).

6 CONCLUSION

We have presented the reactive agent paradigm along with various agent architectures and applications, ranging from simulation to problem solving and games. We have described many issues concerning multiagent systems (i.e., coordination of actions, task allocation, and cooperation) from a reactive point of view. We have shown that reactive agent systems can complete their tasks even in unpredictable worlds, which makes such systems attractive for applications requiring flexible execution.

Works on reactive agents are now concentrated on the issue of emergent functionality, i.e., the way new properties can emerge from interaction of simple behavior-based creatures, and on adaptive behaviors using genetic algorithms to make the structure and behavior of an agent evolve through natural selection [see Meyer and Guillot (1991) and Steels (1994) for general surveys of the field]. Somehow, reactive multiagent systems remain not well understood, because they lack the right formalizations which would permit understanding of the real collective process which is at work and which would allow programmers to be able to design reactive DAI systems with a top-down approach (Zeghal et al., 1993). This is in stark contrast to the deliberative architectures described in Chapter 5 and in part III of this book.

REFERENCES

Agre, P. E., and Chapman, D. (1987). Pengi: An implementation of a theory of activity. *Proc. Am. Assoc. Artif. Intell.*, Seattle, WA, pp. 268–272.

Beer, R. D. (1990). Intelligence as Adaptive Behavior: An Experiment in Computational Ethology, Vol. 6. Academic Press, San Diego, CA.

Belew, R. K., McInerney, J., and Schraudolph, N. N. (1991). Evolving networks: Using the genetic algorithm with connectionist learning. In *Artificial Life II* (C. G. Langton, C. Taylor, J. D. Farmer, and S. Rasmussen, eds.) Addison-Wesley, Santa Fe, NM.

Brooks, R., and Connell, J. H. (1986). Asynchronous distributed control system for a mobile robot. *SPIE* **727.**

Brooks, R. A. (1990). Elephants don't play chess. *Robotics Auton. Syst.* **6,** pp. 3–15.

Bura, S., Drogoul, A., Ferber, J., and Jacopin, E. (1991). Eco-resolution: Un modèle de résolution par interactions. *Proc. Cong. RFIA, 8th,* Lyon, AFCET.

Chapman, D. (1987). Planning for conjunctive goals. *Artif. Intell. J.* **32,** 333–367.

Cliff, D., Harvey, I., and Husbands, P. (1993). Exploration in evolutionary robotics. *Adap. Behav.* **2**(1), 73–110.

Cohen, P. R., and Levesque, H. J. (1990). Intention is choice with commitment. *Artif. Intell.* **42,** 213–261.

Collins, R. J., and Jefferson, D. R. (1991a). Ant farm: Towards simulated evolution. In *Artificial Life II* (C. G. Langton, C. Taylor, J. D. Farmer, and S. Rasmussen, eds.), pp. 579–601. Addison-Wesley, Santa Fe, NM.

Collins, R. J., and Jefferson, D. R. (1991b). Representation for artificial organisms. In *From Animal to Animats* (J.-A. Meyer and S. W. Wilson, eds.), pp. 382–390. MIT Press, Cambridge, MA.

Connah, D. (1991). Why we need a new approach to the design of agents. *AISBQ* **76.**

Conte, R., Miceli, M., and Castelfranchi, C. (1991). Limits and levels of cooperation: Disentangling various types of prosocial interaction. In *Distributed Artificial Intelligence 2* (Y. Demazeau and J.-P. Müller, eds.), pp. 153–166. Elsevier/North-Holland, Amsterdam.

Corbara, B., Lachaud, J. P., and Fresneau, D. (1989). Individual variability, social structure and division of labour in the Ponerine ant Ectatomma Ruidum Roger. *Ethology* **82,** 89–100.

Demazeau, Y., and Müller, J.-P. (1991). From reactive to intentional agents. In *Decentralized Artificial Intelligence 2* (Y. Demazeau and J.-P. Müller, eds.), pp. 3–14. Elsevier/North-Holland, Amsterdam.

Deneubourg, J. L., and Goss, S. (1989). Collective patterns and decision making. *Ecol. Ethol. Evol.* **1,** 295–311.

Deneubourg, J. L., Aron, S., Goss, S., Pasteels, J. M., and Duerinck, G. (1986). Random behaviour, amplification processes and number of participants: How they contribute to the foraging properties of ants. *Physica D* **22,** 176–186.

Deneubourg, J.-L., D. Fresneau, S. Goss, N. Franks, I.-P. Lachand, and J. M. Pasteels (1987). Self-organisation mechanisms in ant societies (II): Learning during foraging and division of labor. *Experientia, Suppl.* **54,** 177–196.

Deneubourg, J.-L., Goss, S., Sendova-Franks, A., Detrain, C., and Chrétien, L. (1991). The dynamics of collective sorting robot-like ants and ant-like robots. In *From Animals to Animats* (J.-A. Meyer and S. W. Wilson, eds.), pp. 356–363. MIT Press, Cambridge, MA.

Doran, J., Palmer, M., and Gilbert, N. (1994). The EOS Project: Modeling upper palaeolithic social change. In *Simulating Societies* (N. Gilbert and J. Doran, eds.), pp. 195–221. UCL Press, London.

Drogoul, A. (1993). De la simulation multi-agents à la résolution collective de problèmes. Une étude de l'émergence de structures d'organisation dans les systèmes multi-agents. Thèse de Doctorat, Université P. & M. Curie, Partis (6).

Drogoul, A., and Ferber, J. (1992a). *Ethomodeling: A Multi-Agent Behavioral Simulation Model*, Res. Rep. 02/92. Laforia, Université Paris (6).

Drogoul, A., and Ferber, J. (1992b). From Tom Thumb to the dockers; Some experiments with foraging robots. In *From Animals to Animats: Second Conference on Simulation of Adaptive Behavior* (J.-A. Meyer, H. Roitblat, and S. Wilson, eds.). MIT Press, Cambridge, MA.

Drogoul, A., and Ferber, J. (1992c). Multi-agent simulation as a tool for modeling societies: Application to social differentiation in ant colonies. *Proc. Eur. Workshop Modell. Auton. Agents Multi-Agent World, 4th*, Rome, Italy, *1992*, pp. 3–23.

Durfee, E. H., Lesser, V. R., and Corkill, D. D. (1987a). Coherent cooperation among communicating problem solvers. *IEEE Trans. Comput.* **C36**, 1275–1291.

Durfee, E. H., Lesser, V. R., and Corkill, D. D. (1987b). Cooperation through communication in a distributed problem solving network. In *Distributed Artificial Intelligence* (M. Huhns, ed.), pp. 29–58. Morgan Kaufmann, San Mateo, CA/Pitman London.

Ferber, J. (1989). Eco problem solving: How to solve a problem by interactions. *Proc. Int. Workshop Distributed Artif. Intell.*, *9th*, Seattle, WA.

Ferber, J., and Drogoul, A. (1992). Using reactive multi-agent systems in simulation and problem solving. In *Distributed Artificial Intelligence: Theory and Practice* (L. Gasser and N. Avouris, eds.), pp. 53–80. Kluwer Academic Publishers, Boston.

Ferber, J., and Jacopin, E. (1991). The framework of eco problem solving. In *Decentralized Artificial Intelligence 2* (Y. Demazeau and J.-P. Müller, eds.), pp. 103–114. Elsevier/North-Holland, Amsterdam.

Gasser, L. (1991). Social conceptions of knowledge and action: DAI foundations and open systems semantics. *Artif. Intell.* **47** (Spec. Issue on Foundations of AI), 107–138.

Gasser, L. (1992). An overview of DAI. In *Distributed Artificial Intelligence: Theory and Praxis* (L. Gasser and N. M. Avouris, eds.), pp. 9–30. Kluwer Academic Publishers, Boston.

Gasser, L., Braganza, C., and Herman, N. (1987). MACE: A flexible testbed for distributed AI research. In *Distributed Artificial Intelligence* (M. N. Huhns, ed.), pp. 119–152. Morgan Kaufmann, San Mateo, CA/Pitman, London.

Hogeweg, P., and Hesper, B. (1985). SocioInformatic processes: MIRROR modeling methodology. *J. Theor. Biol.* **113**, 311–330.

Huberman, B. A., and Hogg, T. (1988). The behavior of computational ecologies. In *The Ecology of Computation* (B. A. Huberman, ed.). North-Holland Publ., Amsterdam.

Jennings, N., and Wittig, T. (1992). ARCHON: Theory and practice. In *Distributed Artificial Intelligence: Theory and Practice* (L. Gasser and N. Avouris, eds.), pp. 179–195. Kluwer Academic Publishers, Boston.

Katz, M. J., and Rosenschein, J. S. (1988). Planning for multiple agents. In *Distributed AI 2* (L. Gaber and H. Huhns, eds.), pp. 197–228.

Korf, R. E. (1985). Depth-first iterative-deepening: An optimal admissible tree search. *Artif. Intell.* **27.**

Korf, R. E. (1988). Real time heuristic search. *Artif. Intell.* **42.**

Koza, J. R. (1990). Evolution and co-evolution of computer programs to control interdependent-acting agents. In *From Animals to Animats* (J.-A. Meyer and S. W. Wilson, eds.), pp. 366–375. MIT Press, Cambridge, MA.

Lyons, D. M., and Arbib, M. A. (1989). A formal model of computation for sensory-based robotics. *IEEE Trans. Robotics Autom.* **RA-5,** 280–293.

Maes, P. (1991). A bottom-up mechanism for behavior selection in an artificial creature. In *From Animals to Animats* (J.-A., Meyer and S. W. Wilson, eds.), pp. 238–246. MIT Press, Cambridge, MA.

Maruichi, T., Uchiki, T., and Tokoro, M. (1987). Behavior simulation based on knowledge objects. *Proc. of European Conference on Object-Oriented Programming*, pp. 257–266.

Mataric, M. (1992). *Designing emergent behaviors: From local interactions to collective intelligence.* In *From Animals to Animats 2* (J.-A. Meyer, H. L. Roitblat, and S. W. Wilson, eds.). MIT Press, Cambridge, MA.

Meyer, J.-A., and Guillot, A. (1991). Simulation of adaptive behavior in animats: Review and prospect. In *From Animals to Animats* (J.-A. Meyer and S. W. Wilson, eds.), pp. 2–14. MIT Press, Cambridge, MA.

Minsky, M. (1986). *The Society of Mind.* Simon & Schuster, New York.

Pfeifer, R., and Verschure, P. (1992). Distributed adaptive control: A paradigm for designing autonomous agents. In *Towards a Practice of Autonomous Systems* (P. Bourgine and F. Varela, eds.), pp. 21–30. MIT Press, Cambridge, MA.

Prigogine, I., and Stengers, I. (1979). *La nouvelle alliance.* Gallimard, Paris.

Rosenschein, S., and Kaelbling, L. (1986). The synthesis of digital machines with provable epistemic properties. In *Theoretical Aspects of Reasoning about Knowledge* (J. Halpern, ed.). Morgan Kaufmann, San Mateo, CA.

Steels, L. (1989). Cooperation between distributed agents through self organisation. *J. Robotics Auton. Syst.* **6.**

Steels, L. (1994). The artificial life roots of artificial intelligence. *Artif. Life* 1(1).

Suchman, L. A. (1987). *Plans and Situated Actions.* Cambridge Univ. Press, Cambridge, UK.

Theraulaz, G. (1991). Morphogenèse et auto-organisation des comportements dans les colonies de Guêpes Polistes Dominilus (Christ). Thèse de Troisiéme Cycle, Université d'Aix-Marseille I.

Theraulaz, G., Goss, S., Gervet, J., and Deneubourg, J. L. (1991). Task differentiation in Polistes wasp colonies: A model for self-organizing groups of robots. In *From Animals to Animats* (J. A. Meyer and S. Wilson, eds.), pp. 346–354. MIT Press, Cambridge, MA.

Travers, M. (1988). Animal construction kit. In *Artificial Life* (C. G. Langton, ed.), pp. 421–442. Addison-Wesley, Santa Fe, NM.

Volterra, V. (1926). Variation and fluctuations of the number of individuals of animal species living together. In *Animal Ecology.* McGraw-Hill, New York.

Wavish, P. (1992). Exploiting emergent behaviour in multi-agent systems. In *Decentralized Artificial Intelligence* (E. Werner and Y. Demazeau, eds.), pp. 129–140. Elsevier/North-Holland, Amsterdam.

Wavish, P. R., and Connah, D. M. (1990). *Representing Multi-Agent Worlds in ABLE*, Tech. Note TN2964. Philips Research Laboratories.

Werner, G. M., and Dyer, M. G. (1991). Evolution of communication in artificial organisms. In *Artificial Life II* (C. G. Langton, C. Taylor, J. D. Farmer, and S. Rasmussen, eds.), pp. 659–687. Addison-Wesley, Sana Fe, NM.

Zeghal, K. (1994). Towards a logic of a multi-intruders collision avoidance system. *Proc. Int. Counc. Aeronaut. Sci./Aircraft Syst. Conf.*, Anaheim, CA.

Zeghal, K., Ferber, J., and Erceau, J. (1993). Symmetrical, transitive and recursive force: A representation of interactions and commitments. *Proc. Int. Jt. Conf. Artif. Intell.*, *13th*, Chambéry, France, *1993*.

PART III

DAI Frameworks and Their Applications

This section describes a representative sample of the diverse approaches which can be employed to build DAI applications. The chapters on ARCHON (Chapter 12), CooperA (Chapter 14), and AGenDA (Chapter 15) describe what is perhaps the most tried and tested approach to building DAI systems, namely, the design and implementation of an agent architecture. The IMAGINE chapter (Chapter 13) is representative of the body of work on developing purpose-built languages for programming DAI systems. TÆMS (Chapter 16) takes yet another approach and offers a framework for modeling computational task environments in which the behavior of both the individual agents and the entire DAI system can be analysed. Finally, the Agent Factory (Chapter 17) describes an approach which supports the construction of DAI systems through their algebraic specification as abstract data types. All of the chapters in this section also describe a more or less real/complex application(s) to which the framework under discussion has been applied—these include management of an electricity distribution and supply network (ARCHON), a meeting scheduler system and management of urban traffic (IMAGINE), chemical emergency management (CooperA), a loading dock scenario and a transportation management system (AGenDA), and management of a distributor sensor network and hospital patient scheduling (TÆMS).

The ARCHON chapter describes the results of Europe's largest ever project on DAI. The ARCHON project devised a general purpose architecture, a software framework, and a methodology which has been used to support the development of DAI systems in a number of real world industrial domains (including electricity distribution and supply, electricity transmission and distribution, control of a cement kiln complex, control of a particle accelerator, and control of a robotics application). The chapter itself describes the rationale for DAI systems in industrial applications and outlines the key design forces of this domain. It then describes the key components of the architecture in more detail, briefly comments on the ARCHON methodology, and then details how the architecture and the methodology were used to construct a DAI system which manages an electricity distribution and supply network.

IMAGINE, like ARCHON, was a large European collaborative project. However, rather than adopting an architecture-based approach, they chose to develop a language which could be used to program DAI systems. The chapter presents each of the project's main results: the language for implementing agents and their interactions, the development environment for constructing cooperative applications, the base language for supporting interaction among processes, and the prototypical applications of urban traffic management and group scheduling which show the usage of the developed concepts.

The CooperA chapter describes an agent architecture for building DAI systems. The start point of this description and the motivation for the original DAI system were the problems encountered when building a monolithic expert system for handling chemical emergencies. The design rationale of the original CooperA multiagent system is given and the agent architecture is discussed and evaluated. As a consequence of the limitations exposed in this evaluation, an updated version (called CooperA-II) was devised to provide more flexible control and cooperation within the system. The key feature of the new architecture is the notion of domain independent cooperative heuristics which, in the form of agent microbehaviors, can be used for flexible programming and experimentation in multiagent systems.

AGenDA is an agent architecture for building DAI systems. Unlike both ARCHON and CooperA, it is composed of a number of rigorously defined layers. These layers each use different types of knowledge representation and different reasoning mechanisms. The choice ranges from very simple reactive mechanisms for dealing with the environment in a real-time manner to the declarative reasoning and modeling of the components which deal with cooperation and interaction with other agents. Accompanying these architectural levels is a system development layer which provides basic knowledge representation and inference mechanisms as well as a toolbox for simulation and experimentation.

All of these frameworks described so far take the agent as the sole unit of analysis—that is, architectures for realizing agents are devised and languages for programming agents are given.

However, the TÆMS framework eschews an exclusively agent centred perspective and places the modeling of the task environment in which the DAI system is situated at its core. The reason for this emphasis is that the author believes that the design of effective coordination mechanisms is heavily dependent on the structure and various other characteristics of the domain (e.g., the presence of uncertainty). The TÆMS framework itself can be used both as a mathematical framework for modeling complex task environments and as a simulation language for executing and experimenting with the models directly.

The Agent Factory similarly provides an environment for the fabrication of agent-based systems. However, it adopts a somewhat different medium through which it tries to achieve this. Agent-based systems are viewed as complex distributed systems whose behavior needs to be specified. Agent Factory adopts an algebraic approach, illustrating how preexisting specification techniques which are amenable to direct execution can usefully form the basis of an environment that supports the development and experimentation with multi-agent systems.

CHAPTER 12

ARCHON: A Distributed Artificial Intelligence System for Industrial Applications

DAVID COCKBURN
NICK R. JENNINGS

1 INTRODUCTION

In many industrial applications a substantial amount of time, effort, and finance has been devoted to developing complex and sophisticated software systems. These systems are often viewed in a piecemeal manner as isolated islands of automation, when, in reality, they should be seen as components of a much larger overall activity (see Chapter 4). The benefit of taking a holistic perspective is that the partial subsystems can be integrated into a coherent community in which they work together to better meet the needs of the entire application. By the very fact that they are integrated, the finite budgets available for information technology development can be made to go further—agents can share a consistent and up-to-date version of the data, basic functionalities need only be implemented in one place, problem solving can make use of timely information which might not otherwise be available, and so on.

Two components are required to devise a well-structured integrated community: a framework which provides assistance for interaction between the constituent subcomponents and a methodology which provides a means of structuring these interactions. ARCHON (*architecture* for *cooperative heterogeneous on*-line systems) addresses both of these facets, providing a decentralized software framework for creating distributed AI (DAI) systems in the domain of industrial applications and devising a methodology which offers guidance on how to decompose an application to best fit with the ARCHON approach (Wittig, 1992) (see also Chapter 3). The former is concerned with

Foundations of Distributed Artificial Intelligence, Edited by G. M. P. O'Hare and N. R. Jennings.
ISBN 0-471-00675-0 © 1996 John Wiley & Sons, Inc.

providing the necessary control and level of integration to help the subcomponents to work together; the latter is concerned with decomposing the overall application goal(s) and with distributing the constituent tasks throughout the community.

ARCHON's individual problem-solving entities are called agents; these agents have the ability to control their own problem solving and to interact with other community members. The interactions typically involve agents cooperating and communicating with one another in order to enhance their individual problem solving and to better solve the overall application problem. Each agent consists of an *ARCHON layer* (AL) and an application program [known as an *intelligent system* (IS)]. Clearly distinguishing between an agent's social know-how and its domain-level problem solving means that the ARCHON approach is both flexible and open, imposing relatively few constraints on the application designer and yet providing many useful facilities. Purpose-built ISs can make use of the ARCHON functionality to enhance their problem solving and to improve their robustness. However preexisting ISs can also be incorporated, with a little adaptation, and can experience similar benefits. This latter point is important because in many cases developing the entire application afresh would be considered too expensive or too large a change away from proven technology (Jennings and Wittig, 1992).

To successfully incorporate both purpose-built and preexisting systems, community design must be carried out from two different perspectives simultaneously (Varga et al., 1994). A top down approach is needed to look at the overall needs of the application and a bottom-up approach is needed to look at the capabilities of the existing systems. Once the gap between what is required and what is available has been identified the system designer can choose to provide the additional functionality through new systems, through additions to the existing systems, or through the ARCHON software itself. This methodology shapes the design process by providing guidelines for problem decomposition and distribution which reduce inefficiencies.

This paper is organized along the following lines: Section 2 provides a detailed view of ARCHON's software framework, covering both interagent interactions and interactions between the AL and its underlying IS. Section 3 outlines the ARCHON methodology, Section 4 describes the electricity distribution application and Section 5 shows how the software and the methodology were applied to this domain. Finally, Section 6 presents the conclusions of this work and outlines some future plans.

2 THE ARCHON SOFTWARE

The ARCHON software has been used to integrate a wide variety of application program types under the general assumption that the ensuing agents will be loosely coupled and semi-autonomous. The agents are loosely coupled since the number of interdependencies between their respective ISs are kept to a minimum; the agents are semiautonomous since their control regime is decentralized (meaning each individual decides which tasks to execute in which order). The ISs themselves can be heterogeneous—in terms of their programming language, their algorithm, their problem-solving paradigm, and their hardware platform (Roda et al., 1991)—as their differences are masked by a standard AL-IS interface. An AL views its IS in a purely functional manner; it expects to invoke functions (*tasks*) which return results—and there is a fixed language for controlling this interaction (see Section 2.1). The design of the tasks invoked by the AL needs careful consideration if the AL is not to be swamped with vast amounts of low-level information which is irrelevant to its job of controlling cooperative problem solving. As a basic guideline, the tasks should be of sufficient granularity to be used as a decision point in the AL's reasoning about local control (further details are contained in Sections 3 and 4). This approach means that some tasks which appear indivisible to the AL may, in fact, be composed of several distinct processes in the IS.

In an ARCHON community there is no centrally located global authority; each agent controls its own IS and mediates its own interactions with other agents. The system's overall objective is expressed in the separate local goals of each community member. Because the agents' goals are usually interrelated, social interactions are required to meet global constraints and provide the necessary services and information. Such interactions are controlled by the agent's AL (Figure 12.1); relevant examples include asking for information from acquaintances, requesting processing services from acquaintances, and spontaneously volunteering information which is believed to be relevant to others. This design is broadly similar to the head-body approach of the IMAGINE project (Chapter 13).

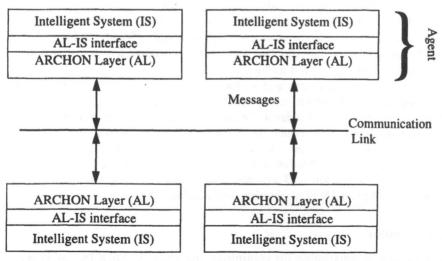

Figure 12.1 Structure of an ARCHON community.

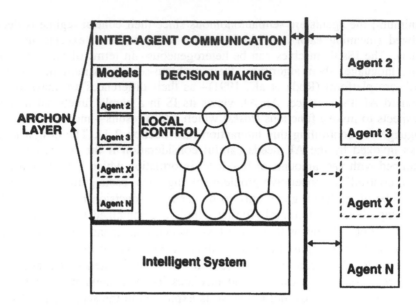

Figure 12.2 *Functional view of an ARCHON agent.*

In more detail, an agent's AL needs to control tasks within its local IS, decide when to interact with other agents (for which it needs to model the capabilities of its own IS and the ISs of the other agents), and communicate with the other agents. The basic functional architecture highlights these four key aspects of local control, decision making, agent modeling, and interagent communication (Figure 12.2). It was decided to embody this functionality in a modular implementation architecture. This architecture contains four modules: monitor (Section 2.1), planning and coordination module (PCM) (Section 2.2), agent information management (AIM) module (Section 2.3), and high-level communication module (Section 2.4), each of which is responsible for one aspect of the functional architecture (Figure 12.3).

In terms of its hardware and software requirements, the ARCHON layer was originally implemented using LISP as a rapid prototyping language. Later it was ported to C++ in order to: improve speed, increase portability between different machines, and reduce the amount of computing resource needed by the AL. The C++ version runs under UNIX on Sun-4 architecture workstations (Sun-4s and SparcStations) and under Linux (a public domain version of UNIX) on i386 machines. Tools are also available which facilitate the construction of ARCHON communities (see Section 4.6).

2.1 Monitor

The monitor is responsible for controlling the local IS. Each IS task is represented in the monitor by a monitoring unit (MU). MUs present a standard

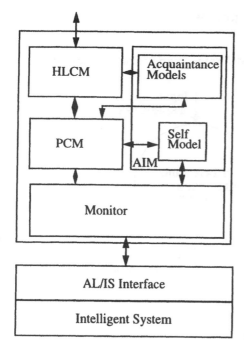

Figure 12.3 *Implementation architecture of an ARCHON agent.*

interface to the monitor whatever the host programming language and hardware platform of the underlying IS. Figure 12.4 shows a graphical representation of an MU called TransformTelemetry which takes TELEMETRY as an input and produces TRANSFORMED-TELEMETRY as an output. The IS task associated with this MU is called TRANSFORM-TELEMETRY in the ARCHON layer.

MUs can send and receive messages (control, confirmations and requests) to/from the IS. All messages have to pass through the AL-IS interface which performs the translation and interpretation required for the IS to understand the AL directives and for the AL to understand the IS messages. For instance, in the above example, the interface functionality involves invoking the IS function transform_telemetry, passing the arguments in the form in which they are expected by the IS's host language, and returning the transformed telemetry in the expected format.

For the IS to be able to react to an AL directive the interface must translate the command into the corresponding local control action(s). However this interpretation is subject to the capabilities of the IS. For example, KILL in a C program may just mean that—kill a process, whereas in a rule-based Prolog system it may mean clear all the facts asserted by the current task and then stop (e.g., before a fault diagnosis process can be terminated any partial hypotheses it has asserted must be removed). This means that the interface has to be specialized to the IS's programming language, although the C language version can be used as foreign code in other programming languages.

Other interface functionalities include specifying how many invocations of

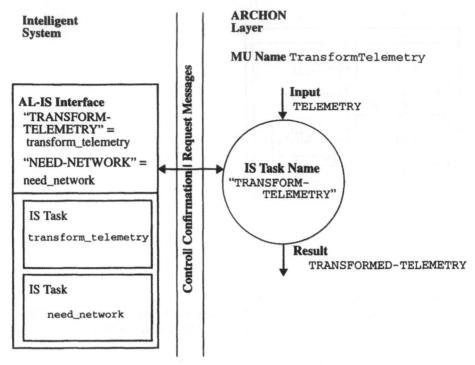

Figure 12.4 *Transform Telemetry monitoring unit.*

a particular task can run in parallel and how many can be queued should that limit be reached. For example, it may be possible to run only one invocation at a time (e.g., updating a global data store), or a task can have multiple instantiations running in parallel but it may be desirable to have a limit and to queue other requests for that task until one has completed.

In more detail, the message format between the AL and its IS is as follows:

```
⟨AL_IS_message⟩ ::=
    (⟨message_type⟩ ⟨urgency⟩ "⟨task_name" ⟨tag⟩
            ⟨argument_or_result⟩))
```

From the AL to the IS it is

```
⟨message_type⟩::= ⟨AL_IS_request⟩ | ⟨AL_IS_response⟩

⟨AL_IS_request⟩ ::=
    start_is_task | kill_is_task | suspend_is_task |
    resume_is_task

⟨AL_IS_response⟩ ::=
    requested_info | requested_info_not_available
```

and from the IS to the AL it is

```
⟨message_type⟩::= ⟨IS_AL_request⟩ | ⟨IS_AL_response⟩

⟨IS_AL_request⟩ ::=
   information_request | intermediate_result

⟨AL_IS_response⟩ ::=
   is_task_started| is_task_killed | is-task-suspended |
   is_task_resumed | is_task_completed
```

It can be seen that the AL can request to start, suspend, resume, or kill any IS task and that the IS will provide an appropriate confirmation. The IS can also make a request to the AL for information, it can send intermediate results, and it can supply final results when a task completes. In this context, an intermediate result is one which is sent before the IS task has been completed. This type of information is particularly useful for a monitoring task where it would be inefficient and disruptive to the IS's normal flow of control to produce a function which has been completed and returned a result.

MUs represent the finest level of control in the ARCHON layer, at the next level of granularity there are plans (cf. Chapter 8). *Plans* are acyclic OR-graphs in which the nodes are MUs and the arcs are conditions. These conditons can

- Depend on data already available from previously executed MUs in the plan
- Depend on data input to the plan when it started
- Use the locking mechanism for part of the plan
- Be used to return intermediate results before a plan has finished

A sample plan which ensures that the electricity network is loaded is shown in Figure 12.5. This plan is activated in a fault diagnosis agent as part of its diagnosis routine. First, the TELEMETRY is transformed into a suitable format by the TransformTelemetry MU. Secondly, the MU NeedNetwork checks whether that portion of the network from which the telemetry originated is available locally. Next there is a decision point: if a network_descriptor was returned by the previous MU, then the relevant portion of the network needs to be obtained; if not, then the network is already available locally and the plan ends. Assuming that the network needs to be loaded, an appropriate request will be sent to the PCM and eventually the network description should arrive. On return of the network the CreateNetworkModel MU is executed and the plan terminates.

The highest level at which the IS's activities are represented is the behavior level (cf. Chapters 11 and 20). *Behaviors* contain a plan, a trigger condition for activating the behavior, descriptions of the inputs needed by the activity

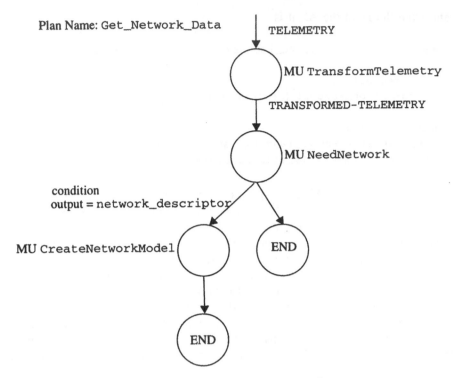

Figure 12.5 Get_Network_Data *plan.*

and the results which will be produced, and any children of the behavior.[1] There are two types of behavior: those that are visible to the PCM (and the other AL components) and those that are purely internal to the monitor (e.g., DiagnoseFault in Figure 12.6). The former type are called *skills* (e.g., DealWithTelemetry in Figure 12.6), and they may be triggered by data arriving from other agents or by direct requests from other agents. Once the PCM activates a skill the monitor is responsible for its execution. This involves testing any plan conditions, activating MUs, and, when appropriate, dealing with messages from the IS. In order to activate an MU the monitor ensures that the necessary inputs are present. They could be available because they were an input to the behavior in the first place or because they were generated by the execution of an earlier MU in the same plan. However, if a piece of information is not available in the local context then a request is forwarded to the PCM (e.g., in the Get_Network_Data plan a request for the network associated with the generated descriptor may not be available in the local context). Finally, the monitor passes the skill's results back to the PCM and then activates any child behaviors.

---

[1]The reason for allowing behaviors to be linked is that it permits greater modularity: a plan can be written to perform one task and can then be incorporated into several different behaviors.

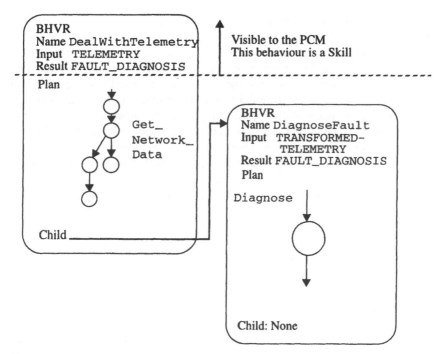

Figure 12.6 DealWithTelemetry *skill with* DiagnoseFault *child behavior.*

2.2 Planning and Coordination Module

The PCM is the reflective part of the ARCHON layer, reasoning about the agent's role in terms of the wider cooperating community (Jennings and Pople, 1993). This module has to assess the agent's current status and decide which actions should be taken in order to exploit interactions with others while ensuring that the agent contributes to the community's overall well-being (see Chapter 8). Specific examples of the PCM's functionality include deciding which skills should be executed locally and which should be delegated to others, directing requests for cooperation to appropriate agents, determining how to respond to requests from other agents, and identifying when to disseminate timely information to acquaintances who would benefit from receiving it.

The PCM is composed of generic rules about cooperation and situation assessment which are applicable in all industrial applications. All the domain-specific information needed to define individual behavior is stored in the self and acquaintance models (Jennings, 1992). The former contains information about the local IS, and the latter contains information about the other agents in the system. The type of information contained in both models is approximately the same, although it varies in the level of detail, and includes the agent's skills, interests, current status, workload, and so on. For example, in order to determine how to process the request to provide the relevant portion of the network which arises from the DealWithTelemetry skill, the PCM will make reference to its self model to see if the information can be provided locally. If the information cannot be provided locally then the acquaintance models are checked to see if another community member can provide it. A second illustration of the interplay between the agent models and the PCM occurs when the monitor provides the results of a recently completed skill: first, the PCM checks the self model to see if the data can be used locally and then it examines its acquaintance models to see if any other agents are believed to be interested in receiving the data. The final major role of the PCM is to deal with requests arriving from other agents. By reference to its self model, it will decide whether to honor the request and will then activate the necessary skill to provide the requested data; when the information is available it will ensure that a reply is directed to the source of the request.

2.3   Agent Information Management Module

The AIM module is a distributed object management system which is designed to provide information management services to cooperating agents (Tuijnman and Afsarmanesh, 1993). Within ARCHON, it is used to store the agent models and the domain-level data.

The self model contains all the definitions of MUs, plans and behaviors. An agent only models those acquaintances with which it will interact; the models themselves contain the agent's name, the information it is interested in (which the local agent can provide), and the skills it can perform (which the local agent may need). As an illustration of the models, consider an agent which is capable of producing information about TELEMETRY. The interest slots of its acquaintance models would contain those agents who are interested in receiving this information. The acquaintance model below specifies that an agent called AVA is interested in TELEMETRY in all cases, that an agent called LVDA is interested when the operation attribute has value autoreclosure, and that the agents called IA and HVDA are interested only if the operation attribute is equal to open or closed:

```
INTEREST-DESCRIPTOR
  INFORMATION-NAME: TELEMETRY
  INFORMATION-CONDITION:
    [("AVA", TRUE);
     ("LVDA", (CONTAIN (TELEMETRY, "OPERATION "Autorec" ")));
     ("IA HVDA",
         (OR (CONTAIN(TELEMETRY, "OPERATION "Open" "))
             (CONTAIN(TELEMETRY, "OPERATION "Closed" "))));]
```

In many industrial applications the domain level data which the agents need to exchange has a complex internal structure. In ARCHON, this structure is specified and maintained by AIM. For example, TELEMETRY is defined in the following manner:

TELEMETRY

Text	STRINGS	Time	INTEGER
Text_time	STRINGS	Substation	STRINGS
Plant	STRINGS	Operation	STRINGS
Source	STRINGS		

and a specific instance is as follows (note this piece of telemetry would be deemed to be of interest to the AVA and LVDA agents but not to the IA or HVDA agents):

```
((Telemetry
    (Text 'ALARM 01JAN94 12.00/12.00 SBSTN1 SUBSTATION1 C1
        CIRCUIT BREAKER AUTOREC')
    (Time 10874390) (Text_time '1JAN94 12.00/12.00')
    (Substation 'SUBSTATION1') (Plant 'SUBSTATION1C1')
    (Operation 'AUTOREC') (Source 'ALARM'))
```

Once domain data has been stored in AIM it is possible for the AL's reasoning and control mechanisms to retrieve it. By giving it a definite structure, it is possible to access the named subparts (e.g., checking that the attribute operation equals open). If the application designer does not require the AL to access these components, then the structure's details need not be given. The scheme is also flexible enough to allow for a halfway house where that part of the data the AL needs to reason about is structured, as above, and that part which is not looked at is left unstructured (e.g., the text field above).

2.4 High-Level Communication Module

The high-level communication module (HLCM) allows agents to communicate with one another using services based on the TCP/IP protocol. The HLCM incorporates the functionality of the ISO/OSI session layer which continuously checks communication links and provides automatic recovery of connection breaks when possible. Information can be sent to named agents or to relevant agents (decided by reference to interests registered in the acquaintance models).

3 THE ARCHON METHODOLOGY

As mentioned, the design of an ARCHON system takes a mixed top-down and bottom-up approach. Taking a top-down approach means the designer must look at the overall problem that the system is being asked to solve and identify the corresponding system-level goals. Next, the tasks necessary to achieve these goals need to be identified and suitably decomposed. Finally, the data flows between the tasks need to be determined. However, this classical design perspective is not the full story in the type of applications with which we were faced—in many cases the system designer wanted to utilize existing ISs to provide some of the functionality. There are sound reasons for doing this: saving development time, familiarity with existing systems, both by the designer and the eventual end user, and proven technology.

For this reason, ARCHON has also been designed to allow preexisting (legacy) systems to be integrated. However, the use of such systems constrains the task decomposition and distribution processes (if these systems are to be used in a similar way to their original stand-alone counterparts). As an example, using an existing IS to provide a particular set of functionality typically implies that all the tasks will be coresident in the same agent, whereas in a totally unconstrained distribution they may have been dispersed into multiple agents. It is at this pragmatic level where the bottom-up considerations are of primary concern. The designer must examine the capabilities of the existing systems (in terms of their goals and tasks) and then compare these tasks with those suggested by the top-down approach. Typically there will be a mismatch, since preexisting systems do not provide all of the necessary functionality, some preexisting system functionality is not required in the cooperating system, and some functionality is duplicated.

Having performed this analysis, the designer must decide which of the preexisting system's functionality should be exploited, which functionality necessitates the creation of new ISs, and which functionality can be supported by the AL. If new systems are to be created it is important that they too have a clear functional role (rather than simply being a collection of tasks which do not fit in elsewhere). Some adaptation of existing systems may be required in order to ensure that the necessary tasks can be invoked by the AL (see Jennings et al., 1993), for a detailed analysis on a real-world example). Typically this process aims to improve the structure of the IS; for example, a stand-alone system may print results to the screen as they are produced and never build up an internal representation. A possibly useful reconceptualization could be to develop a data structure to contain the full result and then return the complete answer from a suitable accessor function.

It may be that preexisting ISs from the same domain can perform the same task but that the systems themselves are at different stages of development. For example, one IS may have been used in the real world and have an existing connection to it to obtain data. Another may require the same data but have only a simple interface (e.g., it is still in a prototype stage and reads data from a file). By integrating these two systems, it is possible to use the better-developed interface for both systems and thus provide a significant improvement to the prototypical IS.

An important aspect of the bottom-up methodology includes a thorough analysis of the data to be exchanged. This is important because the semantics of the data, as well as its syntax, need to be uncovered before meaningful interchange can take place (e.g., it is possible for two similarly named data types to have totally different meanings). This analysis is especially crucial when the cooperating community involves components which have been developed at different times and with which the designer has different levels of familiarity. A common source of such confusion occurs when data from different sources is not entirely compatible in all aspects. As an example consider the notion of "time." There are many reasons why time in one IS differs from time in another: it may be a matter of format (e.g., the time is in seconds rather than minutes from a given base time—the base time might differ too!), or, more importantly, although seemingly related they may measure different attributes (e.g., one could be a measure of CPU time used and the other of system time). This point is worth stressing because when a system is run in stand-alone mode the absolute meaning of the data may not be as important to the user as a comparison between different outputs (e.g., he may have forgotten what the units are but knows what a good reading is and how to compare readings). Problems arise when two systems are integrated and it is thought that two (or more) data types can be easily interchanged because they appear similar.

ARCHON uses a standard data representation mechanism which allows the AL to make decisions based on the contents of the IS data. For example, the interests expressed in the acquaintance models can depend on the value of certain attributes of the data (e.g., agents diagnosing faults on electricity networks are interested in telemetry messages reporting the change of state of switches; see Section 2.3), as might the triggers which activate behaviors. However, this is not to say that the AL representation is imposed on the IS (indeed the IS can represent data in any way that it chooses), but that it can be used as a means of transferring data. New ISs can be designed to use this format and existing ones can be adapted to understand it. If there really is a necessity for an IS to represent data in a totally different way, then this can also be accommodated. For example, data can be left in its original format in the message—this means the AL cannot make decisions based on that part of the data—or a file name can be sent where the data can be accessed. The latter relies on a common file system but is very useful for large amounts of structured data which the AL need not understand.

4 USING ARCHON TO MANAGE ELECTRICITY DISTRIBUTION AND SUPPLY NETWORK

The ARCHON software and methodology have been used to develop real-world DAI systems in industrial domains (see Chapter 4), including

- Electricity distribution and supply (Cockburn et al., 1992; Varga et al., 1994)
- Electricity transmission and distribution (Corera et al., 1993)
- Control of a cement kiln complex (Stassinopoulos and Lembessis, 1993)
- Control of a particle accelerator (Jennings et al., 1993)
- Control of a robotics application (Oliveira et al., 1991)

In this chapter we concentrate on the first of these applications. The DAI system which has been developed is called CIDIM (cooperating intelligent systems for distribution management systems) and its aim is to help control engineers manage electricity distribution and supply networks.

4.1 Application of CIDIM

CIDIM is being developed as an aid to the control engineer who is responsible for ensuring the continuity of electricity supply to customers (see Chapter 21 for a discussion of the issues related to the means by which information is presented to the control engineer). The main jobs to be performed include planning and carrying out maintenance work safely and in coordination with the field engineer, identifying faults on the network, and taking action to restore supply should this be necessary. The electricity network control system allows remote operation of circuit breakers and reports, via telemetry, automatic switching operations in response to faults, alarms and load readings. The control system covers the high-voltage network and part of the low-voltage network, but for much of the low-voltage network switching for maintenance purposes is done manually by the field engineer in radio contact with the control engineer. Due to the lack of telemetred protection equipment, customer telephone calls reporting loss of supply play an important role in decision making about the low-voltage network. The final important source of information used by the control engineer concerns lightning strikes, which may be the cause of a fault and so indicate a good starting point for the field engineer to look for damaged equipment.

CIDIM assists the control engineer by (i) automatically providing a comprehensive range of services such as fault diagnosis, lightning detection, user-driven restoration planning and automatic rechecking of restoration plans; (ii) automatically collating much of the information which is currently collected manually by reference to stand-alone systems. ARCHON also permits information from conventional knowledge sources, such as a data base or the telemetry system, to be shared by more than one agent within the community (thus increasing the degree of consistency).

4.2 Tailoring the ARCHON Methodology to CIDIM

The top-down aspect of the ARCHON methodology for the CIDIM application is obtained by examining the role of the control engineer. The main aspects of this job are

- Ensure continuity of supply to customers.
- Supervise maintenance on the network.
- Restore power after faults.

The tasks which are performed in order to meet the above goals are

- Create safe switching plans for maintenance and repair.
- Diagnose faults on the network.

These are the goals and tasks at the highest level. These activities were then broken down further; descriptions were made of the individual tasks (e.g., fault diagnosis and restoration planning), the data requirements for these tasks (e.g., telemetry, lightning data and network data), and the interrelations between the tasks and the data (e.g., fault diagnosis requires telemetry and network data).

The bottom-up aspect of the methodology for CIDIM was obtained by examining the functionality of the preexisting and stand-alone systems which were currently used in the control room. There were three systems.

1. *High-Voltage Expert System (HVES) (Cockburn et al., 1991a; Cockburn, 1992)*. This system diagnoses the location and type of high-voltage fault on the electricity network. To do this it uses telemetered information from the network protection system (which automatically operates circuit breakers in order to first isolate the faulty section from the rest of the network and then, if possible, restore power). Originally, the HVES had its own network representation and a separate process for accepting telemetry. It was designed so that it could still work if telemetry messages were missing, although sometimes it was unable to discriminate between competing alternatives if it did not have sufficient information.

2. *Switching Schedule Production Assistant (SSPA) (Cross et al., 1992)*. When there is a permanent fault, or a need for maintenance work, a safe switching plan needs to be created. This ensures that the area to be worked on is isolated from the rest of the network and that it is safe for the field engineers to start their work. Originally, the SSPA had its own network representation.

3. *Weather Watch System (Scott, 1988; Lees, 1992)*. The location of lightning strikes can be useful supplementary data to the control engineer. It can help in fault location on overhead lines—on a long line it is best to start to look for damage near to a lightning strike—and can also warn the field engineer that it is unsafe to work in a particular location.

4.3 Applying the ARCHON Methodology to CIDIM: High-Level System Design

By comparing the requirements from the top-down analysis with the functionality of the existing systems, it can be seen that

- There is no assistance for low-voltage fault detection. Telemetry data is only present at the point where the high- and low-voltage networks join and it alone cannot locate the fault or identify its type. However, information from customers' telephone calls which report their loss of supply can be used.

- Sometimes the control engineer will want to operate automatic circuit breakers from the control room in an attempt to restore power by an alternative route. In such cases, a check to see if these operations are safe will help minimize the chance of costly mistakes.
- The overall security of the network is not considered. Rather than just waiting for, and reacting to, faults the control engineer could proactively switch out overloaded lines and reroute power.

In order to provide the missing functionality it was decided that the following additional ISs were required to respectively deal with each of the above points: (i) low-voltage expert system (LVES), (ii) switch checking system (SCS), and (iii) security analysis system. Note that the last two systems have yet to be fully integrated into the CIDIM cooperating community.

With the development of these new ISs, the overall system provides most of the functionality required by the control engineer. As several of the systems make use of telemetry (HVES, LVES) and require network data (HVES, LVES, SSPA, SCS), it was decided to create dedicated agents to provide these services—respectively, the telemetry agent (TA) and the information agent (IA). As the HVES already had a program running as a separate process which accepted telemetry from the network and translated it into a standard format, it was decided to make this program into the TA. The TA could then provide this service, and a standard format, to the other community members. In the UK, different regional electricity companies (RECs) have different telemetry formats and so moving CIDIM to another REC would simply require changes to the IS of the TA program (rather than to all the agents using telemetry). The IA holds the network data base for all agents; again although each REC has a different data base, and a different structure within that data base, this approach only requires changes to the IS of the IA when CIDIM is ported to a different company.

It was decided to provide a common user interface to CIDIM (see Chapter 21) because one of its major functions is to collate and present integrated information from different sources (e.g., when there is relevant information about lightning strikes it needs to be presented in conjunction with the output of the fault diagnosis activity if it is to have the maximum impact). The common interface also means that the control engineer can view CIDIM as a single system and need not be aware of the source of the results (e.g., fault reports from the HVES and the LVES are simply reported as faults. If they are displayed differently it is because they relate to different voltage levels and not because they are produced by different agents).

Both the HVES and the SSPA already had graphical displays of the electricity network, but as the SSPA's interface was more sophisticated it was used as the basis of the system's common interface (named the advisor agent). For reasons of familiarity, it is still possible to use the existing interfaces for some of the systems; for example, the SSPA is user driven and when creating a switching schedule it is easier and more efficient to use the existing display (this is possible because there is no need for interaction with the rest of the CIDIM system when creating a switching schedule). The CIDIM system as it now stands is shown in Figure 12.7.

Integrating these different subsystems in CIDIM allows the agents to interact, this, in turn, gives the following benefits over and above their stand-alone counterparts:

(i) Automatic look-up and cross-referencing of lightning data when there is a fault

(ii) Display of all relevant results in an integrated manner

(iii) Interactions between the high- and low-voltage diagnosis agents and the TA can resolve conflicts in high-voltage diagnosis when telemetry is missing

(iv) Notification of faults in areas where work is planned

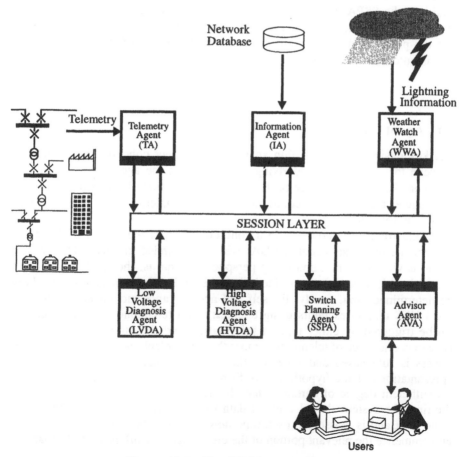

Figure 12.7 *The CIDIM community.*

The first two points are dealt with earlier in this section, so we concentrate on the remaining cases here. Point (iii) illustrates how an integrated system is able to provide the control engineer with better-quality information. The HVES can diagnose faults when some telemetry information is missing; however, in such cases its diagnosis can be less precise about the nature (permanent/transient) or location of the fault. In CIDIM these shortcomings can be minimised in two ways. First, the fact that a permanent fault on the high-voltage network can lead to a loss of supply on the low-voltage network, since the former feeds the latter, can be exploited. In such a case the high-voltage diagnosis agent can ask the low-voltage agent if the low-voltage network has been affected. The second improvement is that the high-voltage agent can ask the TA whether the substation from which the telemetry is missing is working. Replies from each of these agents will assist the high-voltage agent in deciding on the nature and location of the fault.

Point (iv) is one illustration of how information passing betwen agents can trigger useful actions. When the high-voltage agent produces a diagnosis it will send it to the SSPA, which will then recheck any preplanned restoration plans on the updated state of the network. If this analysis results in the conclusion that the plans need to be redone, because of the effect of the fault, then the user is automatically informed.

4.4 Agent Design

The key design decision within an individual agent concerns the interaction between the AL and its underlying IS. Assuming the agent's high-level role has been clearly defined (see Section 4.3), the functionality which is of use to other agents must be identified, as must the appropriately abstract logical grouping of the local functionality.

To illustrate these concepts in a concrete manner, the design of CIDIM's low-voltage diagnosis agent (LVDA) will be expanded in detail. This instantiation is viewed from a bottom-up perspective—that is, the level at which the IS and the AL interact is determined, then the MUs, plans, behaviors and skills are determined, and, finally, the self and acquaintance models are populated. The LVES diagnoses faults using telemetry and telephone calls; a diagnosis can be triggered by either type of information and the outcome may rely on more than one piece of telemetry or more than one telephone call. The diagnosis process is rule based and relies on the incoming data to update its internal representations of the hypotheses. A firm diagnosis is only made when there is a sufficient degree of certainty that all the relevant indicators have arrived. The time the system should wait for data to arrive is dependent on the nature of the fault and is reassessed each time new data arrives. Before the diagnosis can commence the relevant portion of the electricity network needs to be loaded.

IS Tasks and Monitoring Units. ARCHON is designed to have a relatively coarse granularity of interaction between the AL and its IS; indeed it is inefficient to introduce unnecessary interactions. As mentioned in Section 2.1, the IS must be conceptualised as a number of functional units. Even if the IS is rule based, and works by side effect, this is still possible as the following example from the LVDA illustrates.

One of the activities performed by the LVES is to diagnose faults using telemetry information as an input. As shown by Figure 12.8, this activity involves a complex series of actions within the IS: the first thing to check is whether the telemetry relates to an existing hypothesis or whether a new hypothesis is needed. In the latter case, the IS must set a timer to indicate when it can report its final diagnosis. This depends on the information received and an estimation of the time by which the remaining necessary information will arrive. In the former case, there will already be an active behavior concerned with this hypothesis and so a timer will already have been set, but the IS may need to update the hypothesis and possibly reset the timer (e.g., if the new data represents the final piece of expected information then the timer can be set to zero).

Despite this complexity, it was decided to encode this process in a single

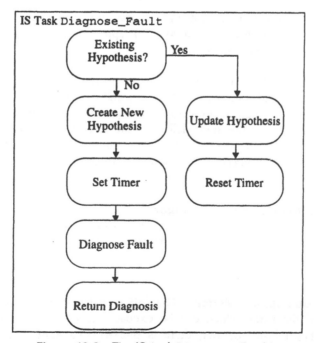

Figure 12.8 *The IS task* Diagnose_Fault.

IS task because there is no further need for interaction with the AL before the task completes. The corresponding MU is represented in the AL as follows:

```
MU DiagnoseFault          ;; MU Name
   "Diagnose_Fault"       ;; IS Task Name (see fig. 12.8)
   (TRANSFORMED-TELEMETRY) ;; mandatory input (see fig. 12.6)
   (FAULT_DIAGNOSIS)      ;; result (see fig. 12.6)
```

Plans. The Diagnose plan which performs the diagnosis is extremely simple and just involves calling the DiagnoseFault MU (see Figure 12.6). In contrast, the Get_Network_Data plan which loads the relevant network before the diagnosis is made is more complex (see Figure 12.5). After the telemetry has been suitably transformed, the MU NeedNetwork checks whether the network from which the telemetry originated is represented internally in the IS. If it is not then the IS extracts a network descriptor, by which the relevant portion of the network can be accessed, from the telemetry message and returns it to the monitor as the result of the MU; if the network is already available then no result is returned. Next there is a decision point: the monitor checks if a network descriptor was returned; if not then the network is already available and the plan ends. However, if a network descriptor was returned then a request is made to the PCM for the network (since it cannot be produced locally). The PCM checks its acquaintance models, sees that the IA can provide the network (see subsequent subsection on acquaintance models). And so sends it a request for assistance. On return of the network, an appropriate model is established by the CreateNetworkModel MU.

Behaviors and Skills. To allow for easier testing and expandability, two behaviors were created, DealWithTelemetry and DiagnoseFault (see Figure 12.6), to control the diagnosis process with respect to telemetered information. DealWithTelemetry is the skill visible to the rest of the ARCHON Layer, being a child behavior DiagnoseFault is internal to the LVDA's monitor. The trigger which fires the DealWithTelemetry skill can be expressed in the following manner:

```
TRIGGER DealWithTelemetry-Trigger
(TELEMETRY)              ;; Arrival of this info is the trigger
[                        ;; Actions associated with trigger
   EXECUTE(DealWithTelemetry);
]
```

Self and Acquaintance Models. The self model of the LVDA contains a description of the skills which can be executed locally. As well as DealWithTelemetry (shown below), there is DealWithTelephoneCalls (which controls fault diagnosis using customer reports of loss of supply), and ResolveHV_Conflict (which the high-voltage agent will request in order to determine whether or not a high-voltage fault has affected the low-voltage network; refer to Section 4.3).

```
Name: DealWithTelemetry
Trigger: DealWithTelemetry-Trigger    (see previous subsection)
Inputs: ((TELEMETRY :mandatory))
Results: (FAULT_DIAGNOSIS)
Plan Name: Get_Network_Data
Children: (DiagnoseFault)
```

In order to perform its designated role in CIDIM, the LVDA only needs to be aware of two other agents: the information agent and the advisor agent. For the IA it represents the fact that it can perform the skill GetNetwork-Substation (which needs to be executed to provide the network required by the CreateNetworkModel MU of the Get_Network_Data plan):

```
Name: GetNetworkSubstation
Trigger: ()
Inputs (network_descriptor)
Results (NETWORK)
```

For the advisor agent, the acquaintance model indicates that it is interested in the outcome of the diagnosis (to show to the control engineer):

```
INTEREST-DESCRIPTOR
   INFORMATION-NAME: FAULT_DIAGNOSIS
   INFORMATION-CONDITION:
      [
         ("AVA", TRUE);
      ]
```

It can be seen that although the LVDA does have interactions with the TA and the high-voltage agent it does not model them. This is because the models are constructed on a need-to-know basis: the LVDA simply receives telemetry from the TA and so does not need to know about its interests and skills; the high-voltage agent makes requests of the LVDA, but not vice versa, so the high-voltage agent models the LVDA but not the other way around. Further details of these models can be found in Cockburn et al. (1991b) and Cockburn (1993).

4.5 An Example Cooperative Scenario

A simple scenario showing how the LVDA interacts with the TA, the information agent (IA), and the advisor agent (AVA) to diagnose and report a fault on the low-voltage network is described. The names of MUs, plans, and behaviors are those used in earlier sections.

The TA is continually receiving telemetry from the electricity network. This is transformed into the standard ARCHON format by its IS and is made available to the PCM as an intermediate result. The TELEMETRY is checked against its acquaintance models, by the PCM, and is sent to the LVDA if its operation is autoreclosure (see Section 2.3).

On arriving at the LVDA, the PCM checks to see if any skills will be triggered by the incoming data. In this case, the skill DealWithTelemetry is triggered and the TELEMETRY data is added to its context. Control then passes from the PCM to the monitor in order to execute the associated plan (Get_Network_Data; see Figure 12.5). The first MU, TransformTelemetry, is invoked; its input, TELEMETRY, is extracted from the context of the behavior. The monitor creates a message containing the name of the IS task (TRANSFORM-TELEMETRY; Figure 12.4) and the TELEMETRY data and sends this to the IS via the interface. The task is performed and the result, TRANSFORMED-TELEMETRY, is added to the context of the behavior. The next MU in the plan, NeedNetwork, is then activated. This checks if the network has been loaded for the TRANS-FORMED-TELEMETRY. Next the plan forks and so, by convention, the leftmost branch is tried first. This branch contains a condition checking on the output of the previous MU. If a network descriptor has been produced then the condition is satisfied and the CreateNetworkModel MU is activated. Assuming this to be the case, CreateNetworkModel has NETWORK as an input. The monitor checks to see if this is available within the behavior's context: it is not, so a request is made to the PCM for the data. The PCM first checks, by referring to the self model, to see if the LVDA can produce the data itself. As it cannot, a check on the acquaintance models is made. It is seen that the IA can provide the data using the GetNetworkSubstation skill and that this skill requires the data network_descriptor to be sent from the behavior's context. The request is passed onto the HLCM where the IA's address is found and the message is actually delivered. The request is dealt with by the IA (with reference to its self model) and the appropriate portion of the network is returned. The LVDA's PCM then makes this result available to the behavior from which the request originated. The CreateNetworkModel MU is then activated and upon its completion the plan ends.

As the DealWithTelemetry behavior has finished, its child behavior DiagnoseFault is called. The plan Diagnose is started and the MU DiagnoseFault is activated with input TRANSFORMED-TELEMETRY. If this produces a new fault diagnosis then it will be some time before the MU returns a result. In the meantime, new telemetry and telephone calls will arrive, some of which will start new diagnoses and some of which will add to the one started by the original behavior. When the DiagnoseFault MU completes the behavior DiagnoseFault terminates, as does its parent DealWithTelemetry. On completion of the behavior, the result (FAULT_DIAGNOSIS) is made available to the PCM. Note that the results of the other MUs (e.g., TRANSFORMED-TELEMETRY) are not specified as a result of the behavior and so are not passed on. The PCM checks the self and acquaintance models to determine whether the diagnosis can be used locally (it cannot) or by another agent (it can—the AVA is interested and so it is sent the result).

4.6 System Debugging

Debugging in a multiagent system is an even more complex and time-consuming process than it is for stand-alone systems since more than one entity is being tested at the same time (see Chapters 3 and 21). In CIDIM, this process was exacerbated by the fact that some of the ISs were still under development when the cooperating community was being designed. To reduce the scope for errors it was decided that dummy ISs would be used for the preliminary testing phase (dummy ISs are stubs which return a result without computation). These stubs were then incrementally replaced with the real programs and a further round of testing was undertaken. The benefits of using this approach are as follows: the possibility of errors is reduced, the IS gives a known response, and the overall time for system testing is decreased. Also this mode of operation is a necessity when an agent is created from the first IS, since checks must be made to ensure that the agent responds properly to requests and volunteered information which arrive from its acquaintances.

An important feature of the ARCHON development environment which made this testing process considerably easier was the ability to trace each of the agent's modules in terms of the flow of messages between them. Figure 12.9 shows telemetry being received from the TA's IS as an intermediate result of the behavior StartUp. The HLCM trace window shows this result being sent to the IA, the AVA and the HVDA as unrequested information because of the contents of their respective acquaintance models.

5 CONCLUSIONS AND FUTURE PLANS

This chapter has outlined the main features of the ARCHON approach to building real-world DAI applications in the industrial supervision and control domain. By necessity, some aspects of this description are lacking in detail, but in such cases we have made reference to more comprehensive literature. Although the ARCHON system has been primarily designed based on our experiences of the supervision and control domain, it is felt that the architecture and the methodology will generalize, in a relatively seamless manner, to new application areas. Indeed this possbility is being actively pursued by a number of organizations.

In its present form, the CIDIM application consists of seven agents: the telemetry agent, the information agent, the weather watch agent, the low-voltage diagnosis agent, the high-voltage diagnosis agent, the switch planning agent, and the advisor agent. The community was tested by providing it with data gathered from a number of actual disturbance episodes. During these trials the agents cooperated with one another, in the manner described, to achieve

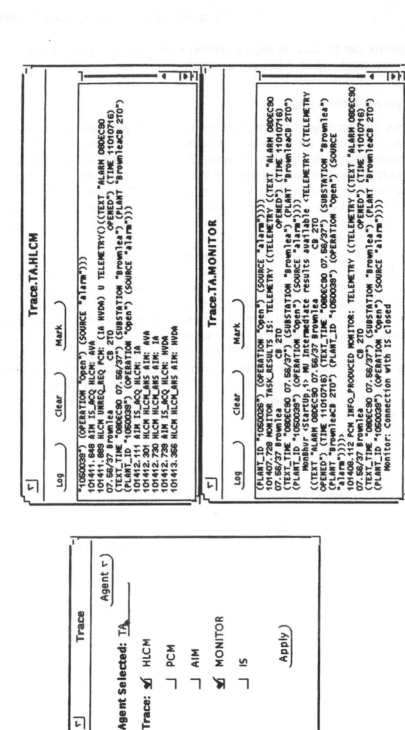

Figure 12.9 Tracing facilities of the ARCHON toolbox.

the goals outlined in this chapter. For the future, two avenues of exploitation are being pursued. First, the possibility of running the CIDIM system in field trials is being investigated. Second, the ARCHON technology and some of CIDIM's intelligent systems are being offered to regional electricity companies as a way of improving the level of integration in their control rooms.

ACKNOWLEDGMENTS

The work described in this chapter has been carried out in the ESPRIT II project ARCHON (P2256), whose partners are Atlas Elektronik, Framentec-Cognitech, Labein, Queen Mary and Westfield College, Iberdrola, EA Technology, Amber, Technical University of Athens, FWI University of Amsterdam, CAP Volmac, CERN, and University of Porto. The concepts reported in this chapter are the result of the consortium's efforts; however, we would particularly like to acknowledge the help provided by László Varga on this application.

REFERENCES

Cockburn, D. (1992). Two model based systems for fault diagnosis in electricity distribution networks. *IEE Collq. Intell. Fault Diagn.*, Part 2, Dig. No. 1992/48.

Cockburn, D. (1993). Intelligent network operation and control systems. *IEE Colloq. Expert Syst. Field Prot. Control*, Dig. No. 1993/193.

Cockburn, D., McDonald, J. B., Brailsford, G., Beaton, J., and Lo, K. (1991a). Expert systems for on-line fault diagnosis in electrical power networks. *Proc. Int. Conf. Elect. Distrib.*, Liege, Belgium, pp. 4.3.1–4.3.7.

Cockburn, D., Corera, J., Cross, A., Echavarri, J., Laresgoiti, I., and Perez, J. (1991b). *Development of Two Large Industrial Applications within A Distributed Artificial Intelligence Framework*, ARCHON Tech. Rep. No. 18. Atlas Elektronik, Bremen, Germany.

Cockburn, D., Varga, L. Z., and Jennings, N. R., (1992). *Cooperating Intelligent Systems for Electricity Distribution*, Proc. Expert Syst. 92 (Appl. Track). Cambridge Univ. Press, Cambridge, UK.

Corera, J., Laresgoiti, I., Cockburn, D., and Cross, A. (1993). A cooperative approach towards the solution of complex decision problems in energy management and electricity networks. *Proc. Int. Conf. Electr. Distrib.*, Birmingham, UK, pp. 4.19.1–4.19.6.

Cross, A., Brailsford, J., and Brint, A. (1992). A KBS for writing safe sequences of operations on a high voltage electricity network. *Proc. Int. Conf. Pract. Appl. Prolog, 1st*, London.

Jennings, N. R. (1992). Using GRATE to build cooperating agents for industrial control. *Proc. IFAC/IFIP/IMACS Int. Symp. Artif. Intell. Real Time Control*, Delft, The Netherlands, pp. 691–696.

Jennings, N. R., and Pople, J. A. (1993). Design and implementation of ARCHON's coordination module. *Proc. Coop. Knowl. Based Syst., SIG Workshop*, University of Keele, Keele, UK, pp. 61–82.

Jennings, N. R., and Wittig, T. (1992). ARCHON: Theory and practice. In *Distributed Artificial Intelligence: Theory and Praxis* (N. M. Avouris and L. Gasser, eds.), pp. 179–195. Kluwer Academic Press, Boston.

Jennings, N. R., Varga, L. Z., Aarnts, R., Fuchs, J., and Skarek, P. (1993). Transforming standalone expert systems into a community of cooperating agents. *Int. J. Eng. Appl. Artif. Intell.* **6**(4), 317–331.

Lees, M. (1992). Measurement of lightning ground strikes in the UK. *Proc. Int. Conf. Lightning Pro.*, London, pp. 2.1.1–2.1.5.

Oliveira, E., Camacho, R., and Ramos, C. (1991). A multi-agent environment in robotics. *Robotica* **4**(9).

Roda, R., Jennings, N. R., and Mamdani, E. H. (1991). The impact of heterogeneity on cooperating agents. *Proc. Am. Assoc. Artif. Intell. Workshop Coop. Heterogeneous Intell. Syst.*, Anaheim, CA.

Scott, L. (1988). A lightning location system for the UK electricity supply industry. *Proc. Int. Conf. Lightning Static Electr.*, Oklahoma.

Stassinopoulos, G., and Lembessis, E. (1993). *Application of a Multi-Agent Cooperative Architecture to Process Control in the Cement Factory*, ARCHON Tech. Rep. No. 43. Atlas Elektronik, Bremen, Germany.

Tuijnman, F., and Afsarmanesh, A. (1993). Distributed objects in a federation of autonomous cooperating agents. *Proc. Int. Conf. Intell. Coop. Inf. Syst.*, Rotterdam, The Netherlands, pp. 256–265.

Varga, L., Jennings, N. R., and Cockburn, D. (1994). Integrating intelligent systems into a cooperating community for electricity distribution management. *Expert Syst. Appl.* **7**(4), 563–579.

Wittig, T., ed. (1992). *ARCHON: An Architecture for Multi-agent Systems*. Ellis Horwood, Chichester, UK.

CHAPTER 13 _____

IMAGINE: An Integrated Environment for Constructing Distributed Artificial Intelligence Systems

DONALD D. STEINER

1 INTRODUCTION

As described in Chapters 1, 19, and 20, many techniques employed in distributed AI (DAI) stem from methods developed in human society. For example, the contract net protocol (Smith, 1980) clearly comes from market economics, and speech acts (Searle, 1969) were originally derived from analysis of human interaction. As these techniques have been formalized and successfully incorporated into artificial intelligence programs, the question naturally arises whether they can, in turn, be applied to the field of computer-supported cooperative work (CSCW) (Greif, 1988), which aims toward computer support of problem solving and task execution by distributed teams of *humans*. Indeed, the question can be expanded by considering the *active* participation of machine elements in such cooperative processes. The development of systems supporting the cooperation processes between humans and actively participating intelligent computers is the focus of the field human computer cooperative work (HCCW) (Steiner et al., 1990).

These questions were among those considered by IMAGINE,[1] which was a three-year project initiated in November 1990 by the Commission of the European Communities as part of the ESPRIT II framework. The participating institutions (along with country and primary contact) were, in alphabetical order, Imperial College (UK, Prof. K. Clark), Intrasoft S.A. (Greece, K. Tze-

_____

[1]Project 5362, Integrated Multi-Agent Interaction Environment.

_____

Foundations of Distributed Artificial Intelligence, Edited by G. M. P. O'Hare and N. R. Jennings.
ISBN 0-471-00675-0 © 1996 John Wiley & Sons, Inc.

lepis), Roke Manor Research (UK, M. Hook), Siemens AG (Germany, H. Haugeneder), Steria (France, C. Koutsoumalis), University of Amsterdam (The Netherlands, P. de Greef), and University of Keele (UK, Prof. S. M. Deen). Siemens acted as primary contractor.

The goal of IMAGINE was to "develop a domain-independent formalism and development environment for modelling and constructing multi-agent systems in the HCCW framework requiring a high degree of cooperation among heterogeneous autonomous agents, including humans" (Haugeneder, 1994). This was accomplished via a unique combination of top-down conceptual analysis and bottom-up platform development along with conceptual prototyping in sample application areas. The primary results of IMAGINE were

- A specification and prototype implementation of a multiagent language for implementation of and interaction among agents (MAIL[2])
- A prototypical multiagent environment for constructing cooperative applications (MECCA)
- Specification and implementation of base languages for supporting interaction among processes (ICP-][and April) (see also Chapter 3)
- Two prototypical applications in the areas of urban traffic management and group scheduling (UTS and MAM, respectively)

In this chapter we provide an overview of each of these results.[3] We begin by examining the underlying concepts adopted by IMAGINE (Steiner et al., 1993).

2   CONCEPTUAL FOUNDATION

We adopted the principle that agents are rational in Newell's sense: if an agent has *knowledge* that one of its *actions* will lead to one of its *goals*, it will select that action. Actions can only achieve goals if they are coordinated by *plans*. In an uncertain world, a rational agent must also be reactive: certain changes in the environment (situations) may activate goals which must be achieved immediately. When a rational agent lacks the skill, knowledge or resources to achieve a goal on its own, it must be able to *cooperate* with other agents. For this purpose, agents must have specialized knowledge about goals, actions, and plans.

2.1   Basic Agent Structure

We also wanted to be able to easily incorporate existing systems as well as different message-passing techniques into the IMAGINE framework. This re-

---

[2]In contexts outside of IMAGINE, often referred to as MAI[2]L.
[3]The results of IMAGINE are presented in more detail in Haugeneder (1994).

TABLE 13.1   Phases of an IMAGINE Agent

Goal Activation	Situation assessment/influence by other agents
Planning	Determining/constructing plans for achieving goals
Scheduling	Committing to the plans and scheduling the required tasks
Execution	Executing tasks, causing a change in the world state

sulted in the structuring of an agent into the following three major components (Steiner et al., 1990): refer to the other contributors in this part of the book for alternative complementary approaches.

Agent Head. The agent head represents that portion of the agent which controls its actions, thus realizing its reactive, rational and cooperative capabilities. The situated rational behavior of each plan-based agent is implemented by a process comprising the basic phases in Table 13.1. Determining the structure of the head was one of the primary concerns of IMAGINE; the next sections describe these phases in more detail.

Agent Communicator. The agent ·communicator performs communicative actions with other agents, thereby releasing the head from managing and controlling the underlying complex communication environment. As we adopted the message-passing paradigm for communication, the communicator's primary actions are send and receive. The messages are represented in the head by *cooperation primitives*: illocutionary speech acts operating upon specified objects. These will be described in Section 3.3.

Agent Body. The agent body performs those actions which observe and influence the external world; it contains the application-oriented processing capabilities of the agent. It may be written in any programming language, provided this has a well-defined functional interface. It is up to the agent programmer to represent body actions in the planning context so that they can be reasoned about by the agent head.

We now direct our attention to the agent head.

2.2   Behavior of Goal-Directed Agents

The agent head represents the knowledge of how the world can be transformed by executing tasks, and which agents can perform which tasks. It processes this knowledge to find out what tasks, when executed by itself or other agents, will bring about a world state described by one of its goals.

In the following, we outline the basic processing schema from a single agent's point of view. Figure 13.1 shows how the basic phases of this schema, first described in Table 13.1, fit together: nodes represent processes; labels on arcs, data passed between processes. This is only a rough sketch of the information flow—all processes interact with each other via an agent's underlying

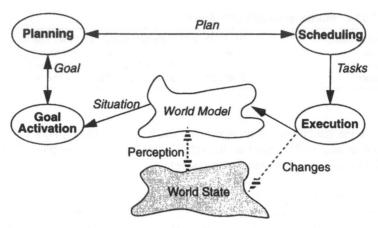

Figure 13.1 *Processes within an agent.*

knowledge. An agent may use a variety of methods to find a plan for achieving a particular goal from its current state. These range from accessing predefined, possibly incomplete, plans from a plan library, to automatically creating full distributed plans (refer to Chapter 8 for a discussion of these alternatives). It may use a combination of backward reasoning from desired goals to forward reasoning from current world states. The use of partial plans allows the interleaving of planning and execution as well as shared multiagent plans (see Chapter 8).

Before a plan can be executed, its tasks must be scheduled by the head, taking into account the other plans of the agent and any resource constraints.

At the heart of an agent is an executor component that runs the schedules, by calling actions and handling interrupts. The actions may be communicative, in which case they are passed to the agent communicator, or domain specific, in which case they are passed to the agent body. The interrupts include incoming messages and "alarm" signals from the body.

It may happen that it is not possible to keep to a schedule: a task may fail, it may take longer than expected, or the agent may be interrupted. Our notions of planning and cooperation allow agents to recover from this situation.

2.3 Cooperation among Agents

How can agents cooperate with each other in an efficient and coordinated way? (See Chapter 6 for a further discussion.) First of all, they need to share a multiagent plan, just as a single agent needs a plan for coordinating the actions to achieve its goals. The multiagent plan is similar to the single-agent plan in that it deals effectively with interdependencies between actions. It is more elaborate since these actions are assigned to different agents and may be communicative in nature.

This leads to the question: how can agents arrive at shared multiagent plans in a flexible way? Our approach is the following:

Agents use *cooperation methods* to create, maintain, and execute multiagent plans.

Cooperation methods themselves are abstract multiagent plan schemas that can be instantiated and thereby customized to fit the problem at hand.

Due to their abstractness the same set of cooperation methods can be used in a wide class of application domains.

Thus, cooperation is simply the process of distributing goals, plans, and tasks across several agents as shown in Figure 13.2.

This process can be described as follows: Assume that changes in the world state, as reflected in the world model, have triggered a goal inside the agent which it is incapable of achieving on its own, because it cannot either find a local plan or execute the required tasks. First, it must convince another agent to adopt its goal. In the case of benevolent agents (see Chapter 1) this will happen as long as the goal does not conflict with any of the other agent's goals. Given such an agent can be found, the initiating agent tries to find a multiagent plan leading to the goal. Each agent involved will schedule its respective parts of the plan and will finally execute the tasks. The effects of task execution should lead to achievement of the initial goal. Obviously, we have described *centralized multiagent planning* (see Chapter 8).

For the process of establishing a multiagent plan other variants are conceivable:

1. An agent is not capable of finding a multiagent plan for a given goal on its own.

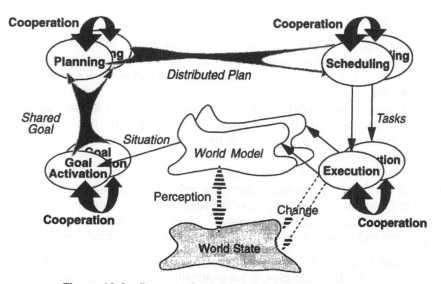

Figure 13.2 *Process view of several distributed agents.*

2. Instead of starting out with a goal at one single agent, several agents might detect changes in their world states that lead to a common, i.e., implicitly shared, goal.

If, in these cases, no predefined plan meets the activated goals, elaboration of a viable distributed plan becomes the subject of negotiation; i.e., planning is carried out as a distributed effort. This is the most general case of *distributed multiagent planning* (see Chapter 8).

A wide spectrum of variants for generating multiagent plans lies between centralised and distributed multiagent planning (see Chapters 1 and 8). The usual way to establish a multiagent plan is a mixture of centralized planning and negotiation about (sub-) plans.

Case 2 shows that cooperation need not be explicitly initiated by one agent alone: A multiagent system as a whole also may have goals. These will be created by the system designer, who will try to ensure that the goals of the individual agents are such that the system goals are achieved. An agent, in general, does not have a record of these global design goals.

3 A MULTIAGENT INTERACTION AND IMPLEMENTATION LANGUAGE

We now turn our attention to the specific language constructs offered by MAIL supporting the above concepts. We progress from the low-level knowledge representation and processing aspects via the single-agent aspects to arrive at the multiagent aspects of MAIL. Note, that all of this occurs in the agent's head. An overview of the MAIL architecture is shown in Figure 13.3.

3.1 Knowledge Representation

The knowledge base (KB) of an agent consists of tuples, called MAIL-*terms*, of aspect-value pairs. Some aspects and their values are provided automatically by the system. The KB is structured by *contexts* which allow for hypothetical reasoning and planning.

MAIL-actions and MAIL-plans are special MAIL-terms as they are compiled into executable MAIL-code when they enter the KB. The execution of plans and actions itself is described in the next section. A value in a plan or an action can be either a constant, a bound variable, or an aspect value. There are some special operators which return frequently used values. The \-operator retrieves the value of a given aspect of a given MAIL-term, the !-operator retrieves the value of a given aspect of the agent itself, !name refers to its name, and the cc-operator represents the context in which the plan or action is running. Plans and actions have four aspects which are of particular interest.

*Characters (*char*).* The characters represent those agents involved in a multiagent action or plan. The plan is automatically compiled into separate plans for each character with appropriate synchronization points.

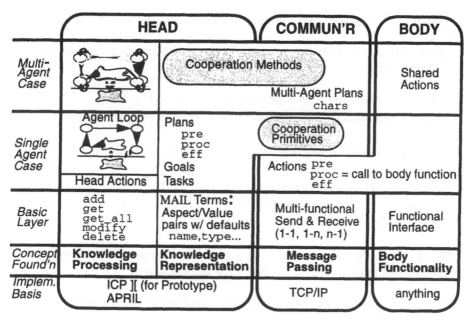

Figure 13.3 MAIL architecture.

Preconditions (pre**).** The preconditions contain operations for knowledge access and for setting conditions on that knowledge. Only when the preconditions are satisfied, may the action or plan be executed. The following constructs can appear in preconditions:

Existential queries (get) for MAIL-terms satisfying given constraints on values.

Negation ($\sim$) of existential queries using *negation-as-failure*.

Universal queries (getall) for all MAIL-terms satisfying given constraints on values.

Simple conditions ($==$, $\==$, $<$, $>$, $<=$, $>=$, in) for comparing two values

Demons ($\rightarrow$) for specifying additional conditions on the evaluation of the precondition, which is delayed until the demon condition holds. These are used for reacting to changes in the world state immediately without having to plan. (Reactive plans are plans already in execution waiting for their demons to be triggered.) Demons may also specify time delays, this is useful for message timeouts.

Procedures (proc**).** An action's procedure consists of a single call to a function which may be in any language, provided there is a suitable interface to MAIL. Currently, functions may be Prolog, C, or Unix calls. The execution of the function takes place either in the body or in the communicator. Arguments to functions are bound in the preconditions and return values in the effects.

Plan procedures allow composing calls to other plans or actions in the following manners:

Sequential execution of two procedures (. . . & . . .)

Parallel execution of two procedures waiting until both are finished
(. . . | . . .)

Forking a procedure and continuing without waiting until it is finished
(fork . . .)

Mapping over lists (foreach . . . in . . . do . . .)

Conditional execution of a procedure (if . . . then . . .)

Looping (while . . . do . . .)

Effects (eff). The effect of a plan or action is to alter the KB upon successful execution of the procedure. This may be a conjunction of

Creation of new terms (+), using local variables to specify aspect values

Deletion of terms (−)

Alteration of terms by adding new aspects or setting different values for existing aspects

The next section describes the execution of actions and plans in detail.

3.2   Knowledge Processing

As alluded to previously, basic knowledge access functions are provided by MAIL, such as assert, get, get_all, delete, etc. Of more importance is the way in which sequences of actions are selected, scheduled, and executed in order to achieve goals.

Execution in MAIL. The basic entity for execution in MAIL is an action. If an action is to be executed it is transformed into an *event* and the event is inserted in the schedule of the agent. Events are special MAIL-terms which are usually not visible to the programmer. The schedule of an agent consists of a set of events and a set of constraints specifying the chronological (partial) order among the events. Each event represents an action or a plan and defines the environment for the execution of the action or plan. The use of the events is twofold. On one hand, they allow for easy yet flexible implementation of the different execution constructs of MAIL, on the other, they enable the agents to reason about their future states. There is one process in every agent that manages the schedule of the agent. If a set of events and their constraints is inserted into the schedule, this process is woken, it finds the next events to execute, and executes the events concurrently, each in a separate process.

The execution of an event is initiated by evaluating the precondition of its corresponding action or plan. If the precondition defines a demon, the event is suspended until the demon condition is valid. Then the rest of the precondition is evaluated. Within the evaluation of the precondition, backtracking is possible. If the entire precondition is satisfied, the local environment is set according to the values gained from the precondition. The next step is to execute the procedure. If the event represents an action, the call to the body or communicator function is executed. If the event is a plan, the procedure's event structure[4] is inserted in the schedule of the agent. The insertion of the new events for the plan wakes up the main process of the agent, which in turn forks processes for each of the executable events in the schedule. The original event is suspended until the last event in the plan's event structure, a special system event, rewakes the event. The knowledge base is then updated according to the effects. If everything went well up to this point, the process is killed, and the event is deleted from the agent's KB and its schedule. The deletion of events from the schedule restarts the main process to find the next candidates for execution. If the event execution process failed at some point, a system exception is raised, the default behavior of which is to remove the event, its parent event, if any, and all the events with the same parent.

Note, that we specify neither how the agent actually arrives at the required actions to achieve its goals nor how the events are scheduled. This can be handled by the programmer's favorite planning[5] and scheduling techniques, as long as they handle MAIL-terms. Also, the basic execution loop described above is represented as a plan itself and, thus, can be modified by the programmer. This allows for customizing an agent's behavior.

3.3 Cooperation in MAIL

Since MAIL is designed to be a multiagent language, it supports distribution of goals, plans, and tasks among agents. This happens via communication on the lowest level, cooperation primitives and cooperation methods at higher levels.

Communication. Upon creation, an agent registers with a given agent directory service (ADS) which itself is an agent (see Chapter 14 for a more detailed discussion). The ADS stores information about the communication details of the agents as well as their types and capabilities. The agent communicator then waits for new connections, executing the predefined send and receive actions as scheduled by the head.

The receive action can be specified with a list of agents and a timeout. The communicator analyses an incoming message and adds the message content

---

[4]The event structure of the plan is computed as soon as it is inserted into the KB.
[5]An effort is currently underway to provide an abductive planner for MAIL based on the event calculus.

(a cooperation primitive) to the corresponding context (creating a new one if necessary) for further processing by the head.

The send action accepts either a single agent or a list of agents. The communicator takes care of generating appropriate MAIL-terms for each message to be sent, determines the address of the agent (querying the ADS if necessary), and sends the message.

On the basis of these actions, the cooperation primitives and cooperation methods can easily be implemented. Some cooperation methods, such as ADS registration and tracing, are executed directly by the communicator.

Cooperation Primitives. Cooperation primitives are the basic building blocks of cooperation (Lux et al., 1993) (see Chapters 1 and 5). They represent a transfer of knowledge from one agent to one or more other agents with a specific intention and, as such, are represented as shared multiagent plans, whose preconditions and effects fix the semantics/intention of the primitives and whose procedures are synchronised calls to the communication actions.[6] A cooperation primitive consists of an illocutionary speech act operating upon a goal, plan, task, or arbitrary knowledge (cooperation object). An initial set of cooperation primitives and their intended use is as follows:

propose A proposal starts or continues a discussion among agents about a cooperation object. The knowledge transferred by a proposal to other agents is in some sense hypothetical as the agents sharing this knowledge have not yet committed to it (e.g., "propose: meeting in Kaiserslautern Wednesday afternoon").

refine An agent proposes a further instantiation of the cooperation object (e.g., "refine: lunch in Kaiserslautern Wednesday at 14.00").

modify A counter-proposal of an altered cooperation object (e.g., "modify: lunch in Saarbrücken Wednesday at 14.00").

accept Indication of commitment to the cooperation object.

reject Indication of failure to commit to the cooperation object.

order The recipient must accept the cooperation object, usually a task. The recipient may still fail to execute the task, in which case a task-failed result is returned. An order is only applicable if either the object has been previously discussed (and committed to) or an appropriate authority link between sender and recipient is established.

request A query for arbitrary knowledge.

tell The answer to a previous information request.

We emphasize that the cooperation object plays an important role in determining the semantics of a cooperation primitive. For example, if an agent has an active goal it cannot itself handle, it must invoke cooperation about the goal

---

[6]The formal specification of the cooperation primitives is in progress.

```
plan(cnet(TaskType,BestBid),
  chars = Mgr, Bdrs,
  proc = (Mgr:cn_make_proposal(TaskType,Specs) &
          Bdrs:CallForBids =
                Mgr:propose(Bdrs,Specs) &
          Mgr:(!timeout -> Bids) =
          Bdrs:(refine_bids(Specs,CallForBids\sender,Bid) &
                 refine(CallForBids\sender,Bid)) &
          Mgr:cn_eval_bids(Bids,BestBid,RestBids,TimeOuts) &
          Bdrs:NotifM =
                Mgr:(accept(BestBid\sender BestBid\object) |
                     (foreach Bid in RestBids do
                        reject(Bid\sender,Bid\object)) |
                     (foreach TOM in TimeOuts do
                        reject(TOM\sender,TOM\object))) &
          Bdrs:(if (NotifM\mtype == reject)
                 then uncommit(NotifM\sender)) &
          Mgr:close_connection &
          Bdrs:close_connection &
          Mgr:new_cooperation(safe_tae(BestBid\sender,TaskType))),
  eff = Mgr:(-cc),Bdrs:(-cc)).
```

Figure 13.4   *Contract net in MAIL.*

in order to get another agent to adopt the same goal. Only when this is accomplished, can it initiate cooperation about the plan for achieving the goal.

In order to provide the flexibility required by human participants in a cooperative process, we allow for dynamic definition of new cooperation primitives. For example, one could introduce message types such as support and oppose in order to more efficiently communicate about intentions (see Chapter 5).

Cooperation Methods. In addition, the semantics of a cooperation primitive can not rest upon the single message alone, rather also upon the history of exchanged messages and the expected replies; i.e., the entire dialogue must be taken into consideration. Such a dialogue consisting of a sequence of cooperation primitives is called a *cooperation method* (see also Chapter 6). Cooperation methods are represented as domain-independent multi-agent plans used to construct and execute domain-specific multiagent plans. An example of contract net in MAIL is given in Figure 13.4. Cooperation methods may be predefined or may be established dynamically. The latter allows for the flexibility required for human agents.

4 TOWARD A MULTIAGENT DEVELOPMENT ENVIRONMENT

The multiagent environment for constructing cooperative applications, (MECCA) provides an implementation of MAIL, the described agent model as well as tools for developing multiagent systems using the model. In this section we first describe the implementational basis of MECCA, then the architecture and capabilities of MECCA agents, some predefined cooperation methods as well as a variety of special agent types available in MECCA.

Distributed Logic-Oriented Programming: ICP-][. ICP-][(Chu, 1993) is a new implementation of Prolog that is particularly suited to distributed applications. It integrates Parlog, a committed-choice nondeterministic concurrent logic programming language, and ICP, an extended Prolog dialect. This allows the coordination of concurrently executing programs on separate workstations communicating via TCP/IP. Important features of ICP-][are its multithreaded capability, allowing for concurrent execution of independent goals, its fine-grained parallelism and high-level primitives providing the means for independent ICP-][processes on different machines on a network to communicate. The combination of the two logic languages offers considerable expressive power since different components of the same application may use either of them or both. Thus, the result of integrating these two paradigms is a new language well suited for network-friendly applications. ICP-][was used for the MAIL conceptual prototyping effort; the first implementation of MECCA was also performed using ICP-][.

Interaction among Processes: April. Based upon the experience gained during the conceptual prototyping effort, April (Agent PRocess Interaction Language) (McCabe and Clark, 1994) was developed in IMAGINE to provide a system tailored for supporting multiagent applications. April allows for the high-level specification of processes and communication among processes. April is based on tuples and sets, and includes a powerful macroprocessing capability, allowing for easy extension of the language. Initial efforts have been made towards mapping MAIL onto April.

4.2   Agents in MECCA

The prototype version of MECCA developed in IMAGINE provides an implementation of MAIL, an agent head, an agent communicator as well as a variety of standard agent types and cooperation methods on ICP-][.

The agent communicator is implemented as an ICP-][thread which opens a TCP/IP server port[7] through which it handles message passing of the agent. The communicator also sends trace messages to the monitor agent, and handles alone (without involving the head) the cooperation with ADS, as the only information exchanged concerns an agents attributes. The cooperation primitives are implemented as procedures in the communicator, which send messages or wait for one depending on the primitive's semantics.

The agent head is an ICP-][thread which accesses the knowledge base,

---

[7]Agents running in the same MAIL process actually use internal channels rather than TCP/IP to communicate.

activates its goals, runs the compiled plans of the agent defining its behavior, and executes cooperation methods via invoking cooperation primitives. The head is provided with predefined cooperation methods for exchanging knowledge with other agents and for requesting task execution from others agents as well as domain-specific multiagent plans.

The agent knowledge base in the head is implemented as a Prolog data base, offering services such assert, retract, find any or all the facts corresponding to some pattern. For instance, it is possible to find all agents having a given skill, or simply to retrieve the agent's information about itself.

The agent body either is programmed directly in ICP-][, in which case the head-body interface is straightforward, or it is a separate Unix process controlled by the head through sockets, pipes, file i/o, or the C interface to ICP-][.

We now describe some of the predefined agent types available in MECCA.

Agent Directory Service. The ADS agents are important in MECCA as they play the role of yellow-page servers throughout the whole network (see Chapter 14). ADSs can be distributed and allocated a partial responsibility over a portion of the multiagent system. They are able to communicate with each other to determine the address of a particular agent or to find all agents of a particular type. Thus, this information is available to any agent in the system (as it is registered with an ADS). They use the cooperation methods update_data and retract_data (see below) among themselves and with other agents to update their knowledge about the current agents.

Machine Agent. Machine agents are skeletal agents equipped with a communicator and head. They serve as a basis for constructing other types of agents, as they provide the minimum functionality a MECCA agent must exhibit in order in order to work in the system. Machine agents (and thus, all agents, by default) are controlled by the following commands:

stop for stopping the agent and removing it from the system

trace for beginning a trace mode (cf. monitor agents below)

untrace for ending trace mode

new for starting a new cooperation with specified parameters

assert for adding to the knowledge base

call for querying a Prolog goal

Monitor Agent. Monitor agents display a trace of all communication to and from a given agent. This is realised by a cooperation method directly in the traced agent's communicator.

User Agent (UA). User agents (Lux and Kolb, 1992) are dedicated to a particular user providing the interface between the user and the rest of the multiagent system (see Chapter 21). They represent knowledge about the user and access the tools a user uses (such as calendar system and e-mail) to provide support in executing tasks and cooperating with other humans (via their respective user agents).

User Interface Agents. Each agent has a graphical user interface displaying its knowledge base and receiving user commands in an agent- and application-specific fashion. In the current version of MECCA, the graphical user interface is implemented in Sun Microsystems' NeWS™, which allows for multithreading and socket communication. Thus, several agents can connect to a single interface by sending appropriate messages (called *tool messages*). The user interface agent (see Figure 13.5) is introduced to collect all such messages from agents within a MAIL process. This allows for only one communication link to the user interface as well as easy distribution of interfaces via cooperation among UIAs.

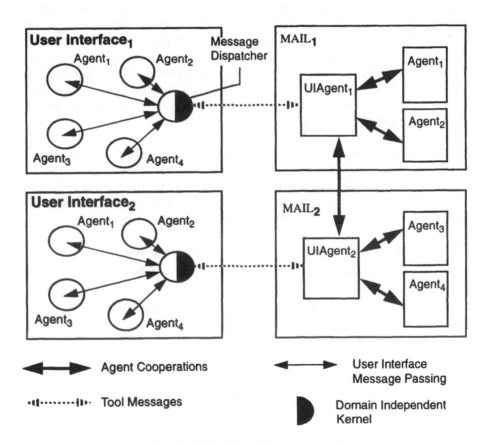

Figure 13.5 *User interface agents.*

4.3 Cooperation Methods in MECCA

A variety of sample cooperation methods are provided with MECCA. Some implement low-level cooperation for knowledge exchange and update, and are used by all agents. Others, while still domain-independent, require the multiagent programmer to define certain internal procedures specified by the method. Domain-dependent multiagent plans defined for a particular MECCA application, such as in the UTS or MAM, will be mentioned in Section 5.

Request Data (`request_data`). Characters: Knowledge Seeker, Knowledge Provider. This method is used by an agent to query another agent for knowledge. The knowledge seeker first determines whether it is requesting knowledge from itself. If so, it consults its own KB. If not, it requests the information from the knowledge provider, indicating in the cooperation object the type of information requested: either any or all data matching a given pattern. On receipt of the request, the recipient may further delegate information retrieval to another agent. The result of the query is passed back to the knowledge seeker.

Update Data (`update_data`). Characters: Knowledge Provider, Knowledge Recipient. This method is used by an agent to assert/retract a fact to/from another agent's KB. The cooperation primitive used is `order`, so that the update is compulsory. Thus, there is no response awaited from the recipient once the order has been sent. Agents may have domain-dependent behavior upon receiving such an update (e.g., the ADS, when receiving new information about a registered agent, redisplays its graphical presentation of agents).

Trial and Error (`tae`). Characters: Initiator, Recipient. This method allows an agent to request another to perform a task. This is done in three steps:

1. The initiator prepares the task, that is, performs any prerequisite action for the task which it is able to do by itself. It may fail in doing so, in which case the cooperation itself fails (only the initiator knows about it, as it did not yet call another agent).
2. The initiator sends a message requesting the other agent to perform the rest of the task. The recipient checks if it can execute the task (check of preconditions), if so performs the task and returns the result of the execution to the initiator. If not, the recipient sends a reject message to the initiator.
3. The initiator evaluates the result.

Safe Trial and Error (`safe_tae`). Characters: As in `tae`. The initiator of `safe_tae` first obtains a commitment from the recipient to execute the task. Upon acceptance of the commitment, the initiator proceeds by preparing the task, and if successful, ordering the recipient to execute it. The recipient executes the task (since it committed, the preconditions already hold), and returns the result which is then evaluated by the initiator.

Contract Net *(c_net)* (cf. Figure 13.4). Characters: Manager, Potential Bidders. The manager sends a request for bids (specifying a task to be performed, criteria for bid evaluation, and a timeout) to a set of potential bidders. Those potential bidders who refine the proposal (customizing the requirements to what they actually offer and possibly committing to the task) are referred to as the bidders. If there are no bidders, the cooperation fails. Otherwise, the manager sorts the bids according to the specified criteria. Based upon the result of this sorting, the set of potential bidders is split in three:

Those who did not answer within the specified timeout

The contractor who submitted the best bid w.r.t. the criteria

The other bidders, known as rejected bidders

The manager sends a reject to the timeouts and rejected bidders causing them to withdraw their (possible) commitment to the task. The last part of the cooperation is of the same form as safe_tae. The manager performs the actions it is able to do by itself, then orders the contractor to perform the task according to its bid. The contractor returns the result, which is then evaluated. Note that the contractor may still fail in execution of the task. This leads us to consider the following method.

Modified Contract Net *(cnet_mod)*. Characters: As in c_net. Here, the manager does not actually reject the bidders until the task is successfully performed. This enhanced version is different from c_net in a specific case: when the contractor fails to execute its task, the manager simply awards the task to the bidder with the next-lowest bid and resumes the cycle: preparing the task, ordering the contractor to execute it, and evaluating the result of the execution. This has the disadvantage that the bidders may remain committed much longer than they need be, and the bids may become invalid; however, the need for calling c_net repeatedly is eliminated.

Transfer Bid *(transfer_bid)*. Characters: Initiator, Associate. If a potential bidder cannot make a suitable bid, it uses this method to ask an associated bidder to assume the bid. If it is the lowest it will automatically be awarded to the associate by the manager. The associate remembers who sent the bid transfer proposal in order to avoid recursively proposing this bid to the initiator.

5 SAMPLE APPLICATIONS

The conceptual prototyping effort of IMAGINE which led to the development of the above-mentioned concepts targeted two demonstration scenarios in urban traffic control and group scheduling. Other applications developed in IMAGINE were in the domains of airport services (catering and air traffic control) and office automation [see Chapter 4 and Haugeneder (1994) for details of other applications].

5.1 Urban Traffic Scenario (UTS)

The MECCA/UTS system (Bomarius, 1992; Haugeneder and Steiner, 1993) targets car park allocation and traffic guidance as specific subdomains of urban traffic control. The system comprises car park allocation according to specific individual needs and route guidance to the selected car park.

The UTS model is based on a marketlike competitive situation, where cars compete for car parks and car parks compete for cars, each ruled by its own private strategy. The initiative for this competition comes from the cars. The route guidance model is based on a distributed problem solving approach toward providing optimal paths. The UTS world itself consists of a traffic area, divided into sectors, each of which has a specific street topology and statically allocated services, such as car parks. In addition, a dynamically changing set of cars using the streets and provided services are allocated to each sector. Adjacent sectors are linked via pairs of so-called sources and sinks which are designated by specific locations in their respective street topology. These sources and sinks constitute the connection points between pairs of sectors via which traffic flow from one sector to the other can be facilitated. Based on the agent architecture described in Section 2 and the domain's ontology, three types of agents are introduced in the UTS application with the following functionality.

Traffic Guidance System (TGS). This agent models the dynamic behavior of its sector by providing sector-specific services, such as route determination. It also acts as a generic agent directory service, as described in Section 4.2.

Driver's Assistant (DA). This user agent constitutes the individual car's (semi-) automatic guidance system, it acts on behalf of the driver to provide car park selection and route-finding services. The former is accomplished by negotiation with car parks, the latter via interaction with the TGS.

Parking Assignment System (PAS). This agent maintains information about its corresponding car park (in particular free and booked spaces, as well as parking fee), which it uses in negotiation with the DA. Two types of PASs are distinguished according to their behavior in making reservations. On the one hand, there are commitment-based PASs which provide a guaranteed reservation if possible. Other PASs only provide an estimated chance of getting a parking space based upon the number of currently available spaces; a space is not guaranteed. However, commitment-based PASs typically have higher fees.

Each parking process is a six-stage event, comprising the following phases:

1. *Negotiation.* The DA selects and initiates a cooperation method for finding an appropriate car park. The method may be one of tae, safe_tae, c_net or cnet_mod, as described in Section 4.3. The DA's bid evaluation function can take into account any combination of three criteria: The fee of the car park under consideration, the distance to this car park and the chance a space will be available upon arrival (guarantee).

2. *Reservation (optional).* In case the DA used a form of contract net, it notifies the PAS that was awarded the bid.

3. *Transfer.* The DA moves to the selected car park, determining the route from the TGS. If the car park is in another sector, then the corresponding TGSs cooperatively determine the best route.

4. *Registration.* The DA notifies the PAS that it has arrived and is requesting a space.

5. *Parking.* The PAS assigns a specific parking space to the DA, to which the DA moves.

6. *Deregistration/Payment.* When the DA desires to leave the car park it must first pay the required parking fee.

Thus, within the UTS system, parking activities in one sector or among several sectors are guided not by a centralized parking allocation system, rather by a robust decentralized, sector-oriented control regime that is sensitive to individual needs. It is based on the individual behavior of different DAs and PASs as well as on the TGS's routing service. The genuine origin of its overall functionality comes from the interaction between the various involved components, i.e., their agentified counterparts.

5.2 MECCA Appointment Manager (MAM)

The primary aim of the MAM system is the implementation of typical cooperative processes to schedule meetings (Lux, 1992). The novelty of MAM is that with the help of a user's associated *user agent* (UA, cf. Section 4.2) not only different semiautomatic meeting scheduling processes are realized but also the integration of different calendar systems. In the current version, interfaces to Sun Microsystems' Calendar Manager™, Calentool, and Emacs Calendar exist, but, in principle, any calendar system can be integrated. The calendar system and a user's personal meeting dates are part of the body of the UA. The head of the UA contains among other things functions to look for and schedule appropriate meeting dates.

Basic Cooperation Strategies. To schedule and manage an appointment a wide variety of different conditions have to be considered. The whole spectrum of making appointments has to be supported, ranging from fully specified proposals up to very vague ones. In the currently implemented MAM system, the intended participants, meeting start time, duration, and subject are taken into account for specification of meetings. The user can instruct his or her UA to use one of two cooperation methods to schedule a meeting.

Within the *optimistic strategy*, the initiator proposes to meet at a specified time. This message is sent by the initiator's UA to the UAs of all invitees. If all UAs accept within a given time constraint, their users are asked for confirmation[8] of the meeting. If a user rejects or is already occupied at the specified time, his or her UA rejects the proposal providing the reason for rejecting. With that knowledge in mind, the initiator will then try another schedule. As is often the case with even a small group of three or four persons, there may be no free time slot. This specific, very constrained meeting proposal has to be relaxed; a more *realistic strategy* has to be tried out.

Within the realistic strategy the initiator proposes a set of time intervals within which the meeting may begin. The corresponding UAs reply by refining the initial proposal with their free time slots within the specified constraints. Upon receipt of the replies, the initiating UA superimposes all the time slots to determine an appropriate start time. If this process yields a list of time slots during which all participants are available, the appointment is proposed for the first time slot in the list. The UAs then ask their respective humans for confirmation; if one human declines, the next available time slot is chosen. If no more time slots are available, the cooperation method fails. This strategy could be extended by asking those UAs with a minimum of conflict to try to reschedule their conflicting meetings. If a time slot is agreed to by all humans, the initiating UA then orders the participating agents to schedule the meeting for the time agreed upon.

The body of the UA thus provides

An interface to the user's calendar tool to perform actions like updating, rereading, or deleting appointments

Transformation of calendar tool specific data to a common time format, and vice versa.

6 CONCLUSION AND OUTLOOK

We have presented an agent model and corresponding language which supports a high-level representation and execution of agents and their cooperation. The MECCA development environment proves the suitability of this approach by supporting two application scenarios. Current work is targeting final specification and implementation of MAIL, and development of plan generation and scheduling techniques customized for this approach. The author gratefully ac-

---

[8]If humans are involved in a cooperation, the final decision should always remain within their responsibility.

knowledges the valuable contributions of Frank Bomarius, Alastair Burt, Hans Haugeneder, Michael Ko, Andreas Lux, Dirk Mahling, and the IMAGINE partners.

REFERENCES

Bomarius, F. (1992). A Multi-agent approach towards modeling urban traffic scenarios. *DFKI Res. Rep.* **RR-92-47.**

Chu, D. (1993). I.C. PROLOG: A language for implementing multi-agent systems. *Proc. Coop. Knowl. Based Syst. SIG Workshop*, University of Keele, Keele, UK, pp. 61–74.

Greif, I. (1988). *Computer-Supported Cooperative Work: A Book of Readings.* Morgan Kaufmann, San Mateo, CA.

Haugeneder, H. (1994). *IMAGINE Final Project Report, IMAGINE*, Esprit Proj. 5362. Siemens, Munich, Germany.

Haugeneder, H., and Steiner, D. (1993). A multi-agent scenario for cooperation in urban traffic. *Proc. Coop. Knowl. Based Syst. SIG Workshop*, University of Keele, Keele, UK, pp. 83–99.

Lux, A. (1992). A multi-agent approach towards group scheduling. *DFKI Res. Rep.* **RR-92-41.**

Lux, A., and Kolb, M. (1992). Linking humans and intelligent systems or: What are user agents good for? *Proc. Ger. Artif. Intell. Conf., 16th*, Springer Lect. Notes Artif. Intell., Vol. 671, pp. 372–385.

Lux, A., de Greef, P., Bomarius, F., and Steiner, D. (1993). A generic framework for human computer cooperation. *Proc. Int. Conf. Intell. Coop. Inf. Systm., 1st*, Rotterdam, The Netherlands, pp. 89–97.

McCabe, F., and Clark, C. (1994). April-Agent process interaction language. *Pre-Proc. Workshop Agent Theor. Archit. Lang.*, Amsterdam, pp. 280–296.

Searle, J. R. (1969). *Speech Acts: An Essay in the Philosophy of Language.* Cambridge Univ. Press, Cambridge, UK.

Smith, R. G. (1980). The contract net protocol: High level communications and control in a distributed problem solver. *IEEE Trans. Comput.* **C-29**(12), 1104–1113.

Steiner, D., Mahling, D., and Haugeneder, H. (1990). Human computer cooperative work. *Proc. Int. Workshop Distributed Artif. Intell., 10th*, Austin, TX, MCC Tech. Rep. ACT-AI-355-90.

Steiner, D., Burt, A., Kolb, M., and Lerin, C. (1993). The conceptual framework of MAIL. *Proc. Eur. Workshop Modell. Auton. Agents Multi-Agent World, 5th*, Springer Lect. Notes Artif. Intell., Vol. 957, pp. 217–230.

CHAPTER 14 _____

The Evolution of the CooperA Platform

LORENZO SOMMARUGA
NIKOS M. AVOURIS
MARC H. VAN LIEDEKERKE

1 INTRODUCTION

Despite the considerable progress of DAI theory and foundations during the recent years, one can observe that there are still many interesting areas for investigation in the field, often described as "the open questions of Distributed Artificial Intelligence" (Gasser, 1992) (see Chapter 1). In addition, the development of DAI experimental platforms (Chapter 3) can often prove to be a long tedious process, involving many phases.

The CooperA platform, described here, has evolved in the frame of such long-standing research effort, during which many diverse research issues have been addressed. These include, among others, multiple-domain experts knowledge acquisition, heterogeneous knowledge representation, interagent communication, user interaction, flexible coordination, and domain-independent cooperation mechanisms.

This chapter presents the major results of the project, which took the form of two experimental prototypes, called CooperA (Sommaruga et al., 1989b) and CooperA-II (Sommaruga and Shadbolt, 1994). The main characteristics of these prototypes are described in an incremental manner, which demonstrates the increased complexity and sophistication of the system in the context of a five-year effort, reflecting in many aspects the shifting interests of the DAI discipline.

The driving force of the reported experimentation has been the need to meet in the most efficient and effective way the requirements of a specific real-life

Foundations of Distributed Artificial Intelligence, Edited by G. M. P. O'Hare and N. R. Jennings.
ISBN 0-471-00675-0 © 1996 John Wiley & Sons, Inc.

application domain of high complexity. This application has provided our effort with a constant point of reference, which has given the status of a testbed to the developed software platform. Hanks et al. (1993) observe that the lack of controlled experimentation in an area of research is an indication of lack of maturity (see also Chapters 3 and 15). The fact that DAI has a long tradition of reported controlled experiments and testbeds since its early days (see Chapter 3), a tradition followed by the reported CooperA system, should be considered as an indication of quality and good prospects of our discipline.

The CooperA experiment took place in the frame of the research project Chemical Emergencies Management (ChEM) of the Commission of the European Community. The main aim of ChEM was the development of tools and techniques for the management of emergency situations involving electrical equipment which contain polychlorinated biphenyls (PCBs), a group of widely used hazardous chemical substances (see Chapter 4 for a discussion of other DAI applications). We investigated various knowledge-based system architectures in this process. We were soon driven to use DAI techniques by the high complexity of the domain, the high modularity of the domain knowledge, the presence of multiple-domain experts, and the requirements of high flexibility in cooperative decision making.

It is, however, outside the scope of this description to provide a detailed presentation of the application domain and its requirements. For more details on this subject one should refer to Sommaruga et al. (1989a) and Avouris et al. (1989), where the DChEM (distributed ChEM) application is presented, and to Avouris (1995), where an analysis of environmental problem solving in relation to DAI techniques can be found.

Instead, more emphasis is provided here to the architectural characteristics of the developed prototypes and the way issues like interagent communication, cooperation, control, heterogeneous knowledge representation, user interaction, and flexibility in agent behavior programming are addressed by CooperA and CooperA-II.

In more detail, we present first the early phases of the project, when the domain knowledge was structured in a rule-based monolithic expert system. Subsequently the multiagent CooperA architecture is presented, through which the knowledge can be distributed in multiple agents and the problem can be solved in a cooperative way. A detailed description of the platform, the structure of the Agent, the communication mechanisms, the user interface, and the CooperA User Agent is offered.

After a discussion of the limitations of this first prototype, we proceed with a description of the CooperA-II experiment results. This phase focuses on dynamic control of the agent's social behavior, through the use of cooperative heuristics. Our models are based on the assumption that cooperative behavior should be considered as a domain-independent characteristic, and therefore the agents should be provided with adequate data structures, mechanisms, and knowledge which support this behavior (see also Chapters 12 and 13). A discussion on how the developed cooperative heuristics can result in programmable macrobehaviors, and how through them agent behavior programming can be affected, is also included.

The final part provides a comparative discussion of the various phases of the project and comments on the final results.

2 BACKGROUND AND RATIONALE FOR CooperA

The first phase of the ChEM project resulted in modelling of the domain of Chemical Emergencies Management and the development of a production-rule-based expert system (ES). The major effort during this phase has been dedicated to knowledge acquisition which involved a group of knowledge engineers, and a community of domain experts.

The ES which was decided to be built in order to support decision makers for threat estimation during management of chemical accidents had to incorporate the knowledge of experts in the various domains involved and had to reason even with uncertain and incomplete information. Relying on this expertise, the system had to provide the user with a picture of the situation at any moment during the emergency, based on the available information at that time.

The KB built during this phase contained knowledge about accidents involving the whole family of polyhalogenated aromatics, and was reported in Argentesi et al. (1987). It contained approximately 1500 production rules. The ES could make an estimation of the threat and produce a relative report. The organization of the KB and the flow of data, which can be seen in Figure 14.1, was based on a two-level structure: in the higher level the semantics of the

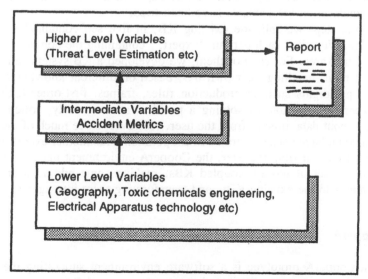

Figure 14.1 Organization of the KB of ChEM.

problem where defined (threat level and intermediate variables), while the lower level contained technical knowledge of the systems involved.

The fact that the knowledge involved could be organized in relatively independent units, which contribute to the solution in a dynamic way, led us to establish that a decoupling of the various modules was a necessary next phase of the project, leading to a distributed ChEM (DChEM).

This decision has been confirmed by the knowledge acquisition experience, which involved experts from different fields and backgrounds with different perspectives and sometimes conflicting contributions. This made it difficult to build one coherent KB.

Various studies and proposed architectures, influenced by the blackboard model and other DAI techniques have been proposed during this design phase (Avouris et al., 1988a,b). However, despite the intense theoretical activity in the DAI area of worldwide, most of the environments developed at that time were experimental and did not provide typical knowledge engineering tools, necessary for eliciting, structuring, and representing the knowledge to build the various modules/agents of the distributed system. Thus, the approach that we took was to extend an existing knowledge engineering environment, by building into it the structures and mechanisms for handling a community of interacting ESs. In this way, multiagent DAI techniques were introduced, also supported by the fact that a collection of cooperating agents corresponding to different domain experts could model more naturally our particular kind of problem solving.

The result of this effort has been the generic testbed for distributed KB applications, called CooperA (cooperating agents) (Sommaruga et al., 1989b).

DChEM has been used for prototyping the CooperA testbed. A community of agents has been developed and various experiments with control structures and communication mechanisms have been tried.

In a first step, we split the existing KB, in five self-contained pieces of knowledge. We called each part an "expert," containing the domain expertise in a particular area. For each of them, we developed a KB system, all ESs in their own right, handling their own I/O, based on different knowledge representation paradigms such as production rules, frames, first-order logic, etc. Each expert was capable of solving a problem autonomously, soliciting the necessary input data directly from the user. However, since much of the solicited data could have been elaborated in cooperation with another expert, instead of merely asking it from the user, the CooperA environment has been used to integrate this set of loosely coupled KBs, making some additions and light modifications to the existing KBs, and transforming them into agents.

3 CooperA

The first CooperA prototype is a software environment supporting the cooperation of heterogeneous, distributed, semiautonomous KB systems presented to the user via a customized user interface.

KB systems or modules are transformed to application agents which can be incrementally and selectively integrated into one system (see Chapters 12 and 13). Each expert module incorporates a self-description mechanism, which allows the shell to integrate it in the community during the group configuration phase. Thus, various alternative expert communities can be tried for the solution of a certain problem.

The user of CooperA can interact with the community of the agents through a special user interface agent. Special attention has been paid to the user interface which incorporates active modeling of the system, so that the user can see the flows of interaction among the agents (see Chapter 21). This satisfies the "comprehension of the problem-solving activity" requirement, a serious problem of the first ChEM prototype.

One of the capabilities of the CooperA user interface is that it can visualize graphically the problem-solving activity in the system and that it can let the user have access to the tools and commands available in a graphical way. For instance, a number of system commands and utilities are available through a graphical representation in the so-called workbench window.

3.1 The CooperA Architecture

The structure of CooperA can be described in terms of layers (see also Chapters 12, 13, and 15). They include

1. *The CooperA Kernel.* It represents the cooperation shell and consists of a collection of initialization procedures and system facilities that each agent can use; it is built on top of an existing language.
2. *The Message-Passing Mechanism.* It supports communication between agents by means of functions which handle and control messages. Messages play an important role in the cooperation: only through them is information exchanged and hence communication made possible.
3. *The Collection of CooperA System Agents.* It is a set of agents created by CooperA independent of the application; they perform basic operations of common interest. For example, one of the CooperA system agents is the user agent which handles all the interaction with the external world.
4. *The Community of Application-Specific Agents.* An agent is the basic computational entity of CooperA; it contains the knowledge to fulfil one or more tasks and knowledge about the external world (other agents, their location, and their capabilities).

On the basis of the CooperA kernel layer and with the help of CooperA system agents, a programmer can define agents, each one representing knowledge in various domains. A community of agents is thus created in which the user is involved through the *user agent,* and can thus interact with the community during problem solving. Message passing has been considered to be the most suitable communication paradigm for the flexible and dynamic creation of distributed systems (Hewitt and Lieberman, 1984).

3.2 Description of a CooperA Agent

CooperA agents are active structures that communicate by means of messages. Each agent exists in its own unique environment: its context. In this context, an agent contains its own specific application knowledge, knowledge about other agents in the external world, and the necessary information to communicate with them.

An agent has a well-defined structure, expressed through a number of attributes enumerated in Table 14.1. The most relevant are described in detail below.

Considering communication, all messages are sent or received through two queues: the *outgoing-messages queue* (*out-q*) from which the outgoing messages are transmitted, and the *incoming-messages queue* (*in-q*) that receives and handles incoming messages. For each of these queues a function is preset in order to coordinate respective actions that have to be undertaken according to the message type. For instance when an agent receives a request, it questions accordingly its own local world of knowledge or activates its rule base using its inference engine, trying to fulfil the request. Then it returns any resulting information to the requesting agent.

In order to facilitate cooperation between agents, each agent contains the attributes *my-skills* and *unsatisfied-goals*. The former contains all the knowledge relative to its own capacities. The latter contains reference to all information that might be needed but is not found in its own world, and to the sources (if known a priori) which can provide this information.

The attribute *Status* of an agent describes the current status of the agent's activity during execution. It can take one of the following values: *new*, *inactive*,

TABLE 14.1 Agent Attributes in CooperA

Context	Used for representing the agent's address
Status	Agent status, changing at run time
Goals	Agent's current goals, used during problem solving
Has tables	Refers to the data structures used for acquaintance modeling and communication
Current message	Message currently being processed
In-q	Input queue where incoming messages are put, awaiting the attention of the agent
Out-q	Output queue where outgoing messages are put, awaiting onward transmission by the kernel
My skills	List of goals that the agent can satisfy, with corresponding methods to achieve them
Unsatisfied goals	List of goals that cannot be reached using the local rule base and the knowledge of the agent
Activation method	Method necessary for the activation of the agent

running, and *waiting*. The value is assigned and handled by the appropriate kernel functions.

Each agent has its own knowledge of the external world (acquaintances) that permits cooperation. This information is contained in data structures local to the agent and created dynamically during the initialization of the system, when the community of agents is defined.

During the execution of a task, an agent can be in one of the following situations: (a) in need for some information, unknown to its own world, it has to decide to what agent to address a request for that information; (b) having calculated some results, it has to decide to what agent to send these.

To solve the first problem, a CooperA agent makes use of a particular structure: the *Yellow-Pages* (see Chapter 13). In this table, for each unsatisfied goal, i.e., information it cannot find or compute in its own world, the agent finds a list of agents in the community who might elaborate that information, or in other words, satisfy the goal in question.

To solve the second problem, the agent consults its *Interested-in-Table*, where it finds a list of agents in the community that could be interested in information it can calculate by itself.

3.3 Communication Mechanism

We have already mentioned the basic role messages play in CooperA: they support communication and hence contribute to agents cooperation. Here, we detail the structure of a message, and how the communication between agents, i.e., their exchange of messages, takes place.

The CooperA message is defined as a data structure containing a number of attributes. They include *identity* which is a unique symbol identifying the message; *type* indicating the kind of message, i.e., whether it is an information request, an answer, etc.; *content* which, in accordance with the message-type, refers to the actions it would like to invoke, or any other knowledge or information (e.g., it can contain the name of a goal, eventually followed by a list of parameters or it can contain an answer to a request, knowledge concerning actions, procedures, plans, allocation of tasks, etc.); *sender* which is the identity of the sender; *receiver* which contains a list of agents to which the message is addressed.

Figure 14.2 shows the communication process in CooperA. Messages are created by a sending agent through appropriate kernel functions and its local knowledge. The created message is put in the out-q of the sender and a kernel demon (*out-q manager*), monitoring the queue, is activated. This kernel service performs the message transmission by copying the message in the in-q of the receiver. Here, an appropriate demon (*in-q manager*) monitoring the in-q is activated and passes control to the receiving agent, if it is available and ready for execution. If the message is tagged as an answer to a previous request, the receiver matches the message with the pending request and reasons about the relevance of the supplied answer, which eventually can update the receiver's

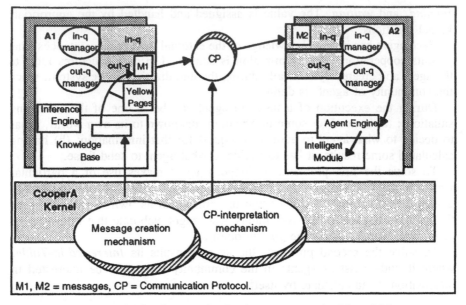

M1, M2 = messages, CP = Communication Protocol.

Figure 14.2 *Communication between agents A1 and A2.*

world of knowledge or begin a new query. If the message is tagged as a request to the receiving agent, the receiver tries to activate the appropriate method in order to satisfy the goal specified by the message. If the message is a request addressed to the user agent, it contains all the necessary information for specifying the dialogue with the user. The actual interaction with the user is managed by a special CooperA agent, called *User Agent*, which transmits the user's reply back to the agents interested in it.

The message receiver will be activated if its status is inactive. If not, the received messages remain in the incoming-messages queue, waiting for the agent to be ready to process them. In general, messages are FIFO processed, but in principle it is possible to introduce some kind of priority handling in the queues.

Agents react upon receiving a message according to the behavior expressed by their procedural activation methods, and the particular type of the received message. The active part of the agent, invoked by its activation method, acts on the local domain knowledge by making inferences on it or modifying it. This knowledge is only locally visible to the agent.

Since CooperA has been designed for interactive systems, there is also provision for communication with the human user. Moreover, there is the possibility of setting alternative communication strategies that can influence the problem-solving activity and the overall convergence to a solution (see Chapter 13).

A message interpretation mechanism is inserted in the transmission phase (see Figure 14.2, CP-interpretation mechanism), in order to provide global understanding in the exchange of message. This is accomplished by means of the communication protocol.

The Communication Protocol CP and the Dictionary. The exchange of information between all agents is done through the *communication protocol* (CP). The CP addresses the problem of defining a common representation for the interleaving parts of KBs. The sender agent creates an outgoing message first in its *local language*, i.e., using symbols which have only a local meaning. During the message-sending operation, a translation into a *global language* message takes place. This global language is part of the CP. The inverse translation, from global to local language, takes place at the receiving agent.

CooperA uses a data structure called *Dictionary* and some relevant kernel functions during the CP-interpretation phase. The *Dictionary* contains a directory of associations between concepts, locally defined and used by an agent, and global terms, defined in the frame of the communication protocol.

The structure of the *Dictionary* for an agent$_x$ is

$$\{Dictionary_x$$

$$. . .$$

$$\text{local-concept}_j : \text{CP-concept}_j \text{ address}_j$$

$$. . . \}$$

where local-concept$_j$ is an attribute referring to a local symbol, CP-concept$_j$ is the globally known name of the local concept and address$_j$ represent the local address where local-concept$_j$ is stored. If the same CP-concept is related to a local-concept$_k$ of an other agent, the two concepts are considered, as referring to the same symbol in a virtual global name-space of the community of the distributed agents.

Figure 14.3 presents an example of the use of the CP-interpretation mechanism together with the corresponding *Dictionary* definitions about an infor-

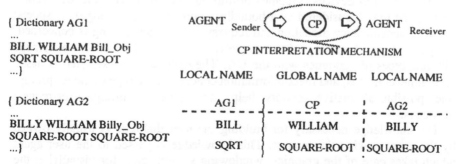

Figure 14.3 *Example of the definition and use of the Dictionary.*

mation (William) and a function (square-root). For instance, if AG1 sends an information about *BILL* to AG2, *BILL* is first translated into *WILLIAM* using AG1's dictionary and then *WILLIAM* converted to *BILLY* using AG2's dictionary. Analogously, if AG2 asks AG1 to compute the square root of a number, SQUARE-ROOT is first translated into SQUARE-ROOT and then into SQRT using respectively AG2's and AG1's dictionaries.

Each agent is provided with a *Dictionary*, in which the part of the agent's local knowledge which could be of interest to the rest of the community is mapped into a global representation. The problem that the CooperA programmer is faced with during the development of the *Dictionary* structure of an agent is not a trivial one. The coherence of the distributed problem-solving activity depends a great deal on an accurate semantic and lexical mapping of the concepts defined in the frame of the various KBs. Once this mapping has been completed the operation of developing structures like *Dictionary* is straightforward. So far, the mapping of the knowledge between agents is entirely left up to the CooperA programmers.

The correct definition of these dictionaries permits coherent communication between heterogeneous agents. This is a necessary (but not sufficient) step toward coherent behavior of the community of agents.

Communication with the User. CooperA is designed as an interactive system. The control over the interaction could be either with the user or with the agent community depending on the control strategy of the particular application. Thus, an agent could ask or notify the user about information, the user could ask for information from an agent, etc.

The user-to-agent interaction has been modeled according to the agent-to-agent communication mechanism. This has been achieved through a CooperA system agent called the *user agent* (UA), which represents the user within the community and handles all communication between the community of agents and the external world. The UA, always present in the system, is structured in the same way as all the other CooperA agents and communicates with them through the same message-passing mechanism. It can be seen as an ordinary agent with no specific domain knowledge, but with some special skills, e.g., it can handle I/O devices, graphics primitives, etc. However, the UA, representing the user (considered as a boundless domain of knowledge), is special as far as acquaintance modeling and request message structuring is concerned. A special type of message (user request) is introduced in order to manage different types of dialogues with the UA. The dialogue style selected is based on multilevel menus, and meta-information concerning the type of menu, prompt line, possible alternative answers, help, etc., is passed through user-request messages.

The knowledge necessary for building the user dialogue is usually owned by the agent making the request. This knowledge is passed to the user agent which takes care of the graphics, windowing system, etc., for visualizing the request and managing the dialogue. After the interaction phase, the user agent will take care of forming the reply message according to the results of the dialogue with the user and passing it to the requesting agent or the agents interested in it. The user agent also manages messages supplying information to the user and answering its requests.

Communication Strategies in CooperA. The CooperA user is given the possibility of experimenting with different communication strategies for solving a problem. The community's behavior can be different, depending on the selections on a set of global switches. The switch *multiple-request* determines whether the set of alternative candidates for satisfying a particular goal could be exhausted before the requesting agent decides about a reply, eventually passing the request directly to the UA. The switch *broadcast-reply* determines how an answer is communicated to the external world of an agent, communicating the result exclusively to the agent who has made the request or to all agents that might be interested in that information.

Different CooperA agents may exchange information involving uncertainty in the form of certainty factors. Meta-knowledge about the uncertainty handling mechanism is essential for an agent in order to interpret a supplied reply. CooperA provides the switch *ask-for-cf* which determines whether the uncertainty management mechanism is active.

3.4 Data Structures for Acquaintances Modeling

In CooperA, some data structures model locally the acquaintances of an agent (see Figure 14.4).

The *Yellow-Pages* structure contains a description of all the acquaintances of the agent who are in a position to satisfy goals that the agent is interested in. The metaphor used is that of a yellow-pages-style directory. This directory is created during the initialization of the agents in a dynamic way, taking into consideration the current participants of the group of agents and the needs of the particular agent. The yellow-pages schema of agent-x therefore have the form

> { *Yellow-Pages$_x$*
>
> goal-1: agent-11 agent-12 . . .
>
> goal-2: agent-21 agent-22 . . .
>
> .   .   . }

The *Interested-in-Table* of an agent contains information about agents who are interested in its skills.

This model is also created dynamically during the phase of the configuration of a community of agents. The form of the interested-in-table for agent-x is

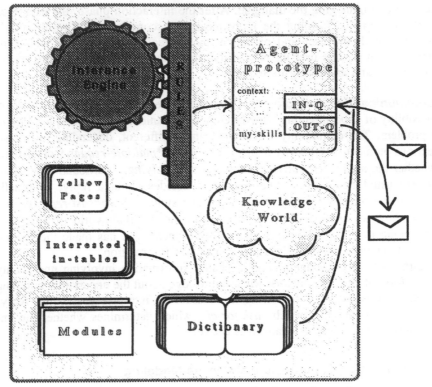

Figure 14.4   *Data structures of a CooperA agent.*

{ *Interested-in-table$_x$*

   skill-1: interested-agent-11 interested-agent-12 . . .

   skill-2: interested-agent-21 interested-agent-22 . . .

    .   .   . }

   Kernel functions take care of creating and updating these acquaintance structures.

3.5   The CooperA Interface

Problem solving in a distributed environment can be a very complex process to explain to the user of the system (see Chapter 21). The design of the CooperA user interface (CUI) has been developed following two requirements: to provide means for configuring in an easy and direct manner a community of agents and to visualize some of the aspects of the distributed problem-solving activity.

   Functionally, the CUI provides the following services: the dynamic configuration of an agents world; the initialization and visualization of a problem-solving activity representing graphically events such as the message exchange or the changing status of the agents; the navigation in the knowledge of the agents and during problem solving; the setting of the CooperA environment where a number of global parameters can be set to influence the problem-solving strategy.

For more details and the representation of the interface one should refer to Sommaruga et al. (1989b).

3.6 CooperA Results

To build CooperA we have borrowed some ideas of previous research activities in the area of DAI, but we have introduced some innovative features. As the most interesting characteristics of CooperA we mention that

CooperA supports the integration of distributed KBs and provides distributed problem-solving building tools.

CooperA has a strong experimental flavor. There is provision for global settings of the environment which permit alternative communication strategies, taking into consideration management of uncertainty, etc.

The concept of knowledge navigation during problem solving represents an useful debugging tool. This allows the user to follow more closely the effects of the agents' activities.

Attempts were made to handle the problem of interaction between the heterogeneous KBs contained in the different agents. The CP has been introduced, establishing a global knowledge representation for the community of agents permitting mutual understanding of agents which still can use their local formalisms.

The search for a solution of a particular subtask during the cooperative problem-solving activity can be performed through an iterative agent invocation mechanism, which allows for the opportunistic and fault-tolerant behavior of the community.

The direct manipulation user interface of CooperA allows visualization of the distributed problem-solving activity and direct access to the commands and options of the system.

The special user interface agent UA in the agents community is responsible for user interaction and for representing the user within the community. This agent has domain knowledge on I/O devices handling, graphical systems, etc. This I/O "expert" takes care of interaction with the user, taking responsibility from the rest of the community, who need only to interact with the UA in a uniform and familiar way.

Concerning the application, DChEM was developed in CooperA as a set of distributed KBs using and refining the existing monolithic ChEM KB. The advantages from doing this were twofold. First, modularization of the knowledge into different KBs corresponding to separate areas of expertise was proficient and made it easier for the knowledge engineer and the expert to follow the problem-solving activity. Second, subsequent modifications to the KBs were easier to perform thanks to this modularization.

At run time DChEM exhibited the expected behavior, one expert agent using the skills of others if needed. The graphical workbench used for an easy configuration and initialization of the system has also proved useful for the visualization of the information flow and for debugging. The ability to configure a limited world of agents, and especially the possibility to set up a world of only one expert agent, together with the UA has proven to be useful for agent debugging.

4   FROM CooperA TO CooperA-II

Some limitations of the CooperA architecture also emerged and suggested starting points for further research:

The lack of concurrence and physical distribution of the agent activities. The main effort has been given over to the design of a distributed KB system, with simulated distribution in problem solving. The use of concurrent processes and computer-networks-based open system hardware platforms should make CooperA more efficient and capable of handling a new range of applications.

The limited flexibility in coordination and cooperation. CooperA provided only implicit cooperation because of the agent's rigid control mechanism.

The limitation of the acquaintance modelling features of the CooperA language. The models were constructed a priori and could not be modified at run time. There was no possibility to reasoning about the skills of the acquaintances and there was no mechanism for any organizational structuring of the community.

Some mechanism for automating the development of the CP. The mapping of the elements of heterogeneous KBs ought to be introduced.

The extension of the UA domain knowledge. This could support dialogues adaptable to different user profiles and characteristics by adding elements of user modelling and so improving the interaction with the user.

These limitations led us to further research resulting in the evolution of the CooperA architecture. In particular, cooperation and control emerged to be the two most pressing issues in the development of cooperative agents (see Chapter 1). As a consequence, the approach used during this phase, was to study first existing theories and experiences in the field of small group interactions and cooperation (Hewstone et al., 1988; Argyle, 1991). In particular, this effort focused on the identification of coordination rules of the members of the group. This resulted in the creation of a knowledge base containing heuristic rules which can drive the cooperation of a group of agents. In addition, the process of defining a generic architecture for cooperative agents has been investigated, also on the basis of previous experiences. The complete analysis is described in detail in Sommaruga (1993). It has been observed that in general this process affects a number of steps. We identify four levels and meta-levels, starting from the lowest level of the real world (*Real World* level), going up to the computational (expert) systems (*Application* level), to the competence abstraction (*Abstraction* level), and finishes at the meta-level of cooperation (*Cooperation* level). The *Real World* level represents a real-life problem, while the *Application* level represents the computer programs which deal with the problem, the *Abstraction* level represents the definition of the agents' skills, needs, etc., and finally the *Cooperation* level represents where the control of the agents resides. The composition of each level of the agent on top of others allows a modular integration of the different levels of functionalities of an agent.

Earlier research has explored many of the issues at lower levels, as mentioned in Gasser (1992). However, a computational understanding of cooperative issues was relatively underresearched. The previous work could be criticized. The major criticism consists of the fact that the attempts at modeling architectures resulted in ad hoc architectures without explicit and distinct control levels for agents. The agent lacked flexibility and generality.

This stratified view offers some advantages, such as a modular and flexible architecture, and independence of the control of the agent from the application domain. On this basis, a new model for a cooperative agent is defined in CooperA-II, and a number of axioms are formalized in a Cooperative Architecture Theory (CATh) according to the level functionalities (Sommaruga, 1993; Sommaruga and Shadbolt, 1994). CATh is a formalization of fundamental premises for defining and obtaining a cooperative architecture of autonomous agent, supported by a language for defining agents and determining their behavior. A number of axioms are dictated by very general constraints on computational (intelligent) systems[1] and others are influenced by more specific DAI and cooperative requirements and refer specifically to our cooperative architecture. They concern issues which deal, for example, with the agent structure, communality requirement for skills and needs, compositionality of local microbehaviors, compositionality of global behaviors (see Section 5.4), group dynamics, communication requirement, and goal induction (see Chapters 2 and 9).

In the next section we are only able to present an overview of the CooperA-II architecture.

[1]An example of which can be found in Newell (1982). For instance, Newell's principle of rationality states that "If an agent has knowledge that one of its actions will lead to one of its goals, then the agent will select that action."

5   CooperA-II

The architectural framework CooperA-II for the cooperation of autonomous agents has been implemented to reflect the principles of the theory and to provide an evaluative testbed. In particular, the problem of coordinating agents' activities in order to achieve cooperative profitable behavior is addressed in CooperA-II. The introduction of a forward-reasoning control mechanism in each agent allows it to plan and coordinate tasks according to heuristic knowledge about cooperation. This has been specified as a cooperative heuristics knowledge base (CH-KB), which pragmatically expresses a number of different possible cooperative behaviors for an agent in the form of rules.

In the following description we focus on a specific overview of the cooperation of agents in the CooperA-II architecture on the basis of the complete agent model introduced in Sommaruga (1993) and Sommaruga and Shadbolt (1994). However, a number of structures and mechanisms which specialize the agent's cooperative attitudes need to be introduced first.

The *agenda* is a new attribute of the agent model. It represents a knowledge structure containing items, called acts, which represent potential actions of the agent. Each agent is autonomously controlled by means of a control loop (control cycle, see below) which uses the agenda to govern the agent's behavior. In particular, acts in the agenda are exploited by the cooperative heuristics rules in order to select the best action to be accomplished.

Only acts of a predefined type and format may be created and put on the agenda. The types of acts, currently considered in CooperA-II, are

DO act, in order to operate on execution of actions

REQUEST act, for requesting information or execution of actions to other agents

REQUESTED-TODO act, in order to adopt an external (act of) request

SUPPLY-INFO act, in order to provide information to others

INFORM act, for being informed about another agent's information

These five types of acts are inspired by Cohen and Perrault's operators (Cohen and Perrault, 1979). The act types are the "conversational" operators which allow agents to interact. An act-based semantics was used and integrated with the agenda mechanism.

Another particular characteristic of CooperA-II is the control cycle of an agent, which begins with the creation of the agent and permanently remains active. It consists of a loop, which is divided into three steps:

Step 1. Situation verifier, which evaluates firstly the current status of knowledge and activities of the agent. If satisfied then go to Step 2; otherwise go to step 1 and the agent remains idle.

Step 2. Select best action, which selects the next action of the agent from the agenda according to the behaviors expressed in the CH-KB. If successful then go to step 3; otherwise go to step 1.

Step 3. Execute best action selected, which possibly produces an output in the form of a message or an action execution. Go to Step 1.

Selecting the best action is a distinctive phase in CooperA-II, and it is the aspect we will turn to later in this chapter.

Considering loci of control in CooperA-II, a number of actions can be asynchronously performed by an agent:

Executing a control cycle

Sending a message

Receiving a message

Executing one or more processes to accomplish tasks

The asynchronous nature of the actions of an agent is an important aspect of a cooperative group of agents. In fact, this could mean, for instance, that sending information (a message) may occur at the same time the agent is executing a task, receiving a message, or deciding what to do next.[2] This aspect is a positive characteristic for cooperation which provides more autonomy in the control of the agent. Moreover, a more open control flow of the agent's actions is allowed by the fact that independent actions are not sequentialized. This extends the limited control of a CooperA agent which was strictly sequential. In CooperA-II, asynchronous actions are obtained by means of distinct processes which manage each type of activity.

In summary, distinctively and differently from MACE's engines, CooperA's start-methods, Actor's script, and other architectures, in CooperA-II an agent behaves entirely in accordance with its control mechanism and its cooperative heuristics.

The communication between the agents is provided by a message-passing mechanism integrated into the agent model. In particular, CooperA's in-q and out-q have been adopted, and other features have been extended in order to guarantee a safe communication (see Section 3.3 and Sommaruga, 1993).

The CooperA-II platform interface is presented in Figure 14.5. A number of facilities, such as tracing of executions, menus for debugging and system commands, continuous updating of the status of agents' tasks, and others, are provided in order to facilitate the agent developer in creating, testing, and running a cooperative application.

A number of attributes of the agent model of CooperA are maintained in CooperA-II, while others are added and extended. Among them, it is interesting to note the dependency between skill/need definition and cooperation. In fact,

---

[2]Here, "at the same time" could mean in parallel or concurrently, depending on the hardware platform used for the implementation.

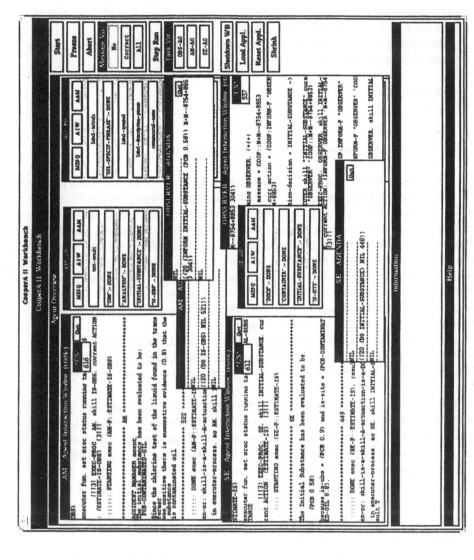

Figure 14.5 The CooperA-II platform with DChEM2 application.

by means of interleaving skills and needs of different agents, cooperation in a group is influenced.

The dynamic composition of a group of agents is another interesting feature which CooperA-II inherits from CooperA. The structure of an agent group can be dynamically changed by adding new computational individuals and hence capabilities (skills). Modules, in the form of agents, can be tested individually before their integration in a group. This allows extreme modularity of the system. Moreover, agents of different granularity may be developed and integrated in CooperA-II. An agent description language is provided in order to support the definition of agents of various complexity ranging from large grain to small grain.

Two applications in different real domains were developed in CooperA-II using the cooperative heuristics approach: the distributed chemical emergencies manager 2 (DChEM2) and Libra.

The DChEM2, a revised version of the DChEM system, is a distributed cooperative agents system prototype which simulates a particular aspect of the management of a chemical accident. The aspect deals with the evaluation of the type of the chemical substance involved in an electrical hazard. DChEM2 consists of a group of three agents which interact with a user in order to determine the nature of a substance involved in a possible chemical accident. We have three agents, each one performing a distinct role. The site-expert (SE) agent, which can estimate the initial substance according to data about the site. The accident-manager (AM) agent, which accomplishes the task of determining the initial substance according to its expertise in managing chemical accidents. Finally, the OBSERVER agent, which allows the user to interact with the system and provides all the input data by means of requests to the user. The task of finding out what kind of substance is involved in a chemical accident is inserted in a more complex system for monitoring such an accident. A request by the user for the computation of the initial substance to one of the agent, starts a sequence of actions of dividing goals into subgoals, of requesting, informing, and computing all the necessary subtasks in order to evaluate the type of the substance. The order of the actions in this sequence is completely determined by the application of the CHs. In Figure 14.5 a session of the DChEM2 application, with the agents previously described, is presented.

The Libra application consists of a group of four cooperating agents which simulate a librarian helping a user to find references about subjects, authors, etc. During a search session in Libra, a number of interleaving tasks are performed by the group of agents. First, the user formulates his or her requests through the user agent. Then these are sent to the other agents. Two kinds of resulting situations are possible after computation by the group of agents. Either an acceptable retrieval strategy is found and applied, or no acceptable retrieval strategy is available. In the first case the user will be provided with either the desired bibliographical items or no acceptable result. In the second case various suggested elaborations are made to the user. The activities each agent performs are determined by the application of sets of CHs, in particular the suggestions are determined by the pro social behavior (see pro-active m-behavior in Section 5.4).

5.1 Cooperation

The coordination of actions of a group of agents is an important issue in designing agent architecture (see Chapter 6). Joint profit should be the main goal of a group. Questions concerning what to do, when to do it and how to achieve it have to be answered. This problem has been only partially addressed in CooperA. It has been successively addressed by means of the CH model which has been integrated in the CooperA-II architecture. A detailed description of this architecture can be found in Sommaruga (1993), where a thorough description of the CH rules is also contained.

Here, we are going to focus on the influence such cooperative rules may have on the cooperative behavior of an agent. First, a general introduction to the cooperative heuristics model is given. Second, the definition of agent behaviors is used to group the cooperative heuristics into subsets according to pragmatic criteria of classification of the rules. Finally, the possibility of the composition of basic behaviors in order to create global or emergent behavior for an agent is discussed.

5.2 Cooperative Heuristics

In the agent model of CooperA-II we organized an agent architecture according to the stratified functional levels presented above. Among other levels, we have justified the introduction of "cooperative mechanisms" at the cooperation level, (see Chapters 12 and 13), in order to enhance meta-level control and coordination. Our attention has been directed to the definition of generic independent cooperative mechanisms. We have already suggested the advantages offered by designing control structures as independent as possible from the other levels of application and communication. The results are improved flexibility and reusability of the architecture.

After having defined the basic architecture and functionalities we need to complete our model, adding inferential meta-level power to each agent. Intelligence has to be encoded in the controller of the agent. In this phase, the previously described control structure and procedures are completed by filling a knowledge base of heuristics which are exploited in the control mechanism of the agent. To this aim a number of heuristic rules relating to the behavior of an agent are defined. These cooperative heuristics derived, in part, from sociology and social psychology (Hewstone et al., 1988; Argyle, 1991) and from previous DAI experience and experiments (CooperA and Wesson et al., 1988). The CHs generally relate to types of act, some of them to communication, and a number of them deal with planning and others with control.

Cooperative heuristics are represented as production rules inside each agent.

They have a left-hand side which describes all the conditions which should be verified in order to fire the rule. The conditions match facts of the agent which reflect mainly the status of knowledge of the agent itself and of its acquaintances. The actions in the right-hand side of rules can both modify the status of control knowledge of the agent and initiate the execution of an action.

Each agent has a local inference engine integrated with its local working memory. Inferences are derived in a forward-chaining fashion by facts declared in the working memory. The control cycle performed inside each agent controls the activity and manages the decision phase (see step 2). The decision phase is the one in which the agent decides what will be the next action to be executed. The choice is entirely determined by the firing of a cooperative heuristic on the basis of the existing agent's situation. In fact, the knowledge corresponding to a situation of the agent (agenda, acquaintances, status of knowledge of skills and needs, etc.) is taken into account in order to make a decision about the best action.

Currently, in CooperA-II the decision making algorithm is implemented in a data-driven way and the cooperative heuristics are implemented as OPS5 rules (Brownston et al., 1985). An OPS5 reasoning mechanism is integrated in step 2 of the controller of each agent. This allows us to define independent sets of rules and to apply them in the control system. Working memories are distinct and inference engines run independently. Therefore each agent reasons in an autonomous way and all interactions are the result of the application of some heuristics.

5.3 Classification of the Cooperative Heuristics

In the context of this description of the evolution of the CooperA platform, it is not relevant to see in detail the definition of each CH. A complete analysis of the semantics of the CHs has been carried out and described in Sommaruga (1993). It is more interesting to consider here an abstraction of the cooperative rules according to their purposes.

The cooperative heuristics so far defined are classified according to some general criteria. A number of properties, such as computational cost, continuity, etc., have been used to create a taxonomy of the CHs rules using a repertory grid method. Groups of similar CHs emerged by comparing the values of the properties. An emerging grouping of most similar cooperative heuristics consider groups and supergroups of heuristics according to their functionalities, as presented in Figure 14.6.

The main groups include

A · *Execute a Task.* This group contains CHs regarding the execution of a skill, in particular the CHs which deal with DO acts.

B · *Acquire Info.* This group contains CHs regarding the acquisition of information which deal with INFORM acts.

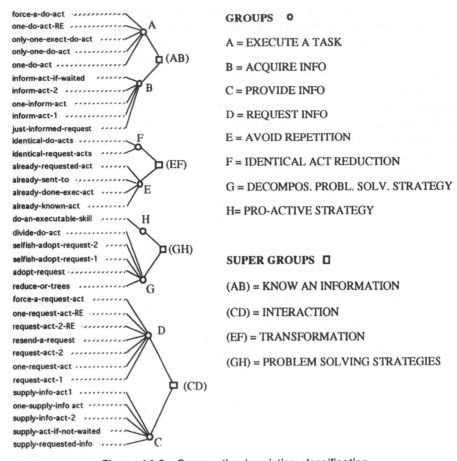

force-a-do-act
one-do-act-RE
only-one-exect-do-act
only-one-do-act
one-do-act
        A
        (AB)
inform-act-if-waited
inform-act-2
one-inform-act
inform-act-1
        B
just-informed-request
identical-do-acts
identical-request-acts
already-requested-act
        F
        (EF)
already-sent-to
already-done-exec-act
already-known-act
        E
do-an-executable-skill
divide-do-act
selfish-adopt-request-2
selfish-adopt-request-1
adopt-request
reduce-or-trees
        H
        (GH)
        G
force-a-request-act
one-request-act-RE
request-act-2-RE
resend-a-request
request-act-2
one-request-act
request-act-1
        D
supply-info-act1
one-supply-info act
supply-info-act-2
supply-act-if-not-waited
supply-requested-info
        (CD)
        C

GROUPS   o

A = EXECUTE A TASK

B = ACQUIRE INFO

C = PROVIDE INFO

D = REQUEST INFO

E = AVOID REPETITION

F = IDENTICAL ACT REDUCTION

G = DECOMPOS. PROBL. SOLV. STRATEGY

H= PRO-ACTIVE STRATEGY

SUPER GROUPS □

(AB) = KNOW AN INFORMATION

(CD) = INTERACTION

(EF) = TRANSFORMATION

(GH) = PROBLEM SOLVING STRATEGIES

Figure 14.6   *Cooperative heuristics classification.*

C · *Provide Info.* It is a group of CHs which concern actions of supplying information to other agents and therefore deal with SUPPLY-INFO acts.

D · *Request Info.* It contains CHs regarding the request for information from other agents and enumerates all the CHs about REQUEST acts.

E · *Avoid Repetition.* This group associates CHs which help the agent to avoid repetition of not advantageous actions.

F · *Identical Act Reduction.* This set associates CHs which help the agent to avoid repetition of the same action.

G · *Decomposition PS Strategy.* This group deals with the accomplishment of a complex skill by means of the decomposition of a goal (namely a skill) into subgoals and their aggregation through a decomposition-synthesis process.

H · *Proactive Strategy*. It deals with the accomplishment of a skill by means of the recognition of a suitable situation in the agent which could allow a successful computation of the skill. Following this strategy the agent under certain conditions can spontaneously activate the execution of an action.

On the basis of the analysis of the groups defined we can compose similar groups into supergroups. We can distinguish the supergroup (AB), about knowing an information, the supergroup (CD), concerning interaction of the agent, the supergroup (EF), dealing with internal transformation, and finally the supergroup (GH), containing specific problem-solving strategies.

It is interesting to note that some groups of CHs express Gricean maxims[3] (Grice, 1975). For example, quantity of information is expressed in the groups provide info (C) and request info (D); quality emerges in most of the groups; relation is considered in avoid repetition (E), identical act reduction (F); and proactive strategy (H); manner is expressed in provide info (C) and request info (D).

5.4 Agent Behaviors and Cooperative Heuristics

Another grouping of the CHs may be created according to the global effects a subset of CHs can produce inside an agent. The global effect a subset of CHs produces in an agent is called the agent micro behavior (*m-behavior*) (Chapters 9, 11, and 20). Various micro behaviors can be composed generating a macro behavior of an agent, which is usually considered as the emergent behavior of the agent. The interaction and coordination of the behaviors of different agents allows the integration of individuals in the form of a cooperative group of agents. In this section we describe a number of *m-behaviors* which have been defined in CooperA-II. A summary is presented in Table 14.2. Finally, examples of their structure are presented.

Micro Behaviors. First, basic functional activities of an agent have to be mapped into default CHs which need to be always present in the agent. They deal with managing simple instances of act types like REQUEST, SUPPLY-INFO, DO, and INFORM. They also manage *forced* actions (actions which may have to be recomputed). They are also used to avoid duplication of identical acts. Such heuristics are referred to as *default* m-behavior.

Second, some CHs reflect the need for an agent not to repeat the execution of actions already accomplished. These mainly regard skills which have been satisfied by the agent when there is no need to evaluate them again. In particular, they consider acts of type REQUEST and DO when the related infor-

---

[3]Gricean maxims can be summarized by the four conversational categories summarized in the "cooperative principle." They deal with quantity, quality, relation, and manner.

TABLE 14.2 Summary of m-Behaviors and Their Composing Cooperative Heuristics

m-Behavior	Cooperative Heuristics Subset
Default	One-inform-act, one-supply-info-act, identical-do-acts, identical-request-acts, just-informed-request, inform-act-1, inform-act-2, supply-info-act-1, supply-info-act-2, inform-act-if-waited, Supply-act-if-not-waited, force-a-do-act, force-a-request-act
Nonrepetitive	One-request-act, only-one-do-act, Only-one-exec-do-act, one-do-act, Already-requested-act, already-known-act, Already-done-exec-act, already-sent-to, request-Act-1, request-act-2
Repetitive	One-request-act-RE, one-do-act-RE, Request-act-2-RE
Reactive	Divide-do-act, reduce-or-trees, Supply-requested-info
Proactive	Do-an-executable-skill
Resend-request	Resend-request
Uncond-goal-adoption	Adopt-request
Selfish-goal-adoption	Selfish-adopt-request-1, Selfish-adopt-request-2

mation is not yet known by the agent. Moreover, they ignore requests to other agents for information which is already available to the agent. The corresponding acts are in this case removed from the agenda. They are here referred to as *nonrepetitive* m-behavior.

Third, some CHs reflect the need for an agent to repeat the execution of actions already accomplished. These regard, for instance, skills which have been already attained by the agent but need to be executed again on different values or arguments. As with the previous group they consider acts of type REQUEST and DO, but they ignore the status of the related information (known or not). They are referred to as *repetitive* m-behavior.

Fourth, the group called *reactive* m-behavior deal with the solution to complex problem by using a decomposition problem-solving strategy. Some CHs manage to split a complex skill of an agent into subactions. Moreover, the reactive m-behavior is also characterized by allowing an agent to answer information which has been previously requested by another agent. For instance, this could be the case where an answer (corresponding to the completion of a skill) needs to be sent back to the requester.

Proactive m-behavior deals with the solution to complex problems by spontaneously activating tasks. The execution of a skill is started spontaneously when the situation of the agent allows it. This behavior reflects the fact that activating a skill whenever possible may generate a generous agent which always tries to do what it can in order to solve a problem.

An agent may need to send again a request for information which has not been answered after a certain time delay. A *resend-request* m-behavior is therefore defined.

Finally, two other m-behaviors regard the adoption of goals of an agent. This problem is associated with managing REQUESTED-TODO acts. It can be approached by two types of solutions: unconditional adoption of goals and conditional adoption of goals. An *uncond-goal-adoption* m-behavior has been defined in order to deal with the direct transformation of a REQUESTED-TODO act into a DO act inside the agenda of an agent. This can be considered as a direct adoption of a goal by the agent. In addition, a *selfish-goal-adoption* m-behavior has been defined in order to deal with the transformation of a REQUESTED-TODO act into a DO act only under certain conditions. In this case a selfish agent is assumed to do the transformation only when there are no other acts of different type. Thus, the selfish agent adopts external requests for a local skill only when it has finished its own activities. We have to note that the approach of conditional adoption of goals is open to a variety of different conditional cases. Only one of them is mentioned above as an example.

Similarly, other m-behaviors which give an agent the possibility of behaving in various ways and coping with different situations could be defined.

In conclusion, some examples of the composition of the m-behaviors so far defined are presented.

During the initialization phase of an agent (i.e., its creation), a behavior can be attributed to an agent by means of a declaration. This will allow the agent to be initialized with some cooperative heuristics sets which will later influence its activity.

For example, the declaration

(ag-behave agent_x 're-active 'non-repetitive 'uncond-goal-adoption)

generates an agent which will behave according to all the CHs corresponding to the reactive, nonrepetitive and uncond-goal-adoption m-behaviors listed in Table 14.2. In particular, the agent will deal with the solution to a complex problem by using a decomposition problem-solving strategy, it will avoid repeat actions like requesting or computing already known information, it will adopt unconditionally external requests for attaining a local skill.

A further example is

(ag-behave agent_y 'pro-active 'repetitive).

This declaration generates an agent which will solve complex problems by spontaneously activating tasks, where the execution of a skill is started spontaneously when the situation allows it, and will allow it to repeat the execution of actions.

Again, by declaring

(ag-behave ag_z 're-active 'repetitive 're-send-request 'uncond-goal-adoption)

the agent being defined will deal with the solution to a complex problem by using a decomposition problem-solving strategy, it will allow repeated actions like requesting or recomputing known information, it can send a request for information which has not been answered after a certain time delay and it will adopt unconditionally external requests for attaining a local skill.

5.5 Examples of Cooperative Heuristics and Their Application

In this section we provide first a description of some cooperative heuristics which are employed in CooperA-II, and successively an example of their application to a real problem-solving session of DChEM2.

Here, some significant CHs have been selected and described in detail just to give an idea of how they can contribute to a particular kind of m-behavior. Each cooperative heuristic is described with a short explanation of its purpose, presenting the effect of the rule triggering. In addition, the conditions for the rule being triggered are given. Moreover, an important property of the cooperative heuristics which affects the continuity of step 2 of the control cycle is underlined for each heuristic. This property distinguishes if a rule is *final* or *intermediate*. A final rule generates the selection of the best action and completes the decision phase of step 2 (see Section 5). An intermediate rule generates modification to the situation of the agent and allows the decision making to proceed until explicitly halted.

The following cooperative heuristics are presented with respect to the groups of m-behaviors in Table 14.2.

Default

identical-request-acts. This rule deletes duplicates of REQUEST acts from the agenda. If two REQUEST acts for the same information are on the agenda, then the most recent REQUEST act, which constitutes a duplicate of the previous one, is removed from the agenda. This is an intermediate heuristic.

just-informed-request. A request for any information that has just arrived to an agent is ignored. If a REQUEST act and an INFORM act about the same information exist on the agenda, then the REQUEST act is removed from the agenda and the INFORM act is immediately executed. This is a final heuristic.

Nonrepetitive

already-requested-act. This rule ignores a request for an information already known by the agent. If the agenda contains a REQUEST act for an information already known by the agent, and the REQUEST act is not forced to be done, then the request is ignored by removing the REQUEST act from the agenda. This is an intermediate heuristic.

already-known-act. This rule avoids doing a skill or requesting information already known by the agent. If the agenda contains a DO act of an already known skill or a REQUEST for already known information, and the act is not forced to be done, then it is ignored removing the DO or the REQUEST act from the agenda. This is an intermediate heuristic.

Reactive

divide-do-act. This rule creates DO or REQUEST acts which are subgoals of a skill. If the agenda contains a DO act about a complex goal which is not yet known and is divisible into subgoals, then the DO act is split into subgoals. These subgoals could be other DO acts, if they refer to (internal) skills of the agent, or REQUEST acts if they refer to (external) needs of the agent. Therefore, other DO or REQUEST acts can possibly appear onto the agenda. This is an intermediate heuristic.

Example of the Application of the CHs. This description completes the explanation of the CHs approach by providing an example of their use in a real application.

We assume that the computation of the initial substance type involved in an accident is the global goal which the DChEM2 group of agents has to reach. We consider that a typical real accidental situation is represented by a set of data values available to the user. They constitute a description of the accident and allow for its simulation. These values may be provided through the OBSERVER agent in any temporal or physical sequence.

The problem-solving method adopts an opportunistic strategy, as follows:

global goal request →

starting skills computation →

combinations of

concurrent actions

$$\left\{ \begin{array}{l} \text{- user providing data,} \\ \text{- agents requests for data to the user} \\ \quad \text{according to the situation and} \\ \text{- skills computations} \end{array} \right. \rightarrow$$

final result.

In this example any input could be initially given to the OBSERVER agent, the initial substance task was directly started, some of the input data values were provided randomly and spontaneously at run time by the user while AM and SE were computing their own skills concurrently.

Details of the main steps are summarized in Figure 14.7, where an overview of a solution to the DChEM2 problem through time, allows the application of the CHs in each problem-solving step to be shown. This is represented in square brackets by the name of the agent followed by the numbers of the CHs used in such step, such as [OBS: CHs 1]. These numbers are listed in the sequence of CHs presented below.

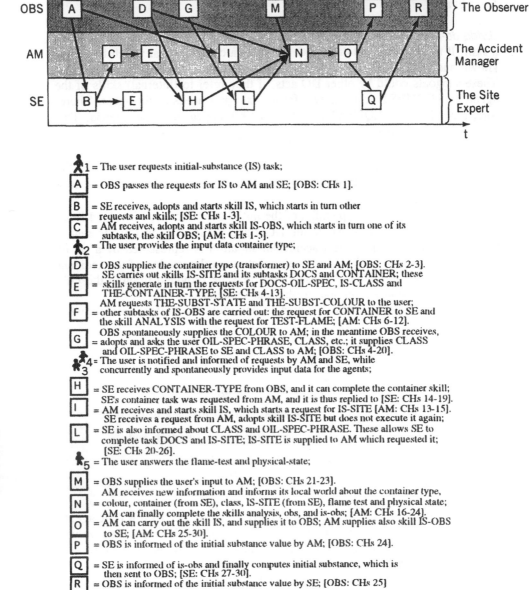

Figure 14.7 _Overview of a solution to DChEM2 problem._

Sequences of CHs Used by Agents in Figure 14.8. We summarize below
for each agent an ordered list of all the CHs used in the sample execution
presented in Figure 14.8. Each CH is paired to the most relevant triggering
information. You should use these lists as a reference to the description presented in the Figure 14.8. The names of the CHs are sufficiently intuitive to
be self explanatory about their effects.

Sequence of CHs Used in Agent SE

1. (ADOPT-REQUEST INITIAL-SUBSTANCE)
2. (DIVIDE-DO-ACT INITIAL-SUBSTANCE)
3. (REQUEST-ACT-1 IS-OBS)
4. (DIVIDE-DO-ACT IS-SITE)
5. (DIVIDE-DO-ACT DOCS)
6. (REDUCE-OR-TREES (IS-CLASS DOCS-OIL-SPEC))
7. (END-RM-OR-TREES DOCS)
8. (REQUEST-ACT-2 DOCS-OIL-SPEC)
9. (REQUEST-ACT-1 IS-CLASS)
10. (DIVIDE-DO-ACT CONTAINER)
11. (REDUCE-OR-TREES (THE-CONTAINER-TYPE)
12. (END-RM-OR-TREES CONTAINER)
13. (REQUEST-ACT-1 THE-CONTAINER-TYPE)
14. (INFORM-ACT-1 CARDS-DATA)
15. (ONLY-ONE-EXEC-DO-ACT CONTAINER)
16. (ADOPT-REQUEST CONTAINER)
17. (ALREADY-KNOWN-ACT CONTAINER)
18. (SUPPLY-REQUESTED-INFO CONTAINER)
19. (SUPPLY-INFO-ACT-1 CONTAINER)
20. (ADOPT-REQUEST IS-SITE)
21. (IDENTICAL-DO-ACTS IS-SITE)
22. (INFORM-ACT-1 CARDS-DATA)
23. (ONLY-ONE-EXEC-DO-ACT DOCS)
24. (ONLY-ONE-EXEC-DO-ACT IS-SITE)
25. (SUPPLY-REQUESTED-INFO IS-SITE)
26. (SUPPLY-INFO-ACT-1 IS-SITE)
27. (INFORM-ACT-1 IS-OBS)
28. (ONLY-ONE-DO-ACT INITIAL-SUBSTANCE)
29. (SUPPLY-REQUESTED-INFO INITIAL-SUBSTANCE)
30. (ONE-SUPPLY-INFO-ACT INITIAL-SUBSTANCE)

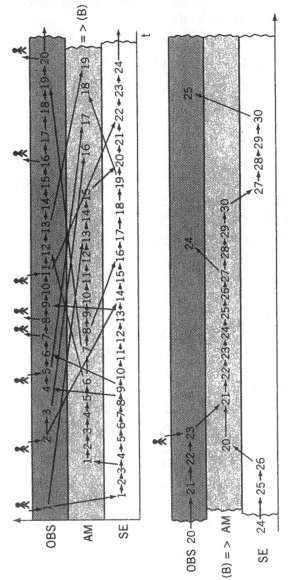

Figure 14.8 Agents and CHs application through time.

Sequence of CHs Used in Agent AM

1. (ADOPT-REQUEST IS-OBS)
2. (DIVIDE-DO-ACT IS-OBS)
3. (DIVIDE-DO-ACT OBS)
4. (REDUCE-OR-TREES (THE-SUBST-COLOUR THE-SUBST-STATE))
5. (END-RM-OR-TREES OBS)
6. (REQUEST-ACT-2 THE-SUBST-STATE)
7. (REQUEST-ACT-2 THE-SUBST-COLOUR)
8. (REQUEST-ACT-1 CONTAINER)
9. (DIVIDE-DO-ACT ANALYSIS)
10. (REDUCE-OR-TREES (TEST-FLAME))
11. (END-RM-OR-TREES ANALYSIS)
12. (REQUEST-ACT-1 TEST-FLAME)
13. (ADOPT-REQUEST INITIAL-SUBSTANCE)
14. (DIVIDE-DO-ACT INITIAL-SUBSTANCE)
15. (REQUEST-ACT-1 IS-SITE)
16. (INFORM-ACT-1 CARDS-DATA)
17. (INFORM-ACT-1 CARDS-DATA)
18. (INFORM-ACT-1 CONTAINER)
19. (INFORM-ACT-1 CARDS-DATA)
20. (INFORM-ACT-1 IS-SITE)
21. (INFORM-ACT-1 CARDS-DATA)
22. (ONE-DO-ACT ANALYSIS)
23. (ONLY-ONE-EXEC-DO-ACT OBS)
24. (ONLY-ONE-EXEC-DO-ACT IS-OBS)
25. (ONLY-ONE-EXEC-DO-ACT INITIAL-SUBSTANCE)
26. (SUPPLY-REQUESTED-INFO INITIAL-SUBSTANCE)
27. (SUPPLY-INFO-ACT-1 INITIAL-SUBSTANCE)
28. (ALREADY-KNOWN-ACT IS-OBS)
29. (SUPPLY-REQUESTED-INFO IS-OBS)
30. (ONE-SUPPLY-INFO-ACT IS-OBS)

Sequence of CHs Used in Agent OBSERVER

1. (REQUEST-ACT-2 INITIAL-SUBSTANCE)
2. (SUPPLY-INFO-ACT-2 CARDS-DATA)
3. (SUPPLY-INFO-ACT-2 CARDS-DATA)
4. (ADOPT-REQUEST CLASS)

5. (SUPPLY-INFO-ACT-1 CARDS-DATA)
6. (ADOPT-REQUEST OIL-SPECIF-PHRASE)
7. (ONE-DO-ACT CLASS)
8. (ONLY-ONE-DO-ACT OIL-SPECIF-PHRASE)
9. (ADOPT-REQUEST CONTAINER-TYPE)
10. (ALREADY-SENT-TO CONTAINER-TYPE)
11. (SUPPLY-INFO-ACT-1 CARDS-DATA)
12. (ADOPT-REQUEST PHYSICAL-STATE)
13. (SUPPLY-INFO-ACT-1 CARDS-DATA)
14. (ADOPT-REQUEST FLAME-TEST)
15. (ONE-DO-ACT PHYSICAL-STATE)
16. (ALREADY-SENT-TO OIL-SPECIF-PHRASE)
17. (ALREADY-SENT-TO CLASS)
18. (ADOPT-REQUEST COLOUR)
19. (ALREADY-SENT-TO COLOUR)
20. (ONE-DO-ACT FLAME-TEST)
21. (ALREADY-SENT-TO PHYSICAL-STATE)
22. (ALREADY-SENT-TO FLAME-TEST)
23. (ONE-SUPPLY-INFO-ACT CARDS-DATA)
24. (ONE-INFORM-ACT INITIAL-SUBSTANCE)
25. (ONE-INFORM-ACT INITIAL-SUBSTANCE)

The example shows the cooperative interactions which occur during the problem-solving process by applying the set of CHs. We can note that the major cooperative interaction happens during the first phases of the problem-solving activities as expressed in Figure 14.8 by the great number of crossing arrows from one agent to others.

It is possible to observe that the agents were aware of the possibility of receiving help from the others. For instance, AM and SE agents requested some of their subtasks of the initial substance skill to SE or AM, respectively, or to the OBSERVER/user. Moreover, some requests were not sent because they were already known or already dispatched, or else were duplications.

In other words, the behaviors of the group of agents reflected the compositions of the m-behaviors assigned to each agent, confirming the cooperative features explicitly designed in the CHs.

The agents adapts their problem-solving strategies to the particular conditions according to the possibilities encapsulated in the set of CHs behaviors. The simplest instance of this adaptation is the case of a need which is requested from the user by an agent, but the user spontaneously provides it in advance to this agent. Thus, the request is no longer necessary and can be removed from the agenda of the agent, saving time and resources. For instance, see CHs number 9 and 10 of agent observer in Figure 14.8.

5.6 CooperA-II Results

An evaluation of our approach, the CooperA-II architecture, and the use of CH-KB was carried out together with a comparative analysis with other well-known DAI architectures (Sommaruga, 1993) and on the basis of the two applications developed, Libra and DChEM2. This analysis highlighted that some ideas of previous CooperA research have been borrowed in CooperA-II, but also that some innovative features have been introduced. We are going to mention the main results.

Good flexible applicability to general domains and environments of the CooperA-II architecture was shown. The resulting model represents a modular and decomposable approach to cooperating autonomous agents, based on co-operative behaviors. In particular, the agent model is sufficiently general to be adopted in various domains and applications. In addition, the use of abstractions of the agents' goals (abstraction level) and the possibility of reasoning about these goals at the meta-level of cooperation provided a more effective cooperation. CooperA-II ranked significantly better than other architectures in providing facilities for agents to act coherently using problem-solving strategies, in using sophisticated group control strategies, in providing effective means to coordinate, organize, control, and reason about control.

In CooperA-II the developer can control the interpretation of events and how an agent should act in certain situations by means of the behaviors expressed in the cooperative heuristics. This explicit heuristic knowledge about cooperation provides agents in the system with a number of cooperative problem-solving strategies in different domains and under different situations within the same domain.

Thanks to the explicit representation of the CH-KB in the form of rules which can express agent m-behaviors, this knowledge could be easily extended or changed, modifying at the same time the global behavior of the agent.

6 CONCLUSIONS

The reported research describes the evolution of the CooperA architecture. In particular, it has investigated cooperative and coordinated problem solving by a set of coarse-grain knowledge-based agents. The agents involved were full-scale expert systems, each of them with distinct area of expertise and problem-solving capabilities. Integration of such knowledge-based components in a multiagent cooperative environment has proved a particularly hard task fulfilled by this research.

During the first phase of experimentation, emphasis was provided in practical issues of multiple agents integration. Thus, interagent communication protocols have been defined, and communication mechanisms devised in order to implement these protocols. The requirement for asynchronous communication has been satisfied through the introduction of message-passing mailbox-like structures and primitives. The requirement for heterogeneous knowledge integration has been met by the introduction of translation mechanisms and semantic mapping dictionaries in the agent communication.

Subsequently, cooperative agent behavior was studied, based on the above communication constructs and mechanisms. Cooperation in this context is seen as a problem of distributed agent control (see Chapter 6). The mechanism for achieving this, during the first phase of experimentation, was a static model of the agent's skills and needs and of the group's characteristics through the "my-skills" and "yellow-pages" structures. This social knowledge is used for the control of the individual agent which executes a simple cycle of "problem-solve, if-goal-not-satisfied seek-support." The control mechanism however introduced during this phase, has proved to be highly inflexible, resulting in predetermined reactive agent behavior.

The introduction of domain-independent cooperation heuristic rules and of an agent control engine provided some remedy to this problem during the second phase of the project. The introduced CHs have been determined through a design process which involved the study of documented interacting groups and the analysis of a wide spectrum of domains with existing patterns of cooperative problem-solving characteristics. After definition and testing of a large group of CHs in the chemical emergencies domain, an analysis of emergent behaviors has been undertaken. As a result, generic agent microbehaviors have been individualized from more (domain) specific ones. Aggregates of these microbehaviors in the form of macro-behaviors have been successively identified. A language has been proposed in order to define these behaviors. In addition, a case-based-like semantics of agent acts has been adopted in order to allow consistent interactions and communications in a group of agents.

The flexibility of the system at run time has increased and a capability of experimentation with alternative agent behaviors has been incorporated in our testbed. In particular, opportunistic adaptation of agent behavior, in terms of control of activities, to different problem-solving situations emerged. In the future, it is expected that experimentation with rich coordination and meta-coordination protocols will be tried in the form of new CHs which could provide the testbed with capabilities of dynamic behavior modification at run time.

Understanding the parallel execution of heterogeneous distributed agents is a desirable feature in DAI systems. Debugging and control become extremely arduous tasks because of concurrency, nondeterminism and uncertainty in problem domain activities (see Chapter 3). A number of facilities are provided in the graphical interface of CooperA-II, such as tracing of executions, continuous updating of the status of agents' tasks, and others.

Issues related with user behavior modeling and user interaction are also expected to be studied in the future. As described above, user interaction has been a matter of experimentation during the first CooperA phase, when the user agent was developed. It is our intention in the future, to introduce the user in the flexible behavior programming environment, by incorporating alternative behaviors in the user agent, permitting the user at run time, implicitly or explicitly, to modify its behavior in relation to the problem-solving task.

Based on these experiences of developing and testing the CooperA architectures, other general results concerning architectural features are worth noting.

First, the characteristics of inherent parallelism and uniform message passing to spawn concurrency are inherited by CooperA-II from Actor languages.

In addition, distinctively and differently from MACE's engines, CooperA's start-methods, Actor's script and other architectures, in CooperA-II an agent behaves entirely in accordance with its complex control mechanism and its CHs. The developer can control the interpretation of events and how an agent should act in certain situations by means of the behaviors expressed in the CHs.

Dynamic composition of a group of agents is another interesting feature which allows, for example, extreme modularity of a system, and the testing of individual modules/agents of various complexity.

Finally, problem-solving computations can be expressed in different languages at the application level, while thanks to the abstraction level the knowledge structure is made transparent to the control level (cooperation level) of an agent.

ACKNOWLEDGMENTS

The CooperA research has been accomplished during the period 1987–1989 at the Joint Research Centre (JRC) of the Commission of European Communities, Centre of Information Technologies and Electronics, Knowledge Based Systems Lab, 21020 Ispra (VA), Italy. The CooperA-II work has been part of Sommaruga's Ph.D., as a joint collaboration of JRC-Ispra and Nottingham University, Psychology Dept., AI Group, University Park, NG9 7RD Nottingham UK, during the period 1990–1993 under CEC-grant cat.21/22.

REFERENCES

Argentesi, F., Bollini, L., Facchetti, S., Nobile, G., Tumiatti, W., Belli, G., Ratti, S., Cerlesi, S., Fortunati, G. U., and La Porta, V. (1987). ChEM: An expert system for the management of chemical accidents involving halogenated aromatic compounds. *Proc. World Chem. Accid. Conf.*, Rome, *1987*, pp. 227–230.

Argyle, M. (1991). *Cooperation, the Basis of Sociability.* Routledge, London.

Avouris, N. M. (1995). Cooperating knowledge based systems for environmental decision support. *Knowl. Based Syst.* **8**(1).

Avouris, N. M., Van Liedekerke, M. H., and Argentesi, F. (1988a). An intelligent information system for management of chemical emergencies. *Eurinfo Proc.*, Athens, *1988*, pp. 990–996.

Avouris, N. M., Van Liedekerke, M. H., Argentesi, F., and Facchetti, S. (1988b). An integrated knowledge based system for the management of emergencies involving PCBs and their pejorative transformation substances (PCDDs-PCDFs). *Ind. Hazards Int. Congr. Proc., 15th*, Firenze, *1988*, pp. 347–357.

Avouris, N. M., Van Liedekerke, M. H., and Sommaruga, L. (1989). Evaluating the CooperA experiment: The transition from the expert system module to a distributed AI testbed for co-operating experts. *Proc. Int. Workshop Distributed Artif. Intell., 9th*, Rosario, WA, *1989*, pp. 351–366.

Brownston, L., Farrel, R., Kant, E., and Martin, N. (1985). *Programming Expert Systems in OPS5*. Addison-Wesley, Reading, MA.

Cohen, P. R., and Perrault, C. R. (1979). Elements of a plan-based theory of speech acts. *Cognit. Sci.* **3**, 177–212.

Gasser, L. (1992). An overview of DAI. In *Distributed Artificial Intelligence: Theory and Praxis* (N. M. Avouris and L. Gasser, eds.), pp. 9–30. Kluwer Academic Publishers, Dordrecht, The Netherlands.

Grice, H. P. (1975). Logic and conversation. In *Syntax and Semantics. III. Speech Acts* (P. Cole and J. L. Morgan, eds.). Academic Press, New York.

Hanks, S., Pollack, M. E., and Cohen, P. R. (1993). Benchmarks, test beds, controlled experimentation and the design of agent architectures. *AI Mag.* **14**(4), 17–42.

Hewitt, C. E., and Lieberman, H. (1984). Design issues in parallel architectures for artificial intelligence. *Proc. IEEE Comput. Soc. Int. Conf., 28th*, San Francisco, *1984*, pp. 418–423.

Hewstone, M., Stroebe, W., Codol, J. P., and Stephenson, G. M. (1988). *Introduction to Social Psychology*. Basil Blackwell, Cambridge, MA.

Newell, A. (1982). The knowledge level. *Artificial Intelligence* **18**, 87–127.

Sommaruga, L. (1993). Cooperative heuristics for autonomous agents: An artificial intelligence perspective. Ph.D. Thesis, Nottingham University, UK.

Sommaruga, L., and Shadbolt, N. (1994). The cooperative heuristics approach for autonomous agents. *Proc. Coop. Knowl. Based Syst. Conf.*, University of Keele, Keele, UK, *1994*, pp. 49–61.

Sommaruga, L., Avouris, N. M., and Van Liedekerke, M. H. (1989a). Studies in Distributed Artificial Intelligence Part I: Development of the testbed environment CooperA. *CEC-JRC*, Ispra, Italy, *1989*, JRC Tech. Rep. I.89.63.

Sommaruga, L., Avouris, N. M., and Van Liedekerke, M. H. (1989b). An environment for experimentation with interactive cooperating knowledge based systems. In *Proceedings of Expert Systems*. Cambridge Press, London.

Wesson, R., Hayes-Roth, F., Burge, J., Stasz, C., and Sunshine, C. (1988). Network structures for distributed situation assessment. In *Readings in Distributed Artificial Intelligence* (A. Bond and L. Gasser, eds.), pp. 71–89. Morgan Kaufmann, Los Altos, CA.

CHAPTER 15 ———————————

AGenDA—A General Testbed for Distributed Artificial Intelligence Applications

KLAUS FISCHER
JÖRG P. MÜLLER
MARKUS PISCHEL

1 INTRODUCTION

Distributed artificial intelligence (DAI) (Bond and Gasser, 1988) explores how a group of intelligent and autonomous computational systems (agents) coordinate their knowledge, goals, plans, and skills in order to achieve certain (local or global) goals.[1] The DAI approach has turned out to be useful for dealing with applications for which a centralized design approach is inappropriate or even impossible, due to either an inherent distribution of knowledge and control or the complexity of the system to be described (see Chapters 1 and 4).

The task of a testbed for DAI application is to provide the designer of such an application with the tools necessary to construct agents, to describe their interaction, to construct the environment in which they are to act, and to support the simulation of the application on a computer (see Chapter 3). Different testbeds for AI systems have been proposed and implemented, most prominently MICE (Durfee and Montgomery, 1989), PHOENIX (Cohen et al., 1990), TRUCKWORLD (Nguyen et al., 1993), and TILEWORLD (Pollack and Ringuette, 1990), imposing more or less severe restrictions on the nature of the agents and the complexity of the environment.

Hanks et al. (1993) drew up a list of requirements for testbeds, relating their ability of

---

[1]See Durfee and Rosenschein (1994) for a detailed discussion of subfields of DAI.

Foundations of Distributed Artificial Intelligence, Edited by G. M. P. O'Hare and N. R. Jennings.
ISBN 0-471-00675-0 © 1996 John Wiley & Sons, Inc.

- Producing and processing exogenous events
- Varying the complexity of the world
- Modeling the cost and quality of sensing and effecting as well as measures for plan quality
- Dealing with multiple agents
- Providing a clean interface between the agents and the testbed world
- Modeling the course of time
- Supporting *controlled experimentation*.

For a DAI testbed, the *multiple agents* requirement should be extended in a sense that it should explicitly support the modeling of interactions among multiple agents. Controlled experimentation, i.e., experimentation ''in which a researcher varies the features of a system or the environment in which it is embedded and measures the effects of these variations on aspects of system performance'' (Hanks et al., 1993, p. 17), is, if carefully used, regarded as an important tool for deriving generalizable, significant results (see Chapter 3).

In this chapter we describe the AGenDA testbed for the design of DAI applications which has been developed in the multiagent research group at DFKI. Our testbed consists of two different levels: the *architectural level* describes a methodology for designing agents in a sense that it provides several important functionalities an agent should have: thus it supports a general template for agents that has to be filled by the designer of a DAI system with the domain-specific instantiation. The *system development level* provides the basic knowledge representation formalism, general inference mechanisms (such as forward and backward reasoning) which are used by the decision-making modules of the architectural layer, as well as a simulation toolbox supporting visualization and monitoring of agents, and the gathering of performance statistics (see also Hanks et al., 1993) for a well-written discussion of properties, problems, and benefits of and examples for testbeds). The interrelationship between the two testbed levels is illustrated in Figure 15.1. The architectural level in the AGenDA testbed is provided by the InteRRaP agent architecture (Müller and Pischel, 1994a,b). It defines the control within an agent as a hierarchical process, mapping different classes of situations to different reactive, deliberative, or cooperative execution mechanisms. The system development level is covered by the MAGSY system (Fischer, 1993). MAGSY provides a frame-based knowledge representation formalism and a set of general-purpose inference mechanisms. Moreover, it provides tools supporting the construction, visualization, evaluation, and debugging of DAI scenarios, including the lower layers of communication, on top of which more complex protocols such as the contract net or bargaining protocols can be defined.

Two applications have been implemented using the AGenDA framework: the first system is FORKS, an interacting robots application. FORKS describes an automated loading dock, where forklift robots load and unload trucks in a coordinated way, while avoiding potential and resolving existing conflicts, and

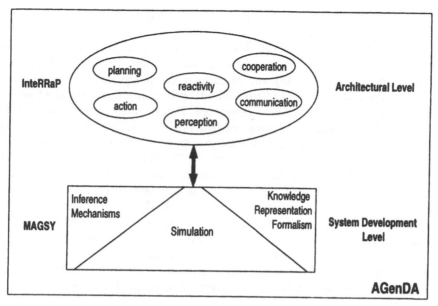

Figure 15.1 *The AGenDA testbed.*

exploiting possibilities to collaborate. The main requirement imposed on the testbed by this application was that it had to support reactivity and deliberation in the decision making of an individual agent as well as perception and manipulation of the physical world. The second system is MARS, which models an agent society consisting of transportation companies and their trucks that have to carry out transportation orders. In the case of the MARS system, the main challenge for our testbed was to provide different cooperation methods based on negotiation, leading to different scheduling mechanisms, and to experimentally evaluate these mechanisms.

The chapter is structured as follows: in Section 2, we describe the InteRRaP agent model which constitutes the architectural level of the AGenDA testbed. The development environment MAGSY which implements the system development level of AGenDA is outlined in Section 3. Section 4 presents the FORKS application. In Section 5, the MARS system is described. Finally, Section 6 contains an evaluation of the current work and a discussion of future research topics.

2 THE ARCHITECTURAL LEVEL: InteRRaP

An autonomous agent acting and interacting in a dynamic environment has to have certain properties, which should be reflected in its underlying design architecture. First, agents are to behave in a *situated* manner, i.e., they have to perceive unexpected events and to react appropriately to them (see, e.g., Brooks, 1986). Second, they are to act in a *goal-directed* fashion in order to achieve their goals (see Chapters 5 and 8). In AI, this is normally achieved by devising plans for certain goals (see, e.g., McDermott, 1991). Third, they are to solve their tasks *efficiently* and often have to satisfy real-time constraints. This requires access to a set of "hard-wired" procedures (Georgeff and Lansky, 1986) with guaranteed execution properties. Fourth, they are to cope with the presence of other agents. Whereas certain types of *interactions* can often be performed by employing local mechanisms (e.g., obstacle or collision avoidance in a robot scenario; see Latombe, 1992; Müller and Pischel, 1994a), others (e.g., collaboration) require the adoption of joint goals, the generation and execution of joint plans, the exchange of relevant information (i.e., about goals and plans) (see Chapter 6 and Kinney et al., 1992), and thus the explicit representation of models of other agents in terms of beliefs, goals, plans, and intentions (Rao and Georgeff, 1991). Finally, agents are to be *adaptive*; i.e., they must learn in order to improve their performance and to survive even if the environment changes. These requirements have led to the development of the agent architecture INTERRAP, a layered architecture describing the individual agent.

In this section, we explain the key ideas of the InteRRaP agent model and its basic functional structure. The main idea of InteRRaP is to define an agent by a set of functional layers, linked by a communication-based control structure and a shared hierarchical knowledge base. The basic design elements of the agent are (1) its world interface facilities, (2) patterns of behavior, as well as (3) local plans and (4) joint, multiagent plans.

Figure 15.2 shows the components of the InteRRaP agent model and their interplay. It consists of five basic parts: the world interface (WIF), the behavior-based component (BBC), the plan-based component (PBC), the cooperation component (CC), the agent knowledge base. The *world interface* holds the agent's facilities for perception, action, and communication. The *BBC* implements the reactive behavior and the procedural knowledge of the agent. Basic building blocks of the BBC are *patterns of behavior* which can be divided into two groups: *reactor patterns* and *procedure patterns*. Reactivity is obtained by providing a set of *reactor patterns* specifying hard-wired condition-action pairs. These are triggered by exogenous events. Procedural knowledge is contained in so-called *procedure patterns* which are activated by the plan-based component; these procedures are basically compiled plans which can be executed by the agent in order to perform some routine tasks. The *PBC* contains a planning mechanism which is able to devise local single-agent plans. In our current implementation, plans are represented as hierarchical skeletal structures[2] whose nodes may be either new subplans, or executable patterns of behavior, or primitive actions. Thus, the plan-based component may activate patterns of behavior in order to achieve certain goals. Finally, the *CC* contains a mecha-

---

[2]Depending on the requirements imposed by the application, the PBC may be instantiated with a suitable planning formalism.

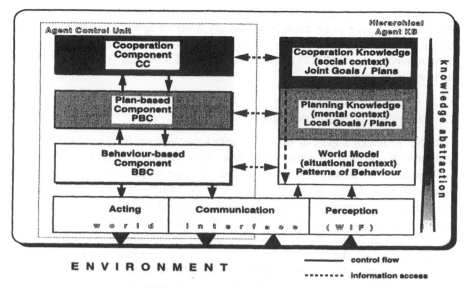

Figure 15.2   The InteRRaP agent model.

nism for devising joint plans (see Kinny et al., 1992; Müller, 1994). It has access to protocols, a joint plan library, and knowledge about communication strategies stored in the cooperation knowledge layer of the KB. CC, PBC, BBC, and the WIF establish the control of the agent. They interact and shift information and control among each other via communication.

The *knowledge base* is structured hierarchically. It consists of three layers which basically correspond to the structure of the agent control. The lowest layer contains facts representing the *world model* of the agent as well as representations of primitive actions and patterns of behavior. The second layer contains the agent's *mental model*, i.e., representation of knowledge the agent has about its goals, skills, and plans. Finally, layer comprises the agent's *social model*, i.e., knowledge of and strategies for cooperation, e.g., beliefs about other agent's goals. The basic idea is to restrict the information access and thus to reduce the practical complexity of reasoning in the lower (more reactive) system layers. For example, the plan-based component can access information about the world model, whereas the behavior-based component does not have access to planning or cooperation information. This is supported by employing different reasoning mechanisms provided by MAGSY (see Section 3) in different InteRRaP layers, namely data-driven forward reasoning in the BBC and goal-driven backward reasoning in the PBC and CC.

3 THE SYSTEM DEVELOPMENT LEVEL: MAGSY

The functionalities like reaction, planning, and cooperation provided by the InteRRaP agent architecture require a knowledge representation formalism as well as a class of basic mechanisms for drawing inferences on this knowledge. Besides, they have to be complemented by a set of specific testbed functionalities for simulation and evaluation. These are provided by the system development environment MAGSY (see also Figure 15.1) which is presented in this section.

3.1   Knowledge Representation

MAGSY provides a general object-centered mechanism for knowledge representation. Knowledge is maintained in a class hierarchy. Knowledge objects are described by means of a frame-based attribute-value structure. Supported relationships between different classes are specialization and generalization. Relationships between classes can be expressed by rules using the set operations union, intersection, subset and superset. Thus, the classes (or concepts) form a simple terminology. The class membership of individual objects may dynamically change, so the given rules are applied to maintain consistency. The knowledge base is an encapsulated component providing synchronization mechanisms needed for concurrent access by various components of the agent architecture. Additionally, there is an active knowledge forwarding service as an interface to supply the forward-chaining situation detection algorithm with changing information. This representation mechanism is a basis for the definition of more abstract knowledge categories such as beliefs, goals, and plans.

3.2   Basic Inference Mechanisms

The implementation of MAGSY started using a forward-chaining rule-based language for the design of each single agent. The rule interpreter was implemented using C++ in a UNIX environment. Recently, the MAGSY system was redesigned on top of the object-oriented concurrent constraint-based language Oz (see Henz et al., 1993). Apart from the reimplementation of the forward reasoning component, a PROLOG-like backward reasoning procedure has been specified. The forward-reasoning mechanism is used in order to evaluate the activation and monitoring conditions of the patterns of behavior in the BBC of the InteRRaP agents. The backward-reasoning mechanism will be used in a from-scratch planning mechanism which is currently being developed as an extension of the script-based planner for the FORKS application.

3.3   Testbed Functionalities

The third major functionality of MAGSY is to provide a simulation environment for DAI applications, supporting communication, visualization, and experimentation. This is detailed in the following.

Communication. MAGSY maintains a communication interface covering the four lowest layers of the OSI/ISO communication model. It uses the stream port/socket interface of TCP/IP for exchanging messages among agents. This allows to distribute the agents of an application on any number of different computers in a local area network. At a higher layer, using a small subset of the KQML language, communication interfaces to the programming languages PROLOG, LISP, and Oz were implemented. MAGSY offers a service concept which can be used in a straightforward manner in order to implement a restricted form of speech-act-like communication, in a sense that agents may request services from other agents.

Simulation. The simulation functionalities supported by MAGSY can be divided into agent-related functionalities, visualization and monitoring services, and experimentation support. They are explained below.

Agent Services. The MAGSY simulation environment offers services which allow to create and to flexibly configure different types of agents either interactively or from predefined descriptions. Agents can be given instructions, and the simulation process can be initiated and suspended. Orders given to agents can be specified relative to the simulation time. MAGSY supports a simple point-based time model. Moreover, agents can be equipped with different cooperation strategies.

Visualization and Monitoring. A graphical user interface based on OSF/MOTIF is used in order to visualize the simulation of the applications. Currently, the testbed support for visualization is restricted to a library of application-independent graphic functions. That means, however, that there is a reduced but still considerable amount of programming necessary in order to provide graphical visualization for new applications. The simulation world is designed as a separate process with clearly defined interfaces to the visualization module and to the agents. When modeling a new application, the effects of the execution of the domain-specific actions on the world as well as certain causal structures and constraints have to be specified in the world process.

The monitoring of agents is provided by a trace tool. A communication interface between the tracer and the agent has been defined. It allows to display the activities of the agents at the different layers of the InteRRaP architecture, e.g., the active patterns of behavior, current goals and plans, as well as communication between different agents.

Experimentation Support. MAGSY provides a statistics module that is able to gather performance statistics, such as the time and cost elapsed for problem solving, information about the frequencies of conflicts and about the results of negotiations, via a communication interface with the agents. Statistical data are prepared and can be graphically displayed. Different system parameters such as the configuration of the simulation world, the configuration and the number of agents can be varied, and exogenous events (for example traffic jams in the transportation scenario) can be triggered. Thus, the system designer is supported in doing controlled experimentation in the sense of Hanks et al. (1993).

4 REACTIVITY AND DELIBERATION IN ROBOT INTERACTION

The FORKS application described in this section deals with the simulation of an automated loading dock. In the loading dock, there are shelves which may contain different types of goods. The agents in the scenario are automated forklifts which have to load and unload incoming trucks. We use a grid-based representation of the loading dock. The primitive actions of the forklifts are moving from one place to another, turning around, getting and storing goods, and communicating with other agents. Each agent has a certain range of perception (for example 3 × 2 squares in front of it). The grid-based representation of the world simplifies many of the problems of mechanical control and geometrical trajectory planning (cf. Latombe, 1992). On the other hand, if we use a grid size of about two meters, the representation is realistic enough to model robots for flexible transport systems (FTS).

In the following, we will demonstrate how the autonomous forklifts in the FORKS application can be designed as InteRRaP agents. In Section 4.1, we will describe the agent's interface to the world. Section 4.2 shows how reactive and deliberate capabilities of the agent are reconciled within the InteRRaP framework by *patterns of behavior* and local plans, and by defining a framework describing the interplay of these two representation and execution layers. Finally, Section 4.3 addresses the implementation of the cooperation layer of the forklifts and shows how joint plans can serve as a means of resolving conflicts in a cooperative manner.

4.1 The World Interface

The *world interface* comprises the agent's facilities for perception, action, and communication. Its individual functionalities are discussed in the following.

The *actions* component controls the effectoric capabilities of the agent. Obviously, these capabilities are very domain dependent. In the case of the forklift robots, these are *walk_ahead*, *turn_left*, *turn_right*, *put_box*, *grasp_box*. The *communication* unit bears the agent's communicative facilities. It controls the physical components for sending and receiving messages. Outgoing messages have to be transformed from the agent's internal language into a knowledge interchange format (often called *interlingua*) which is understood by all agents. Corresponding to this, incoming messages must be transformed into the local agent language. This transformation is done by the *translator module*. The *perception* part of the WIF controls the vision and sensing facilities of the agent. Again the concrete implementation of this module depends strongly on the types of agents we want to model. In the case of a real robot environment, the perception part may include the transformation and processing of the data obtained by a camera. Sensor information can be received for example by infrared, laser, or ultrasonic sensors. In our simulation system, each agent is equipped with a configurable range of perception ($n \times m$ squares). The simulation world computes changes within an agent's range of perception which are caused by actions performed by the agent itself (e.g., by turning around) or by other agents. Perception is then simulated by messages sent by the simulation world to the agent.

4.2 Integrating Reaction and Deliberation

Having defined the interface to the physical world, we now define how the information that is perceived by the agent is processed, how decisions are made based on this information, finally leading to the execution of actions. In the InteRRaP framework, the local behavior of an agent is basically determined by two components and the way they interact: the behavior-based and the plan-based component. In the following, we will describe both components through the FORKS application.

The Behavior-Based Component. The BBC implements an agent's basic reactive behavior (see Chapter 11) as well as its procedural knowledge. It is defined by a set of so-called *patterns of behavior* and by a control mechanism maintaining these patterns.

Patterns of Behavior. Patterns of behavior (PoB) are the essential structural primitives of the behavior-based component. They incorporate the reactive abilities and the procedural knowledge of an agent. The former allow an agent to react quickly, flexibly, and often avoiding explicit replanning, to certain unexpected events, the latter provide the primitives for the plan-based component of an InteRRaP agent.

There are two basic classes of patterns of behavior in our terminology. On the one hand, there is a class of patterns which are basically reactive (*reactor patterns*). On the other hand, certain PoB describe pieces of procedural knowledge, i.e., mechanisms which are not represented in a declarative manner, but which are basically procedures. These *procedure* patterns are compiled plans which can be activated as abstract actions by the planner. They are appropriate for representing *routine behaviors*, which do not require deep reflection or planning. Examples for such routine tasks are starting a car, or walking along a hallway, or moving straight ahead from one landmark to another.

PoB are abstractly defined as frame structures as illustrated in Figure 15.3. The definition of a PoB consists of a description part and an execution part. The description part contains meta-information describing the pattern of behavior which is needed for the control mechanism, such as the activation condition and several monitoring conditions. The execution part contains the executable body of the pattern, which is started if the pattern is selected by the control mechanism. For details of the descriptions within the condition part and for a language describing the execution part of a PoB, we refer to Müller et al. (1994).

Control. The BBC control is implemented in a processing cycle: in each loop, it monitors changes in the world model caused by perception and commands received from the plan-based components. According to the new world state,

```
( PoB
      :name             /* Name of pattern */
      :type             /* reactor, modifier, procedure */
      :args             /* arguments */
      :activation       /* activation condition */
      :monitor          /* conditions monitoring execution */
          :failure      /* failure condition:  stop execution */
          :success      /* condition for successful termination */
          :holding      /* conditions that must hold during execution */
          :exceptions   /* user-definable exceptions */
      :post/* condition that must hold after execution */
      :exec_body        /* actual executable body; e.g. control program */ )
```

Figure 15.3 *Patterns of behavior.*

several PoB may be active because their activation conditions are satisfied or because they have become active in an earlier world state and have not yet been finished. The basic task of the BBC cycle is to determine the active patterns based on the updated world model, then to select one PoB for execution in the current cycle, and to execute it one step further. The control cycle algorithm is displayed in Figure 15.4. At the beginning of each cycle, the agent updates its world model based on its current perception and based on activation messages from the PBC and from other patterns of behavior. The actual processing of the cycle runs in three phases described in the following.

```
/* Variables:                                                           */
/*       POBSET:       set of all patterns of behaviour                 */
/*       ACTᵢ:         set of PoB which are active by the end of cycle i */
/*       INACTᵢ:       set of PoB which are not active by end of cycle i */
/*       PERCᵢ:        perception at start of cycle i                   */
/*       ACT-REQᵢ:     PoB activation requests at start of cycle i       */
/*       PoBᵢ:         pattern of behaviour selected for execution in cycle i*/
/*       WMᵢ:          world model in cycle i                           */

  bbc-cycle(POBSET)
  {
      i := 0;
      ACTᵢ := ∅;
      WMᵢ := init_kb;
      INACTᵢ := POBSET;
      repeat
              WMᵢ₊₁ := update_state(WMᵢ, PERCᵢ₊₁, ACT-REQᵢ₊₁);
              ACTᵢ₊₁ := det_active_pob(ACTᵢ, INACTᵢ, WMᵢ₊₁);
              PoBᵢ₊₁ := select_pattern(ACTᵢ₊₁, WMᵢ₊₁);
              WMᵢ₊₁ := execute_pob(PoBᵢ₊₁, WMᵢ₊₁);

              INACTᵢ₊₁ := POBSET − ACTᵢ₊₁;
              i := i + 1
      forever
  }
```

Figure 15.4 *The BBC control algorithm.*

Active Pattern Determination: In the first phase, a set of active patterns is determined. In the following, let $\mathcal{P}$ denote a set of patterns of behavior, and let $\mathcal{L}$ denote a set of propositions (denoting, e.g., an agent's world model). For a pattern $p \in \mathcal{P}_a$ let $p.AC$, $p.TC$, and $p.FC$ denote p's activation, termination, and failure condition, respectively. A pattern is called active at a certain time if the activation condition of the pattern is satisfied at that time, or if the pattern has been activated at an earlier time and has not yet terminated or failed. Thus, det_active_pob is a function $\delta : 2^{\mathcal{L}} \times 2^{\mathcal{P}} \times 2^{\mathcal{P}} \to 2^{\mathcal{P}}$, where

$$\delta(WM_{i+1}.ACT_i, INACT_i) \overset{\text{def}}{=}$$

$$\{p \in INACT_i | WM_{i+1} \vDash p.AC\} \cup$$

$$\{p' \in ACT_i | \exists j.j < i \wedge WM_j \vDash p.AC$$

$$\wedge \neg \exists k.j < k < i \wedge (WM_k \vDash p.TC \vee WM_k \vDash p.FC)\}$$

Pattern Selection. We see that different PoB may be active at a time. However, our model assumes a sequential model of execution. That means only one pattern may have the control to initiate an action at a certain time. This requires the selection of one pattern in each BBC cycle. Pattern selection has turned out to be the core problem of behavior-based modeling, and the way it is implemented is crucial for the behavior of the agent, for its reactivity as well as for its capability to handle complex situations. A set of mechanisms for solving the pattern selection problem, such as static and dynamic priorities as well as the representation of explicit interrelationships among different PoB have been discussed in Müller et al. (1994).

Pattern Execution. Finally, the PoB which has been chosen before has to be executed. This execution mechanism has to provide stepwise execution of patterns of behavior in order to achieve high-level concurrency of patterns. The main idea behind the stepwise execution algorithm is to define one execution step either as the (computation plus) execution of the next primitive instruction or as the execution of a block defined by the programmer of the pattern. That means, we provide a high-level scheduling mechanism which allows the programmer to define the granularity of execution, and which also forces her or him to take the responsibility for selecting an appropriate choice.

Application in FORKS. Patterns for basic reactive behavior in FORKS have been designed to recognize a new transportation order, recognize when a box has been found, detect a threatening collision, avoid a collision (*step aside* behavior), detect a blocking conflict, or to resolve a blocking conflict (*random move* behavior, *step aside* behavior). Procedural PoB representing abstract routine actions are used for moving to a landmark (variant of potential field using a weighted random function), grasping and storing a box, respectively, searching for a box in a certain area (around a truck, in a shelf), performing a *query* protocol with another agent, e.g., in order to find out the goals of this agents or to get to know the location of a certain box, leaving a narrow shelf corridor and waiting outside, or for returning to the waiting zone.

The Plan-Based Component. The plan-based component of the InteRRaP model contains the agent's local planning facilities. There are two "standard modes" of the PBC: the first is to devise a plan for a goal upon request from the BBC (message do(Goal)) and to control the correct execution of the plan. The second is to interpret the agent's part in a joint plan designed by the CC (message interpret(Plan)). A complete listing of the message types which are defined between BBC and PBC is displayed in Figure 15.5.

In the following, the different subcomponents of the PBC and their interplay are explained. It consists of a planning control module *pbc-control*, of a *plan generator* module, and *plan evaluator* module. The *pbc-control* is the "head" of the PBC. Its main parts are the PBC interface, the plan interpreter, and a set of goal stacks. The interface receives messages from and sends messages to the BBC. The plan interpreter controls the processing and the decomposition of a plan. Furthermore, based on the information brought about by the plan evaluator, it decides which goal to plan next. For this purpose, it maintains a set of goal stacks. This is necessary, because the planner may be called by several concurrent patterns of behavior. Thus, for each goal, one goal stack is maintained. In each cycle, the interpreter chooses one of the goal stacks and processes the top goal of this stack. Processing a goal means either expanding the goal into subgoals or activating a pattern of behavior.

The task of the *plan generator* is to devise a (single-agent) plan for a given input goal of the agent. The plan generator is called by the *pbc-control* by sending a command make_plan(Goal, ?Planlist).

One of our major concerns when modeling the FORKS system was to keep the planning problem as simple as possible by incorporating domain knowledge. Therefore, the main task of the plan generator is to choose and instantiate a

BBC → PBC:

do(Goal)	; derive Plan for Goal and control its execution.
plan(Goal)	; derive Plan for Goal.
evaluate(Plan)	; compute expected local utility for Plan.
interpret(Plan)	; control execution of Plan.
retract(Goal)	; abort planning for a BBC Goal no longer pursued.
done(PoB, Status)	; PoB finished (Status $\in \{success, fail\}$).

PBC → BBC:

done(Goal, Status)	; Goal done/ Plan interpreted (Status $\in \{success, fail\}$).
planned(Goal, Plan)	; returns Plan for Goal.
eval(Plan, Eval)	; returns evaluation for Plan.
activate(PoB)	; activation of a pattern of behaviour.

Figure 15.5   *The interface between BBC and PBC.*

```
lpb_entry(load_truck(T, B), s,
        [do(fetch_box(B)), do(store_box(B, T))])
lpb_entry(fetch_box(B), s,
        [rr(box_position(B, ?Pos)), do(goto_landmark(Pos)), do(get(B))]).
lpb_entry(fetch_box(B), b,
        [pob(random_search(B))]). ;; pattern of behaviour
        ...
lpb_entry(goto_landmark(L₁), b,
        [pob(goto_lm_beh(L₁))])
lpb_entry(goto_landmark(L₁), s,
        [rr(where_am_i(?L₀)), do(gen_moves(L₀, L₁))])
        ...
```

Figure 15.6 *Exemplary plan library.*

suitable plan from a plan library. The plan library consists of a set of entries

$$plan\text{-}lib \ ::= \ (lpb\text{-}entry_1, \ \ldots, \ lpb\text{-}entry_k)$$

Each entry of the plan library is a tuple lpb-entry(Goal, Type, Body). Goal is the reference name of the entry and specifies which goal (or rather: which plan step corresponding to a certain goal) is expanded by the specific entry. Type can be either s for *skeletal plan* or b for *executable pattern of behavior*. For Type = s, the *body* of the entry consists of a list of plan steps, which specify the expansion of the entry plan step. If Type = b, the body denotes the name of an executable pattern of behavior. Figure 15.6 shows an excerpt from the FORKS plan library.

Finally, the *plan evaluator* is able to associate utilities with plans. If it receives a list of alternative plans, it returns a list of evaluated plans. The evaluation is used by the plan interpreter in order to decide which of the alternative plans to pursue.

4.3 Coordination and Cooperative Conflict Resolution

Some situations exceed the problem-solving capacities of the PBC. In these cases, control is shifted to the CC. The main functionality of the CC is that it has to devise a *joint plan* for a certain situation, given a description of the situational context (e.g., type of conflict, position of the conflicting agents) and of the mental context (current goals of the agent). The social context (goals of other agents involved) has to be provided and checked by the cooperation component by evaluating available information about other agents. Currently, goal information is acquired by starting a simple query protocol. This classification process results in a type of interaction, which is used as an index to an entry in a library of joint plans.

The basic parts of the CC are the *CC control*, the *joint plan generator*, the *joint plan evaluator*, and the *joint plan translator*. They are explained in more detail below.

The CC Control. This module firstly serves as an interface between the CC and the PBC. Second, it coordinates the work of the other submodules of the component. Third, it contains a classifier which is able to map a goal description contained in a task do(Goal) received by the PBC to a type of interaction using information from the PBC and the partner model library.

The Joint Plan Generator. The task of this module is to return a set of joint plans for a given situation specification make_plan(Type, OwnGoal, PartnerGoals) so that each of the resulting plan satisfies Own-Goal ∪ PartnerGoals.[3] As mentioned, our objective has been to keep planning tractable by utilizing domain-specific information, and to concentrate on the interplay among the modules. Therefore, the plan generator has to select a set of joint skeletal plans indexed by the situation specification from a joint plan library. This selection is done by pure matching.

The Joint Plan Evaluator. Since joint plans are subject to negotiation (see Chapter 7), the agent must be able to evaluate a joint plan which has been proposed by another agent. On the other hand, in order to generate "reasonable" joint plans itself, the agent must have a measure for what is a reasonable plan. It is the task of the joint plan evaluator to determine whether a plan is reasonable by attributing a utility for the plan. The evaluator accepts as input a list $[P_1, \ldots , P_k]$ of joint plans proposed for achieving a goal, and outputs a list of evaluated plans $[(P_1, u_1), \ldots , (P_k, u_k)]$, where u_i is the utility ascribed to P_i. In the current FORKS implementation, the local utility $u_i(P)$ of a plan P for an agent a_i is determined as $u_i(P) = w_i(P) - c_i(P)$, where $w_i(P)$ is the worth of performing plan P for agent a_i, and $c_i(P)$ denotes the cost caused to agent a_i by performing P. The worth of a plan P is regarded to be the worth of the goal(s) achieved by successfully performing P. The cost c of a plan is defined by inductively extending a domain-specific cost function $\tilde{c}$ given for primitive plan steps according to the structure of the plan language. For example, if we have a plan language that allows to compose plans merely as sequences of primitive actions $p_1, \ldots , p_n$, the cost of a plan P can be defined as $\Sigma_{p \in P}\ \tilde{c}(P), p \in \{p_1, \ldots , p_n\}$. A detailed discussion of joint plan evaluation and different definitions of agent rationality emerging from different ways of relating global and local aspects of cost and worth can be found in Müller (1994).

The Joint Plan Translator. It is the task of the joint plan translator to transform a joint plan into a single-agent plan by projecting the agent's part of the joint plan and by adding synchronization actions which guarantee that the

---

[3]If no such plan could be found, currently the do(Goal) request by the PBC fails. This will in the worst case lead to a failure at the local planning layer, and thus, to the activation of a reactive "emergency" behavior. Future work envisages a more careful analysis of the reasons of failure and the use of goal relaxation techniques (see Zlotkin and Rosenschein, 1991).

constraints contained in the original joint plan are satisfied during plan execution. The organization of the translator depends on the way joint plans and single agent plans are represented. In Section 4.4, we will show the functionality of the translator module by means of the loading dock example.

4.4 Control

As we have seen, the modules of the InteRRaP model exchange information and shift control by communication. In fact, this process can be described in two dimensions, a *bottom-up* dimension and a *top-down* dimension. As tasks get more and more complex, control for this task is shifted from lower layers to higher layers until a suitable one has been found (*bottom-up, competence-driven control*). At the same time, the lower layers remain active and thus can cope with new events. Then, for task execution, control flows back (*top-down, activation-driven*) from higher layers to lower layers, finally resulting in the execution of primitive actions in the WIF.

In the following, we would like to clarify this process by an example. First, we will trace the execution of a transportation order by a forklift agent based on the excerpt of the plan library shown in Figure 15.6. Then, we will see how an unforeseen event, a blocking conflict, can be handled by invoking the cooperation component.

Example: Execution of a Task. Figure 15.7 shows the overall processing of the order request by agent i. The original request re- $\text{quest(agent}_i, \text{ load\_truck}(t_1, b_{23}))$ is handled by a pattern of behavior t reat_order_beh located in the BBC. Due to the limited space, we will not explain the structure of the patterns of behavior and the way they work in more detail. Let us assume here that the pattern of behavior recognizes that the whole goal should be treated by a planner.[4] Thus, as shown in Figure 15.7(1), the BBC sends a request(pbc, do(load_truck(t_1, b_{23}))) to the PBC. Now, the planning process inside the PBC starts (see below for a more detailed description). Since the PBC has been called by a do command, plans are (1) devised and (2) their execution is monitored by the planner.

This monitoring is shown in Figure 15.7(2): whenever the planner has found an executable pattern of behavior or a primitive action, it activates the corresponding pattern of interaction. In the example, the pattern of behavior for moving to a certain landmark is activated by sending a message request(bbc, activate(goto_lm_beh((7, 4)))). The pattern of behavior is executed and reports its (successful) termination by sending a message inform(pbc, done(goto_lm_beh((7, 4)))) to the PBC.

Finally, the PBC has planned and processed the whole load_truck task. It reports this to the calling PoB treat_order_beh. This is shown in Figure 15.7(3). Control shifts back to the BBC, and, as displayed in Figure 15.7(4),

---

[4]In fact, the PoB could call the planner only for a part of the goal.

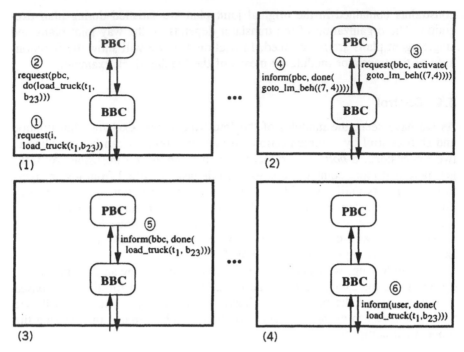

Figure 15.7 *Example: Processing the* load_truck *goal.*

a message is sent to the user denoting that the task has been successfully completed. We refer to Müller and Pischel (1994a) for a complete trace of the planning process for the example.

Coordination in Conflict Resolution. So far, we have seen how InteRRaP agents can perform their tasks using plans and patterns of behavior, and how the use of these concepts can be combined to yield an appropriate overall behavior of the agent. However, what was not included in the example, is how the InteRRaP model supports agent interaction and cooperation. In the following, this issue will be informally discussed by means of the above example.

Let us now assume that another agent, say j, blocks the way of agent i in a narrow corridor between two shelves. In this situation, the BBC recognizes that there is a conflict and calls the PBC by sending a request message

```
do(resolve_shelf_conflict((self, Agent)))
```

to the PBC. The *pbc__control* recognizes that it does not have a plan for solving a blocking conflict in a shelf corridor. Therefore, it calls the cooperation component. This one devises a joint plan, and initiates negotiation with the other agent about the joint plan. The resulting joint plan is translated by the CC to a single-agent plan which is augmented by synchronization commands. For example, a very simple joint plan for two agents *i* and *j* changing places is

```
JP = [[[walk_aside(i, north)], []],
       [[walk_ahead(i)], [walk_ahead(j)]],
       [[walk_aside(i, south)], []]].
```

The plan JP has three phases. Phase one describes that agent *i* must first walk aside. In phase two, *i* and *j* may concurrently walk ahead. Phase three, where agent *i* steps to the other side again, can only start after agent *j* has executed the walk_ahead action. This joint plan is translated into the following single-agent plan *P* for *i*:

```
P = [walk_aside(north), send_synch(j, ready), walk_ahead,
     rec_synch(j, ready), walk_aside(south), send_synch
     (j, ready)].
```

The synchronization commands ensure that the precedence constraints expressed by the joint plan are respected in the execution. This plan is passed to the PBC which interprets it by again activating corresponding patterns of behavior.

5 COOPERATION AND CONTROLLED EXPERIMENTATION

The second application we built using the AGenDA testbed is the MARS system, a simulation of cooperative shipping companies. From the perspective of the testbed, the main challenge in the case of MARS was

- To provide different cooperation methods based on negotiation, which enable the system designer to construct a set of different distributed scheduling strategies
- To supply experimentation in order to evaluate the performance of these strategies and to compare the quality of the solutions found by MARS with that of traditional approaches to these problems

This section is structured as follows: Section 5.1 provides a short introduction into the structure of the MARS system. In Section 5.2, we motivate the tools provided by the AGenDA testbed for modeling different cooperation strategies (so called *cooperation settings*). Finally, Section 5.2 comments on aspects of performing controlled experiments in our testbed.

5.1 The MARS System

The MARS (modeling autonomous cooperating shipping companies) scenario implements a group of shipping companies whose goal it is to deliver a set of dynamically given orders, satisfying a set of given time and/or cost constraints. The complexity of the orders may exceed the capacities of a single company. Therefore, cooperation between companies is required in order to achieve the goal in a satisfactory way. This general setting can be seen in Figure 15.8. Incomplete information about orders and the possibility to share resources allows and requires cooperation among different companies. Although each company has a local, primarily self-interested view, cooperation between the shipping companies is necessary in order to achieve reasonable global plans. Apart from internal *system agents*, which perform tasks such as the representation and visualization of the simulation world, the MARS agent society consists of two sorts of *domain agents*, which correspond to the logical entities in the domain: *shipping companies* and *trucks*. In contrast to other approaches (cf. Falk et al., 1993) we decided to look upon trucks as agents. This view allows to delegate problem-solving skills to them (such as route planning and local plan optimization). Furthermore, we obtain a logical distribution of the system even if we consider only a single company. Patterns of cooperation which can be observed in real transportation business are (i) the exchange and retrieval of information among agents; (ii) task allocation between companies and trucks (contracting) using a *contract-net*-like protocol (see below); (iii) balancing the load of the trucks of different companies by offering or requesting loading space; (iv) negotiating the conditions for orders between companies; (v) having organized the return freight of a truck by a partner company in the destination region; (vi) establishing the connection between long-term and local traffic by

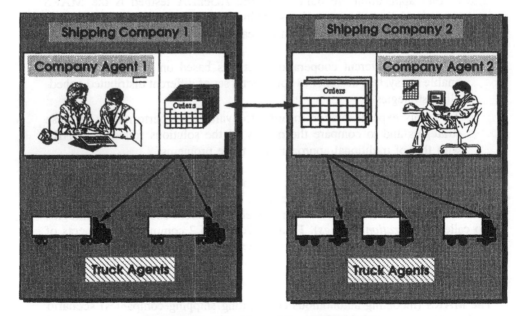

Figure 15.8 Overview of the MARS system.

cooperation. In the next section, we will illustrate two negotiation protocols provided by the AGenDA testbed which were used to model different facets of cooperation in the MARS system.

5.2 Cooperation Settings

Agents in the AGenDA testbed can be equipped with different cooperation capabilities; the different types of cooperative behavior that emerge from different possible configurations are called *cooperation settings*. In this subsection, we introduce two different cooperation settings which are relevant for the transportation domain, namely *vertical cooperation* and *horizontal cooperation*. The former can be used as the standard protocol for the task allocation between a shipping company and its trucks. The latter takes into account the fact that companies are autonomous, self-interested entities, and that they will only cooperate if doing so increases their local utility; the testbed supports horizontal cooperation by providing a general bargaining protocol.

Vertical Cooperation: The Extended Contract Net Protocol. The contract net protocol (CNP) (Smith, 1980) is a well-known DAI problem solving technique which can be used to distribute tasks among a set of agents. However, the pure contract net protocol runs into problems if the tasks exceed the capacity of a single truck. In this case, the manager of the task, i.e., the shipping company agent, has to solve a knapsack problem, which for itself is in general NP hard. To overcome this problem, we decentralized task decomposition by developing and implementing an extension of the CNP, which is called the ECNP protocol. ECNP is available as a standard protocol in AGenDA. In ECNP, the two speech acts *grant* and *reject* are replaced by four new speech acts: *temporal grant*, *temporal reject*, *definitive grant*, and *definitive reject*. The ECNP is a natural, straightforward solution of the task decomposition problem.

A flowchart representation is used to represent the negotiation protocols provided by the AGenDA testbed. The protocols describe the roles played by the individual agents in the protocol. Figure 15.9 shows the flowcharts of the protocol layer of the ECNP protocol (a) from the manager's point of view and (b) from the point of view of the bidders. The main difference to the CNP is that now the bidders, i.e., the trucks, are allowed to bid for only parts of an order.

Communication in the ECNP proceeds as follows. The manager (shipping company) announces an order to its trucks. It then receives bids for the order and selects the best one using an ordering function. The truck which gave the best bid is sent a temporal grant. All other trucks get temporal rejects. If the best bid does not cover the whole amount of an order, the shipping company reannounces the remaining part of the order. This procedure is repeated until the shipping company receives a bid that covers the whole amount of the order which was finally reannounced. At this stage, the shipping company has gath-

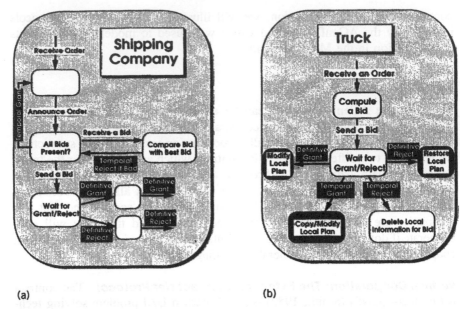

(a)   (b)

Figure 15.9 Description of the ECNP from the point of view of a manager (a) and a bidder (b).

ered a set of bids that covers the whole original order. This set is used to compute a bid for the whole task, that is returned to the broker agent. The latter grants the best of all bids received by the different companies. Based on this answer, the shipping company passes a definitive grant (or definitive reject, respectively) to all trucks which got temporal grants before. One can show that all but the last bid selected are locally optimal choices for the shipping company (Fischer et al., 1994). This provides a valuable hint for further improvements of the ECNP.

On the other hand, the trucks must be able to cope with the temporal and definitive grant or reject messages. When a truck receives a temporal grant for the first time, it has to store a copy of its local situation, i.e., the currently valid plan, because it must be able to restore this situation once it gets a definitive reject. All subsequent temporal grants and temporal rejects are handled like the grants and rejects in the pure contract net protocol. If a truck is sent a definitive grant for an order, it removes the copy created above. If a truck gets a definitive reject, it has to remove all the local information gathered while receiving temporal grants and restore the situation before the first temporal grant.

Horizontal Cooperation by Negotiation. Optimizing the usage of transport capacities is a crucial goal for a shipping company for quite a few economic and ecological reasons. Due to the spatial and temporal distribution of incoming orders, cooperation with other companies may be a beneficial operation for a shipping company. For example, companies may exchange orders and information about free loading capacities, and they may apply for orders offered by other companies. However, in contrast to the coordination between a company and its trucks, cooperation between companies is a peer-to-peer process where a solution (e.g., a price to be paid for an offer) can only be found if all the participants agree, and where the conditions of the solution have to be negotiated among the companies. It is this peer-to-peer negotiation what we call horizontal cooperation.

Negotiation Protocol. AGenDA supports the modeling of horizontal cooperation by providing a parametrized bargaining protocol which can be instantiated with the specific conditions of a negotiation. Figure 15.10 illustrates the protocol by means of a flowchart. It shows both the types of messages exchanged between the companies as well as the connection between local reasoning within a company (represented by its local decision nodes and by the connection to the vertical cooperation protocol with its trucks) and cooperative reasoning in the course of the negotiation. A company (company 1, or c_1, in the example) may decide to announce free transport capacity to another company, let us say, company 2, or c_2. This decision can be made based on information about free capacities c_1 has received by its trucks. Based on its local state, c_2 decides whether it wants to utilize the announcement, and, if so, sends an order to c_1. This instantiates a bargaining protocol where c_1 takes the role of the offering

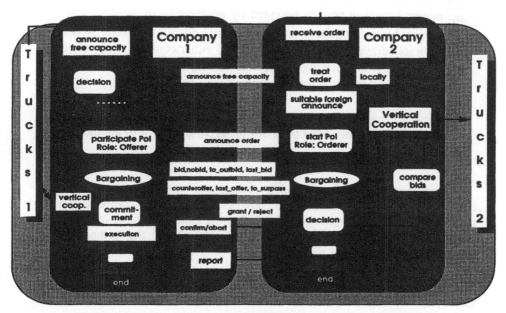

Figure 15.10 *A bargaining protocol for horizontal cooperation.*

agent, c_2 takes the role of the orderer. c_1 will start by sending an offer (bid) to c_2; c_2 will decide whether to accept, reject, or to modify the bid by making a counteroffer. The bargaining process continues either until both parties have agreed on a common solution or until it becomes clear that no compromise can be found.[5]

Decision Making. The decision making of the companies during the negotiation process is based on information they obtain by their trucks, e.g., information about free capacities and costs. This allows a company to determine in how far cooperation will lead to an increase of its local utility, and thus, to determine its range of negotiation. Another important issue for decision making is partner modeling; for example, if all the agents had complete knowledge about the decision criteria of all other agents, each agent could locally compute whether there is a solution accepted by all the partners. In the case where all the agents have the same decision criteria, two agents could directly agree on the mean value of the first bid and the first counteroffer, since negotiation is to converge to this value. However, in reality, agents do not have complete knowledge about each other; this makes the bargaining process interesting. In the current system, *partner modeling* is restricted to agents making simple assumptions on the parameters of other agents; future research will aim at enhancing this model. There are several configurable parameters that can be used to vary the decision-making behavior of an agent, e.g.,

ω_d desired profit in percent for an order

ω_m minimal profit in percent accepted by an agent

Δ function determining the amount to which an agent's next offer is modified given its current offer p; it can be set to either constant k or $max(k, (\omega_d - \omega_m)p/n)$; n is a scaling factor determining the speed of convergence; the *max* function guarantees termination of the negotiation independent of the size of n.

σ_c threshold denoting the agent's cooperation sensitivity (i.e., how uneconomic does an order have to be for an agent to offer it to another agent); $\sigma_c \in [0, 1]$

Providing a set of different configurations and strategies for agents is one important functionality of a testbed; however, it has to be complemented by tools for performing, monitoring, and evaluating experiments in order to derive general properties of the features that are producible by the testbed. This is discussed in the following subsection.

[5]The other communication acts shown in figure 15.10 such as *last_bid*, *to_outbid*, *to_surpass* are special purpose features enabling an auction-like negotiation between more than two agents.

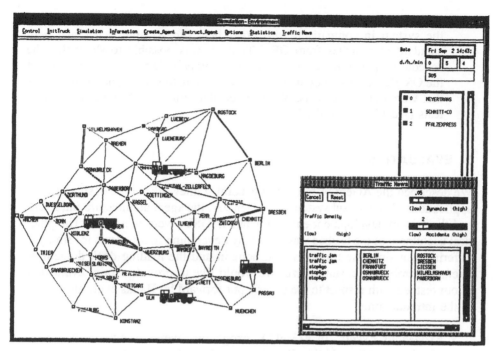

Figure 15.11   *Visualization of the MARS application.*

Controlled Experimentation. As we pointed out in the introduction, the ability of supporting experimentation in a controlled way is a crucial feature of any testbed. In the following, we will provide a brief description of how the AGenDA testbed supports the derivation of empirical results in MARS.

Figure 15.11 displays a snapshot of the simulation environment for the MARS system which is described in Section 5. The testbed allows to vary the characteristics of the agents, e.g., the cooperation methods to be used by the companies and the local planning algorithms used by the plans. Based on these variations, different types of experiments may be run, and statistical data concerning the cost of plans, the number of messages, and the success rate of cooperation processes can be gathered. Two types of experiments were carried through with the MARS system:

- Internal evaluation experiments were used to study the cost and the utility of different negotiation and cooperation strategies developed for the MARS system. They showed the usefulness of horizontal cooperation among different shipping companies, but also that the actual benefit of these methods depends on the cost of cooperation in the application (see Fischer et al., 1993).

- External evaluation experiments were run to evaluate the performance of the system in comparison with other heuristic AI approaches and with standard approaches from OR.[6] Thus, it was possible to show that the scheduling performance of MARS was comparable to the performance of the OR algorithms. Moreover, MARS was able to solve dynamic problems that were out of the scope of the other algorithms used in the benchmark tests (see Fischer et al., 1994).

6 EVALUATION

We described the AGenDA testbed, a general framework for the design of DAI applications. The two subsystems of AGenDA, the agent architecture InteRRaP and the system development environment MAGSY, were presented. The practical usefulness of the testbed was shown by developing two systems for strongly differing domains: the transportation domain and the loading dock domain of interacting robots. To summarize, we would like to provide a brief evaluation of our testbed with respect to the criteria put forward by Hanks et al. mentioned in the introduction.

- *Exogenous Events.* In AGenDA, exogenous events occur due to actions of other agents; additionally, they can be caused by the user, e.g., by initiating traffic jams in the MARS system.
- *Complexity of the World.* Based on the general knowledge representation provided by the MAGSY level, AGenDA allows very general representations of the objects in the world and of causal relationships between them. The other side of the coin is that by not imposing strong restrictions on the structure of the world (as MICE or TILEWORLD do), AGenDA currently does not provide very much active support and guidance for modeling a certain environment.
- *Cost and Quality of Sensing/Effecting/Planning.* The testbed provides a simple utility model for actions and plans. It does currently not support meta-reasoning in the sense of anytime planning (*deliberation scheduling*; Boddy and Dean, 1994). Extending our reaction/deliberation framework by such a model will be an important subject for future work.
- *Multiple Agents.* Coordination and cooperation among agents is supported by low-level communication facilities, predefined negotiation protocols, and cooperative planning facilities.
- *World Interface.* The interface between the InteRRaP agent and the simulation component of MAGSY is clearly defined; there is a clear semantics of actions and perception.

---

[6]For this purpose, a well-known benchmark for the *static vehicle routing problem with time windows* was used.

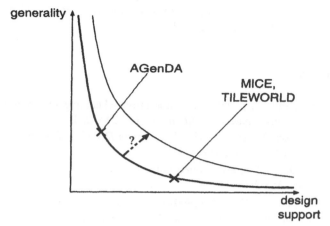

Figure 15.12   *Trade-offs in testbed development.*

- *Time Model.* AGenDA provides a simple point-based time model which is used as a basis for the scheduling algorithms in the MARS system.
- *Experimentation Support.* The testbed offers a rich experimentation environment allowing goal-directed variation of agent and environmental parameters, and providing tools for statistical evaluation.

In conclusion, the development of a helpful testbed for DAI applications as diverse as the ones presented in this chapter is a very difficult task; obviously, there is a trade-off between the generality offered by such a tool and its usefulness for a specific class of applications. This is illustrated in Figure 15.12. Systems such as MICE and the TILEWORLD impose severe restrictions on the admissible scenarios, giving a large amount of guidance to the designer but at the same time limiting the complexity and expressiveness of the systems that can be designed using these testbeds. If we require from a testbed that it support the design of a diversity of different applications, due to the above-mentioned trade-off it becomes very difficult to offer the designer more than a general modular architecture used as templates for building agents, basic knowledge representation and inference mechanisms, and a comfortable simulation environment. What we hope for and what our future work is aiming at is to achieve an improvement of the relationship between generality and the design support in the direction of the arrow in Figure 15.12, starting from a relatively high degree of generality, and a currently lower degree of support.

ACKNOWLEDGMENTS

We would like to thank Thomas Weiser, Michael Thiel, and the two anonymous referees for helpful comments. They greatly improved this chapter. The work presented in this chapter has been supported by the German Ministry of Research and Technology under grant ITW9104.

REFERENCES

Boddy, M., and Dean, T. L. (1994). Deliberation scheduling for problem solving in time-constrained environments. *Artif. Intell.* **67**, 245–285.

Bond, A., and Gasser, L., eds. (1988). *Readings in Distributed Artificial Intelligence.* Morgan Kaufmann, Los Angeles, CA.

Brooks, R. A. (1986). A robust layered control system for a mobile robot. *IEEE J. Robotics Autom.* **RA-2**(1), 14–23.

Cohen, P., Howe, A., and Hart, D. (1990) Intelligent real-time problem solving: Issues and examples. In *Intelligent Real-Time Problem Solving: Workshop Report* (L. Erman, ed.). Palo Alto, CA.

Durfee, E. H., and Montgomery, T. A. (1989). MICE: A flexible testbed for intelligent coordination experiments. *Proc. Int. Workshop Distributed Artif. Intell., 9th,* Rosario, WA.

Durfee, E. H., and Rosenschein, J. (1994). Distributed problem solving and multiagent systems: Comparisons and examples. *Proc. Int. Workshop Distributed Artif. Intell., 13th,* Lake Quinalt, WA, pp. 94–104.

Falk, J., Spieck, S., and Mertens, P. (1993). Unterstützung der Lager- und Transportlogistik durch Teilintelligente Agenten. *Inf. Manage.* **2.**

Fischer, K. The rule-based multi-agent system MAGSY. *Coop. Knowl. Based Syst. SIG Proc. Workshop,* Keele University, Keele, UK, *1993.*

Fischer, K., Kuhn, N., Müller, H. J., Müler, J.-P., and Pischel, M. (1993). Sophisticated and distributed: The transportation domain. *Proc. Eur. Workshop Modell. Auton. Agents Multi-Agent World, 5th,* Neuchatel, Switzerland, *1993.*

Fischer, K., Kuhn, N., and Müller, J.-P. (1994). Distributed, knowledge-based, reactive scheduling in the transportation domain. *Proc. Conf. Artif. Intell. Appl., 10th,* San Antonio, TX, pp. 47–53.

Georgeff, M. P., and Lansky, A. L. (1986). Procedural knowledge. In *Proc. IEEE Spec. Issue Knowl. Represent.* **74**, 1383–1398.

Hanks, S., Pollack, M. E., and Cohen, P. R. (1993). Benchmarks, test beds, controlled experimentation, and the design of agent architectures. *AI Mag.,* Winter, pp. 17–42.

Henz, M., Smolka, G., and Würtz, J. (1993). Oz—A programming language for multi-agent systems. *Proc. Int. Jt. Conf. Artif. Intell., 13th,* Chambéry, France, pp. 404–409.

Kinny, D., Ljungberg, M., Rao, A., Sonenberg, E., Tidhar, G., and Werner, E. (1992). Planned team activity. *Pre-Proc. Eur. Workshop Modell. Auton. Agents Multi-Agent World, 1992.*

Latombe, J. P. (1992). How to move (physically speaking) in a multi-agent world. In *Decentralized Artificial Intelligence* (Y. Demazeau and E. Werner, eds.). Elsevier/North-Holland, Amsterdam.

McDermott, D. (1991). *Robot Planning*, Tech. Rep. No. 861. Department of Computer Science, Yale University, New Haven, CT.

Müller, J.-P., and Pischel, M. (1994a). An architecture for dynamically interacting agents. *Int. J. Intell. Coop. Inf. Syst.* **3**(1), 25–45.

Müller, J.-P., and Pischel, M. (1994b). Integrating agent interaction into a planner-reactor architecture. *Proc. Int. Workshop Distributed Artif. Intell., 13th*, Seattle, WA.

Müller, J.-P., Pischel, M., and Thiel, M. (1994). A pragmatic approach to modeling autonomous interacting systems. In *Working Notes of the ECAI Workshop on Agent Theories, Architectures, and Languages* (N. R. Jennings and M. Wooldridge, eds.). Elsevier, Amsterdam.

Nguyen, D., Hanks, S., and Thomas, C. (1993). *The TRUCKWORLD Manual*, Tech. Rep. 93-09-08. Dept. of Computer Science and Engineering, University of Washington, Seattle.

Pollack, M. E., and Ringuette, M. (1990). Introducing the tile-world: Experimentally evaluating agent architectures. *Proc. Am. Assoc. Artif. Intell.*, Boston, pp. 183–189.

Rao, A. S., and Georgeff, M. P. (1991). Modeling agents within a BDI-architecture. In *Proceedings of the Second International Conference on Principles of Knowledge Representation and Reasoning* (J. Allen, R. Fikes, and E. Sandewall, eds.), pp. 473–484. Morgan Kaufmann, San Mateo, CA.

Smith, R. G. (1980). The contract net protocol: High-level communication and control in a distributed problem solver. *IEEE Trans. Comput.* **C-29**(12), 1104–1113.

Zlotkin, G., and Rosenschein, J. S. (1991). Negotiation and goal relaxation. In *Decentralized Artificial Intelligence* (Y. Demazeau and J.-P. Müller, eds.), pp. 273–286. Elsevier/North-Holland, Amsterdam.

CHAPTER 16

TÆMS: A Framework for Environment Centered Analysis and Design of Coordination Mechanisms

KEITH S. DECKER

1 INTRODUCTION

The design of coordination mechanisms for groups of computational agents, either interacting with one another or with people, depends crucially on the task environment of which they are a part. Such dependencies include the structure of the environment (the particular kinds and patterns of interrelationships that occur between tasks) and the uncertainty in the environment (both in the *a priori* structure of any episode within an environment and in the outcomes of an agent's actions). Designing coordination mechanisms also depends on properties of the agents themselves (arising in turn from the intentional design of their internal architecture)—a large body of work already exists that describes the principled construction of agents that act based on what are variously termed beliefs, desires, intentions, and goals (see Chapters 2 and 5). The central idea presented here is that the design of coordination mechanisms cannot rely on the principled construction of agents alone, but must rely on the structure and other characteristics of the task environment—for example, the presence of uncertainty and concomitant high variance in a structure. Furthermore, this structure can and should be used as the central guide to the design of coordination mechanisms, and thus must be a part of any comprehensive theory of coordination.

This chapter will first present an outline of the TÆMS framework for building models of task environments at multiple levels of abstraction, along with examples of such models. The next two sections will also describe several short

Foundations of Distributed Artificial Intelligence, Edited by G. M. P. O'Hare and N. R. Jennings.
ISBN 0-471-00675-0 © 1996 John Wiley & Sons, Inc.

examples of our experiences in using the framework for modeling domains, analyzing a simple distributed sensor network, and generalizing the partial global planning algorithm. Finally the chapter will step back to discuss the current state of TÆMS, and its strengths and weaknesses.

2 THE TÆMS FRAMEWORK

TÆMS (Task Analysis, Environment Modeling, and Simulation) is a framework with which to model complex computational task environments that is compatible with both formal agent-centered approaches and experimental approaches. The framework allows us to both analyze and quantitatively simulate the behavior of single or multiagent systems with respect to interesting characteristics of the computational task environments of which they are part. We believe that it provides the correct level of abstraction for meaningfully evaluating centralized, parallel, and distributed control algorithms, negotiation strategies, and organizational designs. No previous characterization formally captures the range of features, processes, and especially interrelationships that occur in computationally intensive task environments. TÆMS exists as both a language for stating general hypotheses or theories and as a system for simulation. The simulator supports the graphical display of generated task structures, agent actions, and statistical data collection in CLOS (the common lisp object system) on the TI Explorer Lisp machine and DEC Alpha.

The basic form of the task environment framework—the execution of interrelated computational tasks—is taken from several domain environment simulators (Carver and Lesser, 1991; Cohen et al., 1989; Durfee et al., 1987).[1] If this were the only impetus, the result might have been a simulator like Tileworld (Pollack and Ringuette, 1990). However, formal research into multiagent problem solving has been productive in specifying formal properties, and sometimes algorithms, for the control process by which the mental state of agents (termed variously: beliefs, desires, goals, intentions, etc.) causes the agents to perform particular actions (Cohen and Levesque, 1990; Shoham, 1991; Zlotkin and Rosenschein, 1991). This research has helped to circumscribe the behaviors or actions that agents can produce based on their knowledge or beliefs (see Chapters 2 and 5). The final influence on TÆMS was the desire to avoid the individualistic agent-centered approaches that characterize most AI and distributed AI (cf. work described in Chapters 5 and 9). The concept of agency in TÆMS is based on simple notions of *execution*, *communication*, and *information gathering*. An agent is a locus of belief (state) and action. By separating as much as possible the notion of agency from the model of task environments, we do not have to subscribe to particular agent architectures (which one would assume will be adapted to the task environment at hand), and we may ask questions about the inherent social nature of the task environment at hand

---

[1]See also the discussion in Chapter 3.

(allowing that the concept of society may arise before the concept of individual agents; Gasser, 1991). Thus we might study how the concept and architecture of agents arises naturally from their environment, rather than by starting with a predesigned agent architecture. Another example is the search for so-called social laws (Shoham and Tennenholtz, 1992) (see also Chapter 20 for work on social norms) that can be derived from a task environment to reduce coordination overhead by reducing some forms of uncertainty. The form of our framework is more detailed in structure than many organizational-theoretic models of organizational environments, such as Thompson's notions of pooled, sequential, and reciprocal processes (Thompson, 1967), Burton and Obel's linear programs (Burton and Obel, 1984), or Malone's queueing models (Malone, 1987), but is influenced by them, and by the importance of environmental uncertainty, variance, and dependency that appear in contingency-theoretic and open systems views of organizations (Lawrence and Lorsch, 1967; Galbraith, 1977; Stinchcombe, 1990; Scott, 1987; and Chapter 19).

2.1 General Framework

The principle purpose of a T&MS model is to analyze, explain, or predict the performance of a system or some component. While T&MS does not establish a particular performance criteria, it focuses on providing two kinds of performance information: the temporal intervals of task executions, and the *quality* of the execution or its result. *Quality* is an intentionally vaguely defined term that must be instantiated for a particular environment and performance criteria. Examples of *quality* measures include the precision, belief, or completeness of a task result. We will assume that *quality* is a single numeric term with an absolute scale, although the algebra can be extended to vector terms. In a computationally intensive AI system, several quantities—the quality produced by executing a task, the time taken to perform that task, the time when a task can be started, its deadline, and whether the task is necessary at all—are affected by the execution of other tasks. In real-time problem solving, alternative task execution methods may be available that trade-off time for quality. Agents do not have unlimited access to the environment; what an agent believes and what is really there may be different.

The model of environmental and task characteristics proposed has three levels: *objective*, *subjective*, and *generative*. The *objective* level describes the essential, "real" task structure of a particular problem-solving situation or instance over time. It is roughly equivalent to a formal description of a single problem-solving situation such as those presented in Durfee and Lesser (1991), without the information about particular agents. The *subjective* level describes how agents view and interact with the problem-solving situation over time (e.g., how much does an agent know about what is really going on, and how much does it cost to find out—where the uncertainties are from the agent's point of view). The subjective level is essential for evaluating control algorithms, because while individual behavior and system performance can be measured objectively, agents must make decisions with only subjective information. In organizational-theoretic terms, subjective *perception* can be used to predict agent actions or *outputs*, but unperceived, objective environmental characteristics can still affect performance (or *outcomes*) (Scott, 1987). Finally, the *generative* level describes the statistical characteristics required to generate the objective and subjective situations in a domain. A generative-level model consists of a description of the generative processes or distributions from which the range of alternative problem instances can be derived, and is used to study performance over a range of problems in an environment, avoiding single-instance examples.

2.2 Mathematical Framework

The *objective* level describes the essential structure of a particular problem-solving situation or instance over time. It focuses on how task interrelationships dynamically affect the *quality* and *duration* of each task. The basic model is that *task groups* (problem instances) appear in the environment at some frequency, and induce tasks T to be executed by the agents under study. Task groups are independent of one another (except for the use of computational or physical resources), but tasks within a single task group have interrelationships. Task groups or tasks may have deadlines $D(T)$. The *quality* of the execution or result of each task influences the *quality* of the task group result $Q(T)$ in a precise way; these quantities can be used to evaluate the performance of a system.

An individual task that has no subtasks is called a method M and is the smallest schedulable chunk of work (though some scheduling algorithms will allow some methods to be preempted, and some schedulers will schedule at multiple levels of abstraction). There may be more than one method to accomplish a task, and each method will take some amount of time and produce a result of some *quality*. Quality of an agent's performance on an individual task is a function of the timing and choice of agent actions (local effects), and possibly other (previous or future) task executions (nonlocal effects). When local or nonlocal effects exist between tasks that are known by more than one agent, we call them *coordination relationships* (Decker and Lesser, 1993a). The basic purpose of the objective model is to formally specify how the execution and timing of tasks affect this measure of quality.

Local Effects: The Subtask Relationship.   Task or task group quality [$Q(T)$] is based on the *subtask* relationship. This quality function is constructed recursively—each task group consists of tasks, each of which consists of subtasks, etc.—until individual executable tasks (methods) are reached. Formally, the subtask relationship is defined as subtask(T, **T**, Q), where **T** is the set of all direct subtasks of T and Q is a quality function $Q(T, t)$: [tasks × times] $\mapsto$ [quality] that returns the quality associated with T at time t. In a valid model, the directed graph induced by this relationship is acyclic (no task has itself for a direct or indirect subtask). The semantics of a particular environment are modeled by the appropriate choice of the quality function Q (e.g., minimum when all tasks need to be done, maximum for just one, summation, etc.).

Local Effects: Method Quality. Each method M at a time t will potentially produce (if executed by an agent) some *maximum quality* $q(M, t)$ after some amount of elapsed time $d(M, t)$. The execution of methods is interruptible, and if multiple methods for a single task are available the agent may switch between them (typically, alternative methods trade-off time and quality). We model the effect of interruptions, if any, and the reuse of partial results as non-local effects.

Let Progress(M, t) be the amount of progress at time t on the execution of M. If M were not interruptible and Start(M) and Finish(M) were the execution start time and finish time, respectively, of M, then

$$\text{Progress}(M, t) = \begin{cases} 0 & t \leq \text{Start}(M) \\ t - \text{Start}(M) & \text{Start}(M) < t < \text{Finish}(M) \\ \text{Finish}(M) - \text{Start}(M) & t \geq \text{Finish}(M) \end{cases}$$

We could model the quality produced by a method $Q(M, t)$ using a linear growth function Q_{lin}:

$$Q_{\text{lin}}(M, t) = \begin{cases} \dfrac{\text{Progress}(M, t)}{d(M, t)} (q(M, t)) & \text{Progress}(M, t) < d(M, t) \\ q(M, t) & \text{Progress}(M, t) \geq d(M, t) \end{cases}$$

Other models (besides linear quality functions) have been proposed and are used to represent anytime (Boddy and Dean, 1989), contract anytime (Russell and Zilberstein, 1991), mandatory/optional (Liu et al., 1991), or design-to-time approaches (Garvey and Lesser, 1993).

Nonlocal Effects. Any task T containing a method that starts executing before the execution of another method M finishes may potentially affect M's execution through a *nonlocal effect* e. We write this relation $\text{nle}(T, M, e, p_1, p_2, \ldots)$, where the p's are parameters specific to a class of effects. There are precisely two possible outcomes of the application of a nonlocal effect on M under our model: *duration effects* where $d(M, t)$ (duration) is changed, and *quality effects* where $q(M, t)$ (maximum quality) is changed. An effect class e is thus a function $e(T, M, t, d, q, p_1, p_2, \ldots)$: [task $\times$ method $\times$ time $\times$ duration $\times$ quality $\times$ parameter 1 $\times$ parameter 2 $\times \ldots$] $\mapsto$ [duration $\times$ quality].

Some effects depend on the availability of information to an agent. For defining effects that depend on the availability of information, we define the helper function $Q_{avail}(T, t, A)$ that represents the quality of a task T "available" to agent A at time t. If T was executed at A, $Q_{avail}(T, t, A) = Q(T, t)$. If T was executed (or is being executed) by another agent, then the "available" quality is calculated from the last communication about T received at agent A prior to time t. Thus the local, subjective quality of a task result received by a remote agent may be different from the current quality at another agent—this is one of the important types of environmental uncertainty that our framework can express and for which we can develop coordination algorithm support.

Nonlocal effects are the most important part of the TÆMS framework, since they supply most of the characteristics that make one task environment unique and different from another. Typically a model will define different classes of effects, such as *causes, facilitates, cancels, constrains, inhibits,* and *enables* (Decker and Lesser, 1992). This section contains a definition for one common class of effect that has been useful in modeling different environments; another definition will be presented in Section 2.1.4; see Decker and Lesser (1993e) for a more complete set of definitions. When nonlocal effects occur between methods associated with different agents, we call them *coordination relationships* (Decker and Lesser, 1992, 1993a) (see also Chapter 6).

An important effect, used by the partial global planning (PGP) algorithm (see Chapter 8 and Durfee and Lesser, 1991) but never formally defined, is the *facilitates* effect. Computationally, facilitation occurs when information from one task, often in the form of constraints, is provided that either reduces or changes the search space to make some other task easier to solve. For example, searching for a new book in the library will be faster after the book has been properly shelved, but you could search in the unordered stack of new books if you needed to. In our framework, one task may provide results to another task that *facilitate* the second task by decreasing the duration or increasing the quality of its partial result. Therefore the *facilitates* effect has two parameters (called *power* parameters) $0 \leq \phi_d \leq 1$ and $0 \leq \phi_q \leq 1$, that indicate the effect on duration and quality respectively. The effect varies not only through the power parameters but also through the quality of the *facilitating* task available when work on the *facilitated* task starts (the ratio R). Remember that $q(M, t)$ refers to the maximum quality possible to achieve at method M, and note that before work is started on a method, $Start(M) = t$ (i.e., formulae are evaluated as if execution were about to start).

$$R(T_a, s) = \frac{Q_{avail}(T_a, s)}{q(T_a, s)}$$

facilitates$(T_a, M, t, d, q, \phi_d, \phi_q)$

$$= [d(1 - \phi_d R(T_a, Start(M))), q(1 + \phi_q R(T_a, Start(M)))] \quad (1)$$

So if T_a is completed with maximal quality, and the result is received before M is started, then the duration $d(M, t)$ will be decreased by a percentage equal to the duration power ϕ_d of the *facilitates* effect, and similarly the maximum quality $\mathbf{q}(M, t)$ will be increased by a percentage equal to the quality power ϕ_q. The use of Start(M) in the definition indicates that communications about T_a received after the start of processing have no effect. In other work (Decker and Lesser, 1993a) we explored the effects on coordination of a *facilitates* effect with varying duration power ϕ_d, and with $\phi_q = 0$.

Much more detail on the formal definitions of TÆMS objective, subjective, and generative structures, including the representation of the use of physical resources, can be found in Decker and Lesser (1993e).

2.3 Distributed Sensor Network Example

This example grows out of the set of single-instance examples—distributed vehicle monitoring testbed (DVMT) scenarios—presented in Durfee et al. (1987) (see also the discussion of the DVMT in Chapter 3). The authors of that paper compared the performance of several different coordination algorithms on these examples, and concluded that no one algorithm was always the best—not a very surprising result and one that can be viewed as the central tenet of contingency theory. This is the classic type of result that the TÆMS framework was created to address—we wish to *explain* this result and, better yet, to *predict* which algorithm will do the best in each situation. Here we do this by extending the analysis to take into account a statistical view of the environmental characteristics. The level of detail to which you build a model in TÆMS will depend on the question you wish to answer—here we wish to identify the characteristics of the distributed sensor network (DSN) environment, or the organization of the agents, that cause one coordination algorithm to outperform another.

In a DSN problem like the DVMT (see Chapter 3), the movements of several independent vehicles will be detected over a period of time by one or more distinct sensors, where each sensor is associated with an agent. The performance of agents in such an environment is based on how long it takes them to create complete vehicle tracks, including the cost of communication. The organizational structure of the agents will imply the portions of each vehicle track that are sensed by each agent.

In our model of DSN problems, each vehicle track is modeled as a task group (problem instance). Several task groups (vehicle tracks) may occur simultaneously in a single problem-solving *episode*. The simplest objective model is that each task group $\mathfrak{I}_i$ is associated with a track of length l_i and has the following objective structure, based on a simplified version of the DVMT: (l_i) vehicle location methods (VLM) that represent processing raw signal data at a single location resulting in a single vehicle location hypothesis; ($l_i - 1$) vehicle tracking methods (VTM) that represent short tracks connecting the results of the VLM at time t with the results of the VLM at time $t + 1$; and one vehicle-track completion method (VCM) that represents merging all the VTMs together into a complete vehicle track hypothesis. *Nonlocal effects*, which relate the executions of tasks to one another, exist as shown in Figure 16.1—two VLMs *enable* each VTM, and all VTMs *enable* the lone VCM. This structure is fairly common in many other environments, where a large amount of detailed work needs to be done, the results of which are collected at a single location or agent and processed again (integrated), and so on up a hierarchy. The question is: to achieve a particular level of performance, how many agents are needed and how should they be organized in their unique and/or overlapping capabilities for accomplishing the necessary tasks? Coordination is used not only to accomplish the necessary transfer of results from one agent to another, but to avoid redundant work on the part of agents with overlapping capabilities, and also to potentially balance the workloads.

We have used this model to develop expressions for the expected value of, and confidence intervals on, the time of termination of a set of agents in any arbitrary DSN environment that has a static organizational structure and coordination algorithm (Decker and Lesser, 1993b,d). We have also used this model to analyze a dynamic, one-shot reorganization algorithm (and have shown when the extra overhead is worthwhile versus the static algorithm). In each case we can predict the effects of adding more agents, changing the relative cost of communication and computation, and changing how the agents are organized (in the range and overlap of their capabilities). These results were achieved by direct mathematical analysis of the model and verified through simulation in TÆMS.

Decker and Lesser (1993d) adds significant complexity to this basic model, making it more like the DVMT. For example, it adds the characteristic that

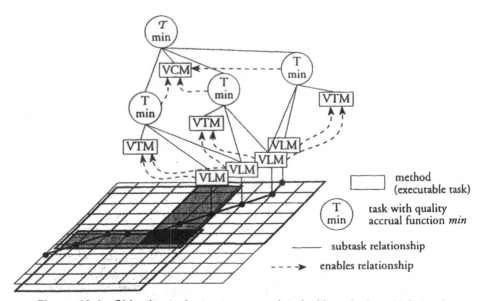

Figure 16.1 *Objective task structure associated with a single vehicle track.*

each agent has two methods with which to deal with sensed data: a normal VLM and a "level-hopping" VLM (the level-hopping VLM produces less quality than the full method but requires less time; see Decker et al., 1990, 1993) for this and other approximate methods; a similar technique can be used to model agents who have different capabilities such as processor speed). It also adds a representation of faulty sensors (a subjective level effect), and result sharing, as well as modeling the relationships that low-quality results early on tend to make things harder to process at higher levels, that the first VLM execution provides information that slightly shortens the executions of other VLMs in the same vehicle track,[2] and that a similar *facilitation* effect occurs at the tracking level (tracking gets easier as more of the track is completed). We can also represent subjective features such as faulty sensors, external noise, and "ghost" tracks (like the example in Chapter 3). In general, having different subjective mappings for different agents or classes of agents allows us to model situations where some agents are more, less, or simply differently "informed" than others.

2.4 Hospital Patient Scheduling Example

Let us look at a second example in a completely different domain, hospital patient scheduling (refer to Chapter 4 for details of other DAI applications). The following description is from an actual case study (Ow et al., 1989):

> Patients in General Hospital reside in *units* that are organized by branches of medicine, such as orthopedics or neurosurgery. Each day, physicians request certain tests and/or therapy to be performed as a part of the diagnosis and treatment of a patient. . . . Tests are performed by separate, independent, and distally located *ancillary departments* in the hospital. The radiology department, for example, provides X-ray services and may receive requests from a number of different units in the hospital.

Furthermore, each test may interact with other tests in relationships such as *enables*, *requires* (must be performed after), and *inhibits* (test A's performance invalidates test B's result if A is performed during specified time period relative to B). Note that the unit secretaries (as scheduling agents) try to minimize the patients' stays in the hospital, while the ancillary secretaries (as scheduling agents) try to maximize equipment use (throughput) and minimize setup times.

Figure 16.2 shows a subjective TÆMS task structure corresponding to an episode in this domain, and the subjective views of the unit and ancillary scheduling agents after four tests have been ordered. Note that quite a bit of detail can be captured in just the "computational" aspects of the environment—in this case, the tasks use people's time, not a computer's. However, TÆMS can model in more detail the physical resources and job shop characteristics of

---

[2]This is because the sensors have been properly configured with the correct signal processing algorithm parameters with which to sense that particular vehicle.

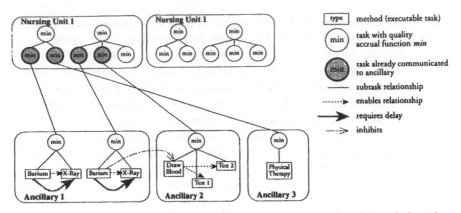

Figure 16.2 *High-level, subjective task structure for a typical hospital patient scheduling episode. The top task in each ancillary is really the same objective entity as the unit task it is linked to in the diagram.*

the ancillaries if necessary (Decker and Lesser, 1993e). Such detail is not necessary to analyze the solution presented by Ow et al. (1989), who propose a primary unit-ancillary protocol and a secondary ancillary-ancillary protocol.

We use *min* (AND) to represent quality accrual because in general neither the nursing units nor ancillaries can change the doctor's orders—all tests must be done as prescribed. We have added two new nonlocal effects: *requires-delay* and *inhibits*. The first effect says that a certain amount δ of time must pass after executing one method before the second is enabled. We could define it mathematically as follows:

$$\textbf{requires-delay}(T_a, M, t, d, q, \delta)$$

$$= \begin{cases} [\mathbf{d}_0(M), 0] & \text{Start}(M) < \text{Finish}(T_A) + \delta \\ [\mathbf{d}_0(M), \mathbf{q}_0(M)] & \text{Start}(M) \geq \text{Finish}(T_A) + \delta \end{cases} \tag{2}$$

The second relationship, *A inhibits B*, means that *B* will not produce any quality if executed in a certain window of time relative to the execution of *A*, and can be defined in a similar manner to the previous example.

3 Using TÆMS: Experiences

The first step in using TÆMS is to build a model of the environment of interest. Often the easiest way to go about this is to first model a single, detailed episode at the objective and subjective levels, and then to use that as a basis for a generative level model. TÆMS supplies several quality accumulation functions (*min, max, mean,* and *sum*) and predefined nonlocal effects (*enables, precedes, facilitates*, and *hinders* for tasks; *uses* and *limits* for resources), but you can extend the set. If you are interested only in general coordination problems, comparing architectures, etc., there is also a random structure generator. It takes parameters such as mean branching factor (Poisson), mean depth (Poisson), mean duration (exponential), user-defined quality accumulation function distributions, etc. This basic structure can then be extended by *patterns*, such as "random but consistent hard nonlocal effects" or "fast fallback methods," each of which will take other parameters. The set of predefined patterns can also be extended. Several different task group templates can be defined with specified interarrival times for each, and the random structures can be recreated for paired-response experiments (running several algorithms or architectures on the same randomly generated episode). At this point the analysis of the endogenous features of individual episodes, given generative parameters, can take place. If the model is of a real domain, a verification phase would also be mandatory.

TÆMS assumes only a simple view of agents as loci of belief (state) and action (see Chapters 2 and 9). A mathematical analysis will usually proceed with a formal specification of what actions an agent will take based on its current beliefs (for example, the agent-oriented programming model of Shoham, 1991; see Chapter 3). TÆMS provides a meta-structure for the agent's state-transition function that is divided into the following four parts: control, information gathering, communication, and method execution. First the control mechanisms assert (commit to) information gathering, communication, and method execution actions and then these actions are computed one at a time, after which the cycle of meta-states repeats. Predefined information gathering actions in TÆMS (which trade computational time for information about the current task structure) include accessing newly arrived subjective task structures and uncovering coordination relationships to other agents' tasks. Predefined communication actions include transmitting the current result of a method execution (or task), transmitting parts of the task structure, and meta-level communications (cf. Chapters 13 and 14). Method execution actions are, of course, the execution of methods in the structure by agents. TÆMS currently supports simple sequential execution, execution with monitoring, suspension, and preemption of methods, and is being extended to interruptable execution and internal agent parallelism.

We will briefly describe some of our experiences with TÆMS in distributed problem solving situations; we have also been using it to examine issues in single agent real-time scheduling and parallel scheduling (Garvey et al., 1993; Garvey and Lesser, 1993).

3.1 Analyzing a Simple Distributed Sensor Network

We have been developing a methodology for analyzing, explaining, and predicting behavior that focuses on chaining models of the environment, of coordination mechanisms, and of principled agent construction together and examining the flow of various uncertainties from the external environment through the models to the collective agent behaviors. We illustrated this with a mathematical analysis of a simplified distributed sensor network problem, verified through simulation (Decker and Lesser, 1993b,c).

The methodology we have been building uses the TÆMS framework and other DAI formalisms to build and chain together statistical models of coordination behavior that focus on the sources of uncertainty or variance in the environment and agents, and their effect on the (potentially multicriteria) performance of the agents. We have used this methodology to develop expressions for the expected value of, and confidence intervals on, the time of termination of a set of agents in any arbitrary simple DSN environment that has a static organizational structure and coordination algorithm (Decker and Lesser, 1993b). This chapter shows how the distributions of objective parameters such as "the number of VLM methods seen by the maximally loaded agent" ($\hat{S}$) and "the max number of task groups seen by the same agent" ($\hat{N}$) can be defined from just the generative parameters $\mathfrak{D} = \langle A, \eta, r, o, \mathfrak{I} \rangle$.[3]

For example, the total time until termination for an agent receiving an initial data set of size $\hat{S}$ is the time to do local work, combine results from other agents, and build the completed results, plus two communication and information gathering actions:

$$\hat{S}\mathbf{d}_0(\text{VLM}) + (\hat{S} - \hat{N})\mathbf{d}_0(\text{VTM}) + (a - 1)\hat{N}\mathbf{d}_0(\text{VTM})$$

$$+ \hat{N}\mathbf{d}_0(\text{VCM}) + 2\mathbf{d}_0(I) + 2\mathbf{d}_0(C) \tag{3}$$

We can use Equation (3) as a predictor by combining it with the probabilities for the values of $\hat{S}$ and $\hat{N}$. Decker and Lesser (1993b) verify this model using the simulation component of TÆMS.

We have also used this model to analyze a dynamic, one-shot negotiated reorganization algorithm (and have shown when the extra overhead is worthwhile versus the static algorithm) (Decker and Lesser, 1993c). In each case we can predict the effects of adding more agents, changing the relative cost of communication and computation, and changing how the agents are organized (in this case, by changing the range and overlap of their capabilities). These results were achieved by direct mathematical analysis of the model and verified through simulation in TÆMS. The interested reader will find the details in our papers (Decker and Lesser, 1993b,c).

3.2 Generalizing the Partial Global Planning Algorithm

The PGP approach to distributed coordination (Durfee and Lesser, 1991), also described in Chapter 8, increased the coordination of agents in a network by such methods as scheduling the timely generation of partial results, avoiding

---

[3]A DSN environment $\mathfrak{D}$ can be described by the following parameters: A, the number of sensor agents; η, the average number of vehicle tracks in an episode; r, the range of the agents' sensors; o, the amount of overlap between agent sensors; $\mathfrak{I}$, which describes the task structure induced by each track given its length (derived from the other parameters).

redundant activities, shifting tasks to idle nodes, and indicating compatibility between goals. It achieved this by recognizing certain *coordination relationships* (nonlocal effects across agents) among tasks in the DVMT environment and producing the appropriate scheduling constraints. In fact, because the local scheduler was so simple, the PGP mechanism supplanted it, recording and responding to many of the appropriate scheduling constraints itself. This work has had the characteristic of showing coordination techniques that are helpful, but not providing a deep analysis of when and why they are appropriate.

Generalized PGP (GPGP) is really a family of algorithms; it is an extendable set of cooperative (team-oriented) coordination mechanisms built of modular components that work in conjunction with, but do not replace, a fully functional agent with a local scheduler. Each component can be added as required in reaction to the environment in which the agents find themselves a part. We have analyzed the performance of several GPGP family members through simulation in conjunction with a heuristic real-time local scheduler and randomly generated abstract task environments.

This approach views the coordination mechanism as *modulating* local control, not supplanting it—a two level process that makes a clear distinction between coordination behavior and local scheduling (Corkill and Lesser, 1983). By concentrating on the creation of local scheduling constraints, we avoid the sequentiality of scheduling in partial global planning that occurs when there are multiple plans. By separating coordination from local scheduling, we can also take advantage of advances in real-time scheduling algorithms to produce CDPS systems that respond to real-time deadlines. We can also take advantage of local schedulers that have a great deal of domain scheduling knowledge already encoded within them. Finally, we can rely on humans as well in making local scheduling decisions. Our approach allows consideration of termination issues that were glossed over in the PGP work (where termination was handled by an external oracle).

The GPGP approach specifies three basic areas of the agent's coordination behavior: how and when to communicate and construct nonlocal views of the current problem-solving situation; how and when to exchange the partial results of problem solving; how and when to make and break *commitments* to other agents about what results will be available and when (see Chapter 6). The GPGP approach of recognizing and reacting to the characteristics of certain coordination relationships is shared with von Martial's work on the *favor* relationship (von Martial, 1992). The use of commitments in the GPGP family of algorithms is based on the ideas of many other researchers (Cohen and Levesque, 1990; Shoham, 1991; Castelfranchi, 1993; Jennings, 1993). Each agent also has a heuristic local scheduler that decides what actions the agent should take and when, based on its current view of the problem-solving situation (including the commitments it has made), and a utility function. The coordination mechanisms supply nonlocal views of problem solving to the local scheduler, including *what* nonlocal results will be available locally, and *when* they will be available. The local scheduler creates (and monitors the execution of) schedules that attempt to maximize systemwide quality through both local action and the use of nonlocal actions (committed to by other agents) without resorting to a complete global problem view.

One question that we have examined in TÆMS is the effects of agents exchanging nonlocal views (one of the GPGP coordination mechanisms; see Figure 16.3), and the decomposability of tasks in the environment (expressed as a probability on nonlocal effects), on system performance in terms of communication, total agent workloads, overall solution quality, and termination time. We showed that there were significant differences in communication and agent workloads due to both task decomposability and exchange of nonlocal views (but no interaction effects).

Another question we have examined is the effect of task structure variance on the performance of load-balancing algorithms. This work is a logical follow-on to the analysis of static and dynamic negotiated reorganization summarized in the last section. A *static* organization divides the load up a priori—in this

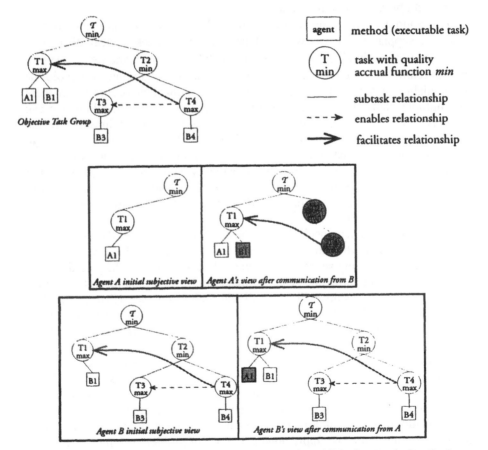

Figure 16.3 *Example of the local view at agents A and B before and after the team shares private information to create a partial nonlocal view. Method boxes are labeled by the name of the agent that has the method.*

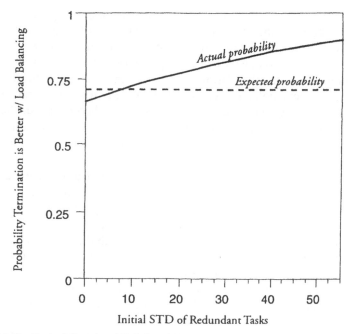

Figure 16.4 *Probability that MLC load balancing will terminate more quickly than static load balancing, fitted using a loglinear model from actual TÆMS simulation data.*

case, by randomly assigning redundant tasks to agents. A *one-shot dynamic* reorganization, like that analyzed by Decker and Lesser (1993c), negotiates the handling of redundant tasks on the basis of the *expected* load on other agents. A *meta-level communication* (MLC) reorganization negotiates the handling of redundant tasks on the basis of actual information about the particular problem-solving episode at hand. Because it requires extra communication, the MLC reorganization is more expensive, but the extra information pays off as the *variance* in static agent loads grows. Figure 16.4 shows how the probability of terminating more quickly with the MLC load-balancing mechanism grows as the standard deviation in the total durations of redundant tasks at each agent grows.

More information about GPGP, including the formal definition of five example coordination mechanisms and experimental methodology for determining when a mechanism is appropriate, can be found in Decker and Lesser (1995).

4 SUMMARY AND FUTURE WORK

TÆMS is a framework for modeling complex task environments. TÆMS exists as both a language for stating general hypotheses or theories and as a system for simulation. The important features of TÆMS include its layered description of environments (*objective* reality, *subjective* mapping to agent beliefs, *generative* description of the other levels across single instances); its acceptance of any performance criteria (based on temporal location and *quality* of task executions); and its non-agent-centered point of view that can be used by researchers working in either formal systems of mental-state-induced behavior or experimental methodologies. TÆMS provides environmental and behavioral structures and features with which to state and test theories about the control of agents in complex computational domains, such as how decisions made in scheduling one task will affect the utility and performance characteristics of other tasks.

TÆMS is not only a mathematical framework, but also a simulation language for executing and experimenting with models directly. The TÆMS simulator supports the graphical display of generated subjective and objective task structures, agent actions, and statistical data collection in CLOS on the TI Explorer and DEC Alpha. These features help in both the model-building stage and the verification stage. The TÆMS simulator is being used not only for research into the coordination of distributed problem solvers but also for research into real-time scheduling of a single agent (Garvey and Lesser, 1993), scheduling at an agent with parallel processing resources available, learning coordination relationships, and computational organizational design.

TÆMS does not at this time automatically learn models or automatically verify them. While we have taken initial steps at designing a methodology for verification (see Decker and Lesser, 1993b), this is still an open area of research (Cohen, 1991). Work now being done includes building new models of different environments that include physical resource constraints, such as hospital patient scheduling and airport resource scheduling. Other extensions we are now working on include more helpful facilities for specifying dynamic objective and subjective models that change structure as the result of agent actions (like the Tower of Babel; Ishida, 1992). Such models add yet another important source of uncertainty that can be a factor in influencing agent organization.

Current applications being developed using TÆMS and the GPGP approach include distributed support for human scheduling in concurrent engineering environments like the ARCADIA software engineering development environment (Taylor et al., 1988). Part of the ARCADIA environment is directly concerned with representing and tracking the state of software development processes (including interrelationships), the products being produced, and the resources available. This information can be used to assist users in task selection by developing a user coordination assistant agent (UCAA) that keeps track of a workstation user's current agenda of tasks and presents a possible schedule (ordering) of these tasks according to user- and domain-directed preferences. Such an agenda is developed not in isolation but through a distributed coordination process using multiple coordination mechanisms triggered by the coordination relationships between the task structures of the different agents involved.

Another application being developed is one using TÆMS to represent and reason about multiagent information retrieval on the Internet. The idea here is to have teams of agents search for useful information. The results of some team member's searchers will have an impact on other team members in a way that can be modeled with TÆMS. Algorithms, such as new GPGP mechanisms, can then be developed to take advantage of these opportunities. Another direction we are pursuing is to use TÆMS to build computational versions of organizational theories, such as Williamson's transaction cost economics (Williamson, 1975). Finally, we wish to expand our analyses beyond the questions of scheduling and coordination to questions about negotiation strategies, emergent agent/society behavior, and organizational self-design.

ACKNOWLEDGMENTS

Many people have worked on the development of TÆMS including Alan J. Garvey, Marty A. Humphrey, and Victor R. Lesser. This work was supported in part by DARPA contract N00014-92-J-1698, Office of Naval Research contract N00014-92-J-1450, and NSF contract CDA 8922572. The content of the information does not necessarily reflect the position or the policy of the U.S. Government and no official endorsement should be inferred.

REFERENCES

Boddy, M., and Dean, T. (1989). Solving time-dependent planning problems. *Proc. Int. Jt. Conf. Artif. Intell., 11th*, Detroit, MI, *1989*, pp. 979–984.

Burton, R. M., and Obel, B. (1984). *Designing Efficient Organizations: Modelling and Experimentation*. North-Holland Publ., Amsterdam.

Carver, N., and Lesser, V. (1991). A new framework for sensor interpretation: Planning to resolve sources of uncertainty. *Proc. Natl. Conf. Artif. Intell., 9th*, Anaheim, CA, pp. 724–731.

Castelfranchi, C. (1993). Commitments: From individual intentions to groups and organizations. In *AI and Theories of Groups and Organizations: Conceptual and Empirical Research* (M. Prietula, ed.), AAAI Workshop, Work. Notes.

Cohen, P. R. (1991). A survey of the Eighth National Conference on Artificial Intelligence: Pulling together or pulling apart? *AI Mag.* **12**(1), 16–41.

Cohen, P. R., Greenberg, M., Hart, D., and Howe, A. (1989). 'Trial by fire: Understanding the design requirements for agents in complex environments. *AI Mag.* **10**(3), 33–48.

Cohen, P. R., and Levesque, H. J. (1990). Intention is choice with commitment. *Artif. Intell.* **42**(3), 213–261.

Corkill, D. D., and Lesser, V. R. (1983). The use of meta-level control for coordination in a distributed problem solving network. *Proc. Intl. Jt. Conf. Artif. Intell., 8th*, Karlsruhe, Germany, *1983*, pp. 748–755.

Decker, K. S., and Lesser, V. R. (1992). Generalizing the partial global planning algorithm. *Int. J. Intell. Coop. Inf. Syst.* **1**(2), 319–346.

Decker, K. S., and Lesser, V. R. (1993a). Analyzing a quantitative coordination relationship. *Group Decis. Negot.* **2**(3), 195–217.

Decker, K. S., and Lesser, V. R. (1993b). An approach to analyzing the need for meta-level communication. *Proc. Int. Jt. Conf. Artif. Intell.*, *13th*, Chambéry, France, *1993*, pp. 360–366.

Decker, K. S., and Lesser, V. R. (1993c). A one-shot dynamic coordination algorithm for distributed sensor networks. *Proc. Natl. Conf. Artif. Intell.*, *11th*, Washington, DC, pp. 210–216.

Decker, K. S., and Lesser, V. R. (1993d). Quantitative modeling of complex computational task environments. *Proc. Natl. Conf. Artif. Intell.*, *11th*, Washington, DC, pp. 217–224.

Decker, K. S., and Lesser, V. R. (1993e). Quantitative modeling of complex environments. *Int. J. Intell. Syst. Acc., Finance, Manage.* **2**(4), 215–234. Special issue on "Mathematical and Computational Models of Organizations: Models and Characteristics of Agent Behavior."

Decker, K. S., and Lesser, V. R. (1995). Designing a family of coordination algorithms. *Proc. First. Int. Conf. on Multi-Agent Systems*, San Francisco, CA, pp. 73–80.

Decker, K. S., Lesser, V. R., and Whitehair, R. C. (1990). Extending a blackboard architecture for approximate processing. *J. Real-Time Syst.* **2**(1/2), 47–79.

Decker, K. S., Garvey, A. J., Humphrey, M. A., and Lesser, V. R. (1993). A real-time control architecture for an approximate processing blackboard system. *Int. J. Pattern Recognition Artif. Intell.* **7**(2), 265–284.

Durfee, E., and Lesser, V. (1991). Partial global planning: A coordination framework for distributed hypothesis formation. *IEEE Trans. Syst. Man Cybernet.* **SMC-21**(5), 1167–1183.

Durfee, E. H., Lesser, V. R., and Corkill, D. D. (1987). Coherent cooperation among communicating problem solvers. *IEEE Trans. Comp.* **36**(11), 1275–1291.

Galbraith, J. (1977). *Organizational Design.* Addison-Wesley, Reading, MA.

Garvey, A., and Lesser, V. (1993). Design-to-time real-time scheduling. *IEEE Trans. Syst. Man Cybernet.* **SMC-23**(6), 1491–1502.

Garvey, A., Humphrey, M., and Lesser, V. (1993). Task interdependencies in design-to-time real-time scheduling. *Proc. Natl. Conf. Artif. Intell.*, *11th*, Washington, DC, pp. 580–585.

Gasser, L. (1991). Social conceptions of knowledge and action. *Artif. Intell.* **47**(1), 107–138.

Ishida, T. (1992). Tower of Babel: Towards organization-centered problem solving. *Proc. Int. Workshop Distributed Artif. Intell.*, *11th*, The Homestead, Glen Arbor, MI, pp. 141–153.

Jennings, N. R. (1993). Commitments and conventions: The foundation of coordination in multi-agent systems. *Knowl. Eng. Rev.* **8**(3), 223–250.

Lawrence, P., and Lorsch, J. (1967). *Organization and Environment.* Harvard Univ. Press, Cambridge, MA.

Liu, J. W. S., Lin, K. J., Shih, W. K., Yu, A. C., Chung, J. Y., and Zhao, W. (1991). Algorithms for scheduling imprecise computations. *IEEE Comput.* **24**(5), 58–68.

Malone, T. W. (1987). Modeling coordination in organizations and markets. *Manage. Sci.* **33,** 1317–1332.

Ow, P. S., Prietula, M. J., and Hsu, W. (1989). Configuring knowledge-based systems to organizational structures: Issues and examples in multiple agent support. In *Expert Systems in Economics, Banking, and Management* (L. F. Pau, J. Motiwalla, Y. H. Pao, and H. H. Teh, eds.), pp. 309–318. North-Holland Publ., Amsterdam.

Pollack, M. E., and Ringuette, M. (1990). Introducing Tileworld: Experimentally evaluating agent architectures. *Proc. Natl. Conf. Artif. Intell., 8th*, Boston, pp. 183–189.

Russell, S. J., and Zilberstein, S. (1991). Composing real-time systems. *Proc. Int. Jt. Conf. Artif. Intell., 12th*, Sydney, Australia, *1991*, pp. 212–217.

Scott, W. R. (1987). *Organizations: Rational, Natural, and Open Systems.* Prentice-Hall, Englewood Cliffs, NJ.

Shoham, Y. (1991). AGENT0: A simple agent language and its interpreter. *Proc. Natl. Conf. Artif. Intell., 9th*, Anaheim, CA, pp. 704–709.

Shoham, Y., and Tennenholtz, M. (1992). On the synthesis of useful social laws for artificial agnet societies (preliminary report). *Proc. Natl. Conf. Artif. Intell., 10th*, San Jose, CA, pp. 276–281.

Stinchcombe, A. L. (1990). *Information and Organizations.* Univ. of California Press, Berkeley.

Taylor, R., Belz, F., Clarke, L., Osterweil, L., Selby, W., Wileden, J., Wolfe, A., and Young, M. (1988). Foundations for the Arcadia environment architecture. *Proc. ACM SIGSOFT/SIGPLAN Software Eng. Symp. Pract. Software Dev. Eviron.*, Boston, pp. 1–12.

Thompson, J. D. (1967). *Organizations in Action.* McGraw-Hill, New York.

von Martial, F. (1992). *Coordinating Plans of Autonomous Agents*, Lect. Notes Artif. Intell. No. 610. Springer-Verlag, Berlin.

Williamson, O. E. (1975). *Markets and Hierarchies: Analysis and Antitrust Implications.* Free Press, New York.

Zlotkin, G., and Rosenschein, J. S. (1991). Incomplete information and deception in multi-agent negotiation. *Proc. Int. Jt. Conf. Artif. Intell., 12th*, Sydney, Australia, *1991*, pp. 225–231.

Agent Factory: An Environment for the Fabrication of Multiagent Systems

GREG M. P. O'HARE

1 INTRODUCTION

It has widely been accepted that the social and private behaviors of agents need to be governed by some theory which facilitates reasoning about such agent communities (see Chapters 1, 2, 6, 7, and 9, and Jennings, 1993). Of late, the subject has witnessed an explosion of such competing theories, many of which are articulated in higher-order logics, epistemic, temporal (see Chapter 10), dynamic, to mention but a few. These logics typically encompass the requisite level of expressiveness but, in so doing, present considerable difficulties for the development of computationally tractable systems that can perform auto-mated deductions based upon them. All too often systems or theories articulated or specified in this manner cannot directly be executed and necessarily they have to be transformed into an alternate formalism. This transformation process can be tortuous and frequently represents an opportunity for the introduction of numerous logical errors whereby the logical content of the theory is not truly captured or is incorrectly captured.

An alternative approach is to adopt a notation that can be directly executed. In embracing this approach there is of course a price to pay, the expressiveness of the medium is typically compromised and it may prove difficult, or almost impossible, to accurately specify certain concepts. Nevertheless, within this chapter it is the approach that we adopt, in an attempt to *actually* realize some of the more abstract concepts described within the multiagent literature. We

Foundations of Distributed Artificial Intelligence, Edited by G. M. P. O'Hare and N. R. Jennings. ISBN 0-471-00675-0 © 1996 John Wiley & Sons, Inc.

seek to get first-hand experience of these ideas in an attempt to gain a more profound understanding.

Specifically this research is based upon the precept that multiagent systems, like complex systems generally, need to be developed in a systematic manner (Cohen et al., 1986). Their behavior needs to be able to be defined in an unambiguous manner and this description must be amenable to inspection. A formal approach is adopted here to the specification of multiagent systems, that of an algebraic technique. Agent Factory like DAI testbeds generally (see Chapter 3) seeks to provide an environment which supports the fabrication of, and subsequent experimentation with, multiagent systems. Complimentary systems are discussed in Part III of this book.

The remainder of this chapter is structured as follows. Section 2 outlines some assumptions inherent in the design of Agent Factory, a system that supports the systematic development of multiagent systems, while Section 3 describes in some detail the design of the system. Section 4 returns to the issue of realizing an implementation, outlining possible alternatives and defending our particular choice. It goes on to explain the systematic development of the software. Section 5 presents the conclusions.

2 SOME BASIC ASSUMPTIONS

Several basic assumptions have been made in the design and development of the Agent Factory system. We shall consider these briefly and outline the motivation behind such assumptions.

The Time Model. The model of time commissioned within the Agent Factory system is that of a linear discrete model of time. Time can thus be visualized as a number line with time commencing at some point, say 0. Thus future time points can be considered as lying to the right of the current time point (*now*), while past time points lie to the left. This model enables time to be mapped on to an enumerated data type and as such represents a very simple and convenient model and its elapse is modeled through the evaluation of a successor function on such a data type.

Message Transmission. The communication medium within which our agents will exist is assumed to be very stable. A *guaranteed delivery* assumption is made which presupposes that messages sent are delivered correctly. By correctly we mean that two important principles are enforced. These are

1. The *content perservance principle*, which states that the content of any given message $m_{a,b}$ remains unaltered during transmission from agent a to agent b.

2. The *privacy principle*, which states that for any given message $m_{a,b1,..,b4}$ is sent to those destinations requested and only those destinations. In the

example above the message *m* would be delivered to *b1*, *b2*, *b3*, and *b4* only.

In reality such assumptions are somewhat presumptuous. In the case of the content preservance principle most systems seek to identify when the content has not successfully been preserved and in such circumstances retransmit. Such detection can easily be achieved through the typing of messages. Type information could be used to impose run-time constraints upon communications that could be checked before transmission or receipt to ensure the correctness of the data. Any corruption could therefore be attributed to the unreliability of the communication medium employed. This kind of approach is adopted within SANDRA (Elshiewy, 1990).

The privacy principle normally involves complex encryption and decryption.

Message Ownership. We also assume that for any given message *m* there is one, and only one, agent from whom the message can be said to have originated.

Benevolence. In general agents within the factory environment are considered as essentially being benevolent in nature. We will later return to this point and illustrate how the degree of benevolence may be adjusted.

Asynchronized Communication. Within our simulation we have assumed that agents communicate in an asynchronous manner. The transfer of data is performed in a buffered manner with the data being deposited and retrieved from the central message pool. The communication protocol is asymmetric, in that the identity of the sender is announced at dispatch time but at retrieval time the receiver typically does not know the sender.

We are aware that this approach to separating communication from process synchronization has been criticized within the distributed systems literature. As Young (1982) states: "The act of divorcing process synchronization from that of process communication is fundamentally unnatural." This separation is enforced through the particular choice of implementation medium that we commissioned. Nevertheless the criticisms are noted and accepted. Agents thus deposit messages in a global buffer,[1] which are typically retrieved by the receiving agent(s) on and when when they are next scheduled.[2]

Static Capabilities. It is assumed that there are no learning capabilities within our agents. Thus the capabilities of any given agent remains static with time. This assumption is enforced in order to simplify certain aspects of system design and in no way represents a cognitive deficiency in our approach. The

---

[1] The global buffer is assumed to have an infinite capacity.
[2] This, however, is not necessarily the case and agent behavior may be specialized such that they exhibit priority to correspondence of a particular type or from a particular source.

simplest form of learning could be equated with the exchange of expertise, through the transmission of capabilities. No concept of capability exchange is permitted at present within Agent Factory.

Community Dynamics. In reality introductions occur in an often ad hoc manner, and as a consequence the social dynamics of agent communities are in a continual state of flux.

Clearly our system seeks not to model such dynamics. For our purposes we presume that our agent communities primarily represent those scenarios where the social structure is well defined and persists over time.

Gullible Agents. It is assumed that all agents within Agent Factory are gullible. We therefore assume that if any given agent is informed of a fact at a given instant in time, then they will believe the information communicated. Each agent presumes that all agents within their community act in good faith. They exhibit an inherent trust of their neighbors.

3 THE DESIGN OF AGENT FACTORY

The design of Agent Factory was approached in a traditional top-down manner. Several key entities were identified as being central to the design; these included the agent, the message pool, and the scheduler (Figures 17.1 and 17.2). The following sections present the main components in a notation akin to VDM (Bjorner and Jones, 1978; Jones, 1980; Jones, 1990).

3.1 Time

As described in Section 2 a discrete linear time model is adopted. Thus a type *Time* is introduced such that it is a member of the set of natural numbers. Hence

$$Time = N$$

where N represents the set of natural numbers.

3.2 Clock

The global system clock is defined in terms of a type called *clock*. Even though we assume that there is only one time zone that applies to our entire agent community, clearly this need not always be the case. Increasingly, organizations, including multiagent organizations, span several time zones, and it is often important that the abstract time within the system directly reflects real-world time. For this reason it may be necessary to differentiate between different

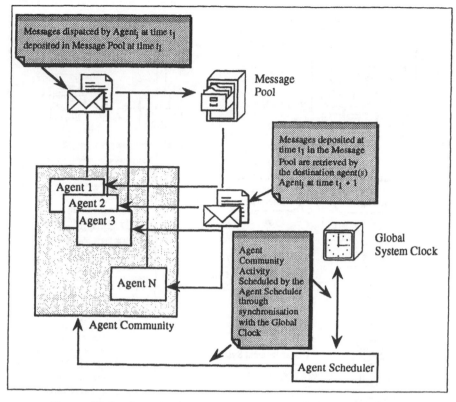

Figure 17.1 *Asynchronous communication via the message pool.*

clocks which act as the temporal frame of reference for varying groups within the agent community. Thus each clock is assigned a unique name drawn from a set of *Clock_name*. The type Clock_name is defined thus:

$$Clock\_name = \{global, cl_2, cl_3, \ldots , cl_n\}$$

We assume a single clock which we will call *global*. The type clock is defined as a triple as follows:

$$Clock = Clock\_name \times Time \times Time$$

It consists of a unique name and two arguments of type time. The first time, *current time*, represents the time at which the system commences from, while the second time refers to the *alarm time*.

Four discrete functions are supported by any given clock *tick*, *now*, *set alarm* and *sound alarm*. Clocks clearly *tick*, and the act of ticking symbolizes and

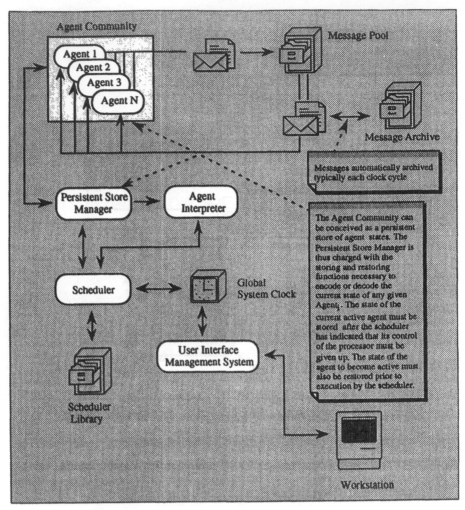

Figure 17.2   *The Agent Factory schematic architecture.*

calibrates the passing of time. A *tick* function can thus be defined such that

$$tick : Clock \rightarrow Clock$$

$$tick \ (clk) \ \triangleq$$

$$\text{let } \langle global, \ t_1, \ t_2 \rangle \ = clk \text{ in}$$

$$t_1 = \bar{t}_1 + 1$$

The *now* function returns the current time and as such constitutes a destructor function. The now function would thus be defined as

$$now : Clock \rightarrow Time$$

$$now \ (clk) \ \triangleq$$

$$\text{let } \langle global, \ t_1, \ t_2 \rangle \ = \ clk \text{ in}$$

$$t_1$$

The final two functions supported are those relating to the alarm. The set alarm function merely specifies a value for the alarm set time. Thus

$$set\_alarm : Clock \times Time \rightarrow Clock$$

$$set\_alarm \ (clk, \ alarm\_time) \ \triangleq$$

$$\text{let } \langle global, \ t_1, \ t_2 \rangle \ = \ clk \text{ in}$$

$$\langle global, \ t_1, \ alarm\_time \rangle$$

Finally the sound_alarm function

$$sound\_alarm : Clock \rightarrow \mathbf{B}$$

$$sound\_alarm \ \ (clk) \ \triangleq$$

$$\text{let } \langle global, \ t_1, \ t_2 \rangle \ = \ clk \text{ in}$$

$$(t_1 \ = \ t_2)$$

3.3 Agent Names

Each agent within Agent Factory is unique at least in the respect that they have a unique identifier. We identify agents by name and consequently we identify a type called *Agt_names*, which includes a set of all agent names. More formally we define Agent_names thus:

$$Agt\_names \ = \ \{n_1, \ n_2, \ \ldots \ , \ n_n\}$$

where each element of the set n_j is an identifier.

3.4 Agent Status

Due to the dynamics of the environment within which agents are situated their epistemic state is typically in a continuous state of flux. Agents within Agent Factory are executed concurrently and consequently their execution is interleaved with that of their peers.

As with most concurrent systems the state of each agent can assist in the opportunistic scheduling of such processes. Each agent within Agent Factory

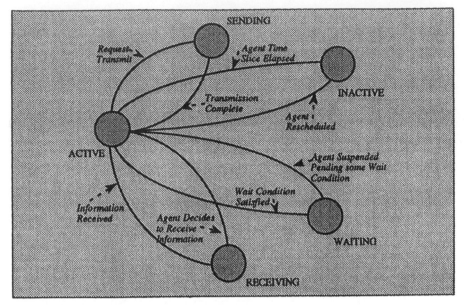

Figure 17.3   *The agent finite state machine.*

at any given can take one of five agent states: active, inactive, sending, receiving, waiting. Agents can migrate from one state to another according to certain conditions and as such can be viewed as finite-state machines. Figure 17.3 depicts a finite-state machine representation of these agent states.

Nodes represent states, while the arcs represent permissible transitions between agent states and the associated events that result in such a state change.

We introduce a new type *state* defined thus

$$state = \{active,\ inactive,\ sending,\ receiving,\ waiting\}$$

At any given instance in time any given agent is said to be in one of these states. The activities of sending and receiving are regarded as indivisible events. Thus an agent who begins sending a message will not be suspended until such a transmission has been effected; likewise with the act of receiving a message or messages.[3]

3.5 Belief

As is traditionally the case we have adopted Konolidge's deductive model of belief. This has in essence become the de facto choice when modelling belief

---

[3]This can be assumed due to the fact that synchronized communication is not supported. Frequently when distributed systems adopt a rendezvous-style communication protocol one process needs to await the other before the necessary exchange of data can occur.

systems. We assume that an agents beliefs can be modelled using some logical formalism. This logical language is referred to by Konolidge as the *internal* language. A set of a beliefs or "Belief Set" can thus be expressed as a set of formula in this logical language L. More formally we introduce a type called *Belset* such that

$$Belset = \text{powerset of Formula}(L)$$

We generally represent belief sets by the symbol Δ. The initial belief set is represented as Δ_0. Like all belief sets ours are dynamic and are subject to revision. The belief set can thus be revised through the disciplined use of belief revision functions. In addition, deductions may be performed on the belief set. Thus an initial belief set could be augmented through the application of deduction rules. This set of deduction rules we will denote by λ. In agent factory such belief sets are subject to closure under such deduction rules. More formally we define a closure function thus:

$$closure : \text{Belset} \times \text{powerset } \lambda \rightarrow \text{Belset}$$

$$closure \ (\Delta, \lambda) \triangleq \{\beta | \Delta >_\lambda \beta\}$$

The closure function adheres to three basic rules (Cohen et al., 1986):

1. Every set of beliefs are contained in its own closure.

$$\forall(\beta) \subset \Delta . \beta \subseteq closure(\beta)$$

2. Monotonity rule, whereby every belief set's closure contains the closure of all its subsets.

$$\forall(\beta)\forall(\chi) \subseteq \Delta . \beta \subseteq \chi \ closure(\beta) \subseteq closure(\chi)$$

3. Closure is maximal.

$$\forall(\beta) \subseteq \Delta . closure(\beta) = closure(closure(\beta))$$

Within agent factory the belief set is considered as a first-order logic and its subsequent manipulation assumes the presence of *complete deduction* unlike true higher-order logics where the *closure* function would have to appeal to *model closure*.

3.6 Messages

Messages represent the fundamental currency of interagent communication. Messages represent packets of information that serves to characterize the communication. Messages in essence can be characterized as being of specific kinds. Typically a message is considered to be either an inform, request, or unrequest. A type can be introduced that defines these options using the normal set notation. We introduce a type called *Mess_kind* which represents this type:

$$Mess\_kind = \{inform, uninform, request, unrequest, refrain\}$$

A new type *message* is defined as a structure

$$\langle s, r, mk, cont, t, p \rangle$$

where

s is the sender such that $s \in Agt\_names$
r is the receiver(s), where

$$r \subseteq Agt\_names \cdot (s \notin r) \wedge (r \neq \{ \ \})$$

mk is the message kind such that $mk \in Mess\_kind$
cont represents the message content which is expressed in some internal
    language L
t is the time that the message is sent by the sender such that $t \in Time$
p is a priority such that $p \in N_l$

These five message types support the informing and requesting of colleagues. Clearly with the dynamics of the system it is necessary that such communications are reversable and as such support is provided for uninform and unrequest. With messages of this type we impose the restriction that if a given agent a_i informs another agent a_j of some fact at some point in time t'. Then only agent a_i can uninform agent a_j of that same fact at some later point in time t''. This same restriction is also imposed on request messages. The refrain message is different, in the sense that it is possible for a given agent a_i to request a particular action ac from a particular agent a_j at some instance in time t' and, at a later instance t'' another agent a_j may ask that agent or a set of agents that contains a_j, to refrain from that very action. For example, an agent may wish at some future point to use a particular resource and may therefore ask all agents that are capable of performing actions that demand the use of the resource to refrain from these actions. The origin of a refrain communication will be prompted by some epistemic input[4] which may result from social behavior or deductive behavior. The symmetric arrangement that must exist with inform-uninform and request-unrequest does not hold with refrain. Of course, some theory or model of authority needs to be included so as to

---

[4]By epistemic input we mean a change to the agents belief set.

compare the relative *position* of the agent who requests a given action with that which seeks the agent to refrain from it. Various distinct *authority models* could arbitrate in such circumstances and the choice ought largely to reflect the particular organization being modeled.[5]

Six selector or deconstructor functions may be defined which each retrieve one of the component fields of the message structure. Three of these are considered below the others *get_mess_kind*, *get_mess_content* and *get_mess_priority* should be intuitive. The recovery of the sender (i.e., agent name) given a particular message is achieved by a function *sender* thus:

$$get\_sender : Mess \rightarrow Agt\_names$$

$$get\_sender(m) \triangleq$$

$$\text{let } \langle s, r, mk, mc, t, p \rangle = m \text{ in}$$

$$\{s | s \in Agt\_names\}$$

The recovery of the receiver(s) [i.e., agent name(s)] given a particular message is achieved by a function *receiver* thus:

$$get\_receiver : Mess \rightarrow Agt\_names$$

$$get\_receiver(m) \triangleq$$

$$\text{let } \langle s, r, mk, mc, t, p \rangle = m \text{ in}$$

$$\{r | r \subseteq Agt\_names \cdot (s \notin r) \wedge (r \neq \{ \ \})\}$$

Another deconstructor function supported is that of *time_sent*. This function retrieves the time at which a given message has been sent.

$$time\_sent : Mess \rightarrow Time$$

$$time\_sent(m) \triangleq$$

$$\text{let } \langle s, r, mk, mc, t, p \rangle = m \text{ in}$$

$$t$$

3.7 Acquaintances

Each agent A_i has an associated set of acquaintances. These acquaintances indicate those colleagues that the given agent is aware of and able or willing to interact with. An *acquaintance* type is defined as a tuple such that it consists of a mapping between agent name and a set of capabilities.

---

[5]Models of authority form the basis of ongoing work at UMIST; however, detailed consideration is beyond the scope of this chapter.

$$Acquaintance = Ag\_names \times Caps$$

$$inv\text{-}Acquaintance \triangleq card(Ag\_names) = 1 \wedge$$

$$card(Caps) \geq 1$$

In turn an set of acquaintances is captured by the type *Acquaintances*:

$$Acquaintances = \text{powerset of } Acquaintance$$

3.8 Capabilities

Capabilities can be ascribed to each agent and represent those activities that the agent is empowered to perform. Two types enable the modeling of such abilities: *Capability* and *Capabilities*, with the latter representing an aggregation of individual capabilities. Each *Capability* represents a mapping between a capability name and a set of *Plans* each of which can support the agent in providing such a capability. An agent can thus be viewed as potentially being able to support its capabilities in a variety of ways. The selection of which plan to invoke would depend upon the particular planner utilized by the Agent Factory system. In essence the planner may commission a given criterion, for example, the availability of resources demanded by a given plan, its degree of refinement, the number of discrete steps required, and so forth. We look at plans in more detail in the subsequent section.

$$Capability = Capability\_name \xrightarrow{m} \text{powerset of } Plans$$

$$Capabilities = \text{powerset of } Capability$$

3.9 Plans

Plans are represented as a sequence of partially ordered actions. A type called *Plan* is described which is comprised of a sequence of *Steps*, where *Steps* in turn are made up of a set of actions that achieve each step. We adopt this convention for two reasons. First each element in the sequence is a set, thus enabling those actions whose ordering is unimportant to be manipulated in an efficient and context-sensitive manner. Second, the sequence enables multiple occurrences of the same action. Thus a plan involving the partial ordering of actions depicted in Figure 17.4 could be represented as [{e}, {c}, {a, b}, {f}]. The declarations are thus:

$$Plan = Steps^*$$

$$Steps = \text{powerset of } Action$$

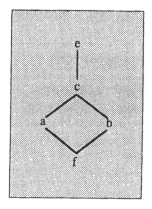

Figure 17.4 *A partially ordered set of actions.*

3.10 Action

Agents are empowered to perform actions. At the simplest level actions can be categorized as being of three discrete classes, namely cognitive, communicative, and physical. Cognitive actions involve actions which result in the revision of the mental state of the agent within which the action is being performed. Communicative actions result in the exchange of a message(s) to other agents within the community.[6]

Physical actions result in the performance of physical events in the actual physical world within which the agents are situated. Physical actions would be effected by some invocation of appropriate robotic functions. Such functions could manifest themselves as a physical movement of the agent itself, as in the case of an autonomous guided vehicle (AGV), movement of parts of the agent as in a robotic arm or merely some form of instruction to separate processes like the automatic increase in pressure thus resulting in the closure of a given pressure valve.

Actions are thus represented as a type *Action*:

$$Action = \langle an, ac, ak, res \rangle$$

where

an represents an action name such that $an \in Action\_names$, where

$$Action\_names = \{a_1, a_2, a_3, \ldots, a_n\}$$

ac represents the action class such that $ac \in Action\_class$, where

$$Action\_class = \{primitive, complex\}$$

---

[6]It is assumed that agents cannot send messages to themselves.

ak represents the type of the particular action such that *ak* ∈ *Action_kind*, where

$$Action\_kind = \{request, unrequest, inform, uninform, do\}$$

(these may be categorized as *cognitive*, *communicative*, and *physical* actions representing the three broad categories of action that an agent is empowered to perform)[7]

res represents a set of resources that the given agent needs access to in order to accomplish the action such that *res* ∈ *Resources*

3.11 Commitments

Commitments are represented as tuples of time and action. The type *commitment* is formally represented as the structure

$$\langle act, men\_c, agt, t \rangle$$

where

act represents the particular action that is committed to such that *act* ∈ *Action*

men_c represents the mental condition that must hold in order that the commitment persist

agt represents the agent to whom the commitment is made such that *agt* ∈ *agt_name*

t represents the time from which the commitment holds such that *t* ∈ *Time*

Clearly not all commitments adopted will be at the bequest of others and any given agent may adopt commitments to self.

In turn a type *Commitment_set* which is represented by a set of commitments:

$$Commitment\_set = \text{powerset of } Commitment$$

Two key functions are supported which manipulate the set of current commitments. These two functions are those of *adopt* and *drop*. When a commitment is adopted it is added to the set of existing commitments.

$$adopt : Commitment \times Commitment\_set \rightarrow Commitment\_set;$$

$$adopt(c, cs) \triangleq \{c \cup cs\}$$

---

[7]Other authors offer similar typologies; for example, Wooldridge (1992) identifies cognitive, communicative, and effectoric while Shoham distinguishes between private/cognitive and communicative acts (Shoham, 1993).

In a similar manner the dropping of a commitment that is currently held involves the removal of the commitment from the current commitment set.

$$drop: Commitment \times Commitment\_set \rightarrow Commitment\_set;$$

$$drop(c, cs) \triangleq \{cs - \{c\}\}$$

It is assumed that the appropriate selector functions exist namely, *get_ com_action*, *get_com_agt*, *get_com_ment_cond* and *get_com_time*. Numerous competing policies exist by which commitments ought to be reevaluated. In a similar vain that belief revision systems have been developed there needs to be complementary *commitment revision systems* (*CRS*), which oversee the application of a given algorithm(s) for charting and tracking the "life" of each commitment. Recent work has addressed the dropping of commitments and numerous authors have proposed different theories for commitment maintenance (Castelfranchi, 1993; Dongha, 1995).

3.12 Commitment Rules

Within Agent Factory as with comparable systems a set of commitment rules associated with each agent encode the criteria which must pertain in order that a given commitment be adopted. The commitment rules adhere crudely to the convention identified within Agent0. Each commitment rule includes a message condition and a mental condition both of which are logically ANDed and as such both must hold true in order for a given commitment to be adopted. Other criteria must also be honored, such as having the capability and access to the necessary resources to accomplish the given action. This issue will be revisited later. The type *commitment rule* is represented by the following structure:

$$\langle mess\_cond, ment\_cond, act, t \rangle$$

where

mess_cond represents the message condition that must hold true at a given instance in order that the particular action *act* may be committed to; it is expressed in the internal language *L*

ment_cond represents the mental condition that must hold true at a given instance in order that the particular action *act* may be committed to, it is expressed in the internal language *L*

act represents an action which is a member of the set of performable actions;

t represents some time such that $t \in Time$

It is assumed that commitment rules are static and thus they will not be revised during the execution of the system. Consequently only a set of deconstructor functions need be identified. Four functions are assumed to exist which support the retrieval of the component fields of the commitment rule structure. These are *get_mess_cond*, *get_ment_cond*, *get_cr_action*, and *get_cr_time*, which respectively recover the message condition, mental condition, action, and time from a given commitment rule.

3.13 Agent

Each agent is considered to be of type *Agent* with an associated structure:

$$\langle \eta, \ St, \ \Delta_0, \ GR, \ acqs, \ Caps, \ Cmts, \ CR, \ res \rangle$$

where

η is a unique identifier for the agent such that $\eta \in ag\_names$

St indicates the current status of the agent such that $St \in leg\_states$

$\Delta_0 \in Belset$ and represents the initial belief set

GR is a record which encapsulates all the graphical information needed by the UIMS in the management of the graphical interface[8]

acqs represents a set of agent acquaintances held by a given agent such that *acqs* $\in$ *Acquaintances*

Caps $\in$ *Capabilities* and represents a set of agent capabilities held by a given agent

Cmts $\in$ *Cmtset* and represents the set of current commitments

CR $\in$ *Cmtruleset* and represents the set of commitment rules held by the given agent

res $\in$ *Resources* and represents the set of resources available to the agent locally and which may be accessible to a subset of its acquaintances

An appropriate range of deconstructor functions are specified which retrieve the appropriate fields within the agent structure.[9] A similar range of constructor functions exist which update the respective fields of the structure. The deconstructor functions are those of *get_name*, *get_status*, *get_graphical_information*, *get_beliefs*, *get_acquaintances*, *get_capabilities*, *get_commit-*

---

[8]The inclusion of such graphical details could be regarded as compromising the purity and generality of the design by allowing such pollutants to be directly represented within the structure. However, our experience indicated that such information was certainly needed and logically it did form part of the type of the agent.

[9]It should be noted that the notation adopted here is somewhat different from that advocated within VDM. We do not make use of the composite object or record facility provided within VDM. While the notation we use provides the same facilities it does not automatically enable specific fields to be retrieved or indeed the constructor function make to be utilized. The notation we adopt is more generic in nature and generally akin to that employed within the multiagent systems community.

ments, *get_commitment_rules*, and *get_resources*. The associated set of constructor operations are *update_name*, *update_status*, *update_graphical_information*, *update_beliefs*, *update_acquaintances*, *update_capabilities*, *update_commitments*, *update_commitment_rules*, and *update_resources*. By way of an example a function *get_status* is thus introduced which supports the retrieval of the state of any given agent a_j at some instance in time.

get_status : $Agent \rightarrow State$

get_status (a_j) $\triangleq$

let $\langle \eta, St, \Delta_0, GR, acqs, Caps, Cmts, CR \rangle = a_j$ in

St

Another function *update_state* performs an update operation on the state of a given agent.

$update\_status$: $Status \times Agent \rightarrow Agent$

$update\_status$ (new_st, a_j) $\triangleq$

let $\langle \eta, St, \Delta_0, GR, acqs, Caps, Cmts, CR \rangle = a_j$ in

$\langle \eta, new\_st, \Delta_0, GR, acqs, Caps, Cmts, CR \rangle$

3.14 Agent Community

Agents are assembled into communities by being introduced to each other. The process of introduction is something that is currently achieved by the system designer statically. Thus at start up the social relationships that define a given community are specified in an a priori manner. Of course dynamic introductions could be performed be some *facilitation agent* or indeed by the agents themselves. The implication of such dynamic introductions would be that a symmetric revision of acquaintance models would occur, of those agents that were being introduced. Such social structures are implicit and are encoded by the acquaintances of each agent A_i within the community.

A type called *Community* is introduced, which is defined as the powerset of agents:

$Community$ = $Community\_names \times$ powerset of $Agent \times Resources$

$inv\text{-}Community$ $\triangleq$ $card$ (community_names) ≥ 1

Several functions exist than manipulate entities of type community. A function Boolean *is_member* returns a Boolean result as to the membership of a given agent a_j within a given community c_j.

$$is\_member : Agent \times Community \rightarrow B$$

$$is\_member\ (a_j,\ c_j) \triangleq$$

$$\text{if } a_j \in c_j \text{ then true}$$

$$\text{else false}$$

As mentioned earlier within Section 3.7 the dynamics of the agent community are such that it is conceivable that agents will join and leave the group from time to time. Two functions those of *join* and *withdraw* are thus defined which support this graceful expansion of the agent community.

$$join : Agent \times Community \rightarrow Community$$

$$joint(a,\ c) \triangleq$$

$$\text{if not } (is\_member\ (a,\ c))$$

$$\text{then } \{c|c = \bar{c} \cup a\}$$

$$\text{else } \{c\}$$

$$withdraw : Agent \times Community \rightarrow Community$$

$$withdraw(a,\ c) \triangleq$$

$$\text{if } is\_member\ (a,\ c)$$

$$\text{then } \{c|c = \bar{c} - \{a\}\}$$

$$\text{else } \{c\}$$

Again the normal deconstructor and constructor functions of *get_agent* and *update_agent* are provided for thus:

$$get\_agent : Agent \times Community \rightarrow Agent$$

$$get\_agent(a_j,\ c_j) \triangleq$$

$$\text{if } (is\_member\ (a_j,\ c_j))$$

$$\text{then } a_j$$

$$update\_agent : Agent \times Community \rightarrow Community$$

$$update\_agent\ (new\_ag,\ old\_ag,\ c_j) \triangleq$$

$$\text{if } (is\_member\ (old\_ag,\ c_j))$$

$$\text{then } \{join(new\_ag,\ withdraw(old\_ag,\ c_j))\}$$

Two further functions called *store_agent* and *restore_agent* would respectively save and retrieve a given agent state within a persistent agent store. These functions are described in more detail in Section 1.2.

3.15 Message Pool

The message pool is assumed to be an infinite repository which can accommodate temporarily message traffic between agents. There exists in fact the possibility of retaining a record of all community communications which may prove useful as a historical record that could be utilized for example, in retrospective analysis of social activity, or in the provision of elaborations as to how particular tasks were performed, or justifications as to how certain answers were derived.

At present the primary requirement is that of providing a shared global data structure that supports asynchronous communication. The message pool consists of a potentially infinite number of messages. For a given system only one message pool exists. Messages can be written to and retrieved from the message pool.

We introduce a new type here namely that of *Message Pool*. *Message Pool* is defined as

$$Message\ Pool = \text{powerset of } Message^{10}$$

The message pool acts as a dynamic resource that continually expands and contracts as the number of messages contained within it increases and decreases.[11] When agents send messages this results in the augmentation of the message pool. Conversely, when agents retrieve messages they retrieve messages from the message pool, thus resulting in the contraction of the pool.

Agents interact with each other by sending and receiving messages. The message pool affords two primitive functions which supports these activities those of *send* and *receive*. Considering the *send* function first:

$$send : Mess \times Mess\_pool \rightarrow Mess\_pool$$

$$send(m, mp) \triangleq$$

$$\text{let } \langle s, r, mk, mc, t \rangle = m \text{ in}$$

$$\{m \cup mp\} \wedge (m = \overline{m})$$

The second conjoined expression enforces the content preservance principle.

---

[10]It would of course be equally valid to declare the *Message Pool* in terms of a sequence such that *Message Pool* = Message*. This would enforce some ordering on the messages in terms of arrival time and would also permit duplicate messages. The occurrence of duplicate messages seems less attractive than one might at first imagine. Given that messages explicitly encode the time at which they are transmitted then the same message (i.e., message content, same source) transmitted twice, would in fact constitute two different messages due to the differing time of dispatch. However, given that the *Message Pool* only houses messages that are in transit and that it is assumed that messages sent at time t are received at time $t + 1$, then ordering or duplicates seem superfluous.

[11]This presupposes that messages are not recorded permanently within the message pool.

In a similar vain then the *receive* function extracts those messages destined for a given agent.[12]

$$receive : Agent\_names \times Mess\_pool \rightarrow Mess\_pool$$

$$receive(a_j, mp) \triangleq$$

$$\text{let } \langle s, r, mk, mc, t \rangle = m \text{ in}$$

$$\{\forall a_j | a_j \in Agent\_names \ \forall m | m \in mp \cdot (r = a_j) \land$$

$$(\forall m | m \notin mp \cdot (r \neq a_j) \land$$

$$(m = \overline{m})$$

$$\}$$

The first two conjunctions ensure the privacy principle, while the last formula, together with the last conjoined sentence in the specification of the send function, enforces the content preservance principle.

A third important function supported by the *Mess_pool* type is the *archive* function which would be invoked by the scheduler either in a systematic manner each clock cycle. The motivation for such an archiving capability is twofold.

- It ensures messages are recorded persistently in another location such that if necessary the evolution of the community interactions can be made subject to scrutiny.
- It ensures that messages are not stored within the message pool with the inevitable consequence of reducing the efficiency of, particularly, the retrieve function.

The archive function would typically be defined thus:

$$archive : Time \times Mess\_pool \rightarrow Mess\_pool$$

$$archive(t, mp) \triangleq$$

$$\overline{mp} = mp - \{archive\ (t, mp)\} \land$$

$$\{\forall m \in mp \cdot (time\_sent\ (m)) \leq t\}$$

Sometimes it is advantageous to be able to introduce a filter when retrieving messages from the message pool. Such filters could be couched in terms of the sender, the message kind, its priority and indeed combinations thereof. One such filter function that we will utilize later retrieves messages of a given type whose destination is a particular agent. We name this function the

---

[12]We assume here that the receive function removes messages from the message pool and does not merely copy them, thereby leaving a history of the community social dynamics.

get_mess_of_kind, which is specified thus:

$$get\_mess\_of\_kind : Mess\_kind \times Mess\_pool \rightarrow Mess\_pool$$

$$get\_mess\_of\_kind \ (mk, \ mp) \ \triangleq$$

$$\{\forall m \in mp \cdot (get\_mess\_kind \ (m) = mk)\}$$

3.16   Systems

The final assemblage that must be presented is the concept of a *system*. Systems are constructed through the judicious assembly of an agent community with a message pool, a clock, an UIMS and an appropriate scheduler.

A type entitled *system* can thus be viewed as a structure, which is defined thus:

$$\langle c, \ mp, \ uims, \ cl, \ s, \ i, \ psm \rangle$$

where

cl represents a clock

c where *c* represents a community

mp represents a message pool

uims represents a user interface management system

s represents a scheduler

i represents an agent interpreter

psm represents some persistent storage manager

It is conceivable that numerous communities may exist and each may be stored persistently. This, however, seems unlikely and reusability would typically take place at the granularity of the agent.

We assume the existence of the normal deconstructor functions like *get_community* and *get_mess_pool*.

3.17   Persistent Store Manager

The persistent store manager supports two functions which enable *agent states* to be stored in a persistent form and restored into their appropriate *mental structures*. Two functions support this encoding and unencoding. The *store* function supports the former, with the *restore* function supporting the latter.

The necessity to capture frequently and store the state of a given agent is a direct consequence of the multiprocessing approach adopted within Agent Factory. Because agents execution is time sliced, their execution often needs to be suspended, their current state frozen and subsequently preserved in order that in some future time slice the mental state is recreated and the execution resumed within an appropriate context. The ability to store and restore agent states thus enables continuity of agent execution. Detailed treatment of these functions is beyond the scope of this chapter. The essence of the functions involves the successive assembly or disassembly of the agent structure into its component parts.

3.18 Scheduler

A scheduler has the responsibility of scheduling the activities of the various agents that exist within the system. Given that Agent Factory simulates the parallel activity of agent communities it needs to ensure that agents are scheduled "fairly" and that each is given access to the processor.

We introduce a type called *scheduler* such that it is comprised as a tuple thus:

$$Scheduler = Scheduler\_name \times Scheduling\_algorithm$$

Three functions are central to the operation of the scheduler: *select_next_agent*, *activate*, and *deactivate*. The *select_next_agent* function selects which agent within the community will next be scheduled.

$$select\_next\_agent : Community \rightarrow Agent;$$

Numerous schedulers may exist and a scheduler that realizes the appropriate scheduling algorithm ought to be selected from a *scheduler library*. We do not define the operation of the function as this is contingent upon the particular scheduling algorithm utilized within the scheduling library. Suffice it to say that a criteria exists by which a *unique* agent is selected.

The second of these functions activates a given agent within the context of a given system, while the third deactivates a given agent, thus releasing control of the processor. The criteria by which agents are adjudged to gain or relinquish control of the processor is the responsibility of an algorithm which is enforced by the scheduler. It is this algorithm that determines the parameter for each of these functions.

$$activate : Agent \rightarrow Agent$$

$$activate\ (a_j,\ s_t)\ \triangleq$$

$$\text{let}\ \langle \eta,\ St,\ \Delta_0,\ GR,\ acqs,\ Caps,\ Cmts,\ CR \rangle = a_j\ \text{in}$$

$$update\_status\ (\text{active},\ a_j)$$

The activation of an agent is thus *synonymous* with the status of the agent becoming active.

deactivate : *Agent* → *Agent*

deactivate (a_j, s_t) $\triangleq$

$\quad\quad\quad$ let $\langle \eta, St, \Delta_0, GR, acqs, Caps, Cmts, CR \rangle = a_j$ in

$\quad\quad\quad$ if *get_status* (a_j) ≠ waiting

$\quad\quad\quad$ then *update_status* (active, a_j)

Numerous different schedulers may exist and a scheduler that realizes the appropriate scheduling algorithm ought to be selected from a *scheduler library*.[13]

3.19 Agent Interpreter

Numerous agent interpreters have been developed and described within the literature. One of the first descriptions was that presented by Rao and Georgeff (1992). They described an abstract architecture for rational agents which they characterized as a BDI (Belief-Desire-Intention) architecture, and which is influenced by earlier work by Cohen and Levesque (1990). The architecture was based upon the attitudes of belief, desire, and intention. Subsequent to this, and, continued work refining and developing the ideas, the community has embraced this model as potentially one of the most profitable avenues through which computationally tractable rational agent societies could be achieved. Chapter 5 considers these issues in more detail.

Numerous researchers have been influenced by this work and several agent-oriented languages have emerged of late whose interpreters are based upon this model (Shoham, 1991, 1993; Thomas, 1993, 1994; Imagine, 1993; McCabe and Clark, 1995).

The agent interpreter which forms an integral part of Agent Factory is similarly derived and grounded within the BDI philosophy. We introduce a new type called *interpreter* such that it consists of a unique name and a given deductive engine.

$$Interpreter = Interpreter\_name \times Deductive\_engine$$

Figure 17.5 gives a high-level description of the discrete stages that the interpreter engages in when a given agent is scheduled. Central to this loop are three functions: *update_beliefs*, *update_commitments*, and *execute_agent*. Within the context of this chapter we focus upon the first two functions only.

---

[13]It is quite conceivable that a single scheduler would be sufficiently generic in order to embrace differing scheduling algorithm selected by the system designer.

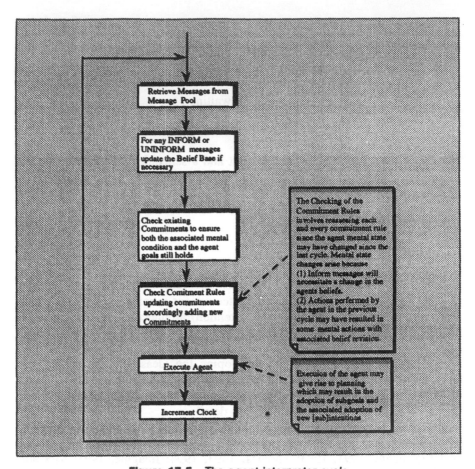

Figure 17.5 *The agent interpreter cycle.*

Update_beliefs as its name suggests results in a change to the belief set of the given agent. Within Agent Factory agents are gullible and, as such, believe all things which they are informed about. Thus any messages of type inform result in a potential update in the agents belief set.

update_beliefs : *Agent* × *Mess_pool* → *Agent*

update_beliefs (a_j, mp) $\triangleq$

    let ⟨*η, St, Δ_j, GR, acqs, Caps, Cmts, CR*⟩ = a_j in

    ⟨*η, St, closure* (($Δj$ ∪ *get_mess_of_kind* (*inform, receive*(a_j, *mp*)))), $λ_{\mathfrak{R}}$),

    GR, acqs, Caps, Cmts, CR⟩

where $\lambda_{\Re}$ represents a set of deduction rules comprised exclusively of Robinson's resolution rule (Robinson, 1965).

This function does not in any way consider the issue of inconsistent belief sets and how they may be avoided. We assume that our agents are gullible thus merely receiving new information and duly incorporating this into their belief set.

Within Agent Factory agents do not blindly commit to the commitments that they adopt. It is recognized that while the conditions might hold at the point in time at which the commitment is adopted, the dynamics of both the agents' mental state and the environment within which they are embedded is such that they may, and indeed probably will, not hold indefinitely. Certainly there is a distinct possibility that they may not hold at the point when the given action to which the agent is commited is due to be performed.

Elsewhere in the literature (Rao and Georgeff, 1992) it is recognized that varying degrees of commitment may be exhibited by agents. Rao and Georgeff (1992, 1992) identify three discrete points on this commitment continuum, namely, *blind commitment, single-minded commitment*, and *open-minded commitment*. Blind commitment is defined as the adherence to a commitment until such time as the agent believes it has achieved the commitment. Single-minded commitment represents a relaxation of blind commitment in that the agent will not drop its commitments unless it believes that they are no longer *achievable*. The computational overhead of ascertaining whether a given goal is achievable can be considerable. Rao and Georgeff suggest that this can be achieved by permitting belief revision but not goal revision. Open-minded commitment offers a further relaxation in that an agent is willing to revise its goals and beliefs, retaining commitments that are still compatible with its goals. Agents within Agent Factory adopt an open-minded commitment scheme they will permit belief revision and the revision of commitments in keeping with these changing mental attitudes. Furthermore, their goals may be revised together with any associated intentions. For example, another agent may cause a change in a given agent's goals through a request or unrequest message.

The task then of updating the agent commitments involves checking that existing commitments are still valid and augmenting the list with any commitments that have become valid as a result of any changes to the mental state of the agent since the last clock cycle, or indeed due to the receipt of *unrequest* statements.

Revising the commitments of each and every agent within a given community is potentially a highly expensive computational process and much consideration ought to be given to the design of such a revision function. In essence three options exist

1. First, each and every commitment rule is reassessed and a new set of commitments generated. This new set will necessarily contain any members of the preexisting set of commitments that are still valid; *or*

2. First, perform a reevaluation of all existing commitments dropping any that are no longer valid. This would involve considering any commitments that a given agent was asked to refrain from and any unrequest messages. Subsequently assess those commitment rules which have not produced any of the commitments in the revised commitment set; *or*

3. Enforce a form of indexing upon commitment rules[14] such that there is a clear causal mapping between commitment rules and entities within the belief set which comprise the mental condition and messages that comprise the message condition. Thus upon the recognition of a change to a given agent's mental state or message state such relationships could cause an intelligent reassessment of *only* those commitment rules whose existence is contingent upon the presence or absence of certain specific beliefs or messages. Differing changes in an agent state could result in the invocation of members of a set of demons which would perform the minimal check necessary.

Each of these approaches has its relative merits. Option one seems at first glance to exhibit a profound degree of simplicity. However, upon further consideration, one realizes that two problems are encountered.

The first involves the need to consider not merely new messages but older messages also. The first difficulty is associated with the fact that existing commitments are not used as a parameter in identifying the next set of commitments. Thus, since all commitment rules are reassessed each cycle, implicit in this is the need to consider not merely new messages but also older messages. By new messages we mean those received in the last clock cycle, while old refer to those that arrived in previous cycles and whose content has not *temporally expired*. For example a message of type *request* for a certain action at some time t' would be said to have temporally expired if the time were now $t' + n$. Thus, old and new messages would need to be recovered each clock cycle. New messages would be retrieved from the message pool while old messages would be retrieved from archive.

The second problem involves being able to recognize when commitments have been honoured. Upon doing so this would necessitate ignoring a proportion of messages relating to these commitments. This introduces the additional computational expense of retrieving potentially large numbers of messages, recognising which are obsolete and filtering these accordingly. Within the other options this recognition process would merely demand the removal or dropping of a commitment from the commitment set, when the requisite action is accomplished, at the required time. When such a commitment set is not main-

---

[14]This approach could be regarded as an enhanced version of option 1. It would similarly be possible to create such a relationship between commitments and beliefs/messages. In this case we would have an enhanced version of option 2.

tained, but rather is recreated each clock cycle, this act of dropping commitments becomes somewhat more involved.

Implicit within option 2 is the inclusion of some relationship between commitment rules and commitments. This causes us to consider more closely this relationship. It is quite possible that the existence of a given commitment may be supported by numerous commitment rules. Conversely, it is quite possible that a given commitment rule may give rise to several commitments. This is due to the potentiality of different unification upon the same commitment rule. By way of example consider two messages from two alternative agents that each might successfully unify against the message condition of a given commitment rule. Two particular commitments to two different agents could conceivably be installed within the commitment set.

Thus a many-to-many relationship exists between commitments and commitment rules. The maintenance of such relationships would introduce an additional computational expense, although this is tempered by the static nature of the commitment rules within Agent Factory. In essence, however, it would seem necessary to evaluate every commitment rule each clock cycle.

It remains to be seen as to the potential performance advantage, if any, of maintaining the links and structuring necessary within options 2 and 3. For this reason, and in the interest of simplicity, we will merely consider option 2 within the remainder of this chapter[15] while ignoring any need to maintain links between commitments and commitment rules.

As a consequence of the many-to-many relationship that exists between commitments and commitment rules, it is necessary to check that duplication of commitments does not occur.

A duplicate commitment would be said to occur if

(i) The same action is commited to *and*
(ii) The commitment is made to the same agent or a set of agents that contains a given agent *and*
(iii) The commitment is due to be realized at the same point in time;

Thus the process of checking for duplicates reduces to that of pattern matching upon the commitment structure. The function *remove_duplicates* filters the commitments accordingly. The *update_commitments* function then takes an agent, the community within which it resides and a message pool and returns an updated agent structure. The approach taken to revision of commitments[16] within Agent Factory is similar in philosophy to that adopted within Agent0.

---

[15]There is no reason why any of the other options could not be encompassed within Agent Factory.
[16]We are aware of the distinction made between the operations of revision and update, by certain researchers. In the context of this chapter we use the terms interchangeably and we will not focus upon the semantic differences.

update_commitments: *Agent* $\times$ *Community* $\times$ *Mess_pool* $\rightarrow$ *Agent*

update_commitments $(a_j,\ com,\ mp)$ $\triangleq$

> let $\langle \eta,\ St,\ \Delta_j,\ GR,\ acqs,\ caps,\ cmts,\ CR \rangle = a_j$ in
>
> $\langle \eta,\ St,\ \Delta_j,\ GR,\ acqs,\ Caps,$
>
> *remove_duplicates*(*check_commitments*(cmts) $\cup$
>
> > *check_commitment_rules*(*get_commitment_rules*(a_j), *com*,
> >
> > > *receive*($a_j,\ mp$))
>
>)
>
> $CR \rangle$

The *removes_duplicate* function is unnecessary within the particular representational scheme that we adopt. We define commitments to be of a set type and as such it is not possible to have duplicate entries. Nevertheless, had an alternative representation been used, this would not have been the case and thus for completeness we include this function.

Considering first the *check_commitments* function. This function takes an input an agent structure together with a set of commitments returning a revised set of commitments as required

check_commitments: *Agent* $\times$ *Commitments* $\rightarrow$ *Commitments*

check_commitments $(a_j,\ cts)$ $\triangleq$

let $\langle \eta,\ St,\ \Delta_j,\ GR,\ Acqs,\ Caps,\ Cmts,\ CR \rangle = a_j$ in

$\{\forall\ c \in cts \cdot (men\_c \in \Delta_j \cup \{true\}) \wedge$

> $(\forall\ m \in (get\_mess\_of\_kind(unrequest,\ receive\ (a_j,\ mp)))$
>
> $get\_mess\_content\ (m) \neq get\_com\_action\ (c))$

$\}$

The function *check_commitment_rules* is defined as follows:

check_commitment_rules : *Agent* $\times$ *Community* $\times$ *Mess_pool* $\rightarrow$ *Commitments*

check_commitment_rules $(a_j,\ com,\ mp)$ $\triangleq$

> let $\langle \eta,\ st,\ \Delta_j,\ GR,\ acqs,\ caps,\ cmts,\ cr \rangle = a_j$ in

{*mk_commitment* (*get_cr_action*(*c*), *get_cr_ment_cond*(*c*),

$\qquad$ *get_requestees*(*c*, *mp*),[17] *get_cr_time*(*c*)

$\qquad$) | ∀ *c* ∈ cr.

$\qquad$ (*check_message_condition* (*a_j*, *get_mess_cond*(*c*)) ∧

$\qquad$ *check_mental_condition*(*get_cr_ment_cond*(*c*)) ∧

$\qquad$ *check_resources* (*a_j*, *com*, *get_resources*(*a_j*)) ∧

$\qquad$ *check_refrainment*(*get_cr_action*(*c*),

$\qquad\qquad\qquad\qquad$ *get_commit_actions*(*cmts*))

$\qquad$)

}

It could be argued that another function *check_capabilities* should form part of this conjunction. Such a function would involve checking that the given agent was in fact capable of performing the action associated with the commitment rule. We assume that this need not be included, since agents will only be permitted to commit to actions that they are capable of achieving. An action can be achieved if there exists a plan or plans they that if executed will realize the desired action. Of course this is not to say that this activity must be achievable individually. This may involve joint activity.

Thus the "programming" of commitment rules is the responsibility of the agent designer and as such commitment rules ought only to exist for those actions that the agent is empowered to perform. It is nevertheless quite conceivable that requests will be made to perform activities of which an individual agent is incapable. In order to address this a "catch-all" commitment rule would merely respond to the sender indicating its inability to assist, where

$$\textit{check\_message\_condition} : \textit{Agent} \times \textit{Mess\_cond} \rightarrow B$$

$$\textit{check\_message\_condition} \ (a_j, \ mes\_c) \ \triangleq$$

$$(mes\_c \in \text{receive}(a_j, \ mp))$$

Evaluating the truth of the message condition involves checking those messages that have been received in this clock cycle. The receive function retrieves the appropriate message pool. If the message condition is satisfied by any of these messages then it evaluates to true.

---

[17]We assume the existence of a function that identifies those agent(s) to which a particular agent is commited given the specific commitment derived from a commitment rule c. We do not consider how this is achieved; however, its operation is made more complex, since within Agent Factory we consider that the same commitment can be made to a team or group of agents.

$$check\_mental\_condition : Agent \times Ment\_cond \rightarrow B$$

$$check\_mental\_condition \ (a_j, \ men\_c) \ \triangleq$$

$$\text{let } \langle \eta, \ St, \ \Delta_j, \ GR, \ Acqs, \ Caps, \ Cmts, \ CR \rangle \ = \ a_j \text{ in}$$

$$(men\_c \in \Delta_j \ \cup \ \{true\})$$

Evaluating the truth of the mental condition involves the current deductive engine utilizing the given set of deductive rules to identify the truth of the Boolean expression via the manipulation and interrogation of the Belief set. The *check_resources* function is a Boolean and is as follows:

$$check\_resources : Agent \times Community \times Resources \rightarrow B$$

$$check\_resources \ (a_j, \ com, \ res) \ \triangleq$$

$$(available\_resources(a_j, \ com) \ \subseteq \ res)$$

where the *available_resources* function checks on the availability of resources to the given agent a_j. Resources may be accessible locally or remotely. The latter case can be subdivided into those resources that are associated with other agents and shared community resources. In the case of the former the *ownership* of the resources is the individual agent in question and their usage is contingent upon collaboration with them. In the case of the latter then access to these resources is merely dependent upon gaining control of the shared resource.

We differentiate between the *accessibility* and *availability* of resources. We assume that resources accessible to a given agent, will at some point in the future, become available to that same agent. Strictly speaking, the function below returns the set of accessible resources.

$$available\_resources : Agent \times Community \rightarrow Resources$$

$$available\_resources \ (a_j, \ com) \ \triangleq$$

$$\text{let } \langle \eta, \ St, \ \Delta_j, \ GR, \ acqs, \ Caps, \ Cmts, \ CR \rangle \ = \ a_j \text{ in}$$

$$\{get\_community\_resources(com) \ \cup \ get\_resources(a_j) \ \cup$$

$$\cup \ \{\forall \ (a_i)|a_i \in get\_acquaintances \ (a_i) \cdot get\_resources(a_i)\}$$

$$\}$$

The function *check_refrainment* checks that the action is not one for which the agent already holds a commitment to refrain from, or, alternatively, if the action to be committed to is a refrain action then it checks that the agent does not hold a commitment to that action. This function would also inforce the particular theory of authority being commissioned checking that the more recent conflicting commitment should in fact override the preexisting commitment.

The evolution of the state of a given agent can be produced through the *agent_next_state* function. This function is defined thus:

agent_next_state : Agent × *System* → *Agent*

agent_next_state(a_j, s_j) $\triangleq$

> let < η, st, Δ, gr, acqs, caps, cmts, cr > =a_j in

> let Δ' = *update_beliefs* (Δ, *get_mess_pool*(s_j))

> let *cmts'* = *update_commitments*(a_j, *get_community*(s_j), *get_mess_pool*(s_j))

> *mk_Agent*(η, t, Δ', gr, acqs, caps, cmts', cr)

4 IMPLEMENTATION OF AGENT FACTORY

In the previous section we outlined the design of agents and systems within Agent Factory. While we have articulated this in a formal notation akin to that of VDM, we have not utilized VDM or its associated language Meta IV, as the medium of implementation. It was felt that while VDM offered an appropriate means for specifying Agent Factory in a highly portable notation, it did not represent an appropriate medium within which to realize the system.

The implementation approach adapted was influenced by two factors:

- Within UMIST a tradition exists in the development of executable algebraic systems (Gallimore et al., 1989) and access to an existing algebraic specification system (UMIST Paradox System) was readily available. This provided a tested and tried environment within which specifications could be developed in a systematic manner employing modular construction techniques.
- We wished to adopt a specification technique that could automatically be implemented.

Thus an alternative formal approach was adopted to the specification of multiagent systems, that of an algebraic technique. All such techniques are underpinned by the theory associated with heterogeneous algebras, which has been developed by Birkoff and Lipson (1970).

Numerous authors have adopted the algebraic approach to the specification of software systems, early pioneering work include (Liskov and Zilles, 1974, 1975), with these ideas subsequently being refined and formalized (Guttag et al., 1982; Bergstra et al., 1989; Ehrig and Mahr, 1985; Ehrig et al., 1992).

Of course, alternative approaches exist such as the use of executable systems based upon temporal logic like Metatem (Barringer et al., 1989), L.0 (Ness, 1993), and the logic of Davies (Davies, 1991). Those less familiar with this subject are directed elswehwer in the literature (Fisher, 1989) and Chapter 10 in this book.

In essence an algebraic specification is a technique where an object is specified in terms of the relationships between a set of operations which act upon that object. The approach has initially been communicated through its usage for the specification of Abstract Data Types (ADT), although latterly the generality of the approach has been described. The reason for this is simply that it is considerably easier to envisage the approach when the objects being specified actually correspond with ADTs in some arbitrary language.

We model agent societies by adopting a simulation approach. This is primarily motivated by the limitations of ADTs in modeling synchronous interprocess communication. This limitation is not applicable to algebraic techniques generally, and several authors have successfully developed languages which express theories of communicating systems through the medium of algebras. These include CSP (Hoare, 1978), CCS (Milner, 1989), EPL (Hennessy, 1988), and TCSP (Theoretical CSP) (Brookes et al., 1984). We identify a base set of ADTs which includes agent, scheduler, clock, and message pool ADTs. We adopt the normal linear discrete model of time, and we assume that messages transmitted take a clock cycle to arrive. Messages are thus presumed to be buffered in a central data structure referred to as the message list or message pool. Our approach embraced software engineering principles at all stages of the development (O'Hare and Wooldridge 1992).

The UMIST Paradox System (Powell, 1987a,b, 1988, 1989) incorporated an algebraic specification component based upon Abstract Data Types, the ADTSPEC (Ozcan, 1993), and supported the modular construction of sytems comprized of both ADTs and modules implemented in an enhanced Pascal language.

Figure 17.6 provides a partial ADT specification for an agent ADT. The Constructor function creates agents comprised of a 5-tuple thus ⟨name, acquaintances, capabilities, beliefs, commitments⟩. As can be seen this illustrates how the basic interpreter cycle of Agent0 could be realized. The normal principles of data enrichment are incorporated and the USES clause enables ADTs to be created through the aggregation of other constituent ADTs. This facilitates the incremental and systematic development of agent communities. Abstraction is further supported through the shielding of axiomatic details contained within the implementation section of the ADT. The paradox system generates actual implementations that adhere to the equational specifications; the system supports the coexistence of both ADT and implementation modules. So in the interests of efficiency when a working prototype has been developed the ADT modules can incrementally be replaced by specific modules enforcing a preferred implementation strategy.

```
ADT_MODULE adt_agent;
INTERFACE


  USES  adt_time,
        adt_fact,
        adt_bel_set,
        adt_cmt_lst,
        adt_mess_lst;


  TYPE  agent;


  CONSTRUCTOR cons_agent(name: string;
                         acqs: adt_acq_lst; caps: adt_skill_lst;
                         bel_set: beliefs; commts: cmt_lst;
                         cmt_rules: cmt_rules
                         ): agent;

  FUNCTION activate_agent(agt: agent): agent;
  FUNCTION deactivate_agent(agt: agent): agent;

SPECIFICATION

  FUNCTION update_bels(old_b: bel_set; m: mess_lst): bel_set;
  FUNCTION update_cmts(b: bel_set; m: mess_lst; cts: cmt_lst): cmt_lst;

  VAR  acqs: acq_lst;
       caps: skill_lst;
       bels: bel_set;
       cmts: cmm_lst;
       mess: mess_lst;

EQUATIONS
  update_cmts(curr_agt, old_bels, cmts) = ....;
  update_bels(curr_agt, old_bels, mess
             ) = IF NOT (is_mess_list_empty(mess)) THEN
                  IF is_inform(head_mess_list(mess)) THEN
                     update_bels(curr_agt, app_bel(old_bels,
                                  get_fact(head_mess_lst(mess))
                                  )
                  ELSE update_bels(curr_agt, old_bels,
                                    tail_mess_lst(mess));
  activate_agent(cons_agent(name, acqs, caps, bels, cmts)
              ) = cons_agent(name, acqs, caps,
                              update_bels(curr_agt,
                                          bels,
                                          get_mess(agt_name,now)
                                          )
                              update_cmts(bels, get_mess(agt_name, now),
                                          cmts
                                          )
                              );

END.
```

Figure 17.6 A partial ADT agent specification.

5 CONCLUSIONS

In this chapter we have outlined the design of Agent Factory and specified its behavior in a formal notation of VDM. Agent Factory exhibits a functionality endemic to all multiagent prototyping systems and like MYWORLD (Wooldridge and Vandekerckhove, 1993; Wooldridge, 1995) is similarly motivated. It supports the rapid instantiation of a central agent component and the aggregation of such components into communities whose model of social interaction is subsequently described. It also provides rudimentary tools for observing the evolution of the community state through inter-agent interactions and inspecting the current (mental) state of each agent. Agent Factory, however, is somewhat different in its adoption of an algebraic specification technique which can be directly executed. This approach has been commissioned with some success and while some difficulties have been encountered, multiagent systems are seen as a specific class of complex distributed systems. The underlying philosophy of this work draws heavily on CSP and views MAS as Communicating Intentional Processes (CIP). On-going work is extending the algebraic approach to model CIPs effectively (O'Hare and Abbas, 1994). Future work is looking at the use of a Synchronous Calculus of Communicating Systems (SCCS) (Milner, 1983) in the specification of multiagent systems.

BIBLIOGRAPHY

Barringer, H., Fisher, M., Gabbay, D., Gough, G., and Owens, R. (1989). *MetateM: A Framework for Programming in Temporal Logic*, Tech. Rep. UMCS-89-10-4. Department of Computer Science, University of Manchester, Manchester, UK.

Bergstra, J. A., Heering, J., and Klint, P., eds. (1989). *Algebraic Specification*. Addison-Wesley, Reading, MA.

Birkoff, G., and Lipson, J. D. (1970). Heterogeneous algebras. *J. Combinatorial Theory, Ser. A* **8**, 115–133.

Bjorner, D., and Jones, C. B., eds. (1978). *The Vienna Development Method: The Meta-Language*, Lect. Notes Comput. Sci., Vol. 61. Springer-Verlag, Berlin.

Brookes, S., Hoare, C. A. R., and Roscoe, A. W. (1984). A theory of communicating sequential processes. *J. Am. Comput. Mach.* **31**(3), 560–599.

Castelfranchi, C. (1993). Commitments: From individual intentions to groups and organizations. In *AAAI '93 Workshop on AI and Theories of Groups and Organizations*.

Cohen, B., Harwood, W. T., and Jackson, M. I. (1986). *The Specification of Complex Reasoning Systems*. Addion-Wesley, Reading, MA.

Cohen, P. R., and Levesque, H. J. (1990). Intention is choice with commitment. *Artif. Intell.* **42**, 213–261.

Davies, N. (1991). A first order logic of truth, knowledge and belief. In *Logics in AI* (J. van Eijck, ed.), Lect. Notes Artif. Intell., Vol. 478, pp. 170–179. Springer-Verlag, Berlin.

Dongha, P. (1995). Toward a formal model of commitment for resource bounded agents. In *Intelligent Agents* (M. J. Wooldridge and N. R. Jennings, eds.), Lecture Notes in Artificial Intelligence, LNAI-890, Springer-Verlag.

Ehrig, H., and Mahr, B. (1985). *Fundamentals of Algebraic Specification 1: Formal: Equations and Initial Semantics*, Monogr. Theor. Comput. Sci. EATCS, Vol. 6. Springer-Verlag, Berlin.

Ehrig, H., Mahr, B., Classen, I., and Orejas, F. (1992). Introduction to algebraic specification. Part 1: Formal methods for software development. *Comput. J.* 35(5), 460–467.

Elshiewy, N. A. (1990). *Robust Coordinated Reactive Computing in Sandra, Swedish Institute of Computer Science*, Tech. Rep. No. SICS/D-90-9003. Royal Institute of Technology (KTH), Sweden.

Fisher, M. (1989). *Characterising Temporal Logic*, Tech. Rep. UMCS-89-10-6. Department of Computer Science, University of Manchester, Manchester, UK.

Gallimore, R. M., Coleman, D., and Stavridou, V. (1989). UMIST OBJ: A language for executable program specifications. *Comput. J.* 32(5).

Guttag, J. V., Horning, J., and Wing, J. (1982). Some notes on putting formal specifications to productive use. *Science Computer Programming*. 2, 53–68.

Hennessy, M. (1988). *Algebraic Theory of Processes*. MIT Press, Cambridge, MA.

Hoare, C. A. R. (1978). Communicating sequential processes. *Commun. ACM* 21(8), 666–677 (reprinted in Hoare and Jones, 1989).

Imagine (1993). *Imagine Final Project Report* (H. Haugeneder, ed.), Esprit Project No. 5362.

Jennings, N. R. (1993). Commitments and conventions: The foundation of coordination in multi-agent systems. *Knowl. Eng. Rev.* 8(3), 223–250.

Jones, C. B. (1980). *Software Development: A Rigorous Approach*. Prentice-Hall, Englewood Cliffs, NJ.

Jones, C. B. (1990). *Systematic Software Development using VDM*, 2nd ed., Prentice-Hall, Englewood Cliffs, NJ.

Liskov, B. H., and Zilles, S. N. (1974). Programming with abstract data types, Proceedings of a Symposium on Very High Level Languages, Santa Monica CA., March 28th–29th, 1974. *ACM SIGPLAN Notices* 9(4), 50–59.

Liskov, B. H., and Zilles, S. N. (1975). Specification techniques for data abstractions. *IEEE Trans. Software Eng.* SE-1(1), 7–19.

McCabe, F. G., and Clark, K. (1995). Agent process interaction language. In *Intelligent Agents* (M. J. Wooldridge and N. R. Jennings, eds.), Lecture Notes in Artificial Intelligence, LNAI-890, Springer-Verlag.

Milner, A. J. R. G. (1983). Calculi for synchrony and asynchrony. *Theoretical Computer Science*. 25, 267–310.

Milner, R. (1989). *Communication and Concurrency*, Int. Comput. Sci. Ser. Prentice-Hall International Publishers, Englewood Cliffs, NJ.

Ness, L. (1993). L.0: A truly concurrent executable temporal logic language for protocols. *IEEE Trans. Software Eng.* SE-19(4), 410–423.

O'Hare, G. M. P., and Abbas, S. (1994). Agent oriented programming: Communicating intentional processes. *18th Gen. Artif. Intell. Conf.*, KI-94 Workshops, Saarbrucken, September 18–23 (J. Kunze and H. Stoyan, eds.), pp. 21–23.

O'Hare, G. M. P., and Wooldridge, M. J. (1992). A software engineering perspective on multi-agent system design: Experience in the development of MADE. In *Distributed Artificial Intelligence: Theory and Praxis* (N. M. Avouris and L. Gasser, eds.), pp. 109–127. Kluwer Academic Publishers, Dordrecht, The Netherlands.

Ozcan, M. B. (1993). An integrated rapid prototyping environment based on executable specifications. Ph.D. Thesis, Department of Computation, University of Manchester, Institute of Science and Technology (UMIST), Manchester, UK.

Powell, M. S. (1987a). Incremental compilation, partial evaluation and persistence. *Proc. Int. Workshop Persistent Objects, 2nd*, Universities of Glasgow and St. Andrews, *1987*, PPRR-44.

Powell, M. S. (1987b). Strongly typed user interfaces in an abstract data store. *Software Pract. Exper.* **17**(4), 241–266.

Powell, M. S. (1988). An input/output primitive for object orientated systems. *Inf. Software Technol.* **30**(1).

Powell, M. S. (1989). A program development environment based on persistence and abstract data types. In *Persistent Object Systems* (I. Rosenberg and D. Koch, eds.). Springer-Verlag, Newcastle, Australia.

Rao, A. S., and Georgeff, M. P. (1991). Modelling rational agents within a BDI-architecture. In *Proceedings of the Second International Conference on Principles of Knowledge Representation and Reasoning* (J. Allen, R. Fikes, and E. Sandwell, eds.), pp. 473–484. Morgan Kaufmann, San Mateo, CA.

Rao, A. S., and Georgeff, M. P. (1992). An abstract architecture for rational agents. In *Proceedings of the Third International Conference on Principles of Knowledge Representation and Reasoning* (B. Nebel, C. Rich, and W. Swartout, eds.). Morgan Kaufmann, San Mateo, CA.

Robinson, J. A. (1965). A machine-oriented logic based on the resolution principle. *J. ACM* **12**(1).

Shoham, Y. (1991). Agent 0: An agent-oriented language and its interpreter. *Proc. Natl. Conf. Artif. Intell., 9th*, Anaheim, CA, pp. 704–709.

Shoham, Y. (1993). Agent-oriented programming. *Artif. Intell.* **60**, 51–90.

Thomas, S. R. (1993). PLACA: An agent programming language. Ph.D. Thesis, Stanford University, Stanford, CA (available as Tech. Rep. STAN-CS-93-1487 Stanford University, Computer Science Department).

Thomas, S. R. (1994). The PLACA agent programming language. *Proc. Eur. Conf. Artif. Intell. Workshop Agent Theor. Archit. Lang.*, Amsterdam, The Netherlands, *1994*.

Wooldridge, W. J. (1995). This is MYWORLD: The logic of an agent-oriented DAI testbed. In *Intelligent Agents* (M. J. Wooldridge and N. R. Jennings, eds.) Lecture Notes in Artificial Intelligence LNAI-890, Springer-Verlag.

Wooldridge, M. J., and Vandekerckhove, D. (1993). MYWORLD: An agent-oriented programming testbed for distributed artificial intelligence, *Pre-Proc. Coop. Knowl. Based Syst. SIG Workshop*, University of Keele, Keele, UK, *1993*.

Young, S. J. (1982). *Real Time Languages Design and Development*. Ellis Horwood, Chichester, UK.

PART IV

Related Disciplines

This final section covers topics that we euphemistically call "related areas." It attempts to show the interdisciplinary nature of distributed artificial intelligence. Many discrete areas of academic pursuit have much to contribute, and it is only through the fostering of a mutual understanding and a bidirectional exchange of research findings that the discipline can truly advance.

The chapter by Tuomela offers insights as to the synergy that exists between philosophy and DAI and which can and needs to be developed further. In particular his chapter looks at the notion of joint intention, an issue that has also been addressed by DAI researchers (see Chapter 6), and argues that such social attitudes are central to all forms of social life.

The second contribution within this section adopts a similar approach only arguing that there is and ought to be a clear interplay between the research areas of organizational theory and distributed artificial intelligence. Kirn postulates that the intelligent organizational capabilities demanded by current and future generations of organizations can be addressed by the incorporation of multiagent concepts. He examines organizational intelligence and considers how it can benefit DAI and how DAI can in turn benefit organizational intelligence.

In the next chapter, Castelfranchi and Conte examine some critical issues within DAI from a social science perspective. They question the current prevailing view of social agenthood that exists within distributed artificial intelligence, focusing particularly upon social actions, including those of shared, joint, and collective actions. They consider collective action as described within the context of joint persistent goals (JPG) and argue that these are neither necessary or sufficient. They present an alternative view of collective action grounded within a theory of social dependence.

The last chapter considers the fundamentally important issue of user interface design. Hall points out that, as with all interactive systems, the ultimate acceptability and efficiency of use of the system is intimately related to the user's perception of the interface. Hall considers the different classes of users that may interact with MASs and their associated needs. She then reviews interactions with existing DAI systems, considering what specific functionality differentiates MAS from other distributed interactive systems. Specifically she focuses upon the key issue of how to represent the DAI system to the user.

This part addresses a diverse range of subject matter, yet demonstrates the pervasive nature of the subject area. Distributed artificial intelligence has much to contribute to and learn from other allied disciplines.

CHAPTER 18 ————————————

Philosophy and Distributed Artificial Intelligence: The Case of Joint Intention

RAIMO TUOMELA

1 PHILOSOPHY AND DAI

In current philosophical research the term "philosophy of social action" can be, and has been, used in a broad sense to encompass the following central research topics: (1) action occurring in a social context; this includes multiagent action; (2) joint attitudes (or "we-attitudes" such as joint intention, mutual belief) and other social attitudes needed for the explication and explanation of social action; (3) social macronotions, such as actions performed by social groups and properties of social groups such as their goals and beliefs; (4) social norms and social institutions (Tuomela, 1984, 1995). The theory of social action understood analogously in a broad sense would then involve not only philosophical but all other relevant theorizing about social action. Thus, in this sense, fields such as artificial intelligence (AI), distributed AI (DAI), and the theory of multiagent systems (MAS) fall within the scope of the theory of social action. DAI studies the social side of computer systems and includes various well-known areas, including human computer interaction (Chapter 21), computer-supported cooperative work (Chapters 1 and 13), organizational processing (Chapter 19), distributed problem solving (Chapter 1), and simulation of social systems (Chapter 20) and organizations. Even if I am a philosopher with a low level artificial intelligence I will below try to say something about what the scope of DAI should be taken to be on conceptual and philosophical grounds. (Later the central notion of joint intention will be the main topic in order to illustrate how philosophers and DAI researchers approach this issue.)

Foundations of Distributed Artificial Intelligence, Edited by G. M. P. O'Hare and N. R. Jennings.
ISBN 0-471-00675-0 © 1996 John Wiley & Sons, Inc.

Let us now consider the relationship between philosophy, especially philosophy of social action, and DAI. Both are concerned with social matters and in this sense seem to have a connection to social science proper. With what kinds of questions should these areas of study be concerned? In principle, ordinary social science should study all aspects of social life (in various societies and cultures), try to describe it, and create general theories to explain it. Philosophers do not create specific social theories, but their task in this context is to create conceptual frameworks for the study of social life, to investigate central social concepts, and to discuss and critically evaluate different fundamental ideas and philosophical views about social life and social systems. What then is the task of DAI? Broadly put, DAI should basically attempt to study and to create "design specifications" for a social world of intelligent robots; it should also be concerned with the actual technical implementation of those specifications. As DAI is basically concerned with intelligent agents it typically adopts rationality assumptions which are stronger than those social scientists can plausibly make (social scientists should also be interested in stupid, clumsy, and mistake-making agents), but because of the end of actually building robots it will have to take into account the resource boundedness of intelligent agents. This concern with bounded resources may also contrast with how philosophers—those prime idealizers—approach these matters.

My most general thesis in this chapter is this: Philosophy is in many ways highly relevant and important for DAI, and, to some extent, vice versa. A sharp borderline between these fields hardly exists, even if philosophers of social action, *qua* philosophers, are interested in somewhat different aspects of social action (and related matters). I argue that, in principle, one of the tasks of philosophy is to specify the research areas and problems of DAI on a general level (but only on a general level). DAI need not be interested in simulating all the inner mechanisms and processes that lead agents to do what they do in a social setting, but it has to be concerned with what people achieve by their actions—with "social outputs"—and various related public matters including social reasons for action. This public output aspect is something that philosophers should specify on a general level: Philosophers ought to say what the output side of social life, and the life of the community of intelligent robots, basically is, or at least they ought to be able to sketch plausible scenarios about it. Here we arrive at fundamental questions such as what general reasons there are for people to form communities and societies at all and what kind of conceptual problems are involved in answers to these questions. This is a broad topic which I can only touch briefly here.

Basically, agents have not only personal needs and wants but also collective ones. Thus we may have as our collective goal to keep our environment clean; no single agent can achieve that collective goal. Or, to mention a small-scale collective or joint goal, we may want to get deer meat, believing that cooperative joint hunting is desirable or even necessary when compared with hunting separately or alone. In this kind of context, especially when a collective goal or "good" is to be achieved, *collective action problems* are central (see Chapter

6). Such problems involve a conflict between individual and collective interests, because there is an in-built incentive to free-ride (e.g., in our example to litter or not to care). Collective action problems typically have the structure of a prisoner's dilemma game or a chicken game (see Chapter 1).

As indicated, in social life there are central tasks that can be solved only collectively: (a) tasks requiring collective goals (e.g., the provision of collective goods in the economist's sense); often but not always there is a collective action problem here—conflict between collective and individual rationality; (b) individual goals (tasks) which, however, require collective cooperation concerning the means (personal goals thus can be satisfied only through collective or joint action). Collective needs and collective goals over and above personal ones thus are central for the formation and maintenance of societies and social institutions, and in this context collective action problems typically occur (norm-based social institutions are supposed to help to solve them). There is of course much more to social life, but basically the above considerations, when spelled out, should cover the most central aspects. As a result we get a conceptual framework of public, output-related social concepts which will include also notions related to social positions, social norms, and social power over and above explicit action notions.

Roughly in this way we then get the needed "output specifications" (understood in the above broad sense), and then also the scope of DAI on a general level becomes determined. As to the question of how to theorize about these matters and how ultimately to create a theory satisfying those output specifications, space does not allow me to say much here, but see Chapter 10 for a discussion of some of these issues. Let me note, however, that here also philosophy has a role to play: it can be assigned the task to create a broad conceptual framework of concepts and basic underlying assumptions for the study of central aspects of social life (Chapter 20). This task, because of its generality and broad scope, goes beyond what social theorists can be expected to do. What kinds of elements does such a conceptual framework contain? Here is a short and incomplete list of notions that philosophers have studied: joint intention (Chapter 6), mutual knowledge (Chapter 2), joint and collective action, joint decision making, social norms of various kinds (Chapters 9 and 20), social institutions, agreement and contract, communication, bargaining, power, strategic interaction, love and caring, morality, social values, and good society [many of these concepts have been investigated in Gilbert (1989), Pettit (1993), and Tuomela (1995)]. These notions—central for the study of social life—will have to be ultimately taken into account also by DAI.

I have claimed thus that philosophers ought to create relevant social conceptual frameworks and show DAI in broad terms where to go, what kind of problems to undertake to solve or at least indicate in what kind of conceptual setting or settings feasibly to work. (It is of course clearly the task of DAI rather than philosophy to determine what its specific research problems ought to be; that depends on the internal development in DAI and in its neighbor sciences.) Let me idealize the situation somewhat and make the following slightly speculative suggestion in terms of the software-hardware distinction: Think of the (or a) public social framework as a kind of software in terms of which to theorize, while the hardware will consist of the agents "realizing" that software and "computing" the programs stated in terms of that software. The present software-hardware distinction is not quite clear-cut: While idiosynchratic psychological states and processes clearly would belong to the hardware side possibly also some nongeneral psychological information should be put on the social software side in a publicly codified form (e.g., in the form psychological types—altruist, free-rider, dominant).

To continue with the tasks of philosophy, it is also expected to sketch the viable philosophical options (or at least arguments pro et con) and investigate their features. For instance, in the case of the mind-body problem it will specify the various versions or monism, materialism (or physicalism) and dualism and discuss their features. (Examples of some recently much discussed mind-body views are identity theory, token physicalism, supervenience physicalism, and functionalism.) Each DAI researcher is committed to, and relies on, some philosophical background assumptions whether he is aware of it or not. The task of philosophy is also to show how DAI connects to other sciences and disciplines such as the brain sciences.

Given the above remarks it should be clear that the social conceptual framework that DAI will ultimately need is quite broad. Thus, for instance, the Belief-Desire-Intention (BDI) architecture (Chapter 5) that has been employed in the study of both single-agent and multiagent action will have to be complemented by other social concepts, as indicated. Over and above helping in the creation of conceptual frameworks and in the critical investigation of underlying assumptions and arguments philosophy can also help DAI in more down-to-earth questions related to actual everyday research. Thus, philosophy can contribute to DAI in the research problems related to logic (see Chapters 4 and 10) in the analysis of specific notions and topics, questions of rationality, and in making choices concerning metaphysical options (e.g., formal ontology, limits of DAI). Analytic philosophers are also good at inventing substantive, unartificial examples, especially counterexamples to specific theses.

As researchers in AI know, they owe much of their logical and exact tools to philosophy. In particular, modal logic, which is so important in AI today, was first developed by philosophers. Possibly most of the research in modal logic is now conducted by researchers within AI, but also philosophers continue to work in that field. I will not present evidence for this; one only needs to open a textbook in AI to see the relevance of the work by philosopher-logicians.

Recent developments within the philosophy of mind and the philosophy of action have helped concept formation in AI, and in part vice versa [cf. the frequent references to books such as Bratman (1987) and the work on belief-kinematics, and in the other direction the influence of AI on the philosophy of mind and even philosophy of science]. As for DAI and multiagent theory, one can find traces of influence, and references, in DAI literature to philosophers' writings, although it must be said that even within philosophy the questions related to the theory of social action were not seriously researched before the 1980s. Some relevant pieces of philosophical work related to joint intention and joint action, cooperation, and communication that also some DAI researchers have noticed are the papers by Bratman (1992, 1993), Grice (1957), Searle (1990), and Tuomela (1991, 1993a), as well as Tuomela and Miller (1988). Other relevant pieces of logical and philosophical work are the works by Belnap (1991), Bratman (1994), Cohen and Levesque (1991), Gilbert (1989), Tuomela and Sandu (1994), Sandu and Tuomela (1994), Tuomela (1984, 1993b, 1995) and Chapter 2. (Relevant works by DAI researchers will be referred to and discussed later in this chapter.) As to questions of rationality and metaphysics, mentioned above, there has not yet been much interaction between philosophy and DAI. It is easy to predict, however, that questions of individual and collective rationality, and rationalization, will have to be tackled also by DAI researchers in the near future when the study of robot communities really gets on its way. Then also all kinds of questions related to the metaphysics of the social realm will have to be confronted (e.g., the reality of groups and social structures).

2 JOINT INTENTION: THE ANALYSANDUM AND CONDITIONS FOR ANALYSIS

To show that there is philosophical research very close to research in DAI, I will in the rest of this chapter discuss the central multiagent notion of joint intention (and to a lesser extent that of joint action). The material I will present is rather concise, and in many places I cannot use space for presenting arguments but refer the reader to other writings. While I will concentrate on my own research below, some representative examples of other theoreticians' work will also be considered toward the end of the chapter. The purpose of the discussion in the rest of the chapter is nevertheless not to give a comprehensive survey. Rather it is to show in a detailed fashion how philosophers and DAI researchers can work hand in hand in this kind of context.

The theoretical view I will present to you has as its intuitive analysandum the following situation. Suppose one of us comes up with the idea of cleaning our backyard. He may express this idea colloquially by saying "Let's clean our backyard! Are you with me?" The others may answer "yes" or "good idea!" Suppose there are three persons involved all of whom in this sense accept the idea of cleaning the backyard. We can say that what they accept is a plan for doing something together. Another way of putting this matter is that they have made an agreement to clean the backyard. The intuitive analysandum here is, anyway, that of accepting—separately or, in some cases, jointly—a plan to do something together (cf. "Here is a plan for joint action. Who accepts it"?).

In my analytic terminology we can say the following about the analysandum. The participants of a joint action to be intentionally performed have publicly accepted a plan for performing that action (or at least a plan somehow implying the performance of that action). The joint action thus is plan-based, and the participants' having and endorsing that plan involves their joint intention to perform the action in question. In my analysis I will accordingly say that the participants conatively endorse a plan involving or entailing the joint-intention expression "We will do X together," X being a joint action. (When applied to a certain participant I will say that he has or shares the "group intention" to do X; what will be called a "we-intention" is a special kind of group intention.) The endorsement of the plan must be public and in standard cases it must also be communicated to the other participants. The acceptance of the plan by the participants can take place purely individually (cf. "This is the plan. Who accepts it?"). The acceptance of the plan, however, commits the participating persons to action. This is commitment in a strong interpersonal sense concerned both with the joint action and the participants' parts or shares, and with responsibility toward the other participants to take part.

I have elsewhere (Tuomela, 1995) argued that joint intentions (Chapters 2 and 6) are central in several respects. As I will below be mainly concerned with analyzing the notion of joint intention, it is useful to present a list of features that indicate the centrality of joint intentions and also serve as a kind of criteria of adequacy that any analysis of joint intention should respect. Consider thus the following list (also cf. Bratman, 1992):

1. Joint intentions figure centrally in participating agents' (social) practical reasoning and resulting joint action. Thus:

   a. Joint intentions, in analogy with single-agent intentions (see Chapter 5), present problems and restrict available action alternatives. Forming a joint intention to go swimming excludes other alternatives and presents problems concerning the means to perform the joint action in question.
   b. Joint intentions serve to initiate, guide, and monitor joint action, creating order—especially interpersonal coordination—in social life. Furthermore, there cannot be intentional joint action without joint intention (at least joint "action-intention").
   c. Joint intentions help to connect the group level with the personal level. Thus it can be argued that a group's intentional action (e.g., a business company's buying another company) must be based on the joint intentions of some authority-possessing members of the group.
   d. Joint intentions have a normative impact on the agents' thinking and acting. (Recall my remarks on joint commitment.)

2. The concept of joint intention is central both in philosophy of social science and in theorizing about the social world (and thus it occurs in some sense in various theorists' heads, so to speak). Thus:

a. The concept of joint intention (a person's we-intention) is needed for a characterization of the social "I" (viz., "I" as "one of us"). It will be argued below that joint intentions, which are necessary ingredients of intentional joint action, are irreducible to personal intentions and other personal notions.

b. The concept of joint intention helps to conceptualize the conflict between the group-level and personal-level interests (cf. collective action dilemmas) and is central for the analysis of group phenomena such as actions performed by groups in terms of what group members think and do,

c. The notion of joint intention (and related jointness notions) can be and should be important in theory formation in the social sciences. The most basic argument for this is simply that people have joint intentions in many central social situations and that therefore social theory, and DAI, must deal with the concept of joint intention.

d. The notion of a social group, in a refined sense, is basically an "authority-involving" system for arriving at joint intentions involving group commitments [see Tuomela (1995) for discussion].

As said, the above features also qualify as a kind of criteria of adequacy for any account of joint intention. [That criteria 1a–d will be fulfilled by the account to be offered should be clear from my presentation in the next section; as for 2a–d I refer the reader to Tuomela (1995).]

3 AN ANALYSIS OF JOINT INTENTION

Suppose that you and I have the joint intention to clean our backyard together, as expressed by the conative sentence "We will clean our backyard together." The content of the intention here involves our performing something together and the pronoun "we" of course refers to our group. A joint intention (expressible by a sentence of the form "We will do X") is something that several agents have among themselves.

In contrast to wants, wishes, hopes, and many other mental states, intentions are, in the last analysis, necessarily related to one's own action. Accordingly, when an agent is said to take part in a joint intention, what he ultimately will have to intend is that he by his own action, by his part or share, contribute to the joint action. A fully intentional joint action X (cf. jointly carrying a table, singing a song) must arguably be based on the participants' relevant joint intention (normally the intention to do X), and we should accordingly require that each participant have the intention to do his part of X. This kind of intention is just an intention that can be called a we-intention.

Intentions being in part cognitive, an agent cannot intend to perform an action unless he believes that this action is possible or at least realizable with some nonnegligible probability. With double analogy, an agent cannot we-intend unless he believes not only that he can perform his part of X but also that he together with his fellow participants can perform the joint action in question: The jointly intending agents must believe that the "joint action opportunities" for an intentional performance of X are (or will be) there. Yet another property of a we-intention is that in each participant's view it must be mutually believed by the participants that the presuppositions for an intentional performance of X hold. Even more must be said, if my plan-view of intention is right: The agents must believe that they have accepted a plan for joint action, and at least in standard cases this must be just the we-intended joint action. What this involves is that the concept of we-intention is conceptually dependent on a preanalytic notion of joint intention. Thus we-intentions cannot be analyzed in terms of personal intentions and mutual beliefs. It can be debated whether the dependence of we-intention on joint intention is of the nature of conceptual presupposition or whether it should be built into the concept of we-intention. If we accept the latter view we must accept that it is a conceptual truth in the case of a we-intending agent A that he we-intends to do X in accordance with and because of the participants' joint intention to do X. This can be argued for by reference to the satisfaction conditions of the we-intention: Unless A performed his part of X because of the participants' plan to do X he surely would not have satisfied his we-intention.

Actually joint intentions must be taken to include also standing intentions. We-intentions directly generate action and do not include all standing joint intentions, e.g., those concerned with future actions about the performance of which ("joint action opportunities") there is no definite belief yet. Group intentions in this sense can be regarded as precisely those intentions which are expressible by locutions of the form "We will do X" (where "will" is conatively used). Arguably, such group intentions are either we-intentions or dispositions to we-intend, and I have argued that joint intentions can be regarded basically as mutually shared we-intentions (or at least dispositions to we-intend) about whose existence the participants have mutual knowledge (or belief) [see Tuomela (1991, 1995, Chapter 3)].

In contrast to joint desires and wants (Chapter 9) we can say the following about joint intentions (shared we-intentions): Based on their various personal and, especially, joint desires and mutual and other beliefs, the agents make up their minds, jointly or separately, and thereby form an intention (or plan, as we may say) to act jointly, attempting to act rationally in a coordinated way so as to fulfil the already formed plan. Joint intentions, in contrast to joint wants and desires, can be regarded as joint commitments to action, viz., the participants' interdependent commitments to perform their parts of the joint action and their responsibility for the total joint action getting performed. (We can also say more generally that the participants are jointly committed to reach a joint goal, such as X's having been performed jointly by them, and their plan to achieve this joint goal, as reflected in their part performances.) Such joint commitments are appropriately persistent and, especially, are not consummated before the agents have jointly achieved what they we-intend (or achieved consensus about the unachievability of the intended goal). However, as in the case of mere personal intentions, the agents can change their minds, and thus joint commitments are not irrevocable. It is nevertheless a rationality condition that the participants preserve their we-intentions as long as the others do or else at least inform the others about their changes of minds in order to become released from their commitment to participate in the intended joint action (see Chapter 6 for more details).

Let us now think of some agents' having accepted "We will jointly clean our backyard" and thus agreed to act jointly. This acceptance must be conative—they must be disposed to contribute to the joint task and also be normatively committed to that task. Joint intentions are formed in such a process of agreement-making (not all agreement-making needs to result in a joint intention). In joint-intention formation each agent also accepts for himself: "I ought to participate in our doing X together." This acceptance means not only that the agent (at least dimly) recognizes the existence of the agreement ("plan") to perform X but also commits himself to performing X together with the others.

The agreement-making that takes place in the context of the formation of a joint intention can take place fully explicitly or only implicitly. Agreement-making, be it explicit or not, is an essentially intentional activity and also a communication-based public activity. Mistakes and errors about the contents of agreements can of course occur, but in the standard cases the participants will share the correct mutual belief not only about that they have made an agreement but also about its content. According to the agreement-view of joint intention and joint action every full-blown or "proper" intentional joint action, and, accordingly, joint intention, must be based on an agreement by the participants. However, this is only the core idea. There are cases of (a) preagreement and (b) institutional cases in which no agreement-making concerning the particular action in question is needed. [I shall not here discuss these issues further; see Tuomela (1995, Chapter 2)].

Let us consider the central notion of we-intention in some more detail. We-intentions are action-generating joint intentions that agents have in situations of joint action, e.g., when they intend to carry a table jointly. The content of a we-intention can (with some reservations) be taken to be "to do X jointly" (or, to emphasize its "we-character," something like "we to do X jointly"). A we-intention involves the intention to perform one's part of the joint action. I will now present a detailed summary analysis of the notion of we-intention (cf. Tuomela, 1995). We consider a member A_i of a collective G ("we" for A_i) assumed to consist of $A_1, \ldots, A_m$, with $i = 1, \ldots, m$ (and allowing the word "agreement" to refer to merely believed agreement).

(*WI*) A member A_i of a collective G *we-intends* to do X if and only if, based on the (explicit or implicit) agreement to perform X jointly made by the agents $A_1, \ldots, A_i, \ldots, A_m$,

(i) A_i intends to do his (agreement-based) part of X (as his part of X);

(ii) A_i has a belief to the effect that the joint action opportunities for an intentional performance of X will obtain (or at least probably will obtain), especially that a right number of the full-fledged and adequately informed members of G, as required for the performance of X, will (or at least probably will) do their parts of X, which will under normal conditions result in an intentional joint performance of X by the participants;

(iii) A_i believes that there is (or will be) a mutual belief among the participating members of G (or at least among those participants who do their parts of X intentionally as their parts of X there is or will be a mutual belief) to the effect that the joint action opportunities for an intentional performance of X will obtain (or at least probably will obtain);

(iv) (i) in part because of (ii) and (iii).

In this analysis clause (i) is the most central one; (ii) and (iii) can be regarded as presupposition-beliefs, whose effectiveness is guaranteed by (iv).

We actually need a general notion of joint intention (or group-intention), viz., a notion which covers not only action-generating but also *standing* joint intentions. Put somewhat differently, we need a characterization of the notion of joint intention satisfying the truth conditions of the conatively used, intention-expressing sentence "We will do X," where X denotes an arbitrary joint action type. While it is rather obvious that we-intentions in the sense of our (*WI*) make this sentence schema true, there are also other truthmakers. I have argued (Tuomela, 1991) that conditional we-intentions with conditions believed by the agent to be satisfied also qualify, and so also do dispositions to we-intend in general. More exactly, I defend essentially the following analysis.

(*GI*) "We will do X" is true of A (relative to A's group G) if and only if, based on the (explicit or implicit) agreement by the members of A's group G to perform X jointly,

1. A we-intends to do X [in the sense of (*WI*)]; or
2. A has formed a standing group-intention to do X, which is a disposition to we-intend to do X (provided X has a part division).

Group-intentions can now be regarded as either we-intentions or dispositions to we-intend. On the basis of our earlier discussion we can now give our analysis of the notion of joint intention.

(*JI*) Agents $A_1, \ldots, A_i, \ldots, A_m$ have the *joint intention to perform a joint action X* if and only if

a. These agents have the group-intention to perform X.
b. There is a mutual belief among them to the effect that (a).

The upshot of our present analysis is this. *Joint intentions* are intentions that several agents among themselves have, and they are expressible by an intention expression of the form "We will do X" endorsed by these agents. When two or more agents have the joint intention to do X each of these agents also accepts the intention expression "We will do X" and essentially because of that they can be said to have the *group-intention* to do X. Furthermore, when the joint action X has a—preassigned or presently agreed-on—part structure, the agent's group-intention to do X is either his *we-intention* to do X or he is *disposed to we-intend* X. Finally, an agent's we-intention to do X amounts to his intention to do his *part* of X (as his part of X) and some relevant beliefs presupposed in this situation. These intention concepts form a family of concepts which cannot be reduced away (e.g., in terms of personal intentions and mutual beliefs). The irreducibility of the notion of joint intention is also indicated by the fact that a person's we-intention contains implicit reference to a preanalytic notion of joint intention: A person cannot we-intend to do X without we-intending in accordance with and because of the agents' joint intention (plan) to do X together.

Up to now I have used both the agreement terminology and the plan terminology to speak about joint intentions. Each of the notions of agreement making and plan-acceptance would suffice as my central analytic concepts. In fact, as I use these notions, they are equivalent in a clear and obvious sense. Thus, the following thesis, or at least its core idea, can be argued to be acceptable.

(*JIP*) Some agents (say $A_1, \ldots, A_i, \ldots, A_m$) have formed the (agreement-based) joint intention to perform X if and only if each of them a) has accepted a plan to perform X jointly, (b) has communicated this acceptance to the others, and (c) because of (a) and (b) it is a true mutual belief among $A_1, \ldots, A_i,$ $\ldots, A_m$ that they are jointly committed to performing X and that there is or will be a part or share (requiring at least potential contribution) of X for each agent to perform that he accordingly is or will be committed to performing.

In other words, while the concept of a joint intention is different from the notion of accepting and endorsing a plan to act jointly, still having a joint intention amounts to accepting and endorsing a plan, provided the agents' have, in the simple core cases at least, communicated their acceptance to each other and have become jointly committed to carrying it out [see Tuomela (1995, Chapter 3) for a discussion].

4 OTHER APPROACHES TO JOINT INTENTION

The study of the notions of joint action and joint intention has not been a popular topic in philosophy. While there is a huge literature on action and intention and related notions in the single-agent case there is relatively little systematic work available concerning the corresponding joint notions. I will briefly consider all the philosophical approaches that are sufficiently precise to be compared with my above account. These are Bratman's and Searle's accounts. From the approaches published by researchers in DAI I will comment on Cohen's and Levesque's account and on a paper by Rao, Georgeff, and Sonenberg.

Recently Michael Bratman, well known in AI for his work on single-agent intention, has begun to investigate multiagent notions. In a recent paper (1993), he analyzes *shared intentions* in terms of the locutions "We intend to J," where J is a joint action. His final analysis is this (for the two-person case):

We intend to J if and only if

1. (a) I intend that we J and (b) you intend that we J;
2. (a) I intend that we J in accordance with and because of 1(a), 1(b), and meshing subplans of 1(a) and 1(b); you intend that we J in accordance with and because of 1(a), 1(b), and meshing subplans of 1(a) and 1(b).
3. (1) and (2) are common knowledge between us.

I shall not discuss Bratman's notions in detail here but only show that it is not only conceptually different but also classifies cases of shared and joint intention differently from my account. Basically his approach operates with mere personal intentions which concern a joint action. The intentions are interdependent (clause 2) and mutual knowledge about the agents' intentions is assumed (clause 3). This conceptually contrasts with my plan conception which regards the concept of joint intention irreducible to personal intentions and mutual knowledge.

The following argument shows that Bratman's shared intentions need not always be joint intentions in my sense. According to him the following example satisfies his analysis: "You and I arrive at a public basketball court and simply begin, without bothering to ensure each other of our intentions, to take turns shooting." According to me, this is best analyzed as a case of mere shared intention based on what I have called a "proper" social norm (one based on mere mutual belief rather than agreement making), not as a case involving a proper joint intention. Both agents shared a turn-taking norm and intend to obey it and there is mutual knowledge about this: this gives the intention to shoot, and Bratman's above conditions for shared intentions are fullfilled, or so Bratman at least assumes. The fulfillment of his clauses does not entail the existence even of an implicit agreement and hence not of a proper joint intention. His analysis accepts the case of shared and suitably interconnected personal intentions, which may be based merely on norm-obeying as above. The basketball example also is a case without strong interpersonal obligations, but there is no joint intention in my plan-sense either. So the case is compatible with my analysis and also serves to show that there are cases of shared intention in Bratman's sense which fail to be cases of joint intention in my sense. I claim that my analysis is more informative as an analysis of joint intention in that it discriminates better between such diverse examples as personal norm-obeying and "true joining of wills" which takes place in the case of agreement-based joint intention. However, Bratman's notion of shared intention is of interest in its own right.[1]

Let me next consider the account by the philosopher John Searle (1990).[2] He adopts a view of collective intentions which is rather close to my view (which I have presented and elaborated, with some changes and corrections, in a number of publications since the late 1970s). His view of the content of we-intention resembles what I have said about the satisfaction conditions of we-intention. According to him the content (satisfaction conditions) of a we-intention is means-relative: A_i intends to perform joint action X by means of his single-agent action X_i. But this idea holds true in my account as well, for the parts X_j, $j = 1, \ldots, m$, are means to the m-agent joint action X. Searle gives the following formula for the satisfaction conditions of a we-intention (intention-in-action, i.a.), B being the joint action of mixing a sauce (p. 414):

> i.a. collective B by means of singular A (this i.a. causes
> A stirred, causes B mixed).

This is not quite right, because it ignores that a participant's part-performance is dependent on the other participants' part-performances. But corrected for this, Searle's account, when corrected also for lack of the resources of "conceptual action generation," more or less amounts to my view. We then get basically this: A_i has a we-intention to perform a joint action X by means of his performing his part X_i (as his part of X), presuming that the other participants perform their parts of X; this we-intention has as its conditions of satisfaction that this very we-intention (causally and/or conceptually) generates A_i's performing his part X_i, which, presuming the other participants' performances of their parts, (causally and/or conceptually) generates an intentional performance of X by the participants.

Let me now briefly consider how researchers in DAI have analyzed joint intention. Actually the only published work I have seen comes from two sources.

[1]In Tuomela (1994) I argue that Bratman's analysis, which is not based on the plan sense of joint intention, is too weak even as an analysis of shared intention. The basic point of the argument is that the agent's intentions in clause 1 of his analysis must be responsive to the mutual knowledge of clause 3. But when corrected for this, Bratman's analysis becomes formally equivalent to the analysis of the notion of an intended collective goal that I advocate in the mentioned book. This notion is wider than the plan-based notion of joint intention and is also reducible to individual intentions and beliefs. It has important applications to the theory of social action.

[2]Searle (1990) presents a criticism of the account of we-intention presented in Tuomela and Miller (1988). I argue in Tuomela (1995), in a long footnote to Chapter 3, that Searle has badly misunderstood our position and that therefore his criticism has very little to do with what our view is. He believes that our position is that joint intentions can be reductively defined in terms of personal intentions and mutual beliefs. As seen above, this is not my view. I take Searle's criticism against that reductive position to be right.

First, Cohen and Levesque and their co-workers have presented a detailed full-blown theory of intention and action both for the single-agent and the multiagent case. Their theory is surely a very fine achievement, although I do have some criticisms concerning its details. Nobody working on joint intention within DAI or in any other field can afford not to study the papers of these authors. I shall sketch in informal terms, used by Cohen and Levesque, some basic features of their complicated theory and I will also present some critical remarks against it.

In Cohen and Levesque (1991) the following definition of joint intention is given (also cf. Cohen et al. (1990) and Levesque et al. (1990)).

Definition. A team of agents *jointly intends*, relative to some escape condition, to do an action, iff the members have a joint persistent goal relative to that condition of their having done that action and, moreover, having done it mutually believing throughout that they were doing it.

The notion of a joint persistent goal used here is analyzed as follows.

Definition: A team of agents have a *joint persistent goal* relative to q to achieve p just in case

1. They mutually believe that p is currently false.
2. They mutually know they all want p to eventually be true.
3. It is true (and mutual knowledge) that until they come to mutually believe either that p is true, that p will never be true, or that q is false, they will continue to mutually believe that they each have p as a weak achievement goal relative to q and with respect to the team.

The notion of a weak achievement goal is this.

Definition: An agent has a *weak achievement goal* relative to q and with respect to a team to bring about p if either of these conditions holds:

(i) The agent has a normal achievement goal to bring about p; that is, the agent does not yet believe that p is true and has p eventually being true as a goal.

(ii) The agent believes that p is true, will never be true, or is irrelevant (that is q is false), but has as a goal that the status of p be mutually believed by all the team members.

The conditions about the existence of joint action and joint-intention opportunities mentioned above seem to be correct. Thus, surely when having a joint goal or intention that p, the participants are assumed not to mutually believe that p or that necessarily $-p$ or that $-q$. (These conditions are also covered in my account, not as conditions in the analysis itself but as presuppositions of analysis.) What is especially valuable in these authors' analysis is that they show what role divergent "private" beliefs about the situation had by the participants may play here. For instance, such a private belief when having the content that the joint action after all faces insurmountable obstacles may lead a participant to switch his original goal of performing his part of the joint action into the goal (or, as we should rather say, obligation) of creating the mutual belief among the participants that the goal of the joint action is not attainable.

However, as seen from the above summary, this account does not refer to either explicit or implicit agreement (not even to believed agreement); nor is obligation or any other normative notion involved in the analysans; finally, communication is not "officially" required in the Cohen-Levesque theory. In Section 5 these features, in contrast, play a central role, and suggest to me that my analysandum may be stronger than in these authors' account. Furthermore, in their theory, joint intention and joint commitment are basically analyzed in terms of goals (chosen, consistent desires) and mutual (and other) beliefs. This analysis problematically reduces away intentions, unless their notion of choice here is a necessarily intentional notion. Their theory also involves the possibility that noncommunicating robots or any similar mechanical devices having beliefs or belief-like states but lacking normative conceptual resources could have joint intentions and commitments. From the point of view of our theory this is implausible at least if full-blown joint intention is meant. Mutual belief surely is necessary in this context, but the normative notion of agreement (at least belief in agreement) is also needed. It seems that cases of mere norm-following with rigid normative constraints for the beginning and end of the instances of norm-following would qualify as joint intentions in the present authors' sense (cf. the Finnish ritual of lighting candles in the evening of Independence Day).[3] From a normative point of view, it can be said that the analysans in the account of Levesque et al., because involving no normative notions, seems not to be fully able to account for the notion of joint commitment no matter how well it may capture the descriptive aspects of commitment.

I have argued above (and in other works) that conceptually the notions joint intention, joint commitment, and joint action can only be based on the normative (viz., joint-commitment entailing) notion of agreement (or believed agreement), implicit or explicit, and that, on factual grounds, recurrently successful joint action would be a surprising phenomenon in cases of several agents trying to act jointly merely on mutual belief, without agreement, about what they and the others should and will do in a joint project. This suggests to me that the Cohen-Levesque approach, no matter how detailed and precise, is not fully adequate.

[3]Castelfranchi et al. (1993) give another kind of counterexample. Two researchers (or, if you prefer, research teams) have the intention to find a vaccine against AIDS. They argue that this shared intention amounts to a joint intention in the sense of Cohen and Levesque. However, as the researchers compete with each other their shared intention cannot be a joint intention.

In a recent paper the DAI researchers Rao, Georgeff, and Sonenberg (1992) present a technical account of joint intention. While in the Cohen-Levesque logical semantics possible worlds are timelines the present authors take possible worlds to be trees. This gives more logical flexibility but also complicates the analysis. However, I cannot here go into technical questions. As to joint intention in the present approach it is a primitive notion which is connected to plans and personal attitudes (intentions, goals, and beliefs).[4] While these authors' work surely is interesting from a logical point of view, it—perhaps because of its preliminary nature—adds relatively little to the conceptual features of joint intention.

5   CONCLUSION

I hope this presentation has shown that work on jointness notions is in full swing both in philosophy and in DAI and that there is genuine interaction between the research done in these two different fields. One would expect that in the near future, possibly in a few years, most of the central social notions mentioned in Section 1 will be topics of interest and, hopefully, of actual work within DAI. There is one good reason for this expectation: As work on multiagent notions gets further it simply has to due to conceptual-theoretical reasons, deal with a number of central, intertwined notions that so far have not been studied by DAI researchers. The BDI paradigm will have to be expanded to deal with, for instance, agreement, joint decision, social power, communication, and various institutional social concepts.

REFERENCES

Belnap, N. (1991). Backwards and forwards in the modal logic of agency. *Philos. Phenomenol. Res.* **51**, 777–807.

Bratman, M. (1987). *Intention, Plans, and Practical Reasoning.* Harvard Univ. Press, Cambridge, MA.

Bratman, M. (1992). Shared cooperative activity. *Philos. Rev.* **101**, 327–341.

Bratman, M. (1993). Shared intention. *Ethics* **104**, 97–113.

---

[4]Rao et al. (1992) give their definition on joint intention on page 68. Let me try to give its basic content verbally: The members of a collection of agents jointly intend that something *p* if and only if everyone in the collection intends that *p* and there is a mutual belief among them that they jointly intend that *p*. Thus we can see that the notion of joint intention occurs irreducibly in the content of the agents' mutual belief. This seems to me to contradict these authors' statement on page 60 according to which "all joint propositional attitudes are defined in terms of the individual propositional attitudes." Rao et al. regard my (and my coauthor Miller's) work as reductive: "Tuomela and Miller [1988] and Grosz and Sidner [1990] regard a joint intention as definable in terms of the conjunction of individual intentions together with mutual beliefs about the intentions of other individuals." As seen, this claim does not hold true of our approach while it may apply to the view of Grosz and Sidner.

Bratman, M. (1994). *Shared Intention and Mutual Obligation*, Cah. epistemol., No. 9319. Université du Québec à Montréal.

Castelfranchi, C., Cesta, A., Conte, R., and Miceli, M. (1993). Foundations for interaction: The dependence theory. In *Advances in Artificial Intelligence. Third Congress of the Italian Association of Artificial Intelligence* (P. Torasso, ed.), 59–64. Springer-Verlag.

Cohen, P., and Levesque, H. (1991). Teamwork. *Noûs* **35,** 487–512.

Gilbert, M. (1989). *On Social Facts.* Routledge, London.

Grice, P. (1957). Meaning. *Philos. Rev.* **66,** 377–388.

Grosz, B., and Sidner, C. (1990). Plans for discourse. In *Intentions in Communication* (P. Cohen, J. Morgan, and M. Pollack, eds.), pp. 417–444. MIT Press, Cambridge, MA.

Levesque, H., Cohen, P., and Nunes, J. (1990). On acting together. In *Proc. Natl. Conf. Artif. Intell., 8th,* Boston, Vol. 1, pp. 94–99.

Pettit, P. (1993). *The Common Mind.* Oxford Univ. Press, New York.

Rao, A., Georgeff, M., and Sonenberg, E. (1992). Social plans: A preliminary report. In *Decentralized Artificial Intelligence 3,* (E. Werner and Y. Demazeau (eds.), pp. 57–76. Elsevier/North-Holland, Amsterdam.

Sandu, G., and Tuomela, R. (1994). Joint action and group action made precise. *Synthese* (to be published).

Searle, J. (1990). Collective intentions and actions. In *Intentions in Communication* (P. Cohen, J. Morgan, and M. Pollack, eds.), pp. 401–415. MIT Press, Cambridge, MA.

Tuomela, R. (1984). *A Theory of Social Action.* Synthese Library, Reidel, Dordrecht and Boston.

Tuomela, R. (1991). We will do it: An analysis of group-intentions. *Philos. Phenomenol. Res.* **51,** 249–277.

Tuomela, R. (1993a). What is cooperation? *Erkenntnis* **38,** 87–101.

Tuomela, R. (1993b). What are joint intentions? In *Philosophy and the Cognitive Sciences* (R. Casati and G. White, eds.), pp. 543–547. Austrian Ludwig Wittgenstein Society, Kirchberg.

Tuomela, R. (1994). *Cooperation: A Philosophical Study.*

Tuomela, R. (1995). *The Importance of Us: A Philosophical Study of Basic Social Notions.* Stanford Univ. Press, Stanford, CA.

Tuomela, R., and Miller, K. (1988). We-intentions. *Philos. Stud.* **53,** 115–137.

Tuomela, R., and Sandu, G. (1994). On seeing to it that something is the case. In *Patrick Suppes: Scientific Philosopher* (P. Humphreys, ed.), Vol. 1, pp. 425–453. Kluwer Academic Publishers, Dordrecht, The Netherlands.

CHAPTER 19 ───────────────

Organizational Intelligence and Distributed Artificial Intelligence

STEFAN KIRN

1 INTRODUCTION

Today, organizations are faced with rapidly changing markets, global competition, decreasing cycles of technological innovations, worldwide (and just in time) availability of information, and dramatic changes in their cultural, social, and political environments.

Most organizational strategies that have been developed to meet these challenges aim to enhance the flexibility (short term) and adaptability (long term) of enterprises. Current "buzz-words" such as downsizing of organizational structures, increased local autonomy, decentralization, cooperation and team work, business process orientation, and workflow management point to the different concepts that are available today (e.g., see Guilfoyle and Warner, 1994; Davenport, 1993; Morton, 1991; Nirenberg, 1993). Also, most organizational experts agree that the ability of an enterprise to achieve competitive advantages in the market and to continuously survive in dynamic, and even hostile, environments largely depends upon its information technology infrastructure, which is required to efficiently support the organizational information processing and problem-solving capabilities (Blanning et al., 1992; Ishida, 1992; Marsden and Pingry, 1988).

Consequently, an increasing number of organizational researchers draw their attention to the design of "intellectual" organizational capabilities such as organizational communication, memory (e.g., Favela and Connor, 1994; Morrison and Olfman, 1994; Paradice, 1988), learning (e.g., Elofson and Kon-

Foundations of Distributed Artificial Intelligence, Edited by G. M. P. O'Hare and N. R. Jennings. ISBN 0-471-00675-0 © 1996 John Wiley & Sons, Inc.

synski, 1993; Niwa, 1992; Sunita, 1992; Watanabe, 1992) cognition, and reasoning (Matsuda, 1988c). At the same time they reshape the scope of their analysis by claiming to explicitly integrate computer-based information processing technology into the body of organizational theory (e.g., Blanning et al., 1992; Favela and Connor, 1994; Huber and McDaniel, 1986; Marsden and Pingry, 1988; Matsuda, 1988a). In essence, the design of computer-based information systems has to follow the rules of organizational design, and this requires as an integrated part to (re-)design machine-based information systems (e.g., Malone, 1988; Petrie, 1992; Morton, 1991).

Within this context, the analysis of this chapter starts from the challenges modern organizations are faced with, and it develops toward what we call "organizational multiagent systems" which are no longer a more or less passive component of the organizational model. Instead, organizational multiagent systems are supposed to play an active, self-contained role, and to form an organizational body on their own right. This differs from current organization theory in that organizational multiagent systems are supposed to establish an additional organizational subsystem which originates from both the social subsystem and the information processing (or technology) subsystem of the organization (see also ACM Computing Surveys, 1994; Guilfoyle and Warner, 1994; Carley and Prietula, 1994). Based on the cooperation paradigm they provide an organizational knowledge processing environment that is particularily well suited to support intelligent organizational capabilities (Matsuda, 1988a; Warnecke, 1993). Organizational multiagent systems are a key technology (Kirn, 1995) to support information and knowledge processing activities in cooperative, networked organizations.[1] This, in turn, requires integrating them with the related human organization (see Chapters 13 and 21). Thus, organizational multiagent systems

1. Must be able to adapt themselves to the organizational aims and objectives, strategies and operations, as well as to the organizational structures, procedures, and constraints.
2. They must actively contribute to an organization's "intellectual" capabilities such as organizational cognition, organizational memory and learning, organizational problem solving, and organizational communication skills.

With respect to the inherent distribution of organizations our basic hypothesis is that there are a lot of interactions between organizational intelligence and the field of distributed AI which urgently need to be investigated. This contribution seeks to initiate such work. To this purpose, and with respect to our interest in distributed AI, we first review how the concept of organizations has emerged from nonorganized "black-box" entities to "computerized" organizations (Section 2). Next, we introduce the concept of organizational intelli-

---

[1]See also the contribution of H. V. D. Parunak in Part I.

gence, which originates from recent work of organizational researchers in Japan and the United States (Section 3). We then ask how organizational intelligence can contribute to the design and research of multiagent systems (Section 4), and how distributed AI can support the design of intelligent organizational skills (Section 5). Finally, we discuss why organizational intelligence is an important application of distributed AI (Section 6).

2 TOWARD THE INFORMATION-INTEGRATED COMPUTERIZED ORGANIZATION

The analysis and description of organizations is one of the major research areas in management science. Organizational designers shape organizational structures so that the resulting organization can pursue the aims and objectives formally introduced, negotiated, and decided upon by the owners of the organization, its members and participants. Organizational theory has developed a diversity of organizational models, each of them with a particular research interest, focus, and practical relevance (see Chapter 1). Within this chapter, we are primarily interested in discovering how the design and research issues involved in distributed AI systems can benefit from recent developments in organizational theory. To this purpose, we have selected five organizational models which demonstrate how the integration of information technology into organizational research has changed over the past 50–70 years. These models are (1) the black-box model originating from economic theory, (2) the production-oriented model of Gutenberg, (3) the sociotechnical approach of organizational theory, (4) the organizational model originating from management of the 1990s Program conducted by the Sloan School of Business of the Massachusetts Institute of Technology (MIT), and (5) the concept of the information-integrated, computerized enterprise.

1. The *black-box model* is still in use in modern macroeconomic theory. It largely ignores the internal organizational structures, procedures and dependencies. The basic idea is that the enterprise as such is the entity which decides, acts and behaves on its own, and that there is no relationship between the actions and the internal structure of an organization. Consequently, there is no need and even no means to study the role of information technology, nor is there any interest in how the information technology of an organization shall be designed in order to improve internal processes, the behavior of the enterprise or the integration of the organization with its environment.

2. The *production-oriented approach* has been developed as a part of Gutenberg's contribution to production theory (Gutenberg, 1951). The basic idea is that the enterprise is just that location where the factors of production (work of various kinds including managerial administration, working capital, and raw materials) are combined and changed into commodities and services. Specifically, organization is a part of the enterprise or, enterprises *have* an organi-

zation. The important contribution of Gutenberg was to relate the internal organizational structure to the efficiency of production processes. However, this model does not support the description and analysis of the motivations, aims and objectives, skills, and actions of human actors. Further, the model is deficient in that it does not investigate how information technology can contribute to organizational issues.

3. From the *sociotechnical* point of view enterprises themselves *are* organizations. This includes the view that any economic activity presupposes decision making which, in turn, requires extensive information processing capabilities (Ginsberg, 1987; Huber and McDaniel, 1986) which comprise the preconditions, the input (data, information, knowledge), the context of decision making, the phases of decision-making processes, and the implementation of decisions. The structure and the results of decision-making processes are dependent upon three different organizational subsystems that together constitute the sociotechnical organizational model:

a. The system of organizational aims and objectives integrates the aims and objectives of the persons, groups, and organizational bodies that are involved in or related to the organization.
b. The information processing system supports the processing of data, information, and knowledge in order to produce decisions that fit with the organizational aims and objectives. The information processing system does not necessarily involve information processing technology.
c. In general, decision making involves more than one person. Thus, it depends upon the social system of an organization, i.e., the social relationships, the balance of power, the availability of information, etc.

These subsystems constitute organizations as goal-driven sociotechnical systems that acquire and process information. Thus, enterprises are organizations where humans collaborate to produce commodities and services. It is interesting that the sociotechnical model provides an "interface" to the technological infrastructure but, up to now, without really integrating information technology with the social system. Within the sociotechnical approach multiagent systems are part of the information processing subsystem of the organization, and as a direct consequence, the goals and intentions of the agents involved are *not* part of the organizational taxonomy of aims and objectives.

4. However, recent organizational research begins to acknowledge the dramatic advances of information technology over the past 15–20 years. The management of the 1990s program has revealed that computer technology does not only provide an infrastructure for communication and data management, but it also enables implementation of new organizational strategies, and it even actively stimulates the development of completely new organzational solution. This has already changed the internal structures of many existing enterprises,

and has resulted in major modifications of worldwide market relationships (Morton, 1991).

5. Recently, the concept of the information-integrated, computerized organization has been suggested (Tapscott and Caston, 1993). The first area concerns the integration of human and machine-based data and knowledge. It addresses the issue that an increasing portion of organizational knowledge is stored in, maintained by, and accessible through electronic services. The second issue is to reduce the dominance of the human factor because due to ongoing process of computer-based automation. More and more, pure computational entities produce commodities and services, interact with suppliers and customers, or deliver data and expertise to software agents which are "members" of a partnership in strategic alliances, of public authorities, or political partys. Thus, the boundaries between the classical human-centered organization and the computer systems become blurred, and we may expect that the organization of the twenty-first century will, as a new organizational submodel, involve an artificial, purely software-based organization which is strongly intertwined with the social system of the organization.

3 ORGANIZATIONAL INTELLIGENCE

Today, organizational experts approach the current market, political and environmental challenges by a set of organizational strategies such as downsizing of hierarchical structures, decentralization of autonomy, business process orientation, networking among more or less mutual independent organizational units, and the implementation of teamwork-like cooperation styles.

These concepts provide the groundwork from which current issues on organizational intelligence has evolved. Within this field two major research communities can be identified. The first one has been established around the annual Hawaii International Conferences on System Sciences (HICSS), starting from a tutorial on intelligent organizations presented by G. P. Huber in 1987. The second has its roots in Japan, where T. Matsuda has developed a holistic approach to what he calls organizational intelligence (OI).

The reader may be aware of the great deal of related work carried out in disciplines such as organizational theory, organizational computing, office information systems, and others. However, while all these disciplines have worked out particular facets such as organizational learning, bounded rationality, or self-organization, they are not providing an overall concept of intelligence from human-centered organizations.

This deficiency has motivated Matsuda (1988a, 1991, 1992) to evolve a model of organizational intelligence that integrates human, and machine-based knowledge processing and problem-solving capabilities. In contrast to others he stresses that machine intelligence is an integral part of the intelligence of an organization. As Matsuda points out, and in conformity with recent work on *user agents* and *personal assistants* in computer science, cooperative organizational work includes both human beings and machine-based problem-solving agents.

In Matsuda's view, OI may provisionally (so long as it is useful for further discussion) be defined as the intellectual capability of an organization as a whole. As such, OI includes two different components: organizational intelligence as a process and organizational intelligence as a product. While *organizational process intelligence* "... provides theoretical analysis of an organisation with a set of subprocesses," *organizational product intelligence* "... supplies the organisation with ... synthetic policy (and design) guidelines for information system design" (Matsuda, 1992). It is clear, and Matsuda outlines it in detail, that these two components are mutually dependent.

Organizational product intelligence considers how information systems must be designed with respect to the needs of organizational intelligence. This requires to develop OI-orientated information system design guidelines. This raises the question: *how can distributed AI systems be designed* so that they effectively support the intellectual capabilities of organizations (Section 4)? On the other hand, modeling organizational process intelligence means to analyze, design, and effectively perform organizational knowledge and information processing and problem-solving activities. This raises a further question: *how can distributed AI benefit organizational process intelligence* (Section 5)?

3.1   Organizational Process Intelligence

Human intelligence as well as machine intelligence (which includes artificial intelligence) represents certain processes (information processing activities) within an organization. These processes can be characterized by three attributes *interaction, aggregation,* and *coordination.* Hence, organizational process intelligence has been defined as "the interactive-aggregative-coordinative complex of human intelligence and machine intelligence of the organization as a whole" (Matsuda, 1992).

Interactions within an organizational body involve different types of actors (humans, and machine agents), which serve very different purposes (e.g., transfer of data and knowledge for remote use, coordination of interrelated activities, etc.). Within a computerised organization interactions involve

1. Human intelligence versus human intelligence
2. Human intelligence versus machine intelligence
3. Machine intelligence versus machine intelligence

The *aggregation* of intelligence "is observed as the process of collection of members proceeds from an individual to the entire organisation via various sizes of groups" (Matsuda, 1992). Thus, individual knowledge is iteratively transformed into group-level knowledge, and in turn, for instance by negotiation (see Chapter 7), it is transformed into organizational knowledge.

Mere human or machine intelligence is not enough. Instead, both are to be coordinated toward the respective organizational objectives (see Chapter 13). *Coordination* provides tools to control interactions as well as the execution of aggregation processes (see Chapters 6 and 8). As such, it involves the human and machine intelligence of an organization, and it aims to speed up organizational processes as much as possible.

Matsuda divides organizational process intelligence into five components: (1) organizational cognition, (2) organizational memory, (3) organizational learning, (4) organizational communication, and (5) organizational reasoning. These five subprocesses can provide a set of powerful tools to analyze and improve organizational decision-making processes (Matsuda, 1992).

3.2 Organizational Product Intelligence

Organizational product intelligence requires the development of design guidelines in order to support the building of organizational information systems. It is one of the most important shortcomings of the work of Matsuda that it does not provide any suggestions to develop these guidelines. This is also the case if we turn our attention to distributed AI. We see that there are no design guidelines that help us to develop multiagent systems with a particular, predefined profile of "organizational" characteristics.

4 HOW ORGANIZATIONAL INTELLIGENCE CAN BENEFIT DISTRIBUTED AI

Current distributed AI is dominated by an "individualistic" approach which mainly focuses on the single member of an agent organization and its local activities (cf. Chapters 16, 18, and 20). As an immediate consequence distributed AI is in a position to further develop a sound understanding of what "organizational" intelligence of a multiagent system should be, and what the relevant components are that contribute to the intellectual skills of the system as a whole. Thus, we adopt the approach of organizational intelligence as a starting point to extend our research into the design of intelligent group-level skills of distributed AI systems.

To this purpose, each subsection below (1) first introduces the current state of the art in organizational theory, and (2) second introduces related work in distributed AI, in order to discuss those issues that are relevant for (3) the design of *organizational intelligent* multiagent systems, and (4) we identify important tasks for future research on group-level intelligence in multiagent systems.

4.1 Organizational Memory

Organizational Theory. Organizational memory enables an enterprise to preserve, remember, and utilize its experience (information about successes and failures in the past) and, thus, to learn from its individual history. Organizational researchers have already spent a great deal of efforts on the question how can important organizational knowledge be identified, how it should be represented, and how an organization can make sure that this knowledge can, and will be accessed in the right way in the future. Traditionally, organizational knowledge is represented in charts representing the division of labor, as descriptions of predefined organizational processes and procedures, and, in addition, as a large body of written material. Thus, organizational memory is completely different to the individual memory of the members of the organization, and organizational knowledge is distinct from the knowledge of the individuals joining the enterprise.

Since the mid-1980s, organizational researchers have learned that recent advances in information technology change the functions, and, thus, the role of organizational memories significantly (Favela and Connor, 1994; Morrison and Olfman, 1994; Paradice, 1988). In the future, a broad range of different types of software systems need to be considered:

1. Data bases and knowledge bases
2. Model bases and case bases
3. Workflow management systems

Apparently, these systems differ in that they use different knowledge representation paradigms, and provide distinct tools for the acquisition, storage, maintenance, and retrieval of information, and implement either more passive (data bases) or more active (cooperative knowledge bases) modes of behavior, etc. However, during the last three to five years we have seen a number of successful attempts to achieve standardization which has demonstrated that very different types of software systems will be able to communicate, and even to cooperate, in the near future. This again will give rise to further enhance the capabilities of organizational memories by knowledge processing technology.

Multiagent Systems—State of the Art. It is commonly agreed in artificial intelligence that the existence of a (mostly supposed long-term) memory is a necessary prerequisite for any type of intelligent skills such as learning, reflection, and rationality. We may expect that this holds for single entities and organizational bodies as well. Thus, it is quite an interesting point that the question remains to be investigated whether multiagent systems as such would need any organizational memory and what such a facility would look like. Instead, most multiagent systems only involve a short-term memory for the single agents involved, without considering any memory function that stands for its own on the multiagent systems' level.

With respect to organizational memory we stress that there is an important difference between the structure of a human organization (which has been designed top-down and which represents the, predefined, division of labor), and the structure of a multiagent system which must be derived (more or less dynamically) (see Chapter 9) from the individual capabilities of the single agents involved. Thus, it is right so far that this structure *may* represent a subsequent division of labor (e.g., see Gasser, 1992). However, as the agents in a multiagent system are autonomous, an agent may not agree to be involved in collaboration, even if she is the only that is capable of solving a particular task. Thus, the structure of a multiagent system as such does not represent organizational knowledge concerning the *division* of labor but only the availability of individual capabilities, and their distribution across the multiagent system.

Design Issues. The design of an organizational memory for a multiagent system involves deciding *where* the respective organizational knowledge should be stored. Subsequently, some additional questions must be addressed. These involve the formal representation of (maybe different types of) organizational knowledge, the creation (and maintenance) of indexes which support knowledge retrieval, and the design of knowledge access mechanisms including database-like transaction concepts in order to coordinate conflicting knowledge access operations. Finally, appropriate role concepts need to be developed in order to enable the system to update and to maintain its own knowledge.

Research Issues. As a direct consequence of not representing organizational memories, there is no real discussion on how multiagent systems can exhibit higher-level intelligent skills, such as learning or reflection. One may feel that this is particularly surprising since distributed AI researchers widely agree that any multiagent system may also be interpreted as a single (complex) entity! Thus, it seems that there is still a great difference between the definition of intelligence in mainstream artificial intelligence and in distributed AI which urgently needs to be resolved by future research.

Another important point concerns the maintenance of distributed knowledge bases and the problem of knowledge base consistency. We may hope that the recently increased collaboration of the data base community with researchers in AI and CSCW (for example, see the Cooperative and Intelligent Information Systems Initiative; Jarke and Ellis, 1993, and Chapter 13) provides for developing transaction-like consistency-preserving mechanisms for distributed knowledge bases.

Finally, if one implements organizational memory within a multiagent system, this does not only affect the static and dynamic structure of the whole system. It also effects the design of role definitions, and of coordination mechanisms. Thus, global search processes will change significantly. This also gives rise to a number of new questions that have not been addressed in the recent distributed AI literature.

4.2 Organizational Cognition

Organizational Theory. According to Matsuda, the collective cognition of an organization is essentially composed of four components (Matsuda, 1992):

1. *Organizational Perception.* Environmental monitoring and self-monitoring by the organization.

2. *Organizational Comprehension.* This includes autoevaluation in the environmental setting, evaluation of other organizations, and, in general, the evaluation of the environmental structure.

3. *Attention Focusing (Matsuda: Mastery Perception).* This is the "mind's eye" of an organization, namely the analytic eye for the relevant process, and the transcendental eye for the "unseen" opportunity.

4. *Generation of Premises.* These are premises for decision making; i.e., they include both value premises and factual premises.

Within this context the information processing activities of an enterprise need to be coordinated toward organizational aims and objectives. As the attention-focusing capabilities are the real scarce resource of an organization (Blanning et al., 1992), it is of particular importance to identify and retrieve all information which is relevant to a problem at hand and to integrate this information in order to develop toward a satisfactory solution. Especially for large organizations this has proven to be a nearly unsolvable challenge.

Multiagent Systems—State of the Art. Distributed AI still lacks an operational description of what the notion of intelligence could mean to a *group* of interacting agents. There is no explanation of what cognition would mean for a multiagent system. If we thus apply to the taxonomy of Matsuda then we may feel that, up to now, distributed AI has mainly concentrated on the ability of comprehension (provisionally defined as ability to analyze and interpret) and on the attention-focusing capabilities of multiagent systems. Little work has been carried out on perception which may not be so important for multiagent systems than for human organizations.

Design Issues. Cognitive abilities are quite well suited to design role concepts and to assign these roles to agents. Depending on the requirements of the respective application one may start from comprehensive, or perceptive capabilities, or one may primarily apply to the design of attention-focusing capabilities of a multiagent system. By this we expect that multiagent systems might be better adapted to (or even embedded into) their current environment. This, in turn, could significantly improve the chance to implement productive multiagent systems applications, especially in domains like business, robotics, and computer-integrated manufacturing.

Research Issues. From the perspective of future research we are convinced that primarily the perceptive abilities of a multiagent system should be addressed. This would also involve the question of how perceived data and information can be evaluated and interpreted internally in such a way that it transforms into the organizational knowledge of the multiagent system. We further believe that enhanced perceptive capabilities will significantly improve the self-adaptation capabilities of multiagent systems.

4.3 Self-Organization, and Organizational Learning Skills

Organizational Theory. Organizational learning refers to an organization's capability to identify and to store knowledge derived from both individual and organizational experiences, and to modify its own behavior according to feedback received from its environment (Teramoto, 1992; Tsuchiya, 1992). Thus, organizational learning supposes that an organization is able to control its behavior with respect to its own aims and objectives, to perform self-monitoring activities, to filter out the relevant information from environmental scanning processes, and to adapt itself to changes in its social, economic, and political environment.

Organizational learning is performed on three interacting levels. *Individual (human) learning* may contribute to an organization if it is not obstructed by organizational constraints, such as responsibilities or well-established information processing procedures. On the *microorganizational level* (the group level) the members of an organization negotiate and integrate their individual experiences in order to build up group-level knowledge. The results of this (permanently evolving) process, i.e., whether the group performs better than the best of its members largely depend upon both the intragroup and the intergroup relationships within an organization. It is important to note that, to a large extent, micro-organizational learning evolves informally, i.e. not primarily determined by fixed organizational rules and procedures. *Macroorganizational learning* evolves on an organization's macrostructure, i.e., its performance, successes and failures are largely determined by the structure of its intergroup relationships.

The ability of an organization to learn from individual knowledge and both individual and organizational experiences assumes that

1. Knowledge to be learned is described in terms of a common ontology.
2. Conflict resolving mechanisms help to decide which knowledge shall be included into the body of organizational knowledge, and which knowledge shall be excluded from it.
3. Knowledge management tools are needed which guarantee, that organizational knowledge is accessible to (and will be accessed by) exactly those members of an organization who need it for doing their work.
4. Pieces of organizational knowledge must be related to each other by a network of relationships in order to provide for organizational reasoning. These are the basic mechanisms within an organization (such as forward or backward chaining in rule-based systems) from which more complex organizational problem-solving procedures are created.

Multiagent Systems—State of the Art. Quite similar to organizational theory, Distributed AI distinguishes between short-term and long-term organizational learning. While the former concerns organizational flexibility, the latter deals with the modification of organizational structures as a result of changes in the environment (Gasser, 1992). The most important approaches work toward self-organization skills of multiagent systems (Corkill 1982, Ishida, 1992; Ishida et al., 1992; Sugawara and Lesser, 1993). Within such work, most researchers are primarily interested in how those systems can be enabled to reorganize themselves in order to meet changing problems or dynamic environments.

However, there is no body of work within distributed AI which deals with organizational learning as such. This is surprising because a number of important distributed AI applications such as business, office procedures, decision processes, and human computer cooperation heavily involve the issue of organizational learning.

Design Issues. To implement organizational learning into a distributed AI system a designer would need to create agents which are responsible for meta-level capabilities such as self-monitoring and self-control. One further needs to develop (explicit, or heuristic) reorganisation strategies, and the respective control and coordination knowledge. Then, two major questions need to be addressed:

1. *What kind of knowledge can, and shall, be learned on the level of the multiagent system?* The most important uses are successes and failures in the past, the usefulness of different pieces of knowledge with respect to different tasks and situations, the capabilities and accountability of other agents in the system, the relationships between the multiagent system and its environment, etc.

2. *What type of learning strategies need to be developed?* We may divide between learning through interaction and learning through introspection, as well as between inductive and deductive learning.

Research Issues. In organizational theory the distinction between individuals, (formal and informal) groups, and organizations is fundamental for the description and analysis of processes of organizational learning. Up to now, there are no similar three-level architectures available in multiagent systems. However, we are convinced that the concept of partial global planning (Durfee and Lesser, 1987) (see also Chapter 8), which divides between nodes, acquaintances, and the whole multiagent organization may provide a platform from which one can start to work toward a similar static and dynamic architecture. Further, if we compare the discussion on learning in mainstream artificial intelligence and distributed AI it seems that the body of knowledge on learning within distributed AI still remains to be integrated with the knowledge already available in mainstream artificial intelligence.

4.4 Interactions between Multiagent Systems and Their Environment

Organizational Theory. Organizational communication refers to the total amount of exchange of data, information, and knowledge which evolves among the human and machine-based actors within an organization and between an organization and its environment. Individual and organizational communication differ in that the latter performs as a set of unobservable processes in the human brain only, while the former occurs as observable interactions among machines, humans, groups, and divisions of an organization, using classical communication structures such as sender, receiver, messages, and channels (Matsuda, 1988a, 1992).

Dynamic environments require an organization to permanently monitor its environment, to filter and to assess the informations received, and to distribute the results of this perceptive activity to other members of the organization (Hammer and Champy, 1993). Thus, organizational communication is closely related to the status (and its changes over time) of the organizational enviroment. On the other hand, organizations are supposed to inform their environment about past and future activities, about their internal status (e.g., accounting, profits, and losses, etc.). This, in turn requires them to represent and to store the respective knowledge in such a way that it can be retrieved and accessed quite easily at any time in the future.

Multiagent Systems—State of the Art. Research in distributed AI mainly addresses the interactions between the agents of a multiagent system (some examples are included in Bond and Gasser, 1988). However, very little work has addressed the issue of communication between a multiagent system and its environment.[2] A well-known example is the unsolved problem of designing user interfaces for cooperative problem solvers (see Chapter 21). Another point is that, in general, a multiagent system can be viewed as a community of interacting agents, or as a single (complex) entity, depending on the current focus of interest. However, from the perspective of communication between a multiagent system and its environment only the former of these two views is supported.

It may be expected, however, that the integration of multiagent systems into other disciplines such as computer-supported cooperative work (CSCW), intelligent user agents (personal assistants) and decision support systems may help to address this issue.

Design Issues. First of all, any interactions between a multiagent system and its environment suppose that the availability of a canonical interaction language. Such an interaction language needs to provide data and knowledge communi-

---

[2]Another point which is not mentioned here are the interactions of agents of a multiagent system with their environment, or with the environment of the whole system. For example, see work on computational ecosystems by Glance et al. (1991).

cation facilities, explanation facilities, and fine-grained dialogue management support. Further, if the user of the system is a human expert, he or she might wish to be actively involved in the global reasoning process. Thus, it becomes evident that we need to develop a "well-shaped" role concept for the multi-agent system which also needs to be able to assign roles to the actors in the environment of the multiagent system.

Research Issues. The ability of a multiagent system to effectively communicate with its environment is one of the most important issues for developing successful applications. This is particularly true for any applications that aim to support human experts' intellectual work. Further, we can see today that research on interaction architectures and languages already involve standardization issues. Two prominent examples are the CORBA standard of the Object Management Group and the Knowledge Sharing Effort which has been launched by DARPA in 1991. It has been argued that an integration of the research, development, and standardization efforts in the related fields of information technology will significantly increase technological competitiveness (Davidow and Malone, 1992; Guilfoyle and Warner, 1994; Kim, 1995; Petrie, 1992; Warnecke, 1993).

4.5 Organizational Reasoning

Organizational Theory. Organizational reasoning does not only include organizational problem solving, it also involves strategies such as problem avoidance, problem evasion, and problem encapsulation (Matsuda, 1992). Typically, organizational reasoning applies to one of the following basic strategies:

1. *Process-orientated reasoning* is performed on the bases of predefined organizational workflows and well-established algorithms, etc.
2. *Case-based reasoning* tackles a problem by accessing a solution that has proven useful for a similar problem which has been solved in the past.
3. *Heuristic reasoning* is used to approach a problem where the necessary information is not available, uncertain, or possibly false.
4. *Explorative reasoning* includes search strategies (goal driven, data driven), trial-and-error concepts, and creativity generating methods such as brainstorming, scenario technique, delphi, etc.
5. *Structural reasoning (adaptation)* evolves whenever an organization modifies its internal structure in order to fit better with (identified or anticipated) changes in its environment.

Organizational problem-solving supposes a set of basic tools such as problem analysis and the selection of critical success factors, the exploration and identification of well-suited organizational competences and resources, the processes of coordinating these resources with respect to the problem at hand, and the ability to focus the attention on the most relevant processes at a time, to name a few.

Thus, it is commonly agreed in organizational theory that the ability to design efficient organizational information processing and reasoning capabilities is one of the key characteristics of successful enterprises.

Multiagent Systems—State of the Art. Reasoning processes within a multiagent system can be studied from two different perspectives. The external perspective considers the multiagent system as a single entity, and it gives descriptions of how the system behaves in its environment. In contrast, the internal view focuses on the description and analysis of the internal processes. This perspective represents the mainstream of work on multiagent reasoning processes (Singh, 1990b; Stephens and Merx, 1989). As a result, we have available today a large body of knowledge on cooperation strategies (Durfee et al., 1987, 1988), coordination mechanisms (e.g., see Fickas and Helm, 1991; Malone, 1987; Malone and Crowston, 1993; von Martial, 1992; Smith, 1979), conflict resolving mechanisms, concepts for modeling intentions and commitment (e.g., see Cohen and Levesque, 1987a,b; Jennings and Mamdani, 1992; Jennings, 1992; Singh, 1990a) and, for example, dependency relationships between different agents of a distributed AI system (see Chapters 6 and 16). However, on the other hand we still lack a sufficient understanding of *how* the design and processing of internal procedures relates to the behavior of the whole system. It is important to realize that this question is of prior importance for any decisions within an enterprise that involve investing money into the development of a distributed AI system.

Design Issues. From the above considerations we learn that whenever we design a multiagent system we should carefully think about adding an organizational layer to the architecture of the system (Kirn, 1994). This organizational layer should include at least the organizational knowledge, the set of available problem-solving strategies and the respective mechanisms to control and monitor cooperative processes within the multiagent system. We also see that this again asks for the development of appropriate role concepts. In other words: step by step we discover that role concepts are of prior importance for the design of fine-grained internal structures of multiagent systems. It should be noted that the organizational layer need not necessarily be a centralized resource within the system; it can also be decentralized.

Research Issues. This subsection has demonstrated the importance of an organizational layer[3] together with the respective role concepts for the design and, as one may want to add, for the expected commercial success of multiagent systems. While the demand for an organizational layer is new in multiagent

---

[3]See also Stary (1993) and Stolze (1991).

systems research, significant research has already been carried out (unfortunately, in splendid isolation) on the development of role concepts. Thus, we still lack an integrated, holistic approach to designing an overall model of roles in multiagent systems in order to provide for a systematic, application-driven design and implementation of future distributed AI systems.

5 HOW DISTRIBUTED AI CAN BENEFIT ORGANIZATIONAL INTELLIGENCE

There is already a large body of literature originating from both the field of organizational research and management science as well as from the community of distributed AI which argues that a lot of business and organizational problems could be solved quite naturally through a multiagent system approach. Some prominent examples are the virtual enterprise (Davidow and Malone, 1992) and the "fractalization" of organizations (Warnecke, 1993), the modeling and simulation of enterprises (Fox, 1981), the efforts toward an integrated theory of coordination (Malone, 1987), support of business processes and work-flows (Malone et al., 1993), and enterprise integration (Petrie, 1992). As we will show, the same holds for some of the components of organizational intelligence.

Distributed AI offers interesting advantages to organizational designers which aim to improve the intelligence of their organizations, and who agree to apply agent-oriented information technology. On a more abstract level we may argue first that distributed AI provides technical facilities (coordination protocols) that support interactions among a set of information servers. Second, it contributes knowledge discovery tools assisting users to identify, select, and access information relevant to their task at hand. Third, many applications require the ability to select data from different nodes of a network and to combine them with respect to a particular "problem profile" (for instance, a set of customer preferences). We will expand on the above discussion in more detail below.

With regard to *organizational memory* we feel that, at the moment, distributed AI may have little to contribute. However, this may change in the future, for example if one starts to integrate results from case-based reasoning.

Distributed AI can benefit *organizational cognition* in that it provides easy-to-use knowledge exchange facilities and collective reasoning capabilities. This, however, involves the question of how to integrate problem solving at the human level (for example, see Newell and Simon, 1972) with problem-solving procedures at the machine level, or, more precisely: Distributed AI technology can be used only if it does not bless the organizational procedures and dependencies that are involved. The reader will remember that this point was the motivation behind our notion of "organizational multiagent systems."

Distributed AI methods can also contribute to *organizational learning* on both the microorganizational and on the macroorganizational level (Nunamaker et al., 1988; Teramoto et al., 1992; Tsuchiya, 1992; Yamamoto et al., 1992). While, primarily, the latter may be supported by the instantiation and maintenance of intergroup relationships, the former may be supported by single- and multistage negotiation, by the instantiation and maintenance of intragroup relationships, and by the availability of sophisticated conflict-resolving mechanisms.

Further, we would like to stress that computerizing an organization also effects the performance of organizational learning. As far as humans are considered[4] individual learning can be supported by local "personal assistants." Thus, organizational learning within a group of software agents may also contribute to the individual learning of the human users. As organizational learning among software agents is part of (and controlled by) those organizational processes that have been established formally, the transfer of the knowledge back to humans establishes a kind of individual learning which is "supervised" by organizational rules and procedures. This is a major issue also within the new of field of human-computer teams (Kirn, 1995).

Typically, distributed AI systems exhibit a more or less decentralized organizational structure. Thus, they can also contribute a great deal to *organizational communication*. This holds for conventional, human-centered organizations, but its effectiveness is directly related to the degree of computerisation of the enterprise (Ginsberg, 1987; Numaoka, 1991). Possible low-level communication support services may include retrieval and identification of addresses, knowledge-based intra- and internetwork communication management (for instance, routing), and intelligent communication control facilities. On a semantically higher level, these services include among others, group-level information filtering, appointment system applications, tools for distributed interpretation, context modeling, knowledge discovery by which the coherence of interactive activities can be improved. As some of these services can also be provided by conventional software, others would benefit a lot more from distributed AI methods (for example, knowledge discovery).

With regard to *organizational reasoning*, distributed AI provides several quite useful tools whenever an organizational problem requires the involvement of distributed expertise to focus the attention of distinct organizational units on a particular task, or if distributed interpretations are to be supported (for example, see Ginsberg, 1987; Guilfoyle and Warner, 1994; Kirn, 1995; Kirn et al., 1992). All these problems assume efficient coordination by which the various types of unilateral or bilateral dependencies among different tasks, activities, objects, and actors can be detected and managed. We feel that coordination techniques of distributed AI are particularily well suited in all cases where the system support of the coordination task is required, and workflow management technology is too rigid.

---

[4]This represents the traditional approach of organizational theory (March and Simon, 1958; Morton, 1991).

6 ORGANIZATIONAL INTELLIGENCE: AN IMPORTANT APPLICATION OF DISTRIBUTED AI

The above discussion developed from organizational theory suggesting (1) that research in distributed AI can benefit a great deal from organizational intelligence, and, in turn, (2) that distributed AI methods can contribute a great deal to implement intelligent organizational skills in human organizations.

From our perspective, this point is quite important for application-oriented distributed AI research. Currently, enterprises worldwide have begun to reengineer their internal processes, and to adapt their structures to the challenges of worldwide competition, and the rapidly increasing dynamics of their political and economical environments. These long-term perspectives have already begun to result in a widespread decentralization of enterprises, which more and more consist of self-contained autonomous organizational units being globally distributed. Such an organizational approach involves two major problems: efficient coordination without having sufficient global knowledge available, and the need to intelligently adapt organizational procedures in such a way to changing environments that the long-term aims and strategies can still be pursued.

Thus, the third important result of our discussion is that organizational intelligence is an important application for distributed AI in that it provides a key technology for the competitiveness of smart, information-integrated organizations in the future (Kim, 1995).

BIBLIOGRAPHY

ACM Computing Surveys (1994). *Special Issue on Intelligent Agents*, Issue 8.

Blanning, R. W., King, D. R., Marden, J. R., and Seror, A. C. (1992). Intelligent models of human organizations: The State of the Art. *J. Organ. Comput.* **2,** 123–130.

Bond, A., and Gasser, L., eds. (1988). *Readings in Distributed Artificial Intelligence.* Morgan Kaufmann, San Mateo, CA.

Carley, K. M., and Prietula, M. J., eds. (1994). *Computational Organization Theory.* Erlbaum, Hillsdale, NJ.

Cohen, P. R., and Levesque, H. J. (1987a). *Persistence, Intention, and Commitment,* Tech. Rep. CSLI-87-88. Center for the Study of Language and Information, Stanford University, Stanford, CA.

Cohen, P. R., and Levesque, H. J. (1987b). Intention = Choice + Commitment. *Proc. Natl. Conf. Artif. Intell., 6th,* pp. 410–415.

Corkill, D. (1982). A framework for organizational self-design in distributed problem solving networks. Ph.D. Thesis, Department of Computer and Information Science, University of Massachusetts at Amherst, (COINS-TR-82-33).

Cyert, R. M., and March, J. G. (1964). The behavioral theory of the firm—A behavioral science-economics amalgam. In *New Perspectives in Organizational Research,* pp. 289–299.

Davenport, T. H. (1993). *Process Innovation: Reengineering Work through Information Technology.* Harvard Business School Press, Boston.

Davidow, W. H., and Malone, M. S. (1992). *The Virtual Corporation. Structuring and Revitalizing the Corporation for the 21st Century.* Harper Collins, New York.

Durfee, E. H., and Lesser, V. R. (1987). Using partial global plans to coordinate distributed problem solvers. *Proc. Int. Jt. Conf. Artif. Intell., 10th, 1987,* p. 875.

Durfee, E. H., Lesser, V. L., and Corkill, D. (1987). Coherent cooperation among communicating problem solvers. *IEEE Trans. Comput.* **C-36,** 1275.

Elofson, G. S., and Konsynski, B. R. (1993). Performing organizational learning with machine apprentices. *Decis. Support Syst.* **10,** 109–119.

Farhoodi, F., Proffitt, J., Woodman, P., and Tunnicliffe, A. (1991). Design of organizations in distributed decision systems. *Am. Assoc. Artif. Intell. Workshop Coop. Heterogeneous Intell. Syst., 1991.*

Favela, J., and Connor, J. J. (1994). Accessing corporate memory in networked organizations. *Proc. Hawaii Int. Conf. Syst. Sci., 27th,* pp. 181–190.

Fickas, S., and Helm, R. (1991). *Acting Responsibly: Reasoning about Agents in a Multi-Agent System,* Tech. Rep. CIS-TR-91-02. Department of Computer and Information Science, University of Oregon, Eugene.

Fox, M. S. (1981). An organizational view of distributed systems. *IEEE Trans. Syst. Man Cybernet.* **SMC-11,** 70–80.

Gasser, L. (1992). DAI approaches to coordination. In *Distributed Artificial Intelligence: Theory and Practice.* (N. M. Avouris and L. Gasser, eds.), pp. 31–52. Kluwer Academic Publishers, Dordrecht, The Netherlands.

Ginsberg, M. (1987). Decision procedures. In *Distributed Artificial Intelligence.* (M. Huhns, ed.), pp. 3–28. Morgan Kaufman, San Mateo, CA/Pitman, London.

Glance, N., Hogg, T., and Huberman, B. A. (1991). *Computational Ecosystems in a Changing Environment,* Tech. Rep. P91-00012. Dynamics of Computation Group, Xerox Palo Alto Research Center, Palo Alto, CA.

Guilfoyle, C., and Warner, E. (1994). *Intelligent Agents: the New Revolution in Software.* Ovum Ltd., London.

Gutenberg, E. (1951). *Grundlagen der Betriebswirtschaftslehre,* vol. 1. Springer-Verlag, Berlin and New York (in German).

Hammer, M., and Champy, J. (1993). *Reengineering the Corporation.* Harper Collins, New York.

Huber, G. P., and McDaniel, R. R. (1986). The decision-making paradigm of organizational design. *Manage. Sci.* **32,** 572–589.

Ishida, T. (1992). The Tower of Babel: Towards organization-centered problem-solving. *Work. Pap., Int. Workshop Distributed Artif. Intell., 11th,* The Homestead, Glen Arbor, MI, pp. 141–153.

Ishida, T., Gasser, L., and Yokoo, M. (1992). Organization self design of distributed production systems. *IEEE Trans. Data Knowl. Eng.* **DKE-4** (Issue 2), 123–134.

Japan Society for Management Information (1992a). *Proceedings of the International Conference on Economics/Management and Information Technology, Tokio, Japan, 1992.* Jpn. Soc. Manage. Inf., Tokyo.

Japan Society for Management Information (1992b). *Proceedings of the Conférence*

Internationale sur l'Economique et l'Intelligence Artificielle, Tokio, Japan, 1992. Jpn. Soc. Manage. Inf., Tokyo.

Jarke, M., and Ellis, C. A. (1993). Distributed cooperation in integrated information systems. *Int. J. Intell. Coop. Inf. Syst.* 2(1), 85–103.

Jennings, N. (1992). Joint intentions as a model of multi-agent cooperation. Ph.D. Thesis, Department of Electronic Engineering, Queen Mary and Westfield College, University of London, UK.

Jennings, N., and Mamdani, E. H. (1992). Using joint responsibility to coordinate collaborative problem solving in dynamic environments. *Proc. Natl. Conf. Artif. Intell., 10th,* San Jose, CA, pp. 269–275.

Keen, P. G. W. (1991). *Shaping the Future—Business Design through Information Technology.* Harvard Business School Press, Cambridge, MA.

Kirn, S. (1994). Supporting human experts collaborative work: Modelling organizational context knowledge in cooperative information systems. In *CSCW and Artificial Intelligence* (J. H. Connolly and E. Edmonds, eds.), Springer Ser. Comput. Supported Coop. Work, pp. 127–139. Springer-Verlag, Berlin and New York.

Kirn, S. (1995). Competitive knowledge processing in banking: State of the art and future developments. In *Cooperative Knowledge Processing: The Competitive Edge in Banking IT. Special Issue of the International Journal of Intelligent Systems in Accounting, Finance and Management,* Issue 2. Wiley, New York (to be published).

Kirn, S., and O'Hare, G., eds. (1995). *Towards the Intelligent Organization: The Coordination Perspective,* Springer Ser. Comput. Supported Coop. Work. Springer-Verlag, London (to be published).

Kirn, S., Scherer, A., and Schlageter, G. (1992). Problem solving in federative environments: The Fresco concept of cooperative agents. In *The Next Generation of Information Systems: From Data to Knowledge.* (M. Papazoglou and J. Zeleznikow, eds.), Lect. Notes Artif. Intell., Vol. 611, pp. 185–203. Springer-Verlag, Berlin and New York.

Malone, T. (1987). Modeling coordination in organizations and markets. *Manage. Sci.* 33(10), 1317–1332.

Malone, T. (1988). Organizing information processing systems: Parallels between human organizations and computer systems. In *Cognition, Cooperation, and Computation* (W. Zachary, S. Robertson, and J. Black, eds.), Ablex, Norwood, NJ.

Malone, T., and Crowston, K. (1993). *The Interdisciplinary Study of Coordination,* CCS WP No. 157, Sloan School WP No. 3630-93. Massachusetts Institute of Technology, Sloan School of Management, Cambridge, MA.

Malone, T., Crowston, K., Lee, J., and Pentland, B. (1993). *Tools for Inventing Organizations: Toward a Handbook of Organizational Processes,* CCS WP No. 141, Sloan School WP No. 3562-93. Massachusetts Institute of Technology, Sloan School of Management, Cambridge, MA.

March, J. G., and Simon, H. A. (1958). *Organizations.* New York.

Marsden, J. R., and Pingry, D. E. (1988). The intelligent organization: Some observations and alternative views. *Proc. 21st Annu. Hawaii Conf. Syst. Sci.,* pp. 19–24.

Matsuda, T. (1988a). Enhancing organizational intelligence through effective information systems management. *EDP Aud. J.* **4,** 17–42.

Matsuda, T. (1988b). OR/MS and information technology for higher organizational intelligence. *Opsearch* **25**(1), 3–27.

Matsuda, T. (1988c). OR/MS, its interaction with and benefit from Japanese organizational intelligence. *OMEGA Int. J. Manage. Sci.* **16**(3), 233–241.

Matsuda, T. (1990). S³-Integration of human and machine for advanced organizational intelligence. In *Human Factors in Organizational Design and Development* (K. Noro and O. Brown, Jr., eds.), pp. 381–384. Elsevier/North-Holland, Amsterdam.

Matsuda, T. (1991). Organizational intelligence: Coordination of human intelligence and machine intelligence. In *Economics and Cognitive Science* (P. Bourgine and B. Walliser, eds.), Sel. Pap. from CECOIA 2, Paris, 1990, pp. 171–180. Pergamon, Oxford.

Matsuda, T. (1992). Organizational intelligence: Its significance as a process and as a product. In *Proceedings of the International Conference on Economics/Management and Information Technology, Tokio, Japan, 1992*, pp. 219–222. Jpn. Soc. Manage. Tokyo.

Morrison, J., and Olfman, L. (1994). Organizational memory. *Proc. 27th Annu. Hawaii Int. Conf. Syst. Sci.*, p. 169.

Morton, M. S. S., ed. (1991). *The Corporation of the 1990s*. Oxford Univ. Press, New York.

Newell, A., and Simon, H. A. (1972). *Human Problem Solving*. Prentice-Hall, Englewood Cliffs, NJ.

Nirenberg, J. (1993). *The Living Organization—Transforming Teams into Workplace Communities*. Business One Irwin, Homewood, IL.

Niwa, K. (1922). Knowledge sharing systems for organizational intelligence. In *Proceedings of the International Conference on Economics/Management and Information Technology, Tokio, Japan, 1992*, pp. 227–230. Jpn. Soc. Manage. Inf., Tokyo.

Numaoka, C. (1991). A conceptual framework for modeling conversation in open distributed systems. Ph.D. Thesis, Department of Electrical Engineering, Keio University, Yokohama, Japan.

Nunamaker, J. F., Jr., Weber, E. S., and Smith, C. A. P. (1988). Crises planning systems: Tools for intelligent action. *Proc. 21st Annu. Hawaii Conf. Syst. Sci.*, pp. 25–34.

Paradice, D. B. (1988). The role of memory in intelligent information systems. *Proc. 21st Annu. Hawaii Conf. Syst. Sci.*, pp. 2–9.

Petrie, Jr., ed. (1992). *Enterprise Integration Modeling. Proceedings of the First International Conference*. MIT Press, Cambridge, MA.

Pondy, L. R., Frost, P. J., Morgan, G., and Dandridge, T. C. (1983). *Organizational Symbolism*. Greenwich, London.

Sheth, A. P., and Larson, J. A. (1990). Federated database management systems for managing distributed, heterogeneous, and autonomous databases. *ACM Comput. Surv.* **22**(3), 183–236.

Simon, H. A. (1969). *The Science of the Artificial*. Harvard Univ. Press, Cambridge, MA.

Singh, M. (1990a). Group intentions. *Proc. Int. Workshop Distributed Artif. Intell., 10th*, Bandera, TX, MCC Tech. Rep. ACT-AI-355-90, Chapter 12.

Singh, M. (1990b). Group ability and structure. In *Decentralized Artificial Intelligence* (Y. Demazeau and J.-P. Müller, eds.), pp. 85–100. Elsevier/North-Holland, Amsterdam.

Smith, R. G. (1979). A framework for distributed problem solving. *Proc. Int. Jt. Conf. Artif. Intell.*, *6th*, Cambridge, MA, pp. 836–841.

Stary, C. (1993). Model-based design bases for task-oriented applications. *Int. Conf. Data Eng.*, Wien, Austria, *1993*.

Stephens, L., Merx, M. (1989). Agent organization as an effector of DAI system performance. *Proc. Int. Workshop Distributed Artif. Intell.*, *9th*, Rosario, WA, pp. 263–292.

Stolze, M. (1991). Task level framework for cooperative expert systems design. *Artif. Intell. Commun.* **4**(2/3), 98.

Sugawara, T., and Lesser, V. (1993). On-line learning of coordination plans. *Proc. Int. Workshop Distributed Artif. Intell.*, *12th*, Hidden Valley, PA, pp. 335–355.

Sunita, T. (1992). A study on measurement of organizational intelligence. In *Proceedings of the International Conference on Economics/Management and Information Technology, Tokio, Japan, 1992*, pp. 207–210. Jpn. Soc. Manage. Info., Tokyo.

Tapscott, D., and Caston, A. (1993). *Paradigm Shift—The New Promise of Information Technology*. McGraw-Hill, New York.

Teramoto, Y., Iwaski, N., and Richter, F.-J. (1992). Inter-organizational learning through strategic alliances—Evolutionary process of corporate networking. In *Proceedings of the International Conference on Economics/Management and Information Technology, Tokio, Japan, 1992*, pp. 239–242. Jpn. Soc. Manag. Inf., Tokyo.

Tsuchiya, S. (1992). Organizational learning and information technology: Information technology improving strategy formation process in a loosely coupled system. In *Proceedings of the International Conference on Economics/Management and Information Technology, Tokio, Japan, 1992*, pp. 249–252. Jpn. Soc. Manage. Inf., Tokyo.

von Martial, F. (1992). *Coordinating Plans of Autonomous Agents*, Lect. Notes Artif. Intell., No. 610. Springer-Verlag, Berlin.

Warnecke, H.-J. (1993). *Revolution der Unternehmenskultur—Das Fraktale Unternehmen*, 2nd ed. Springer-Verlag, Berlin (in German).

Watanabe, Y. A. (1992). The role of Intra-Organization Network (ION) for organizational learning. In *Proceedings of the International Conference on Economics/Management and Information Technology, Tokio, Japan, 1992*, pp. 277–280. Jpn. Soc. Manage. Inf., Tokio.

Yamamoto, B., Nakano, B., and Matsuda, T. (1992). System, information, organizational intelligence and self-dynamics. In *Proceedings of the International Conference on Economics/Management and Information Technology, Tokio, Japan, 1992*, pp. 211–214. Jpn. Soc. Manage. Inf., Tokyo.

CHAPTER 20

Distributed Artificial Intelligence and Social Science: Critical Issues

CRISTIANO CASTELFRANCHI
ROSARIA CONTE

1 INTRODUCTION

In this chapter, the view of social agenthood largely prevailing in DAI and derived from computational models of communication and dialogue is questioned. In the first section of the chapter, some particular features of this view, e.g., a tendency to emphasize the role of cooperation, a hypercognitive view of social agents, a relative indifference for the emergent properties of interaction among cognitive agents, are discussed. Furthermore, the notion of "social" actions and mental states as overlapping with "shared," "joint," and sometimes "collective" ones (see most contributions in Cohen et al., 1990; Levesque et al., 1990; Rao and Georgeff, 1991; Gasser, 1991; Werner, 1988, 1989) is questioned.

In the second section, the notion of collective action and teamwork as based upon joint persistent goals is examined at some length. Joint persistent goals (JPG) are shown to be neither necessary to account for joint action (think of orchestrated cooperation where often the mutual belief condition does not hold) nor sufficient (several examples are given in the chapter where although the conditions for JPG are met, the resulting phenomenon does not correspond to what is usually intended as joint action and teamwork).

In the third section, an alternative view of collective action as based upon an existing theory of social dependence (Castelfranchi et al., 1992b) is presented. The advantages of the notion proposed are briefly discussed.

Foundations of Distributed Artificial Intelligence, Edited by G. M. P. O'Hare and N. R. Jennings. ISBN 0-471-00675-0 © 1996 John Wiley & Sons, Inc.

2 SOCIAL FOUNDATIONS FOR DISTRIBUTED ARTIFICIAL INTELLIGENCE?

"Society or Individual: Which Comes First?": In 1991, with such a question, Les Gasser opened the AAAI workshop on "Knowledge and Action at Social and Organizational Level." Gasser's claim (1991), related to Hewitt's perspective on "open systems," is that we need an adequate foundation for DAI, and that we must begin to lay firm "social foundations" for it. In this perspective, DAI should have autonomous basis with respect to traditional AI: DAI foundation lies in sociology (Durkheim) and in social psychology (Mead), while AI traditionally refers to cognitive science and psychology. DAI constitutes a new paradigm for AI. It is based on a different philosophy of mind in which the mind is seen as a social (not individual, mental) phenomenon. Therefore, Gasser's answer to the original question is "society comes first." The new "social foundation" is opposed to the "individualistic and psychological approach" of (D)AI.

These theses are now very successful in DAI and in the multiagent (MA) domain. However, as social cognitive scientists working in AI, we move some objections against both the dychotomy and this type of social foundation. Three considerations deserve special attention:

First, there are many sociologies and many social psychologies, and many of them are precisely in search of the "individualistic" basis of social action, of the "individualistic" explanation of social phenomena.

Second, the criticism to the supposedly "individualistic" approach of classical (D)AI is mistaken. In AI social studies, the prevailing approach to sociality is top-down: A higher-order unit, a holistic level, whether a social goal, a collective problem or a joint intention, is usually taken for granted. The problem of how to allocate tasks and resources and, more generally, how to coordinate actions is only thereafter raised. Consequently, an overcooperative bias, namely the idea that the structure of sociality *is* cooperative, appears throughout the field. Even in the MA domain, where agents are modeled as autonomous, that is, endowed with their own goals, the unsolved problem is how to coordinate actions, how to reconcile conflicts, how to reach an overall utility, and not simply a local one, etc. In short, *agents and their interests are subordinated to the group* (see Chapters 18 and 19). Gasser is looking for a more systematic and robust foundation of what is already a dominant paradigm in social AI. A world in which artificial agents "will compete with each other for resources in *achieving their selfish aims*" is seen as pure disorder, as a "sorcerer apprentice" scenario. Therefore, "the basis for a social order" is found in intentional cooperation and joint commitments (Levesque et al., 1990). This is what we call *the dominant AI ideology*. On the contrary, the "sorcerer apprentice" scenario is a model of the market: it represents the most efficient device for good resource/task allocation for many collective problems (but not for all!). Echoing Cohen and Levesque, the following question should be formulated: given that actions are performed by individuals, and that it is individuals who ultimately have the beliefs and goals that engender actions, what are the beliefs and goals of the agents involved in a given social phenomenon? In other words, *how is society implemented in the minds of social agents?* Although Gasser considers "individualistic" an approach oriented to solve this question, we think it is a question of primary importance, especially if the following two assumptions are rejected:

a. Agents explicitly know all about their social interaction and society (this will be called "hypercognitive bias", see later).
b. Collective agents and "abstract agents" have "collective beliefs" and "goals," that is, mental states that are necessarily shared by all the individual agents.

The third consideration deserving attention concerns the term "social." This is used in a confused and ambiguous way, and equated to either

a. "Distributed" in the sense of distributed systems;
b. "Collective": the notion of "social" intention or goal (e.g., Werner, 1988) is used to characterize a goal or intention shared by many agents; the notion of "social agent" (e.g., Rao et al., 1992 and Chapters 1, 2, and 6) is used to designate an agent formed by many individual agents, i.e., a group or a team; the notion of "social commitment" (Chapter 6) and "social plan" (Chapter 8) is used to denote the idea of reciprocal commitments within a team of agents.

There is a further important level of "social action," "social agent," and "social mind," where mind and action are directed toward another social entity while remaining "individual." To distinguish between "social" goals or actions of an individual with regard to another individual, and common, mutual, or group's goals is a fundamental task for any scientific discipline dealing with social phenomena.

Therefore, the collective/individual dichotomy, as presented by Gasser, is useless. To search for a logical or historical priority is sterile. A more fruitful solution to the micro-macro (individual-society) link problem lies in a dialectic and co-evolutionary approach.

3 MAIN BIASES

Let us now examine more concretely the main *misconceptions* that can be found in AI social studies.

3.1 Emphasis on Cooperation

On one hand, most applicative work in DAI (from BlackBoard structure systems up to the more recent partial global planning solutions, to say nothing of computer-supported cooperative work, etc.) is aimed at optimizing the allocation of resources and tasks among system units in order to augment the efficiency of their distributed performance. On the other hand, communication systems (cf. Winograd and Flores, 1986) are based upon a benevolence assumption (see Chapter 1). Therefore, the systems' architecture and/or the agent modeling is by default cooperative. The criticism of these models of "benevolent" agents is on the increase, raising among other things the problem of possible conflicts among autonomous agents (Galliers, 1988). However, the "overcooperative" paradigm is so powerful that conflict is admitted only as a reconcilable and socially useful mechanism. That is to say that conflict is introduced not as a possible form of social interaction per se (and having its own justifications) but as useful, in the long run, for cooperation. An appeal is also explicitly made to the tradition of sociological functionalism. In other words, conflict has not the status of an object of analysis and theorizing in its own right; it is studied either in order to find a remedy, to bring it back to cooperation (in line with the tradition of "conflict resolution"), or else in order to demonstrate its validity and cooperative functionality to the community. However, solutions to applicative problems are not necessarily overcooperative: sometimes, competition (and selection) among (groups of) agents which either form or quit relationships in order to maximize the fulfillment of their tasks/goals, may represent alternative and more efficient solutions.

3.2 Hypercognitive Agents

In most agent modeling (be it produced within computational models of communication, cf. Cohen et al., 1990, or within a strategic framework, cf. Rosenschein and Genesereth, 1988), at least the axioms of omniscience and introspection are maintained (see Sections 2 and 10) (and sometimes, even the one of full mental transparence among the agents). Agents are by default omniscient and strategic and likely to take what in a multiagent context is seen as the most rational course of social action, namely negotiation and cooperation. More in general, agents are modelled as having in their minds the representations of their social links. These links seem to hold precisely in virtue of the fact that they are known or intended (subjectivism): *any social phenomenon* (be it global cooperation, the group, or an organization) is represented in the agents' mind and *consists of such representation*. This is an easy way out from the micro-macro problem: global social phenomena are but *idols* produced by the individual minds to facilitate social interaction.

3.3 Lack of Limits on Agents' Autonomy and Freedom

Agents are modeled as completely free to negotiate and establish any sort of commitment with any partner (see Chapter 7). Existing relations of dependence and power among the agents are not expected to set any constraints on their capacity and motivation to negotiate. Analogously, preexisting norms, habits, and procedures are not imposed on the systems and their effects are not considered (Castelfranchi et al., 1992a). In particular:

1. (social) action is explained only on the grounds of (mutual) beliefs and (joint) intentions, that is, in terms of the agents' mental states. Consequently, *the role of objective social conditions* (that is, the factual relations among agents' which form part of the observer's knowledge, but are not necessarily known to the agents themselves) is left unaccounted.

2. Cognitive mediators of the organizational level are relatively neglected (see Chapter 19). In fact, the "implementation" of the organizational level in the agents' minds is allowed through the *cognitive correspondents of norms, values, and roles*, but they are not taken into account in AI social studies (for one exception, see Werner, 1989 and Chapter 2).

3.4 A Monistic View of Communication

Communication is said to be the *glue* of teams and organizations: it serves to reduce divergence among agents' beliefs. In the "teamwork" model (Cohen and Levesque, 1991), the main function of communication is the agents' monitoring one another about the achievements of their mutual goals. In this view, functions and predictions concerning communication are rather poor. In our view, a fundamental social function of communication is to influence others, change their goal-balance, and induce them to adopt one's goals. Several questions arise: who, why, and how to influence others? How can such a goal be predicted (thus predicting a large part of communication)?

In our model (Conte and Castelfranchi, 1994, 1995a), influencing is derivable from dependence and power relations (and their knowledge) (see also Chapters 6 and 16). Therefore, communication is based upon dependence and power and serves to set up commitments and obligations; to assign rewards, etc. Finally, it allows agents to share knowledge and coordinate but only once they have adopted one another's goals.

3.5 Emergent as Opposed to Cognitive

Emergent (extracognitive) functionalities of actions intended and planned by cognitive agents are ignored (Castelfranchi and Conte, 1992). Emergent functionality is allowed only among subcognitive agents (see Chapter 11). Indeed, in some subfields (such as systems acting on a neural network base, reactive systems, etc.) the organizational level is allowed to emerge from spontaneous self-organizing mechanisms acting among subcognitive agents (cf. Steels, 1990).

4 REQUIREMENTS OF A "MIDDLE GROUND" THEORY

To sum up, AI social studies do not show a really "constructivist" approach to social action. Or, if they do, social action is allowed to emerge from interaction among subcognitive agents. As a consequence, the link among the cognitive level and the organizational level of the action control is overlooked.

What is lacking, therefore, is a two-way link between the individual and organizational levels of control of action, namely an integrated approach where the latter level is not only seen as produced by, but also as controlling the individual one.

A so called "middle ground" theory between the individual and organizational aspects should be bidirectional and account for how the latter level emerges from cognitive agents' interactions independent of the agents' acknowledgement and the social and organizational level works through the minds of autonomous agents (cf. Conte, 1991). Notably, the latter process might be seen as a self-contradiction, since autonomous agents are usually defined as totally independent of the influence of external forces. In our terms (cf. Castelfranchi, 1993), however, *for an agent to be autonomous* it is sufficient that it is able to decide whether to "have" a goal proposed by some external authorship. If one agent decides to "accept" such a proposal *on the basis of its own beliefs and its own preferences* (i.e., in order to achieve some of its goals), it is autonomous as much as one that decides not to take it into account.

5 TEAMS, GROUPS, AND JOINT INTENTIONS

Here, the problems presented in the previous sections will be exemplified and illustrated by reference to existing models of teamwork and joint intentions (see Chapters 6 and 18).

Before, however, we should make clear the perspective from which these criticisms are moved. The disciplinary relationship between AI and cognitive and social science still ought to be negotiated. In particular, the possibility for cross-fertilization among those disciplines should be explored, new frontiers ought to be tested.

5.1 Prescriptive versus Descriptive

Sometimes, AI is used for cheating. It is an ambiguous discipline: it is hard to say to what extent it is (or aims to be) a *science* and to what extent it is pure *technology* (engineering). According to the circumstances, AI scientists choose the most convenient self-presentation, the best "facade."

The poor guy intending to discuss (D)AI models from a cognitive and/or social science perspective finds himself in an awkward position: if he objects that the models proposed are "idealized" and do not account for many interesting empirical situations (explained within other disciplines), he will be answered that his arguments are "not pertinent." *AI students* answer/prevent this kind of objections claiming that they *do not intend to describe "natural facts"*: their discipline is not descriptive. However, if (D)AI scientists maintain a "prescriptive," rather than "descriptive," purpose, they will certainly find an audience in such disciplines as operational research, economics, decision theory, and game theory, but they will tell us little about how and why human groups work. *Their contribution to cognitive and social science will be radically limited.* Indeed, *artificial agents* can be designed, and they *should be designed as "rational."* But *they should also be integrated into human organizations*, and be capable to interact with their human partners in an adaptive and understandable way. Is this possible without an understanding of true human interaction, without some representation and reasoning about human cooperative work?

5.2 Current Notions of Teamwork and Joint Activity

Let us take the important analysis of teamwork by Cohen and Levesque (1991; Levesque et al., 1990) as an example of the previous contradiction.

That work proceeds from the following questions: "What is involved when a group of agents decide to do something together? *What motivates agents to form teams and act together?* What benefits do agents expect to derive from their participation in a group effort? We attempt to provide an answer to these questions." *But, in fact, the authors immediately restrict their research to some subquestions, like* "how does a team work? what is a joint intention? how is it translated into an individual one?" These questions widely differ from the initial ones. Many problems relevant for social theory are side stepped. Again, the natural concept of joint activity is said to be irrelevant: "we want to specify an idealized concept that has appropriate consequences . . . , not a descriptive theory. We seek reasonable design specifications . . . that would lead to desirable behaviour" (Cohen and Levesque, 1991). *We claim that "natural facts" should be taken into account and different social situations should be compared*, to rule out situations that by no means we want to equate to "teamwork." We do not mean to provide a comparative analysis of various kinds of "social cooperation" and interaction for the sake of a social-psychological description. Rather, we will endeavor to meet (D)AI on its own ground, arguing from within the discipline and focusing on its internal purposes. However, concepts that do not "grasp" reality will also have an *undesirable impact* on the design of artificial systems. In order both to provide a good definition of teamwork and to design an artificial agent who is able to cooperate, *it is necessary to provide a theory of the agents' motives for participating in a teamwork*; of how cooperation is formed from individual needs and desires; of which rewards one expects and obtains. In other words, not only the *direction of causation from macro to micro* should be accounted for, but also the *way up*. Not only the direction from the group to the individual should be studied but also that from the individual to the group. If agents do not take into account and look after their own advantages, they will behave irrationally, that is, inefficiently.

5.3 Undesirable Applicative Consequences

In the following, we will distinguish two types of undesirable applicative consequences of the model in question.

Too Broad: Teamwork and Exchange. In Cohen and Levesque's (1991) terms, x and y *jointly intend* to do some action if and only if it is mutually known between x and y that

They each intend that the collective action occur.

They each intend to do their share (as long as the other does it).

This mutual knowledge persists until it is mutually known that the activity is over (successful, unachievable, etc.).

The final definition proposed by the authors is somewhat different from this, because this is considered as "too strong." Therefore, the present definition will be refined only to be weakened! On the contrary, we see it as too broad. Since it is not focused on the *specific conditions of teamwork*, it can be applied to several different social situations: to mother-child relationship, a car convoy, and, generally speaking, to social and economic *exchange*. When agents exchange goods or resources, they usually intend that a collective action (exchange) occurs, and each intends to do her share as long as the other does his share of the joint activity. Suppose that in Levesque et al.'s (1990) example of a car convoy, Alice (the convoy leader) leads Bob (the driver of the car behind her) home to gain something in return (Bob has sincerely promised to give her some money). They have come to an agreement and mutually intend to do their share to achieve the goal that Bob reaches home. If the reasons for the collective activity are not specified, it is impossible to distinguish one type of collective activity from another, namely exchange from cooperation.

We prefer to work at definitions that *imply the reasons why agents adopt (and hence share) others' goals*. Motivations are part of the notion of group, or of cooperation, or of joint activity, and allow exchange to be clearly distinguished from cooperation.

DAI researchers, who are essentially interested in the question of "coordination," tend to overlook the question as to *why joint activities are formed*. However, in our view, this question is crucial because it is reflected in the kind of cooperation chosen, in its success, and in the escape conditions: while in cooperation agents intend to do their share of the plan *to reach their own goals*, in exchange they intend to do *so as long as the other is believed to do their share*. In the former case, the agent commits herself to do an action *naturally, intrinsically* expected to achieve her goal. In the latter, the agent commits herself to do an action *artificially, conventionally* expected to achieve her goal. The cognitive capabilities required of the agent widely differ in the two conditions.

In general, a team, a social agent (Rao et al., 1992), etc., are defined in terms of joint persistent goals.

A team of agents have a joint persistent goal relative to q to achieve p (a belief from which, intuitively, the goal originates) just in case:

(1) they mutually believe that p is currently false;

(2) they mutually know they all want p to eventually be true;

(3) it is true (and mutually knowledge) that until they come to believe either that p is true, that p will never be true, or that q is false, they will continue to mutually believe that they each have p as a *weak achievement goal* relative to q and *with respect to the team*

where a weak achievement goal with respect to a team has been defined as ''a goal that the status of p be mutually believed by all the team members'' (Cohen and Levesque, 1991).

Now, it is possible to show that this notion is not sufficient to account for a group or a truly cooperative work.

Let us give another crucial example. Professor Montaigner, of the Institute Pasteur in France, and Professor Gallo in the United States share the final goal p ''vaccine anti-AIDS be found out'' relative to the belief q that ''if vaccine is discovered, AIDS is wiped out.'' They share all three mental attitudes described above as necessary and sufficient conditions for a joint persistent goal and then for a team:

1. They mutually believe that p is currently false: ''vaccine is not already found out.''

2. They mutually know they all want p to eventually be true (to discover the vaccine).

3. It is true (and mutually knowledge) that until they come to believe either that p is true, that p will never be true, or that q is false, they will continue to mutually believe that they each have p as a ''weak achievement goal'' relative to q and with respect to the team: *they want that the status of p* (i.e., whether the vaccine was discovered or not) *be mutually believed by all the team members*, both because this is an expected practice within scientific communities, and because they want to inform their competitor.

But no one would say that Professors Gallo and Montaigner form a team. Indeed, given their ''parallel goals'' (''I discover the vaccine''), they might come to strongly compete with each other.

What else is needed for them to form a team, and carry out a joint action? First, a belief about mutual dependence: without it, the commitment to participate, to do one's own share is unmotivated, irrational. An agent belief that she depends on others to achieve her goals or, in other words, her belief in a ''necessity to collaborate'' is a foundational condition for a really cooperative work (Jennings, 1992; Conte et al., 1991).

Second, obligations are missing in the above definition. Consider the example of the car convoy discussed by Levesque et al. (1990). Alice (the convoy leader) leads Bob (the driver of the car behind) home to gain something in return (Bob has sincerely promised to give her some money). They have come to an agreement and mutually intend to do their share to achieve the goal that Bob reaches home. Alice does her share (which costs her time and resources!). Once Bob has reached home, however, he has no rational reason to give Alice money. The condition for doing so does not hold any longer (the goal is fulfilled). However, according to Cohen and Levesque's analysis, Bob's commitment prevents his abandoning the team: he *must* and will let Alice know that the common plan does not hold any longer.

In such a case, coordination worked rather well, and no misunderstandings occurred. Nonetheless, Alice was cheated! If Alice were fooled by everyone, she would soon become the victim of the group.

A rational agent, whether artificial or natural, cannot run into such risk. Can a group or organization be efficient if some agents spend all their resources without being adequately rewarded, without being able to achieve their own goals (or perform their tasks, jobs, etc.)?

This dilemma is well known within the social sciences. Indeed, it is *the* social dilemma: how can a self-interested agent decide to do something for the group which may cost her more than she gains? How does she cope with possible cheating and free-riding? Social norms and the obligation to reciprocate the benefits received are fundamental mechanisms that prevent cheating. The existence of these obligations motivate self-interested agents to respect the agreement. The motivations to reciprocate the benefits received, or which is the same the costs of defeat, should be considered. *Due to such motivations/ costs, it becomes convenient to carry through one's share of the joint plan even when one's own goals have been achieved.* These motivations/costs must be explicitly accounted for.

This, again, leads us to the necessity for *a theory of the reasons why agents do something useful to others and form joint intentions*. In particular, a typology of groups, cooperation, etc., as well as a typology of the rewards that agents calculate and/or receive, should be provided.

Finally, this entails a (mental) representation of obligations and norms without which there is no true agreement, nor social commitment; and without which the speech act theory itself is vacuous, since a fundamental aspect of speech acts is precisely the formation of obligations in both speaker and hearer.

Too Narrow: Teamwork and Orchestrated Cooperation.

The above definition is not only too broad (lacking necessary conditions for teamwork). It seems also too narrow. It is not clear whether it could be applied to a fundamental case of teamwork that is not only a natural phenomenon but also a *useful coordination* among natural or artificial agents that may have important applications. What we are thinking of is the *outdesigned or orchestrated cooperation* among cognitive systems.

In many cases, the members of a team may not even be aware of the overall plan (for example, the members of an army command during an attack); nor are they always informed about the existence of other participants (think of partisans, guerillas, or comrades of a terrorist organization). Their actions take part in one and the same plan, they are coordinated with one other, necessary to one other, and act deliberately. However, no mutual belief about the plan and its executors can be said to exist.

6 IN SEARCH FOR FOUNDATIONS

The dominant view is always based on purely subjective links, mutual goals and knowledge, and the mental representation of "groupness." No preexisting relationships, no objective bases, no specific motivations for cooperation are supposed in the agents, no obligations and constraints, except their free commitments, are thought to be put on them.

Let us take a different perspective and ground the reasons for social action on some nonsubjective, precognitive structural relations among agents in a common world.

6.1 Social Dependence

Our search for the foundations of social interaction is grounded on few basic concepts all aiming at characterizing the agents' interdependence that rule human relationships in a social context (see Chapters 2 and 6). In the following, x and y denote agents with $x \neq y$ always implicitly stated; a denotes an action, and p a formula representing a state of the world.

An important concept is that of social dependence whose basic definition is as follows (Castelfranchi et al., 1992b):

$$(S - DEP \; x \; y \; a \; p) \equiv (GOAL \; x \; p) \wedge$$
$$\neg (CANDO \; x \; a) \wedge$$
$$(CANDO \; y \; a) \wedge$$
$$((DONE - BY \; y \; a) \supset EVENTUALLY \; p)$$

that is: x depends on y with regard to an act useful for realizing a state p when p is a goal of x's and x is unable to realize p while y is able to do so.

It should be stressed that, unlike what most DAI work seems to take for granted, social dependence is *not fundamentally mental*. It is an *objective* relationship, in that it holds *independently* of the agents' awareness of it. However, many relevant consequences may derive from x and y's (either unilaterally or mutually) becoming aware of it: to mention only the most salient, x may try to *influence* y to pursue p, while y may choose whether to adopt x's goal or not.

Dependence relations may be compound in various ways generating different structures underlying the social context. Such structures are extensively investigated in (Castelfranchi et al., 1992b) where the *OR-dependence*, a disjunctive composition of dependence relations, and the *AND-dependence*, a conjunction of dependence relations, were distinguished. To give a flavor of those distinctions we just detail the case of a two-way dependence between agents (*bilateral dependence*). There are two possible kinds of bilateral dependence:

1. *Mutual Dependence.* This occurs when x and y depend on each other for realizing a *common goal p*, which can be achieved by means of a plan including at least two *different* acts such that x depends on y's doing a_y, and y depends on x's doing a_x:

$$\exists p((S - DEP \; x \; y \; a_y \; p) \wedge (S - DEP \; y \; x \; a_x \; p))$$

As observed in a previous work (Conte et al., 1991), *cooperation* is a function of *mutual dependence*: in cooperation, in the strict sense, agents depend on one another to achieve one and the same goal; they are cointerested in the convergent result of the common activity;

2. *Reciprocal Dependence.* This occurs when x and y depend on each other for realising different goals, that is, when x depends on y for realizing x's goal that p_x, while y depends on x for realizing y's goal that p_y:

$$\exists p_x \exists p_y ((S - DEP \; x \; y \; a_y \; p_x) \wedge (S - DEP \; y \; x \; a_x \; p_y))$$

with $a_x \neq a_y$ implicitly stated. Reciprocal dependence is to *social exchange* what mutual dependence is to cooperation.

6.2   A Dependence-Based Notion of Collective Agent

According to our analysis, a group of agents form a collective entity (in the strictly cooperative sense relevant for MA researchers) when

a. All agents share a *common goal*.
b. Each is required to do its share to achieve the common goal by the group itself or by a subcomponent.
c. Each adopts such request.

It is worth observing that the notion of collective will is more complex: it also includes that of a normative will, that is, an entitled authority which assigns tasks to the group's members (Conte and Castelfranchi, 1995b). In addition a more analytical treatment of various kinds of groups and teams would be required. However, we cannot examine these aspects here.

It is to be noted that by (*GOAL x p*) it is here meant what Cohen and Levesque (1990) define as an achievement goal, that is, x's goal that p will be eventually true and x's belief that p is not currently true. Analogously, our notion of relativized goals draws on Cohen and Levesque's (1990) notion: such goals are relative to an escape condition, namely to a given belief of the agent's. Indeed, this often is used as a device to express a means-end link, an instrumental goal. Here, it will be intended precisely in this sense, although we are aware of the weak expressive power of such use of the notion.

Our definition of a collective agent can be expressed as follows:

$$(COLL - AGT\ x_i\ a) \equiv$$

$$\exists p(\bigwedge_{i=1,n} (C - GOAL\ x_i\ p) \wedge$$

$$(\bigvee_{i=1,n} (z = x_i) \wedge (R - GOAL\ z\ (DONE - BY\ x_i\ a)$$

$$(BEL\ z\ ((DONE - BY\ x_i\ a) \supset$$

$$(EVENTUALLY\ p))))) \wedge$$

$$(ADOPT\ x_i\ z\ (DONE - BY\ x_i\ a)))$$

a common goal (*C-GOAL*) being defined (cf. Conte et al., 1991) as *two or more agents having one and the same goal and being mutually dependent to achieve it.*

$$(C - GOAL\ x_i\ p) \equiv (\bigwedge_{i=1,n} (I - GOAL\ x_i\ p) \wedge$$

$$(\bigvee_{i=1,n} (z = x_i) \supset (\bigwedge_{j=i-z} (S - DEP\ z\ x_j\ a_j\ p))))$$

6.3 Advantages of the Notion Proposed

The present notion of a collective agent ultimately relies upon the objective structure of interdependence among individual agents.

This view seems to provide several advantages over preexisting notions of collective agent and joint intentions:

a. It does not imply mutual belief of the overall plan; therefore *it is applicable to orchestrated cooperation.*

b. It is based upon objective mutual dependence, therefore *it rules out situations of competition* (as in the scientific example examined above: the two scholars do not depend on each other, and therefore they do not need to participate in a teamwork).

c. It is based upon preexisting identical goals, therefore *it rules out situations of exchange*, at least when exchange is not oriented to realize cooperation (as when *x* provides *y* with the paper and *y* does the writing of a common text); in principle, although this is not yet explicitly mentioned in the present definition, *it allows the normative authorship to be ex-*

pressed (as a subcomponent of the group), and therefore obligations and commitments of the members to be taken into account.

7   CONCLUSIONS

In this chapter, the following assumptions have been rejected:

a. AI is concerned with the individual mind (individual intention, action, etc.).
b. DAI is concerned with the social (that, in turn, is equated to the collective) mind (intention, action, etc.).

In our view, the DAI study of the "individual social mind" is much needed. *Even to account for collective minds and activities individual motivations ought to be accounted for, since they have an impact on the nature and quality of groups and interaction.* A social perspective on agenthood does not mean that "the whole (society) is prior to the part (the individual), . . . and the part is explained in terms of the whole . . . " (Mead) (cited in Gasser, 1991). In our terms, a "social perspective" means a theory of action and knowledge of *agents situated in a social word.* Agents can reach their goals if they have the capacities to control and coordinate with (predict, exploit) the actions of other agents.

That of collective agents is an issue of vital importance. However, the glue of a collective agent (formed by cognitive members) is the "social mind" of its members. We share Gasser's view that most social relations preexist to interactions and commitments among the individuals, but *social relations and organizations are not held or created by commitments* (mutual, social) of the individuals. Autonomous agents in a multiagent world (to recall the title of the European DAI workshops) find themselves as "socially situated agents." They find themselves in a network of relations (interference, dependence, concurrence, power, etc.) that are independent of their awareness and choices. But, of course, this "uncommitted" structure presupposes individuals, their goals, needs, capabilities, and resources, especially their *social* goals and capabilities.

REFERENCES

Castelfranchi, C. (1991). *Principles of Bounded Autonomy*, Tech. Rep. TR-IP-PSCS-49. Institute of Psychology, Roma.

Castelfranchi, C. (1992). *AIA'93 Workshop.* ENEA, Roma.

Castelfranchi, C., and Conte, R. (1991). Problemi di rappresentazione mentale delle norme. Le strutture della mente normativa. In *La norma. Mente e regolazione sociale.* (R. Conte, ed.). Editori Riuniti, Roma.

Castelfranchi, C., and Conte, R. (1992). Emergent functionality among intelligent systems: Cooperation within and without minds. *AI Soc.* **6,** 78–93.

Castelfranchi, C., Conte, R., and Cesta, A. (1992a). The organization as a structure of negotiated and non negotiated binds. *Proc. Eur. Conf. Cognit. Ergon., 6th,* Balaton, Hungary, *1992.*

Castelfranchi, C., Miceli, M., and Cesta, A. (1992b). Dependence relations among autonomous agents. In *Decentralized Artificial Intelligence.* (E. Werner and Y. Demazeau, eds.). Elsevier/North-Holland, Amsterdam.

Castelfranchi, R. (1992). No more cooperation, please! In search of the social structure of verbal interaction. In *Artificial Intelligence and Cognitive Science Perspectives on Communication* (A. Ortony, J. Slack, and O. Stock, eds.). Springer-Verlag, Heidelberg.

Cohen, P. R., and Levesque, H. J. (1990). Rational interaction as the basis for communication. In *Intentions in Communication* (P. R. Cohen, J. Morgan, and M. E. Pollack, eds.). MIT Press, Cambridge, MA.

Cohen, P., and Levesque, H. (1991). *Teamwork,* Tech. Rep. SRI-International, Menlo Park, CA.

Cohen, P. R., Morgan, J., and Pollack, M. E., eds. (1990). *Intentions in Communication.* MIT Press, Cambridge, MA.

Conte, R., ed. (1991). *La norma. Mente e regolazione sociale.* Editori Riuniti, Roma.

Conte, R., and Castelfranchi, C. (1995b). Norms as mental objects. From normative beliefs to normative goals. In *From Reaction to Wjnikon* (L. P. Mueller and C. Castelfranchi, eds.). Springer, Berlin.

Conte, R., and Castelfranchi, C. (1994). Mind is not enough. Precognitive bases of social interaction. In *Simulating Societies* (J. Doran and N. Gilbert, eds.). UCLP, London (in press).

Conte, R., and Castelfranchi, C. (1995a). *Cognitive and Social Action.* UCLP, London.

Conte, R., Miceli, M., and Castelfranchi, C. (1991). Limits and levels of cooperation: Disentangling various types of prosocial interaction. In *Decentralized Artificial Intelligence* (Y. Demazeau and J.-P. Müller, eds.). Elsevier/North-Holland, Amsterdam.

Galliers, J. R. (1988). A strategic framework for multi agent cooperative dialogue. *Proc. Eur. Conf. Artif. Intell., 8th,* Munich, Germany, pp. 415–420.

Gasser, L. (1991). Knowledge and action at social and organizational level. *Am. Assoc. Artif. Intell., Fall Symp.,* Asilomar, CA.

Jennings, N. (1992). On being responsible. In *Decentralized Artificial Intelligence 3* (E. Werner and Y. Demazeau, eds.). Elsevier/North-Holland, Amsterdam.

Levesque, H. J., Cohen, P. R., and Nunes, J. H. T. (1990). On acting together. *Proc. Natl. Conf. Artif. Intell., 8th,* Boston, pp. 94–90.

Rao, A. S., and Georgeff, M. P. (1991). Modeling rational agents in a BDI-architecture. *Proc. Conf. Knowl. Representation Reasoning, 2nd, 1991,* pp. 473–484.

Rao, A. S., Georgeff, M. P., and Sonenberg, E. A. (1992) Social plans: A preliminary report. In *Decentralized Artificial Intelligence* (E. Werner and Y. Demazeau, eds.). Elsevier/North-Holland, Amsterdam.

Rosenschein, J. S., and Genesereth, M. R. (1988). Deals among rational agents. In *The Ecology of Computation* (B. A. Huberman, ed.). Elsevier/North-Holland, Amsterdam.

Steels, L. (1990). Cooperation between distributed agents through self-organization. In

Decentralized Artificial Intelligence (Y. Demazeau and J. P. Müller, eds.). Elsevier/North-Holland, Amsterdam.

Werner, E. (1988). Social intentions. *Proc. Eur. Conf. Artif. Intell.*, *8th*, Munich, Germany, *1988*.

Werner, E. (1989). Cooperating agents: A unified theory of communication and social structure. In *Distributed Artificial Intelligence* (M. N. Huhns and L. Gasser, eds.), Vol. 2. Morgan Kaufmann, San Mateo, CA/Pitman, London.

Winograd, T., and Flores, F. (1986). *Understanding Computers and Cognition*. Addison-Wesley, New York.

CHAPTER 21 _____

User Design Issues for Distributed Artificial Intelligence

LYNNE E. HALL

1 INTRODUCTION

This chapter applies factors from human computer interaction (HCI) to DAI systems, through considering issues related to user interaction and user interface design for DAI systems. The main aim of HCI is to enable the development of usable systems. An important aspect of usability relates to user interface design, with the aim to provide software which ensures that computer systems are easy to learn, use and that they perform the functions which their users want. As noted in Sutcliffe (1988) poor interface design can have a number of consequences, such as increasing mistakes in system operation, user frustration, poor system performance, and potential system failure because of user rejection. The importance of the user interface cannot be underestimated, for, as Monk (1985) states, "the design of the user machine interface in any interactive system is crucial for its efficiency and acceptability." However, user interface development has been acknowledged as being one of the most difficult aspects of a system to provide (Myers, 1989).

Here, the aim is to consider user interaction and the design of the user interface for DAI systems. This issue is increasing in importance, as DAI research matures and systems begin to emerge from research laboratories, for example with experimental prototypes for applications (Brandau and Weihmayer, 1989) and large-scale industrial projects such as ARCHON (Wittig, 1992) (see Chapter 12).

Initially, brief details are provided of the range of DAI system users, then

Foundations of Distributed Artificial Intelligence, Edited by G. M. P. O'Hare and N. R. Jennings.
ISBN 0-471-00675-0 © 1996 John Wiley & Sons, Inc.

end users are focused on in more detail. Section 3 provides a number of examples of user interaction and user interfaces to DAI systems, highlighting problems and issues which have emerged. Section 4 discusses factors which are novel in terms of user interaction for DAI systems, and Section 5 considers the implications which these novel aspects have for DAI system user interface requirements. Finally, the issue of representing a DAI system to the user is considered, detailing one of the most important areas of research for future DAI system user interface designers.

2 DAI SYSTEM USERS

As for all computer systems a range of users exist for DAI systems, spanning the entire development process, providing a number of different skills and fulfilling many different roles within the DAI system. Here, using a slightly extended version of the design methodology detailed in Wooldridge et al. (1991) and O'Hare and Wooldridge (1992), the following user groups can be identified, along with the activities and outputs which they provide.

The taxonomy proposed here is based on user relation to the system (see Table 21.1). This identifies eight different user groups, although some users may belong to more than one user group, depending on the resources available for DAI system development.

These eight user groups span the entire development life cycle of a DAI system. Domain experts, knowledge engineers, and agent developers are principally involved in the development of individual agents. Integration platform developers and MAS interface designers are involved with the provision of a multiagent environment. The former focuses on architectural considerations and the latter with the presentation of the DAI system to the user. The MAS developers are involved throughout the development of the DAI system providing a planning and management function, enabling the production of a coherent and cohesive system. The end users and organization are involved in the initial stages to specify needs and requirements, and the final phases of system testing and interface design, to ensure that the DAI system meets user needs and has an acceptable level of usability.

Although a wide range of users can be identified, here the focus is on end users, who are users that require advice about some decision making or problem-solving task, and are using the DAI system for this function. They can be considered to be similar to expert system users, being active agents in the problem-solving process (Kidd and Cooper, 1983), generally having expertise within the domain in which the DAI system is implemented. They use the DAI system to obtain advice and information regarding a decision making or problem-solving activity.

The user can be considered to have a role which involves the sharing of knowledge with other agents within the DAI system and participation in the production of a problem solution (Hall et al., 1994). This user role results in a style of user interaction which differs from that in the majority of information

TABLE 21.1 User Inputs in DAI System Development

Development Phase	Users	Activity	Output
Strategic phase	Domain experts MAS developers organization	Determining applicability of the MAS for both the domain and the problem	Feasibility study
Requirements specification	End users organization MAS developers	Identifying initial user requirements	Requirements specification document
Identification conceptualization	Domain experts	Determining if domain conceptualization will support user needs	Domain support for users
Domain coverage	MAS developers Agent developers Integration platform developers	Identification of existing agents and the integration platform to be used	Development areas identification
Decomposition formalization	Domain experts Knowledge engineers Agent developers	Agent development	Pretested agents
Agent implementation and testing	Domain experts Knowledge engineers Agent developers End users	Agent evaluation	Tested agents
System implementation and testing	Domain experts MAS developers Agent developers	Agent integration and evaluation	Integrated system
Interface phase	MAS developers End users MAS interface designers	Interface design, implementation, and evaluation	Operational system

systems, an issue supported in Berry and Broadbent (1987). They note that with information systems, the user's work is focused on the computer, with computer use needed for the majority of their tasks. Instead, users of intelligent systems usually interact with the computer briefly and sporadically, with their main focus on other people or activities.

Finally, users view the DAI system as a tool, and while they will wish to use the full functionality of the DAI system, no assumptions can be made relating to their level of computer knowledge. Thus, it can be assumed that training will be needed and that the user interface must facilitate user understanding of the system in terms of what it can do and how the user can interact to utilize the system's functionalities.

3 USER INTERACTION WITH DAI SYSTEMS: EXAMPLES

The previous section identified a variety of DAI system users, with the main focus being on end users. In this section, end users are further considered through the examples of several DAI systems which have highlighted user interaction issues.

The DAI systems which are considered consist of coarse-grained autonomous agents (see, for example, Chapters 12, 13, and 14), rather than fine-grained reactive systems (Chapter 11), and this focus relates to the differences which can typically be observed in user interaction with these two types of DAI system. With fine-grained DAI systems, users are relatively passive, having little interaction with the fine-grained agents and minimal involvement in system activity. With coarse-grained DAI systems, users have considerable interaction with agents and are often actively involved in the problem-solving activity of the system (see Chapter 13).

Coarse-grained DAI systems consist of a number of intelligent, autonomous agents with complementary areas of expertise, which exhibit intelligent behavior patterns utilizing cooperation mechanisms in the solution of problems. This section focuses on how the user interface for such systems has been provided and some of the problems which have emerged for users interacting with these systems.

3.1   Initial Attempts at Supporting User Interaction: PUP6

One of the earliest reports of user interaction difficulties with DAI systems is provided by Lenat (1975) in relation to PUP6. This system was designed to imitate the dialogue involved in designing programs, with the dialogue being provided by BEINGS (the agents in PUP6), which simulated the behavior of expert programmers. It was tested in the domain of automatic programming, with the agents attempting to build a program by interacting with the user. However, this interaction with the user resulted in a number of problems. In Lenat (1975) it is observed that users rarely understood what was wanted by the BEINGS, having to interrupt them and ask questions about who was in control, why, what they were trying to do, etc. To alleviate this problem, the user was given the possibility of interrupting the agents during the problem solving. However, the BEINGS were incapable of widely varied dialogue with the user, with the abilities of users having to coincide with those of the user who was simulated in the protocol.

3.2   Shielding the User from Complexity: The Pilot's Associate

A more successful example in terms of user interaction, is provided by the Pilot's Associate project. This aimed to design a prototype of an expert pilot aid, based on the distributed system development environment ABE (Smith and Broadwell, 1988; Hayes-Roth et al., 1988). A set of fairly complex modules interact among themselves and with the pilot in order to perform monitoring and assessment of the situation inside and outside of the aeroplane, planning of the mission, tactics planning, etc. A module has the responsibility of interacting with the pilot and other agents to perform monitoring and continuous assessment of the pilot's responses.

In the development system prototype there are a number of features of considerable interest in terms of user interaction, including the capacity of the designed system to handle the complexity of such a system. This is achieved by partitioning and hiding the complexity of the system's components and by uncovering portions selectively, according to the needs of the dialogue.

3.3 The User Agent: CooperA, FELINE, and CooperA-II

The inclusion of a user agent (an intelligent agent similar to all other agents within the DAI system) which deals with user interaction, has recently gained considerable popularity (see Chapters 12, 13, and 14). The user agent provides a pragmatic solution to the issue of user interaction with DAI systems, with a number of mitigating factors within DAI system design making this a useful and implementable solution for the interface. These include the existence of agents without user interface facilities, the need to partially hide the complexity of the DAI system, and the need for a mechanism to shield the user from disconcerting inconsistency and irregularity among the various agents.

One of the earliest examples of a user agent is provided by CooperA (Sommaruga et al., 1989; Chapter 14, this volume), as detailed in the application DChEM (distributed chemical emergencies manager) (Avouris et al., 1989). DChEM contains a number of heterogeneous expert systems covering distinct areas of expertise. These agents interact cooperatively among themselves and with the user to establish the threat level of an emergency. Interaction with the user is performed by the user agent, which is structured in the same way as all other CooperA agents and communicates with them through the same message-passing mechanism. This user agent represents the user to other agents and is considered to be a boundless domain of knowledge in the problem solving. It does not contain application-specific knowledge, thus when it needs to satisfy a goal, it must be supplied with information on how to establish a dialogue with the user. This interaction meta-knowledge is supplied by the agent involved in the interaction, enabling different dialogue styles to be used for interaction with different agents.

However, user interaction with CooperA highlights a number of issues for DAI system user interface design. First, the lack of uniformity produced by different interaction styles can be disturbing for the user, as she may become confused by differences in agent styles, an effect which seems to be caused by the lack of an accurate conceptual model of the system. Another major problem with the CooperA user agent is that it is intended for use both by the end user and the developer. Thus, the user is subjected to information relating to agent communications, which is difficult to interpret and understand. In addition, the user is unable to ask for information relating to CooperA activity, which is frustrating and means that interaction is limited. Further, CooperA explanation facilities provide the user with the means to enter the knowledge base of agents, thus a user (who is potentially unfamiliar with computer programming) has to attempt to understand the intricacies of LISP code.

The initial agent of FELINE (Wooldridge et al., 1991) has the same structure as other agents within the system, and provides the DAI system with information which the user has entered, as if the user was another agent. It provides the user with relatively basic interaction features, using a form-filling style interface with simplistic explanation facilities. Although this interface is usable, it is fairly limited, providing an outdated interface which fails to utilize direct manipulation or windowing technology. In addition, no consideration has been given as to the mental representation which the user has of FELINE.

CooperA-II (Sommaruga, 1993) also enables user interaction through a user agent (see Chapter 14). However, similar to a number of other DAI systems, this use of the user agent reveals the addition of a user interface at the end of the development process, without real consideration of human factors issues, with the result of a low-quality though serviceable end user interface.

3.4   Supporting the DAI System User ARCHON

These latter examples reveal the trend of providing low-quality user interfaces which are intended to provide a basic, pragmatic solution to the issue of user interaction, without actually considering in any great detail user needs in terms of the interaction. Recently, there has been a move away from this approach, to one where the needs and requirements of users are actually considered in some detail.

One of the most positive attempts to support user interaction has been provided within the ARCHON project (Wittig, 1992), which has focused on a wide range of issues related to DAI system design and development (see Chapter 12). However, this project has also given considerable importance and effort to the issue of user interaction. One reason which can be suggested for this, is that the DAI systems which are developed within ARCHON are real-life in the sense that they are being developed for use in work environments, rather than as applications which illustrate architectural advances in research laboratories.

ARCHON also utilizes the concept of the user agent, however, this issue has been considered from a number of perspectives. These include the issue of the design and development of the user agent (Hall et al., 1990); the facilities which should be provided by a user agent (Avouris et al., 1993); representing the DAI system to the user (Hall and Avouris, 1992) and the need to separate the developer and end user interfaces (Lekkas and Van Liedekerke, 1992).

The main focus in ARCHON has been in the domain of process supervision and control, however, a wide range of issues have been considered relating to how the user can be inserted into the problem-solving environment and supported within this. The user agents support the user in playing an active role in problem solving, while protecting her from unnecessary and overwhelming information, abilities which are essential to enable productive interaction (Norman, 1994). Additionally, through following ideas dominant in software engineering, the ARCHON project has considered users throughout the development process, identifying user needs and requirements. The user agents produced within the ARCHON project reveal considerable user involvement, and the resulting designs provide high standard interfaces which adequately support their users in cognitively complex situations.

4 DAI USER INTERFACE DESIGN ISSUES

The previous section has highlighted a number of factors relating to user interaction and the design of the user interface for a number of DAI systems. This section focuses on the general issues which need to be considered in terms of the design of the user interface, to facilitate and support user interaction.

Interface design is particularly important for many application domains in which DAI systems are introduced, since these systems can be highly interactive, involving sharing of problem-solving tasks between the agents and the user, aiming to provide users with support to enhance their work capability. The multifaceted abilities of these systems, related to the diversity of the agents incorporated in them, can provide a wide range of facilities for users. Complex cognitive tasks such as fault detection and diagnosis can be enhanced through the provision of expert information and support as discussed in Jennings and Wittig (1992).

Although DAI system use provides a number of new requirements for user interaction and thus for interface design, many factors relating to interface design for information systems and expert systems are of relevance. Issues such as screen design and dialogue facilities, explanation, help, etc., are all areas which are important for enabling DAI systems to be usable and effective systems. However, the issues which are further considered here, are those which are felt to be novel for user interaction with DAI systems.

4.1 Control Issues

A number of different mechanisms can be implemented within a DAI system to promote coordination and coherence, thus resulting in a variety of different control strategies. These can be of importance to the user, for her understanding of how the DAI system functions and in terms of her own interactions. Particularly relevant are factors such as the organizational structure used by the DAI system, which provide a framework of constraints and expectations to the agents. In a DAI system where explicit organizational relationships between the agents exist, user interactions with the DAI system will be affected by these relationships.

In a DAI system with a strict hierarchy, user requests to the DAI system may not be performed immediately, due to the fact that an agent may already be occupied with a task which has come from an agent at a higher level within the hierarchy. Therefore, the user would need to be aware of her place, and the place of her tasks in this hierarchy to understand the DAI system's response.

A second example is of a DAI system which uses a contract net approach, where agents bid for tasks. In this case, the user may find that she is interacting with different agents (possibly with different interaction styles), to perform the same task. Without any understanding of the DAI system's control protocols this situation would be difficult to comprehend. From these examples, it can be that it may be beneficial to make control relationships explicit to the user, to help her understanding of DAI system activity and to facilitate interaction.

4.2 Cooperative Nature of the Interaction

The cooperation strategy which exists in a DAI system, can be of importance, particularly in relation to the nature of problem solving. The main division is that of task and result sharing (see Chapter 1), the former involves the independent solution of subproblems, with agents solving diverse subtasks. The latter involves the production of results for the same task, thus providing several views of the same result.

In a DAI system which uses task sharing, the user may benefit from knowledge of task progression to determine when the task will be completed. Further to this, mechanisms may also need to be provided which clarify user understanding of how a task is performed. For example, factors such as how the task has been decomposed and which agents are fulfilling the task may need to be explained to the user. For DAI systems which use result sharing, the user may be confronted with a number of different agent responses to the same demand. This could be extremely confusing, unless the DAI system facilitated her interactions with a mechanism to view and understand the different results obtained for the same problem.

The mechanism for producing the general solution can also vary, with a number of strategies available, ranging from master/slave to negotiation. To enable the user to interact efficiently and easily it may be necessary to explicitly detail such factors.

4.3 Heterogeneity of the Problem-Solving Agents

Many DAI systems are formed from agents which have existed as standalone expert systems, with the result that agents present various degrees of heterogeneity (see Chapter 12). Roda et al. (1991) present a classification of heterogeneity through the dimensions of semantic, architecture, type, language, and computer environment. The first three categories are of particular relevance to user interaction.

Agent heterogeneity results in a variety of agent types existing within the same environment, which can perform a variety of skills, including diagnosis, interpretation, and monitoring. These differing types of agents will demand different interaction patterns and provide varying information, a factor which may need to be understood by the user. Related to this is the heterogeneity of the end-user interfaces, although consistency has been identified as one of the most desirable attributes of user interfaces (Nielsen, 1989), this may be extremely difficult if not impossible to provide in a DAI system; thus inconsistencies across different agent user interfaces must be minimized, and those which exist must be explained to the user.

In relation to this, is agent architecture heterogeneity, which refers to the knowledge representation and control which can be different from agent to agent. These aspects can affect the user interaction, especially if the agent interfaces are significantly different.

Also problematic for the users is semantic heterogeneity, which is the means of enabling interagent cooperation. If a common protocol is used it may be beneficial to utilize this for user interaction, this would facilitate interaction between the user and the agents, removing the need to translate agent messages, and requests involving cooperation. However, this common protocol would have to be explicitly detailed to the user to enable her to understand how cooperation occurs between herself and other agents.

4.4 Explanation of System Reasoning

A major problem for user interaction with DAI systems is that of the explanation of system reasoning, which is one of the major features of intelligent system interaction. In certain cases this presents considerable difficulties, particularly when the semiautonomous agents have distinct knowledge organization and problem-solving behavior. Explanation of the structure and of the reasoning process provides several new issues. Almost all of the aspects of DAI systems as detailed in the introduction to Bond and Gasser (1988), for example, description, decomposition, distribution, and allocation of tasks; interaction, language, and communication; coherence and coordination; modeling other agents and organized activity; interagent disparities: uncertainty and conflict, etc., will complicate the explanation of system behavior especially in the case of loosely coupled distributed networks of autonomous problem-solving agents.

5 DAI SYSTEM USER INTERFACE DESIGN REQUIREMENTS

From the description of issues for user interaction which relate specifically to the particular features of DAI systems detailed in the previous section, it can be stated that the DAI system end-user interface demands a number of facilities to enable user interaction (see Chapters 1 and 3).

- *An Environment Which Enables the User to Be Inserted in the Problem-Solving Arena of the Multiagent World (Hall et al., 1994).* The construction of this environment determines how the user views the system, which relates to the understanding and knowledge which the user has of the underlying architecture. This has considerable effect on user participation in the problem-solving activities of the DAI system.

- *A Mechanism to Clarify Agents' Activities and Reasoning.* For example, as detailed in relation to PUP6, specific problems were identified, including the need to inform the user about the reasoning of the individual agents as well as about the overall problem-solving progress.

- *Reduction of Complexity of the Multiagent World to Facilitate Interaction.* This was achieved in the Pilot's Associate project where certain agents were hidden from user view to make interaction easier.

- *Multithread Dialogue.* This enables the user interface to support the interaction of the user with more than one task at any one time. For example, DAI systems in process supervision and control usually provide monitoring as well as other activities. This occurs continually in the background, only becoming of interest in a fault situation. The appearance of a fault can result in user information requests from several agents, and the user wishing to receive updates, history, forecasts, etc., thus necessitating many dialogues occurring within a single phase.

- *Facilities to Support User Interaction.* Mechanisms which enable the user to cooperate and communicate with the DAI system (see, for example, Avouris, 1992), including information display, error handling, and explanation. Facilities are also needed to enable the user interface to deal with speculative user input (not tied to a specific task), which must be directed to an appropriate agent.

- *Filtering Information.* The user interface will need to ensure that excessive information is not presented to the user at any one time. Thus the user interface will have to manage presented information to ensure that cognitive overload does not occur.

- *Maintaining a Consistent Information Interface to the User.* Situations will arise when the response to a user question, or information presented to the user is an amalgamation of several pieces of information from several different agents. In these cases the user interface must ascertain that this information is presented in a consistent and coherent manner.

This description of user interface requirements and the factors identified in earlier sections highlight the features and issues that differentiate a DAI system from other intelligent systems, in terms of user interaction. Emerging from this discussion is the fact that in general users will have to be at least partially aware of the underlying architecture of the DAI system. To facilitate interaction, and to understand the inconsistencies between agent reasoning, knowledge, and interface styles, users need to have at least some awareness of the fact that they are interacting with a system composed of a number of separate agents. Further to this, users may also need to be aware at a high level of protocols used for cooperation and control to enable them to understand DAI system activity.

6 REPRESENTING THE DAI SYSTEM TO THE USER

The issues considered in the previous sections highlight the need to support the user in their interaction with DAI systems, a factor that can be achieved through an adequate representation of the DAI system to the user. Research within HCI has demonstrated that a mechanism to provide this type of support is a mental model. This provides an appropriate, accurate, consistent mental representation of the system which both supports the user and facilitates interaction (see, for example, Ackermann and Tauber, 1990). Such models provide "a representation or metaphor that a user adopts to guide his actions and help him interpret the device's behavior" (Young, 1983). A mental model provides a rich and elaborate structure, which reflects the users knowledge of what the system contains, how it works and why it works in a certain way. It is seen as containing knowledge which is sufficient to permit the user to mentally try out actions before choosing one to execute, and enables the user to rationalize and explain system behavior.

The mental model for a DAI system user would be a conceptual machine whose simulated function matches the DAI system. The mental model would be designed in such a way as to insert the user into the problem-solving world, yet protect her from excessive complexity and overwhelming information, thus enabling her to interact effectively with the DAI system. Use of a mental model would enable the underlying system to be simplified, masking system complexity, while retaining functionality. Thus statements such as that of (Moran, 1981) that the mental model developed by developers should be a complete and self-consistent model of the system, have a different perspective in DAI systems. The mental model must provide to the user a model which appears to be complete and self-consistent rather than an accurate model of the DAI system.

Issues of heterogeneity highlight that users will generally have to be aware that they are interacting with a system composed of different intelligent agents. Agent heterogeneity resulting in different functionalities and interface styles would be difficult to explain as a single monolithic system. Although users may not need to be aware of all agents, in the majority of DAI systems, user interaction would be facilitated by some user knowledge of the underlying architecture of the DAI system. This knowledge would enable the user to understand differing interaction styles and agent knowledge areas and facilitate her interactions with the DAI system.

An appropriate mental model of the DAI system should enable the user to understand the nature of the DAI system. The model used for expert systems is based on the metaphor of a human expert. In DAI systems a similar model can be applied, considering the system as a group of cooperating experts. This metaphor is easily understandable for a user who can view each of the agents as an expert in a separate domain, and the DAI system as a whole is viewed as a group of experts interacting with one another in the solution of a global problem. Using this type of mental model a number of factors relating to the

DAI system can be made explicit to the user including the group-solving process; the distributed expertise; and the functionality of the individual experts, with an explanation of their capacities and dependencies. This knowledge is necessary to support the user if participation in the problem solving is required. If agent relations can be mapped to some human problem-solving approach, the organization could be explicitly represented in the mental model as causal relationships can be deduced from this structure (see Chapter 19). These causal relations can be used for instance in order to link individual agents explanations, or to derive the high-level explanation if required.

Initial attempts to provide an interface design which incorporates this type of model have been provided within the ARCHON project (see, for example, Wittig, 1992; Hall and Avouris, 1992). These attempts focus on the abstraction, omission, and amalgamation of agents, providing users with a limited number of agents with whom they will interact. This approach has focused on an application in the electricity supply industry, and a preliminary user interface agent design has been produced. Through extensive analysis the agents and features of these which are essential to user activity have been identified. These are then revealed to the user in the form of conceptual agents, and users are aware of a limited subset of agents and their activities. This approach, while still at an early stage, appears promising, with the complexity of a large DAI system being reduced through limiting user attention and knowledge to a subset of agents with whom she will interact.

7 CONCLUSIONS

This chapter has considered the issues of user interface design and user interaction with DAI systems. Although a number of DAI system users were identified, the focus has been on end users and their requirements in terms of the novel features which DAI systems possess. These requirements are quite extensive, and it can be seen that DAI system user interfaces must be designed through a careful consideration of a variety of issues.

The current trend in DAI systems of implementing the user interface as a separate agent can be considered to be of benefit as it enables concentration on issues relating to user interaction. However, as identified in this chapter, it is essential that the user agent is given the same level of importance as other agents rather than providing a pragmatic solution which enables interaction, but fails to utilize available technology or fully satisfy user requirements. The user agent needs to contain a wide range of facilities to support user interaction with agents within the DAI system. It will generally need to provide mechanisms which at least partially reveal the underlying architecture of the DAI system to the user. The use of such mechanisms will enable the user to develop an appropriate conceptualization of the DAI system.

The issue of DAI system representation to the user has received limited attention in DAI research, although this is one of the most crucial issues which face designers of the DAI system user interface. Determining how such models could be developed and designed is of considerable importance to enable users to interact effectively, efficiently and enjoyably with DAI systems, and forms one of the main future research areas for DAI system user interface designers.

The issues discussed here, relating to user interaction and user interface design, are of considerable relevance for DAI systems. Well-designed user interfaces for DAI systems will facilitate the transition from research environments into the real world and will enable users to fully utilize the power of these systems.

REFERENCES

Ackermann, D., and Tauber, M. J., eds. (1990). *Mental Models and Human-Computer Interaction 1.* North-Holland Publ., Amsterdam.

Avouris, N. M. (1992). User interface design for DAI applications: An overview. In *Distributed Artificial Intelligence: Theory and Praxis* (N. Avouris and L. Gasser, eds.), pp. 141–162. Kluwer Academic Publishers, Dordrecht, The Netherlands.

Avouris, N. M., Van Liedekerke, M. H., and Sommaruga, L. (1989). Evaluating the CooperA experiment: The transition from an expert system module to a distributed A.I. testbed for cooperating experts. *Proc. Int. Workshop Distributed Artif. Intell., 9th*, Rosario, Washington, *1989*.

Avouris, N. M., Van Liedekerke, M. H., Lekkas, G. P., and Hall, L. E. (1993). User interface design for co-operating agents in industrial process supervision and control applications. *Int. J. Man-Mach. Stud.* **MMS-38**, 873–890.

Berry, D. C., and Broadbent, D. E. (1987). Expert systems and the man-machine interface. Part II: The user interface. *Expert Syst.* **4.**

Bond, A. H., and Gasser, L., eds. (1988). *Readings in Distributed Artificial Intelligence.* Morgan-Kaufmann, San Mateo, CA.

Brandau, R., and Weihmayer, R. (1989). Heterogeneous multiagent cooperative problem solving in a telecommunication network management domain. *Proc. Int. Workshop Distributed Artif. Intell., 9th*, Rosario, Washington, *1989*.

Drogoul, A., and Ferber, J. (1992). Multi-agent simulation as a tool for modelling societies: Application to social differentiation in ant colonies. *Pre-Proc. Eur. Workshop Modell. Auton. Agents Multi-Agent World*, Viterbo, Italy, *1992*.

Hall, L. E., and Avouris, N. M. (1992). Methodological issues of DAI applications design: Transparency analysis. In *Distributed Artificial Intelligence: Theory and Praxis* (N. Avouris and L. Gasser, eds.), pp. 163–178. Kluwer Academic Publishers, Dordrecht, The Netherlands.

Hall, L. E., Avouris, N. M., and Cross, D. A. (1990). Interface design issues for cooperating expert systems. *Proc. Avignon Conf. Expert Syst.*, Avignon, France, *1990*.

Hall, L. E., Macaulay, L., and O'Hare, G. (1994). User role in problem solving with distributed artificial intelligent systems. *Artificial Social Systems.* Springer-Verlag, Berlin, pp. 324–337.

Hayes-Roth, F., Erman, L. D., Fouse, S., Lark, J. S., and Davidson, J. (1988). ABE: A cooperative operating system and development environment. In *Artificial Intelligence Tools and Techniques* (M. Richer, ed.), Ablex, Norwood, NJ.

Jennings, N., and Wittig, T. (1992). ARCHON: Theory and Practice. In *Distributed Artificial Intelligence: Theory and Praxis* (N. Avouris and L. Gasser, eds.), pp. 179–195. Kluwer Academic Publishers, Dordrecht, The Netherlands.

Kidd, A. L., and Cooper, M. B. (1983). Man-machine interface for an expert system. In *Proceedings of the British Computer Specialist Group for Expert Systems*. Cambridge Univ. Press, Cambridge, UK.

Lekkas, G., and Van Liedekerke, M. (1992). Prototyping multi-agent systems: A case study. In *Distributed Artificial Intelligence: Theory and Praxis* (N. Avouris and L. Gasser, eds.), pp. 129–140. Kluwer Academic Publishers, Dordrecht, The Netherlands.

Lenat, D. B. (1975). Beings: Knowledge as interacting experts. *Proc. Int. Jt. Conf. Artif. Intell., 1975.*

Monk, A., ed. (1985). *Fundamentals of Human-Computer Interaction.* Academic Press, London.

Moran, T. P. (1981). The command language grammar: A representation for the user interface of interactive Computer systems. *Int. J. Man-Mach. Stud.* **15.**

Myers, B. (1989). User interface tools: Introduction and survey. In

Nielsen, J. (1989). *Coordinating User Interfaces for Consistency.* Academic Press, San Diego, CA.

Norman, D. A. (1994). How might people interact with agents. *Commun. ACM* **37**(7).

O'Hare, G. M. P., and Wooldridge, M. J. (1992). A software engineering perspective on multi-agent system design: Experience in the development of MADE. In *Distributed Artificial Intelligence: Theory and Praxis,* (N. Avouris and L. Gasser, eds.), pp. 109–128. Kluwer Academic Publishers, Dordrecht, The Netherlands.

Roda, C., Jennings, N. R., and Mamdani, E. H. (1991). The impact of heterogeneity on cooperating agents. *Proc. Natl. Conf. Artif. Intell., 9th,* Anaheim, CA.

Smith, D., and Broadwell, M. (1988). The pilots associate: An overview. *SAE Aerotech Conf.,* Los Angeles, *1988.*

Sommaruga, L. (1993). Ph.D. Thesis, University of Nottingham, UK.

Sommaruga, L., Avouris, N. M., and Van Liedekerke, M. H. (1989). *Studies in Distributed A.I.: Development of the Testbed Environment CooperA,* JRC Tech. Note. JRC, Ispra, Italy.

Sutcliffe, A. (1988). *Human-Computer Interface Design.* Macmillan Education, London.

Wittig, T., ed. (1992). *ARCHON: An Architecture for Multi-Agent Systems.* Ellis Horwood, London.

Wooldridge, M. J., O'Hare, G., and Elks, R. (1991). FELINE—A case study in the design and implementation of a co-operating expert system. *Proc. Avignon Conf. Expert Syst.,* Avignon, France, *1991.*

Young, R. M. (1983). Surrogates and mappings: Two kinds of conceptual models for interactive devices. In *Mental Models* (D. Gentner and A. Stevens, eds.). Erlbaum, Hillsdale, NJ.

APPENDIX _____

Distributed Artificial Intelligence References and Resources

DENNIS KWEK
SUSANNE KALENKA

1 INTRODUCTION

For the past 10 years, there has been increasing interest in the area of distributed artificial intelligence (DAI). This steadfast growth in DAI-related research activity has resulted in the publication of numerous books on DAI and related areas, as well as the conception of several key conferences and workshops. In addition, to provide a forum for DAI researchers to exchange their ideas, Internet mailing lists were created to facilitate intellectual discussion. For researchers interested in papers and software from their colleagues, repositories were established to allow easy retrieval of relevant files. All these sources of information have given DAI researchers an abundance of knowledge to refer to, but they have also resulted in confusion for the uninitiated researcher as to where to begin. In addition, a lack of a common updated source of DAI references and resources means it becomes increasingly difficult for the active DAI researcher to search for the relevant information in an efficient and rapid manner.

This appendix establishes a comprehensive list of references and resources for new as well as active DAI researchers. The purpose of this endeavor is twofold. First, it guides new researchers in an appropriate direction, by providing frequently cited reference books to start on, as well as instructions on accessing popular Internet resources. Second, the paper will appeal to active DAI researchers as a useful and easily accessible reference.

This information is abstracted from the frequently asked questions (FAQ)

Foundations of Distributed Artificial Intelligence, Edited by G. M. P. O'Hare and N. R. Jennings.
ISBN 0-471-00675-0 © 1996 John Wiley & Sons, Inc.

for the DAI mailing list, of which the first author is the creator and maintainer. It does not include references or resources which are transient: for example, workshops which do not appear on a regular basis or FTP sites which are unstable. Neither does it contain the majority of paper references; to do so would be impossible as there are now in excess of 600 papers. Instead, pointers are given to DAI bibliographical indices. The aim is not to swamp the reader with too much information, but to selectively choose information that is deemed to be stable (as in the case of DAI conferences and internet resources) or frequently used (as in the case of DAI references), which will provide a suitable reference point. For the complete FAQ, please contact the first author via email. Alternatively, the FAQ is available on the World Wide Web (in short WWW, W^3 or Web), regularly updated in the DAI FTP Site, and posted on the DAI mailing lists (see below for more detailed information[1]).

This chapter is organized as follows. Section 2 contains a list of Internet mailing lists for the DAI community, including instructions on how to subscribe to them. Section 3 lists DAI-related conferences and workshops, with brief descriptions of their agenda and topics of interest. Section 4 lists reference books in the area of DAI, as well as several related subfields. Finally, Section 5 points the reader to several Internet resources that are available on the World Wide Web.

2 DAI-RELATED INTERNET MAILING LISTS

A mailing list is a single email address that redistributes all messages sent to it to a list of addresses. Most mailing lists have two email addresses, one for administrative tasks and the other for usual list discussions. Take note that emails meant for administration should be sent to the appropriate email address; otherwise the administrative request will be sent to the entire list of users. To join a mailing list, it must be subscribed to, typically by asking for permission from the list moderator or by sending a standard format request to the listserver. Certain mailing lists may be moderated, which means that submissions to the list may be vetted by a moderator for distribution suitability.

With regards to the selection criteria for inclusion into this section, we have chosen only those mailing lists which are of interest to the DAI community, and have a long-term broad-based agenda. We did not include mailing lists which discuss specific projects or languages, although they may be related to DAI; neither did we include mailing lists which are peripheral to DAI. These can be found in the DAI FAQ.

The alphabetical list below is structured as follows: *mailing list name* indicates the name of the respective mailing list; *description* contains a brief summary of the purpose of the mailing list; *moderator* is the name(s) of the people in charge of the mailing list; *administrative requests* contains the email address for administrative tasks (e.g., subscriptions, cancellation, list queries,

---

[1]We assume the reader is knowledgeable in the use of WWW browsers.

administrivia, etc.); *submissions* is the email address one should post to for circulation among list recipients; *miscellaneous* contains information that does not fall into any particular heading. With regards to *administrative requests*, we have indicated whether the requests are addressed to a human moderator or an automated listserver, the latter case requiring a particular format for email requests; this is detailed in the respective areas.

Mailing List Name: *Computational Organization Research Mailing List (COR-List)*

Description: COR-List is established to provide an international forum for discussion and dissemination of information about activities and research in the area of computational organization research. The list is concerned with research in the area of explicitly computational approaches to organizational phenomena and is the result of recent meetings and growing interest in the interdisciplinary organization-studies community. Examples of research topics might include computational models and representations of organizational knowledge, computational approaches to organization design, study of computational organizations, simulations of organizational activity or structuring, as well as agent-oriented, societal-level, and organization-level phenomena.

Moderators: Ingemar Hulthage and Les Gasser, University of Southern California (hulthage@usc.edu, gasser@usc.edu)

Administrative Requests: COR-List-Request@usc.edu (Human; Send email address)

Submissions: COR-List@usc.edu

Mailing List Name: *Cooperating Knowledge Based Systems Special Interest Group*

Description: The Cooperation Knowledge Based Systems Special Interest Group (CKBS-SIG) manages a mailing list offering distribution to nearly 500 academic and industrial researchers worldwide. The list is aimed at disseminating information relating to conference calls, availability of technical reports and research job announcements, etc. within the CKBS area. A CKBS is considered to be an applied multiagent system with an emphasis on real-world problems.

Moderator: Martyn Fletcher (martyn@cs.keele.ac.uk)

Administrative Requests: ckbs@cs.keele.ac.uk (Human; Send email address)

Submissions: For UK only distribution, send to ckbs-uk@cs.keele.ac.uk
For Europe distribution, send to ckbs-europe@cs.keele.ac.uk
For worldwide distribution, send to ckbs-int@cs.keele.ac.uk

Mailing List Name: *DAI-List*

Description: This is the definitive DAI Mailing List, and is frequently an international forum for discussing various DAI-related topics. It also contains announcements of interest to the DAI community (e.g., conferences, books, Internet resources), as well as DAI-related queries. This mailing list is moderated.

Moderator: Mike Huhns, South Carolina (Huhns@ece.sc.edu)

Administrative Requests: DAI-List-Request@ece.sc.edu (Human; Send email address)

Submissions: DAI-List@ece.sc.edu

Miscellaneous: Back issues of the DAI-List can be obtained via anonymous FTP from the DAI Archives at ftp.mcc.com (128.62.130.101)

Mailing List Name: *Distributed-AI Discussion List*

Description: An unmoderated forum with international subscribers, this list serves to facilitate the exchange of research ideas in the DAI community.

Moderator: Lyndon Lee (lyndon@essex.ac.uk)

Administrative Requests: mailbase@mailbase.ac.uk (Computerized; Send HELP or COMMAND for subscription/help details)

Submissions: distributed-ai@mailbase.ac.uk

Mailing List Name: *MAAMAW Blackboard*

Description: In conjunction with the European Workshops on "Modeling an Autonomous Agent in a Multi-Agent World" (MAAMAW), this mailing list is dedicated to the field of multiagent systems, including multiagent paradigms, their development, their application, and their evaluation. The purpose of this mailing list is to stimulate exchange and discussion of research in the multiagent area. This list is moderated.

Moderator: Yves Demazeau (Yves.Demazeau@imag.fr)

Administrative Requests: Yves.Demazeau@imag.fr (Human; Send address, phone number, fax number, email)

Submissions: maamaw@imag.fr

Miscellaneous: Information can also be retrieved from the WWW page "The virtual MAAMAW Blackboard" (URL:http://cosmos.imag.fr/MAGMA/maamaw.html)

Mailing List Name: *Simulating Societies Mailing List*

Description: A distribution list for those interested in the computer simulation of societies and social phenomena. Simulating societies shows how computer simulations can help to clarify theoretical approaches, contribute to the evaluation of alternative theories, and illuminate how social phenomena can emerge from individual action.

Moderator: Nigel Gilbert (gng@soc.surrey.ac.uk)

Administrative Requests: simsoc-request@soc.surrey.ac.uk (Human; Send email address)

Submissions: simsoc@soc.surrey.ac.uk

Mailing List Name: *Software Agents Mailing List*

Description: This mailing list is devoted to the issues concerning software agents. The term "agent" is ill-defined and because of this the scope of this mailing list will also be somewhat ill-defined. It should be restricted to software agents as opposed to hardware (robots) and human agents; however, the interface from software agents to other agents can be included in the scope. This mailing list is managed by listserv software.

Moderator: Ray Johnson (Raymond.Johnson@Eng.Sun.COM)

Administrative Requests:

To join: email to listserv@sunlabs.sun.com (Computerized) with "subscribe agents ⟨FirstName⟩ ⟨LastName⟩" in body of message.

For help: email to listserv@sunlabs.sun.com with "help" in body of message.

To quit: email to listserv@sunlabs.sun.com with "unsubscribe agents" in body of message.

Submissions: agents@sun.com

Miscellaneous: All posted messages of this mailing list are archived and made available via the WWW at http://www.smli.com/research/tcl/lists/agents-list.html. The Software Agents Mailing List FAQ is maintained at http://www.ee.mcgill.ca/~belmarc/agent-faq.html

3 DAI-RELATED CONFERENCES, WORKSHOPS, AND SYMPOSIA

This section contains an alphabetical listing of DAI-related conferences, workshops and symposia.[2] We include all the major international DAI gatherings, including several conferences which have strong DAI themes. However, we have excluded transitory workshops and symposia, that is, those workshops or symposia that do not appear on a regular basis. We have also excluded conferences which offer DAI as a subtheme area, for example, the International Joint Conference on Artificial Intelligence, the National Conference on Artificial Intelligence, or the Conference on Theoretical Aspects of Reasoning about Knowledge, etc.

Almost all the information given below is based on the latest gatherings (in 1994–1995), and we should also bear in mind that most gatherings will have special themes which vary from year to year (or biannually in certain cases). As such, readers are advised to use this information only as an approximate gauge of the general content of the gatherings. We have included the contact persons for these gatherings who can assist in general enquiries. Further details for each gathering, and other gatherings not listed within this section, can be found in the DAI FAQ.

Title: *European Workshop on Modelling Autonomous Agents in a Multi-Agent World (MAAMAW)*

General Theme and Topics of Interest: The purpose of this workshop is to bring together academic and industrial researchers in the fields of DAI and multiagent systems to stimulate discussion and exchange of ideas.

---

[2]Henceforth, conferences, workshops, and symposia will be collectively known as "gatherings."

MAAMAW can be regarded as a generalisation of classical DAI beyond distributed problem solving and task allocation to the problems arising when several autonomous agents, endowed with their own goals, knowledge and abilities share a common environment and pursue either shared or competing goals.

Topics of interest include classical DAI problems, artificial life from a multiagent perspective, conceptual and theoretical foundations of multiagent systems, distributed planning and group work, learning of cooperation and coordination, social simulation and formalization of social concepts, agent-agent and agent-environment interaction, multiagent architectures and testbeds, and applications of multiagent systems.

Contact Person: Yves Demazeau of the LIFIA, Grenoble, France (Yves.Demazeau@imag.fr)

Title: *International Conference on Cooperative Information Systems (CoopIS)*

General Theme and Topics of Interest: The CoopIS conferences provide a forum for the presentation and dissemination of research covering all aspects of cooperative information systems (CIS) design, requirements, functionality, implementation, deployment, and evolution.

Topics of interest include CIS systems issues, CIS architectures and communication protocols including multiagent planning frameworks, core technology for CIS including open distributed computing architectures, CIS implementation techniques including interoperability issues in distributed heterogeneous information bases, integration challenges, CIS modeling, migration, and evolution, CIS applications, information modeling and reasoning techniques for CISs including multiagent planning and problem solving, advanced CIS programming, information engineering for CIS including information sharing and management, reengineering including reengineering legacy and new information systems into CISs, CIS evolution, information agents including novel models and organizations, application of information agent technology in virtual laboratories, concurrent engineering, and other groupware frameworks.

Contact Person: Mike Papazoglou of the Queensland University of Technology, Australia (mikep@icis.qut.edu.au)

Title: *International Conference on Multiagent Systems (ICMAS)*

General Theme and Topics of Interest: This international conference is a collaborative effort of the North American DAI community, the Japanese Multi-Agent and Cooperative Computing (MACC) community, and the European Modeling Autonomous Agents in a Multi-Agent World (MAA-MAW) community. The central theme of the conference is multiagent systems, whereby human or computational agents may interact to perform tasks or satisfy some goals (which themselves may be common or distinct) in a common environment.

Topics of interest include agent architectures, artificial life (from a multiagent perspective), conceptual and theoretical foundations of MAS, development and engineering methodologies, distributed artificial intelligence, distributed consensus and algorithms for MA interaction, distributed search, evaluation of MAS, integrated testbeds and development environments, intelligent agents in enterprise integration systems and similar types of applications, multiagent cooperative reasoning from distributed heterogeneous databases, multiagent planning, and planning for multiagent worlds, negotiation strategies, organizational aspects of MAS, practical applications of multiagent systems, social structures and their significance in multiagent systems, user interface issues for multiagent systems.

Contact Person: Victor R. Lesser of the University of Massachusetts at Amherst (lesser@cs.umass.edu)

Title: *International Working Conference on Cooperating Knowledge Based Systems (CKBS)*

General Theme and Topics of Interest: The objective of the CKBS series of conferences is to bring the researchers from DAI, distributed databases (DDB), and industry together to discuss issues and solutions to problems that are inherently distributed. A CKBS may be viewed as an applied multiagent system, which distinguishes itself from the traditional multiagent systems by having a stronger emphasis on real-world problems, where issues such as performance, reliability, consistency, organisational constraints, security and end-user facility are important. In this sense, a CKBS type approach amalgamates ideas from DAI and DDB for solving distributed problems, such as those encountered in intelligent manufacturing systems, air traffic control, telecommunications network management, distributed sensor networks, distributed decision-making systems, distributed banking systems, distributed office procedures, and distributed fault diagnosis.

Contact Person: S. Misbah Deen of the University of Keele, UK (deen@cs.keele.ac.uk)

Title: *International Workshop on Distributed Artificial Intelligence (IWDAI)*

General Theme and Topics of Interest: The workshop is dedicated to advancing the state of the art in the field of DAI. For over a decade now the workshop has gathered a relatively small group of active researchers for intensive discussions on the state of the art, as well as fruitful directions for future exploration. Recent attention has been drawn to making attempts to connect with other research communities and improving DAI awareness in such communities, as well as trying to understand the relationships between DAI and other related research areas including real-world problems. The workshop aims at helping participants develop a better understanding of the differences between current theory and potential applications, and identify future research directions that integrate multidisciplinary efforts to address these differences.

Topics of interest include real-world DAI systems, design of coordination-capable agents, multiagent learning, societies of agents, agent design and behavior, implementational approaches such as languages, frameworks, infrastructures, and integration of heterogeneous systems.

Contact Person: Victor R. Lesser of the University of Massachusetts at Amherst (lesser@cs.umass.edu)

Title: *Multiagent and Cooperative Computing Workshop (MACC)*
General Theme and Topics of Interest: The workshop covers the issues in multiagent and cooperative computing, such as formal models and architectures of agents, cooperative computing models/systems, social models/systems, agent autonomy and reflection, modeling of communication and discourse, distributed planning, learning in multiagent environment, and applications (robotics, simulation, network/distributed system management, etc.).

Contact Person: Koiti Hasida of the Electro Technical Laboratory, Tsukuba-shi, Ibaragi, Japan (hasida@etl.go.jp)

Title: *Simulating Societies Symposium—The Simulation of Social Phenomena and Social Processes*
General Theme and Topics of Interest: Although the value of simulating complex phenomena in order to come to a better understanding of their nature is well recognized, it is still rare for simulation to be used to understand social processes. This symposium is intended to present original research, review current ideas, compare alternative approaches and suggest directions for future work on the simulation of social processes. "Social process" may be interpreted widely to include, for example, the rise and fall of nation states, the behavior of households, the evolution of animal societies, and social interaction.

Topics of interest include discussions of approaches to the simulation of social processes such as those based on multiagent systems, distributed artificial intelligence, cellular automata, genetic algorithms and neural networks, nonlinear systems, general purpose stochastic simulation systems, etc. Accounts of specific simulations of social processes and phenomena, reviews of simulation work in anthropology, archeology, economics, political science, psychology, geography, demography, game theory, etc., with lessons for the simulation of social processes, Simulations of human, animal, and "possible" societies, Considerations of the relevance of concepts such as emergence, complexity, coalitions, and self-organization to the simulation of social phenomena.

Contact Person: Nigel Gilbert of the University of Surrey, UK (gng@soc.survey.ac.uk)

4 DAI REFERENCES

This section contains a comprehensive list of published material on DAI and several related areas. With the exception of certain parts of this section, we have excluded references to individual papers as there are now in excess of 600 published papers on DAI.[3] Instead, the purpose of this section is to provide pointers to all available collections of work on DAI, including books and journals with special themes. The list of references are sorted by year, then by title.

4.1 DAI Introductory Texts

Most DAI texts come in the form of a collection of research papers. However, readers uninitiated in DAI may choose, in addition to the current book, the following as starting points for an introduction into DAI:

1. "An Analysis of Problems and Research in Distributed Artificial Intelligence" by A. H. Bond and L. Gasser, in *Readings in Distributed Artificial Intelligence*, A. H. Bond and L. Gasser (eds.), Morgan Kaufmann 1988, ISBN 093461363X

2. "Cooperative Distributed Problem Solving" by E. H. Durfee, V. R. Lesser, and D. D. Corkill, in *The Handbook of Artificial Intelligence Volume 4*, A. Barr, P. R. Cohen, and E. A. Feigenbaum (eds.), Addison-Wesley 1989, pp 83–148, ISBN 0201518198

3. "Distributed Problem Solving" by E. H. Durfee, V. R. Lesser and D. D. Corkill, in *Encyclopedia of Artificial Intelligence (2nd Edition)*, S. C. Shapiro (ed.), John Wiley 1992, pp 379–388, ISBN 047150307X

4.2 DAI Reference Books

1. *Distributed Artificial Intelligence* by M. N. Huhns (ed.), Pitman/Morgan Kaufmann 1987, ISBN 0273087789

2. *Readings in Distributed Artificial Intelligence* by A. H. Bond and L. Gasser (eds.), Morgan Kaufmann 1988, ISBN 093461363X

3. *Distributed Artificial Intelligence 2* by L. Gasser and M. N. Huhns (eds.), Pitman/Morgan Kaufmann 1989, ISBN 0273088106

4. *Decentralized Artificial Intelligence: Proceedings of the First European Workshop on Modelling Autonomous Agents in a Multi-Agent (MAA-MAW), Cambridge, UK, 1989* by Y. Demazeau and J. P. Muller (eds.), North-Holland 1990, ISBN 0444887059

---

[3]The only exception to this rule is when the paper contains either a survey, overview, or bibliographical index to DAI.

5. *Decentralized Artificial Intelligence: Proceedings of the Second European Workshop on Modelling Autonomous Agents in a Multi-Agent World (MAAMAW)—Saint Quentin en Yvelines, France, 13–16 August 1990* by Y. Demazeau, and J. P. Muller (eds.), Elsevier Science 1991, ISBN 0444890513

6. *Decentralized Artificial Intelligence: Proceedings of the Third European Workshop on Modelling Autonomous Agents in a Multi-Agent World (MAAMAW), Kaiserslautern, Germany, 5–7 August 1991*, by E. Werner and Y. Demazeau, Elsevier Science 1992, ISBN 0444896619

7. *Distributed Artificial Intelligence: Theory and Praxis* by N. M. Avouris and L. Gasser (eds.), Kluwer Academic 1992, ISBN 0792315855

8. *Artificial Social Systems: Proceedings of the Fourth European Workshop on Modelling Autonomous Agents in a Multi-Agent (MAAMAW), S. Martino al Cimino, July 1992* by C. Castelfranchi and E. Werner (eds.), Springer Verlag Lecture Notes in Artificial Intelligence 830, 1994, ISBN 3-540-58266-5 Springer-Verlag Berlin Heidelberg New York and ISBN 0-387-58266-5 Springer-Verlag New York Berlin Heidelberg

4.3 Books on Distributed Problem Solving and Multiagent Systems

1. *Cognition, Computation, and Cooperation* by W. Zachary, S. Robertson, and J. Black (eds.), Ablex 1988, ISBN 089391536X

2. *Coordination of Distributed Problem Solvers* by E. H. Durfee, Kluwer Academic 1988, ISBN 089838284X

3. *Coordinating Plans of Autonomous Agents* by F. von Martial, Springer-Verlag Lecture Notes in Artificial Intelligence 610, 1992, ISBN 354055615X

4. *Multiagent Systems: A Theoretical Framework for Intentions, Know-How, and Communications* by M. P. Singh, Springer-Verlag Lecture Notes in Artificial Intelligence 799, 1994, ISBN 3540580263

5. *Intelligent Agents* by M. J. Wooldridge and N. R. Jennings (eds.), Springer-Verlag Lecture Notes in Artifical Intelligence 890, 1995, ISBN 3540588558

4.4 Books on Cooperating Knowledge Based Systems

1. *CKBS-90 Proceedings of the International Working Conference on Cooperating Knowledge Based Systems, 3–5 October 90, University of Keele, UK* by S. M. Deen (ed.), Springer-Verlag 1991, ISBN 3540196498

2. *CKBS-SIG Proceedings 1992: Proceedings of the Special Interest Group on Cooperating Knowledge Based Systems* by S. M. Deen (ed.), DAKE Centre, Keele University, September 1992, ISBN 0952178907

3. *CKBS-SIG Proceedings 1993: Proceedings of the Special Interest Group on Cooperating Knowledge Based Systems* by S. M. Deen (ed.), DAKE Centre, Keele University, September 1993, ISBN 0952178915

4. *CKBS'94 Proceedings of the Second International Working Conference on Cooperating Knowledge Based Systems, 14–17 June 94, University of Keele, UK* by S. M. Deen (ed.), DAKE Centre, University of Keele, 1994, ISBN 0952178923

4.5 Books on DAI Applications

1. *ARCHON: An Architecture for Multi-Agent Systems* by T. Wittig (Ed), Ellis Horwood 1992, ISBN 0130444626
2. *Cooperation in Industrial Multi-Agent Systems* by N. R. Jennings, World Scientific Series in Computer Science Vol 43, 1994, ISBN 981-02-1652-1

4.6 Books on DAI Negotiation

Rules of Encounter: Designing Conventions for Automated Negotiation among Computers by J. Rosenschein and G. Zlotkin, MIT Press 1994, ISBN 0262181592

4.7 Books on Blackboard Systems

1. *Blackboard Systems: Theory and Practice* by R. Engelmore and T. Morgan, Addison-Wesley 1988, ISBN 0201174316
2. *Blackboard Architectures and Applications* by V. Jagannathan, R. Dodhiawala, L. S. Baum, Academic Press, 1989, ISBN 0123799406
3. *Blackboard Systems* by Ian D. Criag, Ablex 1992, ISBN 0893915947

4.8 Books on Modeling Societies

1. *Simulating Societies: The Computer Simulation of Social Phenomena Proceedings of the Symposium on Simulating Societies* by N. Gilbert and J. E. Doran (eds.), University College Press, 1994, ISBN 1857280822
2. *Artificial Societies: Computer Simulation of Social Life* by N. Gilbert and R. Conte (eds.), University College Press 1995, ISBN 1857283058.
3. *Cognitive And Social Action* by R. Conte and C. Castelfranchi, UCL Press 1995, ISBN 1857281861

4.9 Books on AI and Organization Theory

1. *Artificial Intelligence in Organization and Management Theory* by M. Masuch and M. Warglien (eds.), Elsevier Science 1991, ISBN 0444890424
2. *Computational Organization Theory* by K. M. Carley and M. J. Prietula (eds.), Lawrence Erlbaum 1994, ISBN 080581406X

3. *Cooperative Knowledge Processing* by S. Kirn, G. M. P. O'Hare (eds.), Springer-Verlag 1996, ISBN 3540199519

4.10 Books on Actor Models and Concurrent Object-Oriented Programming

1. *Actors: A Model of Concurrent Computation in Distributed Systems* by G. Agha, MIT Press 1986, ISBN 0262010925
2. *Object-Oriented Concurrent Programming* by A. Yonezawa and M. Tokoro (eds.), MIT Press 1987, ISBN 0262240262
3. *Concurrent Aggregates: Supporting Modularity in Massively Parallel Programs* by A. Chien, MIT Press 1993, ISBN 0262032066
4. *Research Directions in Concurrent Object-Oriented Programming* by G. Agha, P. Wegner, A. Yonezawa (eds.), MIT Press 1993, ISBN 0262011395

4.11 Books on Models of Distributed System Behavior

The Ecology of Computation by B. A. Huberman (ed.), Elsevier Science/North-Holland 1988, ISBN 0444703756

4.12 DAI Special Issue Journals and Periodicals

1. Special Issue on Distributed Artificial Intelligence by B. Chandrasekaran (Guest Ed.), in *IEEE Transactions on Systems, Man, and Cybernetics*, Vol. SMC-11, January 1981, IEEE Press
2. Special Issue on Distributed Artificial Intelligence by E. H. Durfee (Guest Ed.), in *IEEE Transactions on Systems, Man, and Cybernetics*, Vol. 21, No. 6, November 1991, IEEE Press
3. Special Feature on Distributed Artificial Intelligence by N. Seel (Guest Ed.), in *AISB: Quarterly Newsletter of the Society for the Study of Artificial Intelligence and the Simulation of Behaviour*, Spring 1991, Number 76, AISB
4. Special Issue on Distributed Sensor Networks, in *IEEE Transactions on Systems, Man, and Cybernetics*, Vol. 21, No. 5, 1991, IEEE Press
5. Special Issue on Intelligent and Cooperative Problem Solving, in *International Journal of Intelligent and Cooperative Information Systems*, Vol. 1, No. 2, June 1992, World Scientific Publishers
6. Special Issue on Distributed Artificial Intelligence (Selected Papers from 1992 11th DAI Workshop), by K. P. Sycara and L. Gasser (Guest Eds.), in *Group Decision and Negotiation*, Vol. 2, No. 3, 1993, Kluwer Academic Publishers
7. Special Issue on Intelligent Agents by D. Riecken (Guest Ed.), in *Communications of the ACM*, Vol. 37, No. 7, July 1994, ACM Press

8. Special Volume Computational Research on Interaction and Agency by P. E. Agre and S. J. Rosenschein (Guest Eds.), in *Artificial Intelligence*, Vol. 72–73, No. 1–2, January–February 1995, Elsevier Science.

9. Special Issue on Intelligent Agents and Multi-Agent Systems by M. J. Wooldridge and N. R. Jennings (Guest Eds.), in *Applied Artificial Intelligence Journal*, Vol. 9, No. 4, July/August 1995, and Vol. 10, No. 1, January/February 1996, Francis & Taylor.

4.13 DAI Surveys and Overviews

1. "Natural and Social System Metaphors for Distributed Problem Solving: Introduction to the Issue" by B. Chandrasekaran, in *IEEE Transactions on Systems, Man, and Cybernetics*, Vol. SMC-11, Jan. 1981, pp. 1–5, IEEE Press.

2. "Distributed Problem Solving Techniques: A Survey" by K. S. Decker, in *IEEE Transactions on Systems, Man, and Cybernetics*, Vol. SMC-17, 1987, pp. 729–740, IEEE Press

3. "An Analysis of Problems and Research in Distributed Artificial Intelligence" by A. H. Bond and L. Gasser, in *Readings in Distributed Artificial Intelligence*, A. H. Bond and L. Gasser (eds.), Morgan Kaufmann 1988, pp. 1–35, ISBN 093461363X.

4. "On Distributed Artificial Intelligence" by LEC Hern, in *The Knowledge Engineering Review*, Vol. 3, Pt. 1, Mar. 1988, pp. 21–57, Cambridge University Press

5. "Cooperative Distributed Problem Solving" by E. H. Durfee, V. R. Lesser, and D. D. Corkill, in *The Handbook of Artificial Intelligence Volume 4*, A. Barr, P. R. Cohen, and E. A. Feigenbaum (eds.), Addison-Wesley 1989, pp. 83–148, ISBN 0201518198.

6. "Evaluating Research in Cooperative Distributed Problem Solving" by K. S. Decker, E. H. Durfee, and V. R. Lesser, in *Distributed Artificial Intelligence Vol. II*, L. Gasser and M. N. Huhns (eds.), Pitman/Morgan Kaufmann 1989, pp. 487–519, ISBN 0273088106.

7. "Themes in Distributed Artificial Intelligence Research" by L. Gasser and M. N. Huhns, in *Distributed Artificial Intelligence Vol II*, L. Gasser and M. N. Huhns (eds.), Pitman/Morgan Kaufmann 1989, pp. vii–xv, ISBN 0273088106

8. "Trends in Cooperative Distributed Problem Solving" by E. H. Durfee, in *IEEE Transaction on Knowledge and Data Engineering*, Vol. KDE-1, 1989, pp. 63–83, IEEE Press

9. "Engineering Coordinated Problem Solvers" by L. Gasser and R. W. Hill, in *Annual Review of Computer Science Vol. 4*, Annual Reviews Inc., 1990

10. "Overview of DAI: Viewing DAI as Distributed Search" by V. R.

Lesser, in *Journal Japanese Society of Artificial Intelligence*, Vol. 5, No. 4, 1990, pp. 392–400, JSAI

11. "The Distributed Artificial Intelligence Melting Pot" by E. H. Durfee, in *IEEE Transactions on Systems, Man, and Cybernetics*, Vol. 21, No. 6, November 1991, pp. 1301–1306, IEEE Press

12. "Distributed Problem Solving" by E. H. Durfee, V. R. Lesser and D. D. Corkill, in *Encyclopedia of Artificial Intelligence, 2nd Edition*, S. C. Shapiro (ed.), John Wiley 1992, pp. 379–388, ISBN 047150307X

13. "Trends in Distributed Artificial Intelligence" by B. Chaib-draa, B. Moulin, R. Mandiau, and P. Millot, in *Artificial Intelligence Review*, Vol. 6, No. 1, 1992, Kluwer Academic Press

14. "Intelligent Agents: Theory and Practice" by M. Wooldridge and N. R. Jennings, in *The Knowledge Engineering Review*, Vol. 10, No. 2, 1995, pp. 115–152, Cambridge University Press

4.14   DAI Bibliographies

1. "Distributed Artificial Intelligence: An Annotated Bibliography" by V. Jagannathan and R. Dodhiawalla, in *Distributed Artificial Intelligence*, M. N. Huhns, ed., Pitman/Morgan Kaufmann 1987, pp. 341–390, ISBN 0273087789

2. "A Subject-Indexed Bibliography of Distributed Artificial Intelligence" by A. H. Bond and L. Gasser, in *IEEE Transactions on Systems, Man, and Cybernetics*, November/December 1992, Volume 22, Number 6, pp. 1260–1281, IEEE Press

5   DAI INTERNET RESOURCES

One of the functions of the Internet is to serve as the communication backbone of the international research community. In recent years, tools have become available that facilitate fast information transfer and browsing. The Internet is now home to thousands of libraries of research papers, and immediate access to the works of other colleagues has invariably helped to push forward the frontiers of research even faster. User interfaces to the Internet, in particular the World Wide Web with browsers like Netscape and Mosaic, have provided easier and more intuitive methods of navigating the Internet. WWW links now allow users to search for and retrieve published papers by DAI researchers in an efficient manner, as well as transferring software from various DAI research groups to test them out.

The nature of the WWW is the easy access of distributed information without a specific "top" entry page. Individual WWW sites contain particular information and links to further information on the Web. Therefore, almost every WWW page can be used to start searching the Web interactively. We have chosen to include just a few WWW sites in this section—the ones listed are well established and are the ones most likely to have a long-term stable address and be maintained and updated frequently. These sites provide a comprehensive list of DAI resources and are therefore good starting points to browse around and discover the DAI world on the Web. The sites are classified either as general respositories (Section 5.1), meaning they contain links to numerous DAI-related WWW sites, or as home pages of specific institutions (Section 5.2) who are prominent in the DAI field.

5.1 General Repositories

Name: Agent-Based Computing
URL: http://www.sics.se/ps/abc/survey.html
Description: Sverker Janson collects pointers to WWW pages on Agent-Based Computing. His subdivision into several categories (i.e., Cooperating agents, Mobile agents) simplifies navigation on specific kinds of "Software Agent."

Name: Intelligent Software Agents
URL: http://www.cl.cam.ac.uk/users/rwabl/agents.html
Description: The WWW pages of Ralph Becket are intended as a repository for information about research into fields of AI concerning intelligent software agents. It includes information about other related pages on the Web, research papers, and short descriptions of people working on agents.

Name: Multiagent Systems
URL: http://www.ift.ulaval.ca/recherche/profs/chaib/MAS/multiagents/E__index.html
Description: Brahim Chiab-draa provides a collection of WWW links related to Multiagent Systems. In particular the list of related projects and testbeds is wide-ranging.

Name: UMBC Intelligent Software Agents Resources
URL: http://www.cs.umbc.edu/agents/
Description: Tim Finin maintains a well-organised set of WWW pages with comprehensive pointers to information and resources concerning intelligent information agents (a.k.a. software agents, softbots, knowbots, etc.), KQML, and knowledge sharing technology.

Name: The Agency
URL: http://www.info.unicaen.fr/ ~ serge/sma.html
Description: Serge Stinckwich's archive of DAI and Multiagent Systems contains a detailed list of hypertext links to numerous other related pages organiszed into categories like Agent Definitions, Calls for Papers and Languages/Testbeds. Remarkable are his pages on Related Topics (i.e., Concurrent Object-Oriented Programming), which he organised along similar categories.

5.2 R&D Institutions and Corporations

Name: Carnegie Mellon University Robotic Institute (Katia Sycara)
URL: http://www.cs.cmu.edu/afs/cs.cmu.edu/user/katia/www/katia-home-page.html

Name: Hebrew University of Jerusalem DAI Group (Jeff Rosenschein)
URL: http://www.cs.huji.ac.il/labs/dai/Index.html

Name: LIFIA/IMAG MAGMA Group (Yves Demazeau)
URL: http://cosmos.imag.fr/MAGMA/home.html

Name: Manchester Metropolitan University (Mike Wooldridge)
URL: http://www.doc.mmu.ac.uk/STAFF/mike/mikew.html

Name: MIT Media Lab Autonomous Agents Group (Pattie Maes)
URL: http://agents.www.media.mit.edu/groups/agents/

Name: QMW Distributed Artificial Intelligence Research Unit (Nick Jennings)
URL: http://www.elec.qmw.ac.uk/dai/

Name: Stanford University Logic Group (Michael Genesereth)
URL: http://logic.stanford.edu/group/technology.html

Name: Stanford University Nobotics Group (Yoav Shoham)
URL: http://robotics.stanford.edu/groups/nobotics/home.html

Name: Univ. Essex DAI Group (Jim Doran)
URL: http://cswww.essex.ac.uk/AI/DAI/Welcome.html

Name: Univ. Massachusetts DAI Laboratory (Victor Lesser)
URL: http://dis.cs.umass.edu/

Name: Univ. Maine CDPS Research Group (Roy and Elise Turner)
URL: http://cdps.umcs.maine.edu/

Name: Univ. Michigan DAI Group (Edmund Durfee)
URL: http://ai.eecs.umich.edu/diag/homepage.html

ACKNOWLEDGMENTS

Most information gathered here has been solicited from responses via the DAI-List, as well as previous postings from the various DAI mailing lists. All information given was correct at the time of publication, and we apologize to all those who have contributed to the FAQ but were not included in this appendix. The authors would like to thank Nick Jennings and Daniel Mack for their useful comments and feedback.

INDEX

Printed and bound by CPI Group (UK) Ltd, Croydon, CR0 4YY

27/10/2024

14580256-0003